BEETHOVEN

Beethoven's birthplace, Bonngasse 515. View from the garden.

From Verein Beethovenhaus in Bonn, 1889–1904 *(Bonn, 1904). Beethovenhaus, Bonn.*

BEETHOVEN

Second, Revised Edition

Maynard Solomon

SCHIRMER
TRADE
BOOKS

NEW YORK LONDON SYDNEY MADRID TOKYO COPENHAGEN

Schirmer Trade Books
A Division of Music Sales Corporation, New York

Exclusive Distributors:
Music Sales Corporation
257 Park Avenue South, New York, NY 10010 USA
Music Sales Limited
8/9 Frith Street, London W1D 3JB England
Music Sales Pty. Limited
120 Rothschild Street, Rosebery, Sydney, NSW 2018, Australia

Order No. SCH 10106
International Standard Book Number: 0.8256.7268.6

Printed in the United States of America

Extracts from *The Letters of Beethoven*, edited by Emily Anderson, are reprinted by
permission of Macmillan London and Basingstoke.

A pictorial chronology of Beethoven's life follows p. 234.

For Eva

and for Mark, Nina, and Maury

Contents

IV. THE FINAL PHASE

Preface to the First Edition

GREAT MEN ARE UNDERSTANDABLY ambivalent about the prospect of their posthumous biographies. Some have attempted to dissuade potential biographers or even to prevent them from obtaining data of an intimate nature, arguing that their creative achievement should be evaluated without regard to its biographical sources. Beethoven, however, had been raised on Plutarch's *Lives*, in which the heroes' flaws are given a weight equal to their redeeming qualities. There is no sign of fear that the assessment of his music would be adversely affected by a full knowledge of the facts of his life. True, in 1820 he declined an offer by one of his literary friends to furnish an accurate biographical sketch to a German encyclopedia that had published misinformation about his ancestry.[1] But as his life drew to a close he apparently overcame whatever inhibitions he may have had on this score, for in August 1826 he authorized his friend the violinist Karl Holz to undertake "the publication of my biography," adding, "I am fully confident that he will not hand down to posterity in a garbled form the information which I have given him for that purpose."[2]

Precisely what he gave to Holz is not quite clear, but we do know that at his death Beethoven left as rich a mass of documentary material as any composer in history. Included were a large number of manuscript scores of works, both published and unpublished; a profusion of sketch-leaves and sketchbooks, the study of which has led to a clearer understanding of Beethoven's creative process; his library, which included several books in which he had underscored favorite and meaningful passages; and the unparalleled collection of 137 notebooks—the Conversation Books—containing uncensored personal conversations between the deaf composer and his associates during his final decade.[3]

More dramatic than these, perhaps, were several other documents found in his effects, such as the Heiligenstadt Testament of October 6–10, 1802, in which Beethoven exorcised his suicidal impulses and declared his determination to resist adversity; his Tagebuch (diary) of 1812–18, in which we may observe Beethoven in his most vulnerable and self-questioning moods; and his passionate letter to an unidentified woman (whom he called "my Immortal Beloved"), written on July 6 and 7 of an unspecified year. Regrettably, he preserved relatively few of the letters that he received over the years, but this is most likely because he considered them superfluous; we have no reason to suspect that Beethoven prepared bonfires analogous to those that Charles Dickens and Henry James lit to keep their personal correspondence from reaching posterity.[4]

It is a reasonable assumption, then, that Beethoven wished us to know something more about him than a mere chronology of his life and work. He wanted understanding as well, as though sensing that both forgiveness and sympathy inevitably follow in its train. As an artist and as a man, he knew the healing power of communication and the cathartic effect of shared fears. "All evil is mysterious and appears greater when viewed alone," he wrote in a diary entry of 1817. "It is all the more ordinary, the more one talks about it with others; it is easier to endure because that which we fear becomes totally known; it seems as if one has overcome some great evil."[5]

Unfortunately—and inevitably—Beethoven's hope that the facts of his life would be presented in an ungarbled and unvarnished form was not soon to be fulfilled. Before the year of his death was over, a hasty and error-filled biography, by Johann Aloys Schlosser, was published in Prague.[6] More fatefully, Anton Schindler, his former assistant and secretary, removed many of the most important documents, which lay unguarded in Beethoven's lodgings, and converted them into his private property, until, in 1845, he sold most of the collection to the King of Prussia in exchange for a large sum in cash and a lifetime annuity. His much-translated and often-reprinted biography of Beethoven (1840, with revised and enlarged editions in 1845 and 1860) largely shaped the nineteenth-century conception of the composer, and it has continued to exert its influence in our own time. It was not until the publication between 1866 and 1879 of the first three volumes of a biography by the American writer Alexander Wheelock Thayer (1817–97) that Schindler's unreliable portrait was seriously challenged and the main outlines of Beethoven's life faithfully reconstructed. After Thayer's death, his biography of Beethoven—which had been published only in German translation—was completed and revised by Hermann Deiters and Hugo Riemann (1901–17); the original English manuscript was edited and completed by Henry E. Krehbiel (1921), and was reedited by Elliot Forbes (1964; revised edition, 1967), who skillfully incorporated into it many of the findings of modern research, while paring away some of Thayer's misconceptions and digressions. Thayer remains the indispensable biography of Beethoven, but his strictly chronological, year-by-year method of documentation—and his avoidance of any discussion of the music other than the details of Beethoven's productivity—did not permit him or his editors to illuminate the composer's psychological development, to deal with his personal relationships in their evolution, or to demonstrate any significant connections between his life and his works.

The reader who consults the bibliographical essay that closes this book will discover that the work of Beethoven documentation began rather than ended with the work of Thayer and his scholarly contemporaries Ludwig Nohl and Gustav Nottebohm. (Indeed, the accurate reconstruction of the chronology of Beethoven's works has been made possible only in recent decades through the careful study of his sketches and autograph manuscripts.) Scholars such as A. C. Kalischer, Theodor von Frimmel, Ludwig Schiedermair, Romain Rolland, Max Unger, Jacques-Gabriel Prod'homme, Stephan Ley, Joseph Schmidt-Görg, Georg Kinsky, Hans Halm, Donald W. MacArdle, Emily Anderson, and Alan Tyson—to name only a few—devoted decades of their lives to the accumulation of data and to the careful construction of a factual foundation for Beethoven studies.

The proper study of Beethoven is based on contemporary documents—on letters, diaries, Conversation Books, court and parish records, autograph manuscripts and sketches, music publications, reviews, concert programs, and similar materials. These may be utilized by a biographer with relative confidence as to their authenticity, although even they, as we shall see, must be approached with some caution. A second major source of material bearing significantly on Beethoven's life and personality consists of the reminiscences of his contemporaries. Here more serious questions arise as to the validity of anecdotes, reports, and memoirs that were written down long after the fact by a wide variety of individuals. The extent of the dangers involved in the use of contemporary documents was dramatically illustrated in March 1977 at the Berlin Beethoven-Kongress, where a long-held suspicion was finally confirmed.

Working with handwriting analysis, Grita Herre and Dagmar Beck
proved that Schindler had fabricated more than 150 of his own entries in
the Conversation Books.[7] Until then these entries had been unhesitatingly accepted as authentic by Beethoven scholars; some of Schindler's
forgeries had formed the basis for extensive biographical and musical
interpretations. It is true that Thayer had little confidence in Schindler's
testimony, and ever since Thayer published his *Ein kritischer Beitrag zur
Beethoven-Literatur* (*A critical contribution to the Beethoven literature*) in
1877, Schindler had been seen as an unreliable, biased, and self-serving
witness. Nevertheless, even Thayer relied heavily on Schindler, and the
latter, who was in intimate contact with Beethoven for a number of
years and who personally interviewed many of his friends, cannot wholly be dismissed. It will not be an easy task to separate his facts from his
fictions.

We have no such extreme problem with regard to other contemporary observers. But each of their reports must also be verified, where
possible, and their reminiscences as a whole evaluated as to their reliability and possible bias. Of the leading sources, it is my judgment that
the reminiscences of Ignaz von Seyfried, Carl Czerny, Gerhard von
Breuning, Fanny Giannattasio del Rio, and Karl Holz are generally
trustworthy insofar as they reflect personal observations, and that the
Biographische Notizen (*Biographical Notes*) of Franz Wegeler and
Ferdinand Ries reveal some curious lapses and factual errors but are in
the main unbiased and accurate. More difficult to evaluate is the so-
called Fischer Manuscript, which consists of the reminiscences of
Cäcilia and Gottfried Fischer, written down by the latter more than a
half century after the Beethoven family had rented a flat in their parents' home. This manuscript is the most important single fund of information on Beethoven's family background and on his early years in
Bonn. Thayer regarded it as somewhat suspect, but Hermann Deiters
and Joseph Schmidt-Görg, each of whom published editions of portions of the manuscript, concluded that wherever parallel evidence was
available from other sources, the Fischer memoirs were found to be
quite reliable. Nevertheless, as I have observed elsewhere,[8] even the
simple Fischers had an ax to grind—viz., the desire to prove that
Beethoven had been born in their parents' house—and this led them
into a number of deliberate falsifications concerning the dates of the

Fischer family's association with the Beethovens. On the whole, however, I have accepted as valid their homely, keenly observed anecdotes concerning Beethoven's youth, his family, and his early experiences.

Another important document is the Fischhof Manuscript, a copy of a collection of materials for a projected but never completed early biography. Along with a miscellany of documents, including Beethoven's Bonn "farewell album" (Stammbuch), his baptismal certificate, and Heiligenstadt Testament, it contains interesting anecdotes, memoirs, and letters, as well as a third-generation transcription of the Tagebuch of 1812–18.[9] The last is an extraordinary document containing Beethoven's intimate musings during a critical period of his life, along with his transcriptions of a wide variety of philosophical, literary, and theological texts that enrich our knowledge of his intellectual and religious strivings. Unfortunately, Beethoven's original manuscript has disappeared and scholars now rely upon a copy made directly from it by Anton Gräffer that is inaccurate in several details, owing mainly to the copyist's difficulty in deciphering Beethoven's handwriting.[10]

The present book is an attempt to provide an accurate account of Beethoven's life and works based on authentic documents and reminiscences and on the accumulated discoveries of Beethoven scholarship. But no new biography of Beethoven is needed that does not also try to come to grips with at least a few of the many unanswered questions concerning his personality and his creativity. I do not entertain the illusion that it is possible to explain all such questions, or even to give more than provisional answers to the major ones. But I believe that I have successfully resisted the temptation to fashion an uncontradictory and consistent portrait of Beethoven—to construct a safe, clear, well-ordered design, for such a portrait can be purchased only at the price of truth, by avoiding the obscurities that riddle the documentary material. I will recount the salient facts and describe the significant relationships of Beethoven's life in some detail, but I will pause at those junctures where we are suddenly confronted with opaque and seemingly inexplicable events and situations—where we discover delusions and even pathological actions. "There is a grain of truth concealed in every delusion," Freud observed: "There is something in it that really deserves belief."[11] At the least, every delusion deserves an attempt—however imperfect—at clarification. In this sense, my book is an essay in interpretation and meaning: I will try to discover the meaning of several of the ambiguities and delusions in Beethoven's life and to offer some indications of their possible significance for his creative quest.

It is my belief that neither a work of art nor a person's life can be fully understood through any single category of analysis. Accordingly I have utilized a rather wide variety of categories—aesthetic, historical, psychoanalytic, sociological—in a search for the manifold origins of Beethoven's personality and of his music. And I have tried to place Beethoven simultaneously within the contexts of social events, of his family constellation, of the history of ideas, and of the evolution of musical styles and forms. The reader will soon discover which of these categories and contexts I lean most heavily upon, but it should not be supposed that I regard any of these—or all of them taken together—as sufficient to exhaust the meaning of a series of creative events unique in the history of mankind.

NEW YORK

JULY 1977

(revised)

Introduction to the Revised Edition

WITHOUT, I HOPE, DISTURBING the essential character of the original edition, I have revised the text in many small details where necessary to bring it into line with my current understanding of Beethoven's biography and to correct infelicities of style. Substantial changes have been made in a few areas where I now have more information than was available to me in the 1970s. For example, my recent study of the documents bearing on Beethoven's family's earnings during the Bonn years has led me to a reappraisal of the economic situation in which he spent his childhood and adolescence. Similarly, from my readings of the nineteenth-century Austrian musical press I have discovered numerous performances of Beethoven's music that were previously unknown or neglected, and these have caused me to alter my picture of the fluctuations in his popularity and public reputation after 1815. I have also included in either the text or the footnotes brief discussions of several issues that have been raised by my colleagues or in my own later writings: about the existence of a compositional "moratorium" in Bonn in the later 1780s; the personal relationship between Beethoven and Haydn; the lingering advocacy of Josephine Deym-Stackelberg as Beethoven's Immortal Beloved; and the significance of his sister-in-law Johanna van Beethoven's conviction in 1811 for misappropriation of an expensive necklace. The reader will find that in the revision I have also benefited from suggestions offered by several of my generous reviewers and colleagues, notably Lewis Lockwood, Robert S. Winter, Michael Steinberg, Elliot Forbes, Barry Cooper, William Drabkin, Douglas Johnson, Harry Goldschmidt, and Frank Kermode.

The Selected Bibliography has been updated and expanded to include listings of many recent contributions to the Beethoven literature, and the indexes have been thoroughly redone. The footnotes have been revised to take account of recent editions of several major primary sources, such as the authoritative editions of Beethoven's correspondence and Conversation Books (*Konversationshefte*); Beethoven's Tagebuch (diary) of 1812–18; the Fischhof manuscript; and English translations of such standard biographical studies as Franz Wegeler and Ferdinand Ries's *Biographische Notizen über Ludwig van Beethoven* (*Biographical Notes on Ludwig van Beethoven*) and Gerhard von Breuning's *Aus dem Schwarzspanierhause* (*From the House of the Black-Robed Spaniards*). In all but a handful of instances I have adopted the numerous new datings and addressee attributions given in the Beethovenhaus collected edition of Beethoven's correspondence, meticulously edited by Sieghard Brandenburg. The footnotes now provide references both to the Beethovenhaus edition (*Briefe*) and to Anderson's standard English-language edition (*Letters*) of the letters, the latter in several instances supplemented by Theodore Albrecht's translation of letters from Beeethoven's correspondents (*Letters to Beethoven*). However, no such cross-references are given for documents such as legal instruments, petitions, receipts, contracts, and press announcements, which are to be included in the as-yet-unpublished volume 8 of *Briefe*.

Where appropriate, the datings of some of Beethoven's compositions have also been adjusted to reflect the latest researches into the autographs, sketches, contemporary manuscript copies, and published editions, as reflected in the writings of such scholars as Brandenburg, Barry Cooper, Kurt Dorfmüller, Douglas Johnson, William Kinderman, Seow-Chin Ong, Nicholas Marston, Michael C. Tusa, Alan Tyson, and Robert Winter. Without any attempt to be exhaustive, I have also called attention to several ongoing controversies over the precise chronology of the works.

My discussions of Beethoven's personality, inner conflicts, patronage affiliations, intellectual tenets, religious beliefs, and the dynamics of his family constellation have not been significantly altered. Similarly, I have not found it necessary to realign my views concerning such topics as Beethoven's deafness, his marriage project, the Immortal Beloved, the proposed move to Paris, the "return" to Bonn, or those involving the cluster of fantasies that center on issues of birth, lineage, and ancestry, such as his Family Romance, nobility pretense, and birth-year delusion. I remain convinced that there is something of value in my reperiodization of Beethoven's life and music; in my proposals of a connection between biographical crisis and musical creativity; in my articulation of Beethoven's ambivalence toward Haydn, Lichnowsky, and Bonaparte, among others; and in my speculations on the psychological sources of the guardianship of his nephew, Karl, the nature of the entanglement with his sister-in-law Johanna, his conflicts with his brothers, and his succession of surrogate siblings, beloved women, and paternal figures. With due allowance for alternative hypotheses, my views on all of these seem to me to be well grounded in the documentary record. As for my critical remarks on the music, in all but one or two instances I have resisted the very strong temptation to bring them into line with my present outlook or with the formulations of recent scholars and commentators.

There are several important topics that I have not attempted to deal with in any systematic way here, for to do so would require a more comprehensive presentation than is possible within the framework of this biography. I have written—or hope to write—about them in other contexts. Perhaps foremost among these subjects is Beethoven's turn toward a sui generis modernism in his last decades, a modernism that may be related to ideas, attitudes, projects, and imaginative tropes of emergent romanticism. Closely connected to this trend may be a necessary rethinking of the significance of the so-called "heroic style," which is said to characterize certain emblematic works of Beethoven's middle Vienna years. I now think it might be fruitful to consider the designation "Eroica" and its attendant rhetorical style elements as expressive in the first place of Beethoven's identification with the Classical norms of ancient Greek and Roman culture, perhaps along lines laid down in Schiller's aesthetic writings. It also seems to me that it may be time to take stock of the threads that connect Beethoven directly or indirectly to Freemasonry; there is now sufficient evidence to hypothesize that Beethoven remained influenced by Illuminist and esoteric trends in Freemasonry after his departure from Bonn, even though there is no indication that he actually belonged to a Masonic lodge. Finally, Beethoven's attraction to certain aspects of utopian thought has been the subject of several of my more recent papers, in which I also raise the related issue of the authoritarian implications of such utopian perspectives and ideals, including a pressure toward conformity and the suppression of individuality in the name of fraternity and altruism.

Another group of revisions arises from my reevaluation of several early documentary sources, in particular, materials by untrustworthy memoirists or biographers. Although Anton Schindler's extensive, deliberate forgeries in the Conversation Books became known in 1977, the extent of his unreliability in every other respect was not yet fully grasped.[1] Accordingly, in the first edition I relied upon his testimony in several instances: I have now combed this book in an attempt to eliminate interpretations based on "evidence" provided by Schindler, except where there may be supporting documentation or independent confirmation. In the meanwhile, the trustworthiness of other memoirs has also come into question: in a paper entitled "Beethoven's Creative Process: A Two-Part Invention," published in 1981, I tried to show that the Beethoven reminiscences of two other influential memoirists, Johann Friedrich Rochlitz and Louis Schlösser, were fabricated, or at least are so dubious that they, too, should be largely eliminated from consideration.[2] These materials have now been deleted or included with an appropriate caveat. One can, of course, carry a skepticism about contemporary documents too far. In 1993 the editors of the definitive edition of Beethoven's Conversation Books suggested that his letter to Karl Holz of August 30, 1826—the text of which is in Holz's handwriting above an authentic signature of Beethoven's—authorizing him to be the composer's official biographer, might have been fabricated by Holz in the 1840s to strengthen his hand against his archrival, Schindler. The editors regarded its authenticity as "rather improbable" because there are no references to the authorization in the Conversation Books of summer 1826 and because Holz may have "had available a blank sheet of paper on which Beethoven had written his signature."[3] The evidence, however, does not support their hypothesis: Holz's handwriting is consistent with his handwriting on other documents of the 1820s; the official stamped sheet of paper on which it was written is of a type available in 1826; and there is no reason to expect that every document would be the subject of conversations preserved in the Conversation Books.[4]

Still, it gives one pause to be so forcefully reminded of the fragility of the documentary foundation of biographical work, to know that today's apparent certainty may become tomorrow's apparent fallacy. And if historians must constantly be on their guard, readers also would do well to refrain from placing their entire trust in a scholar's hands, no matter how persuasively the evidence is presented. A biographer's understanding is always imperfect, in process, ongoing. If the job is done well, some of the potential meanings of a biographical issue may emerge, and pathways of interpretation may be illuminated. But mysteries and obscurities will always abound. I do not expect ever fully to understand why Beethoven, with his powerful, synthesizing mind, remained incapable of finding the product of any two numbers; what he meant when he wrote that he came "into the world with an obbligato accompaniment," presumably a caul;[5] why he set down the phrase "A weeping willow or acacia tree on my brother's grave" on the sketches for the first Razumovsky Quartet; what the actual causes of his deafness were, for which he offered so many conflicting explanations; what really happened during his visit to Mozart in 1787.

The enigmas of Beethoven's personality and creativity will always simultaneously thwart and encourage his biographers, who seek to wrest some fragment of meaning from the documentary materials. Nevertheless, even if what we do know about Beethoven remains partial, provisional, and contingent, that in itself may be a small step toward understanding.

NEW YORK
JANUARY 1998

Acknowledgments

GRATEFUL ACKNOWLEDGMENT AND THANKS to the following for their helpful assistance and for providing photocopies of manuscript and/or scarce materials: Columbia University libraries; New York Public Library; Library of Congress; Harvard University music library; Bibliothèque nationale, Paris; Stadtarchiv, Frankfurt; Goethe Museum (Freies Deutsches Hochstift), Frankfurt; Deutsche Staatsbibliothek, Berlin; Universitätsbibliothek, Münster; Universitätsbibliothek, Mainz; Beethovenhaus, Bonn; Mugar Memorial Library, Boston University. Thanks to George Marek for permitting me access to his photocopies of the Karlsbad guest lists and police registers for 1812 and of the *Prager Oberpostamts-Zeitung* for June–July 1812; to Ruth MacArdle for permitting the microfilming of the typescript of her late husband's monumental guide to the periodical literature, *Beethoven Abstracts,* some years before its publication; to my friend Harry Goldschmidt for a highly interesting correspondence concerning the Immortal Beloved, for guiding me to several sources that I would otherwise have overlooked, and (through his assistant Clemens Brenneis) for transcripts of hitherto unpublished sections of Beethoven's Conversation Books; to Joseph Schmidt-Görg and Hans Schmidt, formerly of the Beethovenhaus, for replying to several queries; to Josef Braunstein, Douglas Johnson, Christa Landon, Peter Riethus, William Drabkin, and Nathan Fishman for clarifying particular factual or bibliographical questions; to Achim von Brentano for kindly permitting reproduction of the 1798 miniature portrait of Antonie Brentano; to Martin Staehelin, present director of the Beethoven-Archiv, for generously providing newly acquired materials on Frau Brentano; to Ingrid Scheib of the Goethe House, New York, for her help in deciphering and translating the Brentano manuscript correspondence; to the many antiquarian booksellers who helped me to obtain rare materials on Beethoven, and especially to Samuel Orlinick of the Scientific Library Service (New York), Theodore Front (Los Angeles), H. Baron (London), and Walter Ricke (Munich); to Muriel Bennett for typing the manuscript; to Ken Stuart, editor of Schirmer Books, for his confidence in this project; and to Abbie Meyer, Eileen Fitzgerald DeWald, Valerie Klima, and Robert Cohen for their care in editing the typescript and seeing it through the press.

The chapter on Haydn was read by James Webster, who generously corrected a number of factual errors. The section on the Immortal Beloved was read in an earlier manuscript version by Elliot Forbes and Leon Plantinga; I have greatly benefited from their comments.

My profoundest gratitude goes to my friends Joseph Kerman, William S. Newman, Harry Slochower, and Alan Tyson—each of whom read the typed manuscript in its entirety—for their keen criticisms; their extensive corrections of fact, interpretation, and style; their insistence upon an unattainable standard of excellence; and also for their extremely lively hostilities, which confirmed my feeling (and my hope) that I had written a book that might spark some small controversies. But this does not sufficiently express my debt to each of these men. Harry Slochower set me on the path of biographical exploration and patiently provided me with the equipment to attempt the task. William S. Newman encouraged my Beethoven studies in their early stages and prompted me to deal with the nature and the causes of Beethoven's profound style shifts. Alan Tyson generously shared with me his inexhaustible store of knowledge about Beethoven. And Joseph Kerman's extremely detailed critique of the manuscript served as my indispensable guide to its final revision. Naturally, the errors of fact and extravagances of interpretation that the reader will doubtless encounter in the following pages are wholly my responsibility.

Several sections of this book appeared in different form in *The Musical Quarterly, Music Review, Music & Letters, Beethoven Studies, Telos,* and *American Imago.* I am grateful to the editors of these publications for their encouragement and for their permission to reprint these materials.

My wife, Eva, helped me to revise a number of the most problematical chapters of this book. Even more crucially, she provided a sane sounding board for my speculations on Beethoven over these past twelve years.

For the Revised Edition, additional grateful acknowledgements to my valued colleague and correspondent Sieghard Brandenburg of the Beethoven-Archiv, Bonn; Lothar Bangert, Historisches Archiv des

Erzbistums Küln; Grita Herre of the Staatsbibliothek zu Berlin, Preussischer Kulturbesitz, Musikabteilung; Deirdre Donohue of the Costume Institute at the Metropolitan Museum of Art, New York; Mary Sue Morrow of Loyola University; Mr. Theo Molberg; Otto Biba of the Gesellschaft der Musikfreunde; J. Joester of the Nordrhein-Westfälisches Hauptstaatsarchiv; Doris Schneider-Wagenbichler and the very helpful staff of the Österreichische National-Bibliothek; the Universität-Bibliothek of Karl-Franzens-Universität, Graz; Stadtarchiv und Stadthistorische Bibliothek of the Bundesstadt, Bonn; and to the music librarians of the New York Public Library, Harvard University, Yale University, Columbia University, and the Library of Congress. Also to the *Journal of the American Musicological Society* for permission to reprint passages from my "Economic Circumstances of the Beethoven Household in Bonn." Credits and/or locations of illustrations are given in the individual captions.

Thanks also to Schirmer Books editor Richard Carlin and production supervisor Jane Andrassi for gracefully shepherding the book into print; to Louise Fili for the cover design; to Lisa Chovnik and Kevin Hanek for the interior design; and to copy editor Katherine Scott, for her thoughtful efforts to improve the revised manuscript in matters both stylistic and substantive.

I
BONN

Kapellmeister Ludwig van Beethoven. Portrait in oils by Radoux.

Private collection.

CHAPTER ONE

FAMILY BACKGROUND

L UDWIG VAN BEETHOVEN WAS BORN INTO A FAMILY of court musicians at the electorate of Cologne, one of the ecclesiastical principalities of the Holy Roman Empire, whose court was situated in Bonn. His grandfather, whose name he bore, was bass singer and kapellmeister at the electoral court; his father, Johann, was a court tenor and music teacher of moderate talent. Johann married the widowed Maria Magdalena Leym (née Keverich) on November 12, 1767. Their first child, Ludwig Maria, baptized on April 2, 1769, lived for six days. Their second son, Ludwig, was baptized on December 17, 1770.

One would expect that so straightforward a sequence of events could generate no biographical difficulties. Yet this tiny nucleus of incontrovertible, documented facts gave rise to a complex series of misconceptions that shaped many of Beethoven's emotional attitudes and actions throughout his life.

The first misconception concerned the year of Beethoven's birth, and on this point he was so inaccessible to reason that it may well be more accurate to say that he was in the grip of delusion. For most of his life, Beethoven believed that he had been born in December 1772 rather than December 1770. (In his Heiligenstadt Testament, an impassioned document written in October 1802, he implied that he was three to five years younger than his actual age.)[1] His friends Ferdinand Ries, Franz Gerhard Wegeler, and Wilhelm Christian Müller provided him with three separate copies of his baptismal certificate, but in each case he refused to accept the document's validity. In some obscure way, Beethoven convinced himself that the baptismal certificates were those of his older brother, Ludwig Maria. He warned his childhood friend Wegeler to be on the alert for this possibility when he wrote him on May 2, 1810, asking that he obtain a "correct" certificate of baptism:

But one thing must be borne in mind, namely that there was a brother *born before me*, who was also named Ludwig with the addition *Maria*, but who died. To fix my age beyond doubt, this brother must first be found, inasmuch as I already know that in this respect a mistake has been made by others, and I have been said to be older than I am. Unfortunately I myself lived for a time without knowing my age. . . . I urge you to attend to this matter, to find Ludwig Maria and the present Ludwig, who was born after him.[2]

When the certificate arrived, duly signed by the "mayor's office of Bonn," giving December 17, 1770, as the baptismal date, Beethoven still would not accept it as valid. He wrote on the back of it: "1772. The baptismal certificate seems to be incorrect, since there was a Ludwig born before me."[3]

How is this to be explained? It was long believed that Beethoven merely adopted as his own a misconception about his age that had been current during his years in Bonn. Some biographers blamed Beethoven's father for the two-year discrepancy, claiming that he may purposely have falsified the boy's age in order to promote his possibilities as a wunderkind along the lines of the Mozart children. Others gave Johann the benefit of the doubt, stressing the widespread laxity at that time in keeping family records. A hard look at the evidence, however, shows that Johann van Beethoven never deducted two years from his son's age, that at no time prior to 1790 was Beethoven's age understated by two years; rather there was a consistent pattern of deducting one year from his age during his first two decades.[4] Apparently Beethoven and his associates (and perhaps his parents as well) all then believed that he had been born in December 1771. Therefore, Beethoven's persistent belief that he was born in December 1772 (or later) originated in his own mind. In view of the unmistakable ways by which he could have tested and confirmed the accuracy of the baptismal certificates, it seems clear that he was unwilling or unable to subject the issue of his birth year to rational consideration. The birth-year delusion was Beethoven's own. Its possible meaning and ramifications will become clearer only after we have learned more about his life and personality.

A related matter of even greater emotional significance is Beethoven's uncertainty about the facts of his parentage itself. Reports that Beethoven was the illegitimate son of a king of Prussia—variously Friedrich Wilhelm II (1744–97) and his uncle, Frederick the Great (1712–86)—first appeared in print in 1810 and were repeated in encyclopedias, music dictionaries, and music periodicals throughout the remainder of his lifetime. At precisely what date Beethoven became aware of these reports is not known; probably they came to his attention almost immediately. Beginning in 1819, his friends and his nephew, Karl, urged him to deny the reports. The Conversation Books repeatedly contain such entreaties as "Such things must be corrected, because you do not need to borrow glory from the king—rather the reverse is the case," or "It is written that you are a bastard of Frederick the Great. . . . We must insert a notice in the *Allgemeine Zeitung*."[5] But the composer would not be moved to action, nor did he authorize or even permit any of his friends to refute the story of his royal ancestry, which had by this time gained wide currency in France, England, and Italy as well as in Germany and Austria. Wegeler, in a letter of December 28, 1825, sounded a note of anger and disappointment with Beethoven for having permitted the story to flourish for so long without contradiction: "Why do you not avenge the honor of your mother when, in the *Konversations-Lexikon* and in France, it is given that you are a love-child? . . . Only your natural reluctance to occupy yourself with anything other than music is the cause of this culpable indifference. If you wish, I will let the world know the truth about this. This is the least point on which you should respond to me."[6]

That neither the accusation of "culpable indifference" nor his old friend's challenge to avenge his mother's honor called forth an immediate response is in itself remarkable. It was almost a full year later, and only after the onset of the illness that was to result in his death, that Beethoven belatedly replied to Wegeler, in a letter of December 7, 1826: "You say that I have been mentioned somewhere as being the natural son of the late king of Prussia. Well, the same thing was said to me a long time ago. But I have adopted the principle of neither writing anything about myself nor replying to anything that has been written about me. Hence I gladly leave it to you to make known to the world the integrity of my parents, and especially of my mother."[7] Yet, having written the

letter, he neglected to have it posted. Evidently he still had a great reluctance to refute the rumor. When Wegeler again wrote to him reproach-
fully, Beethoven replied on February 17, 1827: "But indeed I was
surprised to read in your last letter that you had not yet received anything. From the letter which you are now receiving you will see that
I wrote to you as long ago as December 10th of last year. . . . [It was] left
lying about until today."[8]

Here, as in Beethoven's delusion about his birth year, we are confronted with a difficult question: What were the forces and events in
Beethoven's life that caused him thus to deny his father and to dishonor
his mother's memory? And here, too, an interpretation of this extraordinary matter can be attempted only after we have laid a foundation of
fact concerning Beethoven's earliest experiences in Bonn.

Kapellmeister Ludwig van Beethoven strongly opposed the marriage of
his son, Johann, to Maria Magdalena Keverich Leym in 1767. He
claimed to have made inquiries and discovered that she had been a
chambermaid. His reproaches were sufficiently loud to reach the ears of
his landlord's family, the Fischers, who lived downstairs: "I never
believed or expected that you would so degrade yourself," they reported
that he said to Johann.[9] Such was the first confrontation involving the
three main characters in the early life of Ludwig van Beethoven: his
grandfather, his father, and his mother.

Maria Magdalena Keverich was born on December 19, 1746, the
daughter of Heinrich Keverich, chief overseer of the kitchen at the
palace of the elector of Trier at Ehrenbreitstein. At sixteen she married
Johann Leym (born August 9, 1733; he was a valet of the elector of
Trier), bore him a son who died an infant, and was widowed in 1765,
before she was nineteen. Johann van Beethoven brought his intended
bride home to Bonn from Ehrenbreitstein, and they were married on
November 12, 1767, despite the elder Ludwig's opposition. "Madame
van Beethoven later said," Gottfried Fischer tells us, "that her family
would have given her a good wedding celebration, but her father-in-
law stubbornly refused to be present unless the thing were quickly
over with."[10]

The kapellmeister was mistaken in his claim that Maria
Magdalena had been a housemaid. Actually, her family included a

number of wealthy merchants, court councillors, and senators. Hence, as Schiedermair remarks, it was not Johann van Beethoven but rather Maria Magdalena Keverich Leym "who contracted a marriage beneath her station."[11] Why, then, did the elder Beethoven oppose the marriage? Perhaps because it threatened to disturb the carefully ordered, precise, and comfortable existence that he had led for many years with his son in the second-story apartment at Rheingasse 934, a building owned by Theodor Fischer, the most recent in a family line of master bakers. The memoirs of Fischer's children described the apartment: "Everything was so beautiful and proper and well arranged, with valuables, all six rooms were provided with beautiful furniture, many paintings and cupboards, a cupboard of silver service, a cupboard with fine gilded porcelain and glass, an assortment of the most beautiful linens which could be drawn through a ring; everything from the smallest article sparkled like silver."[12] A household so meticulously maintained reflected the equally well-ordered life of its strong-willed owner, who was used to his own ways and had no desire to be separated from his only son.

Ludwig van Beethoven the elder, Beethoven's grandfather, had been baptized on January 5, 1712, at Malines (Mechlin) in Belgium, the third son of Michael and Mary. At the age of five he became a student at the choir school of the church of St. Rombaut, where he remained until 1725. In that year he began to receive instruction on the organ and in the art of accompanying and realizing figured bass at the keyboard; soon he was playing at services in various churches. In 1731 he was appointed choir director at the church of St. Pierre at Louvain, and by 1732 he was singing bass at the Cathedral of St. Lambert in Liège. In March of the following year—perhaps at the request of Elector Clemens August, archbishop of Cologne, who is thought to have met him in Liège—he made his way to Cologne and thence to Bonn, where he was to spend the rest of his life, first as bass soloist and singer in the choir (a post he retained until his last year of life) and in addition, from 1761 until his death, as court kapellmeister in charge of music at the chapel, the concert hall, the theater, and the court ballroom. He died on December 24, 1773, following a stroke early in the year.

His starting salary was 200 thalers per annum, which was increased by an additional 100 thalers on August 22, 1746; when he was appointed court kapellmeister in a decree dated July 16, 1761, the total was raised to almost 400 thalers, a very substantial sum. Moreover, in addition to his court duties, he had sufficient cash and time to establish a profitable wine business, evidently started soon after he arrived in Bonn. As early as 1738 he took a six-year lease on two apartments, a cellar, and part of a storehouse in a building in the Wenzelgasse.[13] He and his family lived in one of the apartments and rented out the other, reserving the cellar and storehouse for commercial use. In later years, he also had enough spare capital that he was able to lend out considerable amounts of money. Contemporary documents, dated between 1769 and 1773, refer to three loans totaling some 500 thalers, equivalent to the kapellmeister's salary for more than a year.

The kapellmeister's commercial activities were quite in the family tradition. His father, Michael (1684–1749), had been indentured as a baker's apprentice in 1700 and became a master baker in 1707; he later prospered in real estate and, after 1720, as a dealer in laces, paintings, and furniture. By 1739 his fortunes had suffered a reversal and rumors of bankruptcy spread, causing him to begin selling off his estate. By 1741 he was indeed bankrupt, with unpaid judgments of approximately 10,000 florins (an amount equivalent to a small fortune today) against him. He and his wife accordingly joined their sons, Ludwig and Cornelius, in Bonn, where, beyond the jurisdiction of the Flemish courts, they lived peacefully until their deaths in 1749. Cornelius (1708–64), who arrived in Bonn circa 1731–32, was a chandler by trade and became purveyor of candles to the electoral court. He married a widow of the Bonn bourgeoisie in 1734, and from 1736 onward his name appeared on the list of the burghers of Bonn. After the death of his first wife in 1755, Cornelius married a relative of hers, Anna Barbara Marx, under a special papal dispensation overriding the proscription on marriages within the restricted bounds of consanguinity.[14]

On September 7 or 17, 1733, Ludwig married Maria Josepha Poll (or Pols; nothing is known of her background; she was born ca. 1714), and they had three children, of whom only Johann, born in 1739 or 1740, survived (no record of his baptism has ever been found).[15] Maria Josepha reportedly was an alcoholic, and her condition became such that she was placed in a cloister, where she remained until her death on

September 30, 1775. The date of her removal to the cloister is not known.[16] The Fischer memoirs describe her husband at the wedding of Theodor Fischer, on June 24, 1761: "During the ceremony, tears streamed from his eyes, and when asked about it, he answered that he was thinking about his own marriage and wedding ceremony."[17] Presumably he was thinking also of his marital tragedy, and so his wife may have been absent as early as 1761. The testimony as to her alcoholism comes from the Fischer children, Gottfried and Cäcilia, who would have learned of it from their parents. There is nothing to indicate that any member of the Beethoven family visited her at the cloister. In later years the composer never mentioned his grandmother's existence, although her death took place when he was almost five years old. There is no indication that the elder Beethoven entered into a relationship with another woman after his wife's removal; according to the little that is known, he remained alone in the Fischer house with his son. His subsequent resistance to his son's marriage may have been in part an unwillingness to reintroduce a discordant female element into his totally self-sufficient bachelor existence.

Within Maria Magdalena Leym's family, the attitude toward the marriage seems to have been equally unenthusiastic; the wedding was held in Bonn rather than in the bride's hometown, perhaps because of family opposition. Maria Magdalena's father (born January 14, 1702) had died on August 3, 1759, when she was only twelve years old. Her mother, born on November 8, 1707, was married on August 14, 1731, and had six children, of whom four seem to have died in infancy. After the death of Herr Keverich in 1759 the mother became the family breadwinner, working as a cook at the court. Toward the year 1768 Frau Keverich suffered a psychological breakdown, to which her daughter's second marriage may have contributed. A petition on her behalf to the elector of Trier, dated March 26, 1768, reports that "through an ill-turned marriage of her only daughter up to 300 Thalers disappeared," and although one scholar generously takes this to mean that she had given her daughter a substantial dowry, other observers conclude that Johann van Beethoven relieved his mother-in-law of almost all her savings.[18] Because of her poverty, and because she was allegedly "feeble-minded," a guardian was appointed. The petition continues: "She has imposed upon herself a life of such severe and unusual penitence that it is hard to understand how she can survive, living as she does in this unnatural manner, taking little food, and that of the worst quality, and sometimes lying almost the whole night through in the bitterest cold, wind, and rain, outside the churches in the open air."[19] Indeed, she did not survive for very long: she died in September of the same year.

Maria Magdalena's reaction to her mother's death and the contributing role her own marriage may have played in it is not known, but we may reasonably surmise that this was one of the first links in the "chain of sorrows" that she described to Cäcilia Fischer, one of the Fischer children, as constituting her married state. In a discussion concerning a suitor of Cäcilia's, Frau van Beethoven remarked to the young woman: "If you want to take my good advice, remain single, and then you will have the most tranquil, most beautiful, most pleasurable life. For what is marriage? A little joy, but then a chain of sorrows. And you are still young." Frau van Beethoven often elaborated on this theme, remarking "how thoughtlessly so many young people get married without knowing what [sorrows] await them." She knew of few happy marriages and of fewer happy women: "One should weep when a girl is brought into the world," she said.[20]

Her first son by Johann, named Ludwig Maria, was baptized on April 2, 1769, and died after six days. The next child, Ludwig, was baptized on December 17, 1770, and therefore was probably born on December 15 or 16. She had five more children, of whom two, Caspar Anton Carl, baptized on April 8, 1774, and Nikolaus Johann, baptized on October 2, 1776, survived. Anna Maria Franziska, baptized on February 23, 1779, lived only a few days; Franz Georg, baptized on January 17, 1781, survived until August 16, 1783; and Maria Margaretha Josepha, baptized on May 5, 1786, died on November 26, 1787, at the age of a year and a half.

We have, then, a sketch of the beginnings of an inauspicious marriage, one that had been opposed by the parents, that was to be marked by precarious economic circumstances, conflict, and tragedy throughout its relatively brief span, and that was apparently regretted by the wife soon after the ceremony. Maria Magdalena's disappointment at her marriage cannot be ascribed simply to the deaths of her mother and her first child, nor to poverty. Three of her first four children survived and in the early years of the marriage her family was under the protection of the elder Ludwig, who was earning a high salary from his post as kapellmeister supplemented by income from other enterprises, and who turned out to be not at all averse to helping his son's family. Clearly, the marriage did not fulfill the threat that he had anticipated. His orderly existence continued as before; his daughter-in-law recognized his authority as the patriarchal head of her family; his relationship to his son underwent no profound change; and he gained a grandson as well, who bore his name.

Nor was Maria Magdalena's husband incapable of providing for his new family. Contrary to widespread assertions in the earlier biographical literature, Beethoven did not spend his entire childhood and youth in highly straitened circumstances, let alone in what A. W. Thayer and other biographers called "great poverty."[21] Johann van Beethoven's typically modest annual salary of 100 thalers as court tenor was increased in 1769 by a token 25 florins, but he received a further 50 florins more under a decree of April 3, 1772, and in January 1774 he was granted 60 thalers per annum for the maintenance of his mother, a sum that was transferred to him as a permanent addition to his salary following her death the following year. Thus, by 1774, Johann's income from the court was fixed at 210 thalers, which at the prevailing rate of exchange was equivalent to 315 florins. This salary was in line with salaries paid to other court musicians.[22] Later, after June 1784, when Beethoven began to receive a salary for his services in the court orchestra, the family's income from the court reached 450 florins (300 thalers)—in those days a not insignificant salary in a German principality, more than double the salary of the most poorly paid musicians and exceeded only by the salaries of the kapellmeister and the kapelldirektor.

Johann also earned something as a music teacher, for he was regarded, at least throughout the 1770s, as a competent musician. There is no reason not to accept Gottfried Fischer's statement that during these years Johann "performed his duties punctually; he gave clavier and voice lessons to the sons and daughters of the English, French, and Imperial embassies, to the gentlemen and young ladies of the local nobility, as well as to those of esteemed burghers; he often had more to do than he could do."[23] He was said to be so well liked by his students that he received many favors and presents from their families. (Among the gifts were supplies of good wines; Beethoven scholar Theodor Frimmel wryly comments that even at this early time, "one must notice that the talk is already about wine.")[24] He was also frequently called on to prepare young musicians for service in the chapel.

Thus, the young court musician earned amounts normally sufficient to support a family in a modest way. Furthermore, with the death of his father on December 24, 1773, when Beethoven was just three years old, Johann became the sole heir to a sizable estate consisting of a substantial legacy in cash, household possessions, accounts receivable, and outstanding loans, cash advances, and mortgages. He pursued the collection of debts owed to his father, several of which were for significant amounts and one of which—a loan to one Johannes Curth—was for the large sum of 1,000 florins, an amount sufficient for a Bonn family to live on for more than two years.[25] The kapellmeister's bequest lifted his son out of the category of a hard-pressed court employee. It was not, therefore, as a family provider that Johann failed, at least in the early years.

Changes in the Beethoven family's lodgings over the years help to chart some of the fluctuations in their fortunes.[26] Soon after marrying, in 1767, Johann and Maria Magdalena found lodgings appropriate for a young couple of modest income setting up its first residence and moved to the simple garden house behind Bonngasse 515 (now no. 20) where Beethoven was born. Six years later, however, upon inheriting the kapellmeister's property, the growing family swapped those cramped quarters for superior lodgings in the Dreieckplatz. By 1775 or the fall of 1776 at the latest they returned to the Fischer house in the Rheingasse, near the banks of the Rhine, where Beethoven's grandfather and father had lived from 1760 to the end of 1767. There they remained for nine years or thereabouts, with two brief interruptions, one in 1776–77, when they stayed at lodgings in the Neugasse, and a second in February 1784, when the Rhine overflowed, flooding many sections of Bonn, and the Beethovens briefly lived at Stockenstrasse 9 until the waters receded.[27] The lodgings in the Fischer house, although reportedly in a plainer section of Bonn, were both comfortable and spacious. The Beethoven family occupied six rooms—two large ones facing the street and four facing the courtyard—plus a maid's room."[28] The Neugasse apartment was smaller and had a less congenial view, but was centrally located; supposedly it was taken because Frau von Beethoven wanted lodgings closer to the court, the church, and the market.[29] Probably in early 1785 they rented their last apartment, in an attractive house at a desirable location at Wenzelgasse 462, and it was there that a housekeeper was engaged to attend the family after the death of Frau van Beethoven.[30]

Johann van Beethoven had received an elementary education and had been placed in a preparatory class of the College of Jesuits in Bonn, where he failed to make any progress. At twelve he had entered the court chapel as a soprano. His father had taught him to sing and to play the clavier, and he learned to play the violin capably as well. After his voice changed, he was, by a decree of 1756, accepted into the electoral choir, in which he remained until his last years, when his "stale voice" and notoriously drunken behavior compelled his retirement. He had faithfully followed the pattern that his father had set out for him; and he had remained under his father's wing—both at home and in the choir—evidently without demur, until, in what must have been a major act of defiance for so amiable and submissive a young man, he decided upon marriage in 1767.

Actually, he had spoken of marriage for many years prior to that time. He and Theodor Fischer, the landlord's son, were close friends, played the zither and sang songs together, and decided in approximately 1760 that the time had finally come for them to start families—to "ship out onto the sea of love."[31] Theodor Fischer was married in 1761, but "Johann der Läufer" ("Johann the sprinter"), as his father derisively called him, was off to a slow start; it would be another six years before he summoned sufficient courage. When the time finally came, he found a bride in a distant city and brought the news of his betrothal to his father as a *fait accompli:* "When Johann van Beethoven presented his loved one to his father in person," relate the Fischers, "he said that this is what I wish, and he stood fast and declared that he would not be swayed from his determination that she would be his bride."[32]

Thayer believed that Johann's alcoholism was probably inherited from his mother, and Gottfried Fischer naively attributed it to the wine trade that the kapellmeister maintained. Biographers have had their theories: Prod'homme hazards that the court tenor began to drift "little by little" into drunkenness as the family's "resources diminished, after the death of his father."[33] Schiedermair assumes that the alcoholic haze in which Johann spent his final years was somehow intensified by the death of Maria Magdalena.

The etiology of alcoholism, however, has deeper roots than these. As the British psychoanalyst Edward Glover has observed: "All the primary features of alcoholism represent fundamentally the individual's attempt to extricate himself from an impasse."[34] An alcoholic may find in drink a temporary surcease from an unhappy life situation or an unbearable psychological conflict. We may speculate that the impasse from which Johann could not extricate himself was the conflict concerning his relationship to his father, a domineering personality who brooked no opposition from either his family or his musicians. Where Ludwig could not control by persuasion he did not hesitate to seek to compel; unable to enforce obedience by his musicians on one occasion, he petitioned the elector, who thereupon commanded the unruly court musicians "to obey all the commands given by our Kapellmeister" upon threat of dismissal.[35] Johann's domination by his father is readily evident: the elder Ludwig had chosen his son's profession, taught him music, introduced him to the court chapel, obtained his appointment as court singer, and functioned simultaneously as his employer, protector, and sole parent. The absence of Johann's mother both necessitated and intensified this protective role and perhaps contributed to resentments on both sides. The Fischer memoirs portray a father who was convinced that his son would never amount to anything and broadcast this conviction in contemptuous tones. The elder Ludwig's opposition to his son's marriage apparently reflected his belief that Johann—who was by then twenty-seven or twenty-eight—was incapable of becoming a husband and a father, let alone of choosing a suitable bride. Johann's marriage, then, seems to have represented a rare moment of rebellion against a demeaning relationship.

But Johann was not to find in marriage release from the powerful influence of his father. Although the kapellmeister moved out, it was only down the street, a little way from his son's lodgings at 515 Bonngasse, and he remained a dominant force within Johann's new household. Johann had found his own woman, had started a family, and was carrying out his duties and obligations—he was doing the best he could. But it was still not enough. Nothing had changed, really. To his father he remained "Johann der Läufer," the Johann van Beethoven who "had a flighty spirit," who, when his father was called away from home, would take advantage of his absence to leave Bonn, traveling to Cologne, Deutz, Andernach, Coblenz, Ehrenbreitstein, "and who knows where else." "Keep running, keep running," said his father, sarcastically. "You will some day run to your final destination."[36]

The death of his father brought to the surface signs of Johann's competitive and even hostile feelings. (Surely it was no desperate need

for money that caused him to pawn his departed father's portrait.) The
mediocrity of his own career should have made Johann aware of the gulf
that separated his capabilities from those of his father, but his only
recorded reaction to the elder Ludwig's death shows that he thought
otherwise. Within two weeks of his father's death, in early January
1774, he petitioned the elector for a salary increase, writing:

> Will your Electoral Grace be pleased to hear that my father has
> passed away from this world, to whom it was granted to serve His
> Electoral Grace Clemens August and Your Electoral Grace and glo-
> riously reigning Lord . . . 42 years, as Kapellmeister with great honor,
> whose position I have been found capable of filling, but nevertheless
> I would not venture to offer my capacity to Your Electoral Grace.[37]

The thought that he could become kapellmeister was doubtless only the
most grandiose of Johann's notions, but it was an enduring one that he
would try to convert into reality a decade later. In general, however, he
lacked the energy to pursue his fantasies. The Fischers remembered
him often lounging next to the window, staring out at the rain or making faces at his drinking companion, the fish dealer Klein, who was similarly wont to recline in the window across the street. He spent an
increasing amount of time away from home, as well as many nights in
the taverns or wandering through the town with his friends, arriving
home in the middle of the night or early in the morning—a sure way of
avoiding his family and conjugal responsibilities and leaving the leadership of the family to his wife. When the Rhine flooded in 1784, it was
not Johann but his wife who showed heroism and bravery, calming the
residents with encouraging words and waiting until others had been
evacuated to make her escape into the Giergasse across the roofs and
down improvised ladders.

In later years, Johann came to be regarded as a person of uncertain
reputation. An official report to Archduke Maximilian Franz, immediately after he reached Bonn in the summer of 1784 as successor to the
deceased elector Maximilian Friedrich, reflected the general opinion:
"Johann Beethoven has a very stale voice, has been long in the service,
very poor, of fair deportment and married."[38] Until 1784, he had been
tolerated because of the protection first of his father and then of the
powerful electoral minister Count Kaspar Anton von Belderbusch. (We

may assume that Belderbusch's protection was a transference from a friendly and long-standing relationship with the court kapellmeister, who was a fellow Fleming.) The count served as godfather to Johann's third son and was a frequent visitor to the Beethoven lodgings, one of the few members of the titled nobility so recorded. Johann became so closely identified as a protégé of Belderbusch's that he earned the ill will of the minister's many enemies. An anonymous contemporary document prepared by opponents of Belderbusch includes Johann van Beethoven on a list of "good sleuthhounds and spies who may be hired for a cheap price,"[39] suggesting that Johann may have been regarded as an agent or informer for Belderbusch.

The death of the minister in 1784, a few months after the passing of Elector Maximilian Friedrich, left Johann van Beethoven without a protector or friends of influence at the court. To compound his difficulties, in late 1785 or early 1786 he attempted to defraud the heirs of Belderbusch through a false claim on their estate.[40] He claimed, in a petition to the elector, that he had given many valuable gifts to the count and to his mistress, the abbess of Vilich, in return for an alleged promise that he would be appointed kapellmeister. He demanded that the Belderbusch heirs return the gifts, which were detailed in Johann van Beethoven's petition under a forged signature. He claimed that it had been suggested to him that "his late father's inheritance could perform faithful service and release him from his poverty." Thereby, the document alleged, his father's inheritance had melted away—"the largest part of his wealth sacrificed to the man upon whom he at that time depended"—with disastrous consequences for his wife and children. Though no legal action was taken against him when the scheme collapsed, his status in the court and in Bonn reached its nadir, perhaps hastening the downward-spiraling course of his dissolution. A report on a petition by young Ludwig van Beethoven of February 15, 1784, requesting that he receive a formal appointment as assistant court organist with increased remuneration bluntly states that his father was no longer able to support his family. Thereafter, Johann was tolerated on the electoral rolls as an act of charity, and he became something of a comic figure. On January 1, 1793, the elector wrote to Court Marshal von Schall that "the revenues from the liquor excise have suffered a loss" by the recent death of Johann van Beethoven.[41]

At home, Maria Magdalena complained about her husband's drinking debts and often lamented being left alone so often in the house. But it seems clear that both she and Johann were content to have her run the family's affairs. This is implied in an episode reported from their early married life:

> When he received his monthly salary or money from his pupils, he would play a joke upon returning home: he would throw the money in his wife's lap and say: "Now woman, manage with that." Then she would give him a flask of wine, saying: "One cannot let men return home with *empty* hands." . . . He said: "Yes, *empty* hands!" She responded: "Yes, *so empty,* but I know that you prefer a full glass to an empty one." "Yes, yes, the woman is right, she is always right."[42]

Essentially nothing changed in later years. Johann would walk conspicuously through the neighborhood drinking wine from a flask. Once Frau van Beethoven called to him from the window and he responded: "It is such hot weather that I have a great thirst." She said, "That's true, but you often have a thirst without a summer heat," to which he replied amiably, "You are right, I agree with you. I thank you, it will soon be time to eat; don't worry, I will come right away."[43] When he was in his cups, he was prone to lose his sense of propriety. Jokingly, he addressed young Cäcilia as "our patroness of music" and asked her for a kiss. She objected, telling him, "I am not a kissing girl, you already have a wife, go kiss her, not me," to which he responded, "You are a clever witch and you know well how to reply." When, some years after this, he again made advances to her, "She pushed him away, he hit the oven and knocked it over, pulling the stove and stovepipe from the wall." Everyone supposedly took the episode in good fun, Johann saying, "That taught me a good lesson," and his wife praising Cäcilia Fischer: "That was the right thing to do; that's how it should turn out."[44]

Such embarrassed attempts at levity aside, it might not be unfair to conclude from these and similar reports that Maria Magdalena assumed the role of the pained, suffering, righteous wife of a ne'er-do-well drunkard and played it in high tragic style until she herself succumbed to a lingering illness. Surely that is not the whole story, but the surviving documents do not encourage an image of a hopeful and confident marital partnership. Cäcilia Fischer could not remember ever having seen Frau van Beethoven laugh ("She was always serious"), and the widow Karth described her as "a quiet, suffering woman."[45] She was said to be "a clever woman [who] could give converse and reply aptly, politely, and modestly to high and low, and for this reason she was much liked and respected."[46] Apparently she was not withdrawn, for it was reported that she became "hot-tempered and argumentative" on occasion, and Gottfried Fischer observed that "she knew how to give and take in a manner that is becoming to all people of honest thoughts."[47] Cäcilia also recalled that Beethoven's mother would often speak about her travels and about the "dangers she had undergone,"[48] which, taken together with her warnings about marriage, may indicate a fearful and imaginative disposition, perhaps one quite similar to that which Beethoven evinced in his Heiligenstadt Testament, his letter to the Immortal Beloved, and elsewhere in his correspondence and diaries. We may safely assume that, directly or by implication, Maria Magdalena imparted to her children, and particularly to her oldest son, many of the same thoughts she passed on to Cäcilia Fischer. Indeed, the Fischers assert that Beethoven was present when his mother warned Cäcilia against marriage, which, if true, may explain why we find an almost literal echo of those feelings in a report by Fanny Giannattasio of Beethoven's opinions in 1817 on the same subject.[49]

On Maria Magdalena's birthday the family momentarily set aside its troubles and conflicts. The scene is described by Cäcilia Fischer:

> Each year, the feast of St. Mary Magdalene (her birthday and name day) was kept with due solemnity. The music stands were brought from the *Tucksaal* and placed in the two sitting rooms overlooking the street, and a canopy, embellished with flowers, leaves, and laurel, was put up in the room containing Grandfather Ludwig's portrait. On the eve of the day, Madame van Beethoven was induced to retire betimes. By ten o'clock all was in readiness. The silence was broken by the tuning up of instruments; Madame van Beethoven was awakened [and] requested to dress, and was then led to a beautifully draped chair beneath the canopy. An outburst of music roused the neighbors, the most drowsy soon catching the infectious gaiety. When the music was

over the table was spread and, after food and drink, the merry company fell to dancing (but in stockinged feet to lessen the noise), and so
the festivities came to an end.[50]

No equivalent respect or honor was shown the father of the family, for it
was his role to play the amiable and ineffectual Dionysian, heir to the
weaknesses of the flesh, as a foil for Maria Magdalena's suffering transcendence of life's tribulations.

Title page, "An einen Säugling," WoO 108 (1783).

First edition, Neue Blumenlese für Klavierliebhaber *(1784).*

CHAPTER TWO

CHILDHOOD

HERE IS AMPLE EVIDENCE of the crucial effect upon Beethoven's
early life of the stresses and conflicts within his family constellation. In a home in which the son's natural role model, the
father, had been toppled from his pedestal, the monumentalization of
the grandfather took on heroic proportions, and this deeply affected
Johann's attitude toward his oldest son, with, in turn, rich implications
for the latter's course of development.

Beethoven's admiration for his grandfather bordered on hero worship; his desire to emulate the kapellmeister remained with him
throughout his life. In 1801 he wrote from Vienna to his friend Wegeler
in Bonn, asking him to forward "by the mail coach as soon as possible"[1]
one object—the portrait of his grandfather, painted by Radoux—which
he treasured until his death.[2] Wegeler is, perhaps, the best witness to the
earliest manifestations of this reverence: "Little Ludwig clung with the
greatest ardor to the grandfather, who, we are told, was at the same time
his godfather; despite his tender age when he lost him, he vividly retained
the early impressions. He spoke readily about his grandfather to his
childhood friends, and his pious and sweet mother—whom he loved
more than his harsh father—had to tell him much about his grandfather."[3] In 1816 Fanny Giannattasio wrote in her diary that Beethoven
often spoke of his grandfather in glowing terms, describing "what a true
and honorable man he had been."[4] We have to make some allowances for
exaggeration in these anecdotes, for the kapellmeister was "incapacitated"
by a stroke early in 1773, when his grandson was just turned two years
old.[5] Whatever his actual memories may have been, Beethoven's psychological identification with the old man was so powerful that on August 1,
1824, he wrote his attorney, Johann Baptist Bach: "I think that I might
have a stroke some day, like my worthy grandfather, whom I take after."[6]

It was only natural that Beethoven should strive to emulate the kapellmeister, who had been the most powerful force in Bonn's musical life. (Beethoven himself retained a lifelong aspiration to become a kapellmeister.) It is worth noting, however, that a strong psychological identification with a grandfather may well go hand in hand with a repudiation of the father; a boy may try to come to terms with an unsatisfactory image of his father by idealizing a male grandparent. In Beethoven's case, as we have seen, the kapellmeister's death failed to restore Johann to a position of eminence in the household; on the contrary, recollections of the grandfather's talent, position, and power, contrasted painfully with the father's hapless mediocrity. Moreover, Johann's resentments against the kapellmeister, already deeply rooted, were intensified by what may have appeared to him as his wife's attempt to mold Beethoven in the grandfather's image, an attempt that Johann was bound to resist.

The issue was joined when Beethoven reached the age at which he could be taught music, when he was about four or five years old. Johann used the occasion as a means of establishing his supremacy in the family as well as an opportunity to instruct a supremely gifted child in the art of playing clavier and violin. He conducted his son's musical education in a brutal and willful manner. There is unequivocal testimony on this. Head Burgomaster Windeck "saw the little Louis van Beethoven in [the] house standing in front of the clavier and weeping."[7] Cäcilia Fischer remembered him as "a tiny boy, standing on a little footstool in front of the clavier, to which the implacable severity of his father had so early condemned him."[8] The Belgian music historian François-Joseph Fétis interviewed a childhood companion of Beethoven's who reported that "Beethoven's father used violence when it came to making him start his musical studies, and . . . there were few days when he was not beaten in order to compel him to set himself at the piano."[9] Wegeler claimed to have witnessed "the same thing," recalling that on his visits to a neighboring house, "The doings and sufferings of Louis were visible."[10] The father was not merely strict, but cruel. "He treated him harshly," wrote Court Councillor Krupp many years later to the musician Nikolaus Simrock, "and sometimes shut him up in the cellar."[11]

After several years, Johann, finding his own knowledge insufficient to the task of Ludwig's musical education, enlisted the aid of an eccentric actor-musician, Tobias Pfeiffer, who had come to Bonn in the summer of 1779 with the Grossman and Helmuth theatrical company. Pfeiffer and Johann soon became tavern companions; Pfeiffer was invited to stay in the Beethoven apartment, and it evidently appeared only natural to Johann that he share his pedagogical duties with the twenty-eight-year-old Pfeiffer until the latter's departure the following spring. Bernhard Mäurer, a cellist in Bonn at the time, relates the story: "Often, when Pfeiffer had been boozing with Beethoven's father in a wine-tavern until 11 or 12 o'clock, he went home with him, where [they found] Louis . . . in bed sleeping. The father roughly shook him awake, the boy gathered his wits and, weeping, went to the piano, where he remained, with Pfeiffer seated next to him, until morning."[12]

Johann naturally viewed the boy's talents both as a potentially significant source of extra income and as a means of self-glorification: reports that he rejoiced in his son's accomplishments indicate that he welcomed credit for having fathered such a being. In the early years, at least, his primary goal was to train Beethoven as a competent musician who would in due course take his place in the family line of electoral court musicians. Although he presented the seven-year-old in a concert in Cologne on March 26, 1778, which also featured his pupil the soprano Helene Averdonck,[13] Johann promoted no further public concerts for some years, which may be an indication that Beethoven was not yet ready to be hailed as a keyboard prodigy of the first rank. Perhaps that is why Johann's pedagogy took an unusual turn, if we can credit the Fischers on this point. They recalled that Beethoven's first steps toward expression of his genius were manifested in free fantasies on the violin and clavier, improvisations that were quickly silenced by his father: "Once he was playing without notes; his father happened in and said: 'What silly trash are you scraping away at now? You know that I can't bear that; scrape according to the notes; otherwise your scraping won't be of much use.'" This was not an isolated incident. "When Johann van Beethoven happened to have visitors and Ludwig came into the room, he was wont to edge up to the piano and play chords with his right hand. Then his father would say: 'More of your fooling around? Go away, or I'll box your ears.'" On another occasion, he was again playing according to his own invention, without notes. "His father said: 'Haven't you heard anything of what I've told you?' He played again, then said to his father: 'Now isn't that beautiful?' Whereupon his father said: 'That is something else, which you made up yourself. You are not to do that yet. . . . I won't have you doing it now, you're not ready for it yet.'"[14]

One wonders when Johann might have considered his son to be ready. Mastery of the art of improvisation was the hallmark of the eighteenth-century virtuoso and composer. At the age of six, Leopold Mozart's son created "utter amazement" with his ability to "improvise for hours on end out of his own head, now *cantabile,* now in chords, producing the best of ideas according to the taste of today."[15] An impulse to express his talent through improvisation manifested itself in Beethoven, too, during his first decade, but his father did not take kindly to attempts to stray from the narrow path that he had set for his son.

It would be natural for a child, in confusion and despair over so tangled a relationship with his father, to turn to his mother for solace and love. However, it is nowhere recorded that Maria Magdalena protested her husband's treatment of her oldest son. (We may surmise that Johann insisted that his harsh methods were merely good pedagogy.) Furthermore, there are indications that her care for her son was insufficient to offset the negative implications of her husband's actions. Thayer found contemporary reports implying "that the mother's care in externals was not always of the best";[16] Cäcilia Fischer related that the "Beethoven children were not delicately brought up; they were often left with the maids."[17] And she confirmed that Beethoven was "often dirty and negligent."[18] The only anecdote of Beethoven's childhood directly expressive of his mother's love for him dates from their trip to Holland in 1783; a young neighbor (later the widow Karth) heard Maria Magdalena relate that during a cold spell en route she "had to hold his feet in her lap to prevent them from being frostbitten."[19]

In later years, Beethoven shrouded his first decade in a veil of silence. He rarely spoke of family, his school years, his early experiences.[20] At the same time, he protected himself from his memories of childhood trauma by repeated expressions of love and respect for his mother, and avoidance of derogatory remarks about his father. All who knew Beethoven agree that he remembered his mother "with filial affection and fervent gratitude" and always referred to her "with love and feeling, calling her often an honest, good-hearted woman."[21] The first preserved letter by Beethoven, dated September 15, 1787, to an acquaintance in Augsburg, surely expresses deep feelings of love for his mother, who had died on July 17: "She was such a good, kind mother to me and indeed my best friend. Oh! who was happier than I, when I could still utter the sweet name of mother and it was heard and answered; and to whom can I say it now? To the dumb likenesses of her which my imagination fashions for me?"[22]

Although the material we have bearing on Beethoven's relationship to his father is extremely meager, it is sufficient to indicate, not only the expected resentments and shame, but the presence of a strong tender strain toward him as well. The Fischers recalled that Johann's three sons, led by Beethoven, would go in search of their father when he "had a little too much to drink" and "induce their papa to go quietly home with them."[23] Two men who knew Beethoven intimately commented on his relationship with his father. Stephan von Breuning saw Beethoven "desperately" intervene with the police to prevent his father's arrest.[24] And Ferdinand Ries related that "he spoke seldom and with reluctance" about his father, "but any harsh word by a third person made him angry."[25] Beethoven complained about the inadequacy of his early musical training, but he never directly criticized his father.[26] In a rare written reference to his father, found on a fair copy of Carl Philipp Emanuel Bach's "Morgengesang" that had been made by Johann van Beethoven, Beethoven devotedly wrote in the upper corner: "Written down by my dear father."[27]

This matrix of family circumstances, actions, and attitudes might well have led to permanent disillusionment and despair. It is testimony to Beethoven's strength and resiliency of character that he was able to withstand these stresses. Nevertheless, their effects were readily discernible to many of his contemporaries. Apparently abandoning hope of establishing warm and loving relationships, Beethoven largely withdrew from the society of his fellows and playmates, and from his parents as well. Gottfried Fischer reports that Beethoven's "happiest hours were those when he was free from the company of his parents, which was seldom the case—when all the family were away and he was alone by himself."[28] "He remained shy and monosyllabic," wrote author Wilhelm Christian Müller, who interviewed Ferdinand Ries and Nikolaus Simrock, "because he had little thought of communication with others."[29] Mäurer also noticed the early signs of withdrawal in Beethoven, who "remained indifferent to all praise, retreated, and practiced best when he was alone, when his father was not at home."[30] Thayer, summarizing his researches among Beethoven's former schoolmates, wrote: "Of those who were his school-fellows and who in after years recorded their reminiscences of him, not one speaks of him as a playfellow, none has anecdotes to relate of games with him, rambles on the hills, or adventures upon the Rhine and its shores in which he bore a part."[31]

Even the most withdrawn child, of course, has his bright moments: we hear a few pathetic tales of young Beethoven stealing Frau Fischer's chicken eggs and a neighbor's hen, or reacting with excitement to piggyback rides by his cousins. But essentially his was a lonely, withdrawn childhood. Mäurer described him in the year 1780: "Outside of music he understood nothing of social life; consequently he was ill-humored with other people, did not know how to converse with them, and withdrew into himself, so that he was looked upon as a misanthrope."[32] His schoolmates recalled him as isolated and neglected. Electoral Councillor Joseph Würzer, who like Beethoven attended the Bonn Tirocinium, wrote these devastating words in his memoirs: "In all probability his mother was already dead at the time, for Louis van Beethoven's external appearance was marked in a quite extraordinary way by uncleanliness, negligence, etc."[33]

It is possible that Beethoven's unclean and uncared-for appearance was a mute cry for help, an expression of a tormenting need that he could not express in words. A less equivocal distress signal was his inability to make progress at school. Funck, another classmate at the Tirocinium, wrote bluntly: "What was striking about Louis, to which I can testify, is that he learned absolutely nothing in school."[34] The Fischers remember Johann saying that Beethoven "wasn't learning very much in school."[35] And Councillor Würzer marveled that "not a sign was to be discovered in him of that spark of genius which glowed so brilliantly in him afterwards."[36] Most unusual was his lifelong inability to learn arithmetic beyond addition.

Now, the child of genius or potential genius is inevitably said to be a lonely child, for, as one authority on the psychology of creativity Phyllis Greenacre has observed, "He is a child who senses his own difference [and] feels isolated and inferior thereby."[37] In his second decade, strengthened by the constantly growing consciousness of his creative powers, Beethoven emerged from his isolation with the assistance of teachers, friends, and patrons. In the 1770s, however, when both his creativity and his emotional survival were at risk, he seems to have found sustenance in inwardness, in fantasy. Cäcilia Fischer recalled Beethoven "leaning in the window with his head in both hands and staring fixedly at one spot." When she interrupted his reverie, he said: "I was just occupied with such a lovely deep thought, I couldn't bear to be disturbed."[38] In the attic of the Fischer house in the Rheingasse were two telescopes, with which one could see twenty miles. It was Beethoven's delight to seclude himself in the attic and look out across the Rhine toward the Siebengebirge range.

The center of Beethoven's fantasy life, however, was his music, which occupied virtually all his waking hours. School and friendship counted for little compared with the gratification and sense of accomplishment that he received from making music. Later he told his student Carl Czerny that he practiced "prodigiously," usually until well past midnight, perfecting the technique that was to mark him as one of the outstanding keyboard virtuosos of his day, testing and expanding his improvisatory powers, giving expression in his solitude to his luxuriant musical imagination, tapping creative currents that must have stirred their originator as deeply as they did his listeners in later years. He hungered for instruction and sought it outside his home. The court organist Gilles van den Eeden (ca. 1710–82) taught him briefly in the late 1770s, perhaps in composition as well as organ technique, and according to tradition, Beethoven had organ lessons from Friar Willibald Koch and from Zensen, the organist of Bonn's Münsterkirche. Van den Eeden is said to have sent the boy to play organ at High Mass, and one Pater Hanzmann arranged for him to play at six o'clock morning Mass at the monastery of the Minorites. His musical interests were not limited to the keyboard: he had lessons on violin from his mother's distant cousin Franz Rovantini, and later, from Franz Ries, Bonn's leading violinist; and he also studied horn with Nikolaus Simrock.

With the aid of his music, Beethoven wrapped himself in a protective cloak of his own daydreams. Freud writes that "unsatisfied wishes are the driving power behind fantasies; every separate fantasy contains the fulfillment of a wish, and improves on unsatisfactory reality."[39] And Beethoven's reality paled in comparison with his ideal world. When Cäcilia Fischer reproached him: "How dirty you are again—you ought to keep yourself clean," he replied: "What's the difference—when I become a gentleman [*ein Herr*] no one will pay that any mind."[40] We seem to be in the presence of a fantasy life of rich and unusual dimensions.

Under ordinary circumstances, the topography of this fantasy life could not be mapped. However, Beethoven left us several trails to his psychic interior in his birth-year delusion and in his refusal to deny the reports of his royal parentage. Perhaps we are now in a position to offer some highly tentative interpretations of these matters.

In the fantasy that Freud and his disciple Otto Rank named the "Family Romance," the child replaces one or both of its parents with elevated surrogates—heroes, celebrities, kings, or nobles.[41] Freud found that this fantasy, which is universal in myth, religion, fairy tales, and imaginative fiction, is widespread in the daydreams of ordinary people, and appears in a more intense and enduring form among the creative and the talented.[42] Usually it is a fantasy that arises during childhood or adolescence and thereafter recedes into an amnesia, from which it can be recovered only by analysis. With Beethoven, on the contrary, the fantasy apparently gained in strength and tenacity as he grew to maturity. But its roots were in the conditions of his childhood.

In Beethoven's Family Romance, as with many others, only the father is replaced by an elevated substitute, while the actual mother is retained. This is so for several reasons, but primarily because the identity of the mother as a rule is readily ascertainable, whereas, as the mythologist Johann Jakob Bachofen wrote, "The father as begetter presents an entirely different aspect. Standing in no visible relation to the child, he can never, even in the marital relation, cast off a certain fictive character."[43] *Pater semper incertus est.* Or, in Telemachus's words to Athene, which Beethoven underscored in his copy of the *Odyssey:*

> My mother saith that he is my father;
> For myself I know it not,
> For no man knoweth who hath begotten him.[44]

For this reason, the Family Romance fantasy may unwittingly be fostered in a child by a mother, especially by one who is dissatisfied in marriage, who demeans her husband in the presence of the child, or who feels that she deserved a more worthy mate. The contrast in status between Beethoven's father and grandfather was already sufficient to underscore the former's inadequacies. Added to this, Maria Magdalena's frequent, and justified, complaints about Johann's alcoholism and ineffectuality may well have had an unexpected effect on her son. At some point he may have come to feel that another man was (or should have been) his father, ultimately leading to Johann's being supplanted as the father in Beethoven's inner world. For the denial that Johann van Beethoven was his real father is the central "fact" in Beethoven's Family Romance.

The ramifications of the Family Romance are extremely tangled, and its possible meanings cannot be exhausted. The father is at once slain and elevated; the mother is retained, raised to the rank of king's mistress, but simultaneously degraded for her infidelity. The father may be removed in order to give the child access to the mother; siblings may be illegitimized to assuage incestuous feelings or to satisfy rivalrous impulses. The Family Romance permits the imaginary seizure of parental power, a seizure that we will encounter on more than one occasion in Beethoven's later life. Patricidal implications are on the surface: the Family Romance neutralizes the father's power by setting a more powerful figure in his place. At the same time it relieves guilt over the death or transcendence of the father. ("The man whose death I desired was not my father," reasons the child, "it was a stranger who was slain.") In a sense, Beethoven had split his father into real and illusory images, suppressing the all-too-painful knowledge of his father as wastrel, second-rate musician, toady, possible police agent, drunkard, and hapless extortionist and resurrecting him as a noble, royal figure or as the beloved paragon of childhood. In the recesses of Beethoven's mind, his real father vied for supremacy with his desired, ideal father.

Beethoven was forced to carry a multiple burden, consisting not only of the patterns of father rejection that his mother's attitudes and his father's actions had instilled in him, but a matrix of negative feelings toward his mother as well, for she had caused him to become complicit in Johann's downfall. Yet he could not identify with his father, for this would have entailed, in addition to a rejection of his grandfather's example and his mother's precepts, the suppression of his genius. (Otto Rank wrote, "There seems to be a certain necessity for the prophet to deny his parents.")[45] Surely, as he began to grow up, Beethoven must have wondered about the disparity between his own creative gifts and his father's mediocrity. Perhaps this is why he underlined another meaningful passage in the *Odyssey:*

> Few sons are like
> Their fathers; most are worse, a very few
> Excel their fathers.[46]

A person of Beethoven's creative endowments may find it difficult to reconcile his gifts with his parentage. He may be imbued with a sense of his superiority over others, perhaps even over those who gave him life. This may lead toward an overweening self-sufficiency, a feeling of omnipotent self-creation, or it may lead to thoughts of having been begotten by more suitable—noble, royal, even divine—parents. The fantasy of royal descent satisfied Beethoven's passion for grandeur, his hunger for greatness.

Let us consider the simplest, the most touching, and, I believe, the bedrock level of Beethoven's Family Romance: the fantasy that he was an illegitimate child. Beethoven's Family Romance was fed by, and perhaps had its origin in, his birth-year delusion. This, too, was a fantasy of illegitimacy. Here we may recall the confusion concerning his birth year and particularly the widespread belief that he was born in December 1771. Beethoven's difficulty was this: if he was born in December 1771 at the earliest, then the certificate documenting the baptism of a Ludwig van Beethoven on December 17, 1770, must have belonged, as in fact he insisted it did, to his older brother, Ludwig Maria. And if this were the case, Beethoven's own, "true" baptismal certificate had disappeared from the archives. It could not be found by Beethoven or by any of his friends—Wegeler, Ries, Müller—all of whom had procured copies of the "wrong" certificate. It follows, therefore, that his own baptismal certificate—the evidence of his birth and the proof of his parentage—either never existed or had been concealed or destroyed. What (he may well have wondered) could have been the reason for this mysterious suppression of the facts of his birth?

Following from this, other crucial questions arose, focusing superficially on the mystery of his correct age but in fact, and more poignantly, centering on the impenetrable secret: "Who is my real father?" The text of what was perhaps Beethoven's first song, "An einen Säugling" ("To an

Infant"), WoO 108, which he set to music when he was but twelve years old, holds out the hope of an answer:

> You still do not know whose child you are. You do not know who pre-pares the swaddling clothes, who it is that warms you and gives you milk. You grow in peace nevertheless. Within a few years, among all those who have cared for you, you will learn to distinguish your moth-er. Nonetheless there is some occult giver who cares for all of us—our thanks go to him—with food and drink. My dim intelligence does not yet comprehend this; but after the years have gone by, if I am pious and a believer, even he will be revealed.

From here it was but a short step to the Family Romance fantasy.

The fantasy can take deep root, however, only when the child is (or imagines himself to be) neglected, maltreated, and unloved. The rarely assuaged, tragic family circumstances of his youth placed Beethoven's personal "golden age" not in his earliest childhood but in the period before he was born, immediately after the marriage of his parents in 1767 and up to the death of their first son, Ludwig Maria. "What is marriage?" his mother asked, as Beethoven overheard: "A little joy, and then a chain of sorrows." Surrounded by sadness, withdrawing into iso-lation and daydreaming, Ludwig van Beethoven may have inwardly felt that the first link in that chain of sorrows was forged at the time of his own conception and birth. He looked back in anguish to an Eden that he could not reach except by sharing the identity of his more favored older brother.

Ultimately, Beethoven's Family Romance signified his belief that he was the "false" son, who could never take the place of his dead brother. His fantasy of ennoblement was not merely the assertion of a desired nobility, or the delusory rejection of his humble parents; most of all, it was the admission of a pathetic longing to be the firstborn, who was mourned but not forgotten by his parents. All of these inter-woven fantasies, then, may have a single, transparent source: they may be the expression, denial, and symbolic transcendence of the feeling that he was unloved and unwanted. They are the rectification of a pre-sumed illegitimacy. They are the heartfelt—and unanswered—cry of a child for his parents' love.

Christian Gottlob Neefe. Unsigned portrait in oils.

Collection Marie Greinert. From Irmgard Leux, Christian Gottlob Neefe
(Leipzig, 1925).

CHAPTER THREE

THE SECOND DECADE

A T THE BEGINNING OF HIS SECOND DECADE, Beethoven's career as a musician began to establish itself. Though he was not to become a prodigy like Mozart, at a respectably early age he was seen as an able young professional, something in which he took great pride. The Fischers describe him when he "came forward as a composer and . . . organist, and in token of rank wore a sword on his left side when he went up to the rood loft in the court church with his father." No longer unkempt and ill clothed, he wore the gala dress of the court musician: "Sea-green frock coat, green knee breeches with buckles, stockings of white or black silk, shoes with black bowknots, embroidered vest with pocket flaps, the vest bound with real gold cord, hair curled and with queue, crush hat under the left arm, sword on the left side with silver belt."[1]

Beethoven was now engaged in the work of the world, seeking to establish for himself a settled place both in his family and in society at large. He was imbued with a new sense of his inner worth. Indeed, according to the Fischers, he "now believed himself to be the equal of his father in music."[2] The relationship between father and son was undergoing an inevitable realignment, coinciding with the final separation of Beethoven's musical education from his father's supervision as well as the beginning of his training in composition. In short order, his musical abilities were recognized, so that he became assistant court organist at the electoral court (without salary) in 1782, when he was only eleven, and "cembalist in the orchestra" in 1783. In June 1784 he received an official appointment as deputy court organist, at a salary of 150 florins. These events mark the end of Beethoven's childhood and the beginning of his "first period" as a composer.

The pivotal figure in this transition was Christian Gottlob Neefe (1748–98), a German composer, organist, and conductor who had come to Bonn in October 1779 to join the Grossman and Helmuth theatrical company and was named successor to van den Eeden as court organist on February 15, 1781. He became Beethoven's composition instructor in 1780 or 1781 and remained his only significant teacher until Beethoven left Bonn in November 1792.

Neefe at once recognized and encouraged Beethoven's genius and provided him with his earliest professional experience. He trained him as assistant court organist and left him temporarily in full charge as early as June 1782; shortly thereafter he turned over to his twelve-year-old student his position as "cembalist," which involved direction of the orchestra from the keyboard and playing at sight from the score. Furthermore—and indicative of the quality of his concern for the young composer—he arranged for publication of Beethoven's early works, and he wrote the first public notice about him, in a communication dated March 2, 1783, to C. F. Cramer's *Magazin der Musik,* describing the electoral court musical establishment:

> Louis van Betthoven [*sic*], . . . a boy of eleven years and of most promising talent. He plays the clavier very skillfully and with power, reads at sight very well, and—to put it in a nutshell—he plays chiefly *The Well-Tempered Clavichord* of Sebastian Bach, which Herr Neefe put into his hands. Whoever knows this collection of preludes and fugues in all the keys—which might almost be called the *non plus ultra* of our art—will know what this means. So far as his duties permitted, Herr Neefe has also given him instruction in thoroughbass. He is now training him in composition and for his encouragement has had nine variations for the pianoforte, written by him on a march—by Ernst Christoph Dressler—engraved at Mannheim. This youthful genius is deserving of help to enable him to travel. He would surely become a second Wolfgang Amadeus Mozart were he to continue as he has begun.[3]

Later, from Vienna in 1792 or 1793, Beethoven was to write appreciatively (if rather stiffly) to Neefe: "I thank you for the advice you have very often given me about making progress in my divine art. Should I ever become a great man, you too will have a share in my success."[4] Clearly, Neefe hoped to be associated with the discovery of a second Mozart, and in fact his claim to fame rests in large part on his tutelage of Beethoven.[5] Whatever his motivations, Neefe's teaching and encouragement provided the springboard for Beethoven's rapid development in the early 1780s. Moreover, by virtue of his own intellectual background and moral code, Neefe was someone whom Beethoven could look up to, and even emulate, at this critical juncture of his life. During his Leipzig years (1769–76), Neefe had been drawn toward the German Sturm und Drang movement, as well as to the poets Christian F. Gellert, Friedrich Gottlieb Klopstock, and the young Goethe, and he had become sympathetic to the ideals of the German Enlightenment (*die Aufklärung*) as well. In Bonn, Neefe was a leader (*Lokaloberer*) of the Order of Illuminati and active in the city's intellectual circles. Although there is no direct evidence of his influence on Beethoven's subsequent attraction to Enlightenment literature and ideals, it is probable that it was at least partially through Neefe that Beethoven first made their acquaintance.

Neefe's ethical outlook was evidently shaped by his own early conflicts with his father, who wished his son to follow him in the legal profession. He enrolled in 1769 at the University of Leipzig as a student of jurisprudence, but he was ridden with hypochondria and thoughts of suicide. His dissertation was, transparently, devoted to the question of whether a father could disinherit a son who wanted to enter the theater.[6] Neefe opted for the negative on this issue, and turned from law to music in 1771. His moral code, as revealed in his *Lebenslauf* (*Autobiography*) of 1782, was marked by a striving for ethical perfection and for the suppression of sensual desire through sublimated activity.[7] Clearly, Beethoven had found a kindred spirit and a moral mentor in Neefe, whose puritanical presence and ethical imperatives were a superb counterbalance to the behavior and character of Johann van Beethoven.

Beethoven's first known compositions were produced under Neefe's guidance. From 1782 to 1785 his works include the set of Nine Variations in C minor on a March by Dressler, WoO 63 (1782); Three Clavier Sonatas ("Electoral"), WoO 47 (1782–83), dedicated to Elector Maximilian Friedrich; a Piano Concerto in E-flat, WoO 4 (1784); Three Quartets for Piano and Strings, WoO 36 (1785); as well as several lieder and small keyboard works. The variations, sonatas, and lieder were quickly published, with attention pointedly drawn to their composer's tender age. In a brief space of time Beethoven had entered the lists as a

young, emerging prodigy, industriously applying himself to the vocation of composer.

Until recently it was assumed that his progress as a composer continued uninterruptedly throughout the remainder of the decade. A cold
look at the evidence, however, reveals that, apart from these compositions, not a single one of the thirty-odd later Bonn pieces can with certainty be placed in the second half of the 1780s either by documentary
evidence or by the testimony of contemporaries. No surviving autograph bears a date between 1785 and 1790; no contemporary review,
correspondence, biographical notice, concert program, or dedicatory letter exists to confirm that a given work was written in that half decade.[8]
Of course, inasmuch as the dates of Beethoven's Bonn compositions are
very inexactly known, the absence of such documentation does not
prove that none of them belongs to that period, but it does suggest that
Beethoven composed at most a handful of works in a period of about
four or five years after 1785. He apparently resumed composition with
renewed seriousness and an increased level of productivity only as he
was entering his twentieth year, in late 1789 or early 1790.

To confirm the existence of such a compositional hiatus would help
answer several vexing questions about the graph of Beethoven's productivity and perhaps explain why his grasp of the techniques of composition was insufficient until a rather advanced age, so that, after his arrival
in late 1792 in Vienna, he found himself obliged to study counterpoint,
at which point it took the combined efforts of a number of teachers to
ground him in the rudiments of the art. The hiatus itself, however,
which delayed his development as a composer during the crucial adolescent years, remains unexplained.

External factors surely played some role in Beethoven's failure to
compose a great deal between 1785 and 1790. His first publications evidently failed to create sufficient interest to warrant the assumption that
he would emerge as a major composer. A devastating contemporary
notice in Forkel's *Musikalischer Almanach* of 1784 unfavorably compared
several of Beethoven's first publications with the work of beginning students ("[They] perhaps could be respected as the first attempts of a
beginner in music, like an exercise by a third- or fourth-form student in
our schools").[9] By the time the three Piano Quartets, WoO 36, were
completed in 1785, it is possible that Beethoven's sponsors had given up

hope of creating a prodigy of Mozartian proportions; perhaps this is one reason why the quartets remained unpublished. In fact, it is note-worthy that from 1784 until his departure from Bonn, there was only one publication, in 1791, of a Beethoven work.[10] The successive deaths of Elector Maximilian Friedrich and Minister von Belderbusch in 1784 deprived the young composer of those who undoubtedly had been his most powerful friends at Bonn. A mid-1784 report to the new elector, Maximilian Franz, does not even refer to Beethoven as a composer, but merely as a young keyboard player of "good capability."[11] At least tem-porarily, Beethoven seems to have lost ground at the electoral court.

Moreover, his relationship with Neefe may well have gone through something of a crisis in mid-1784. As a foreigner, a radical, and a Protestant, Neefe was considered dispensable and the court tried to effect economies by replacing him with Beethoven. Neefe's wages were in fact halved in June; as Forbes noted, Beethoven's first payments "had clearly been taken out of the salary of his teacher."[12] The matter was resolved in early 1785, however, with the restoration of Neefe's full salary.

The catastrophes that enveloped Beethoven's family during the sec-ond half of the 1780s increased Beethoven's responsibilities as financial provider and virtual head of the family. He was thoroughly occupied with multiple activities as court musician—with, from 1788, additional duties as violist in the court and theater orchestras—as music teacher, and, increasingly, as a solo performer. Starting from perhaps as early as 1781 he began to emerge as a regional keyboard virtuoso. During sum-mers when the electoral court was on vacation, Beethoven frequently played for music lovers and art patrons in the towns and palaces of the Rhine countryside, so much so that Madame van Beethoven became a self-described "grass widow" (*Strohwitwe*).[13] He ventured farther afield on only one known occasion, a voyage to Holland that, it is worth not-ing, was made wholly under his mother's supervision. On November 23, 1783, he was featured (probably playing his Concerto in E-flat, WoO 4) in an orchestral concert at The Hague at the court of Prince Willem V of Orange-Nassau, for which he received the sum of 63 florins.[14] Further details of Beethoven's performances in Holland are sparse, but the widow Karth recalled Frau van Beethoven's saying that "Ludwig played a great deal in great houses, astonished people by his skill and received valuable presents."[15] Perhaps expenses outstripped anticipated income, for the Beethovens, who hoped "they would make a lot of money" in Holland, evidently were disappointed by the takings, as may be gathered from Beethoven's famous remark "The Dutch are penny pinchers who love money too much."[16]

In Bonn, Beethoven gave private concerts at the family's lodgings at the Fischer house: the two front rooms were joined to form an improvised concert hall and there "they held large concerts,"[17] which were so well attended by a broad cross-section of Bonn's music lovers—theater and university people, intellectuals, the bureaucracy, and nobility, and strangers attracted by news of the young pianist's phenomenal gifts—that the landlord, Theodor Fischer, found his rest disturbed and eventually saw fit to give notice. The Fischers recalled how some of the concerts came about:

> As Herr Ludwig van Beethoven progressed day by day in music and composing and sold his compositions to strangers, his fame thereby spread so far and wide that many of those who had visited him reported to others that, although he was still a youngster, he had already held his ground against all composers, so that many music lovers came here from far away foreign places out of curiosity and asked that he allow them to hear him play in a small concert. Then Herr Johann van Beethoven, when it was possible, sent out for musicians and organized a concert in his room. However, the gentlemen must have paid him well for this—we do not know.[18]

Presumably, similar concerts were held at the Beethoven family's other lodgings and perhaps at the homes of friends and fellow musicians as well. As the foremost young virtuoso in Bonn Beethoven certainly performed from time to time at the electoral court, as well as in the salons of the high nobility and leading burghers and officials. It was not long before he gained the support of the new elector, Maximilian Franz, of Count Ferdinand Waldstein, and of the families of Count Westerholt-Gysenberg and Count Hatzfeld as well. Additionally, in his capacity as a composer, he would normally expect to receive valuable gifts in return for dedications of published works, such as the Nine Variations in C minor on a March by Dressler, WoO 63, dedicated to Countess Wolf-Metternich in 1782, the Three Clavier Sonatas, WoO 47, dedicated to Elector Maximilian Friedrich in 1783, and the Twenty-four Variations in D on Righini's "Venni amore," WoO 65, dedicated to Countess Hatzfeld in 1791. Similarly, there is no doubt that Beethoven was rewarded for music written to a patron's order, such as the Trio in G for Piano, Flute, and Bassoon, WoO 37, for the Westerholt-Gysenberg family, and the Musik zu einem *Ritterballett* (Music for a Knight's Ballet), WoO 1, for Count Waldstein. The latter's generosity was observed by contemporaries, Wegeler reporting that in Beethoven's later Bonn years the young musician "often received financial support" from the count, "bestowed with such consideration for his easily wounded feelings that Beethoven usually assumed they were small gratuities from the elector."[19]

So far as we know, Beethoven's earnings in Bonn were always dedicated to the family interests, something that remained a matter of pride to him in later years. Naturally, it would be prudent not to overestimate how much money he might have earned from such sources, but there is no reason to think that the aggregate payments to him as composer and virtuoso performer were negligible. On the contrary, it is very likely that the patrons of the arts in the electorate of Cologne appropriately demonstrated their appreciation to the most prodigiously gifted of Bonn's musicians. Thus, even after the exhaustion of the bulk of his grandfather Ludwig's legacy, the family's earnings were sufficient—when Beethoven's auxiliary income was added to his and his father's combined salary of 450 florins—to keep the family in relative security under normal circumstances.

Even in the later 1780s the documentary record is not altogether consistent with a picture of a family in need, let alone poverty. Nevertheless, the family endured occasionally straitened circumstances, living beyond their means, and experienced times when household expenses exceeded income. The main source of these difficulties was Johann van Beethoven's decline into notorious alcoholism, accompanied by debt, wasteful expenditures, and reckless ventures. Clearly, by 1784 Johann had lost his moorings, the respect of his peers, and the capacity to support his family in a dependable manner, regardless of his income. Not outright poverty but a perpetual state of precariousness is what gives Beethoven's early family circumstances their special poignancy. The Beethovens seem to have lived in a state of relative

comfort, but at the same time were perched hazardously on the edge
of calamity. They surely went through periodic cash shortages and
temporary slumps, and the possibility of further setbacks or even of
economic shipwreck was a source of perpetual anxiety, perhaps intense-
ly felt by a family that had become accustomed to a privileged status by
the history of their forebears, whose chief members included respected
court employees, wealthy tradespeople, and entrepreneurs.

It may not have been the pressure of his extremely varied activities
alone that limited Beethoven's productivity as a composer in the second
half of the 1780s; he found much time for leisure, social contact, and
entertainment during precisely this period. And in the subsequent, very
productive years of 1790–92 he found it possible to combine essentially
identical duties as court musician and family provider with a very
respectable output as a composer. Perhaps, after all, it was beneficial for
Beethoven's creative powers to lie fallow for a while; his later career contains several such "silent" periods, which were followed by heightened
creativity. Lockwood rightly observes that "Beethoven's development as
a pianist and improviser, in the late 1780s, was not entirely a retreat
from composition but a diversion of some of his energy into keyboard
practice and improvisation that would soon after produce results in his
most fruitful field of composition."[20]

His apparent withdrawal from formal composition does, however,
inevitably carry overtones of diminished ambitions, or even of defeat.
And these implications were reinforced by the failure of his journey to
Vienna in the spring of 1787. It is thought that he was sent there by the
elector to enable the Viennese to hear and judge a gifted Bonn pianist,
and perhaps to play for (or even to take lessons from) Mozart. But his
stay lasted not more than two weeks: almost immediately following his
arrival in early April his father notified him that his mother's consump-
tive condition had worsened and requested that he return to Bonn at
once. Beethoven immediately set out for home; yet even as he was on
his way home his father urged him on: "The nearer I came to my native
town, the more frequently did I receive from my father letters urging
me to travel more quickly than usual, because my mother was not in
very good health. So I made as much haste as I could."[21] He had not
remained in Vienna long enough to accomplish his purpose, and he did

not return there after his mother's death—she lingered until July 17—to take up where he had left off. The trip to Vienna, as the elector later caustically pointed out in a letter to Haydn, was a total failure, with Beethoven bringing back "nothing but debts."[22]

These events would have been sufficient to wound the self-esteem of any sixteen-year-old. The death of his mother, followed by that of his baby sister in November, was of a different order: these losses and the ensuing mourning process may well have blocked Beethoven's creative development and contributed to the prolongation of his moratorium. Moreover, his mother's death had the effect of placing Beethoven in charge of the family, a responsibility that soon became a restrictive factor in his development, even as it forced him prematurely into an adult role.

After a parent's death, a child's position in the family may undergo a radical change, and sometimes there is a desperate, pathetic attempt to put the child in the place of the missing parent. It was now Beethoven rather than Maria Magdalena who was in charge of the family finances, Beethoven who had to deal with the consequences of Johann's alcoholism, Beethoven who had to intervene with the police to prevent his father from being taken into custody. Events had combined to compel Beethoven to assume the role that first the kapellmeister and then Maria Magdalena had played throughout Johann's life. In effect, Beethoven became his father's guardian, thus restoring the infantile relationship of domination and care from which Johann had never been able to free himself.

During these last years, Johann van Beethoven largely gave up his grip upon reality and abandoned himself to a narcotized existence. Nevertheless, he was now able to exercise an even more profound control over his son's life, based upon his ability to manipulate Beethoven's sense of pity and guilt, which apparently grew as Johann's fortunes declined. In fact, it seems that Johann's strength lay in his very weakness, in his ability to compel others—successively his father, his wife, and his oldest son—to rescue him from himself. He had become Anchises on the back of Aeneas. (Ernest Simmel wrote of the alcoholic that "by his alcoholism he tortures those who care for him. . . . His addiction is chronic murder and chronic suicide.")[23] For Beethoven the burden of Johann would ultimately become insupportable. He would have to set aside the parasitical father whom he simultaneously loved and despised, who had transformed him into a surrogate wife and father, and who had become an impediment to his fulfillment as a composer and as an individual.

The turning point in this poignant entanglement occurred in late 1789, when Beethoven addressed a petition to the elector asking that half his father's salary be paid to him, coupled with the condition that his father be retired from service and perhaps exiled from Bonn as well. Beethoven's petition has disappeared, but the answering decree of November 20, 1789, survives:

> His Electoral Highness having graciously granted the prayer of the petitioner and dispensed henceforth wholly with the services of his father, who is to withdraw to a village in the electorate, it is graciously commanded that he be paid in accordance with his wish only 100 rthr. [Reichsthalers] of the annual salary which he has had heretofore, beginning with the approaching new year, and that the other 100 thlr. [thalers] be paid to the petitioning son, besides the salary which he now draws and the three measures of grain for the support of his brothers.[24]

Thayer refers to Beethoven's petition as "the extraordinary step of placing himself at the head of the family."[25] Actually, that step had been taken long before. Now he was attempting to free himself from a paralyzing embrace.

In order for the decree to become effective, Beethoven was to present the document to the elector's Inland Revenue Office and Exchequer (*Landrentmeisterei*). He did not do this during his father's lifetime, because, as Beethoven wrote in a petition to the elector in the spring of 1793, "My father earnestly besought me not to do this, lest he should be publicly regarded as incapable of supporting his family by his own efforts. He added that he himself would pay me the 25 Reichsthalers every quarter; and this was always punctually done."[26] Beethoven's 1789 petition had clearly been warranted by circumstances, but he was incapable of fully carrying through the action, perhaps because of its patricidal implications. It is a measure of his devotion to his father (and of his inner strength) that Beethoven granted Johann's plea that he be permitted to retain a fragment of personal dignity.

That Beethoven was ridden with conflicts concerning this momentous event in his life is shown by the remainder of his 1793 petition to the elector. It is the only record we have of Beethoven's reaction to his father's death:

> MOST WORTHY AND MOST EXCELLENT ELECTOR:
> MOST GRACIOUS LORD!
>
> A few years ago Your Electoral Excellency was pleased to retire my father, the court tenor van Beethoven, and by a most gracious decree to allow me out of his salary 100 Reichsthalers so as to enable me to have my two younger brothers clothed, fed, and educated and also to discharge the debts which our father had incurred. . . .
>
> After his death, which took place in December of last year, I wanted to avail myself of your most precious favor by presenting the aforementioned most gracious decree. I was horrified, however, to find that he had suppressed it.
>
> Hence with the most dutiful reverence I beg Your Excellency graciously to renew this decree and also to instruct Your Excellency's *Landrentmeisterei* to send me the previous quarterly amount which fell due at the beginning of February.
>
> > Your Electoral Excellency's most humble and
> > most faithfully obedient
> > LUDWIG VAN BEETHOVEN,
> > Court Organist[27]

It is striking that here, as in Johann's petition to the elector of January 1774 in which he had asserted his ability to take his father's place as kapellmeister, there is not the slightest hint of filial piety, let alone of grief. Instead, Beethoven expresses his "horror" that his father had done away with the electoral decree. This does not mean that Beethoven did not love his father. In earlier years, they had shared the pleasures of summer journeys visiting music lovers in the Rhine countryside. In later years, he had favored his father with the opportunity to bask in the reflected glory of his achievements, and permitting him vicariously to realize some of Johann's frustrated ambitions. Beethoven had listened with undoubted embarrassment to the sentimental and drunken cadences in which Johann boasted, "My son Ludwig, he is now my only joy, he has become so accomplished in music and composition that he is looked upon with wonder by everyone. My Ludwig, my Ludwig, I foresee that he will in time become a great man in the world."[28]

It was not the absence of love that prevented Beethoven from revealing either his love or his grief; rather, I suspect, it was his unwillingness to loosen the powerful ties that bound him to his father. Helene Deutsch has written: "As long as the early libidinal or aggressive attachments persist, the painful affect continues to flourish, and vice versa, the attachments are unresolved as long as the affective process of mourning has not been accomplished."[29] The inability to verbalize his sense of loss at the deaths of those he loved—such as certain of his patrons, friends, and teachers—was characteristic of Beethoven throughout his life.

The documentary record provides copious material for the construction of narratives about Beethoven's deeply conflicted attachment to his father, including narratives of loss and restitution, of a prosperous golden age presided over by a productive and respected father, giving way to a dismal picture of that same father, now inebriated and hapless, stumbling home from the taverns; of an eldest son standing between his father and the night-watch; of an adolescent musician forced to petition for control of his father's salary; of a forlorn, bereft, leaderless family still mourning the death of a mother. One will want to think about the possible effects on the young Beethoven of his father's dreams and delusions, of his deterioration into helplessness and obloquy, his grandiosity, his disastrous attempt to defraud the electoral minister's estate. Perhaps there was a time when Beethoven shared his father's dreams of a turn for the better, of a windfall, and he wanted to help realize those ambitions. Eventually, though, he came to realize that he had to take resolute action in order to protect the family as a whole, to protect it, that is, from his father's wayward fantasies as well as his extravagances.

Be that as it may, the audacious petition of 1789 coincided with the liberation of Beethoven's creative force as a composer. The period of his diminished creativity was over. A sudden and sustained burst of activity began around late 1789 or in the first months of 1790 and continued until his departure for Vienna in November 1792. Among the many works composed in this period were four or five sets of piano variations (WoO 64, WoO 65, WoO 66, WoO 67, and perhaps WoO 40 as well); two full-scale cantatas (WoO 87 and WoO 88); incidental music for a ballet (WoO 1); a number of works for piano solo and for various combinations of wind instruments; and a piano trio (WoO 38), along with other chamber music, several concert arias, and a substantial number of songs, including almost all of the eight lieder that were published in 1805 as opus 52.

Simultaneously, we begin to find after 1790 Beethoven's first glowing notices as an interpreter and improvisor on the keyboard. In 1791 he improvised with great effect for the famous pianist Abbé Sterkel; later in the year, a report by author Carl Ludwig Junker in an important contemporary journal, H. P. C. Bossler's *Musikalische Correspondenz*, published at Speyer, described the high esteem in which Beethoven was held: "I heard also one of the greatest of pianists—the dear, good Bethofen. . . . Even the members of this remarkable orchestra are, without exception, his admirers, and all ears when he plays."[30]

Maximilian Franz, Elector of Cologne and Grandmaster
of the Teutonic Order. Engraving by J. F. Beer.

Stadtarchiv Bonn, Portrait Collection.

CHAPTER FOUR

LAST YEARS IN BONN: ENLIGHTENMENT

GERMANY IN THE EIGHTEENTH CENTURY consisted of a multiplicity of small feudal territories and dominions, so-called *Kleinstaaten,* ruled by hundreds of lesser and greater sovereigns. These nearly three hundred ministates, along with other lands of the Habsburg empire, constituted the splintered, motley, decaying entity, the Holy Roman Empire, whose political and cultural life tended to orbit around the twin centers of Berlin and Vienna.

Bonn, the residence of the prince elector of Cologne, owed its main allegiance to Vienna, seat of the Holy Roman Empire and headquarters of the Habsburg monarchy. The prince electors were simultaneously the ecclesiastical and secular rulers of the fairly sizable territory on the Rhine, adjoining France. A contemporary traveler, Baron Caspar Riesbeck, described Bonn in 1780 as "the largest and handsomest town betwixt Coblentz and Cologne."[1] As for its political and cultural life, he reported: "The present government of the archbishoprick of Cologne and the bishoprick of Münster is without a doubt the most active and most enlightened of all the ecclesiastical governments of Germany. The ministry of the court of Bonn is excellently composed. . . . The cabinet of Bonn is singularly happy in the establishment of seminaries of education, the improvement of agriculture and industry, and the extirpation of every species of monkery."[2] Riesbeck was writing of the Bonn of Maximilian Friedrich, who was elector from 1761 until his death in 1784. Under his rule the Jesuits were suppressed (1774) and their educational institutions liquidated, an academy was founded (1777), and despite the harsh economies of his powerful minister of state, Count Belderbusch, cultural activities, especially theater and opera, flourished. There was a remarkably broad dissemination of Enlightened literature and thought in Bonn. Booksellers in the 1770s and

47

Bartholomäus Fischenich.
Unsigned miniature locket
portrait.

*Private collection. From Max
Brauback,* Die erste Bonner
Universität und ihre Professoren
(Bonn, 1947).

1780s sold the latest editions of the works of Rousseau and Montesquieu alongside the writings of Klopstock, Herder, Schiller, and Goethe.

Under the rule of Elector Maximilian Franz, which began in 1784, the ideas of the Enlightenment became virtually the official principles of the electorate. The regime of Maximilian Franz, a son of Empress Maria Theresia, was the reflection in Bonn of the attitudes and ideology of his brother, the Habsburg emperor Joseph II, who was a follower of Voltaire, Frederick the Great, and the encyclopedists. Upon the death of Maria Theresia, in 1780, Joseph launched a headlong and unparalleled program of internal reform that included steps toward the emancipation of the serfs, the spread of education, secularization of church lands, tax and juridical reforms, and the founding of numerous charitable institutions. This program brought him into conflict with the high clergy and segments of the nobility as well as with neighboring states and sovereigns. Ultimately, in 1790, the year of Joseph's death, major portions of his reforms were retracted, although the land reforms remained relatively intact. Riesbeck believed that Joseph's "principles of government [were] as republican as those of most of the states who at this day call themselves republics."[3] The historian A. J. P. Taylor calls Joseph's undertaking "an astonishing achievement of Enlightened phi-

Euloglus Schneider.
Unsigned engraving.

From Max Braubach, Die erste Bonner
Universität und ihre Professoren
(Bonn, 1947).

losophy, witness to the force of the Imperial structure." But he also remarks that "his revolutionary policy did not have the support of a revolutionary class.... His aim could be completed only by revolution; and revolution would destroy the dynasty."[4]

In Bonn, Maximilian Franz tried to keep pace with developments in Vienna, and enlarged the scope of intellectual freedom in his tiny electorate. Wilhelm von Humboldt, a distinguished scholar who visited Bonn in October 1788, noted that the court library contained "the best periodical writings as well as learned and political newspapers and books."[5] Of great significance was the elector's decree of August 9, 1785, raising the Bonn academy to the rank of university. Here Kantian philosophy was taught by Elias van der Schüren and Johannes Neeb, while such professors as the revolutionary Eulogius Schneider lectured on theology and classical literature and Schiller's friend Bartholomäus Ludwig Fischenich lectured on natural law and human rights.

Despite the receptivity to Enlightenment ideas, advanced and radical thinkers were constantly on the alert for signs of repression. Freemason's lodges had been founded in Cologne and Bonn in 1775–76 under Maximilian Friedrich and flourished under Emperor Joseph II's restrictive Freimaurerpatent of December 11, 1785, which stringently limited the growth of the movement and placed it under increased surveillance and control of the authorities. During much of that period, the most radical branch of Freemasonry, the anticlerical Order of Illuminati, founded in 1776 in Bavaria, played an influential role in Bonn, and even for a brief time beginning in April 1784, published its own weekly newspaper, *Beiträge zur Ausbreitung nützlicher Kenntnisse* (*Contributions to the Dissemination of Useful Knowledge*), to which Neefe was a main contributor.[6] In addition to Neefe, Bonn's Illuminati included many who were associated with Beethoven: two of his instrument teachers, Nikolaus Simrock and Franz Ries, Clemens August von Schall, Johann Peter Eichhoff, and Johann Joseph Eichhoff.[7] In 1784–85, when the order was suppressed in Bavaria, where it had originated, the Bonn Illuminati, anticipating a similar prohibition, dissolved in favor of a less perilous forum, the Lesegesellschaft (Reading Society), which was founded in 1787 by thirteen "friends of literature," who included most of the former Illuminati.[8] Though it shared the same ideals, the Lesegesellschaft "was by no means merely a camouflaged continuation" of the Illuminati; its close ties to the governing circles are an indication that it did not threaten to go into political opposition.[9] Soon its membership exceeded one hundred, including Neefe, J. J. Eichhoff, Franz Ries, Count Waldstein, Karl August von Malchus, Schneider, and numerous other older colleagues and friends of Beethoven. After the dissolution of the Order of Illuminati, activities of Masonic lodges were also restricted, and ultimately suspended: clearly, the Lesegesellschaft provided a home for both displaced Illuminati and Freemasons during that period.

Ultimately, as we know, the representatives of Enlightened thought were hounded in and out of the capitals of anti-Napoleonic Europe by many of the former adherents of Enlightened despotism. In the later 1780s, however, though there were a few hints of future repression, its depth could not have been predicted, nor were there premonitions that the dissolution of the electorate itself would take place in 1794, following the occupation of the Rhineland by the French armies and its subsequent annexation by Napoleonic France (1798–1814).

Within this atmosphere Beethoven's social and cultural attitudes took shape. He adopted as his own the leading principles of the European Enlightenment under conditions in which it was unnecessary for him to step outside of society as a rebel or apostate. As far as we know, his behavior at Bonn was that of an exemplary young court musician, a dutiful servant of the electorate. An official report of 1784 described him from the court's viewpoint as being "of good capability" and "of good and quiet deportment."[10] Of course he was only thirteen then, but there is no later recorded instance of his dissatisfaction with or rebellion against the requirements of Bonn's feudal aristocratic patronage. Perhaps he was grateful to the court, which acted favorably on his various petitions for partial amelioration of his family's financial situation. (As late as 1801, long after he had left the court's service, Beethoven intended to dedicate a major work, his Symphony No. 1 in C, op. 21, to Maximilian Franz.) It was surely a mark of extreme favor that the elector twice underwrote Beethoven's journeys to Vienna; from afar he observed his court organist's progress with a nice mixture of concern and irony. The elector's "favorite and constant companion,"[11] Count Ferdinand Waldstein (1762–1823), who arrived in Bonn in 1788, also became Beethoven's patron, and was the first to link his name with those of both Mozart and Haydn.

Beethoven's daily routine reflected his adherence to an exemplary standard of behavior. In addition to fulfilling his family responsibilities and court duties he gave lessons to augment the family income, suppressing to some degree what Wegeler called his "extraordinary aversion" to teaching.[12] In overcoming this aversion, he had the assistance of the widowed Frau Helene von Breuning, the mother of his friends Stephan, Christoph, Lorenz, and Eleonore. He clearly seems to have turned to Frau von Breuning as a mother surrogate in these years, spending a good deal of time in the Breuning household. Wegeler remembered that she "had great power over the boy, who was frequently stubborn and sullen."[13] She possessed the capacity, as Thayer wrote with such approval, to "compel him to the performance of his duties."[14]

It is a striking fact that in later years Beethoven repeatedly recalled his dedication to virtue as emanating from his childhood. Thus, in a letter of 1811 he wrote, "From my earliest childhood my zeal to serve our poor suffering humanity in any way whatsoever by means of my art has made no compromise with any lower motive."[15] Similar sentiments were expressed in a letter of 1824: "Since I was a child my greatest happiness and pleasure have been to be able to do something for others."[16] He emphatically rejected any implication that he might have fallen short of the highest ethical standards: "*Never, never* will you find me dishonorable. Since my childhood I have learnt to love virtue—and everything beautiful and good."[17] It would appear, then, that virtue and service to humanity were Beethoven's conscious goals from a very early age.

These private imperatives readily found ideological clothing in the humanistic and virtuous precepts of Enlightened thought: Beethoven adopted as his own the ideals of fraternity, freedom of thought, social justice, and moral improvement that were prevalent in the cities of the Rhineland, where advanced French and German intellectual trends intersected. During the later 1780s, Beethoven came into contact with the most distinguished minds of Bonn. His participation in the city's intellectual life took place on many levels; the tendency of biographers (following Franz Wegeler, who introduced Beethoven to the Breuning family and married Eleonore, called Lorchen) to ascribe his cultural blossoming primarily to his relationship with the Breunings is surely exaggerated. Beethoven was not an actual member of the Lesegesellschaft because, by statute, students were "excluded, for their own benefit";[18] its commission from him in 1790 of a cantata on the death of Emperor Joseph II was clearly a sign of his close connection and affinity with the society as well as of the high regard in which he was held. He established a close rapport with several of its leading members: Fischenich watched his progress and predicted greatness for him; Eulogius Schneider's *Gedichte* (1790) bore the name of the nineteen-year-old composer on its list of subscribers. In his later years at Bonn, Beethoven spent many of his evenings at the Zehrgarten, a tavern with an adjoining bookshop, run by the widowed Anna Maria Koch, which was the favorite meeting place for radicals, university professors, and intellectuals of all classes and ages, without regard to rank. And in 1789, together with his close friends Anton Reicha and Karl Kügelgen, he actually enrolled at the university. Further details—which lectures he attended and the length of his matriculation—are not known.

The university experience was not to be repeated. Wegeler informs us that when a series of lectures on the philosophy of Immanuel Kant was organized in Vienna in the 1790s, "Beethoven didn't want to attend even once, even under my urging."[19] Rather, Beethoven preferred self-education through voracious reading in everything from Greek and

Roman literature to esoteric writings on theology and science to popularizations of the works of the major thinkers; through rich encounters with poetry, drama, and opera; and, most happily, through discourse and conversation with good minds in congenial surroundings—whether in the salon or the tavern, the palace or the coffeehouse. In 1809 he wrote to Gottfried Christoph Härtel, head of the Leipzig music publisher Breitkopf & Härtel: "There is hardly any treatise which could be too learned *for me.* I have not the slightest pretension to what is properly called erudition. Yet from my childhood I have striven to understand *what the better and wiser people* of every age were driving at in their works."²⁰ This is no pose, even if the first sentence may be overstated. In the Conversation Books of his last years, he jotted down the titles of scores of books that he wished to buy or consult.

Although he was unwilling to attend the Kant lectures in Vienna, Kant's ideas had their impact on Beethoven, as they did on virtually all of the composer's educated contemporaries. The poet Heinrich Heine wrote, "In the year 1789 . . . nothing else was talked of in Germany but the philosophy of Kant, about which were poured forth in abundance commentaries, chrestomathies, interpretations, estimates, apologies, and so forth."²¹ Beethoven's was, of course, a popularized conception of Kant, one that had no room for Kant's epistemology or his exploration of the faculties of knowledge but that centered, rather, on basic moral concepts. Beethoven had no training or aptitude for discussions of the distinctions between the world of phenomena and the world of "noumena"; the Kantian idea of time and space as a priori forms of perception was beyond the grasp and probably beyond the interest of the young composer who, some university lectures aside, had never gone past grade school and had been a backward student at that. As did most of his contemporaries, Beethoven understood Kant in a sloganized and simplified form; his was the Kant of the categorical imperative who, in a paraphrase of the Golden Rule, wrote, "Act so that the maxim of thy action may be a principle of universal legislation," the Kant of "Two things fill the soul with ever new and increasing wonder and reverence the oftener the mind dwells upon them—the starry sky above me and the moral law within me." This image found its way into Beethoven's Conversation Book of February 1820 as "The moral law in us, and the starry sky above us—Kant!!!"²² Beethoven was surely familiar with the opening words of Kant's preface to his 1794 treatise *Religion innerhalb der Grenzen der blossen Vernunft* (*Religion in the Light of Reason Alone*): "So far as morality is based upon the conception of man as a free agent who, just because he is free, binds himself through his reason to unconditioned laws, it stands in need neither of the idea of another Being over him, for him to apprehend his duty, nor of an incentive other than the law itself, for him to do his duty."[23]

We know very little about the nature or extent of Beethoven's religious beliefs during his Bonn years. However, there is in fact no hint that he practiced the Catholic religion into which he had been born. Apart from the Fischers' conventional references to his mother's piety, there are no reports that his parents were active Catholics or that they instructed their sons in religious observance. It seems clear that Enlightened and especially Kantian conceptions of morality served Beethoven and many of his compatriots in Bonn as a substitute theology during this period. True, the external forms of Catholicism were observed at court. But this Enlightened "electoral Catholicism" was really a compromise ideology that permitted a relatively peaceful coexistence between the Church and rationalism. Bonn's leading intellectuals and artists were not avowed atheists by any means: Neefe, after a period of youthful questioning, had returned to belief in God; even Eulogius Schneider, the professor and poet who took up the cause of the French Revolution (and fell in the Terror), argued against hierarchical religion not as a disbeliever but as a proponent of a rationalist portrait of Christ in which Jesus is seen as a teacher of mankind. Nevertheless, many intellectuals turned away from the traditional religions during this period, indeed until a variety of neo-Christian forms and beliefs revived in the aftermath of the Napoleonic Wars. As a practical matter, religion was relegated to a subordinate position, and where it was not altogether rejected as inimical to reason, it was viewed as but a special case of the Kantian moral law.

Beethoven's superficial Kantianism and his worship of Schiller were fully consistent with service to the nobility and the court. His presumed sympathy with the French Revolution (of which, in fact, there is no sure early sign on Beethoven's part) was not inconsistent with acceptance of the given state of affairs at home. Such men as Schneider were rare indeed. Most German intellectuals hailed the revolution but condemned its consequences. Germany fought its revolutionary battles not in the political arena but on the stage and in the study. Germany's philosophers occupied themselves with the notion of freedom at the very moment that the French were bloodying their streets and their soil in search of the reality of freedom. But this political somnolence was not without its compensations. Marcuse observed that the isolation of the German educated classes from practical affairs may have rendered them impotent to reshape their society but that it simultaneously led to extraordinary achievements in science, art, and philosophy. "Culture," he wrote, "set freedom *of thought* before freedom *of action,* morality before practical justice, the inner life before the social life of man. This idealistic culture, however, just because It stood aloof from an intolerable reality and thereby maintained itself intact and unsullied, served, despite its false consolations and glorifications, as the repository for truths which had not been realized in the history of mankind."[24]

The Sturm und Drang movement, which briefly dominated German drama of a somewhat earlier period, had occasionally inveighed against absolutism as such, but as Paul Henry Lang has remarked, "Its revolutionary tendencies usually flickered out with the exhaustion of the pathos that engendered them."[25] Beethoven, too, despised tyranny, but he did not visualize—let alone advocate—the abolition of kingship. His reverence for Schiller was primarily for the author of *Die Räuber* and *Don Carlos,* dramas that center on generational and oedipal conflicts between prince and monarch. Beethoven's Schiller heroes are those princes who struggle with oppressive absolutism as representatives of Enlightened monarchy, whose goal is not conquest but reconciliation. The historical Saint Joan gives way to Schiller's (and Beethoven's, to judge from his fondness for quoting from *The Maid of Orleans*) Johanna, who rises from defeat on the battlefield not to face inquisition and immolation, but rather to receive ennoblement by the king, quite in the tradition of Enlightened absolutism and archaic wish fulfillment:

> Kneel down! and rise
> A Noble! thy monarch, from the dust
> Of thy mean birth exalts thee.
> (*Die Jungfrau von Orleans,* Act III, scene 4)

At bottom, Beethoven's Schiller is the Schiller of "An die Freude" ("To Joy"), the elevated Masonic *Trinklied* of 1785 that so profoundly captured the composer's imagination that he planned to set it to music even before his departure from Bonn. In 1793, Bartholomäus Fischenich wrote to Schiller's wife, Charlotte: "He intends to compose Schiller's '*Freude*' verse by verse."[26] It was a long way from conception to fulfillment of the "Ode to Joy" project: its musical setting in the Ninth Symphony represents the clearest statement of Beethoven's desire for harmony and reconciliation.

Utopian currents of the eighteenth century revolved around the idea of a *bon prince*, a wish-fulfilling hero who could dissolve the tangled problems of the relations between masters and men. It was such heroes—represented in German drama by Wallenstein, Karl Moor, and Count Egmont—who bore the accumulated weight of messianic hopes and strivings. We will meet their counterparts in Beethoven's *Fidelio* and his Incidental Music to Goethe's *Egmont*, op. 84, and perhaps in the symphony that he intended to call *Bonaparte*. Those who shared the hope for a noble savior did not see themselves in the role of servants of aristocratic masters; rather, they wished to preserve aristocratic ideals through the realization of what they envisioned as Enlightened rule. Their desire was to purge society of those elements within the absolutist framework that were base and "ignoble." Even Frederick the Great himself, in his *Considérations sur l'état du corps politique de l'Europe* (*Thoughts on the State of the Body Politic in Europe*), insisted that the Enlightened leader must reform the tyrannical princes. (That Frederick's version of the social contract did not altogether square with the realities of his own rule is attested to by Lessing, who wrote, "Let some one appear in Berlin and raise his voice for the rights of the subjects and against exploitation and despotism . . . and you would find out very soon which is the most enslaved country of Europe."[27])

The figure of a princely savior entered Beethoven's music with a cantata composed in 1790 in mournful celebration of Joseph II, the *Aufklärer* emperor whose idealized memory was cherished for decades after his death by many of his subjects. And reliance upon the notion of an aristocratic redeemer remained central to Beethoven's beliefs until his last years. This may enable us to understand some of the contradictions in his later political utterances, which included Caesaristic formulations along with lofty humanistic statements, apparent support of Napoleon during the Consulate along with glorification of the monarchs assembled at the Congress of Vienna, and condemnation of the restoration of hereditary monarchy under the French imperium side by side with admiration of constitutional monarchy along British lines.[28] We will see later that Beethoven's veneration for ideal Enlightened leaders—be they prince, king, or First Consul—is countered by a process of disillusionment with such leaders in reality. In his early years, however, this erosion of belief has yet to make its appearance.

Beethoven had found his place in society and had accepted—evidently without question—the current, advanced ideology of his community. Thereafter, throughout his life, he was to be unfailingly guided by a conscious adherence to the principles of political liberty, personal excellence, and ethical action. His devotion to art and beauty and his acceptance of the main notions of the Enlightenment—virtue, reason, freedom, progress, universal brotherhood—may have served to contain the eruptive forces within him that had been engendered by the conditions of his childhood and the predicaments of his adolescent years.

But of course these forces could not be wholly contained. It seems to be in the nature of adolescence that the personality undergoes a liquefying process, in the course of which the individual strives to discover new creative goals and to seek their realization. Forces previously bound up within the personality structure are liberated, new identifications and interests are formed, and hidden potentialities rise to the surface. At the same time, regressive features may well emerge, and there may be a bewildering dissolution of prior identifications and beliefs. Surely we can make out Beethoven's silhouette, if not his portrait, in Anna Freud's sketch of the mood swings characteristic of many creative adolescents: "the height of elation or depth of despair, the quickly rising enthusiasms, the utter hopelessness, the burning . . . intellectual and philosophical preoccupations, the yearning for freedom, the sense of loneliness, the feeling of oppression by the parents, the impotent rages or active hates directed against the adult world, the erotic crushes, . . . [and] the suicidal fantasies."[29]

We cannot fail to note the conflict-ridden side of Beethoven's character during his adolescent years. "Since my return to Bonn I have as yet enjoyed very few happy hours," he wrote to Joseph Wilhelm von Schaden in September 1787. "I have been suffering from melancholia, which in my case is almost as great a torture as my illness."[30] To Frau von Breuning he revealed "his obstinate and passionate moods," his occasional willfulness or irrationality. "He has his *raptus* again," she would say with a shrug of her shoulders, when he was especially recalcitrant.[31] More painfully, the young Beethoven was unable to establish a love relationship with any woman—perhaps in part because he was invariably drawn to women who were attached or pledged to others. This pattern—of intense passion for the unavailable—continued throughout his life. Beethoven's reputed first love, Jeannette d'Honrath, who was also the object of Stephan von Breuning's affections, was already devoted to an Austrian recruiting officer. Bernhard Romberg (an outstanding cellist) described Beethoven's passion for his student Maria Anna von Westerholt as a hopeless attachment like that of Goethe's Werther for Lotte; Fräulein Westerholt married a member of the nobility in 1792. Beethoven may also have been attracted to Barbara, daughter of the widow Koch, but she neglected to answer the letters he wrote from Vienna and later became Countess Anton von Belderbusch. It seems clear that he was especially drawn to Eleonore von Breuning, who later became Wegeler's wife; a letter written in the summer of 1792, in a vein remarkably similar to that in later letters to Josephine von Deym and Therese Malfatti, reveals a melancholy mixture of affection and resentment, evidently stemming from her unwillingness to be more than a friend to him:

> However little, in your opinion, I may deserve to be believed, yet I beg you to believe, *my friend* (please let me continue to call you friend), that I have suffered greatly, and am still suffering, from the loss of your friendship. . . . However little I may mean to you, please believe that I entertain just as great a regard for you and your mother as I

have always done. . . . Think now and then of your true friend, who
still cherishes a great regard for you.[32]

On at least one occasion, Beethoven's sexual timidity made him the
unhappy target of the younger orchestra players. While dining in a
restaurant in 1791, several musicians prompted the waitress "to play off
her charms upon Beethoven. He received her advances and familiarities
with repellent coldness; and as she, encouraged by the others, still per-
severed, he lost his patience and put an end to her importunities by a
smart box on the ear."[33] It must have been a desperate trial of his chastity that caused Beethoven to strike a woman.

His romantic misadventures notwithstanding, Beethoven formed
many rich relationships during his later Bonn years. Among his intimate friends were the brothers Christoph, Lorenz, and Stephan von
Breuning; Franz Gerhard Wegeler; the twins Gerhard and Karl
Kügelgen; the cousins Andreas and Bernhard Romberg; Karl August
von Malchus; and the budding composer Anton Reicha. And he was
fully at home among the members of the court orchestra. Nikolaus
Simrock, the horn player who later became Beethoven's Bonn publisher, told C. L. Junker that "the utmost harmony reigns among us, and we
love each other as brothers."[34] During the two-month stay of the electoral orchestra in Mergentheim in the fall of 1791, the twenty-year-old
Beethoven and cellist Bernhard Romberg happily served as scullions for
their fellows in the orchestra, and this journey remained for Beethoven
an "abundant source of the loveliest memories."[35] Indicative of his
friends' warm affection for him are the fifteen entries in Beethoven's
autograph album dating from October 24 to November 1, 1792, on the
eve of his departure for Vienna.[36]

His situation at Bonn gave Beethoven a relative freedom from
material want. Feudal patronage provided those whom it favored with
the necessities of life, in addition to fine uniforms and powdered wigs,
which engendered illusions of social superiority, and with a relative
peace of mind that would rarely have been obtained in a "free" market-
place. But the circumstances of musical patronage in Bonn made it difficult for Beethoven to venture outside the bounds of conventional
musical expression. Viewing Beethoven's career in retrospect, it seems

clear that a rupture with or radical reshaping of tradition was to be a necessary precondition for the emergence of his genius.

A crucial figure in this development was Franz Joseph Haydn, who was himself newly liberated from the more extreme modes of feudal patronage. In 1790, following the death of his patron, the Hungarian Prince Nicholas Esterházy, Haydn accepted an offer from the Bonn-born London impresario, Johann Peter Salomon, to visit England. In December he set out for London, where for the first time he was to achieve a full consciousness of standing upon the world musical stage. On the way there, accompanied by Salomon, he stopped at Bonn, arriving during Christmas. He was feted by the elector and the leading musicians—perhaps including Beethoven and certainly including Neefe, who was a keen admirer of Haydn's music. He is reported to have stopped in Bonn once more, en route to Vienna on his return from his triumphal English stay, in the late spring of 1792.[37] It was on one of these occasions that Beethoven showed him one of the cantatas he had written (it is not known which). Haydn was sufficiently impressed that, upon the elector's request, he accepted Beethoven as a student. A day or two after November 1, 1792, Beethoven set out for Vienna. Writing to Charlotte von Schiller in Jena from Bonn on January 26, 1793, Bartholomäus Fischenich referred to Beethoven as "a young man of this place whose musical talents are universally praised and whom the elector has sent to Haydn in Vienna. . . . Haydn has written here that he would put him at grand operas and soon be obliged to [himself] quit composing."[38]

On December 18, 1792, barely seven weeks after Beethoven's departure, Johann van Beethoven died. The Fischers must have thought of him as an old man, for they overstated his age by more than a decade; they remembered the cause of death as what we now call heart failure: "In 1792, Johann van Beethoven lay sick . . . with dropsy of the chest [*Brustwasser*], and died in the said year, aged sixty-three."[39] How long he lay dying we do not know, but from the characteristically lingering nature of heart failure, it now seems clear that Beethoven was aware of his father's terminal illness. We cannot tell whether his departure in these circumstances is to be regarded as an abandonment or as a means of absenting himself because he could not face the prospect of his father's death; perhaps both factors were at play. In any event, this separation, with all its poignancy, was a part of the process by which Beethoven passed from adolescence to maturity.

No doubt it was Beethoven's intention eventually to return to Bonn and take a leading role in the city's musical life (perhaps as kapellmeister) following the completion of his course of study with Haydn.[40] He never fulfilled this wish, however. Despite repeated declarations of his desire to visit his birthplace and the graves of his parents, Beethoven never saw Bonn again. But he was to make a symbolic, spiritual return to his birthplace in his last years, in which he once again took up the unresolved problems of his youth and arrived at a new mode of self-understanding.

Title page, Three Clavier Sonatas ("Electoral"), WoO 47.

First edition, Bossler (1783).

CHAPTER FIVE

THE MUSIC

ONN'S MUSICAL LIFE IN THE 1780S was that of a miniature Vienna, a cosmopolitan crossroads in which a wealth of Classical styles competed freely and without restriction. Beethoven had an opportunity to hear or perform the widest imaginable variety of the most important secular works of the age, from the solo sonata and chamber music repertory to large-scale compositions for the stage. Operas by Mozart, Gluck, Cimarosa, Sacchini, Benda, Neefe, Salieri, Paisiello, Grétry, Pergolesi, Gossec, and many others were staged in the early 1780s. The repertory of the seasons from 1789 through 1792 similarly included music from the leading schools of the day (excepting that of Berlin), with a heightened concentration on the operas of Mozart, plus works by such men as Paisiello, Dalayrac, Cimarosa, Holzbauer, Dittersdorf, and Pergolesi. As for instrumental music, publications by most of the outstanding contemporary composers were on sale in Bonn, including many symphonies, sonatas, concertos, and chamber works by Haydn and Mozart, and even more by Haydn's pupil, the popular and accessible Ignaz Pleyel. Furthermore, the electoral court library contained a vast amount of religious music, along with symphonic and chamber music by many composers.[1]

Neefe, to his credit, apparently made no special attempt to impose upon his student his own predilections for the music of the North German masters, but instead permitted or even encouraged Beethoven to absorb influences from a variety of sources. Beethoven's Bonn works, although they do not yet reflect an achieved personal style, reveal a broad-ranging eclecticism in which French, Franco-Rhenish, North German, South German, Viennese, and Italian influences are at play. Scholarship has succeeded in tracing many of the musical sources of his early style, but has not succeeded in establishing a single, dominant influence, partly because of the intermingling of styles in his early music

and also because the elements of the Classical style appeared simultaneously in many European centers. In any event, Beethoven's music from
this period shows the almost unvarying adoption of conventional formulas. He fully accepted the language and styles of his contemporaries
and predecessors. Nor did his first compositions impress his peers as the
works of an exceptional composer. As late as mid-1791 he does not
even appear as a composer on the list of "Cabinet, Chapel, and Court
Musicians of the Elector of Cologne" printed in Bossler's *Musikalische
Correspondenz,* although Joseph Reicha, Andreas Perner, and the
Romberg cousins are so listed.[2]

Beethoven's Bonn works explore a good many of the standard genres of his time. The piano music includes at least five sonatas, several
sets of variations, and a concerto, along with rondos and miscellaneous
compositions. His chamber music consists of three quartets for piano
and strings; a trio for keyboard, violin, and cello; and a number of works
for various combinations of wind instruments. He also composed a
good deal of vocal music, including about eighteen lieder, three concert
arias, and two full-scale cantatas for soloists, chorus, and orchestra.
Finally, there were incidental music to a ballet and fragments of a violin
concerto and of a C-minor symphony. In all there are more than fifty
separate Bonn works, two-thirds of which were composed between
1790 and 1792.

The works for winds, such as the Octet, op. 103, the Rondino,
WoO 25, and the Trio for Piano, Flute, and Bassoon, WoO 37, all heavily indebted to Mozart, were quite unabashedly music for court entertainment. Maximilian Franz's digestion evidently was helped by music
for wind instrument ensembles, and, like his brother, Emperor Joseph,
he was regularly entertained at table by a small band consisting of pairs
of oboes, clarinets, horns, and bassoons. The Octet and the Rondino
were scored for this combination. The Octet is a diverting and agreeable
work, with an Andante lightly touched by melancholy, a trenchant
Minuet, and a cheerful finale. The Rondino, a one-movement work that
leans on Mozart's melodic invention, shows equal sureness in its handling of the instrumentation. (It was probably intended as the original
finale of the Octet.) It may be that Beethoven was contented with his
easy mastery of this genre—or dissatisfied with its potentialities—for
he wrote few works for winds alone in later years.

The potentialities of the variation form were far greater, but the courtly pursuit of pleasure under the aegis of Enlightenment music theory encouraged a fashionable, *galant* style of variation characterized by pleasing but superficial embroidery of the thematic material. The sets of variations Beethoven wrote in Bonn are largely in this prevailing manner. The Variations on a March by Dressler, WoO 63, are figural variations of a fairly simple kind. The Variations for Piano on a Theme from Dittersdorf's *Das rote Käppchen*, WoO 66; for Piano and Violin on Mozart's "Se vuol ballare," WoO 40 (completed in Vienna in 1793); and for Piano Four Hands, WoO 67, on a theme by Count Waldstein, are characteristic and charming ornamental variations, although the Waldstein set is also of interest for its quasi-orchestral colors and the Dittersdorf set contains fine humorous moments as well as a beautiful slow variation in minor, marked *Espressivo* (variation 6), which plumbs the inner structure of the theme. (These last sets are said to be modeled on a set by Neefe on another theme from Dittersdorf's opera.) The brilliant set of variations on Righini's "Venni amore," WoO 65, is of superior quality, so much so that some earlier scholars wrongly believed it had been thoroughly recomposed prior to its Vienna publication in 1802.[3]

None of Beethoven's Bonn works in sonata form are studied as landmarks in the development of the form. They are essentially imitative examples of contemporary Classical sonata-style works, to which we listen in the hope of catching a glimpse of the mature Beethoven, a motif utilized in a later work, an intimation of future greatness. Nor are we disappointed in these respects. The three Sonatas for Piano ("Electoral"), WoO 47 (1782–83), are unadventurous three-movement works, with little development, utilizing simple rondo and variation techniques. Some claim they are modeled on the music of C. P. E. Bach; others hear in them echoes of Neefe, Haydn, Stamitz, or Sterkel. However, in the Sonata in F minor, WoO 47, no. 2, can be heard anticipations of the Piano Sonata in C minor ("Pathétique"), op. 13 (1798–99), and Schiedermair noted that the main theme of its third movement contains an idea that reappears in the Sonata, op. 10, no. 2, as well as in the scherzos of the Third and Fifth Symphonies.[4] In the third "Electoral" Sonata, in D, Prod'homme observed a motif reminiscent of the introduction to the Seventh Symphony of three decades later.[5] The fragmentary Sonata in C, WoO 51, composed for Eleonore von Breuning,[6] makes little attempt at thematic development; it is transparent and undemanding, with the lovely ornamental passagework of its Allegro reminiscent of the Italian style of Baldassare Galuppi or Domenico Scarlatti. The graceful Adagio, however, recalls early sonatas of the Viennese school.

The Three Quartets for Piano and Strings, WoO 36 (1785), are in the style of Mozart, whose music became increasingly popular after the installation of Maximilian Franz as elector in 1784. The Quartet in E-flat is frankly modeled on, and owes some of its most beautiful passages to, Mozart's Violin Sonata, K. 379/373a, while, as Douglas Johnson has shown, those in C and D are more subtly based on Mozart's K. 296 and K. 380/374f sonatas, respectively.[7] Each of the quartets is in three movements, with quick outer movements enclosing a slow movement in the dominant or subdominant key; the finales are in rondo form. Beethoven never published these works, possibly because of their indebtedness to Mozart, or because the piano so completely dominates the scoring. He evidently held them dear, however, for they contain a number of original melodic ideas upon which he drew in Vienna for the Sonatas in F minor and C, op. 2, nos. 1 and 3, the "Pathétique," in C minor, op. 13, and the finale of the Sonata in E-flat, op. 27, no. 1. The cheerful Trio in E-flat for Piano, Violin, and Cello, WoO 38 (1791), may, as Deiters says, be more advanced than the quartets (it is Beethoven's first work with a scherzo and the first to use a coda in a sonata-form movement), but it is lacking in depth and character.

Rounding out Beethoven's instrumental music from this period are fragments of a violin concerto and two other orchestral works. The Concerto for Piano and Orchestra in E-flat, WoO 4, of 1784 is formally diffuse and melodically uninteresting despite moments of folklike gaiety in the closing movement; although composed in emulation of the early Classical style of J. C. Bach and the South Germans, it lacks their customary craftsmanship and elegance. The Incidental Music for a *Ritterballett,* WoO 1, is of interest largely for extramusical reasons: at its performance on March 6, 1791, Count Waldstein was named as its composer. It is unlikely that Beethoven resented this appropriation of his work by his patron; more likely he agreed to act as Waldstein's ghostwriter. (Even Mozart understood that his Requiem, K. 626, was to be presented as the composition of Count Walsegg, the nobleman who had commissioned it as a memorial to his wife.)

Beethoven's propensity for instrumental music is often exaggerated. More than 40 percent of his Bonn works are for voice, a percentage that corresponds closely to the proportion governing his entire output: approximately half of his 600 works are vocal.[8] Naturally, statistics do not properly express the relative importance of various works, but they do indicate that Beethoven was drawn to the voice throughout his career. His lieder compare favorably with those of his contemporaries, although, as with most pre-Romantic lieder, few have entered the modern repertory. Most of them are in simple strophic form, but several—perhaps as a result of Beethoven's absorption of style elements from Italian opera—utilize contrasting sections, recitative passages, and through-composed techniques. Especially touching are the "Elegie auf den Tod eines Pudels" ("Elegy on the Death of a Poodle"), WoO 110, and "Klage" ("Lament"), WoO 113, the latter featuring contrasting major and minor sections and touches of chromaticism. The songs are important in revealing Beethoven's literary leanings, which largely reflect the humanist sentiments and aesthetic tastes of the intellectual circles in which he moved. He set to music poems by Ludwig Hölty, Gottlieb Konrad Pfeffel, J. W. L. Gleim, Friedrich Matthisson, Sophie Mereau, Goethe, Lessing, and Gottfried August Bürger, many of which he found in contemporary almanacs and journals. Two Arias for Bass and Orchestra, WoO 89 and 90, in the Italian opera buffa style have touches of humor, expressive writing for the voice, and skillful orchestration. Of equal facility is "Primo amore," WoO 92, a scene for soprano and orchestra, which, although long thought to have been written in Vienna, has been established as a Bonn work.[9]

In these works Beethoven remained within the traditional patterns of musical expression. His Bonn compositions rarely penetrate the surface of the emotions, perhaps because they correspond so harmoniously with the ideal of the benevolent principality in which they were created: an untroubled aestheticism that exalted abstract beauty and found pleasure in the predictable repetition of graceful patterns and forms.

All of this would make for a straightforward and wholly consistent view of Beethoven's music during the Bonn period were it not for the existence of the Cantata on the Death of Emperor Joseph II, WoO 87, and its companion work, the Cantata on the Elevation of Leopold II to the Imperial Dignity, WoO 88. These works, especially the "Joseph" Cantata, reveal what would otherwise be quite unexpected—the existence, even at so early a stage, of many of those dramatic and transcendent elements that were to form the basis of Beethoven's post-1800, so-called heroic style. It is as though the elements of the "heroic" manner existed embryonically and were waiting only for the processes of time—the conjunction of outward events and inner daring—to manifest themselves.

The news of Emperor Joseph II's death on February 20, 1790, reached Bonn within a few days. Severin Anton Averdonk's text for a memorial cantata was soon completed, and at a meeting of the Lesegesellschaft, Eulogius Schneider proposed that it be set to music by Beethoven. The Cantata on the Death of Emperor Joseph II was completed probably sometime in March; the Cantata on the Elevation of Leopold II followed shortly after Leopold's election as emperor on September 30, 1790. Although a memorial meeting of the Lesegesellschaft was held in honor of Emperor Joseph II on March 19, the minutes of a March 17 meeting state that "for various reasons the proposed cantata cannot be performed."[10] In the fall of 1791, one of the cantatas (probably the "Joseph" Cantata) was scheduled for a performance during the court's visit to Mergentheim, but was canceled after an acrimonious rehearsal: "We had all manner of protests over the difficult places [in the score]," wrote Simrock, "and [Beethoven] asserted that each player must be able to perform his part correctly; we proved we couldn't, simply because all the figures were completely unusual . . . and so it was not performed at court, and we have never seen anything more of it since."[11]

Neither work was performed during Beethoven's lifetime, nor did he ever bring the cantatas to public notice or offer them for publication; no doubt they were regarded as too closely bound up with the occasions that had given rise to them. Thus, the music remained unknown until the rediscovery of copies of the scores at an auction in 1884. In a letter to critic Eduard Hanslick in May 1884, Brahms wrote of the "Joseph" Cantata, "Even if there were no name on the title page, none other could be conjectured—it is Beethoven through and through! The beautiful and noble pathos, sublime in its feeling and imagination; the intensity, perhaps violent in its expression; moreover, the voice leading and declamation, and in the two outer sections all the characteristics which we may observe in and associate with his later works."[12]

The significance of the cantatas lies less in their strength as independent works than in the clues they provide to the formation of Beethoven's musical vocabulary. Motifs, passages, and dramatic ideas from the "Joseph" Cantata recur in the middle-period symphonies— the *Eroica*, the Sixth, and the Seventh—and in the overtures to *Coriolan* and *Egmont*. Of particular interest are several anticipations of passages in the Funeral March of the *Eroica* Symphony that reveal Beethoven's association of certain musical ideas with the concept of death. For example, the extramusical meaning of the "disintegrating" passage in the closing measures of the Funeral March movement is confirmed by the composer's use of a similar passage in the cantata to accompany the word "Todt" (dead).[13] Beethoven used one section of the cantata—the soprano aria with chorus, "Then mankind mounts toward the light"—as the basis for the second finale of *Fidelio*. The beautiful arched melody of the aria has been called Beethoven's *Humanitätsmelodie*, his "humanity melody," expressive of the yearning for freedom and brotherhood.[14] These anticipations even reach beyond Beethoven's middle years: the opening of the cantata's second section, preceding the words "A monstrous creature, named Fanaticism, rose up from the caverns of Hell," finds its fulfillment in the opening of the Ninth Symphony's finale, and in both instances the passages are followed by bass recitatives of quite similar shape and purpose.

The "Leopold" Cantata is not equally inspired—although the addition of trumpets and drums to the scoring and the martial, festive character of several sections provide a propulsive character significantly lacking in the earlier work—nor does it contain as many notable foreshadowings of the later Beethoven. Nevertheless, it has its own importance in Beethoven's development. Whereas the funeral cantata represents a stage in the formation of Beethoven's musical vocabulary for the portrayal of death, sorrow, strife, heroic defiance, grief, and tranquillity, the "Leopold" Cantata expands the vocabulary for the representation of victory and joyful conclusion. All the more significant, because this was one of the major musical problems for which Beethoven could find no single adequate solution. The "Joseph" Cantata avoids the issue of transcendent closure by circularity of form, repeating the opening "death" chorus as its finale; the "Leopold" Cantata, because of its affirmative subject matter, is forced to come to grips with the issue. Its final section, "Stürzet nieder, Millionen" ("Prostrate yourselves, ye multitudes"), anticipates in rudimentary form the section of the finale of the Ninth Symphony in which the chorus interrupts the variations and intones "Seid umschlungen, Millionen" ("Embrace, ye multitudes").

Numerous influences of other composers upon the "Joseph" Cantata can be traced: of Gluck, in the orchestral timbres and the character of the writing for strings and winds; of Mozart, whose style is echoed in both the soprano and bass arias; and of the school of Rameau, with its *tombeaux* and *apothéoses* for deceased composers. Schiedermair has also posited the influence of the Mannheim composer Ignaz Holzbauer in the introductory unison chords and in the second soprano aria, as well as in several sections of the "Leopold" Cantata. Such influences are far outweighed, however, by uniquely Beethovenian elements: the orchestral underlinings, dynamic contrasts, sudden *pianissimos* or *fortissimos*, and, above all, the first emergence of Beethoven's special kind of "absolute melody," which Hans Gál described as characterized by broad rhythms, eight-measure groupings, clear melodic curves, and diatonic movement without suspensions.[15] These *cantabile*, expressive, *legato*, sustained melodies appear in the soprano aria with chorus of the "Joseph" Cantata and reappear in *Fidelio*, the *Missa Solemnis*, the adagios of the greater instrumental works, and the "Ode to Joy" of the Ninth Symphony. They signify Beethoven's emancipation from the Mannheim style and his sublimation of the Classical melodic style of Mozart and Haydn.

It is not far-fetched to see in the "Joseph" Cantata in particular one of those extraordinary leaps in Beethoven's creative powers such as we encounter in the *Eroica* Symphony of 1803–4 and the "Hammerklavier" Sonata of 1817–18. Ultimately, such an event is not fully explicable, but it may be worthwhile to sketch the confluence of biographical and historical factors that played some role in its genesis.

The form in which the work is cast is essentially a product of the Enlightenment. For this is not a cantata in Bach's sense or an echo of the early-eighteenth-century, Neoclassical French cantata. In the late eighteenth century, the cantata was revived as a large-scale secular hymn of virtuous character for public celebration. Examples of the form, such as the Cantata for the Funeral of Gustavus III of Sweden by the German-Swedish composer Joseph Martin Kraus confirm its function as a secular requiem for Enlightened leaders, and indicate that cantatas of this type may have been current in European courts of the 1780s. Its main examples, however, were created by the composers of the French Revolution.

The Revolution sought to transform French music into a moral weapon in the service of a momentous historical mission. The frivolities and sensuousness of *galant* music were abjured, and the "scholastic" contrivances of Baroque and Classical forms were done away with; music was assigned, in the words of music historian Jules Combarieu, "a serious character which it had not had since antiquity outside of the Church."[16] In brief, the Revolution introduced an explicit ideological and ethical function into music, which was later to become one of the characteristics of Beethoven's "public" compositions. Revolutionary music was utilized in official ceremonies and celebrations of various abstract Revolutionary ideals. And one of its major functions was the apotheosis of its fallen heroes through funeral hymns, marches, and cantatas. The French were ever ready to compose such works on short notice. For example, Luigi Cherubini, a transplanted Italian composer, wrote several such works, including a Hymne et marche funèbre sur la mort de général Hoche (Hymn and Funeral March on the Death of General Hoche) in 1797, and even a premature Chant sur la morte de Haydn (Hymn on the Death of Haydn) inspired by a false rumor in 1805. François-Joseph Étienne-Nicolas Gossec and Méhul, among others, wrote similar works, with Gossec using what was perhaps the best title: Chant funèbre sur la mort de Féraud, représantant du peuple, assassiné, l'an II, dans la convention nationale (Funeral Chant on the Death of Féraud, Representative of the People, Assassinated in the Year Two in the National Convention).

The death of the hero, a theme that was to become a prime component of Beethoven's musical vocabulary and was central to the subject matter of Revolutionary music, makes its first major appearance in Beethoven's funeral cantata. We will meet it again in the slow movement marked "Marcia funebre sulla morte d'un Eroe" ("Funeral March on the Death of a Hero") of the Piano Sonata in A-flat, op. 26; the oratorio

Christus am Ölberge (*Christ on the Mount of Olives*), op. 85; the *Eroica* Symphony in E-flat, marked "composta per festeggiare il sovvenire di un grand Uomo" ("Composed to Celebrate the Memory of a Great Man"); *Fidelio;* and the Incidental Music to Goethe's *Egmont,* op. 84. Intimations that as a young composer he was already attracted to the subject of death itself were evident in several of his Bonn lieder and perhaps in the choice of a pathetic funeral march as a theme for his first published work, the Nine Variations for Piano on a March by Dressler, WoO 63. This inclination may even have been present in Beethoven's first reported composition, the lost "Funeral" Cantata of 1781, said to have been written in memory of George Cressener, the English ambassador to the electoral court who was a friend of the Beethoven family.[17]

The "Joseph" Cantata's dramatic theme, the death of a good prince, seems also to have given Beethoven leave to express deeper feelings than those possible within the manner and modes of his imitative and "obedient" instrumental music. The cantata speaks of shared grief, of love between a ruler and his subjects, of the battle of reason against ignorance and fanaticism, of a hero who dies in humanity's service. Moreover, it was a commissioned work, sanctioned and approved by Beethoven's patrons, teachers, and social superiors—a work consciously dedicated to a collective and humanistic purpose. Hence, in it Beethoven could freely give expression to his deeper impulses, including his passion for heroism. And indeed, he could simultaneously appear as a devoted son honoring his father—the kaiser being the ultimate authority figure of the Habsburg realms—and as a mournful but triumphant disciple who has survived to tell the tale.

Whether the "Joseph" Cantata also indirectly provided an outlet for Beethoven's conflict-ridden feelings toward his father, who was at this time reduced to a shadowy and feeble existence, is impossible to say. But apart from the speculative question of Beethoven's psychological predisposition to this subject matter, there is a striking timeliness about the appearance of his first major work. The "Joseph" Cantata came into existence at a critical juncture in European history, one that would soon have fateful consequences for the electorate in which it was created. Until the French Revolution, the chief German courts, whether at Berlin, Vienna, Bonn, or Weimar, had presented a relatively placid and harmonious surface; the aristocracy that presided over them was imbued with an unshakable belief in its own benevolence and in the value of its way of life and culture. Above all, it was persuaded of the immutability of its future. The storming of the Bastille on July 14, 1789, effectively undermined this pervasive confidence, which was supplanted by a sense of loss, disruption, and unrootedness. The Revolution set in motion impulses of nostalgia, even homesickness, stimulating widespread yearnings to restore an earlier historical condition. This trend deepened as the destructive Napoleonic Wars continued well into the nineteenth century. An image of an idealized aristocratic "golden age" of heroism and beauty was conjured into being. Of course, the Germans and Austrians were not unique in this: all societies undergoing disintegration, violent transformation, or repression tend to locate such mythic periods in their national past. (For segments of the French aristocracy, the seventeenth century became "*le grand siècle.*") It was only natural that some inhabitants of Bonn should yearn for the pre-Revolutionary period, before the currents of history washed away the electorate itself. And to many Enlightened citizens of the Habsburg monarchy, including Beethoven, the "golden age" was now seen to be the period of the reign of Emperor Joseph II, which became the focus of nostalgic longings. The actualities of the past were submerged in a golden glow of mythological re-creation. Beethoven's personal mythology—his revision of the facts of his own parentage—seems here to have found its social equivalent.

Whatever its biographical and historical sources may have been, the Cantata on the Death of Emperor Joseph II inaugurated a new and highly productive phase in Beethoven's career as a composer. Today, however, despite the grandness of its conception, the rhetorical dynamism of its style, and the beauty of many of its details, the work has little impact. The loosely structured cantata form was sufficient to strike ideological poses and to express conventional feelings of piety and mourning, but it proved inadequate to explore the concepts of heroism or tragedy. The "Joseph" Cantata's incipient "heroic" style elements themselves disappeared from Beethoven's musical palette for more than a decade, while he developed the technical and formal equipment necessary adequately to express these new contents.

Belatedly, Beethoven now had to master counterpoint and the forms and styles of the Viennese school.

II

VIENNA:
EARLY YEARS

Prince Karl Lichnowsky.
Unsigned portrait in oils.

Hradec u Opavy, Czechoslovakia.

Princess Marie Christiane
Lichnowsky. Unsigned portrait in oils.

Hradec u Opary, Czechoslovakia.

CHAPTER SIX

A PIANIST
AND HIS PATRONS

HERE BEETHOVEN'S EARLIER JOURNEY to Vienna had been an abject failure, his second was an unqualified success. His first decade in the Austrian capital consisted of an unbroken series of professional triumphs. He arrived in the second week of November 1792, bearing introductions from Count Waldstein along with the invitation to study with Haydn. Through Waldstein's family connections and Haydn's musical connections he gained access to the houses of the hereditary nobility, including several that had played significant roles in furthering the careers of Gluck, Haydn, and Mozart. Moreover, his reputation as a notable pianist in the employ of the uncle of the Holy Roman emperor Franz II (after 1804, Habsburg emperor Franz I) had preceded him. He was received in the palaces and salons of aristocratic connoisseurs, amateurs, and music lovers, who sought to nourish and encourage the young Beethoven as a worthy successor to the masters of the Viennese musical tradition. Upon Beethoven's departure from Bonn, Waldstein had written in his autograph album: "The Genius of Mozart is mourning and weeping over the death of her pupil. She found a refuge but no occupation with the inexhaustible Haydn; through him she wishes to form a union with another. With the help of assiduous labor you shall receive *Mozart's spirit from Haydn's hands*."[1] This prophecy was fulfilled more rapidly than could have been expected.

Beethoven was initially regarded primarily as a virtuoso pianist but as only a student of composition, despite the rather large body of works he had created during his last years in Bonn. He arrived in Vienna at a propitious moment for a virtuoso pianist. Potential rivals had vacated the scene: Muzio Clementi and Johann Baptist Cramer had settled in

London; Joseph Wölffl was just beginning his career in Warsaw. Mozart, who in his last years did not play frequently in public, had been dead for twelve months, leaving no pianistic successor of the first rank in Vienna. From all accounts, Beethoven was a remarkable pianist; his historic importance is that he bridged the Classic and emergent Romantic styles of performance. His powerful, brilliant, and imaginative style contrasted strongly with the fashionably sweet and delicate style of earlier keyboard virtuosos, although when he wished to, Beethoven could imitate their cloying and fastidiously refined manner with devastating accuracy.[2] Musicians who were attached to the earlier style allegedly found his playing harsh and disturbing, but most musicians and connoisseurs, especially those of the younger generation, were profoundly moved. His extraordinary effect on audiences was described by Beethoven's pupil, the pianist and composer Carl Czerny:

> In whatever company he might chance to be, he knew how to produce such an effect upon every hearer that frequently not an eye remained dry, while many would break out into loud sobs; for there was something wonderful in his expression in addition to the beauty and originality of his ideas and his spirited style of rendering them. After ending an improvisation of this kind he would burst into loud laughter and banter his hearers on the emotion he had caused in them. "You are fools!" he would say. . . . "Who can live among such spoiled children!" he would cry.[3]

Beethoven was concerned to maintain his preeminent position and regarded any accomplished pianist as a potential rival. In late 1793 he wrote to Eleonore von Breuning of his "desire to embarrass" and "revenge myself on" the "Viennese pianists, some of whom are my sworn enemies."[4] Vienna was a city of pianists. In the 1790s there were more than 300 pianists there, most of whom were engaged in teaching piano to the children of the best families. (According to Arthur Loesser, there may have been as many as 6,000 piano students in Vienna at the time.) Beethoven feared that other pianists might hear him extemporize and then copy down the "several peculiarities of my style and palm them off with pride as their own."[5] A few years later, he indeed encountered contenders for his position as the leading pianist of Vienna. These included Wölffl and Cramer (both of whom had returned to Vienna), Johann Nepomuk Hummel, Abbé Joseph Gelinek, and Daniel Steibelt. So keen were several of these rivalries that patrons and devotees of these men formed opposing camps and set their favorites against each other in competitions.

Gelinek remembered one such pianistic duel, in which he was quickly bested by "that young fellow [Beethoven, who] must be in league with the devil."[6] In 1799 a series of contests between Beethoven and Wölffl was held at the villa of Baron Raimund von Wetzler, a member of a banking family who was Wölffl's patron. The composer Ignaz von Seyfried described the duels between the two "athletes" as though he were reporting one of those contests between wild animals at the Hetz Amphitheater—a favorite amusement of the Viennese until the mid-1790s. (In fact, the virtuoso was indeed considered something of a freak of nature, and eighteenth-century fairs throughout Germany featured virtuosos and musical child prodigies alongside itinerant jugglers and ropewalkers.) In 1800, a similar contest took place between Beethoven and the flamboyant Daniel Steibelt at the home of Count Fries, and shortly thereafter, when Hummel was at the peak of his pianistic proficiency, Czerny wrote that the general public preferred him to Beethoven. "Soon," he reported, "the two masters formed parties which opposed one another with bitter enmity."[7] Beethoven, like Bach and Mozart before him, seems to have participated in such keyboard contests as a matter of course.

Beethoven's reputation as a virtuoso performer soon spread beyond the confines of the aristocratic salons, although these remained his primary forum. From March 1795 to October 1798 he played in at least ten separate public performances in Vienna, mostly in concerts given by other musicians (Haydn, the Romberg cousins, the singers Josepha Duschek and Maria Bolla) or in concerts for the benefit of the Tonkünstler-Societät (Society of Musicians) and other worthy causes.[8] His name was prominently featured at several of these, and the reviews were favorable. From February to July 1796 he undertook a tour to Prague, Dresden, Leipzig, and Berlin culminating in a performance at the Prussian court for King Friedrich Wilhelm II. Along with the famed cellist Jean-Louis Duport, he played his Two Sonatas for Cello and Piano in F and G minor, op. 5, for the king, who was himself an amateur cellist. Beethoven was delighted when the king gave him a gold snuffbox filled with louis d'ors; he "declared with pride that it was not an ordinary snuffbox, but such a one as it might have been customary to give to an ambassador."[9] Later in the same year he performed at Pressburg (present-day Bratislava) and perhaps at Pest as well, although it is probable that his only concert performance there dates from 1800. He also gave several successful concerts in Prague in 1798.

If Beethoven's initial reputation rested on his abilities as a performer, it was not long before he made his presence felt as a composer. His first major Viennese compositions began to appear in 1795, and within a few years several of his early publications—such as "Adelaide" (later numbered opus 46), the Sonata in C minor ("Pathétique"), op. 13, and many of his sets of variations—achieved a wide sale, so that in short order music publishers were bidding competitively for his next works. By 1799 his music was being circulated by five publishers in Vienna alone, with others waiting in the wings. Beethoven was rapidly gaining a consciousness of addressing a continental audience and achieving a measure of international fame. "My art is winning me friends and renown, and what more do I want?" wrote Beethoven to his brother Nikolaus Johann on February 19, 1796, adding, on a blunter note, "And this time I shall make a good deal of money."[10]

Czerny reported that as a youth, Beethoven "received all manner of support from our high aristocracy and enjoyed as much care and respect as ever fell to the lot of a young artist."[11] Schindler wrote that Beethoven himself "frequently declared that at this time he was best appreciated, and best comprehended as an artist, by noble and other high personages."[12] It is impossible to tell whether this unreliable witness actually heard Beethoven say this or merely deduced it, but Beethoven certainly was lionized by the aristocracy, petted and spoiled by the sensitive and the wealthy. So great was their passion for music, and so important was it to their sense of social status that they be known as patrons of an important artist, that they lavished money and gifts on him. During the initial Vienna years, he was simultaneously sponsored by a number of individual nobles. Several of these, including Prince Joseph Lobkowitz (1772–1816), Count Andreas Razumovsky (1752–1836), and Count Moritz Fries (1777–1826—"Good Count Fries," Beethoven called him), began to play a more significant role in his commissions and performances during the following decade. The most influential of the earlier patrons were Baron Gottfried van Swieten (1733 or 1734–1803), Count Johann Georg von Browne-Camus (1767–1827), and, above all, Prince Karl Lichnowsky (1756–1814) and his wife, Princess Christiane (1765–1841).

Baron van Swieten, formerly of the imperial diplomatic service and later director of the Hofbibliothek (court library) and chief of the Studien- und Zensurshofkommission (Commission for Education and Censorship), was a musical connoisseur of the first order. He founded and from the 1780s on presided (rather autocratically) over the Gesellschaft der associierten Cavaliere (Society of Associated Cavaliers), a consortium of nobles dedicated to the performance and preservation of "old" music, particularly the choral music of Handel, Bach, and the Renaissance masters. He figured prominently in the biographies of C. P. E. Bach, Mozart, and Haydn, and is well remembered as the librettist for Haydn's oratorios *The Seasons* and *The Creation* as well as the revised text for the vocal version of the "Seven Last Words from the Cross." He organized frequent concerts, usually held at his residence in the Renngasse or in the great hall of the court library, which were high points of Viennese musical life. Swieten, who had the demeanor of a *grand seigneur* and who, according to Haydn, wrote symphonies "as stiff as he himself,"[13] became one of Beethoven's staunchest supporters. Beethoven preserved one of the notes Swieten wrote to him, which suggests real affection on the composer's part. The note, dated December 15, 1794, also hints at a whimsicality (lightly concealed behind a peremptory facade) not otherwise attributed to the old connoisseur, who was to receive the dedication of the Symphony No. 1 in C, op. 21:

Herr Beethoven Alstergasse, No. 45, care of Prince Lichnowsky
If you are not hindered this coming Wednesday, I wish to see you at my home at 8:30 in the evening with your nightcap in your bag. Give me your immediate answer. Swieten.[14]

The Count von Browne-Camus, descended from an old Irish family, was in the Russian imperial service at Vienna. His great wealth derived from landholdings in the Baltic region Livonia, but he eventually squandered his income—like many other passionate devotees of the arts. His generosity toward Beethoven between 1797–98 and 1803 was rewarded by Beethoven's dedication to him of the Three String Trios in G, D, and C minor, op. 9, which the composer regarded very highly; the Sonata in B-flat Major, op. 22; and the six Gellert Lieder, op. 48. In addition, Beethoven dedicated to Countess Browne-Camus the set of Three Piano Sonatas, op. 10, and the Twelve Variations for Piano on a Russian Dance, WoO 71. In his dedication of the String Trios, Beethoven called Count Browne-Camus "the foremost Maecenas of my muse."[15]

Beethoven's foremost patron, in actuality, was Prince Karl Lichnowsky, and he remained so for more than a dozen years. His home was the center of a circle of musicians, composers, and connoisseurs, and it was at his musical parties that many of Beethoven's works were first performed. At the Lichnowsky home Beethoven met those youthful musicians who were to become famous as the outstanding players of the day, including the members of the Schuppanzigh Quartet (later renamed the Razumovsky Quartet for a time), led by the violinist Ignaz Schuppanzigh. There he formed lifelong friendships with the prince's brother, Count Moritz Lichnowsky, and with Baron Nikolaus von Zmeskall, an official in the Hungarian chancellery who remained perhaps Beethoven's most constant Viennese friend.

When he first arrived in Vienna, Beethoven stayed briefly in a small attic room, where "he had a miserable time."[16] Then he was invited to live with the Lichnowskys in their quarters in the Alserstrasse, and he remained with them as "a guest" or even as "a member of the family" for several years.[17] So close were his ties to the prince that for many years after he took his own, separate lodgings, he chose his rooms with a view to remaining in close proximity to the Lichnowskys.[18] According to Carl Czerny, Lichnowsky treated Beethoven "as a friend and brother, and induced the entire nobility to support him."[19]

The relationship was quite a coup on Beethoven's part, for the Lichnowsky family had been a leading force in Viennese musical life for several generations. The prince's mother-in-law, Countess Maria Wilhelmine Thun, had been a patron of Gluck, Haydn, and Mozart, and it was Mozart who wrote, on March 24, 1781, "She is the most charming and most lovable lady I have ever met, and I am very high in her favor."[20] Two of her daughters married patrons of Beethoven—Lichnowsky and Count Razumovsky—and she herself was one of his devotees. Lichnowsky was Mozart's pupil, patron, and Masonic brother; in 1789 he had accompanied Mozart on a tour of Bohemia and northern Germany almost identical to that which he arranged for Beethoven in 1796. Lichnowsky's wife, Princess Christiane, was one of the better pianists among the Viennese nobility.

Lichnowsky gained Beethoven's deepest affection and gratitude, and his wife, although she was only five years older than Beethoven, reportedly became a "second mother" to him.[21] The couple also earned the unusual (perhaps unique) right to suggest and even demand changes or improvements in his compositions, including *Fidelio*. They were utterly persuaded of Beethoven's genius, so much so that in 1804–5 the prince interfered in Beethoven's love affair with Countess Josephine Deym, apparently on the grounds that it would have a detrimental effect on the composer's career.[22]

In return for his patronage, Lichnowsky received the dedications of Beethoven's first major Vienna works, the Piano Trios, op. 1, and later those of the Sonata in C minor ("Pathétique"), op. 13, the Sonata in A-flat, op. 26, the Symphony No. 2 in D, op. 36, and the Variations on "Quant' è più bello," WoO 69. His wife was honored with the dedication of the Variations on a Theme from *Judas Maccabeus*, WoO 45, and of Beethoven's ballet score *Die Geschöpfe des Prometheus* (*The Creatures of Prometheus*), op. 43. In addition, Beethoven dedicated his Rondo in G, op. 51, no. 2, to the prince's sister, Countess Henriette, and the Fifteen Variations and Fugue in E-Flat, op. 35, as well as the Sonata in E minor, op. 90, to Count Moritz Lichnowsky. Countess Thun received the dedication of the Clarinet Trio in B-flat, op. 11.

But the depth of their association went far beyond this rich harvest of dedications—in fact, their relationship cannot be considered typical of that which generally obtained between patron and composer. It seems clear that Prince and Princess Lichnowsky regarded Beethoven almost as a son[23] and that he in turn experienced considerable emotional conflict in relation to them. He wanted their affection and favor, but he had an equally strong wish to be free of their custody, which sometimes had the effect of a suffocating protectiveness. His every need or want was anticipated, including (and this must have been infuriating) his desire to liberate himself from their protectiveness. The prince, Wegeler recalled, "once directed his serving man that if ever he and Beethoven should ring at the same time the latter was to be first served. Beethoven heard this, and the same day engaged a servant for himself."[24] When Beethoven was learning to ride horseback, the prince's stable was put at his disposal, but Beethoven bought a horse of his own to avoid the feeling of dependency that came with the acceptance of such a gift. (Count Browne-Camus also gave him a horse, which he subsequently abandoned.) Sometimes, as had occurred earlier with Waldstein, the prince's gifts were made circuitously in order to avoid Beethoven's rejection. Thus, Lichnowsky seems to have secretly subsidized the publication of the Trios, op. 1, from which Beethoven reaped a profit of 843 florins—equivalent to almost two years of his salary from the Bonn court.

Apparently, Beethoven was unable freely to accept these evidences of favor and affection. He would eat away from his home at the Lichnowskys in order to assert his independence: "The dinner hour at the prince's was four o'clock. 'Am I supposed,' said Beethoven, 'to come home every day at half-past three, change my clothes, shave, and all that? I'll have none of it!' And so he would very often eat at a tavern."[25] At the same time he delighted in their gifts. Lichnowsky gave Beethoven a quartet of rare Italian instruments (preserved in the Beethovenhaus at Bonn), which he prized throughout his life. And in 1800, perceiving Beethoven's need to be both secure and independent, he granted him an annuity of 600 florins, to be continued for an indefinite period (it was paid at least until 1806).

Beethoven's gratitude is expressed in several letters of 1801. He wrote to Wegeler, "Lichnowsky, who, although you may find it hard to believe what I say, was always, and still is, my warmest friend (of course we have had some slight misunderstandings, but these have only strengthened our friendship), has disbursed for my benefit a fixed sum of 600 gulden, on which I can draw until I obtain a suitable appointment."[26] To Karl Amenda he wrote, "I may say that of all of them Lichnowsky has best stood the test."[27] There were other gifts as well, of a more personal nature. Resting on Beethoven's desk until his death was a pendulum clock in the shape of an inverted pyramid on which was engraved in alabaster the head of a woman; it had been given to him by Princess Lichnowsky. And perhaps most important of all was a bust of the prince, which Beethoven kept in a place of honor in his lodgings until 1806.

If we can credit a report by Schindler, the difficulty of the matter was summed up by Beethoven himself, who supposedly said, "They treated me like a grandson. The princess's affection became at times so oversolicitous that she would have made a glass shade to put over me, so that no unworthy person might touch or breathe upon me."[28] To be put under glass was to be made a passive object—carefully preserved and beloved, true, but an object nevertheless—whereas Beethoven needed to become an active force making his mark on the world. It would be some time, however, before Beethoven would be able to loosen his bond to the Lichnowskys.

Similar conflicts developed between Beethoven and other patrons and friends. It troubled him to think that he was admired primarily for his talents rather than for his qualities as a person. When Countess Susanna Guicciardi gave him a gift, he took this as "payment" for his lessons to her daughter, Giullietta, and was deeply hurt: "I'm not exaggerating when I say that your present gave me a shock. . . . It immediately put the little I had done for dear [Giulietta] on a par with your present."[29] Typifying his anxieties on this point, he once wrote angrily to a friend, "Am I then nothing more than a music maker for yourself or the others?"[30]

This may be why Beethoven developed a reluctance to playing the piano for his patrons. Wegeler, referring to the years 1794–96, wrote that "his aversion to playing for an audience had become so strong that every time he was urged to play he would fly into a rage. He often came to me then, gloomy and out of sorts, complaining that they had made him play, even though his fingers ached and the blood under his nails burned."[31] It even became his custom to play in a room adjoining the main salon, where he could be heard but not observed. On one such occasion, when a member of the audience tried to look into the room, Beethoven promptly "left the piano, took his hat, and ran out without yielding to pleas and importunities."[32] Wegeler writes that Beethoven's resistance to playing "was frequently the source of bitter quarrels with his closest friends and patrons."[33] One of the most startling of these incidents was recounted by a certain Frau Bernhard; when she was a young visitor at the Lichnowsky residence in the late 1790s she witnessed the elderly Countess Thun "on her knees in front of Beethoven who reclined on the sofa, begging him to play something, which he refused to do."[34]

Ernest Newman thought of such incidents as "exhibitions of ill-breeding" rather than as "evidences of a noble democratic spirit."[35] Certainly, Beethoven was not an English gentleman, but neither was he a Jacobin teaching dissipated nobles a lesson. His boorishness, *hauteur*, and many eccentricities cannot be explained solely in terms of his need to demonstrate his independence and assert his equality with his patrons as a human being. The very nature of personal patronage seems inevitably to arouse in artists contradictory emotions of gratitude and resentment, submission and rebelliousness, love and hostility. And where the tie is of an especially intimate character—as was the case with Beethoven and patrons such as the Lichnowskys—these conflicts quickly become intensified. Moreover, several of Beethoven's patrons were hardly themselves free of personality difficulties and even bizarre tendencies. Count Browne-Camus was described by his tutor, Johannes Büel (a warm friend of Beethoven's), as "one of the strangest men, full of excellent talents and beautiful qualities of heart and spirit on the one hand, and on the other full of weakness and depravity."[36] He suffered a mental breakdown and was committed for a time to an institution. According to one source, Prince Lobkowitz was also highly eccentric: he would leave his correspondence unanswered, even unopened, for years, and he would sometimes spend weeks in absolute seclusion. He installed in his room a great mirror opposite the window so that he could watch passersby without himself being seen, and he is reported to have gazed into this mirror for hours on end.[37]

The Lichnowskys, too, were scarcely a normal couple. Lichnowsky, despite being a rationalist, a Freemason, and a disciple of Voltaire, was described by one contemporary as "a cynical lecher," while the princess, whose breasts had been surgically removed, was "very withdrawn" and anguished by doubts concerning her husband's fidelity. She accused him of fathering an illegitimate daughter and insisted upon adopting the child as her own. And, however unlikely, it was rumored by a contemporary scandalmonger that she once disguised herself as a prostitute and arranged to meet her own husband at a brothel.[38] ("They did not seem to live happily together," Frau Bernhard wrote. "Her face always bore such a melancholy expression.")[39]

At this time, powerful economic pressures were placing great strains on the finances of the nobility, and its drive toward ostentation and luxury was now being slowed, with a consequent curtailment of the more lavish forms of patronage of the arts. Especially in the years following the French Revolution, there were attempts to restrict expenditures on music at the palaces and the courts, which led to the disbanding of many private orchestras and theater or opera companies. When Beethoven arrived in Vienna, only a handful of the standing orchestras formerly employed in aristocratic houses remained; instead, the higher nobility kept groups of chamber players and instrumental soloists, some of whom doubled as servants. Beethoven's patrons were among those whose fortunes began to erode: eventually, Count Waldstein died in poverty, Prince Lobkowitz and Count Fries went bankrupt, and Prince Kinsky became financially embarrassed. Even Prince Lichnowsky was reported by Frau von Bernhard to have lived well beyond his means. These impoverishments, however, belong to a somewhat later period; in Beethoven's early years in Vienna, the aristocratic houses remained relatively intact despite the encroachment of debts and the necessity of liquidating portions of their estates.

The source of Beethoven's patronage had been transferred from the Bonn electoral court to segments of the Viennese high nobility. He was now a "freelance" semifeudal composer and virtuoso, moving toward relative independence from aristocratic sponsorship. But hand in hand with the growth of Beethoven's personal freedom went the loss of much of the security that had sustained three generations of musicians in his family. Throughout his life Beethoven never abandoned the hope of obtaining a permanent court position that would relieve his ever-increasing—if often exaggerated—financial anxieties. His expectation of soon returning to Bonn evaporated with the French occupation of the Rhineland in 1794. Whatever hopes he may have entertained of receiving an appointment at the Prussian court also failed to materialize. Thereafter, it remained one of his most profound wishes to obtain an imperial post in Vienna, an ambition fueled not only by his need for security and appreciation but—it may be—by his desire to emulate the great kapellmeister of his childhood. In any event, these ambitions were not to be fulfilled;

furthermore, Beethoven was not altogether free of inner conflict about obtaining the position to which his father had aspired. In the last analysis, Beethoven's desire to be his own master remained in perpetual and irreconcilable conflict with his desire for status and financial stability.

Half a century earlier, in 1749, Joseph Haydn had been expelled from the choir of Vienna's St. Stephen's Cathedral because his soprano voice was changing, whereupon he became a "free" musician, earning a living by playing at dances, writing arrangements, giving music lessons, and participating in outdoor serenades. After a decade of economic uncertainty, Haydn was relieved to secure a regular post, first as music director to Count Karl Joseph Franz Morzin in Vienna and Lukavec, and, in 1761, as assistant kapellmeister to the court of Esterházy at Eisenstadt. He remained there, as Prince Nikolaus Esterházy's leading musician and conductor, for almost thirty years, under conditions that permitted the abundant development of his creativity. Haydn was well aware of the advantages of court patronage. He told the Saxon diplomat and memoirist Georg August von Griesinger, "My prince was always satisfied with my works. Not only did I have the encouragement of constant approval, but as conductor of an orchestra I could make experiments, observe what produced an effect and what weakened it, and was thus in a position to improve, to alter, make additions or omissions, and be as bold as I pleased. I was cut off from the world; there was no one to confuse or torment me, and I was forced to become original."[40] In his autobiographical sketch of 1778 he described himself as "*Kapellmeister* to his Highness Prince Esterházy, in whose service I hope to live and die."[41]

In the service of the Esterházys he retained his nimble ability to weather all kinds of storms. "Haydn did not fight," writes biographer Karl Geiringer; "he was apparently never in opposition; nevertheless, he succeeded in having things done exactly the way he wanted."[42] By 1790, however, he began to chafe at the restrictions and isolation of life at the Esterházy palace. He wrote: "I am doomed to stay at home. It is indeed sad always to be a slave."[43]

Now, in the closing days of 1792, just returned from his first, triumphal London residence, Haydn was charged with completing the musical education of a brilliant, sensitive, and uncontrollable composer from the Rhineland.

CHAPTER SEVEN

HAYDN

I T IS SAID THAT HAYDN, IN A FIT OF PIQUE, once called Beethoven
an "atheist."[1] Although Haydn's statement may have reflected the
then prevailing view of Beethoven's religiosity, more likely it merely expressed Haydn's resentment at his pupil's reluctance to acknowledge a musical rather than a heavenly deity. Haydn was agreeable to
training a disciple who would ultimately equal or transcend him (and he
surely knew that this would be the case with Beethoven) but understandably he wanted to obtain from him the frank concession that he
was a "pupil of Haydn." Indeed, Ries reported that Haydn asked
Beethoven to place those very words on the title page of his first works,
but that Beethoven disdainfully refused to do so, unlike Haydn's more
compliant pupils like Ignaz Pleyel, Anton Kraft, Paul Struck, and
Anton Wranitzky, all of whom included phrases to that effect on their
title pages.[2] (When Ries questioned him about this, Beethoven became
so angry—even in retrospect—that he exclaimed that "he had never
learned anything from [Haydn].")[3] Public acknowledgment of their
relationship as one of master and pupil was precisely what Beethoven
could not grant Haydn. Perhaps he did not wish to be regarded as
another Ignaz Pleyel, who remained a "pupil of Haydn" throughout his
life. Even Pleyel was evidently not content with this designation, for
when Haydn arrived in London to give concerts sponsored by impres-
sario Johann Peter Salomon, he found that Pleyel had consented to
compete with him under the auspices of a rival musical society, the
Professional Concerts. "So now a bloody, harmonious war will com-
mence between master and pupil," Haydn wrote from London.[4] On the
surface, he and Pleyel remained friends, but on one occasion when
Pleyel was being praised, Haydn burst out, "But I hope it will be
remembered that he was my pupil." He wrote to Marianne von
Genzinger, "Pleyel's presumption is criticized everywhere."[5]

Franz Joseph Haydn. Portrait in oils by Thomas Hardy (1791).

Royal College of Music, London.

Beethoven began studying with Haydn in November 1792 and was his pupil for fourteen months, until January 1794, when Haydn departed for his second journey to London. The relationship between the two took on a complex and tangled character from the very start. Almost immediately after the start of his lessons, Beethoven conceived the notion that Haydn was envious of him, or unconcerned about his progress. Whether this was Beethoven's motivation (and I believe there is a better explanation), it is striking that he is said to have commenced secret lessons in early 1793 with another teacher, Johann Schenk (1761–1830). Schenk tells the story, unfortunately in somewhat garbled form and with inconsistent dates:

> Towards the end of July [*sic!*], Abbé Gelinek informed me that he had made the acquaintance of a young man who displayed extraordinary virtuosity on the pianoforte, such, indeed, as he had not observed since Mozart. In passing he said that Beethoven had been studying counterpoint with Haydn for more than six months [*sic!*] and was still at work on the first [counterpoint] species; also that His Excellency Baron van Swieten had earnestly recommended the study of counterpoint and frequently inquired of him how far he had advanced in his studies. As a result of these frequent incitations and the fact that he was still in the first stages of his instruction, Beethoven, eager to learn, became discontented and often gave expression to his dissatisfaction to his friend. Gelinek took the matter much to heart and came to me with the question whether I felt disposed to assist his friend in the study of counterpoint.[6]

A meeting was arranged, at which Beethoven improvised to great effect for Schenk and then showed him his first exercise in counterpoint, which "disclosed the fact that . . . there were mistakes in every mode."[7] Schenk claims he agreed to help him. Naturally, it was all-important that Haydn not find out. Schenk wrote, quite candidly, "I recommended that he copy every exercise which I corrected in order that Haydn should not recognize the handwriting of a stranger when the exercise was submitted to him."[8] (It seems possible that Beethoven engaged Schenk not only to check on Haydn but to help him with his homework.) According to Schindler's probably exaggerated story, Beethoven and Schenk met in 1824 and reminisced about the secret instruction: they "burst out laughing to think how they had fooled Haydn, who never once had guessed what was going on."[9]

Although Schenk's story is surely inaccurate in some details, his specific knowledge of Haydn's deficient instruction of Beethoven in counterpoint suggests that Beethoven did consult him about his exercises, and his account is confirmed in its essence by the noted musicologist Gustav Nottebohm, who reviewed the exercises written under Haydn's supervision and came to the conclusion that Haydn was not a systematic or sufficiently conscientious teacher. Only a sixth of the exercises had been to any extent corrected, numerous errors remained uncorrected, and in some cases Haydn, while attempting to correct one error, would make another in his own solution.[10] These lapses are perhaps understandable, given Haydn's circumstances at the time. The deaths of Mozart in 1791 and of Haydn's esteemed friend Marianne von Genzinger in 1793 had affected him deeply. Furthermore, Haydn was conducting more-or-less simultaneous love affairs with a London widow, Rebecca Schroeter, and the singer Luigia Polzelli. He had returned from the heady English experience to the usual and painful relationship with his wife, whose death he wished for in the most candid way; writing to Polzelli from London, he congratulated her on the death of her husband: "Dear Polzelli, perhaps, perhaps the time will come, which we both so often dreamt of, when four eyes shall be closed. Two are closed, but the other two. . . ."[11] Haydn was, moreover, preoccupied with preparations for a return trip to London in early 1794, for which he was planning six new symphonies and for which, in 1793, he wrote the set of six String Quartets, opp. 71 and 74. Perhaps Haydn also resented Beethoven because the newcomer had obtained such immediate and easy access to the highest plane of Viennese society. It should be remembered that although Haydn had influential early supporters among the nobility and its connoisseurs, it was not until after his London triumphs that his music met with universal admiration in the Habsburg capital. True, he had achieved a considerable reputation even in the 1770s, but Emperor Joseph II had described his work as "tricks and nonsense," and in 1778–79 his application for membership in the charitable organization for musicians, the Tonkünstler-Societät, had failed to find a hospitable reception.

Geiringer dates the Viennese apotheosis of Haydn from the second London residence, and he observes—perhaps with some degree of overstatement—that even as late as the years 1792–95 Haydn was still regarded by some as "nothing more than the court conductor of a Hungarian magnate."[12] Hence, there may have been some simple jealousy on Haydn's part toward the pianist-composer who was so quickly accepted and adored by many among the Viennese nobility. But this is conjecture, for we also know that it was substantially through the influence of Haydn that Beethoven was able to make his initial impact upon Vienna. Many of Haydn's pupils became Beethoven's friends or patrons, including Countess Thun, the Erdödy family, Pleyel, the violinist Wenzel Krumpholz, the cellist Anton Kraft, and the composer Paul Wranitsky. And Haydn apparently presented Beethoven to Prince Paul Anton Esterházy at Eisenstadt in 1793, surely a sign of pride in his pupil.

In any event, Nottebohm's conclusion about the insufficiency of Haydn's instruction of Beethoven is at best a partial view of the matter.[13] Countless schoolteachers and *Kleinmeister*, proficient in the craft of counterpoint, could have corrected the infringements of the rules in Beethoven's studies; it did not require a Joseph Haydn to point out parallel fifths in Beethoven's exercises. And if we look at the development of Beethoven's music during the period immediately following his studies with Haydn, we see that this was not Haydn's main function or contribution. Furthermore, the fact that errors in the exercises examined by Nottebohm remained uncorrected does not mean that Haydn did not correct them verbally or urge Beethoven (who was in his twenty-third year and already the composer of numerous works) to uncover and repair his own errors. To study with Haydn was to learn not merely textbook rules of counterpoint and part writing, but the principles of formal organization, the nature of sonata writing, the handling of tonal forces, the techniques by which dynamic contrasts could be achieved, the alternation of emotional moods consistent with artistic unity, thematic development, harmonic structure—in short, the whole range of ideas and techniques of the Classical style. There is no evidence that Haydn formally instructed Beethoven in such matters; he did not need to, for Beethoven took Haydn as his musical model and absorbed these lessons by his presence and his example.

There was no shortcut from the "Joseph" Cantata to the *Eroica* Symphony. Men like Schenk and the music theorist Johann Georg Albrechtsberger could teach Beethoven counterpoint, but they could not convey to him the heritage of Mozart and Haydn. Beethoven's difficulty with Haydn was that he learned too much from him—more than he could acknowledge. And this may partly explain why he was less than forthright in his dealings with the older man. First there was the secret instruction with Schenk, which did not remain a secret from Haydn for very long: "After a year," wrote Schenk, "Beethoven and Gelinek had a falling out. . . . As a result, Gelinek got angry and betrayed my secret. Beethoven and his brothers made a secret of it no longer."[14] But this was not the only reason for Haydn's disenchantment with his student during the fourteen months of formal instruction. Beethoven took cash advances from his teacher, misinformed him about the amount of his subsistence allowance from Bonn, and led him to believe that a number of works written before his departure from Bonn were new compositions.

Beethoven's motives in this last regard were by no means malevolent. Perhaps he had hoped to impress Haydn with his productivity. But the fact was that he had not been able to complete a single work of importance during 1793;[15] the year had been almost wholly given over to revisions of such Bonn compositions as the Octet, op. 103, and the Piano Concerto No. 2 in B-flat, op. 19. Although it was long believed that the Trios, op. 1, had been written or completed in 1793 and performed for Haydn prior to his departure for London in January 1794, it now seems fairly certain from the investigations of Douglas Johnson that nos. 2 and 3 were sketched and composed only after Haydn's departure and that the final autograph of no. 1 also dates from late 1794 or early 1795. The date of the Trio no. 1 "cannot be conclusively established," but the evidence suggests that it was begun somewhat earlier, perhaps in Bonn, and touched up in Vienna.[16] The only other works that may have been completed in 1793 were the Variations for Piano and Violin on "Se vuol ballare," WoO 40, the Rondo for Wind Octet, WoO 25, the lost Oboe Concerto, Hess 12, and a few lieder.[17]

Beethoven's productivity in the year 1793 showed that he was not yet ready to consolidate his gains as a composer. Very possibly the move to Vienna, the demands of his virtuoso career, the death of his father, and his need for time to absorb Haydn's profound precepts all contributed temporarily to retard Beethoven's productivity as a composer. Perhaps there was also a loss of creative confidence, which led Beethoven to pretend that some Bonn works (perhaps partly rewritten in some cases) were new compositions. In his last years, Beethoven came to realize that occasional periods of standstill were to be expected. ("Many times I haven't been able to compose for long periods of time, but it always comes back sooner or later," he reportedly said.)[18] But the young Beethoven may have been deeply troubled by such creative difficulties.

On November 23, 1793, almost one year after his work with Beethoven had begun, Haydn wrote a letter to Elector Maximilian Franz in Bonn on behalf of his student that reveals his paternal affection for Beethoven, the high regard in which he held him as a composer, the pride he took in being his teacher, and his total unawareness that Beethoven was anything other than a devoted pupil:

MOST REVEREND ARCHBISHOP AND ELECTOR,

I am taking the liberty of sending to your Reverence in all humility a few pieces of music—a quintet, an eight-voice "Parthie," an oboe concerto, a set of variations for the piano, and a fugue—composed by my dear pupil Beethoven, who was so graciously entrusted to me. They will, I flatter myself, be graciously accepted by your Reverence as evidence of his diligence beyond the scope of his own studies. On the basis of these pieces, expert and amateur alike cannot but admit that Beethoven will in time become one of the greatest musical artists in Europe, and I shall be proud to call myself his teacher. I only wish that he might remain with me for some time yet.

While I am on the subject of Beethoven, may your Reverence permit me to say a few words concerning his financial affairs. For the past year he was allotted 100# [ducats]. That this sum was insufficient even for mere living expenses your Reverence will, I am sure, be well aware. Your Reverence, however, may have had good reasons for sending him out into the great world with so small a sum. On this assumption and in order to prevent him from falling into the hands of usurers, I have on the one hand vouched for him and on the other advanced him cash, so that he owes me 500 fl., of which not a kreutzer has been spent unnecessarily. I now request that this sum be paid him. And since to work on borrowed money increases the interest, and what is more is very burdensome for an artist like Beethoven, I thought that if your Reverence would allot him 1000 fl. for the coming year, your Reverence would be showing him the highest favor, and at the same time would free him of all anxiety. For the teachers which are absolutely indispensable to him and the expenses which are unavoidable if he is to be admitted to some of the houses here, take so much that the barest minimum that he needs comes close to 1000 fl. As to the extravagance that is to be feared in a young man going out into the great world, I think I can reassure your Reverence. For in hundreds of situations I have always found that he is prepared, of his own accord, to sacrifice everything for his art. This is particularly admirable in view of the many tempting opportunities and should give your Reverence the assurance that your gracious kindness to Beethoven will not fall into the hands of usurers. In the hopes that your Reverence will graciously accept this request of mine in behalf of my dear pupil, I am, with deepest respect, your Reverence's most humble and obedient servant

JOSEPH HAYDN

Kapellmeister of Prince Nicholas Esterházy

Vienna, November 23, 1793[19]

The elector's reply was, at the very least, disillusioning:

The music of young Beethoven which you sent me I received with your letter. Since, however, this music, with the exception of the fugue, was composed and performed here in Bonn before he departed on his second journey to Vienna, I cannot regard it as progress made in Vienna.

As far as the allotment which he has had for his subsistence in Vienna is concerned, it does indeed amount to only 500 fl. But in addition to this 500 fl. his salary here of 400 fl. has been continuously paid to him; he received 900 fl. for the year. I cannot, therefore, very well see why he is as much in arrears in his finances as you say.

I am wondering, therefore, whether he had not better come back here in order to resume his work. For I very much doubt that he has made any important progress in composition and in the development of his musical taste during his present stay, and I fear that, as in the case of his first journey to Vienna, he will bring back nothing but debts.[20]

Doubtless knowing that a storm was impending, Beethoven wrote to the elector on the same day that Haydn's letter was dispatched, begging "that your Electoral Highness will not deprive me of the kindness once granted" and assuring him of his eternal respect for his "kindness" and "nobility."[21] Clearly, Haydn had been deceived by Beethoven, both as to the provenance of these works he so proudly sent to the elector and as to his pupil's income from the electoral court. He had unwittingly been led by Beethoven to understate the income by 400 florins, to the chagrin of all the parties—especially Haydn, who now understood that he had dim prospects of recovering the 500 florins he had lent Beethoven. Perhaps it was as a result of this episode that Haydn's reported plan to take Beethoven to London with him was abandoned, and that there was no formal resumption of lessons after Haydn returned to Vienna in early September 1795. Haydn arranged for the continuation of Beethoven's studies in counterpoint with the composer and renowned pedagogue Johann Georg Albrechtsberger (1736–1809), a course of instruction that began soon after Haydn's departure and continued until approximately the spring of 1795.

Beethoven's tendency to arouse in his Vienna teachers conflicting reactions compounded of affection and resentment, admiration and enmity, was not restricted to Haydn. The noted Italian opera composer and imperial kapellmeister Antonio Salieri (1750–1825) was Beethoven's teacher in dramatic and vocal composition for a number of years in Vienna, starting perhaps as early as 1798.[22] The young Ignaz Moscheles, who in 1808 moved to Vienna to study with Salieri and Albrechtsberger, remembered "how astonished I was one day when calling upon Hofkapellmeister Salieri, who was not at home, to see on his table a sheet of paper on which was written, in large, bold characters, 'The pupil Beethoven has been here.'"[23] This evidently took place in 1808 or 1809 and seems to indicate a warm relationship between the teacher and his former student. Yet in January of 1809 Beethoven described Salieri as "my most active opponent."[24] In 1799 Beethoven dedicated to Salieri his Three Sonatas for Violin and Piano, op. 12, but when his teacher criticized *Fidelio,* Beethoven refused to make the suggested changes and remained angry for some time. For his part, Salieri could not accept Beethoven's later works, and it was during Salieri's tutelage of Schubert that the young composer became for a short while so heated an opponent of Beethoven's music.[25]

Albrechtsberger, too, seems to have had mixed feelings about his student. He wrote three extremely friendly letters to Beethoven in 1796 and 1797,[26] but Jan Emanuel Doležálek, a contemporary musician whom Thayer considered a reliable witness, claimed that Albrechtsberger called one of Beethoven's opus 18 quartets "trash" and advised him not "to have anything to do with [Beethoven]; he learned absolutely nothing and will never accomplish anything decent."[27] For his part, Beethoven referred to Albrechtsberger as a "musical pedant" and creator of "musical skeletons." Nevertheless, he cherished Albrechtsberger's course of instruction, returned to it for self-study, and in later years rendered assistance to his former teacher's nephew. Nottebohm reported on Albrechtsberger's instruction of Beethoven in a totally favorable light.

Beethoven's difficulty in crediting his teachers extended to Albrechtsberger and Salieri as well as Haydn. According to Ries, "All three thought very highly of Beethoven but were of one opinion of him as a student. Each said Beethoven was always so stubborn and so bent on having his own way that he had had to learn many things through hard experience which he had refused earlier to accept through instruction. Albrechtsberger and Salieri in particular were of this opinion."[28] Another central figure in Viennese musical life, the piano manufacturer Andreas Streicher, similarly commented on what he saw as his friend Beethoven's failure generously to credit his teachers, according to Mary and Vincent Novello, who interviewed him in 1829: "Beethoven is considered very ungrateful by Mr. Streicher, he was a pupil of both Haydn and Albrechtsberger, yet never acknowledged it, either in his publications or by speech."[29]

In any case, Haydn appears to have forgiven Beethoven after returning from his second residence in London; certainly, they renewed their association and it would be nice to think that Haydn even continued, perhaps informally, to instruct his pupil and comment on his works. On December 18, 1795, Beethoven was the sole featured instrumentalist at a Haydn concert in the small Redoutensaal of the imperial palace in which three of the "London" symphonies were featured, surely a sign of great favor by Haydn and an indication that he considered Beethoven his protégé. And Beethoven in turn dedicated to Haydn his important set of three Piano Sonatas, op. 2, in 1796, and improvised publicly on Haydn themes. In addition, he scored one of Haydn's quartets (opus 20, no. 1, in E-flat) and in later years obtained and carefully preserved the autograph of one of the "London" symphonies.

Why, then, do we find Beethoven expressing hostility toward his former teacher? Ries related that "Haydn seldom escaped without a few digs in the ribs, for Beethoven cherished a grudge against him from earlier days."[30] Beethoven reportedly told Ries that the reason for his "grudge" against Haydn was that Haydn had severely criticized the third of the opus 1 Trios:

> This astonished Beethoven, inasmuch as he considered the third the best of the Trios, as it is still the one which gives the greatest pleasure and makes the greatest effect. Consequently, Haydn's remark left a bad impression on Beethoven and led him to think that Haydn was envious, jealous, and ill-disposed toward him. I confess that when Beethoven told me of this I gave it little credence. I therefore took occasion to ask Haydn himself about it. His answer, however, confirmed Beethoven's statement; he said he had not believed that this Trio would be so quickly and easily understood and so favorably received by the public.[31]

Despite the reasonableness of his teacher's explanation, Beethoven did not forgive the criticism, which he may have interpreted to mean that Haydn had set boundaries upon his creativity.

Thayer marked 1800 as a critical year for Beethoven: "It is the year in which, cutting loose from the pianoforte, he asserted his claims to a position with Mozart and the still living and productive Haydn in the higher forms of chamber and orchestral composition—the quartet and the symphony."[32] It is therefore not very surprising to find that

Beethoven's conflicts with Haydn reached their peak at around this time. Ries's report of Beethoven's "grudge" against Haydn describes events that postdate 1800, as does a famous anecdote that indicates how strained relations between them had become at this time. Haydn, meeting Beethoven on the street, complimented him on his ballet music for *The Creatures of Prometheus*. "Oh, dear Papa," Beethoven responded, "you are too good; but it is no *Creation* by a long shot." Startled by the unnecessary comparison with his own masterpiece, Haydn retorted, "You are right. It is no *Creation*, and I hardly think it ever will be!"[33] Beethoven made no secret of his competition with Haydn at this time. Doležálek reports that when the Septet, op. 20 (completed in 1799), was first played Beethoven exclaimed, "This is my *Creation*."[34]

It seems possible, then, that by the turn of the century Beethoven felt the weight of Haydn's influence (as well as that of the Viennese school, of which Haydn was the greatest surviving representative) as an impediment to the attainment of his own musical individuality.[35] It should be noted, however, that although Haydn was clearly Beethoven's major (though far from his only) musical influence, in addition to being his teacher, there are already many wholly individual characteristics in Beethoven's compositions of this period. In any event, it seems to have been necessary for Beethoven's further development that having absorbed some of the precepts of Mozart and Haydn, he now begin to move toward a new synthesis of styles that would make his future works a thoroughgoing departure from those of his predecessors and contemporaries.

To be sure, this process was already under way in the later 1790s. Indeed, some connoisseurs were not ready wholly to accept the early Beethoven as an authentic inheritor of the Mozart-Haydn tradition. If we are to believe the recollections of Carl Czerny, it was at this very time that "all the followers of the old Mozart-Haydn school opposed [Beethoven] bitterly."[36] We know that this is not altogether accurate, for Prince Lichnowsky, Count Thun, Prince Lobkowitz, Count Anton Georg Apponyi, Baron van Swieten, and other patrons of Beethoven were also among the significant enthusiasts of his predecessors' music. But it was surely a source of disappointment to Beethoven that Swieten, writing in the first volume of the *Allgemeine musikalische Zeitung* in 1799, failed to mention his name among those contemporary composers "who tread firmly in the footsteps of the truly great and good."[37] Furthermore, early critics were apparently more sensitive than we are to the extent of Beethoven's departures from the tradition, especially those of a harmonic nature. Reviewers in the *Allgemeine musikalische Zeitung* complained of "clumsy, harsh modulations" in his early sets of variations, and they found in his elegant Violin Sonatas, op. 12, "a forced attempt at strange modulations, an aversion to the conventional key relationships, a piling up of difficulty upon difficulty."[38]

If these signs of Beethoven's revolutionary style shift were perceptible to his contemporaries several years before the *Eroica* Symphony, they certainly had long been apparent to Joseph Haydn. Thus, it became evident to Beethoven that, unless he was willing to write numerous works like the Septet and First Symphony, his "new path" (as he termed it) would mean creating music that might not be to Haydn's taste or meet with his approval. Ignaz von Seyfried, who was close to both Beethoven and Haydn during this period, makes this explicit when he writes that Beethoven suffered from "a sort of apprehension, because he was aware that he had struck out a path for himself which Haydn did not approve of."[39] To protect himself from the feelings of sorrow and guilt that accompanied this process of professional separation, Beethoven began to loosen the personal tie as well, and he visited the increasingly infirm Haydn "less and less."[40]

Haydn missed Beethoven. Seyfried writes that he frequently inquired after him, asking, "Well, how goes it with our Grand Mogul?" knowing that Seyfried would tell his friend that Haydn had asked after him.[41] In 1803, Haydn (almost humbly) submitted a text to Beethoven through their mutual friend Griesinger, asking for his opinion as to whether it was a fit subject for an oratorio setting. Griesinger, who was acting as a Viennese agent for Breitkopf & Härtel, wrote to the Leipzig music publisher, "Papa's [request] will surprise you not less than it did me; but that is really what happened! . . . It is likely that Haydn's decision will depend on Beethoven's pronouncement."[42] In due course, Beethoven reported unfavorably on the text, but of course it was not the text that primarily concerned Haydn, who "was delighted that Beethoven was so well disposed toward him, for he had the feeling that Beethoven was guilty of a great arrogance toward him."[43] The older man longed for contact and friendship with Beethoven, and one would like to believe that Beethoven's desire was equally great, that his withdrawal from Haydn was painful to him, arousing feelings of remorse over being young and productive at a time when Haydn was unable to work and was approaching death.

Beethoven attended the March 27, 1808, concert in honor of Haydn's seventy-sixth birthday, which featured a performance of *The Creation*. He stood with members of the high nobility "at the door of the hall of the university to receive the venerable guest on his arrival there in Prince Esterházy's coach," and accompanied him as he was carried in an armchair into the hall, to the sound of trumpets and drums.[44] It is said that Beethoven "knelt down before Haydn and fervently kissed the hands and forehead of his old teacher."[45] After Haydn's death, which is nowhere mentioned in Beethoven's correspondence, all residual traces of resentment and bitterness disappeared, to be replaced by unlimited expressions of praise and affection.

In later years, Beethoven unfailingly referred to his old master in terms of reverence, recognizing him as the equal of Handel, Bach, Gluck, and Mozart. And on one occasion he even refused to acknowledge that he himself merited a place alongside these men. "Do not rob Handel, Haydn and Mozart of their laurel wreaths," he wrote to a young admirer in 1812. "They are entitled to theirs, but I am not yet entitled to one."[46] But in his earlier years he had not yet achieved this level of confidence, and he felt the need to insist upon his equality with the Viennese masters; writing to Breitkopf & Härtel about Haydn's and Mozart's talent for arranging their own sonatas, he observed, "Without wishing to force my company on those two great men, I make the same statement about my own pianoforte sonatas also. . . . I am quite convinced that nobody else could do the same thing with ease."[47]

Viewed in the light of the conflict both of generations and of styles, it is not surprising that Haydn should have been unable to follow Beethoven beyond the limits of the Classical style that he himself had perfected. A number of reports allege that Haydn was hostile to Beethoven's post-1800 music. For example, one contemporary musician recalled that Haydn "could not quite reconcile himself with Beethoven's music,"[48] and the writer Giuseppe Carpani quoted Haydn as saying of Beethoven's compositions, "The first works pleased me very much; but I confess that I do not understand the later ones. It seems to me that he writes more and more fantastically."[49] No single one of these reports can be confirmed by documentary evidence, and the reliability of the most detailed of them has been questioned.[50] But the sheer number of these recollections—and the total absence of reports of praise by Haydn for any of Beethoven's compositions following the Septet and *The Creatures of Prometheus*—make it rather probable that Haydn was unable or unwilling to embrace Beethoven's greater achievements.[51] This must have been a source of pain to the younger composer. Certainly it reinforced his feeling that he had to make his own way—even without the appreciation and encouragement of the man whom he venerated above all other living composers.[52]

Title page, Trios, op. 1.

First edition, Artaria & Co. (1795). Courtesy of Gesellschaft der Musikfreunde, Vienna.

CHAPTER EIGHT

PORTRAIT
OF A YOUNG COMPOSER

BEETHOVEN WAS SHORT OF STATURE, with a large head and thick, bristly coal-black hair framing a pockmarked and ruddy-complexioned face. His forehead was broad and heavily underlined by bushy eyebrows. Some contemporaries report that he was "ugly" and even "repulsive," but many remarked the animation and expressiveness of his eyes, which reflected his inner feelings to an extraordinary extent—now flashing and brilliant, at other times filled with an indefinable sadness. His mouth was small and delicately shaped. He had white teeth, which he habitually rubbed with a napkin or handkerchief. His chin was broad and divided by a deep cleft. He was powerfully built, with wide shoulders, strong hands overgrown with hair, and short, thick fingers. It was to be some years before his frame filled out and became robust; he remained lean until his mid-thirties. He was wholly lacking in physical grace: his movements were awkward and clumsy, and he constantly overturned or broke things and tended to spill his inkwell into the piano. Ries wondered how Beethoven ever managed to shave himself, for his cheeks were covered with cuts. Although, upon his arrival in Vienna, Beethoven noted down in his diary the name and address of a dance master, he never learned to dance in time to music. His "entire deportment," Frau von Bernhard wrote, "showed no signs of exterior polish; on the contrary he was unmannerly in both demeanor and behavior."[1]

His outer dress was altogether variable and often reflected his inner moods. As the years progressed he tended to go about, as the dramatist Franz Grillparzer noted, "dressed in a most negligent, indeed even slovenly way."[2] But in the early Vienna years he was neatly and on occasion even modishly dressed. Naturally he abjured the pre-1789 courtly gentleman's costume, with its knee breeches and wigs, which by the 1790s had become a mere anachronism. Frau von Bernhard vividly remembered a study in contrasts at the Lichnowsky residence: "Haydn and Salieri sat on the sofa on one side of the little music room, both most carefully dressed in the old-fashioned style with bagwig, shoes, and silk stockings, while Beethoven used to appear even here in the freer, ultra-Rhenish garb, almost carelessly dressed."[3] In accord with the imitation of Roman styles under the influence of the French, Beethoven at this time wore his hair cut "à la Titus." Later, he let it grow as it would.

In the company of strangers, Beethoven was "reserved, stiff, and seemingly haughty."[4] Haydn was not the only one who regarded him as arrogant and overbearing. One report recalled his "studied rudeness" and thought this suggested that he was "acting a part."[5] Beethoven's defensive exterior masked a fragile sensitivity to slights, real or imagined. He would storm away from an aristocratic dinner in fury because he had not been seated at the main table. Exaggerated or false attentiveness equally disturbed him; on one occasion he suddenly quit the country house of a certain baron because the latter "annoyed him with his excessive politeness, and he could not bear to be asked, every morning, if he were quite well."[6] Cherubini called him "an unlicked bear"; Goethe regarded him as "an utterly untamed personality."[7] His closest friends suffered his moods and sudden rages—most often followed by expressions of boundless penitence. Occasionally his temper crossed the boundary into physical violence. He was seen to throw an unwanted entrée at a waiter's head, and to pelt a housekeeper with eggs that he found insufficiently fresh.

Among his close friends he could be exuberant, lively, and talkative, even garrulous. Czerny remembered that in the early years, apart from his inevitable melancholic moods, Beethoven was "always merry, mischievous, full of witticisms and jokes."[8] His correspondence with certain friends crackles with zany metaphors, satire, exuberant jests, and occasionally scatological wordplay. In company, or when listening to mediocre music, he would often unaccountably break into a loud, hearty laugh, as though he had attained a Homeric insight into an indefinable drollery. His friends, wrote Seyfried, "seldom learned the why and wherefore of an explosion of this kind, since as a rule he laughed at his own secret thoughts and imaginings without condescending to explain them."⁹ Rarely, however, could he sustain one mood for any extended time. He wrote to Bettina Brentano that he had attended "a bacchanalia, where I really had to laugh a great deal, with the result that today I have had to cry as heartily." "Exuberant jollity," he explained, "often drives me back most violently into myself."¹⁰

Beethoven's daily life was organized so as to maximize his creative productivity. He arose at daybreak, breakfasted, and went directly to his desk, where he normally worked—with occasional time out for a short walk—until midday. His dinner concluded, he generally took a long walk ("twice around the city," according to Seyfried),¹¹ which could occupy much of the afternoon. Toward nightfall he often repaired to a favorite tavern to meet with friends and read the newspapers. Evenings were typically spent in company, at the theater, or making music. He retired early, usually at ten o'clock, but would sometimes continue to write for many more hours through the night until a creative surge was exhausted.

He sketched musical ideas constantly, whether at home, on the street, in a tavern, lying on his side in a meadow, or perched in the crook of a branched tree. "I always have a notebook . . . with me, and when an idea comes to me, I put it down at once," he told young Gerhard von Breuning, the son of his friend Stephan von Breuning. "I even get up in the middle of the night when a thought comes, because otherwise I might forget it."¹² He filled a large number of sketchbooks during his lifetime, and retained them for very occasional reference (and perhaps because he hesitated to discard any evidence of his creativity) until his death. "I dare not go without my banner," he said, quoting Schiller's Joan of Arc, when asked why he always carried a sketchbook with him.¹³

Beethoven's productivity was generally richer during the warmer months, which he spent, like most Viennese of means, in rural districts and spas outside the capital. In the 1790s he probably passed his summers at the country estates of his patrons and admirers. After becoming financially more secure, he took his own summer lodgings, with rare exceptions, each year from 1800 on, staying in places like Baden, Mödling, Döbling, Hetzendorf, and Heiligenstadt. In the countryside he was better able to find tranquillity, seclusion, and contact with nature, which he worshiped in an almost religious fashion: "It is indeed," he wrote in stammering phrases, "as if every tree in the countryside spoke to me, saying 'Holy! Holy!' In the forest, enchantment! Who can express it all?"[14] In a letter of 1810 he wrote that he looked forward to the country with "childish excitement": "How delighted I shall be to ramble for a while through bushes, woods, under trees, through grass and around rocks. No one can love the country as much as I do. For surely woods, trees, and rocks produce the echo which man desires to hear."[15] Beethoven's creativity required peaceful, conflict-free external surroundings. This may be why he wrote in his diary that "tranquillity and freedom are the greatest treasures."[16]

Perhaps in the pursuit of an unattainable tranquillity, Beethoven changed his lodgings almost as readily as his moods. "Scarcely was he established in a new dwelling," Seyfried wrote, "when something or other displeased him, and he walked himself footsore to find another."[17] It was said that the slightest provocation led him to pack his belongings, and at times it became difficult to find an apartment for so unreliable a lodger. (This was especially true of the years 1799–1804 and of Beethoven's last decade: for he remained a faithful lodger at the Pasqualati house—with only several interruptions—from late 1804 until 1814.) Perhaps Beethoven's restlessness reflected his unsatisfied desire to establish a real home, a desire unrealizable in view of his bachelorhood, to which he never became fully reconciled.

If he did not establish his own family, he repeatedly attempted to participate, by reflected light as it were, in the family life of others. Frequently, so much so that it became one of the basic patterns of Beethoven's life until his final decade, he attached himself to a series of families as a surrogate son or brother. This pattern first became visible in Bonn, with the Breuning, Koch, and Westerholt families, and continued in Vienna, with the Lichnowskys for some years, as we have seen. The Lichnowskys were followed by the Brunsvik, Guicciardi, and Deym families, the Bigots, the Erdödys, the Malfattis, the Brentanos, the Giannattasios, and the Streichers. It can fairly be said that Beethoven's happiest personal moments—music making aside—were spent in these home settings, where he could experience some of the joys, pleasures, and fellowship of family life. It was at the hearths of these surrogate families that most of his love interests were kindled— sometimes unwittingly. Consequently, it is not surprising that these quasi-familial relationships developed stresses that undermined each of them, whereupon Beethoven, after a period of mourning mingled with distress, would take up his peregrinations in search of another "ideal" family or a reasonable facsimile thereof.

Of his own family, only his two younger brothers, Caspar Carl and Nikolaus Johann, were still alive. The former arrived in Vienna in 1794 and, after a brief career as a music teacher, obtained a minor position as bank cashier in the state bureaucracy, which he held until his death in 1815. He occasionally served his brother, rather ineptly, as unpaid secretary and business agent. Beethoven had less contact during the early years with Nikolaus Johann, who followed his brothers to Vienna in 1795. He was employed as a pharmacist's assistant in Vienna until 1808, when he started a shop of his own in Linz and became wealthy, perhaps in good part from war profits made during the French occupation of 1809. Beethoven's relations with his brothers alternated freely between effusive fraternal affection and rivalry, which on more than one occasion led to physical violence. It never occurred to him that his brothers knew how to conduct their own lives: he repeatedly interfered in their affairs, asserting his supposed prerogatives as the eldest brother and guardian.

Perhaps in partial compensation for his fraternal conflicts, Beethoven entered into intimate association with a series of idealized brother figures. This, too, was a continuation of a Bonn pattern, which began with the Breuning brothers, the Romberg cousins, Anton Reicha, Karl August von Malchus, the Kügelgen twins, and others. Typifying the tone of these relationships is Malchus's entry in Beethoven's autograph album, upon the composer's departure from Bonn:

> The heaven of my deep love ties our hearts with bonds which cannot be untied—and only death can sunder them.—Reach out your hand, my beloved, and so until death
>
> THY MALCHUS[18]

In Vienna, this series of exaggeratedly romantic friendships continued, first with Lorenz von Breuning (1777–98), who arrived there in 1794 for a stay of three years, and then with Karl Friedrich Amenda (1771–1836), a violinist and theology student who arrived in the spring

of 1798, just in time to fill the void left by Lorenz's departure the previous fall. As a talented young violinist, who was also employed as a reader and music teacher by Princess Karoline Lobkowitz and Constanze
Mozart respectively, he quickly made Beethoven's acquaintance and
soon, in the words of a contemporary document, "captured Beethoven's
heart." They became such inseparable companions that when one was
seen alone people would call out, "'Where is the other one?'"[19]
Beethoven gave Amenda a manuscript copy of the String Quartet in F,
op. 18, no. 1, with a warm dedicatory message and, prior to Amenda's
permanent return to his native Latvia in the fall of 1799 to become a
pastor, he played the Adagio of the quartet for him. "'It pictured for me
the parting of two lovers,'" said Amenda. "'Good!'" said Beethoven,
"'I thought of the scene in the burial vault in *Romeo and Juliet*.'"[20] For
Amenda it brought to mind a parting; for Beethoven the music carried
implications of a final separation and of death. Beethoven wrote of
Amenda to Ferdinand Ries in 1804, "Although for almost six years neither of us has had news of the other, yet I know that I hold the first
place in his heart, just as he holds it in mine."[21]

Amenda was succeeded by Stephan von Breuning, who took up
residence in Vienna around 1801, and, to a lesser extent, by Count
Franz von Brunsvik, recipient of the dedication of the Piano Sonata
in F minor, op. 57 ("Appassionata"). Breuning remained Beethoven's
closest friend until 1808 or 1809; after a long hiatus, they resumed
their friendship in Beethoven's last year. In 1807, perhaps in anticipation of Breuning's impending marriage to Julie von Vering, Beethoven
began to transfer his affection to Baron Ignaz von Gleichenstein
(1778–1828), and this young cellist, who hailed from Freiburg im
Breisgau, became Beethoven's most faithful friend for several years. He
handled many of Beethoven's business affairs during these years, and
received in return the dedication of the Cello Sonata in A, op. 69. In
1809, Beethoven enlisted Gleichenstein's aid in a matrimonial project,
writing, "Now you can help me to look for a wife. Indeed you might
find some beautiful girl at F[reiburg]. . . . If you do find one, however,
please form the connection in advance."[22] Later in that year, indeed, we
find both of them courting the Malfatti sisters, Anna and Therese,
Gleichenstein successfully and Beethoven unsuccessfully. The strains of
their intimacy, along with Gleichenstein's decision to marry, ended the

relationship in ca. 1810. (He reappeared on the scene only when Beethoven was on his deathbed.) "Again and again your friendship only causes me fresh irritation and pain," wrote Beethoven in 1810. "My cold friend, I send you all good wishes—Whatever is wrong with you you are not really my friend—not by far as much as I am yours."[23]

Beethoven's early difficulties in establishing an enduring love relationship with a woman carried over into his early Vienna period. He wrote home to Nikolaus Simrock in 1794, "If your daughters are now grown up, do fashion one to be my bride. For if I have to live at Bonn as a bachelor, I will certainly not stay there for long—Surely you too must now feel rather anxious."[24] Beethoven's own anxiety may be operating here, mingled with the desire that the older man assist him in entering the forbidding world of marriage.

His first known "flame" in Vienna was the singer Magdalena Willmann, one of whose attractions may have been her Bonn origins—a link to Beethoven's childhood home. She arrived in Vienna in 1794. Beethoven is said to have proposed marriage to her unsuccessfully—evidently without any encouragement or preparation. She refused him, it was said, because he was "ugly and half-crazy."[25]

Beethoven's name has also been loosely, and unconvincingly, linked with several other women whom he knew during the early Vienna years—with Countess Josephine Clary, an amateur singer, who married Count Christian Clam-Gallas in 1797; with Christine Gerhardi, another singer whom Beethoven frequently accompanied at the keyboard, who married the physician Joseph Frank in 1798; and with Anna Luise Barbara Keglevich, who became Princess Odescalchi in 1801 and who received the dedications of four of Beethoven's significant piano compositions (opuses 7, 15, 34, WoO 73). But there is no hard evidence of an attachment to any of these, and in any event it certainly constitutes a meager list for a young man in his twenties. This makes it difficult fully to accept Wegeler's frequently quoted statement "In Vienna, at all events so long as I lived there, Beethoven was perpetually engrossed in a love affair, and occasionally he made conquests which an Adonis would have found difficult if not impossible."[26] Wegeler was in Vienna for about eighteen months, until mid-1796, and therefore was probably present during Magdalena Willmann's rebuff of Beethoven. Evidently

Announcement of Beethoven's first academy, April 2, 1800.

Private collection.

it took more (or less) than an Adonis to win her. It was not until after 1800 that Beethoven began a more determined pursuit of what Goethe called the "eternal feminine." As for less ethereal relationships, Beethoven during this period seems to have had a powerful aversion to prostitutes. He warned his brother Nikolaus Johann in 1794, "Do be on your guard against the whole tribe of bad women."[27] He, too, was on his guard. It was said that the Falstaffian violinist Ignaz Schuppanzigh "once, after a merry party, took Beethoven to a girl, and then had to avoid Beethoven for weeks."[28]

This surely represents the continuation of a pattern that had been formed years earlier. From his Bonn days onward Beethoven was imbued with the ideal of exemplary behavior, and he consciously patterned his life in emulation of a noble paradigm. He proudly told his friends that he had been educated with proverbs; in a Conversation Book he wrote, "*Socrates* and *Jesus* were my models."²⁹ Seyfried summed up Beethoven's moral outlook: "Rectitude of principle, high morality, propriety of feeling, and pure natural religion were his distinctions. These virtues reigned within himself, and he required them at the hands of others. 'As good as his word' was his favorite saying, and nothing angered him more than a broken promise."³⁰

Naturally, few people could live up to Beethoven's high standards of morality, and many of his relationships were undermined by a suspiciousness that in later years took on a somewhat ominous cast. To overemphasize the latter aspect of the young Beethoven's personality, however, would be a mistake. His trusting qualities predominated to such an extent that when the composer Friedrich Himmel slyly wrote him from Berlin that a lamp for the blind had been invented, Beethoven unhesitatingly broadcast the remarkable news to all his friends. The organist Wilhelm Karl Rust, who got to know Beethoven in 1808, observed that although he was "always satirical and bitter," he was also "very childlike and certainly very sincere. He is a great lover of truth and in this goes too far very often."³¹ It is the child in Beethoven that emerges in these early Vienna years, the child whose desires for self-indulgence and play had been largely suppressed by the conditions of his life in Bonn.

Overall, Beethoven's first Vienna decade was a period of growth, challenge, and achievement. He had carried the Viennese salons and concert halls as a virtuoso, launched a major career as a composer, and forged for himself a significant place in the greatest musical tradition of his time. Whatever fears he might have entertained of a repetition of the failure of 1787 proved unfounded; Beethoven had left home, traveled to the city of the emperor, and conquered it. He rejoiced in his liberation, both from the rigors of feudal service and from the weight of family responsibilities that had burdened him in Bonn. He had loosened the reins on his creative powers and attained a consciousness of his own potentialities. To be sure, there were stresses—external and internal—that would inexorably lead to later crisis, but in the main, he was well contented by his rich productivity, public appreciation, and financial reward. It was a time in his life when Beethoven could unre-strainedly take pleasure in friendships and his newfound fame and try to become, as he wrote Eleonore von Breuning, "a happier man, from whose visage time and a kindlier fate shall have smoothed out all the furrows of a hateful past."[32]

During this period Beethoven appears to have temporarily eased the burden of the imperative that he subordinate his own needs for gratifica-tion to those of others. Beethoven's main impulse was now toward self-fulfillment. On or about January 1, 1794, he wrote in his diary: "Courage! In spite of all bodily weaknesses my spirit shall rule. . . . This year must determine the complete man. Nothing must remain undone."[33] He had acquired an unshakable faith in his ability and had become imperiously aware of the quality of his genius. As early as 1793, in a letter to his Bonn teacher, Christian Neefe, he wrote, immodestly, of "my divine art."[34] On another occasion he exhibited withering scorn toward a man who would not automatically grant him a place beside Handel and Goethe in the pantheon of genius. In later years, on hearing that one of his works had failed to please, he impatiently responded, "It will please one day," a remark that would be difficult to imagine coming from Haydn or Mozart, as Ernest Walker noted.[35] Nevertheless, the desire for acknowledgment—now, not later—was as deeply rooted in Beethoven as in anyone, and he took unalloyed pleasure in receiving the accoutrements of recognition: medals, honors, money, fame, and applause. As Thayer gently noted, "Beethoven was not always as indif-ferent to distinctions of all kinds as he sometimes professed."[36] Nor was he unconcerned about reviews. He wrote to Gottfried Härtel on April 22, 1801, broadly intimating that he expected better treatment (it was indeed forthcoming) in the publisher's influential music journal:

> Advise your reviewers to be more circumspect and intelligent, partic-
> ularly in regard to the productions of younger composers. For many a
> one, who perhaps might go far, may take fright. As for myself, far be it
> from me to think that I have achieved a perfection which suffers no
> adverse criticism. But your reviewer's outcry against me was at first
> very mortifying.[37]

But these are secondary aspects of Beethoven's personality and do not touch on the central motivations of his creativity. Beethoven was possessed of an unswerving sense of "mission," of "vocation," filled with a deep conviction concerning the significance of his art. All else was subordinated to the fulfillment of this mission. Clearly, the categorical imperative is not absent here, but rather has taken a new and proudly exultant form. Whereas in early 1793 Beethoven could take as his own Schiller's precept "To do good whenever one can, to love liberty above all else, never to deny the truth, even though it be before the throne," by 1798 an elitist, almost autocratic element had entered his thought.[38] In that year, he wrote to his friend Nikolaus von Zmeskall, "The devil take you. I refuse to hear anything about your whole moral outlook. *Power* is the moral principle of those who excel others, and it is also mine."[39] And in 1801, he referred to two of his friends as "merely . . . instruments on which to play when I feel inclined. . . . I value them merely for what they do for me."[40] One need not take such utterances literally, but in them one may see the strengthening of a boundless self-esteem, which was surely a necessary precondition for the formation of Beethoven's sense of mission and, consequently, it may be, of his "heroic" style.

Though we have no reason to believe that Beethoven inwardly abandoned his beliefs in Enlightened and humanistic principles, it is a curious fact that there is virtually no reflection of these beliefs in his actions, correspondence, or creative work during the first years in Vienna. Nor is there any manifestation of Beethoven's sympathy with the French Revolution, apart from his supposed—and unconfirmed— friendship with the French ambassador, General Jean Baptiste Bernadotte (who eventually became Charles XIV of Norway and Sweden), for two months in 1798. Beethoven's radicalism, it seems, was strongly tempered by discretion after his arrival in Vienna. In 1794 he wrote to Simrock:

We are having very hot weather here; and the Viennese are afraid that soon they will not be able to get any more *ice cream*. For, as the winter was so mild, ice is scarce. Here various *important* people have been locked up; it is said that a revolution was about to break out—But I believe that so long as an Austrian can get his *brown ale* and his *little sausages,* he is not likely to revolt. People say that the gates leading to the suburbs are to be closed at 10 P.M. The soldiers have loaded their muskets with ball. You dare not raise your voice here or the police will take you into custody.[41]

Beethoven was one of those who did not raise his voice—nor did he necessarily feel any powerful compulsion to do so. During these years there is no expression of his dissatisfaction with the Habsburg court or with the repressive imperial regime. Just as in Bonn he had readily adopted as his own the advanced ideology and outlook of that society, in the capital he tended to merge his views and interests with those of his patrons and with those of Vienna as a whole. Beethoven's ambivalence with respect to Vienna, his rages against his adopted city, begins to emerge in the following decade. In these earlier years, his desire to belong may have been predominant. In 1796 he set a patriotic anti-Napoleonic text by J. Friedelberg, "Abschiedsgesang an Wiens Bürger" ("Farewell Song to Vienna's Citizens"), WoO 121; the following year he wrote music for another war song by the same writer, "Ein grosses, deutsches Volk sind wir" ("We Are a Great German People"), WoO 122. In 1800 he dedicated his Septet, op. 20, to Empress Maria Theresia, and on April 5, 1803, he closed a triumphal concert with a series of improvisations on Haydn's "Gott, erhalte Franz den Kaiser" ("God Save Emperor Franz").

But we should beware of overstressing what appear to be signs of Beethoven's conformism. In large part his ability to express his views was profoundly restricted by a repressive social context in the aftermath of the French Revolution, when the full weight of Austrian police power was directed to supress local dissent. For example, several frankly Masonic references in his letters and diaries make it clear that Beethoven was well disposed toward Freemasonry, starting in his early years, when so many of his friends, patrons, and teachers belonged to the Order of Illuminati, the Masonic lodges, and the Lesegesellschaft, and continuing throughout his Vienna years, when Masonic ideas led a subterranean existence among Habsburg intellectuals.[42] It is doubtful, however, that he ever belonged to a lodge, despite the violinist Karl Holz's statement that "Beethoven was a Freemason, but not active in later years."[43] His name does not appear on any documented lists of Masons and Illuminati of the period. This is not surprising, because in his later Bonn years there were no active lodges in the electorate of Cologne, and soon after his arrival in Vienna, Freemasonry was prohibited as an allegedly conspiratorial secret society and the lodges were dissolved, except for one or two "official," pseudo-Masonic lodges.

Thus, if Beethoven's allegiance to Enlightened ideals was not altogether visible during these years, it does not mean that his faith in reason and freedom had given way to cynicism or that his ethical precepts had yielded to self-serving opportunism. Rather, strivings that could not find an outlet in the spheres of politics or everyday discourse were transmuted into an attempt to capture and transform the realm of the aesthetic, where he could give free rein to his world-shaping ambitions. His innermost beliefs and private quests were metamorphosed, as I have written elsewhere, "into a complex quarrel with artistic tradition, into a propulsive tension between conformity and originality, Classicism and modernism."[44]

During Beethoven's first Vienna years, both the continuation and the modification of patterns of thought and behavior that had been established in Bonn are readily discernible. There is one significant matter, however, that at first glance has no obvious earlier antecedents and that provides a dramatic insight into Beethoven's personality. This is the certainty that he encouraged, or at the very least permitted to pass unchallenged, the widespread assumption among the Viennese that he was of noble birth. This "nobility pretense" was effective for more than a quarter of a century after his arrival in Vienna, until December 1818, when, in a moment of "confusion," Beethoven confessed his lack of a patent of nobility in a legal proceeding held before the Imperial and Royal *Landrecht*, a court that was reserved for the nobility, and thereby brought the deception to an end—outwardly, at any rate.[45]

We have no way of knowing whether Beethoven set out to commit a deliberate imposture. Most likely, the nobility pretense was tacitly inaugurated when he permitted the assumption that he was an aristocrat, which flowed from the "van" in his name, to pass unchallenged. The "van," no sure sign of nobility in the Netherlands, was transformed into the noble "von" on numerous occasions, even in the early years. For example, the announcements and a review of the March 29, 1795, benefit concert for the widows of the Tonkünstler-Societät refer to "Herr Ludwig von Beethoven," as does the announcement of the concert given by Andreas and Bernhard Romberg at which Beethoven appeared in 1796 or 1797. Later, in a letter to his wife, Goethe wrote of "von Beethoven," and during the Congress of Vienna the police filed a secret report on this same "Herr von Beethoven."[46] So there was a ready and widespread belief in Beethoven's presumed nobility (though naturally not among those who had known him in Bonn), raising the ever-present possibility of exposure and embarrassment. Soon it may have been too late, and too inconvenient, to correct the belief.

There was surely no economic necessity involved in this deception. Haydn had risen to the rank of a revered national composer despite his humble origins, and without benefit of nobility patent. No pretense was required for Beethoven to gain entrée as a musician and composer to the homes and salons of the nobility, for these were open to talented men and women of less than noble rank.[47] But if the nobility pretense didn't rise from a desire for economic advantage, it was clearly a matter of some psychological urgency. It seems probable that Beethoven's growing confidence in his genius and in his personal worth could have overcome any sense of social inferiority based upon ancestry had not his identification with the aristocracy been deeply rooted.

This is not to say that Beethoven overvalued the aristocrats with whom he associated. Quite the contrary. Frequently he criticized his high-born friends, often in the most impolite and scornful language. And in later years he railed imprudently—but with impunity—against the imperial court and even against the kaiser. Clearly, Beethoven ideal- ized not actual nobles, but the concept of nobility itself. Conversely, he despised the common citizen—the burgher—with an aristocrat's dis- dain for the lowborn and the moneygrubbing. One day in 1820 his friend Karl Peters wrote in a Conversation Book, "You are as discon- tented today as I." Beethoven took up the pencil and responded, "The burgher ought to be excluded from the society of higher men, and here am I fallen among them."[48] When his deception was exposed in 1818, the nobles' court transferred Beethoven's legal proceeding to the *Magistrat*, a civil court with jurisdiction over issues involving common- ers. This had a devastating effect on the composer. He wanted nothing to do with such lower courts, which were suited, he wrote, only for "innkeepers, cobblers, and tailors."[49]

The equation of power and nobility was inevitable to one who had grown up in a hierarchical German principality. The nobility did, in fact, hold the reins of power in the Habsburg realms: it controlled the means by which one made a living, and it daily demonstrated its omnipotence in relation to those—Beethoven's father and grandfather, his teachers—who were the young composer's authority figures. The psychoanalyst Otto Fenichel has observed, "Human beings have only two ways of facing a power which restricts them: revolt; or else a (more or less illusory) participation, which makes it possible for them to bear their suppression."[50] Beethoven, through his nobility pretense, was able to put himself in the place of the mighty, to partake of aristocratic power, to share the insignia of social supremacy, and to "conquer" the nobility by pretending to be of it. (He once said, "It is good to go around with the nobility, but one must have something with which to impress them.")[51] At the same time, he was thereby asserting his equality with the aristocrats. In this he comes close to a number of contemporary thinkers—typified by Rousseau in France and the dramatist August von Kotzebue in Germany—who maintained that aristocracy should be elective rather than hereditary, based on merit rather than birth; Beethoven (who owned Kotzebue's book on the subject) probably shared this view. In an 1823 letter to Schindler he wrote, "As for the question of 'being noble,' I think I have given sufficient proof to you that I am so on principle."[52] Actually, Schindler's famous though discredited tale of Beethoven defying the *Landrecht* with the words "My nobility is *here* and *here*," as he pointed to his head and heart, is not far from the psychological truth of the matter.[53]

Central to the nobility pretense is the wish for acceptance by those in command of society: the leaders and shapers, the royalty and nobility. That Beethoven felt he had to pretend nobility in order to obtain such acceptance may be a poignant indication of the depth of this need in him. The matter only begins here, however. For not even his "confession" before the *Landrecht* in 1818, when he acknowledged his lack of an aristocratic genealogy, was able to persuade Beethoven that he did not indeed belong to the nobility. His claim of nobility was no simple pretense, nor did it rest on a theoretical definition of nobility. At bottom, it was a claim of equality of birth. Moreover, Beethoven seemed to be genuinely unsettled about the facts of the matter. In a Conversation Book of 1820, he wrote that the courts had "learned my brother was not of the nobility," and added, in apparent puzzlement, "It is singular, as far as I know, that there is a hiatus here which ought to be filled, for my nature shows that I do not belong with this plebeian M[agistrat]."[54] In thus acknowledging his brother's non-nobility and simultaneously stating that his own "nature" was that of a noble, Beethoven seems to be expressing the fantasy that he and his brother had different parents—this seems to be the only way in which the "singular hiatus" could have been filled.

The nobility pretense leads, then, back to Beethoven's Family Romance. By means of the pretense he sought transcendence of his parentage and his humble origins; through it, he could perhaps pursue his quest for a mythical, noble father to replace the mediocre court tenor who had begotten him. Thus, the pretense may well have been a medium by which Beethoven "lived out" his Family Romance. Perhaps we have here the materialization of an archaic daydream, an attempt to transform reality as the only "sure" way of fulfilling a deeply held wish.

The mythic hero fulfills his quest in a distant city—Thebes, Troy, Jerusalem, or Rome. Similarly, the creative genius often must leave home in order to find his destiny. Handel travels to London; Mozart must escape to Vienna to dissolve the ties that bind him to Salzburg; Chopin and Stravinsky settle in Paris; Beethoven and Brahms leave Germany for Vienna. Perhaps certain forms of genius can flower only under conditions of exile or alienation. Perhaps, too, the genius needs to take on a new identity congruent with his creative accomplishments and capabilities, an identity possible only in a city of strangers who are unaware of the facts of his birth and the circumstances of his past. In the new city his origins are clouded, thus becoming the subject first of speculation and then of a variety of legends. With Beethoven, the conquest of the new city was accompanied by his adoption of a new persona and by the fabrication of a noble lineage.

On some level, the nobility probably sensed all along that Beethoven was not one of them; his manners, education, and speech surely marked him as a commoner, despite his best efforts to achieve an aristocratic polish through dancing lessons, horseback riding, and self-education. It is conceivable that members of the aristocracy tolerated the great composer's pretense with a fine combination of tact and secret amusement.

But Vienna would have tolerated much more from Beethoven: for he and his music played an increasingly vital role not only in Viennese musical life but in the shaping of a people's image of itself at a crucial moment in its history.

CHAPTER NINE

VIENNA:
CITY OF DREAMS

T HE DEATH OF EMPEROR JOSEPH II IN 1790, and the reversal of
most of his Enlightened, anticlerical, and antifeudal reforms,
resulted in the withdrawal of Austria from the evolutionary
currents of European history. Two decades before minister of state
Prince Metternich and his adviser Friedrich von Gentz developed
police surveillance and political repression into a fine art, Emperor
Franz (who ruled from 1792 to 1835) had established a regime wholly
devoted to the preservation of privilege. One leading historian calls his
empire "the classic example of the police state."[1] There was an official,
controlled press; correspondence was monitored; passports were
required for travel within the Austrian realm; a network of spies penetrated all levels of society, inhibiting the expression of criticism and of
"dangerous thoughts"; and there was heavy censorship of all reading
matter and an arbitrary prohibition of all manner of foreign books. The
secret police kept guard against all signs of social ferment; the execution
or imprisonment of leaders of dissident groups of officials and military
men in mid-1795 stifled vocal criticism.

These measures, as Beethoven pointed out to Simrock, had not
created a sullen, rebellious, seething populace. The fortunes of the
trading middle class were bound up with the welfare of the court and
the imperial administration. As for Vienna's so-called sub-nobility—
the well-educated members of the state bureaucracy and the profes-
sionals who rendered personal or cultural services to the high
aristocracy—its members felt excluded from the main circles of power
and resented imperial privilege but nonetheless cherished their position
in the social order and maintained as their ideal an empire organized on
Enlightened principles.[2] (Many of Beethoven's closest friends are to be

Michaelerplatz, Vienna. Colored engraving by Karl Postl (1810).

Private collection.

found among these lesser aristocrats. Their egalitarianism did not extend very far; they had no discernible sympathy for the artisans and unskilled workers who from time to time after 1792 demonstrated, struck, rioted, and were flogged and jailed by "Papa" Franz's armed forces. Nor did the industrial and financial classes seriously challenge existing privilege; rather, their goal was to emulate the high aristocracy and share in its prerogatives. The wholesale ennoblement of bankers and financiers was sufficient to defuse most resentments based on hierarchical differences. As for the peasantry, which constituted more than 60 percent of the Austrian population, it lived securely on the fertile agricultural lands of the entailed estates.

The Austrian national character had been imbued with a spirit of outward piety leavened by prudent conformism ever since the savage suppression of the Reformation in the sixteenth and seventeenth centuries. Actually, the regimes of Maria Theresa and Joseph II, however benevolent, had also been despotisms that conditioned most of the populace to accept arbitrary government. A German visitor in 1780 wrote that there were then six hundred spies in Vienna, and that "the police of this place [are] entirely taken up with the object of suppressing everything that indicates vigor and manly strength."[3] Nevertheless, the decade of the 1780s under Joseph II had been a liberating experience for many Viennese, who glimpsed the possibilities of a more humane and rational organization of society. For them the reinstitution and intensification of repressive measures of rule were all the more devastating, because these measures were seen against the background of those hopeful possibilities.

Though the portrait of sybaritic Vienna painted by prudish English and German observers in the later eighteenth century may have been overdrawn, it is largely true that the Viennese gave the impression of a people dedicated to entertainment rather than enlightenment, to escapism rather than involvement in the affairs of the world. "What succeeds most here is buffoonery, and even the bettermost part of the reading public is satisfied with plays, romances, and fairy tales," wrote Baron Caspar Riesbeck in 1780,[4] while another traveler, John Owen, noted in 1792 that "good cheer is, indeed, pursued here in every quarter, and mirth is worshipped in every form."[5] "Serious" topics of conversation were generally avoided by most Viennese: *traurig* (sad), they were wont to say, as they turned to matters of amusement and gossip.[6] "Desperate but not serious" became an unofficial Viennese motto. Rope dancers and jugglers, puppeteers and charlatans, competed for attention on the public squares. The theaters were filled with entertainments of the widest variety, while at the Hetz Amphitheater equestrians and acrobats served as curtain-raisers for the main events: bloody battles to the death between wild animals for the diversion of the populace. In fair weather, the people walked upon the ramparts that surrounded the inner city or strolled in the Prater or the Augarten, and always they gathered in the lavish coffeehouses, inns, and *Weinstuben* that proliferated throughout Vienna. Dancing was a universal amusement, and there were numerous houses appropriate to this purpose at which members of all classes mingled, often wearing masks to disguise their identity and increase their fascination. It was said that "many of these dancing halls are institutions for infamous purposes."[7] Whether this was true or not, prostitution was widespread in Vienna. When it was proposed to Joseph II to construct licensed brothels, he reportedly replied, "The walls would cost me nothing, but the expense of roofing would be ruinous, for it would just be necessary to put a roof over the whole city."[8] The number of illegitimate births was not far short of the number of those within wedlock.

Another British visitor to Vienna may well have exaggerated when he wrote, "No city perhaps can present such scenes of affected sanctity and real licentiousness,"[9] but it surely is not unfair to assert that most Viennese had accepted a life of bread and circuses rather than one of high principle and deep feeling. Nor were the police unaware of the pacifying advantages of these Viennese proclivities. A police memorandum preventing the proposed closing of the Theater-an-der-Wien in 1805 observed: "The people are accustomed to theatrical shows. . . . In times like these, when the character of individuals is affected by so many sufferings, the police are more than ever obliged to cooperate in the diversion of the citizens by every moral means. The most dangerous hours of the day are the evening hours. They cannot be filled more innocently than in the theater."[10] If the police winked at the political jokes that were frequently interspersed in popular farces they did so because they understood that such diversion was an escape valve for social resentments and pressures.

Viennese life may have presented a surface of gaiety, but "at its heart," wrote A. J. P. Taylor, "was a despairing frivolity."[11] The determination to savor the present masked a desire to forget or revise the past and a hopelessness concerning the future. The vaunted Viennese idealization of womanhood went hand in hand with a pernicious, commercialized view of sex and marriage. The easy rejection of *"traurige"* politics arose from fear of reprisal; love for the kaiser was thoroughly intertwined with dread of his secret police. And for many members of Viennese society—those who had not forgotten the Josephinian ideal of a benevolent monarchy devoted to rationality and social advancement—the reversion to irrationality and terror interwoven with hedonistic gratification was a source of profound dismay.

In some ultimately inexplicable way, the Classical style of the late Mozart, the later Haydn, and the early Beethoven seemed perfectly to embody and to crystallize the moods and sentiments of such Viennese during the post-Josephinian period. Though the conditions of Viennese life in the Napoleonic era led to a failure of political nerve, to a withdrawal from philosophical inquiry, and to a diminution in avowedly humanistic concerns, Enlightened sentiments and rational tendencies nevertheless had to find their outlet. Apparently they found one in the realm of Viennese instrumental music—the most immediate, most abstract, and least censorable of the arts. In a sense, we may view the masterpieces of the high-Classic style as a music into which flowed the thwarted impulses of the Josephinian *Aufklärung,* a music of meditative cast that refuses to give way to superficiality and pretense, a music that is "Classic" by virtue of its avoidance of the extremes of triviality and grandiosity. At the same time, this music expressed a utopian ideal: the creation of a self-contained world symbolic of the higher values of rationality, play, and beauty. In the greater works of Mozart, Haydn, and the early Beethoven are condensed some of the contradictory feelings of Viennese life. Gaiety is undermined by a sense of loss, courtly grace is penetrated by brusque and dissonant elements, and profound meditation is intermingled with fantasy.

The rituals of benevolence and reconciliation of opera seria had largely worn out their effectiveness through overuse: Rococo aestheticism, the *galant* style and overworked early-Classic formulas had too large an admixture of transparent narcoticism to satisfy the needs of the more discriminating and enlightened members of society. Within a few short years, Viennese music underwent a stunning alteration through the crystallization of the mature Classical style, which began to take shape as a "national" art. Mozart, who had labored so painfully to make his mark in Vienna, was suddenly (and posthumously) its favorite son, and both his person and his works were lauded as the embodiment of the Viennese spirit. Haydn was now monumentalized by the city that had rather neglected him for several decades.

At first, Beethoven deliberately chose for himself the role of their successor, mastering their genres, styles, and tradition, attempting to bring these to further maturity. Beethoven's role in Viennese life, however, was to be quite different from that of his predecessors. Despite, or perhaps because of, his iconoclasm and rebelliousness, Vienna was to find in Beethoven its mythmaker, the creator of its new "sacred history," one who was prepared to furnish it with a model of heroism as well as beauty during an age of revolution and destruction and to hold out the image of an era of reconciliation and freedom to come. In the 1790s Beethoven was merging his most intimate desires with the collective strivings of Vienna and its aristocracy, finding collaborators in what Hanns Sachs terms the "community of daydreams."[12] Later he would supply citizens of his adopted city with a consistent body of emotional attitudes and with a conception of the world that would symbolically legitimize their very existence and give them hope of a future in which their place might be secure.

CHAPTER TEN

THE MUSIC

A LTHOUGH A MULTIPLICITY OF INFLUENCES converged in
Beethoven's early Vienna works, they did not—as had been
the case with his Bonn music—result in an unfocused eclecticism, but came under the control of an increasingly forceful musical
personality. Beethoven listened to and studied an enormous amount of
the music of his contemporaries, sometimes with admiration and sometimes bursting into laughter—perhaps because he perceived missed
connections and unfulfilled possibilities. Always he was receptive to
new ideas, trying to master, as he wrote in another connection, "what
the better and wiser people of every age were driving at in their works."[1]

Scholars have long delighted in tracing Beethoven's style to a wide
variety of sources. His primary models, of course, were the creators and
masters of the Viennese Classical style. He revered Gluck as one of the
supreme composers, ranking him with Handel, Bach, Mozart, and
Haydn. Romain Rolland rightly says that insufficient attention is paid
to Gluck's influence on the young Beethoven with respect to "dramatic
expression, energy of accent, concision of musical speech, breadth and
clarity of design."[2] Donald Francis Tovey, however, did not overlook
Gluck's significance; he wrote that the whole of Beethoven's "aesthetic
system has arisen from the sonata style, which is . . . intimately connected with the revolution, or rather the birth, of dramatic music style in the
operas of Gluck."[3] Mozart's influence, which had shaped many of the
Bonn works, remained fundamental during the early Vienna years,
especially in Beethoven's chamber music for strings and for winds. The
absence of personal competition in relation to Mozart permitted
Beethoven to express sublimated adoration for the Salzburg master,
seeking to become his musical heir, while still sensing the futility of
striving for a perfection that had already been attained. On hearing a
performance of Mozart's C-minor Piano Concerto, K. 491, Beethoven

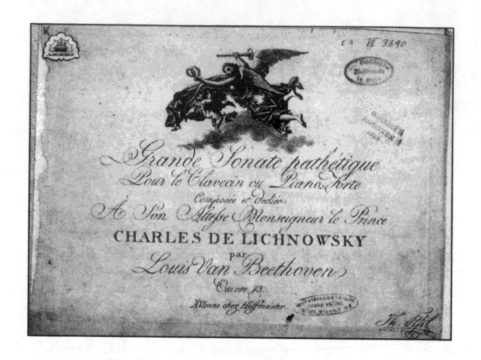

Title page, Sonata in C minor ("Pathétique"), op. 13.

First edition, Hoffmeister, Vienna (1799).
Courtesy of Gesellschaft der Musikfreunde, Vienna.

exclaimed to a fellow pianist and composer, "Cramer! Cramer! We shall never be able to do anything like that!"[4]

Haydn was the main focus of Beethoven's anxieties, for he was seeking to find a personal voice in a world thoroughly dominated by the older master. Muzio Clementi, too, seems to have caused Beethoven some disquiet: on Clementi's visit to Vienna in 1804 Beethoven refused to make a first call on the Italian-born English composer and keyboard player, with the result that the two composers studiously avoided each other. Ries remembered that Beethoven and Clementi, along with their respective pupils, would eat in a tavern at the same table, but that "the one did not speak to the other, or if he did, he confined himself to a greeting."[5] Still later, Beethoven evinced anxiety over Luigi Cherubini's influence as well; this lasted until Beethoven mastered Cherubini's rhetorical "grand manner," and eventually subsided following his clear transcendence of the Italian-French master.

The main genres Beethoven explored during his first Vienna period, which lasted until about 1802, were the piano sonata, the duo sonata, the piano trio, the string trio, the string quartet, chamber music for winds, the concerto, and the symphony. In addition he wrote a good many occasional pieces (mostly dance music), almost two dozen lieder, several arias, a concert scene, and numerous sets of variations. Conspicuously absent (or minimally present) are choral music, music for the church, and (with the exception of *The Creatures of Prometheus*, op. 43, which we will leave for a later chapter) music for the stage. He applied himself to developing the implications of the various sonata forms in three- and four-movement cycles and, continuing the Bonn trend, the variation form, both within and outside of the sonata cycle.

The piano was the central vehicle of Beethoven's musical development during these years, both as composer and as virtuoso. With his removal to Vienna, his emergence as a virtuoso, and his tutelage under Haydn, he became increasingly aware of the expressive possibilities of the piano in contrast to those of earlier keyboard instruments. From early on he interested himself in piano construction, seeking instruments of increased range, heavier action, bigger tone, and more versatile pedals. "One can also make the pianoforte sing," he wrote in 1796 to his piano manufacturer friend Johann Andreas Streicher. "I hope the time will come when the harp and the pianoforte will be treated as two entirely different instruments."[6] In 1802, he wrote to Zmeskall that piano manufacturers were "swarming around me in their anxiety . . . to make me a pianoforte exactly as I should like it."[7]

There was a ready market for piano variations among Vienna's multitude of pianists and piano students. Beethoven wrote more than a dozen sets of variations for piano (some with accompanying violin or cello) between 1793 and 1801; each of them was promptly published, usually within a few months of its composition. They were for the most part skillfully wrought sets of ornamental variations on themes from popular or familiar operas—entertaining, brilliant, and often deliberately superficial, although few are without beautiful moments. Meanwhile, in slow movements of sonata-cycle works such as the Trio, op. 1, no. 3; the String Quartet in A, op. 18, no. 5; the Septet, op. 20; the Sonata in G, op. 14, no. 2; and the first movement of the Sonata in A-flat, op. 26, Beethoven was progressing from the external variation manner to more complex and imaginative principles of variation technique. The Variations on Salieri's "La stessa, la stessissima," WoO 73, written in early 1799, still rely on ornamental techniques, but their harmonic plan and carefully designed tempo alternations create a more organic structure. The significant advance in this form, which constitutes part of the transition to Beethoven's next style period, took place in 1802 with the Six Variations on an Original Theme in F, op. 34, and the Fifteen Variations and Fugue in E-flat, op. 35, later known as the "Eroica" Variations. Beethoven wrote to Gottfried Härtel asking that the printed edition include an introductory note, written by the composer, calling attention to their innovative character:

> As the v[ariations] are distinctly different from my earlier ones, instead of indicating them like my *previous ones* . . . I have included them in the proper numerical series *of my greater musical works,* the more so as the themes have been composed by me.[8]

In the opus 34 set, the first five variations are arranged in a harmonic scheme of descending thirds, alternating between minor and major, and the fifth variation ends in C major, the dominant of the opening key, preparing a direct return to the tonic. An epilogue restates the theme of the opening Adagio in its simplest form and offers a new, highly ornamented treatment of it that is less a new variation than a transfiguration of the theme, now shown to have been "incomplete" earlier. Beethoven appears to be trying to convey something like the vicissitudes of a human journey, inscribing a musical metaphor for a circuitous route: as in the later Piano Sonata in E-flat ("Lebewohl"), op. 81a, a pattern of departure, extension, and return is implicit in Beethoven's formal plan.

The opus 35 Variations are of particular interest by virtue of their use of compositional procedures—fugue, chaconne, harmonic variation—identified with the Baroque composers. "The introduction to these grand variations, . . ." wrote Beethoven, "begins with the bass of the theme and eventually develops into two, three, and four parts; and not till then does the theme appear, which again cannot be called a variation."[9] It remains tantalizingly ambiguous whether the grotesque bass melody is the theme or the harmony of a theme that has yet to materialize.

Beethoven's first works to bear an opus number were the three Trios for Piano, Violin, and Cello, op. 1, published in 1795. They were a great success, commanding "extraordinary attention" and receiving—except for Haydn's caveat concerning the C-minor Trio—the "undivided applause" of connoisseurs and music lovers.[10] (Yet, a few arrangements aside, Beethoven did not return to the form until his Trios, op. 70, in 1808.) Like his first Viennese piano sonatas, the opus 1 Trios are fashioned on a grand scale, each in four movements and of considerable length, averaging almost 1,100 measures. From the first, Beethoven was thinking in terms of formal expansion, long-range harmonic action, and heightened rhetoric. Noteworthy in the trios is the independent and occasionally florid writing for the cello: here, Beethoven had considerable precedent in Mozart's trios, but little in Haydn's. In the Cello Sonatas, op. 5, written in the spring of 1796 for himself and Jean-Louis Duport to play for the sonatas' dedicatee, Friedrich Wilhelm II of Prussia,[11] Beethoven had no such precedent, for neither Mozart nor Haydn had composed sonatas for the cello, which was only recently emancipating itself from its traditional role as a continuo instrument and beginning to assert its prerogatives as a virtuoso vehicle. Beethoven's ambitiously scaled, sonorous sonatas, with their spacious Adagio sostenuto introductions, were the first important sonatas for this combination to contain a fully written-out piano part. Beethoven's next effort in this genre dates from 1807–8; in the early Vienna years, however, he also wrote three sets of accessible variations for cello and piano, opus 66, WoO 45, and WoO 46.

Beethoven's ten sonatas for violin and piano have always been cornerstones of the violin sonata repertory, though they have received far less critical attention than the piano sonatas. Beethoven, himself a violinist in Bonn, took lessons with Schuppanzigh and Krumpholz after arriving in Vienna and had, if no remarkable skill, a special love for the instrument; he composed for it some of his most contented, graceful, and perfectly proportioned music. All but two of the sonatas were composed within the five years ending in 1802. The set of Three Sonatas in D, A, and E-flat, op. 12, dates from 1797–98; the Sonatas in A minor and F ("Spring"), opp. 23 and 24 , from 1800–1801 (they were originally intended to be published as a unit); and the Three Sonatas in A, C minor, and G, op. 30, which were dedicated to Czar Alexander, 1801–2. Of these, only opus 24 and opus 30, no. 2, are in four movements, the others using the customary three movement layout. Commentators have remarked of the first five violin sonatas that they are less ambitious and individual than the piano sonatas of the same period.[12] Nevertheless, there are innovative and even experimental touches—especially in opus 23, with its unusual Presto first movement, foreshadowing the Sonata in A ("Kreutzer"), op. 47, and in the Rondo-finale of opus 24, with its unexpected digressions into distant tonalities in the passage preceding the fourth refrain. The opus 30 Sonatas for Violin and Piano are a clear departure, with an expansion of tonal sonorities and moments of heroic pathos clearly signaling that Beethoven was pressing at the outer limits of the Mozartian model. Indeed, what is now the finale of the "Kreutzer" was originally intended as the finale of opus 30, no. 1. Beethoven had by this time dramatically extended the expressive range of his piano writing. Now he was in the process of shaping a new, dynamic, and declamatory voice for the violin to complement this unprecedented pianistic style.

Beethoven's chamber music for strings, which includes three string trios, six string quartets, and two string quintets, marks a stage in the gradual loosening of his reliance on the piano as the anchor of his compositional style. The String Trios in G, D, and C minor, op. 9, were written in 1797–98 and published by the Viennese publisher Johann Traeg in July 1798. In his dedicatory message to Count Browne-Camus, Beethoven called them "la meilleure de [mes] oeuvres" ("the best of my works") up to that point, and more than one critic has agreed with his judgment.[13] Like the Piano Trios, op. 1, each of them is in four movements and each elaborates somewhat different possibilities of the sonata cycle. Opus 9, no. 1, opens with an Adagio introduction and closes with a movement in sonata form rather than the more usual rondo. Opus 9, no. 2, substitutes an Andante quasi allegretto for the traditional slow movement, a shift in balance that recurs most famously in the Eighth Symphony in 1812. Where the first two trios are expansive and luxuriant, the third, in C minor, is considerably condensed, striving for the sense of inevitability and logic that characterizes Beethoven's later symphonic C-minor projects. Beethoven did not return to the string trio in subsequent years, perhaps because of the greater expressiveness and textural interest of the string quartet, which ultimately superseded other chamber music genres for him.

It was to the set of Six String Quartets, op. 18, that Beethoven turned for the most ambitious single project of his early Vienna years. Begun in 1798, the set was composed primarily in 1799 and 1800 and was published in 1801 in two installments with a dedication to Prince Lobkowitz. The string quartet, the most elevated, expressive, and learned genre of the Classical style, had flourished in Vienna since the 1770s; with the death of Mozart, Haydn remained as the unrivaled practitioner of the form. During the years 1793–99 he composed fourteen of his sixty-eight quartets, dedicating them to members of the same group of aristocratic patrons whose names are frequently encountered in Beethoven's early biography: Count Apponyi (op. 71 and op. 74), Count Erdödy (op. 76), and Prince Lobkowitz (op. 77). Beethoven's opus 18 carried overtones of both emulation and competition.[14]

The probable original order of composition of the opus 18 String Quartets was established (somewhat erroneously) by Nottebohm and clarified by Brandenburg: the now-accepted order is 3, 1, 2, 5, 4, and 6.[15] Several were partially rewritten prior to publication. All of them essentially accept the usual four-movement structure and all exemplify the

Viennese Classical style, with an occasional pre-Romantic touch and an admixture of Italianate melody—perhaps under the influence of Salieri, to whom Beethoven had just dedicated his Violin Sonatas, op. 12.

The adherence to tradition is somewhat more evident in the first three quartets than in the later ones, where Beethoven began to alter the weights and textures of the movements within the usual structure. Kerman writes that in these, "Beethoven seems suddenly to have thrown the classical framework in doubt. These pieces all entertain experiments with different types and arrangements of movements."[16] The opening movements are lightened, and since the finales are composed in sonata form rather than in the characteristic rondo form, the climax tends to be transferred to the close of each work. The Andante scherzoso quasi Allegretto of no. 4, like the similarly designated second movement of the String Trio, op. 9, no. 2, signals Beethoven's willingness to dispense with the traditional slow movement. The insertion of an allegro passage in the Adagio cantabile of no. 2—this apparently occurred late in the compositional process—is another example of the flexibility with which Beethoven was now handling the traditional forms. Most striking, perhaps, is the mystical forty-four-measure second Adagio, entitled "La Malinconia," that prefaces the finale of no. 6 and returns briefly to arrest the climax of the Allegretto quasi Allegro before the final statement and coda.

This is not to say, however, that the opus 18 String Quartets can be regarded as experimental works comparable to Beethoven's most impressive contemporary piano sonatas. Many of Beethoven's "unusual" touches—the reversal of the inner movements in no. 5 and the use of variation form in the Andante cantabile of the same work—have precedents in Haydn and Mozart. If there are in these works occasional anticipations of the rhetoric and textures of Beethoven's later chamber music styles, the opus 18 String Quartets essentially remain traditional and even conservative, reflecting Beethoven's main ambition: to master the most prestigious genre of the Classical style.

Beethoven showed his authority in the string quintet medium (string quartet, with added viola) with only two efforts. In late 1795 he arranged for string quintet his then unpublished Octet for Winds (later published as opus 103), with revisions sufficient to warrant calling it a new composition (opus 4). It is, however, the String Quintet in C, op. 29, written in 1801 and published the following year, that is his most accomplished work in this genre, worthy of a place alongside Mozart's works for this combination of instruments. It is a characteristically spacious, sonorous, and fully controlled work, with smoothly flowing thematic development, a lyrical Adagio molto espressivo, an inventive and unflagging Scherzo, and—with much tremolo accompaniment—one of the most successful "stormy" finales (the first was in opus 2, no. 1) of Beethoven's early years.

Completing this brief survey of Beethoven's chamber music are three works for piano and winds: the Quintet in E-flat, op. 16, written in 1796 or 1797 and modeled on Mozart's Quintet, K. 452, for the same instrumentation; the Sonata in F for French Horn (or Cello) and Piano, op. 17, written in haste (according to Ries, in one day) for performance by Beethoven and Johann Wenzel Stich at the latter's concert of April 18, 1800 (it was repeated at another concert shortly thereafter in Pest); and the Trio in B-flat for Clarinet, Cello, and Piano, op. 11, composed in 1798. Beethoven also wrote several works for winds and strings: the slight Serenade in D, op. 25, for flute, violin, and viola; and the popular Septet in E-flat, op. 20, for clarinet, horn, bassoon, and strings, written for Empress Maria Theresia at the turn of the century.[17] Also composed during this period, but not published until 1810, were a Sextet for String Quartet and Horns, op. 81b, and a Sextet for Clarinets, Horns, and Bassoons, op. 71. Rosen makes the interesting point that works such as the Septet and the Quintet are "classicizing" rather than "Classic" in style: "They are reproductions of classical forms . . . based upon the exterior models, the results of the classical impulse, and not upon the impulse itself."[18] This style also leads, however, toward the tenuous and amiable pre-Romantic "Biedermeier" manner of Ludwig Spohr and other composers of the following decades.

Beethoven completed three concertos for piano and orchestra in these early Vienna years. The Concerto No. 2 in B-flat, although of Bonn origin, and perhaps first drafted as early as 1785, was rewritten at least twice in Vienna and was published in 1801 as opus 19.[19] The sparkling Concerto No. 1 in C, op. 15, also published in 1801, bears an earlier opus number than the Second Concerto but was written later, most likely at the end of 1795, with cadenzas and further sketches from 1798 for an October 27, 1798, concert at the Theater-an-der-Wien.[20] It is scored for full orchestra, including trumpets and timpani. Perhaps to forestall negative criticism in Breitkopf & Härtel's *Allgemeine musikalische Zeitung*, Beethoven warned the Leipzig publisher that neither work was among his better compositions in the form.[21] He wrote out three cadenzas for the First Concerto, the last of which dates from 1804 or even somewhat later. Both concertos are fairly unadventurous in formal organization, in the balance between solo and orchestra, and in the nature of the piano writing. The Concerto No. 3 in C minor, op. 37, which was written over a period of time extending from as early as 1799 to 1802–3,[22] represents a marked advance over its predecessors, and it became an established model of Classic-Romantic concerto form for the nineteenth century. Where the First Concerto has elements of what Tovey calls the music equivalent of the "comedy of manners," and the Second reveals a more intimate, if not fully realized, chamber music quality, the Third represents Beethoven's first effort in this genre to record something far beyond merely exterior wit or refinement, and to move toward dramatic oratory. Beethoven had earlier (e.g., in the Trio, op. 1, no. 3; the String Trio, op. 9, no. 3; the Piano Sonatas, opp. 10, no. 1, and 13; and the String Quartet, op. 18, no. 4) enlisted the key of C minor in his search for the expression of "*pathétique*" sentiments; in his middle Vienna years, C minor would become his "heroic" key, as in the Fifth Symphony, the Funeral March of the *Eroica* Symphony, and the overture to *Coriolan*. This direction is foreshadowed to some extent in the Third Piano Concerto as well as in the Violin Sonata, op. 30, no. 2.

Sketches from 1795–96 for an unfinished Symphony in C survive,[23] but it was not until 1800 that Beethoven ventured to complete his First Symphony, op. 21. Beethoven's entry into symphonic music had to await the emergence of appropriate performance opportunities, which were rare enough in this genre. It was then five years after Haydn's final effort in the form, and twelve years after Mozart's *Jupiter* Symphony. In the interim, symphonies by such minor composers as Wranitsky, Eybler, and Cartellieri occasionally found their way onto concert programs in Vienna, but failed to make any lasting impression.[24] In light of the risks involved, as well as the newness of the task, it was natural that Beethoven's Symphony No. 1 in C, op. 21, scored for the standard orchestra of Haydn and Mozart with added clarinets, should lean heavily on the traditional inheritance. Tovey, who calls it Beethoven's "fitting farewell to the eighteenth century," stresses that it "shows a characteristic caution in handling sonata form for the first time with a full orchestra."[25] Contemporary critics, however, did not by any means regard it as a timid or imitative work. The reviewer in the *Allgemeine musikalische Zeitung* spoke of its "considerable art, novelty and . . . wealth of ideas,"[26] thinking no doubt of the audacious "off-key" opening; the striking use of the timpani in the Andante cantabile, which foreshadows similar passages in Beethoven's later works; and the teasing scale figure that initiates the closing Allegro molto e vivace.

Completed in 1802, during a turbulent period in Beethoven's life, the Second Symphony in D, op. 36, is already the work of a mature master who is settling accounts—or making peace—with the existing symphonic tradition before embarking on an unprecedented musical voyage. It is a work that has both retrospective and prospective characteristics, firmly rooted in Mozart's and Haydn's last symphonies while anticipating Beethoven's later development by its dynamic contrasts, unexpected modulations, and propulsive movement, all of which are controlled by a confident and flowing classicism.

Thirty-two piano sonatas bear Beethoven's opus numbers. The first twenty were composed in the eight years up to 1802, and it is in them that Beethoven's first unquestioned masterpieces are to be found. These sonatas fall readily into two groups: thirteen sonatas written between late 1794 and mid 1800—op. 2 to op. 22, plus two "easy sonatas," op. 49— that explore and expand the possibilities of sonata form; and seven sonatas, op. 26 to op. 31, that constitute a new line of development and experimentation. Even the earliest sonatas, however, are spacious in design and rich in detail and invention, and were clearly intended as major efforts. Where Haydn and Mozart had relied almost exclusively on a three-movement layout, six of Beethoven's first sonatas (including his first four) used the four-movement scheme—by means of an added minuet or scherzo—usually reserved for symphonies and quartets. These sonatas were on the average almost one and a half times as long as those written by his predecessors. The sonatas run the full gamut of Sturm und Drang sentiment—passion, reverie, exuberance, heroism, solemnity, nobility, and dramatic pathos—but they are also full of abrupt harmonic and dynamic effects, piquant episodes, unusual rhythms, syncopations, and brief departures for distant keys, all of which signify that this young composer was not content to remain a dutiful exponent of a great tradition. It is Beethoven's unification of two opposing trends, what Tovey calls his "epigrammatic" manner along with an overall striving for spaciousness, that is a distinguishing characteristic of his early Vienna style.

Beethoven had a special regard for the Sonata in E-flat, op. 7, written in 1796–97, for he entitled it "Grande Sonate" and issued it as a separate opus rather than as one of a set. The first two of the set of Three Sonatas, op. 10 (1796–98), are filled with imaginative ideas, but are overshadowed by the third sonata (also designated "Grande" by the composer), with its eloquent and sombre Largo e mesto, which foreshadows the disintegrating passage at the close of the *Eroica* Symphony's Funeral March movement. The Sonata in C minor ("Pathétique"), op. 13, of 1798–99 was the most dynamically propulsive of Beethoven's piano sonatas yet written, the first to utilize a slow, dramatic introduction, and the first whose movements are clearly and unmistakably linked through the use of related thematic material and flashbacks or reminiscences. In its ardent, youthful way, it opens up the path to the "fantasy sonatas" of the following years.

The Sonatas in E and G, op. 14 (1798–99), mark a turn toward less dramatic subject matter. The "Grande" Sonata in B-flat, op. 22, composed in 1799–1800, closes out this mature Classical phase of Beethoven's sonata development on a note of absolute confidence in his mastery of the form. Beethoven was especially proud of it: "This sonata is really something," he wrote to his publisher.[27]

The next group of sonatas belongs to the years 1800–1801. In the Sonatas in A-flat ("Funeral March"), op. 26, and in E-flat and C-sharp minor, op. 27, nos. 1 and 2 (the latter dubbed "Moonlight"), Beethoven appeared to take leave of the customary sonata-cycle form in favor of a more flexible construction that permitted the freer expression of improvisatory ideas and displaced the climax of the cycle to the final movement. Beethoven gave the title "Sonata quasi una Fantasia" to each of the opus 27 sonatas, a designation that has no readily apparent precedent. The unusual innovation is that none of these three sonatas contains an opening sonata-form allegro movement. Paul Bekker, the eminent

German music critic who analyzed this important stage in Beethoven's sonata evolution, wrote that he must have found first-movement sonata form a hindrance to his desire "to give free rein to his fancy, to improvise, not only in a single movement, but with absolute freedom throughout a multiple form." The opening sonata-allegro movement, writes Bekker,

> gave the work a definite character from the beginning . . . which succeeding movements could supplement but not change. Beethoven rebelled against this determinative quality in the first movement. He wanted a prelude, an introduction, not a proposition. He did not wish to commit himself in the first movement to a certain sequence of thought.[28]

Nor, we may add, did he wish to exhaust the dramatic essence of the cycle in its first movement. The Sonata in A-flat, op. 26, initiates this development with its opening Andante con variazioni movement, but fails thereafter to pursue the movement's architectural implications. It remained for the opus 27 Sonatas to fulfill those implications. Each work begins with a slow introductory movement with the character of a dreamlike improvisation, followed by a scherzo interlude (and, in opus 27, no. 1, a lyrical Adagio con espressione), and each closes with a climactic fast movement. In opus 27, no. 2, the finale is no longer a rondo, but a fully developed sonata-form movement with driving fugato passages. Jürgen Uhde sees the opus 27 Sonatas as standing at the crossroads of eighteenth-century optimism and emergent Romantic pessimism, and the "quintessence" of these sonatas as a "breakthrough from meditation to activity," providing a metaphor for the improvement of the world.[29]

Beethoven's exploration of the potentialities of the fantasy sonata did not end in 1801; he would take up this thread again in his later years. At this moment in his creative journey, however, he was setting himself other tasks. With the calm and reflective Sonata in D ("Pastoral"), op. 28, Beethoven reverted to the typical distribution of emotional weights and emphases of four-movement sonata form. Like so many of Beethoven's works that follow hard upon a dramatic achievement, opus 28 celebrates the peace that comes from the fulfillment of a difficult creative effort and withdraws to a relative traditionalism, from which Beethoven will gain strength for a new creative surge.

It is difficult to say whether the Three Piano Sonatas, op. 31 (composed in 1802; published 1803–4 by Hans Georg Nägeli in Zürich), opened an era or closed one. Bekker saw the first two sonatas as the culmination of the fantasy-sonata form, and the third as the beginning of a new virtuoso style that would later come to fruition in the "Waldstein" and "Appassionata" Sonatas. Blom calls the first—a three-movement piece in G major—"a somewhat reactionary work for its time" and one that leans heavily on pianistic devices.[30] The cheerful and witty third sonata, in E-flat, is in four movements, using both a Scherzo and a Menuetto between the two sonata-form outer movements. But it is the impassioned second sonata, in D minor and in three movements, that is the best known of the set. The first movement of the D-minor Sonata opens with an unusual alternation of an arpeggiated recitative-Largo and an agitated Allegro and omits the traditional second theme; this has given rise to debate as to its underlying structural principle. Ludwig Misch believes that the Largo and the Allegro, taken together, constitute the theme, and he finds in this mixture a daring innovation, "far more novel and simple, more daring and logical" than had previously been supposed.[31] The dancing, triumphant Allegretto is one of Beethoven's most successful finales, foreshadowing the transfigured waltz movement that closes the String Quartet in A minor, op. 132.

One senses during these years, and especially in the years 1798 to 1802, Beethoven's determination to achieve a mastery of the Viennese Classical style within each of its major instrumental genres. The challenge of the piano trio was met earliest, with opus 1 in 1795; the string trio with opus 9 in 1798; the string quartet with opus 18 in 1799 and 1800; the string quintet with opus 29 in 1801; the duo sonata with opuses 23, 24, and 30 in 1801–2; the piano sonata with opuses 22–28 in 1800 and 1801; the symphony with the Symphony in D in 1802; and the piano concerto with the Third Concerto between 1799 and 1803. It was Beethoven's tendency, having mastered a genre, to withdraw for a time from a further expansion of the implications of his advance and turn elsewhere. Until 1802, Beethoven seems to have restrained the pull of his imagination each time it threatened to move him beyond the limits of the Classical style and, with what appears to have been conscious deliberation, occupied himself in less dangerous terrain. This may be why several works of this period—such as the two symphonies and the Sonatas, op. 28 and op. 31, no. 1—have a somewhat conservative cast when viewed alongside several of the String Quartets, op. 18, and the Piano Sonatas, op. 27 and op. 31, no. 2.

Beethoven had gained the high ground of the Viennese tradition; he was now faced with the choice of repetition of his conquests or casting out in an uncharted direction. According to Czerny, it was soon after the composition of the Sonata in D, op. 28, that Beethoven said to his friend the violinist Wenzel Krumpholz, "I am only a little satisfied with my previous works. From today on I will take a new path."[32] Several paths were open to Beethoven. One of these lay in the direction of romanticism, toward the loosening and imaginative extension of classical designs and the consolidation of an internal, probing, transcendent style. For reasons that are necessarily obscure, he did not immediately pursue this path, perhaps because in the years around 1801 and 1802 he found within sonata form new, unexplored possibilities: thematic condensation; more intense, extended, and dramatic development; and the infusion of richer fantasy and improvisatory materials into an even more highly structured classicism.

Beethoven was now well launched upon his "new path"—a qualitative change in his style that would become a turning point in the history of music itself. It was a transformation of great magnitude, and it coincided with a biographical crisis of major proportions.

III
THE
HEROIC PERIOD

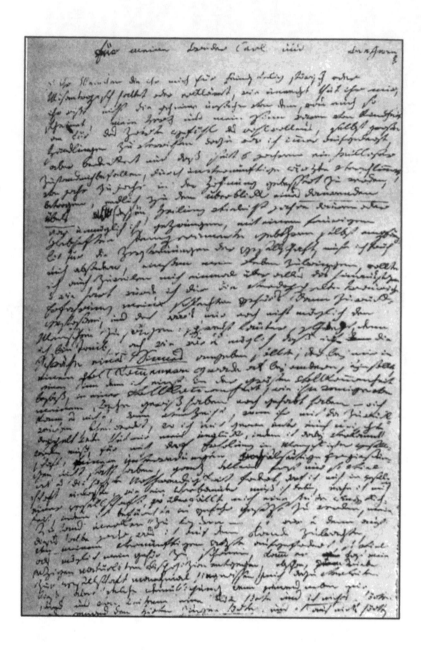

Heiligenstadt Testament, page 1.

Staats- und Universitätsbibliothek, Hamburg.

CHAPTER ELEVEN

CRISIS AND CREATIVITY

THE YEARS 1800 AND 1801 MARKED AN IMPORTANT advance in
Beethoven's career. In 1800 he began to receive a sizable
annuity from Prince Lichnowsky—600 florins per annum—
which gave him a relative degree of independence from the more
restrictive forms of aristocratic patronage and encouraged him to pursue aesthetic projects of greater magnitude. On April 2, 1800, he gave
his first *Akademie* (academy), a public concert for his own benefit, at
which were performed, in addition to works by Mozart and Haydn,
Beethoven's Symphony No. 1 in C, op. 21, the Septet, and his Piano
Concerto No. 1 in C, op. 15, with the composer at the keyboard. Even
though the Viennese critics inexplicably ignored the concert, and a
review in Breitkopf & Härtel's music journal, *Allgemeine musikalische
Zeitung,* was not altogether favorable, the event symbolized Beethoven's
emergence as a major creative personality. Shortly thereafter, the ballet
Die Geschöpfe des Prometheus (*The Creatures of Prometheus*), op. 43, for
which he had written the score, was a resounding success, performed
twenty-three times in 1801–2. Foreign publishers increasingly began
to bid for his works (which clearly had enjoyed an excellent sale in
Viennese editions), thereby giving Beethoven a sense of his international stature and, perhaps, a glimpse of the possibilities of immortality
as well. The year 1801 saw the richest publishing harvest of his career so
far, both in quantity and in musical scope.

Beneath this surface of accomplishment, however, inner conflicts
were converging to generate a crisis of major proportions. Beethoven
was fulfilling many of his most deeply rooted wishes. Why, then, do we
now find an undercurrent of malaise, a feeling of anxiety mingled with
the apprehension of some unknown yet dreaded misfortune? It is as
though he worried that he might be destroyed by success itself. (Indeed,
at a later time he actually wrote to Zmeskall, "Sometimes I feel that I

shall soon go mad in consequence of my unmerited fame; fortune is seeking me out and for that very reason I almost dread some fresh calamity.")[1]

This contradiction in Beethoven's existence—an outward appearance of accomplishment, productivity, and gratification permeated by a sense of impending personal shipwreck—is reflected in his famous letter of June 29, 1801, to Franz Wegeler in Bonn:

> You want to know something about my present situation. Well, on the whole it is not at all bad. . . . My compositions bring me in a good deal; and I may say that I am offered more commissions than it is possible for me to carry out. Moreover for every composition I can count on six or seven publishers, and even more, if I want them; people no longer come to an arrangement with me, I state my price and they pay. So you see how pleasantly situated I am. For instance, I see a friend in need and it so happens that the state of my purse does not allow me to help him immediately; well then, I have only to sit down and compose and in a short time I can come to his aid. Moreover, I live more economically than I used to; and if I remain in Vienna for good, no doubt I shall contrive to obtain one day for a *concert* (*Akademie*) every year. I have given a few concerts.

Now Beethoven changes his mood and gives a detailed account of his medical symptoms, perhaps hoping to obtain some advice from his friend, who is a physician:

> But that jealous demon, my wretched health, has put a nasty spoke in my wheel; and it amounts to this, that for the last three years my hearing has become weaker and weaker. The trouble is supposed to have been caused by the condition of my *abdomen*, which, as you know, was wretched even before I left Bonn, but has become worse in Vienna, where I have been constantly afflicted with diarrhea and have been suffering in consequence from an extraordinary debility. Frank tried to *tone up* my constitution with strengthening medicines and my hearing with almond oil, but much good did it do me! His treatment had no effect; my deafness became even worse and my

abdomen continued to be in the same state as before. Such was my condition until the autumn of last year; and sometimes I gave way to despair. Then a medical *ass* advised me to take cold baths to improve my condition. A more sensible doctor, however, prescribed the usual tepid baths in the Danube. The result was miraculous, and my insides improved. But my deafness persisted—or, I should say, became even worse. During this last winter I was truly wretched, for I had really dreadful attacks of colic and again relapsed completely into my former condition. And thus I remained until about four weeks ago when I went to see *Vering*. For I began to think that my condition demanded the attention of a surgeon as well; and in any case I had confidence in him. Well, he succeeded in checking almost completely this violent diarrhea. He prescribed tepid baths in the Danube, to which I had always to add a bottle of strengthening ingredients. He ordered no medicines until about four days ago, when he prescribed pills for my stomach and an infusion for my ear. As a result I have been feeling, I may say, stronger and better; but my ears continue to hum and buzz day and night. I must confess that I lead a miserable life. For almost two years I have ceased to attend any social functions, just because I find it impossible to say to people: I am deaf. If I had any other profession I might be able to cope with my infirmity; but in my profession it is a terrible handicap. And if my enemies, of whom I have a fair number, were to hear about it, what would they say? In order to give you some idea of this strange deafness, let me tell you that in the theater I have to place myself quite close to the orchestra in order to understand what the actor is saying, and that at a distance I cannot hear the high notes of instruments or voices. As for the spoken voice, it is surprising that some people have never noticed my deafness; but since I have always been liable to fits of absentmindedness, they attribute my hardness of hearing to that. Sometimes, too, I can scarcely hear a person who speaks softly; I can hear sounds, it is true, but cannot make out the words. But if anyone shouts, I can't bear it. Heaven alone knows what is to become of me. *Vering tells me that my hearing will certainly improve, although my deafness may not be completely cured.* Already I have often cursed my Creator and my existence. *Plutarch* has shown me the path of *resignation*.

If it is at all possible, I will bid defiance to my fate, though I feel that as long as I live there will be moments when I shall be God's most unhappy creature. . . . *Resignation*, what a wretched resource! Yet it is all that is left to me. . . .[2]

Two days later, on July 1, Beethoven wrote a similar letter to Karl Amenda in Latvia:

How often would I like to have you here with me, for your B[eethoven] is leading a very unhappy life and is at variance with Nature and his Creator. Many times already I have cursed Him for exposing His creatures to the slightest hazard, so that the most beautiful blossom is thereby often crushed and destroyed. Let me tell you that my most prized possession, *my hearing*, has greatly deteriorated. When you were still with me, I already felt the symptoms; but I said nothing about them. Now they have become very much worse. . . . You will realize what a sad life I must now lead, seeing that I am cut off from everything that is dear and precious to me. . . . I must withdraw from everything; and my best years will rapidly pass away without my being able to achieve all that my talent and my strength have commanded me to do. Sad *resignation*, to which I am forced to have recourse. Needless to say, I am resolved to overcome all this, but how is it going to be done?[3]

Despite the ominous portents in these letters, Beethoven's anxiety receded in the subsequent months. This was partly due to his good fortune in obtaining a new physician, with whom he developed a strong personal bond. The first symptoms of deafness had given rise to panic, sending Beethoven from one doctor to another in search of relief. But shortly after mid–1801 he turned to Johann Adam Schmidt, professor of general pathology and therapy at the Josephine Academy, who inspired Beethoven's confidence and allayed his fears to an extraordinary extent. Replying to Wegeler's inquiry about the ongoing state of his health, Beethoven wrote, on November 16, 1801, "True enough, I cannot deny it, the humming and buzzing is slightly less than it used to be, particularly in my left ear, where my deafness really began." Fearful of overstating the improvement, he continued, "But so far my hearing is certainly not a bit better; and I am inclined to think, although I do not dare to say so definitely, that it is a little weaker." However, optimism then gets the better of Beethoven's caution: "I am now leading a slightly more pleasant life, for I am mixing more with my fellow creatures.... This change has been brought about by a dear, charming girl who loves me and whom I love. After two years I am again enjoying a few blissful moments; and for the first time I feel that—marriage might bring me happiness. Unfortunately she is not my class—and at the moment—I certainly could not marry—I must still bustle about a good deal." (The reference is almost certainly to Countess Giulietta Guicciardi, one of Beethoven's piano students, aged sixteen, to whom he was strongly attracted at this time.) And finally, he abandons the pessimistic tone: "For some time now my physical strength has been increasing more and more, and therefore my mental powers also. Every day brings me nearer to the goal which I feel but cannot describe.... I will seize Fate by the throat; it shall certainly not bend and crush me completely."[4] Resignation was now tempered by the determination to resist.

We gather, then, that Beethoven had endured several years of considerable anxiety. Yet these were years of extremely high productivity and creative accomplishment, years that gave rise to the works that exhibit Beethoven's increasing mastery of the Classic style as well as the clearest signs that he was in transition toward a radically new style. Unlike the apparent compositional hiatus between 1786 and 1790, the brief creative impasse of 1793, and the long crisis that would inaugurate his last period, there was here no interruption of productivity, but rather a remarkable acceleration in Beethoven's stylistic evolution, in which new and superseded styles were thoroughly intermingled. "I live entirely in my music," he wrote to Wegeler, in the very same letter in which he announced his deafness, "and hardly have I completed one composition when I have already begun another. At my present rate of composing, I often produce three or four works at the same time."[5]

His July 1, 1801, letter to Amenda was even more exuberant on this score: "Why, at the moment I feel equal to anything. Since your departure I have been composing all types of music, except *operas* and sacred works."[6] One begins to suspect that Beethoven's crisis and his extraordinary creativity were somehow related, and even that the former may have been the necessary precondition of the latter.

In 1800 alone, Beethoven completed the Six String Quartets, op. 18; the First Symphony in C, op. 21; the Septet, op. 20; the Third Piano Concerto in C minor, op. 37; and the Sonata in B-flat, op. 22, as well as a number of lesser works. The list of his compositions in 1801 was even more impressive, including *The Creatures of Prometheus,* op. 43 (originally numbered opus 24); the String Quintet in C, op. 29; the Violin Sonatas in A minor, op. 23, and F, op. 24; and four Piano Sonatas, op. 26; op. 27, nos. 1 and 2; and op. 28. Major works of the year 1802 included the Second Symphony in D, op. 36; the Three Violin Sonatas in A, C minor, and G, op. 30; the sets of Variations, opp. 34 and 35; and the Three Piano Sonatas, in G, D minor, and E-flat, op. 31. Clearly there is every sign of a creative acceleration rather than of a slowdown.

At this time, moreover, Beethoven was apparently leading an active social life. He was increasingly on close terms with his brother Caspar Carl. Stephan von Breuning had arrived from Bonn in 1801, and he and Beethoven met almost every day. Beethoven wrote of him to Wegeler, "It does me good to revive the old feelings of friendship."[7] Another Bonn friend, the composer Anton Reicha, arrived from Paris in 1802 to resume an intimate friendship ("like that of Orestes and Pylades," Reicha claimed).[8] Beethoven continued to spend much time in Zmeskall's company and kept up his amusing correspondence with this friend whom he variously dubbed "Most Excellent Count of Music," "Baron Muck-Driver," and "Plenipotentiary of Beethoven's Kingdom."

Moreover, it was during these years of crisis that Beethoven developed close relationships with two aristocratic families that were to play a major role in his social and emotional life: the Brunsviks, a Hungarian family, and the Guicciardis. Countess Anna Elisabeth Brunsvik and the Countess Susanna Guicciardi were sisters, and Beethoven gave piano lessons to the young Josephine and Therese Brunsvik (perhaps to Charlotte Brunsvik as well) and to their cousin Giulietta Guicciardi. He was a frequent guest at the Brunsviks' Vienna residence and a welcome visitor to their Hungarian estates in Martonvásár. Their brother Franz "adored" Beethoven,[9] and the two men used the intimate "Du" form in addressing each other.

Such warm friendships notwithstanding, it appears that Beethoven's malaise had returned by the spring of 1802. Certainly his deafness was the prime factor in this discontent, but impediments to the progress of his career also played some part. He had hoped to give a major academy during the previous winter but had been unable to obtain the use of the much sought-after court theater. Furthermore, his overtures to the imperial court had not brought his desire for a permanent court position any closer to fruition. In a letter of April 8 to the publisher and composer Franz Anton Hoffmeister he expressed his anger in surprisingly strong—even dangerous—terms, writing, "There are rascals in the Imperial City as there are at the Imperial Court—."[10] A few weeks later he wrote to Gottfried Härtel, "A good deal of business—and also a great many worries—have rendered me for a time quite useless for some things."[11] Dr. Schmidt recommended seclusion in the countryside as a refuge from the vexations of ordinary life. Accordingly, probably in late April, Beethoven repaired to the quiet village of Heiligenstadt, just north of Vienna, on the Danube, and seems to have remained there for a full half year, an unusually extended vacation for him. His student Ferdinand Ries—the son of his Bonn colleague and neighbor Franz Ries—who had visited Vienna in the spring of 1800 and returned there from Munich in late 1801 or early 1802,[12] joined him in Heiligenstadt, and later on described both his apparent deafness and his moods. "I called his attention to a shepherd who was piping very agreeably in the woods on a flute made of a twig of elder. For half an hour Beethoven could hear nothing, and though I assured him that it was the same with me (which was not the case), he became extremely quiet and morose. When occasionally he seemed to be merry, it was generally to the extreme of boisterousness; but this happened seldom."[13] Perhaps these swings between melancholia and exuberance reflected the depths of the pain he was enduring—a pain sufficient to cause him to consider ending his life. We learn of this from a celebrated document, dated October 6 and 10, 1802, that was found among his papers after his death and that is now known as the Heiligenstadt Testament. It is addressed to his brothers:

FOR MY BROTHERS CARL AND BEETHOVEN
Oh you men who think or say that I am malevolent, stubborn, or misanthropic, how greatly do you wrong me. You do not know the secret cause which makes me seem that way to you. From childhood

on, my heart and soul have been full of the tender feeling of goodwill, and I was ever inclined to accomplish great things. But, think that for six years now I have been hopelessly afflicted, made worse by senseless physicians, from year to year deceived with hopes of improvement, finally compelled to face the prospect of *a lasting malady* (whose cure will take years or, perhaps, be impossible). Though born with a fiery, active temperament, even susceptible to the diversions of society, I was soon compelled to withdraw myself, to live life alone. If at times I tried to forget all this, oh how harshly was I flung back by the doubly sad experience of my bad hearing. Yet it was impossible for me to say to people, "Speak louder, shout, for I am deaf." Ah, how could I possibly admit an infirmity in the *one sense* which ought to be more perfect in me than in others, a sense which I once possessed in the highest perfection, a perfection such as few in my profession enjoy or ever have enjoyed.—Oh I cannot do it; therefore forgive me when you see me draw back when I would have gladly mingled with you. My misfortune is doubly painful to me because I am bound to be misunderstood; for me there can be no relaxation with my fellow men, no refined conversations, no mutual exchange of ideas. I must live almost alone, like one who has been banished; I can mix with society only as much as true necessity demands. If I approach near to people a hot terror seizes upon me, and I fear being exposed to the danger that my condition might be noticed. Thus it has been during the last six months which I have spent in the country. By ordering me to spare my hearing as much as possible, my intelligent doctor almost fell in with my own present frame of mind, though sometimes I ran counter to it by yielding to my desire for companionship. But what a humiliation for me when someone standing next to me heard a flute in the distance and *I heard nothing*, or someone heard a *shepherd singing* and again I heard nothing. Such incidents drove me almost to despair; a little more of that and I would have ended my life—it was only *my art* that held me back. Ah, it seemed to me impossible to leave the world until I had brought forth all that I felt was within me. So I endured this wretched existence—truly wretched for so susceptible a body, which can be thrown by a sudden change from the best condition to the very worst.—*Patience,* they say, is what I must now choose for my guide, and I have done so—I hope my determination will remain firm to endure until it pleases the inexorable Parcae to break the thread.

Perhaps I shall get better, perhaps not; I am ready.—Forced to become a philosopher already in my twenty-eighth year,—oh it is not easy, and for the artist much more difficult than for anyone else.—Divine One, thou seest my inmost soul; thou knowest that therein dwells the love of mankind and the desire to do good.—Oh fellow men, when at some point you read this, consider then that you have done me an injustice; someone who has had misfortune may console himself to find a similar case to his, who despite all the limitations of Nature nevertheless did everything within his powers to become accepted among worthy artists and men.—You, my brothers *Carl* and

as soon as I am dead, if Dr. Schmidt is still alive, ask him in my name to describe my malady, and attach this written document to his account of my illness so that so far as is possible at least the world may become reconciled to me after my death.—At the same time, I declare you two to be the heirs to my small fortune (if so it can be called); divide it fairly; bear with and help each other. What injury you have done me you know was long ago forgiven. To you, brother Carl, I give special thanks for the attachment you have shown me of late. It is my wish that you may have a better and freer life than I have had. Recommend *virtue* to your children; it alone, not money, can make them happy. I speak from experience; this was what upheld me in time of misery. Thanks to it and to my art, I did not end my life by suicide—Farewell and love each other—I thank all my friends, particularly *Prince Lichnowsky* and *Professor Schmidt*—I would like the instruments from Prince L. to be preserved by one of you, but not to be the cause of strife between you, and as soon as they can serve you a better purpose, then sell them. How happy I shall be if I can still be helpful to you in my grave—so be it.—With joy I hasten to meet death.—If it comes before I have had the chance to develop all my artistic capacities, it will still be coming too soon despite my harsh fate, and I should probably wish it later—yet even so I should be happy, for would it not free me from a state of endless suffering?—Come *when* thou wilt, I shall meet thee bravely.—Farewell and do not wholly forget me when I am dead; I deserve this from you, for during my lifetime I was thinking of you often and of ways to make you happy—please be so—

LUDWIG VAN BEETHOVEN

(seal)

HEIGLNSTADT, [HEILIGENSTADT]
October 6th,
1802

FOR MY BROTHERS CARL AND   TO BE READ AND EXECUT-
ED AFTER MY DEATH.

Heiglnstadt, *October* 10th, 1802, thus I bid thee farewell—and indeed sadly.—Yes, that fond hope—which I brought here with me, to be cured to a degree at least—this I must now wholly abandon. As the leaves of autumn fall and are withered—so likewise has my hope been blighted—I leave here—almost as I came—even the high courage—which often inspired me in the beautiful days of summer—has disappeared—Oh Providence—grant me at last but one day of pure *joy*—it is so long since real joy echoed in my heart—Oh when—Oh when, Oh Divine One—shall I feel it again in the temple of nature and of mankind—Never? No Oh that would be too hard.[14]

The emotional tone of the Heiligenstadt Testament, the most striking confessional statement in the biography of Beethoven, is curiously uneven, alternating between touching expressions of Beethoven's feelings of despair at his encroaching deafness and stilted, even literary formulations emphasizing his adherence to virtue. There are passages of real pathos, but these are so intertwined with self-conscious dramatics that one begins to realize that this neatly written document is a carefully revised "fair copy" that has been scrubbed clean of much of its original emotion. In particular, one remains unpersuaded by the references to suicide: "I would have ended my life—it was only *my art* that held me back"; "Thanks to [virtue] and to my art, I did not end my life by suicide." It is as though Beethoven were being deliberately laconic in order to avoid reviving distressful feelings.

Probably the testament was written after the passions that gave rise to it had begun to cool. Nevertheless, these underlying passions are evident despite Beethoven's redrafting, and they are so because Beethoven failed in his apparent goal—to present a coherent and "rational" explanation of his troubled state. For three years, perhaps more, he had been subject to attacks of severe anxiety, bordering on panic; he sought in the Heiligenstadt Testament to explain this suffering and anguish, which, he avowed, left him lonely, discontented, and suicidal. He believed that he had found in his deafness the sole "secret cause" of his torments, and he offered the testament as an essay in self-justification, asking that after his death it be made public so that "the world may become reconciled to me" and will understand why he was thought to be "malevolent, stubborn, or misanthropic."

Of course, we know that this is a great oversimplification, for these traits in Beethoven's character existed long before the onset of his deafness. Frau von Breuning was already familiar with his stubborness and wayward moods in Bonn; his tendencies toward misanthropy and withdrawal were also evident in his earliest years; and patrons, teachers, and rival pianists had felt the force of his aggressiveness long before this time. Naturally, the awareness of advancing deafness had a traumatic effect, but one senses that there is much more at work here than a mere reiteration of sentiments he had already voiced to Wegeler and Amenda fifteen months earlier.

It is both singular and striking, as biographers have not failed to observe, that Beethoven three times left portentous blank spaces in the testament where the name of his youngest brother should have appeared. But no one has seriously tried to explain these omissions.[15] Seemingly, the spaces hint at some peculiarity in Beethoven's relations with his brothers. But it really isn't unambiguous that the testament was intended only for his brothers. Several times Beethoven addresses not his brothers, but mankind at large: "Oh you men who think or say that I am malevolent"; "Oh fellow men, when at some point you read this, consider then that you have done me an injustice." This confusion is further compounded in the postscript, where, as George Grove observed, the change from "you" to "thee" would "seem to indicate that Beethoven is there addressing a single person."[16] Is there, we wonder, another, perhaps unspecified, addressee?

Clearly, there is no way of determining Beethoven's inner motives for omitting Nikolaus Johann's name. But it may help us reach a preliminary understanding to observe that there were other occasions when Beethoven failed to write the name of his youngest brother. Of the hundreds of references to Nikolaus Johann in Beethoven's letters and Conversation Books, there are only a few in which his name is written. Two are on the addresses of Beethoven's letters of February 19,

1796 ("To my brother Nikolaus Beethoven, to be delivered at the chemist's shop near the Kärntnertor") and July 30, 1822 ("To Johann *van Beethoven*, Esq., landowner in Gneixendorf").[17] Another is in a legal document dated March 6, 1823, addressed to and prepared under the supervision of Beethoven's attorney, Johann Baptist Bach, whom Beethoven instructs, "You are entitled and requested to find for my beloved nephew K[arl] v. Beethoven a guardian, who must not be, however, my brother Johann van Beethoven."[18] In the former instances the name is given not in the letters but only in the addresses; in the last, Beethoven, seeking to exclude his brother from the guardianship of their nephew, could not legally avoid writing the name "Johann van Beethoven." Even then, the sentence that includes his name was added as an afterthought, at the foot of the page.

Beethoven addressed his youngest brother by every imaginable circumlocution. At best he called him "my brother the chemist," "my brother, the bearer of this letter," or "the civil pharmaceutical chemist"; at worst, "pseudo-brother," "brother Cain," "brain eater," "my ass of a brother," or "Signor Fratello." In some instances, Beethoven had to employ considerable ingenuity to avoid the use of the name. We may reasonably conclude from this that he had a powerful reluctance to use his brother's name. And this reluctance of Beethoven's extended also to Caspar Carl's name: apart from the Heiligenstadt Testament, his name is written only in four legal documents pertaining to the guardianship of his son,[19] as well as in the aforementioned letter of February 19, 1796, where his name is written ("My greetings to our brother Caspar") and then obliterated, followed by "stet." Here, too, Beethoven occasionally had to go to some lengths to avoid using Caspar Carl's name, for example in a letter to Nikolaus Johann, where Beethoven wrote, "If only God would give to our other worthy brother instead of his heartlessness—some feeling."[20] Surely it would have been more natural to have given Caspar Carl's name here.

Beethoven apparently was loath to grant either of his brothers a name. And it is tempting to connect this with his disinclination to accept their independence from him, which is strikingly illustrated in later years by his interference in Nikolaus Johann's marriage and by his forcible alteration of Caspar Carl's last will. Nevertheless, the name of one brother is written four times in the Heiligenstadt Testament. It does seem, therefore, that Beethoven specifically could not there bring himself to write the name "Johann."

Of course, there is a possible commonsense explanation of the omission of Nikolaus Johann's name—that Beethoven, perhaps for legal purposes, was unsure whether to call Nikolaus Johann by his first name, by his middle name, or by both. For, as Ludwig Nohl observed, around the time of his move from Bonn to Vienna Nikolaus Johann dropped his first name and began to call himself simply Johann.[21] More remotely, Beethoven may have regarded his brother's adoption of this name as in some way a usurpation of the name of their father. We cannot tell, but our speculations would be incomplete if we failed to mention that nowhere in the surviving documents does Beethoven refer to his father by either his first or his full name. Only one document, indeed, includes even a portion of his name, and it contains a most curious and offhand reference to the composer's departed father. This is the already cited petition to the elector of Cologne, dated May 3, 1793, which begins, "A few years ago Your Electoral Excellency was pleased to retire my father, the court tenor van Beethoven. . . . [22] Here too the name Johann is omitted. One possibility, then, is that the memory of Johann van Beethoven *père* may still have aroused such piercing feelings in Beethoven that he could not readily bring himself to inscribe his father's name on paper.

Just as we will never really know the reasons for the omissions, the identity of the "thee" of the postscript, from whom Beethoven takes his leave, will always remain enigmatic. It would make sense in a document that utilizes the prescriptions of classical rhetoric[23] for Beethoven to revert at the close to the subject of his opening lines, that is, to his brothers, or to one of them, or to mankind at large ("O ihr Menschen"), but none of these is quite satisfactory, if only on grammatical grounds. It could also be a farewell to Heiligenstadt (as Brandenburg suggests), or to life, Providence, Nature, or some unspecified agency or addressee.

"Thus I bid thee farewell." What can be said is that the Heiligenstadt Testament is a leavetaking—which is to say, a fresh start. Beethoven here metaphorically enacted his own death in order that he might live again. He recreated himself in a new guise, self-sufficient and heroic. The testament is a funeral work, like the "Joseph" Cantata and *Christ on the Mount of Olives*. In a sense, it is the literary prototype of

the *Eroica* Symphony, a portrait of the artist as hero, stricken by deafness, withdrawn from mankind, conquering his impulses to suicide,
struggling against fate, hoping to find "but one day of pure joy." It is a
daydream compounded of heroism, death, and rebirth, a reaffirmation
of Beethoven's adherence to virtue and to the categorical imperative.

In view of its centrality in the Heiligenstadt Testament, this may be the
place to review briefly the history of Beethoven's deafness. After
Beethoven's death the autopsy report stated that "the auditory nerves ...
were shriveled and destitute of neurina; the accompanying arteries were
dilated to more than the size of a crow quill and cartilaginous."[24]
Specialists disagree as to a diagnosis; some lean toward "otosclerosis";
others claim that it was a disease of the inner ear ("neuritis acoustica" or
"labyrinthitis"); while still others favor "otitis media," a disease of the
middle ear.[25] The onset of his hearing difficulty dates from approximately 1796 at the earliest, and the first troublesome symptoms appear
in 1798 or 1799. In the years leading up to the Heiligenstadt crisis,
1801–2, the fact is that Beethoven's physical deafness had not progressed very far. He experienced intermittent symptoms of tinnitus,
such as humming, ringing, buzzing, and other discordant sounds in the
ears; there was a partial loss of his ability to distinguish high frequencies; and sudden loud noises caused discomfort and even pain.
Beethoven sought treatment from various doctors—Johann Peter Frank,
Gerhard von Vering, and an unknown whom he dubbed a "medical
ass"—before he found the firmly sympathetic Dr. Schmidt in 1801.
Czerny remembered that in that year "he did not give the least evidence
of deafness."[26] Seyfried, who for long stretches of time between 1803
and 1806 lived in the same building as Beethoven and often dined with
him, confirmed, "No physical ill had then afflicted him; no loss of the
sense which is peculiarly indispensable to the musician had darkened
his life."[27] Even Ries, who learned of Beethoven's deafness in 1802,
believed that "the trouble soon disappeared again."[28]

By 1804, to be sure, there is a report that Beethoven had difficulty
hearing the wind instruments during a rehearsal of the *Eroica*
Symphony, and in the same year Stephan von Breuning wrote to
Wegeler, "You cannot believe, dear Wegeler, what an indescribable—I
should say terrifying—impression the waning of his hearing has had

upon him. . . . He has become very withdrawn and often mistrustful of his best friends, and irresolute in many things!"[29] But Beethoven was far from incapacitated: in 1805 he conducted the rehearsals of *Fidelio*, and in 1808 he called attention to subtle nuances in Wilhelm Rust's playing, indicative of the keenness of his hearing. By the decade's end he no longer performed in concerts as a solo pianist; by 1814 his hearing was only barely adequate for him to participate in performances of the "Archduke" Trio, op. 97. It was actually after 1812 that his deafness progressed more rapidly, and increasingly it became necessary to raise one's voice when speaking to him. However, Czerny told Otto Jahn, Mozart's biographer who had gathered material for a life of Beethoven, that "it was not until 1817 that the deafness became so extreme that he could no longer hear music either."[30] Beethoven began to use an ear trumpet around 1816, and by 1818 the Conversation Books came into existence, so that visitors could communicate with him in writing.

In his last decade, Beethoven became more markedly deaf, and he was apparently totally so in his right ear. Even then, traces of hearing persisted throughout the 1820s. Several visitors in 1822 and 1823 were able to converse with him, and Schindler described Beethoven listening intently to the overture to Cherubini's *Medea* on a music box. On October 3, 1822, he conducted (with assistants) at the opening of the Josephstadt Theater, but the following month he attempted in vain to conduct a revival of *Fidelio* and was forced to quit the theater. As late as 1825 and 1826, Sir George Smart, Stephan von Breuning, and Samuel Spiker reported that Beethoven could occasionally still understand loud speech. Holz confirmed that "Beethoven undertook the rehearsals of his quartets up to the last." He could hear high tones: "When one yelled powerfully into his left ear one could make oneself understood."[31] He could also still distinguish certain low frequencies, such as the clatter of wagon wheels, the rumble of thunder, and the sounds of gunfire.[32]

The data strongly suggest a pattern of progressive, though uneven, deterioration of Beethoven's hearing, which reached a state of almost total deafness only in his final decade. This pattern is clearly quite different from the popular conception—that the onset of Beethoven's deafness was sudden and dramatic. To take the 1801 letters and the Heiligenstadt Testament at face value gave currency, in Thayer's words, "to a very exaggerated idea of the progress of his infirmity."[33] Beethoven shared that idea: the terrifying anxieties that were generated by the probability that he would ultimately become totally deaf led him to dramatize the extent of his earlier hearing problems. In his despair and panic he felt himself to be more deaf than he actually was at the time.

Throughout his life Beethoven and his friends were mystified as to the cause of his deafness. They attributed it to a wide variety of possibilities—to the violent digestive disorders that plagued him; to a "frightful attack of typhus"; to his having become drenched while composing music outdoors during a driving rain; to exposure in a draft on a hot summer day; to rheumatism; and to a congenital "weakness" in his auditory canals.[34] At one time, Beethoven even thought his deafness had been induced by frustration and rage. An English pianist, Charles Neate, who visited Beethoven in 1815, urged him to come to England to seek treatment for his deafness. Neate gave Thayer the following account of Beethoven's strange reply:

> BEETHOVEN: No; I have already had all sorts of medical advice. I shall never be cured—I will tell you how it happened. "I was once busy writing an opera . . .
> NEATE: *Fidelio?*
> BEETHOVEN: No. It was not *Fidelio.* I had a very ill-tempered, troublesome *primo tenore* to deal with. I had already written two grand airs to the same text, with which he was dissatisfied, and now a third, which, upon trial, he seemed to approve and took away with him. I sat down immediately to a work which I had laid aside for those airs and which I was anxious to finish. I had not been half an hour at work when I heard a knock at my door, which I at once recognized as that of my *primo tenore.* I sprang up from my table under such an excitement of rage that, as the man entered the room, I threw myself upon the floor as they do upon the stage, coming down upon my hands. When I arose I found myself deaf and have been so ever since. The physicians say the nerve is injured.[35]

One would love to interpret this fascinating story (or fantasy), which Thayer rightly calls "extraordinary and inexplicable," but this might lead us into speculative regions from which we could return only with difficulty to the known facts of Beethoven's life. This much, at least, can be said: Beethoven imagined that he had induced his own deafness (though there was, and is, no evidence of this), and he attributed it to his own rage in response to what he considered persecutory behavior by a *primo tenore*. (One cannot help wondering if this tenor is not a screen for another *primo tenore* in Beethoven's earlier life.)

The gradual closing off of Beethoven's aural contact with the world inevitably led to feelings of painful isolation and encouraged his tendencies toward misanthropy and suspiciousness. But deafness did not impair and indeed may even have heightened his abilities as a composer, perhaps by its exclusion of piano virtuosity as a competing outlet for his creativity, perhaps by permitting a total concentration upon composition within a world of increasing auditory seclusion. In his deaf world, Beethoven could experiment with new forms of experience, free from the intrusive sounds of the external environment; free from the rigidities of the material world; free, like a dreamer, to combine and recombine the stuff of reality, in accordance with his desires, into previously undreamed-of forms and structures. Perhaps this is a clue as to why, in the Heiligenstadt Testament, Beethoven expresses his acquiescence in his affliction. Surely, encroaching deafness was not a condition to be desired; he regarded it as a retaliation, a curse visited upon him by his Creator or by "Fate." But throughout the testament one senses a note of acceptance: "*Patience*, they say, is what I must now choose for my guide, and I have done so"; or, to Wegeler, "*Resignation*, what a wretched resource! Yet it is all that is left to me." Beethoven once referred to his hearing as "my noblest faculty," and to its deterioration as the cause of his withdrawal into a self-imposed isolation. "If I approach near to people," the testament reads, "a hot terror seizes upon me and I fear being exposed to the danger that my condition might be noticed." The lonely void was filled by his music: "Live only in your art, for you are so limited by your senses," he wrote in his Tagebuch in 1816; "this is nevertheless the *only existence* for you."[36] This reparative view of music may partly explain his striking remark to Amenda, "When I am playing and composing, my affliction . . . hampers me least; it affects me most when I am in company."[37]

Ultimately, Beethoven turned all his defeats into victories. Like Henry James's "obscure hurt" and Dostoevsky's "holy disease," even his loss of hearing was in some indefinable sense necessary (or at least useful) to the fulfillment of his creative quest. The onset of his deafness was the painful chrysalis within which his "heroic" style came to maturity. "I am staying in the country and leading a rather lazy life," he wrote from Heiligenstadt to Hoffmeister in Leipzig, "in order, however, to lead again later on—an all the more active one."[38] As his shift in style asserted itself and the advances in his art were consolidated, the symptoms themselves receded for him into a different perspective and were no longer the subject of lamentation. Between the writing of the Heiligenstadt Testament, in October 1802, and 1810 there are only two or three passing references to his deafness in Beethoven's correspondence, along with one revealing note on a leaf of sketches for the "Razumovsky" Quartets in 1806: "Let your deafness no longer be a secret—even in art."[39] Beethoven had come to terms with his deafness.

THE HEROIC DECADE (I)

T HROUGHOUT THE COURSE OF BEETHOVEN'S LIFE, each of his psychological crises was followed by a period of reconstruction. He could not permanently rid himself of deep internal conflicts, but he was able temporarily to surmount them by immersion in his work and through posing and solving increasingly intricate and profound creative problems. The end of the Heiligenstadt crisis in late 1802 ushered in a long period of relative equilibrium during which he reached the highest order of creativity, which remained remarkably secure for a full eight years and was not significantly undermined until 1813. Beethoven's remarkable productivity during these years included an opera, an oratorio, a Mass, six symphonies, four concertos, five string quartets, three piano trios, three string sonatas, and six piano sonatas, plus incidental music for a number of stage works, many lieder, four sets of piano variations, and several symphonic concert overtures. Every year saw the completion of a cluster of masterpieces, each of a highly individual character. Only toward the end of this period, in 1811, did the quality of his output falter somewhat, a situation impressively remedied in 1812 with the composition of the Seventh and Eighth Symphonies, opp. 92 and 93, and the Violin Sonata in G, op. 96.

This steady and rich productivity took place against a background of expanding reputation and international fame. So innovative a composer necessarily met resistance from those who were emotionally bound to familiar and less demanding musical styles, but even these resistances were counterbalanced by what Moscheles called the "Beethoven fever" that raged among connoisseurs and especially among musicians and music lovers of the younger generation.[1] There were many among older composers and music pedagogues who could not readily accept what appeared to them "fantastic" (Haydn) and "hare-brained" (Moscheles' teacher, Dionys Weber) departures from tradition.[2] Czerny reported that

"Marcia funebre sulla morte d'un Eroe," Sonata in A, op. 26.
First page of the autograph score.

Staatsbibliothek Preussischer Kulturbesitz, Berlin.

the *Eroica* Symphony was "considered too long, elaborate, incomprehensible, and much too noisy," and the *Allgemeine musikalische Zeitung* wrote that it contained "an excess of whimsicalities and novelties."[3] (Beethoven angrily responded, "If you fancy you can injure *me* by publishing articles of that kind, you are very much mistaken. On the contrary, by so doing you merely bring your journal into disrepute.")[4]

Arthur Loesser may well be right when he asserts that "for most people, Beethoven's fame was an article of superstition; for the most part they much preferred the works of his less assertive, less inspired contemporaries."[5] Certainly, although his standing as a composer was steadily on the rise and eventually came to eclipse his reputation as a virtuoso performer, Beethoven was not the most popular composer of the age during his first ten or twelve years in Vienna. In the crucial world of opera he was scarcely in the running, and a look at the programs of Viennese public concerts up to 1806 shows that Mozart, Haydn, Paer, Cherubini, Mayer, Righini, and several other fashionable composers were more frequently played than was Beethoven. Although he retained the loyalty of what we have called the connoisseur aristocracy, that group could not altogether compensate with its enthusiasm and refinement for its relatively small numbers, so that their favorite's works did not dominate musical life in the salons and residences of the wealthy—whether aristocratic, imperial, or bourgeois—during those years.

As early as 1804, however, publications of Beethoven's music came to be more widely circulated in the Habsburg realms than those of any other young composer, and within a few years his works were so much in demand that they appeared on concert programs even more frequently than those of Mozart and Haydn. True, during this period, Beethoven was able to obtain permission for only two public orchestral concerts for his own benefit—those of April 5, 1803, and December 22, 1808—but major public concerts by other musicians increasingly scheduled his music. During the period 1803–6 the number of such concerts featuring his works averaged four per year, but there was an explosive increase in the number of performances of music by Beethoven in the years 1807 and 1808, perhaps comparable only to Mozart's domination of Viennese concert life in 1784 and 1785. In 1807 alone, Beethoven's music was heard at three academies by other artists; the first four symphonies, the

Piano Concerto No. 4 in G, op. 58, and other works were played at major concerts at the Lobkowitz Palace; and at six of the series of newly established *Liebhaber* concerts, reserved for audiences of the aristocracy and foreign notables, Beethoven's works were the main attractions, performed often under his own direction. Even more striking, in the following year his music was played at eight academies, five *Liebhaber* concerts, three concerts in a series promoted by Schuppanzigh (which had moved indoors from the Augarten to the Razumovsky Palace), two chamber music recitals at Countess Erdödy's residence, and, climactically, at Beethoven's academy of December 22, at the Theater-an-der-Wien. As Thayer observed, by 1808 "it was Beethoven's popularity that must insure success to the grand concerts for the public charities; it was his name that was known to be more attractive to the Vienna public than any other, save that of the venerable Haydn."[6]

The quantity of Beethoven performances declined during 1809 and 1810, owing in large part to the disruption of musical life during the French occupation of Vienna, only to increase once again in the years 1811 and 1812. Meanwhile, performances in other cities in the Habsburg empire—Graz, Prague, Pest—became commonplace. In Graz, which was emerging as a musical center of great importance, Beethoven's rise to eminence started as early as 1805 in programs presented in the local *Liebhaber* concert series, with performances of the *Prometheus* Overture, op. 43, and a symphony (probably No. 2 in D, op. 36); in 1808, the *Coriolan* Overture, op. 62, and a piano concerto (probably the G-major, op. 58) were heard; and in 1809 two *"grosse Sinfonien"* by Beethoven—apparently the *Eroica* and *Pastoral*—were played in the *Liebhaber* concerts, and one of the opus 5 Cello Sonatas was offered at a virtuoso recital.[7]

Abroad, Beethoven's music was rapidly making its way in several major countries. In Germany, his earlier piano concertos quickly entered the repertory, and the Septet, op. 20, and the First Symphony, op. 21, had a sensational success. His compositions found an especially welcome reception in his native Rhineland. It was in England, however, that Beethoven gained his greatest popularity outside Austria. There the Septet was performed several times in 1801, and two of his symphonies were played in 1803. In 1804–5 there were ten performances of major Beethoven works in England, and thereafter an increasing number of his compositions was heard.[8] Beethoven was much impressed by his British reception. Perhaps it was partly in gratitude that in 1803 he wrote his Variations on "God Save the King," WoO 78, and on "Rule Britannia," WoO 79.

France, however, long proved insusceptible to Beethoven's innovations. ("The French find my music beyond their powers of performance," remarked the composer.)[9] Following a few performances at the Paris Conservatory in 1802, his music went unheard in the French capital until 1807, and thereafter there were but a few performances until the late 1820s. Only one Beethoven symphony, the First, seems to have been played in France before 1811. Nevertheless, many of Beethoven's earlier works were rapidly published there, indicating that amateur performers, at least, found his music to their liking.

Of course, public performances were not a wholly accurate index of a composer's popularity, for public concerts featuring chamber music or lieder were then in their infancy and solo keyboard recitals were not given. Such music was usually performed in salons and at private concerts, and accordingly is rarely noted in print. Thus it is not really surprising that there were only two known public performances of Beethoven solo piano sonatas during his lifetime—of opus 90 or opus 101 in Vienna in 1816, and of the "Funeral March" Sonata in A-flat, op. 26, in Boston in 1819.[10]

New publications of Beethoven's music continued to be issued at a very good rate, including editions of all of his major symphonic works, for which there was a smaller market than for piano sonatas and variations. In the years between 1803 and 1812 an average of almost eight separate new publications of his works appeared annually, from publishers in Vienna, Bonn, Leipzig, and Zürich. New editions, often pirated, of previously published works appeared in other countries. In England, half a dozen of Beethoven's works were published prior to 1810; in that year, the composer-publisher Muzio Clementi issued thirteen works by Beethoven in London, including two concertos; the String Quartet in E-flat, op. 74; the "Choral Fantasia," op. 80; a number of lieder, and several piano works.[11] During this same period there were numerous unauthorized English reprints of his works.

Naturally, Beethoven also encountered disappointments during this productive decade. Many of his works did not please, and others essentially disappeared from the repertory during his lifetime. The failure of his only opera in its first two versions was an especially bitter disappointment.

Conflicts with both of his brothers also marked this decade. Caspar Carl's marriage in 1806 led to a partial estrangement, and Nikolaus Johann's insistence in 1807 that Beethoven pay him back a loan of 1,500 florins was met with angry resistance by the composer, so that Nikolaus Johann's departure for Linz in 1808 was not the occasion for a fond, fraternal separation. In addition, the vicissitudes of Beethoven's amorous life—or, more precisely, the absence of one—were a constant source of pain. Beethoven also had his normal share of bad notices, quarrels with patrons, perpetual postponements of his cherished benefit concerts, delayed publications, and contract difficulties, and he could not have remained unaffected—though he is essentially silent on the matter—by the progress of his deafness throughout this period. Nevertheless, his personality was at this time sufficiently resilient that he could withstand these and other pressures with relative equanimity.

Following his stay in Heiligenstadt in 1802, Beethoven returned to Vienna by mid-October bearing a thick sheaf of manuscripts, for it had been a remarkably productive summer. Almost immediately he became involved in a quarrel with Artaria & Co., until then his most devoted Viennese publisher, concerning its publication of his String Quintet in C, op. 29, the rights to which he had sold to Breitkopf & Härtel, but which Artaria had received, apparently with Beethoven's consent, from Count Fries, the dedicatee of the Quintet. He thus inaugurated the series of legal entanglements that drained his energies (and through which he worked off his aggressions?) during the next two decades. Despite his later admission that he himself had corrected Artaria's proofs, he denied that there was any verbal commitment and accused the firm of having stolen the Quintet. In February 1803, Artaria filed a court petition demanding a public apology. Beethoven stubbornly refused to issue a retraction, however, even in the face of a court order.[12]

At the beginning of 1803, the impresario Emanuel Schikaneder's lavish new Theater-an-der-Wien, which had opened in June 1801 and was in fierce competition with the two Imperial Royal Court Theaters (Burgtheater and Kärntnertortheater), engaged Beethoven to compose an opera, and he and his brother Caspar Carl soon took up lodgings at the theater. Beethoven remained occupied with other matters until late in the year, however, probably because of the late delivery of the opera text by Schikaneder (who had been the librettist of Mozart's *Die Zauberflöte*). Beethoven's oratorio *Christus am Ölberge* (*Christ on the Mount of Olives*), op. 85, was written out in a few weeks during March 1803 and performed, along with the First and Second Symphonies and the Third Piano Concerto, at his successful academy on April 5. Immediately after the completion of *Christus*, Beethoven sketched and rapidly completed the Violin Sonata in A ("Kreutzer"), op. 47, for a performance by himself and the violinist George Bridgetower, on May 24. The months from May until November a good portion of which were spent at the summer resorts of Baden and Oberdöbling near Vienna—were devoted to composing the first draft of the *Eroica* Symphony; by December he had completed the Piano Sonata in C ("Waldstein"), op. 53, dedicated to his former patron Count Ferdinand Waldstein.

Beethoven's correspondence for this year reflects little of his inner life; most of his letters are devoted to negotiations with publishers, rehearsals, performances, copying, proofreading, and other business details. One letter, however, written in September to Hoffmeister, shows that, despite his burgeoning success, he was far from reconciled to his freelance existence in Vienna: "Please remember that all my acquaintances hold appointments and know exactly what they have to live on," he wrote. "But Heaven help us! What appointment at the Imperial Court could be given to such a *parvum talentum com ego* [mediocre talent like myself]?"[13]

His dissatisfaction was such that he seriously began to consider leaving Vienna. On August 6, 1803, Ries wrote to Simrock that "Beethoven will stay here [in Vienna] at most for another year and a half. He is then going to Paris, which makes me extraordinarily sorrowful."[14] On October 22, Ries wrote again to advise Simrock that Beethoven wanted to title his new symphony *Bonaparte* and that he also wanted to dedicate his new sonata for violin and piano jointly to Rodolphe Kreutzer and Louis Adam, "as the foremost violinist and pianist in Paris." He added the news that Beethoven would soon begin work on his opera and would leave Vienna upon its completion. By December, Beethoven had decided not to permit publication of the new symphony prior to his Paris trip: "He now doesn't want to sell it and will reserve it for his journey." Early in 1804, in a letter to the secretary of the court theaters Joseph Sonnleithner, he wrote, "I received yesterday another letter about my journey, and this one has made my decision to travel *irrevocable*."[15] We can only speculate on the motives behind this intended move (or lengthy visit). Clearly, Beethoven felt that he deserved a position commensurate with his talents; perhaps, too, he had received some indication that his arrival in Paris would be warmly welcomed. And perhaps his disappointment at Giulietta Guicciardi's impending marriage to Count Gallenberg was greater than has been supposed.

In November Beethoven commenced work on Schikaneder's *Vestas Feuer* (*The Vestal Flame*), Hess 115, and by year's end he had almost completely drafted the first scene. Not finding the libretto to his liking, however, he returned the text and settled instead upon a more sympathetic topic—the rescue of an imprisoned husband by his loving wife—to be adapted and translated by Joseph Sonnleithner from J. N. Bouilly's French libretto *Léonore; ou, l'amour conjugal*. Its choice may not be altogether unrelated to Beethoven's intended journey to Paris, for he had chosen a libretto that had originated in and found favor in post–Revolutionary France, and had begun to compose an opera in a genre, the rescue opera, that had originated in and was wildly popular in Paris.

He began work on the first act, but a change on February 11 in the ownership and management of the Theater-an-der-Wien led, according to Thayer, to the suspension or even annulment of his contract, which was not reinstated until late in 1804. It seems reasonable to think that Beethoven interrupted work on the opera because he no longer had the certainty of a production at the Theater-an-der-Wien. Moreover, the libretto was not altogether ready and Beethoven had other urgent projects on hand: in the intervening months he revised the *Eroica* Symphony into final form after private rehearsals of it and of a preliminary draft of the Concerto for Piano, Violin, and Cello in C ("Triple Concerto"), op. 56, at the Lobkowitz Palace, utilizing an orchestra placed at his disposal by Prince Lobkowitz;[16] wrote the Sonata in F, op. 54; and perhaps began planning, and possibly actually sketching, the Sonata in F minor ("Appassionata"), op. 57. At the same time, however, despite the apparent nullification of his contract and a conflict with the management that led to his moving out of his quarters at the Theater-an-der-Wien, the sketchbooks show that Beethoven continued working on the opera and by the end of March had entered sketches for the first five numbers. The remainder of the opera except for the overture was fully sketched by June 1805, and the opera was ready for production early in the following autumn.[17]

In a letter of July 6, 1804, Beethoven disclosed to a German musician, Gottlob Wiedebein, "I shall probably leave here next winter."[18] And on December 21, Charlotte Brunsvik wrote to her brother, Franz, "Beethoven will write to you; he hopes to travel to Paris with Lichnowsky this coming spring."[19] Nevertheless, at some point during those very months Beethoven drew back from the drastic idea of moving to the French capital, and eventually also abandoned any plans for a concert tour to Paris.

Beethoven's decision to remain in Vienna is closely related to the most dramatic incident of 1804, one that bears upon his political and ideological outlook: his destruction of the "Bonaparte" inscription of the Third Symphony upon hearing the news, in May 1804, that Napoleon had proclaimed himself emperor of France.

Napoleon Bonaparte. Portrait in oils by Anne Louis Girodet-Troison.

Arenenberg Castle, Switzerland.

Eroica Symphony. Title page of corrected copy of full score
with Beethoven's alterations and remarks.

Courtesy of Gesellschaft der Musikfreunde, Vienna.

CHAPTER THIRTEEN

BONAPARTE:
THE CRISIS OF BELIEF

In this symphony Beethoven had Buonaparte in mind, but as he was when he was First Consul. Beethoven esteemed him greatly at the time and likened him to the greatest Roman consuls. I as well as several of his more intimate friends saw a copy of the score lying upon his table with the word "Buonaparte" at the extreme top of the title page, and at the extreme bottom "Luigi van Beethoven," but not another word. Whether and with what the space between was to be filled out, I do not know. I was the first to bring him the intelligence that Buonaparte had proclaimed himself emperor, whereupon he flew into a rage and cried out: "Is he then, too, nothing more than an ordinary human being? Now he, too, will trample on all the rights of man and indulge only his ambition. He will exalt himself above all others, become a tyrant!" Beethoven went to the table, took hold of the title page by the top, tore it in two, and threw it on the floor. The first page was rewritten and only then did the symphony receive the title *Sinfonia eroica*.[1]

This simple anecdote, told by Ferdinand Ries, is one of the more Promethean of the Beethoven legends, popular with chroniclers of romanticism and revolution. Although it describes a largely rhetorical and wholly symbolic action, it has, with the passage of time, become a monumentalized example of the artist's resistance to tyranny, of the antagonism between art and politics, of the individual against the state. But a closer examination reveals that the process by which the French leader's name was removed from Beethoven's Third Symphony was more complex than has been supposed. Furthermore, and more important, it shows that a crisis of belief was centrally involved in the crisis that precipitated and accompanied Beethoven's "new path," which he had announced to Krumpholz a few years earlier.

The accuracy of Ries's account of Beethoven's reaction to the news that Napoleon had been proclaimed emperor is not in question.[2] Obviously, we may make allowances for Ries's rendering of Beethoven's actual words, and we know he was incorrect in saying that the symphony was thereupon or shortly thereafter retitled *Eroica,* for this name was not used before October 1806, when the first edition of the orchestral parts was published by the Bureau des Arts et d'Industrie (also called Kunst- und Industrie Comtoir) in Vienna.[3] But what Ries did not know was that in the interim Beethoven decided to restore Bonaparte's name to the symphony. On August 26, 1804, Beethoven wrote to Gottfried Härtel of Breitkopf & Härtel:

> I have now finished several compositions . . . my oratorio—a *new grand symphony*—a concertante for violin, violoncello, and pianoforte with full orchestra—three new sonatas for pianoforte solo. . . . The title of the symphony is really *Bonaparte.*[4]

Perhaps even more significant in illuminating Beethoven's indecision is the title page of his own copy of the score of the symphony. It is filled with erasures and corrections in the composer's hand:

[AT THE TOP]

N.B. 1.   Cues for the other instruments are to be written into the first violin part.

[1]   Sinfonia Grande

[2]   Intitulata Bonaparte

[3]   [1804] im August

[4]   Del [or de] Sigr.

[5]   Louis van Beethoven

[6]   Geschrieben

[7]   auf Bonaparte

[8]   Sinfonia [or Sinfonie] 3 Op. 55

[AT THE BOTTOM]

N.B. 2.   The third horn [part] is so written that it can be played by a primario as well as a secundario.

The original title consisted of lines 1, 2, 4, and 5, written by the copyist; lines 3 and 8 were added by unknown hands.[5] Line 2—*Intitulata Bonaparte*—was later crossed out, so that it is barely legible, but lines 6 and 7—*Geschrieben auf Bonaparte*—were added in pencil by Beethoven and were never erased.

Actually, even while he was writing the symphony, Beethoven had begun to dilute his commitment to France's First Consul. Ries wrote to Simrock on October 22, 1803: "He wants very much to dedicate it to Bonaparte; if not, since Lobkowitz wants [the rights to] it for half a year and is willing to give 400 ducats for it, he will title it Bonaparte."[6] It seems then that Beethoven initially planned to dedicate the symphony to Bonaparte. However, finding that this would deprive him of a large fee, he conceived the alternative idea of entitling it *Bonaparte*, and it was this alternative that he confronted in May 1804 when Ries arrived, bringing the latest news from Paris. In the end, Bonaparte was to receive neither the dedication to nor the inscription of the *Eroica* Symphony.

To its participants, the central issue of the post-Revolutionary age appeared to be the issue of Bonapartism, around which ideological responses to historical movements revolved. Émile Zola, in his essay on Stendhal, wrote that "Napoleon's destiny acted like a hammer-blow on the heads of his contemporaries.... All ambitions waxed large, all undertakings took on a gigantic air, ... all dreams turned on universal kingship."[7] For Beethoven's German and Austrian contemporaries, the Napoleonic image was especially potent: Bonaparte's admirers included Kant, Herder, Fichte, Schelling, Hegel, Schiller, Goethe, Hölderlin, Wieland, and Klopstock. The dramatist Franz Grillparzer wrote in his *Autobiography*, "I myself was no less an enemy of the French than my father, and yet Napoleon fascinated me with a magic power. . . . He put me under a spell, as a snake does a bird."[8] Goethe, who kept a bust of Napoleon in his room, said to his literary assistant, Johann Peter Eckermann, in 1829, "Napoleon managed the world as Hummel his piano; both achievements appear wonderful, we do not understand one more than the other, yet so it is, and the whole is done before our eyes." Hegel, in 1806, called Napoleon a "soul of worldwide significance ... an individual who ... encompasses the world and rules it."[9]

Soon, however, the difficulty of reconciling the Napoleonic ideal with the French wars of conquest—or with the Napoleonic substitution of permanent war for permanent revolution—led to confusion if not disillusionment among many European intellectuals and artists. Heinrich Heine observed that the German democrats "wrapped their thoughts in profound silence," being "too republican in their sentiments to do homage to Napoleon, and too magnanimous to ally themselves with a foreign domination."[10] Napoleon himself noted that "everybody has loved me and hated me: everybody has taken me up, dropped me, and taken me up again. . . . I was like the sun, which crosses the equator as it describes the ecliptic; as soon as I entered each man's clime, I kindled every hope, I was blessed, I was adored; but as soon as I left it, I no longer was understood and contrary sentiments replaced the old ones."[11]

Bonaparte's coronation was widely regarded as a subordination of principle to personal ambition. Beethoven's dismay was shared by intellectuals everywhere. Shelley wrote, in his introduction to *The Revolt of Islam*, that "the revulsion occasioned by the atrocities of the demagogues and the reëstablishment of successive tyrannies in France was terrible, and felt in the remotest corner of the civilized world."[12] But where Shelley optimistically continued to listen to Reason's plea for political and economic justice, and Goethe and Jefferson maintained an aloof objectivity that forbore to take sides on issues where morality was unable to choose, others, such as Coleridge and Wordsworth, became obsessed with fears of the Jacobin danger and opted for a restoration of the ancien régime. For his part, Beethoven neither gave way to spiritual melancholia over this issue nor abandoned his belief in the secular, fraternal utopia that Bonaparte—one *bon prince*—had betrayed.

The Revolution was over, dissolved in war and petrified in the stultifying bureaucratic forms that sooner or later overtake all social transformations. But this was a process that had begun well before 1804. Beethoven's rending of the title page therefore cannot be accepted as a simple act of angry defiance at a new development in Napoleonic politics, for these regressive tendencies had already been apparent for some years, and Beethoven was aware of them. His equivocal attitude toward the French leader neither started nor ended with the Imperium. Beethoven's composition of two patriotic songs in 1796 and 1797 was inspired by Habsburg anti-Napoleonic campaigns, and Beethoven had even explicitly expressed his disillusionment with Napoleon in 1802, when Hoffmeister, the Leipzig publisher, transmitted a suggestion that

Beethoven compose a sonata in celebration of Napoleon or of the Revolution. Beethoven's reply to Hoffmeister of April 8, 1802, indicates that even then—shortly before the *Eroica* Symphony was begun—he considered Bonaparte to have betrayed the Revolution by virtue of his concordat with the Vatican (signed in July 1801), which reestablished Catholic worship in France:

> Has the devil got hold of you all, Gentlemen?—that you suggest that *I should compose such a sonata.* Well, perhaps at the time of the *Revolutionary* fever—such a thing might have been possible, but now, when everything is trying to slip back into the old rut, now that *Buonaparte* has concluded his *Concordat* with the Pope—to write a sonata of that kind? . . . But good Heavens, such a sonata—in these newly developing Christian times—Ho ho—there you must leave me out—you won't get anything from me—.[13]

Why, then, did Beethoven decide to write a *Bonaparte* symphony shortly after this letter to Hoffmeister?

Beethoven's projected move to Paris provides an apparently simple motive: the *Bonaparte* Symphony and the proposed dedication of the Violin Sonata, op. 47, to Adam and Kreutzer may have been intended to smooth Beethoven's entry into the French capital.[14] And the cancellation of the tour coincided rather closely with the final removal of Bonaparte's name from the Third Symphony. Yet it would be an oversimplification to counter the Promethean interpretations of this story by reducing the entire matter to a musician's desire to advance his career. It was during this period that Beethoven began openly to reaffirm his adherence to enlightened ideals, signs of which had, certainly for reasons of discretion, almost disappeared from his letters and his music of the preceding decade. The composition of nationalist battle songs in 1796–97, the dedication of the Septet to Empress Maria Theresia in 1800, and the improvisation on "God Save Emperor Franz" in April 1803 had not seemed to be the actions of an independent and defiant thinker, but of an apparently faithful servant of the state. Private acts of rebellion against his patrons were insufficient to offset the implications of such public avowals. True, Beethoven was reported by Schindler—though there is no confirmation of this—to have associated with the circle that gathered at the house of the French ambassador Bernadotte between February and April of 1798. If this association indeed had political overtones, it may have been a sign of the chaotic nature of Beethoven's allegiances, of the depth of his conflict with Vienna, and perhaps even of his vacillation between opposing political forces. Only after 1800 do we find the first indications of a rehabilitation of his political and ideological indepen- dence. In 1801 he wrote to Wegeler that he wished his art to be "exer- cised only for the benefit of the poor,"[15] and to Hoffmeister in the same year he proposed a quasi-socialist system of artistic patronage: "There ought to be in the world a *market for art [Magazin der Kunst]* where the artist would only have to bring his works and take as much money as he needed. But, as it is, an artist has to be to a certain extent a businessman as well."[16] Remarkably, the 1802 letter to Hoffmeister concerning the proposed "Revolutionary sonata" is the first seriously political reference in his correspondence in eight years.

Beethoven was emerging from what seemed to be a period of ideo- logical quiescence. Perhaps this is one reason why, in the opening years of the nineteenth century, he began a series of apparently disinterested dedications of his works to leading exponents of enlightened views. Thus, in December 1801 he inscribed his Symphony No. 1 in C, op. 21, to Baron Gottfried van Swieten, reformer, presumed Freemason, and a guardian to Mozart's orphaned sons; next, the revered Austrian- Jewish *Aufklärer*, Freemason, and Illuminist Joseph von Sonnenfels (favorite of and adviser to Emperor Joseph II) received the dedication of the Piano Sonata in D, op. 28, in August 1802; and the young Czar Alexander, who had instituted a program of reform in the tradition of Enlightened despotism, received that of the three Sonatas for Violin and Piano, op. 30, in 1803. Because dedications for Beethoven were either a major source of patronage and income or a means of express- ing gratitude or friendship, these unpaid, honorary dedications are all the more significant.[17]

The culmination of this series was the proposed dedication to Bonaparte of the Third Symphony. This dedication, along with the con- sideration of a move to Paris, may, therefore, have been a dramatic sign of Beethoven's desire to break with Habsburg Vienna and its political system as well as with its modes of musical patronage. If this is true, then the rending of the inscription may constitute an equally dramatic turning point—Beethoven's abandonment of his identification with France and his decision henceforth to view himself as a citizen of Vienna.

The idea of a symphonic apotheosis of Napoleon had been worked out during the relatively long period of peace that followed Napoleon's defeat of Austria in late 1800, as codified by the February 9, 1801, Treaty of Lunéville. That peace was unraveling in 1804, and war was to erupt once again in 1805. To have kept "Bonaparte" either as title or as dedication at a moment when renewed war between France and Austria was imminent would have marked Beethoven as a philo-Jacobin, a supporter of a radical cause and of a hostile power. It would have led not merely to the loss of a patron—Lobkowitz was an ardent patriot who later raised a battalion of troops to fight the French—but to the probability of reprisals in anti-Revolutionary Austria as well.

Of all the European nations, writes Eric Hobsbawm, "Austria, whose family links with the Bourbons were reinforced by the direct French threat to her possessions and areas of influence in Italy, and her leading position in Germany, was the most consistently anti-French, and took part in every major coalition against France."[18] Austria suffered heavier defeats and territorial losses than any other continental power during the Napoleonic Wars. We saw earlier how the Viennese authorities kept constant watch on all expression of social or political dissent. And of all forms of dissent, support for France was considered the most dangerous.

In light of these circumstances, Beethoven's obliteration of the Bonaparte inscription and the consequent merging of his heroic ideal with the Habsburg national outlook can be seen as his passport to Viennese citizenship.

Beethoven needed musical collaborators to help create a revolutionary, "heroic" music. The Viennese Classical style had essentially been completed (or exhausted) with Mozart, Haydn, and the early Beethoven. It would require an infusion of fresh elements from a previously untapped source to transcend this style and to open up new avenues for exploration. Beethoven discovered some of these elements in contemporary French music.

The influence of French Revolutionary music on Beethoven was no secret to his contemporaries and early admirers. Beethoven's most brilliant critic, E. T. A. Hoffmann, pointed to Cherubini's presence in the Overture to *Coriolan;* another German music critic, Amadeus Wendt, likewise heard echoes of Cherubini in the *Leonore* Overture; and Robert Schumann recognized the influence of Méhul's Symphony in G minor on Beethoven's Fifth Symphony. That *Fidelio* was adapted from a French post-Revolutionary opera subject and that the opera was a German example of French "rescue opera" has long been known. But it took the researches of twentieth-century scholars—Hermann Kretzschmar, Ernst Bücken, Hugo Botstiber, Adolf Sandberger, Ludwig Schiedermair, Arnold Schmitz, Alfred Einstein, Boris Schwarz, and others—to establish and trace in some detail the breadth of these influences in the formation of Beethoven's post–1800 style. For example, Schmitz unearthed many examples of parallels between Beethoven's music and the works of Gossec, Grétry, Kreutzer, Berton, Méhul, Catel, and Cherubini and wrote an important study, "The Influence of Cherubini on Beethoven's Overtures."[19] He documented the use of French material in such works as Beethoven's First, Fifth, and Seventh Symphonies, the *Egmont* and *Leonore* overtures, the "Funeral March" Sonata, op. 26, and the Violin Sonata, op. 30, no. 2. Schwarz revealed the surprising origins of many of Beethoven's stylistic idiosyncrasies in the music of the French violin school, and he underlined the influence of Kreutzer, Rode, Baillot, and Viotti on the middle-period Violin Concerto in D, op. 61.[20]

The highly ordered yet flexible structure of sonata form readily expanded to embrace the driving, ethically exalted, "grand style" elements of French music, which had itself lacked that kind of formal concentration and intensive development.[21] In a number of his "public" compositions over the next decade, Beethoven would continue to explore the potentialities of this mixture of styles. Ironically, Beethoven's "heroic" style, which came into being as a collaboration between Vienna and France, expired in the years 1813–14 as a vehicle celebrating victory over Bonaparte and France.

Beethoven's conflicts with Napoleon did not end with the *Eroica* incident. In succeeding years he was regarded as a Francophobe because he was given to expressions of defiance against France and Napoleon. After Bonaparte's victory at Jena, Beethoven reputedly said to violinist

Wenzel Krumpholz, "It's a pity that I do not understand the art of war as well as I do the art of music. I would conquer him!"[22] Nevertheless, the astute Baron Louis-Philippe de Trémont, a member of Napoleon's council of state, became friendly with Beethoven in 1809 and noted the composer's preoccupation "with the greatness of Napoleon." Trémont observed that "through all his resentment I could see that he admired his [Bonaparte's] rise from such obscure beginnings; his democratic ideas were flattered by it. One day he remarked, 'If I go to Paris, shall I be obliged to salute your emperor?' I assured him that he would not, unless commanded for an audience. 'And do you think he would command me?'" This caused Trémont to conclude that Beethoven "would have felt flattered by any mark of distinction from Napoleon." That Beethoven welcomed a member of Napoleon's council at the very moment that Napoleon was bombarding Vienna was itself a curious matter, and Trémont reported that everyone "was astonished."[23]

At about the same time, Napoleon's brother Jérôme, whom he had installed as king of the newly created kingdom of Westphalia, offered Beethoven the post of kapellmeister at a substantial salary. Despite his anti-Bonapartist views, Beethoven was at one point on the verge of accepting the post. The entire affair remains clouded in ambiguities. Thayer wondered what "could have induced this half-educated, frivolous, prodigal and effeminate young satrap and sybarite to sanction an invitation" to Beethoven, and comments that it "is one of those small mysteries which seem impenetrable."[24] For his part, Beethoven used the offer as a lever to acquire an annuity from Archduke Rudolph and the Princes Lobkowitz and Ferdinand Kinsky, which guaranteed him lifelong financial support in return for his promise to make his domicile in Vienna a permanent one. The matter is surely more complex than this, however, and one of the factors involved may have been Beethoven's desire for just that "mark of distinction from Napoleon" which Baron de Trémont had remarked. Later, in 1813, Beethoven once again hoped for some "reward" from a Bonaparte—this time Louis, another brother of Napoleon, who had been appointed king of Holland. He is rather abashed and defensive about the matter when he writes to Joseph von Varena (an ardent promoter of Beethoven's music) in Graz, "I thought perhaps that the third person you mentioned was the former *king of Holland*, and—well, after all, from him, who has perhaps taken a good deal from the Dutch in a less legitimate way, I would not have scrupled to take something on account of my present situation."[25]

From May 13 to November 20, 1809, Vienna was occupied by the French. Napoleon's eagle perched on the masthead of the *Wiener Zeitung;* a cantata, *Sieg der Eintracht,* was written by Ignaz Castelli and Joseph Weigl to celebrate the marriage of Napoleon to the Habsburg princess Maria Louise; the best artists of Vienna were called to Schönbrunn to perform for Bonaparte. Beethoven was not called. On September 8, he conducted his *Eroica* Symphony at a charity concert at the Theater-an-der-Wien for the theatrical poor fund (*Theaterarmen*). Thayer asks, "Was this selected, in the expectation that Napoleon would be present, to do him homage? If so it failed of its aim. The day before, Napoleon journeyed from Schönbrunn. . . . Or was it in bitter sarcasm that Beethoven chose it?"[26] The latter possibility is unlikely, for Max Unger has turned up Beethoven's extraordinary note to himself of October 8, 1810: "The Mass [in C, op. 86] could perhaps be dedicated to Napoleon."[27] It is a pity that we have only the insufficient word "ambivalence" to describe such total reversals of emotional attitude— surely too tame a word for so turbulent a set of feelings. What is involved, actually, is not merely a series of reversals but an insoluble conflict that can be resolved, if at all, only through a change in the balance of forces. This was to come later, with Napoleon's defeat at Waterloo, his exile to St. Helena, and his death.

But even after those events it is doubtful that Beethoven ever came to terms with Bonaparte. On hearing of Napoleon's death on May 5, 1821, Beethoven remarked, rather enigmatically, "I have already composed the proper music for that catastrophe";[28] and in 1824 he said to Czerny, "Napoleon, I could not tolerate him earlier. Now I think quite differently."[29]

Perhaps it is in Beethoven's ambivalence itself that we have a clue to a deeper meaning of Bonaparte's connection with the *Eroica.* As we have seen, it is a curious fact that there is no evidence whatever that Beethoven had anything other than negative feelings toward Bonaparte prior to 1803. His reported brief association with the French ambassador Bernadotte in 1798 does not contradict this, for Bernadotte was himself on extremely bad terms with Bonaparte. (Schindler, who mistakenly believed that Bernadotte was still ambassador in 1804, thus was probably equally mistaken in claiming that Bernadotte suggested that Beethoven write a composition in honor of Bonaparte.)[30] The *Eroica* Symphony, therefore, may not, after all, have been conceived in a spirit of homage, which was then superseded by disillusionment. Rather, it is possible that Beethoven chose as his subject one toward whom he already felt an unconquerable ambivalence containing a strong component of hostility. The symphony, with its Funeral March movement, is centrally concerned with the death of the hero as well as with his birth and resurrection: "Composed," Beethoven eventually wrote on the title page, "to celebrate the memory of a great man." Striving to free himself from his lifelong pattern of submission to the domination of authority figures, Beethoven was drawn to the conqueror who had confounded the venerable leaders of Europe and set himself in their place. If homage is on the surface, the underlying themes are patricide and fratricide, mingled with the survivor's sense of triumph. As in the "Joseph" Cantata, piety toward the departed hero may mask feelings of an opposite kind.

According to one of his physicians, Joseph Bertolini, Beethoven's original plan had been to compose the Funeral March of the *Eroica* on a British topic, either the wounding of Lord Nelson at the Battle of the Nile in 1798 or the death of General Ralph Abercromby at Alexandria in 1801.[31] In view of Beethoven's steadfast admiration for the British (which dated back to his family's friendship with George Cressener, the British ambassador to Bonn), Nelson or Abercromby could not serve as appropriate subjects of the conflicting emotions that are condensed in the *Eroica*. And so Beethoven may have fixed upon one toward whom he had mixed feelings, one whom he had already rejected as an ideal prince/legislator. Thus, the choice of Bonaparte as his subject and the rending of the inscription may have been part of the same process: of establishing parity with and hegemony over the most powerful figure of the era. Beethoven disposed of Bonaparte twice—once in composing the symphony and again in removing his name from the title.

Georg Brandes described German romanticism's glorification of desire, of wish, as "impotence itself conceived as a power."[32] A sense of national impotence lay just behind the facade of Viennese life after the death of Joseph II, with whom were interred the thwarted hopes for

Enlightened absolutism. These feelings of futility were reinforced by the Habsburgs' abject submission to Napoleon following the succession of crushing military defeats between 1797 and 1809.

That Beethoven was capable of producing the ultimate musical definition of heroism in this context is itself extraordinary, for he was able to evoke a dream heroism that neither he nor his native Germany nor his adopted Vienna could express in reality. Perhaps we can only measure the heroism of the *Eroica* by the depths of fear and uncertainty from which it emerged.

There was a component of caution, an excess of discretion, even a failure of nerve, in Beethoven's removal of the Bonaparte inscription. This should not, however, lead us to reject other levels of motivation and meaning. As we have seen, Beethoven regarded Bonaparte as an embodiment of Enlightened leadership, but, simultaneously, he felt betrayed by Bonaparte's Caesarist deeds. Beethoven's ambivalence mirrored a central contradiction of his age, and it is this contradiction that finds expression in the *Eroica* Symphony. The *Eroica* arose from the conflict between Enlightened faith in the savior-prince and the reality of Bonapartism. Bonaparte—whose image replaced Christ's in myriads of European homes—had inherited the displaced messianism of his time; Beethoven, who rejected blind faith and hierarchical orthodoxy in his personal theology, now rejected its secular equivalents. As an artist and a man, Beethoven could no longer accept unmediated conceptions of progress, innate human goodness, reason, and faith. His affirmations were now leavened by an acknowledgment of the frailty of human leadership and a consciousness of the regressive and brutalizing components in all forward-thrusting stages in social evolution.

Beethoven, ever questioning, spurred by doubt, rejecting the passivity of superstition and the false confidence of ideological certainty, never abandoned his central faith in the values of the Enlightenment—altruistic love, reason, and humanistic ideals. The Enlightenment abjured superstition and dogma and supplanted theological pessimism about the possibilities of earthly salvation with a harmonious and optimistic view of mankind's freedom to develop its potentialities within a framework of natural law and political reconstruction. This is not to say that its philosophers were unaware of the problem of evil or that its views were predicated upon a banal rejection of skepticism. Nevertheless, as Ernst Cassirer observed, "This era is permeated by genuine creative feeling and an unquestionable faith in the reformation of the world"; and he quoted Voltaire's maxim "*Some day all will be well,* is our hope; *all is well today,* is illusion."[33] Beethoven rejected the latter illusion, and cleaved to the principle of hope.

Beethoven could not have "journeyed to Paris," which is to say, transferred his allegiance to France, without becoming a musical conformist working in conventional formulas, as Gossec, Méhul, and Spontini had done. French Revolutionary music (and painting) largely ignored both the Revolution and the Terror, stressing instead nobility of motivation and action and substituting heroic portraiture and triumphal rhetoric for conflict and tragedy. Idealism and simple faith alone, however, are insufficient grounds for greatness. Conflict is absent from such ideological formulations, and the artworks that result accordingly require no formal containment, but merely craftsmanlike expression. For it is the conflict between faith and skepticism, the struggle between belief and disbelief—which Goethe described as the most important theme of world history[34]—that creates those dynamic tensions that tend to expand and threaten to burst the bonds of form. The *Eroica* Symphony is Beethoven's elaboration of that theme in the closing hours of the Enlightenment.

Fidelio, Act II, scene 3 ("Er sterbe").

From Wiener Hoftheater Almanach *(1815).*

CHAPTER FOURTEEN

THE HEROIC DECADE (II)

TOWARD THE END OF 1804, BEETHOVEN RESUMED his lodgings at the Theater-an-der-Wien. He sketched the balance of *Leonore* (retitled *Fidelio* by the theater management) by June 1805 and completed it at Hetzendorf, a village near Vienna, where he spent the summer. It was ready for rehearsal early in the fall, but difficulties with the censor led to a postponement. In the interim, Napoleon's armies occupied Vienna, so that *Fidelio* received its premiere under extremely inauspicious conditions, on November 20.[1] According to the tenor Joseph August Röckel, "Only a few friends of Beethoven had ventured to hear the opera,"[2] and the presence of French officers in the audience was an inhibiting factor. After performances on the twenty-first and twenty-second, *Fidelio* was withdrawn. A visiting Englishman left a record of the November 21 performance in his journal:

> Went to the Wieden Theatre [the name of Schikaneder's former theater] to the new opera *Fidelio*, the music composed by Beethoven. The story and plan of the piece are a miserable mixture of low manner and romantic situations; the airs, duets, and choruses equal to any praise. . . . Intricacy is the character of Beethoven's music, and it requires a well-practised ear, or a frequent repetition of the same piece, to understand and distinguish its beauties. This is the first opera he ever composed, and it was much applauded; a copy of complimentary verses [by Stephan von Breuning] was showered down from the upper gallery at the end of the piece. Beethoven presided at the pianoforte and directed the performance himself. He is a small dark young-looking man [who] wears spectacles. . . . Few people present, though the house would have been crowded in every part but for the present state of public affairs.[3]

The critics did not respond favorably to the opera, and Beethoven's friends, led by the Lichnowskys, urged drastic revisions—especially in the long, undramatic first act—preparatory to a revival. Beethoven and Breuning now took up the libretto and, as Breuning recalled, "remodeled the whole book . . . quickening and enlivening the action."[4] (Beethoven later claimed the entire credit for the libretto's revision.) Acts 1 and 2 were combined; several numbers were omitted and others abridged. Winton Dean writes, "While the effect of these alterations must have been beneficial in speeding up the action, they did not go to the root of the problem, the undue prominence of Marzelline, and some of them were ill-judged."[5] The new version was performed on March 29, 1806, and repeated on April 10. According to Röckel, who now sang the role of Florestan, it was well received "by a select public."[6] It did not find favor, however, with such eminences as Cherubini and Salieri, and we may assume that Beethoven himself was not pleased, for he undiplomatically accused the theater management of cheating him on the receipts and, following a quarrel with the theater director, Baron Peter von Braun, peremptorily withdrew the opera from production. A private performance may have been given at the Lobkowitz Palace toward midyear. Lichnowsky sent the score to the queen of Prussia for a proposed Berlin production, and there was talk of a Prague production to be mounted in 1807. But these did not materialize and the opera was set aside until 1814. It was only then that Beethoven finally completed it to the public's satisfaction, if not to his own, for even after the last revision he wrote to his new librettist, Georg Friedrich Treitschke: "Let me add that this whole *opera* business is the most tiresome affair in the world, for I am dissatisfied with most of it, and there is hardly a number in it which *my present dissatisfaction would not have to patch up here and there with some satisfaction.*"[7]

The explosive inauguration of Beethoven's post-Heiligenstadt style gave rise to a multitude of ideas for compositions. Sketches of ideas for the Fifth and Sixth Symphonies appear in the *Eroica* sketchbook of 1803–4, and several string quartets were apparently germinating as early as the fall of 1804.[8] The termination in March 1806 of Beethoven's long operatic labors seems to have unleashed a flood of important instrumental compositions, which were now written out simultaneously or in rapid succession during the remainder of 1806. As though to make up for lost time, Beethoven rapidly completed the Piano Concerto in G, op. 58; the Symphony No. 4 in B-flat, op. 60; Thirty-two Variations for Piano in C minor, WoO 80; the Violin Concerto in D, op. 61; and the Three String Quartets in F, E minor, and C ("Razumovsky"), op. 59 . (In this year, too, he put the finishing touches on his "Appassionata" Sonata in F minor, op. 57, which had been started in 1804.) On the autograph of opus 59, no. 1, he wrote, "begun on the 26th of May—1806."[9] On May 25, Beethoven's brother Caspar Carl married Johanna Reiss, who was then three months pregnant, and at least one commentator believes that this accounts for the strange inscription on a leaf of the sketches for the very emotional Adagio of this quartet, "A weeping willow or acacia tree on my brother's grave."[10]

The quartets were dedicated to Count Razumovsky—Lichnowsky's brother-in-law, the czar's envoy to Vienna, and an acquaintance of both Mozart's and Haydn's—who in 1808 took over the patronage of Schuppanzigh's quartet after Prince Lichnowsky became financially pinched. Razumovsky now emerged as one of Beethoven's leading patrons, sharing with Prince Lobkowitz the dedications of the Fifth and Sixth Symphonies. According to Seyfried, "Beethoven was as much at home in the Razumovsky establishment as a hen in her coop. Everything he wrote was taken warm from the nest and tried out in the frying pan."[11] In contrast to his pattern of familiar intimacy with Lichnowsky and Lobkowitz, however, Beethoven maintained a rather formal reserve vis-à-vis the Russian music lover and art collector, whom French musicologist Jacques-Gabriel Prod'homme succinctly described as "enemy of the Revolution, but good friend of the fair sex."[12] (It may have been of some importance to Beethoven that Razumovsky was intimate with such powerful political officials as Prince Metternich and Friedrich von Gentz.) Apparently at Razumovsky's request, Beethoven included a *thème russe* in at least two of the quartets. Extramusical factors may have been operative in those inclusions, for there had been great battles between the French and the Russians at Austerlitz in the last months of 1805, and thousands of Russian prisoners ("poor, miserable, ragged, wretched objects," a contemporary wrote[13]) filled Vienna's hospitals, convents, and schools.

The composer's patronage relationships had continued their rapid evolution. Ties based on his pianistic virtuosity alone had largely disappeared, and he had achieved an unusual degree of independence as a freelance composer. New forms of patronage—the public theater, members of the financial nobility, and a consortium of connoisseurs— had emerged. Beethoven had been catapulted into the unaccustomed and, for him, burdensome role of business entrepreneur: seeking and sifting offers, negotiating fees and contracts, shipping merchandise, and collecting overdue accounts.

Although other aristocrats, especially Prince Lobkowitz, Count Razumovsky, Count Franz von Oppersdorff, and young Archduke Rudolph, were playing important roles in Beethoven's career, Prince Lichnowsky, who surely regarded his stewardship as indispensable to Beethoven's welfare, was not ready to yield his prerogatives. In 1805 he had meddled in Beethoven's love affair with the widowed Josephine Deym, and he and his wife pressed him to make changes in *Fidelio* that were not necessarily beneficial. Beethoven now tried to loosen the tie: Röckel was present on one occasion in 1805 when the prince and princess were refused admission to the composer's lodgings, and it was only after much urging—and with a gloomy countenance—that Beethoven agreed to accompany them on a drive in the country.

The matter came to a head in late October or early November 1806, when Beethoven refused Prince Lichnowsky's request that he perform for a group of French officers at his Silesian country estate. Seyfried reported that Beethoven "grew angry and refused to do what he denounced as menial labor," and there ensued a violent confrontation. Count Oppersdorff may have made his greatest contribution to Beethoven's welfare on that occasion, for, according to Ries, he threw himself between the two combatants just at the moment when Beethoven "picked up a chair and was about to break it over the head of Prince Lichnowsky, who had had the door forced of the room in which Beethoven had bolted himself."[14] Beethoven angrily left the estate, returned to Vienna, and dashed the bust of his patron to the floor.[15] The personal rupture was soon healed; within a year, indeed, Beethoven actually considered dedicating the opus 59 String Quartets to Lichnowsky, but the relationship had now been restructured.[16] In later years, Lichnowsky would visit Beethoven in his study, quietly sit watching his protégé at work, and then depart with a brief "Adieu." On occasion Beethoven would lock him out, and the prince, uncomplaining, would descend the three flights of stairs to the street.

Beethoven undoubtedly continued to receive his annuity from Lichnowsky until 1806 or 1807; his income was augmented by the sale of his works not only to a wide variety of publishers but also, in the case of major new works, to noble patrons for a fixed sum, in return for dedications and, sometimes, exclusive performance rights for a fixed period. Thus, he was making an extremely good living up to this time. He had long since ceased giving piano lessons to young ladies of the aristocracy; now he was able to give up teaching almost entirely.[17] Gone was the pressing need to write potboilers, such as the many frankly ephemeral works—contredanses, *Ländler,* and minuets for orchestra; pieces for mandolin or for mechanical instruments—that he had produced in his first Vienna decade. However, his violent break with Lichnowsky, which followed hard upon his rupture with the Theater-an-der-Wien, surely also coincided with the prince's withdrawal from his role as Beethoven's chief patron and financial mainstay. The state of Beethoven's finances therefore had become a matter of great concern. Perhaps this accounts in part for Stephan von Breuning's remark to a Bonn friend in the fall that "Beethoven's frame of mind is generally of a melancholy turn."[18] In the spring of 1807 Beethoven concluded an advantageous contract with Clementi & Co. for the British publication of a number of his works, but the guaranteed payment of 200 pounds was delayed for three years. In the fall of 1807, Beethoven addressed a formal petition to the Imperial Royal Court Theater—now headed by a directorate of noblemen that included Princes Lobkowitz, Joseph Johann Schwarzenberg, and Nikolaus Esterházy—in which he applied for an employment contract at a fixed annual income of 2,400 florins, in return for which he would undertake to compose one opera per year, plus other works. To emphasize the seriousness of his situation, he strongly implied that he would be compelled to leave Vienna in the absence of a favorable response:

> Admittedly the undersigned may flatter himself that so far during the period of his stay in Vienna he has won a certain amount of favor and appreciation not only from the distinguished aristocracy but also from the rest of the public, and that his works have been given an honorable reception both at home and abroad.
>
> Nevertheless, he has had to contend with all kinds of difficulties, and as yet he has not been fortunate enough to establish himself here

in a position compatible with his desire to live entirely for art, to develop his talents to an even higher degree of perfection, which must be the aim of every true artist, and to secure for an independent future the advantages which hitherto have been merely incidental.

Since on the whole the aim which he has ever pursued in his career has been much less to earn his daily bread than to raise the taste of the public and to let his genius *soar* to greater heights and even to perfection, the inevitable result has been that the undersigned has sacrificed to the Muse both material profit and his own advantage. Nevertheless, works of this kind have won him in distant countries a reputation which in several important centers guarantees to him the most favorable reception and a future suited to his talents and his knowledge.

Yet the undersigned must confess that the many years he has spent in Vienna, the favor and appreciation of high and low which he has enjoyed, his desire to see completely fulfilled the expectations which hitherto he has been so fortunate as to awaken, and, he ventures to add, the patriotism of a German make his present place of residence more to be valued and desired than any other.[19]

The written reply to this petition has not survived. Clearly, however, Beethoven's application was not accepted. The minutes of the Imperial Royal Court Theater for December 4, 1804, read, succinctly, "Beethoven is not to be engaged."[20] In May he wrote to Franz von Brunsvik, "I shall never come to an arrangement with this princely rabble connected with the theaters."[21] Moreover, his urgent request to use the theater for an academy in 1807 was denied, which increased his malaise. This was counterbalanced by the great academy of December 22, 1808, at the Theater-an-der-Wien, which saw the first performances of a group of masterpieces that had been completed during 1807 and 1808: the Symphony No. 5 in C minor, op. 67, the Symphony No. 6 in F (*Pastoral*), op. 68, excerpts from the C-major Mass, op. 86, the "Choral Fantasia," op. 80 (which had been rapidly composed as a finale for the concert), and, for good measure, the Piano Concerto in G, op. 58. Even that event was not an unalloyed triumph, for by its very magnitude it seems to have taxed the patience of the most knowledgeable music lovers, like Johann Friedrich Reichardt, who complained of the length, the performance, and the weather. "There we sat from 6:30 till

10:30 in the most bitter cold," he wrote, "and found by experience that one might easily have too much even of a good thing," adding that he wished he had had the courage to leave but was prevented by being placed in a prominent box seated next to Prince Lobkowitz.[22]

It was an immensely prolific time for Beethoven: in addition to the works on this mammoth program, he had in 1807 composed the *Coriolan* Overture and in 1808 completed such masterworks of chamber music as the two Piano Trios in D ("Ghost") and E-flat, op. 70, and the Cello Sonata in A, op. 69. Beethoven's productivity was clearly at flood tide, and his popularity in concerts public and private was similarly reaching its crest. Nevertheless, he often insisted during 1808 that he would soon quit Vienna. "They are forcing me to it," he told the organist Wilhelm Rust.[23] In the summer he wrote to Gottfried Härtel: "For the last two years I have suffered a great many misfortunes, and, what is more, here in V[ienna]."[24] And to the poet Heinrich Collin he wrote, "The thought that I shall certainly have to leave Vienna and become a wanderer haunts me persistently."[25]

The issue was joined in October, when King Jérôme Bonaparte invited Beethoven to come to Kassel in Westphalia as his kapellmeister at an annual salary of 600 ducats (equivalent to almost 3,000 florins). As noted earlier, Beethoven used this offer to conclude an annuity agreement—negotiated on his behalf by Baron von Gleichenstein and his close friend and patron Countess Marie Erdödy—with three young members of the high nobility, Princes Lobkowitz and Kinsky and Archduke Rudolph. Under its terms he pledged himself to "make his domicile in Vienna" or "one of the other hereditary countries of His Austrian Imperial Majesty," in return for which they bound themselves to pay to him the sum of 4,000 florins annually "until Herr van Beethoven receives an appointment which shall yield him the equivalent of the above sum"—or, in the absence of such an appointment, for life. The noblemen wrote:

> As it has been demonstrated that only one who is as free from care as possible can devote himself to a single department of activity and create works of magnitude which are great, sublime, and which ennoble art, the undersigned have decided to place Herr Ludwig van Beethoven in a position where obtaining the necessaries of life shall not cause him embarrassment or hinder his powerful genius.[26]

The annuity agreement was dated March 1, 1809. With it
Beethoven had attained the highest degree of independence and security possible within a semifeudal mode of patronage. Between him and
his patrons there was no longer a relationship of personal dependency,
let alone the slightest hint of subservience. Indeed, the contract did not
even require that Beethoven compose a given number of works or that
he render services of any kind as a musician. (His work as Archduke
Rudolph's teacher was unrelated to the annuity.) Beethoven hoped,
vainly, that an appropriate title would follow—"the title of an Imperial
Kapellmeister would make [me] very happy," he wrote—but the failure
for such a title to materialize was a comparatively small disappointment.[27] (Later, Beethoven's expectation of lifelong security was temporarily shattered, first by the March 15, 1811, devaluation of the
Austrian currency, which raised the possibility that the real value of the
annuity would be reduced by 60 percent, and still later by the bankruptcy of Lobkowitz and the death of Kinsky. These events led to a tangle of
threatened legal actions that were not resolved until early 1815, but then
matters turned out almost wholly in Beethoven's favor.) A tone of elation
entered Beethoven's correspondence in 1809, and his thoughts turned to
the possibilities of travel and marriage. In March he wrote to
Gleichenstein, enclosing a copy of the annuity agreement:

> You will see from the enclosed document, my dear, kind
> Gleichenstein, how honorable my remaining here has now become
> for me. Moreover, the title of Imperial *Kapellmeister* is to follow, and
> so forth. Now let me know as soon as possible whether you think that
> in the present warlike conditions I ought to travel. . . . Now you can
> help me to look for a wife. Indeed you might find some beautiful girl
> at F[reiburg] where you are at present, and one who would perhaps
> now and then grant a sigh to my harmonies.[28]

Neither hope was to be fulfilled, however. The siege and renewed
occupation of Vienna by Napoleon's armies intervened, beginning in
May 1809. Those who could—including the entire nobility, their
entourages, and many public officials—fled the capital. Of the composer's close friends, it is said that only Breuning remained in Vienna.
Beethoven himself took refuge in the house where his brother Caspar

Carl and his wife, Johanna, lived with their two-year-old son, Karl. He described his disquieted state of mind in a letter of July 26 to Härtel in Leipzig:

> You are indeed mistaken in supposing that I have been very well. For in the meantime we have been suffering misery in a most concentrated form. Let me tell you that since May 4th I have produced very little coherent work, at most a fragment here and there. The whole course of events has in my case affected both body and soul. . . . The existence I had built up only a short time ago rests on shaky foundations. . . . What a destructive, disorderly life I see and hear around me: nothing but drums, cannons, and human misery in every form.[29]

The deaths of his physician, Johann Schmidt, on February 19 and of Haydn on May 31 surely deepened Beethoven's gloom.

In September Beethoven conducted the *Eroica* Symphony at a charity concert. Vienna gradually returned to relative normalcy, and on October 14 Austria concluded a peace treaty with France. Writing once again to his Leipzig publisher, on November 22, Beethoven noted:

> We are enjoying a little peace after violent destruction, after suffering every hardship that one could conceivably endure. I worked for a few weeks in succession, but it seemed to me more *for death* than for *immortality*. . . .
>
> What do you say to this *dead peace?* I no longer expect to see any stability in this age. The only *certainty* we can rely on is *blind chance*.[30]

Despite his somber mood, and an indisposition to work seriously that lasted several months, Beethoven was able to compose a cluster of major works during the invasion year, including the Piano Concerto in E-flat ("Emperor"), op. 73, the String Quartet in E-flat ("Harp"), op. 74, and three Piano Sonatas, in F-sharp, G, and E-flat, opp. 78, 79, and 81a, plus several lieder and some lesser works. His productivity fell off somewhat in 1810, a year whose main completed works were the Incidental Music to Goethe's *Egmont*, op. 84, and the String Quartet in F minor, op. 95. One senses not that Beethoven was slowing down, but that he no longer felt driven to compose at so prodigious a pace.

AFTER JOHANN ADAM SCHMIDT DIED IN 1808, Beethoven was treated by Dr. Johann Baptist Malfatti, a renowned physician in Vienna. In 1810 Beethoven proposed marriage to Malfatti's niece Therese, who was then nineteen; it was his first such known offer since that made to Magdalena Willmann in the mid-1790s, and it, too, was rejected. Despite the proposal, however, Therese Malfatti was not the most significant of Beethoven's romantic attachments during this decade.

To retrace our steps a bit: at the beginning of the decade, Beethoven's friendly contacts with women were largely confined to the Brunsvik and Guicciardi families. Contrary to legend, there was no romantic involvement with Therese Brunsvik. Instead, by the fall of 1801, Beethoven settled his affections upon Countess Giulietta Guicciardi. From Giulietta's correspondence and from a drawing that she made picturing Beethoven as a lovestruck Romeo who gazed up at her balcony while she peeked out from behind a curtain, it is evident that she delighted in her control over him, knowing that she could coax him through scolding and flirtation into becoming her gallant servant. "I have spoken to Beethoven about his variations for four hands," she wrote to her cousin Therese Brunsvik. "I scolded him over them; and then he promised me everything."[31]

At the same time that she was flirting with Beethoven, Guicciardi was involved on a more serious level with a young composer, Count Wenzel Robert Gallenberg, with whom she had been intimate since soon after her family's arrival in Vienna in 1800 from Trieste; they married in November 1803. Beethoven was well aware of her affair with Gallenberg. In a Conversation Book entry of 1823, he revealed to Schindler the triangular nature of the relationship. "She loved me very much, far more than ever she did her husband. He, however, rather than I was her lover, but I learned of his poverty from her, and I found a rich man who gave me the sum of 500 florins to relieve him. He was always my enemy; it is for that reason that I was as good to him as possible."[32]

This is, in sharply delineated form, an example of the standard pattern of Beethoven's love affairs: his attraction to a woman who is firmly attached to another man, evidently so that he may participate vicariously in their relationship. Beethoven's unacknowledged libidinal ties with Gallenberg (his "enemy," whom he nevertheless lavishly assisted), which were implicit in this triangle, may have placed great strains on his perception of his own sexuality. And Giulietta's rejection of him in favor of Gallenberg may well have revived more archaic issues—thwarted desires for his mother's love, attitudes toward his father compounded of submissiveness and rancor, resentment of more "favored" siblings—which intensified Beethoven's anxieties during this critical period.

The pursuit of unattainable women, however, had great advantages to one for whom bachelorhood was apparently a necessary (though painful) condition of artistic achievement. (As Brahms quipped of his own bachelorhood, "Unfortunately I never married and am, thank God! still single.")[33] For Beethoven seems to have regarded love relationships as impediments to his creative mission. He wrote to Wegeler in 1801, "I certainly could not marry. . . . For to me there is no greater pleasure than to practice and exercise my art."[34] In his conversation with Schindler about Giulietta Guicciardi, he wrote that she "sought me out, crying, but I scorned her." To this, Schindler tritely but accurately observed, "*Hercules* at the crossroads!" whereupon Beethoven closed the conversation with the pungent observation: "And if I had wanted to sacrifice my vital powers and my life in such a way, what would have remained for the nobler, the better?"[35]

It was not long before Giulietta's place was taken by her cousin Josephine von Brunsvik, the second of the three Brunsvik sisters. In 1799, she had been compelled by her mother, Countess Anna von Brunsvik, to marry Count Joseph Deym, who was thirty years her senior. Deym died in January 1804, and Josephine gave birth to their fourth child a few weeks thereafter. Later in the year she suffered an emotional collapse, causing her younger sister, Charlotte, to write to Therese of Josephine's "dreadful nervous breakdown; sometimes she laughed, sometimes wept, after which came utter fatigue and exhaustion."[36] The first evidence of Beethoven's love for Josephine surfaces shortly after this, in late 1804. On December 19 Charlotte wrote to Therese, "Beethoven comes very often, he gives lessons to Pepi [Josephine]—that's just a little dangerous, I confess to you." Therese in turn warned Charlotte on January 20, 1805, "But tell me, Pepi and Beethoven, that's something. May she be on her guard. . . . Her heart must have the strength to say no!"[37]

Therese's diaries and memoirs are rich in details of her sister's love interests and conflicted family life after the death of Count Deym—her courtships by Beethoven, then by Count Anton Maria von Wolkenstein-Trostburg from early 1806 until his death in 1808, and thereafter by Baron Christoph von Stackelberg, whom she eventually married in February 1810, inaugurating a period in which, in Rolland's words, she was "overwhelmed with domestic and financial anxieties."[38] A police report on Josephine dated July 12, 1815, reads, "The morality of the Countess does not appear to enjoy a good reputation, and it is stated that she cannot be absolved from having given ground for conjugal quarrels."[39] But even apart from the notorious unreliability of police dossiers, this refers to later times. She claimed to have taken vows of chastity after her husband's death, and she did not give herself to Beethoven. That Beethoven pressed her rather urgently, though unavailingly, on this issue is clear from the following draft of an undated letter to him:

> This favor which you have accorded me, the pleasure of your company, would have been the finest ornament of my life if you had been able to love me less sensuously. That I cannot satisfy this sensuous love, does this cause you anger? I would have to break holy vows were I to listen to your desire. Believe me—it is I, through the fulfillment of my duty, who suffer the most—and my actions have been surely dictated by noble motives.[40]

It seems that Josephine did not fully reciprocate Beethoven's love, preferring "the pleasure of [his] company" to a fulfilled relationship. Her letters speak of her "affection," her "deep interest," her "enthusiasm" for Beethoven, but rarely of her love, and never of that in an unqualified way. But if Beethoven's desire for Josephine was of a passionate nature at the beginning, he nevertheless readily withdrew in the face of her resistance. He advised her that he was content with the relationship. "Oh, beloved J[osephine], it is no desire for the other sex that draws me to you, no *it is just you, your whole self* with all your individual qualities—this has compelled my regard."[41] He acquiesced in a spiritual relationship in which he was able to pour out his heart to her, seeking solace and comfort. "As soon as we are together again with no one to disturb us, you shall hear all about my real sorrows and the struggle with myself between death and life, a struggle in which I was engaged for some time."[42] The goals of physical gratification and marriage were set aside. "You have conquered me," he wrote, and he accepted the relationship on her terms, best expressed in her draft letter: "I love you inexpressibly—as one devout mind loves another."[43]

Soon, however, Beethoven began to torment Josephine with suspicions that she was carrying on a secret affair. "*Do not doubt me,*" she wrote; "I cannot express how deeply wounding it is to be equated with low creatures, even if only in thought and slight suspicion. . . . This suspicion which you impart to me so frequently, that is it which pains me beyond all expression."[44] Josephine was no stranger to such behavior; according to Therese, Deym had "watched her every turn with the greatest jealousy."[45] Hence she was once again subjected to morbid suspicion, at a time when she was recovering from an emotional breakdown.

By the summer of 1805, Beethoven's letters took on an aloof, and somewhat false, character. He asked for the return of music he had given or lent to her, and when "An die Hoffnung," op. 32, which he composed for her, was published in September, her name had been removed from the dedication. In the fall, Josephine left Vienna with her children, returning sometime in 1806. By the winter of 1805–6, Josephine had turned away from Beethoven to Count Wolkenstein.[46] She moved to Budapest in the latter part of 1806.

Some months after her return to Vienna in mid-1807 Beethoven attempted to renew their friendship, but was refused admittance to her house by her servants ("I was not so fortunate as to see you—That hurt me deeply").[47] Finally, he acknowledged that it would be wiser if they were no longer to meet: "How sorry I am not to be able to see you. But it is better for your peace of mind and mine not to see you."[48] As Forbes notes, Beethoven's extremely reserved final letter ("I thank you for wishing still to appear as if I were not altogether banished from your memory"[49]) provides "a wistful close to the affair."[50]

This was not the only feminine rebuff that Beethoven received at this time. Early in the same year, he invited the pianist Marie Bigot (the wife of Count Razumovsky's librarian) and her infant daughter for a drive, in her husband's absence. This invitation, which probably merely expressed Beethoven's yearning to join the Bigots' family circle, was misread by them as an attempted seduction of Madame Bigot, or at least a breach of propriety. It led to a painful rejection, which called forth two heartfelt and heavily underlined letters of apology and explanation. In the first of these, addressed jointly to the couple, he wrote:

> It is one of my chief principles *never to stand in any other relationship than that of friendship with the wife of another man. For I should not wish by forming any other kind of relationship to fill my heart with distrust of that woman who some day will perhaps share my fate.* . . . Possibly once or twice I did indulge with Bigot in some jokes which were not quite refined. But I myself told you that sometimes I am very naughty. . . .
>
> If I said that *something dreadful* would result from my going to see you, that was certainly meant rather as a *jest,* the purpose of which was to show you that everything connected with you attracts me more and more, so that my dearest wish is to be able to live with you both for ever. That too is the truth. . . . For *never, never* will you find me dishonorable. Since my childhood I have learnt to love virtue—and everything beautiful and good.[51]

Whether or not Marie Bigot should be tentatively listed as the successor to Josephine Deym in the chronology of Beethoven's love interests, it is clear that any love he may have had for her was not reciprocated.[52] Beethoven's association with the Bigots soon came to an end. They resided in Paris after 1809.

These rejections may have caused Beethoven to avoid any further romantic involvement with women for a while. His attachment to Julie von Vering, the daughter of the physician Gerhard von Vering, was primarily an attempt somehow to take part in the love between Julie and his dear friend Stephan von Breuning. "Often," wrote Stephan's son Gerhard, repeating a family tradition, "Beethoven improvised for the young couple until deep into the night."[53] Julie and Stephan were married in April 1808. She died, at the age of nineteen, on March 21, 1809. In later years, Beethoven—whether truthfully or as fantasy we will never know—told the Giannattasio del Rio family "about one of his friends, who loved the same girl as he did, but the girl preferred Beethoven. . . . Beethoven left the field to his friend and retired. The girl did not live very long. I believe she died soon after marrying Beethoven's friend."[54]

In the fall of 1808, Beethoven took lodgings with his friend Countess Marie Erdödy at 1074 Krugerstrasse. (The Lichnowskys lived upstairs in the same building.) It is doubtful that there was any romantic element in his relationship with the countess, whom he called his "father confessor" (*Beichtvater*) and who was his adviser in personal and business affairs. He dedicated to her the Two Piano Trios in D and E-flat, op. 70, in 1809, and the Cello Sonatas in C and D, op. 102, in 1817. Despite their devotion to one another, his experiment as Countess Erdödy's lodger ended in failure. Early in 1809, the composer learned that the countess secretly had been paying not inconsiderable sums of money to his manservant. As I reconstruct the matter, Beethoven apparently believed that the countess, or Joseph X. Brauchle—her close companion, chamberlain, and tutor to her children—was paying his servant for sexual favors. On leaves of sketches for the Fifth Piano Concerto, then in progress, he wrote: "What more can you want? You have received *the servant* from me instead of *the master*. . . . What a substitution! ! ! ! What a glorious exchange! ! ! !" "Beethoven is no servant. . . . You wanted a servant, now you have one."[55] In a rage, Beethoven moved out and took rooms at 1087 Walfischgasse, which he knew housed a brothel. It seems that he had taken the countess's action as an affront, not only to his prerogatives as an employer, but to his sexuality. The breach with the countess was healed for a time by her assurance that she had given the money only "in order that he shall stay with me." "I am now *compelled* to believe in this generosity," he wrote, not quite persuaded, to Zmeskall.[56] But the relationship had been undermined and there ensued a period of estrangement until 1810. A temporary reconciliation in that year was soon followed by a further breach, which lasted until early 1815.[57]

Beethoven's courtship of Therese Malfatti was a hopeless one—opposed by her parents, conducted through an unwilling intermediary (Baron von Gleichenstein, who successfully courted her sister Anna), and without the slightest encouragement from the intended bride. In his only surviving letter to her, the rather embarrassed Beethoven wished to close the unsuccessful affair on a friendly note:

It so happens that I have an acquaintance who lives near you. So perhaps you will see me at your home early one morning for half an hour; and then I'll be off again. You see, that I want to bore you for as

short a time as possible—. Commend me to the goodwill of your
father and your mother, although as yet I can rightly make no claim
to it—My remembrances also to your Cousin M.—Well, farewell,
esteemed T[herese], I would like you to have everything that is good
and beautiful in life. Remember me and do so with pleasure—Forget
my mad behavior.[58]

The courtship had probably run its course by the spring of 1810. (Later,
in August, Stephan von Breuning wrote to Wegeler: "I believe his marriage project has fallen through.")[59]

As always when wounded, Beethoven retreated to a defensive and
self-sufficient posture. Resigned to Therese Malfatti's rejection, he
wrote to Gleichenstein:

> I can therefore seek support only in my own heart; there is none for
> me outside of it. No, nothing but wounds have come to me from
> friendship and such kindred feelings—So be it then: for you, poor
> B[eethoven], there is no happiness in the outer world, you must create
> it in yourself. Only in the ideal world can you find friends.[60]

From early 1810 until his love affair with the Immortal Beloved, which
culminated in July 1812, Beethoven's only known amorous pursuits
were a flirtation with Bettina Brentano for a few weeks in the spring of
1810 and, perhaps, several days of affectionate teasing with the singer
Amalie Sebald at Teplitz, now Teplice-Sanoy, a spa about fifty miles
northwest of Prague, in the summer of 1811.

We cannot measure the suffering that the series of rejections caused
Beethoven. According to the mid-nineteenth-century French music
critic Paul Scudo, who did not disclose the source of his information,
Beethoven tried to take his own life in despair over his failure to win
Countess Guicciardi's heart:

> Then, like a wounded lion who carried a poisoned arrow in his flanks,
> he absented himself from Vienna, and went to Hungary seeking
> refuge with his old friend, Countess Erdödy, but, unable to overcome
> his restlessness, he suddenly disappeared from the castle, and for three
> days wandered about alone on the estate, a prey to his grief, which

nothing could appease. He was found lying alongside the banks of a ditch by the wife of Countess Erdödy's piano teacher, who led him back to the castle. Beethoven confessed to that woman that he wanted to let himself die of starvation.[61]

Schindler included the story in the 1860 edition of his biography of Beethoven, and indeed now claimed to have related the incident to Scudo, but he, too, was vague about his own source, nor did he explain why he had neglected to mention these melodramatic events in the earlier editions of his book.

> In his despair he sought comfort with his approved and particularly respected friend Countess Marie Erdödy—at her country seat in Jedlersee, in order to spend a few days in her company. Thence, however, he disappeared and the Countess thought he had returned to Vienna, when, three days later, her music master, Brauchle, discovered him in a distant part of the palace gardens. This incident was long kept a close secret, and only after several years did those familiar with it confide it to the more intimate friends of Beethoven, long after the love affair had been forgotten. It was associated with a suspicion that it had been the purpose of the unhappy man to starve himself to death.[62]

Thayer did not credit Schindler's story and showed that its connection to Countess Guicciardi was particularly implausible. "Indeed the whole story . . . ," he wrote impatiently, "is told on such mere hearsay evidence as would not justify the police in arresting a beggar."[63] A modern biographer would be prudent to suspend judgment altogether, and to offer the account only for whatever it may be worth, bearing in mind that one of Beethoven's colleagues, the tenor Joseph August Röckel, when interviewed by Ludwig Nohl in 1867, claimed that he knew of such a suicide attempt.[64]

In May 1810, perhaps in connection with his marriage plans, Beethoven wrote to Wegeler, who lived in Coblenz, for the first time since 1801, asking that he furnish a copy of Beethoven's baptismal certificate (see Chapter 1) from neighboring Bonn. Perhaps it was the revival of his birth-year mystery and the thoughts of his older brother,

Ludwig Maria, that led Beethoven to speak once more of his hearing affliction—and of suicide:

> For about two years I have had to give up my rather quiet and peaceful way of life and have been forced to move in society. So far I have noticed no *beneficial* result; on the contrary, perhaps a rather unfavorable one—But who can escape the onslaughts of tempests raging around him? Yet I should be happy, perhaps one of the happiest of mortals, if that demon had not settled in my ears—If I had not read somewhere that a man should not voluntarily quit this life so long as he can still perform a good deed, I would have left this earth long ago—and, what is more, by my own hand. Oh, this life is indeed beautiful, but for me it is poisoned for ever.[65]

Around this same time, Beethoven wrote a letter to his dear friend Zmeskall that has a pathetic and despairing quality:

> DEAR Z,
> Don't be vexed with me for sending you this little sheet of paper—Are you not aware of the kind of situation in which I am placed, just as Hercules was formerly with Queen Omphale??? I asked you to buy me a looking glass like yours. When you no longer require yours, which I am sending you with this note, please return it to me today, for mine is smashed. All good wishes, and don't describe me any more as "the great man"—for never have I felt so deeply as I do now the strength or the weakness of human nature. Be fond of me—[66]

The "great man" had once again been blocked from entering the fearful world of marriage and fatherhood. Yet, as we saw earlier, it may have been the very nature of Beethoven's creative impulse that barred his way. Indeed, it may well have been necessary that all competing outlets—his virtuosity, his hearing, politics, love, and marriage—be sacrificed to his composer's vocation. In Schopenhauer's words, "If Petrarch's passion had been gratified, his song would have fallen silent."

From Schiller's essay of 1791, "Die Sendung Moses" ("The Mission of Moses"), Beethoven copied out three ancient Egyptian inscriptions

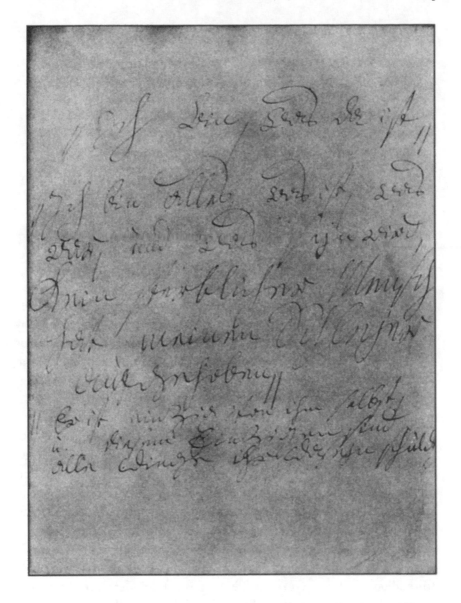

Egyptian inscriptions

Wegeler Collection, Beethoven-Haus, Bonn.

"and kept them framed and mounted under glass, on his work table."
The first two of these read:

> I AM THAT WHICH IS.

> I AM EVERYTHING THAT IS, THAT WAS,
> AND THAT WILL BE.
> NO MORTAL MAN HAS LIFTED MY VEIL.

And the third:

> HE IS OF HIMSELF ALONE, AND IT IS TO
> THIS ALONENESS
> THAT ALL THINGS OWE THEIR BEING.[67]

Precisely what these inscriptions meant to him we cannot know. They
seem to have both a Masonic and a theological significance, and may
have some bearing on Beethoven's deep attraction to exotic formulations
on the attributes of divinity; perhaps, too, they are somehow related to
Beethoven's feelings of isolation from the world. But he knew from
Schiller that the first two were found on monuments of the Egyptian
mother goddesses. In these matriarchal inscriptions, the goddess asserts
her capacity to conceive and give birth without the cooperation of man.
(In the full transcription by Champollion, the second passage is followed
by the phrase "The fruit I have borne is the Sun.") The third inscription
derives from an Egyptian initiation rite current at a later, patriarchal
stage of development, but it, too, contains precisely the same privileging
of the solitary, except that it denies the necessity for a woman to participate in the act of generation. These irreconcilable matriarchal and patriarchal inscriptions remained in plain view on Beethoven's worktable
throughout the later part of his life, poignant reminders of the composer's withdrawal to an impregnable self-sufficiency, a self-sufficiency that
ultimately prevailed against his longings for love.

THE IMMORTAL BELOVED

THE RIDDLE

FERDINAND RIES WAS THE FIRST TO OBSERVE that although Beethoven was "very often in love," his "attachments were mostly of very brief duration."[1] Thayer also noticed this pattern. "One all-absorbing but temporary passion, lasting until its object is married to a more favored lover, is forgotten in another destined to end in like manner, until, at length, all faith in the possibility of a permanent, constant attachment to one person is lost."[2] Elliot Forbes wryly commented on the composer's frequent "decision to plunge into work when faced with the possibility of a permanent attachment with a woman."[3] It seems clear that there was some element of pretense or at least self-deception in Beethoven's continual series of flirtations, which bordered on but never became love affairs. The turbulent relationship with Josephine Deym may constitute an exception to this pattern, but with his other infatuations there seems to have been little possibility of their evolving into serious relationships. Either the woman was firmly attached to another man (as were Giulietta Guicciardi, Julie von Vering, Bettina Brentano, Marie Bigot, and perhaps Elizabeth Röckel), or she exhibited little or no feeling for him (Magdalena Willmann, Therese Malfatti).

The affair with the woman known as the Immortal Beloved was of a different order. Found among Beethoven's personal effects after his death was the only unalloyed love letter of his bachelor existence—an uncontrolled outburst of passionate feeling, exalted in tone, confused

Antonie Brentano

FIG. 1. Unsigned minature
on ivory (ca. 1798). Attributed
to Friedrich Heinrich Fuger.

Brentano Collection, Winkel/Rheingau, Germany.

FIG. 2. Unsigned minature
on ivory (ca. 1802–5).

*By permission of the Beethoven-Haus, Bonn.
Collection H. C. Bodmer.*

FIG. 3. Portrait in oils
by Joseph Carl Stieler (1808).

Brentano Collection, Winkel/Rheingau, Germany.

FIG. 4. With her children Georg
and Franziska. Portrait in pastels
attributed to Nikolaus Lauer (1809).

By permission of the Beethoven-Haus, Bonn.

in thought, and ridden with conflicting emotions. There was no tinge of amorous charade here; Beethoven, for the first and as far as we know the only time in his life, had found a woman whom he loved and who fully reciprocated his love. The letter was written over the course of two days.

July 6, in the morning.

My angel, my all, my very self—Only a few words today and at that with pencil (with yours)—Not till tomorrow will my lodgings be definitely determined upon—what a useless waste of time— Why this deep sorrow when necessity speaks—can our love endure except through sacrifices, through not demanding everything from one another; can you change the fact that you are not wholly mine, I not wholly thine—Oh God, look out into the beauties of nature and comfort your heart with that which must be—Love demands everything and that very justly—thus it is *to me with you, and to you with me.* But you forget so easily that I must live *for me and for you;* if we were wholly united you would feel the pain of it as little as I—My journey was a fearful one; I did not reach here until 4 o'clock yesterday morning. Lacking horses the post coach chose another route, but what an awful one; at the stage before the last I was warned not to travel at night; I was made fearful of a forest, but that only made me the more eager—and I was wrong. The coach must needs break down on the wretched road, a bottomless mud road. Without such postilions as I had with me I should have remained stuck in the road. Esterházy, traveling the usual road here, had the same fate with eight horses that I had with four—Yet I got some pleasure out of it, as I always do when I successfully overcome difficulties—Now a quick change to things internal from things external. We shall surely see each other soon; moreover, today I cannot share with you the thoughts I have had during these last few days touching my own life—If our hearts were always close together, I would have none of these. My heart is full of so many things to say to you—ah—there are moments when I feel that speech amounts to nothing at all—Cheer up—remain my true, my only treasure, my all as I am yours. The gods must send us the rest, what for us must and shall be—

Your faithful LUDWIG

Evening, Monday, July 6

You are suffering, my dearest creature—only now have I learned that letters must be posted very early in the morning on Mondays—Thursdays—the only days on which the post coach goes from here to K.—You are suffering—Ah, wherever I am, you are with me, I will arrange it with you and me that I can live with you. What a life!!!! thus!!!! without you—pursued by the goodness of mankind hither and thither—which I as little want to deserve as I deserve it—Humility of man towards man—it pains me—and when I consider myself in relation to the universe, what am I and what is He—whom we call the greatest—and yet—herein lies the divine in man—I weep when I reflect that you will probably not receive the first report from me until Saturday—Much as you love me—I love you more—But do not ever conceal yourself from me—good night—As I am taking the baths I must to go bed—Oh God—so near! so far! Is not our love truly a heavenly structure, and also as firm as the vault of Heaven?—

Good morning, on July 7.

Though still in bed, my thoughts go out to you, my Immortal Beloved, now and then joyfully, then sadly, waiting to learn whether or not fate will hear us—I can live only wholly with you or not at all—Yes, I am resolved to wander so long in distant lands from you until I can fly to your arms and say that I am really at home with you, and can send my soul enwrapped in you into the land of spirits—Yes, unhappily it must be so—You will be the more composed since you know my fidelity to you. No one else can ever possess my heart—never—never—Oh God, why must one be parted from one whom one so loves. And yet my life in V[ienna] is now a wretched life—Your love makes me at once the happiest and the unhappiest of men—At my age I need a steady, quiet life—can that be so in our connection? My angel, I have just been told that the post coach goes every day—therefore I must close at once so that you may receive the l[etter] at once.—Be calm, only by a calm consideration of our existence can we achieve our purpose to live together—Be calm—love me—today—yesterday—what tearful longings for

you—you—you—my life—my all—farewell.—Oh continue to
love me—never misjudge the most faithful heart of your beloved.

    ever thine

    ever mine   L.[4]

    ever ours

Missing from the letter were the year and place of its composition
and the name of its intended recipient. The fact of these omissions was
hidden for several decades, because when the letter was first published,
in 1840, Schindler confidently identified its addressee as Countess
Guicciardi and asserted that it had been written in the summer of 1806
from a Hungarian spa where Beethoven had gone "on account of his
gradually increasing deafness."[5] The unsuspecting reader could know
neither that Schindler had thrice inserted the date "1806" in the letter,
nor that he was simply guessing the beloved's identity. By the time
he completed the enlarged edition of his Beethoven biography in
1860, Schindler had doubtless learned that Giulietta married Count
Gallenberg in November 1803 and immediately left Vienna for Naples,
where the couple made their home. Therefore in 1860 he stated, "I cannot give [the] exact date," and speculated that the letter had been written in or prior to 1803.[6] In the second volume (1867) of his Beethoven
biography, Ludwig Nohl continued to accept Schindler's identification
of Giulietta as the Immortal Beloved, but he also began to subject the
claim to scrutiny for the first time. He ruled out all possible years
between 1800 and 1806 except 1801, and found even this date difficult
because of Beethoven's presumed stay in Hetzendorf during the summer of that year.[7] There the matter rested until 1872, when Thayer
shattered the entire basis for Schindler's bland assertions. The publication of the second volume of Thayer's *Ludwig van Beethovens Leben*
revealed for the first time the existence of a genuine riddle with respect
to the actual identity of the Immortal Beloved. Thereupon the quest for
a solution commenced, and the subject became a matter of intense con-
troversy among Beethoven scholars.

At first this debate tended to obscure more than it revealed, for
most nineteenth-century biographers failed to pursue the material
clues within the letter itself. Instead they first sought to demonstrate

that Beethoven had been (or might have been) in love with one or another woman at some time during his life, following which they attempted to fit the letter to the affair as best they could. Even Thayer fell victim to this tendency. Not content merely to demolish Schindler's claim for Giulietta, he proposed Therese von Brunsvik as the beloved in volume 3 of his life of Beethoven (1879). This was a strange case of biographical matchmaking, for no hard evidence of any kind existed to indicate a love affair between Beethoven and Therese. The only supporting data consisted of Therese's apparent gift to Beethoven of a copy of her portrait in oils; his retention of the portrait until his death; a letter to her brother Franz in which Beethoven wrote, "Kiss your sister Therese";[8] his dedication of the Sonata in F-sharp, op. 78, to her in 1810; and Giulietta's comment to the biographer Otto Jahn: "Count Brunsvik . . . adored [Beethoven] as did his sisters, Therese and Countess Deym."[9]

On the basis of this flimsy evidence, along with an unwarranted predating of Beethoven's 1810 marriage project to 1807, Thayer decided that the letter had been written in 1806 to Countess Brunsvik. But 1806 was a year in which July 6 did not fall upon a Monday. As the American Scholar O. G. Sonneck noted, "Something snapped"[10] in Thayer's reasoning, for Thayer had been the first to establish that the only years that should be considered were 1795, 1801, 1807, 1812, and 1818, because these were the only ones in which July 6 fell on a Monday. To support his thesis, however, Thayer abandoned the evidence of the letter itself and pleaded that "there is an error of one day in Beethoven's date."[11] This most scrupulously objective of all of Beethoven's biographers fell victim to his desire to protect Beethoven from the accusation that he might have fallen in love with a woman whose character, age, or marital status did not suit the standards of Victorian morality. He chose Therese to counter two possibilities: that the beloved was the married Giulietta, or that she might have been the then fourteen-year-old Therese Malfatti. Thayer's motive became quite transparent when he wrote, "Our contention has a much more serious purpose than the determination of the date of a love letter; it is to serve as the foundation for a highly necessary justification of Beethoven's character at this period in his life."[12]

Objectively, Thayer's candidate possessed fewer credentials than Giulietta as the addressee of the letter. It was, therefore, most heartening to Therese's supporters to learn that she had left a full and melodramatic account of her love affair with Beethoven, including details of their secret betrothal in 1806, an account that was published in 1890 under the name of Mariam Tenger (pseudonym for Maria Hrussoczy) as a book entitled *Beethovens unsterbliche Geliebte, Nach persönlichen Erinnerungen* (*Beethoven's Immortal Beloved: From Personal Reminiscences*).[13] The book was enthusiastically received, translations were immediately undertaken, and a second edition was called for. Although A. C. Kalischer exposed it as a fiction and a forgery in 1891, it was some time before Thayer's followers could acknowledge this.[14] In the interim, Sir George Grove had the misfortune to interpret the Fourth and Fifth Symphonies as program works precisely congruent with Tenger's narrative.[15] (The Fifth Symphony, he wrote, contains, in its main themes, "actual portraits of the two chief actors in the drama.")

Only Thayer's extraordinary authority in Beethoven studies permitted his hypothesis to be taken seriously for a number of years. The disintegration of the case for Therese Brunsvik was largely completed by 1909, when it was established that Beethoven had been in Vienna and Therese in Transylvania on the crucial dates in 1806. Moreover, examination of the extensive Brunsvik papers uncovered several of Therese's love affairs, but no hint of one with Beethoven. Most decisively, it turned out that in her later years Therese, believing Schindler's misdating of the love letter to be correct, thought her sister Josephine to have been the Immortal Beloved. The long debate "Therese or Giulietta?" had come to an end, with both candidates discarded and their advocates in disarray, somewhat abashed at the shoddy scholarship that had led them astray. Later books on Beethoven continued to repeat the old speculations, but they had lost their conviction.

Despite—or perhaps because of—the high seriousness with which the debate was carried on, its comic aspects were never far from the surface. In August 1911 Paul Bekker, the then editor of the influential periodical *Die Musik*, published in that journal a "new" letter to the Immortal Beloved that he accepted as authentic. Several leading scholars were wholly taken in by this forgery, which included the following delicious song fragment, supposedly written by Beethoven to his beloved:[16]

Ich lie - be Dich ___ von gantz - em Her - zen ich lie - be

Da capo ad infinitum

ein - zig Dich al - lein,   ja!

THE SUMMER OF 1812

In 1909, music biographer Wolfgang A. Thomas-San-Galli published a small book entitled *Die unsterbliche Geliebte Beethovens: Amalie Sebald* (*Beethoven's Immortal Beloved: Amalie Sebald*), which for the first time put the study of this question on a scientific basis.[17] Proceeding from the evidence contained within the letter and from the accumulated knowledge of Beethoven's movements during his Vienna residence, Thomas-San-Galli eliminated from consideration as the year in which the letter could have been written every year between 1795 and 1818 with the sole exception of 1812, one of the five years on which July 6 fell on a Monday. Thayer, too, had gone over this ground, but had passed over this year in what Sonneck called a "strange oversight."[18] Thayer mistakenly wrote that "1812 must be rejected because [Beethoven] wrote a letter to [Ignaz] Baumeister on June 28 from Vienna and arrived in Teplitz on July 7th."[19] In fairness to Thayer, he had received an extract from the Teplitz guest lists showing Beethoven's registration date as July 7, 1812, a correct but deceptive date, as we shall see; nor did he have access to Beethoven's letter of July 17, 1812, to Breitkopf & Härtel, which correctly gave his arrival date as July 5.[20] In any event, Thayer's unqualified rejection of the year 1812 was the foundation of two generations of pyramiding errors, until Thomas-San-Galli fixed that year as the correct one, at which point a wealth of corroborative detail immediately came to the surface. It was documented in Thomas-San-Galli's brochure and, shortly thereafter, in an even keener study by Max Unger entitled *Auf Spuren von Beethovens "Unsterblicher Geliebten"* (*On the Trail of Beethoven's "Immortal Beloved"*).[21] These, together with a 1910 sister volume on the same subject by Thomas-San-Galli, solved most of the substantive questions relating to the letter and laid the groundwork for the identification of its intended recipient.[22] Later researchers have added minor supporting details to the reconstruction of the events of late June and early July 1812, which may be summarized as follows.

Each year Beethoven customarily left Vienna for some time during the summer months. Ordinarily, he took a summer house in one of the spas or resorts surrounding Vienna. In the years 1811 and 1812, however, he traveled to Bohemia, where the cultural eminences, the wealthy, and the ranking nobility of the German-speaking lands vacationed at such spas as Karlsbad, Teplitz, and Franzensbrunn. In 1812, Beethoven left Vienna on June 28 or June 29 on the first part of his journey. He arrived in Prague on July 1.[23] His arrival was noted in a contemporary newspaper supplement listing prominent persons entering Prague, as was his registration at the Schwarzen Ross (Black Horse Inn).[24] While there, he discussed financial matters with Prince Kinsky and received a partial payment of 60 ducats on the amount due him under the 1809 annuity agreement. On July 2, he saw the writer Karl August Varnhagen von Ense (who reported the visit in a letter to his future wife, Rahel Levin) and made an appointment to meet him on the following evening, but the meeting did not take place, for unexplained reasons. "I was sorry, dear V[arnhagen], not to have been able to spend the last evening at Prague with you, and I myself found that inappropriate [*unanständig*], but a circumstance which I could not foresee prevented me from doing so. . . . Verbally more about it."[25] Varnhagen's memoirs are silent on this matter; apparently he never received the promised explanation.

Before noon on Saturday, July 4, Beethoven took the post coach to Teplitz.[26] Simultaneously, in a separate carriage, Prince Paul Anton Esterházy, the Austrian ambassador to Dresden, left Prague, headed for the same destination.[27] It had rained continuously on July 1, and after a single day of clear weather, there was heavy rain on July 3, which continued through noon of July 4. The rain then stopped, but the skies remained overcast and the weather cold through July 5.[28] According to

Unger, the usual post route passed through Schlan, Budin, and Lobositz and across a high pass through the Mittelgebirge range to Teplitz.[29] If that is so, Esterházy's eight-horse coach followed the normal route, but Beethoven's driver, having only four horses, decided to avoid the mountain road: "Lacking horses, the post coach chose another route—but what an awful one," wrote Beethoven to the Immortal Beloved. Instead, they went by way of Schlan, Laun, and Bilin. "At the stage before the last [i.e., in Laun], I was warned not to travel at night—made fearful of a forest [the large forest that lay between Laun and Bilin] . . . ; the coach must needs break down on the wretched road." Beethoven arrived in Teplitz at four A.M. on July 5. There he learned that the Esterházy coach had experienced similar difficulties. "We say to you only that we have been here since the 5th of July," he wrote to Breitkopf & Härtel.[30] He was given temporary quarters on that day, no doubt on account of the lateness of his arrival ("Not till tomorrow will my lodgings be definitely determined upon"), and on July 7 he was formally registered on the Teplitz guest list as "Herr Ludwig van Beethoven, Kompositeur, Wien, wohnt in der Eiche, Nr. 62" ("Ludwig van Beethoven, composer, Vienna, staying at the Oak, No. 62").[31]

On the next day, "July 6, in the morning," Beethoven began the letter, probably in response to a letter from the beloved, which he may have received in the morning mail. "Why this deep sorrow where necessity speaks," he wrote, in what appears to be a reference to her letter. Assuming that they had met in Prague, a letter mailed by her on the fourth would have been placed on the July 5 post coach for delivery on the following morning.

His letter completed, Beethoven found that he had missed the morning post. "Only now have I learned that letters must be posted very early in the morning on Mondays—Thursdays—the only days on which the mail-coach goes from here to K." Therefore, he went on, "I weep when I reflect that you will probably not receive the first report from me until Saturday." It is clear from this that Beethoven knew "K" to be two days or less distance from Teplitz. The clues in these postal references led to the identification of "K" as Karlsbad, another fashionable spa one and a half days distance away, which Beethoven elsewhere abbreviated as "K."[32] Goethe, who made the trip between the two towns several times, and who often received mail sent from one to the other, repeatedly confirmed the travel time in his diary.[33] Of striking significance was a contemporary Teplitz postal notice (dated 1815) discovered by Unger, which reads as follows:

OUTGOING MAIL:
MONDAY. Early, about 8:00 o'clock, the Reichspost goes to Saaz, Karlsbad, and Eger. After midday, about 4:00 o'clock, to Prague, Vienna, Silesia, Moravia, Italy, Hungary, Bavaria, France, etc.
TUESDAY. After midday, about 3:00 o'clock, to Dresden, Leipzig, Prussia, and the other northern countries.
THURSDAY. Early, about 8:00 o'clock, same as early Monday.
FRIDAY. After midday, about 4:00 o'clock, same as Monday afternoon.
SATURDAY. Same as Tuesday.[34]

Beethoven presumably saw this notice and concluded that he could not mail his letter until Thursday, July 9, for arrival on July 11. Evidently, however, he later learned that he had overlooked the following in small type at the bottom of the postal notice:

NOTE:
From May 15 until September 15, the mail arrives daily early in the morning from all the Austrian imperial dominions, and also leaves daily before noon about 11:00 o'clock to the same.[35]

So in the second postscript he wrote, "My angel, I have just been told that the post coach goes every day—therefore, I must close at once so that you may receive the l[etter] at once."

In this way it was proved that the letter to the Immortal Beloved was written in Teplitz, Bohemia, on July 6 and 7 in the year 1812.[36] The evidence for this was soon accepted as definitive by almost all serious Beethoven scholars. It was similarly established beyond a reasonable doubt that the place ("K") to which the letter was to be sent was Karlsbad. Ineluctably following from this is the virtual certainty that Beethoven's beloved was in (or about to arrive in) Karlsbad during the week of July 6.[37] To simplify matters, it was noted by Thomas-San-Galli that the Karlsbad police required formal registration of all arrivals.[38]

Another clue was to prove useful in the identification of the intended recipient. Most Beethoven biographers believe that the following entry on the first page of Beethoven's Tagebuch of 1812–18, dated 1812, contains a reference to the Immortal Beloved:

> For you there is no longer any happiness except within yourself, in your art. O God! give me strength to conquer myself, nothing at all must fetter me to life. In this manner with A everything goes to ruin.[39]

Finally, another lead flows from a conversation overheard by Fanny Giannattasio in September 1816 between Beethoven and her father, the educator Cajetan Giannattasio. She recorded the following in her diary:

> Five years ago Beethoven had made the acquaintance of a person, a union with whom he would have considered the greatest happiness of his life. It was not to be thought of, almost an impossibility, a chimera—"Nevertheless it is now as on the first day."[40]

The riddle was on the brink of solution early in this century. All substantive questions relating to the letter had been resolved—with the sole exception of the identity of its addressee. The quest continued. What was required was to test every woman of Beethoven's acquaintance who might be the Immortal Beloved against the requirements of the evidence.

THE SOLUTION OF THE RIDDLE

The requirements were, first, that the Immortal Beloved be a woman closely acquainted with Beethoven during the period in question, so that a love relationship could have developed, culminating in early July of 1812. It is most unlikely that the love affair was brought to its evident fever pitch via prior correspondence alone. Nor is it likely that a momentary encounter could have sparked the conflicts concerning the lovers' future plans that are so manifest in the letter of July 6–7. The Immortal Beloved, therefore, almost certainly lived in proximity to Beethoven in Vienna. Some evidence of an intimate association in Vienna during the months prior to July 1812 is an important material requirement.

Next, the letter gives rise to the powerful implication that Beethoven and his beloved had met in Prague immediately prior to July 6. He has her pencil; he does not refer to the journey from Vienna to Prague or to any events during his stay in Prague, but refers only to events from July 4 to July 7. He alludes to events of "these last few days"; he despairingly writes, "Today—yesterday—what tearful longings for you." (This last implies that they parted on July 4.) The Immortal Beloved, therefore, must be a woman whom Beethoven had seen and spoken to—almost certainly in Prague, although possibly in Vienna—during the week or two preceding July 6. Evidence that a candidate for the Immortal Beloved had been in Vienna during the last days of June 1812 would count in her favor. If it could be demonstrated that she had actually been in Prague between July 1 and July 4, when Beethoven was also there, it would be extremely compelling evidence. If, in addition, it could be shown that she was actually in contact with Beethoven in either city, this would strengthen her case even more.

Finally the sine qua non for identification of the Immortal Beloved is that she must have been in Karlsbad during the week of July 6, 1812. This test eliminates all but four women—the daughter of a noted Viennese family Antonie Brentano, the outstanding pianist Dorothea von Ertmann, the poet Elise von der Recke, and Princess Marie Liechtenstein—all of whose names are entered on the Karlsbad police registers for that week. The other indispensable circumstance eliminates three of these women: the Immortal Beloved must not only have been in Karlsbad during that week, she must have *arrived* in Karlsbad very recently, en route from Vienna and/or Prague. Otherwise, she and Beethoven could not have had the meeting that necessarily preceded the letter.

(Clearly, there is no possibility of absolute certainty here, and the researcher should not exclude even the most remote possibilities. For example, it is conceivable that the letter was written to a woman in Karlsbad whose name is on the guest lists or police registers but who is wholly unknown to Beethoven researchers; or she may meet all of the requirements of time and place without our being aware of her doing so. And it is possible that the letter arose from a Prague or Vienna meeting with a woman who informed Beethoven that she was going to Karlsbad and then failed to carry out her declared intention. Despite such cautions, any inquiry into the identity of the Immortal Beloved must base itself on the most reasonable reading of the existing evidence.)

Turning now to the secondary requirements, the beloved would most probably be a woman whom Beethoven had met or become closely acquainted with approximately five years prior to 1816, which is when Fanny Giannattasio recorded in her diary that Beethoven remained in love with a woman whom he had met five years earlier. Ever since the date of the Immortal Beloved letter was established as 1812, it has become an overwhelming probability that the Immortal Beloved and the woman Fanny Giannattasio referred to were one and the same. Fanny's diary entry should be read in conjunction with the closing lines of Beethoven's letter to Ferdinand Ries, written on May 8 of the same year, 1816: "Unfortunately I have no wife. I found *only one,* whom no doubt I shall *never possess.*"[41] (Both Fanny's diary entry and Beethoven's letter to Ries suggest a continuing association in 1816 between the composer and the Immortal Beloved.) "*Only one.*" The emphasis is Beethoven's. Those who have remained proponents of one or another woman as the Immortal Beloved have been forced by Fanny's reference to "five years" to assume two loved ones, because even if we take the reference to "five years" as an approximation, all of the leading candidates—Giulietta Guicciardi, Josephine Deym, Therese Brunsvik, Marie Erdödy, and Dorothea von Ertmann—are eliminated from contention. Other previously considered candidates who do meet the "five years" test are Therese Malfatti (1809–10), Bettina Brentano (1810), Antonie Adamberger (1810), the singer Amalie Sebald (1811), Elise von der Recke (1811), and the poet Rahel Levin (1811). But none of these women meets any of the primary requirements.

Other possible criteria arise from veiled references by Beethoven to possibly beloved women whose names are designated by various initials. These are the "A" in the Tagebuch reference of late 1812, the "T" in two Tagebuch references of 1816, and the "M" in a note that was actually written between 1807 and 1810 but that Beethoven researchers long believed to have been written during the following decade. The Immortal Beloved need not have had the initials *A* or *T*; the opacity of Beethoven's diary entries precludes certainty in this regard. A woman having one or both of these initials would not be proved to be the

Immortal Beloved unless she met the necessary requirements of time and place. However, if a woman who met all or most of these requirements also possessed one or both of these initials, it would appear to increase the probability that she was the beloved.

Another possible precondition for identification of the Immortal Beloved is that she be someone whom Beethoven believed he would shortly reencounter. The expectation of an impending meeting arises from Beethoven's remark "We shall surely see each other soon." The expected or actual place of the reunion is not significant. What is important is the probability that the Immortal Beloved was a woman whom Beethoven expected to see again "soon" after the letter of July 6–7.

These, then, are the requirements for the identification of the Immortal Beloved. A century of research, however, has excluded from consideration all of those who were once seriously considered (Giulietta Guicciardi, Therese Brunsvik, Magdalena Willmann, Amalie Sebald, Bettina Brentano). Similarly, no meaningful evidence in favor of Therese Malfatti or Dorothea von Ertmann has been introduced, and their names have been put forward most tentatively even by their supporters. Also set aside were the more remote possibilities—Marie Bigot, Countess Marie Erdödy, Rahel Levin, the Graz pianist Marie Pachler-Koschak, and the actress Antonie Adamberger, who was betrothed to poet Theodor Körner. The case for Josephine Deym— advanced in 1920 by La Mara, enlarged by Siegmund Kaznelson, and later revived by the Massins, Harry Goldschmidt, and others— had its day in the sun, but the disclosure in 1957 of her correspondence with Beethoven, which began in 1804, indicated an early (and chilly) end to an unconsummated romance by autumn 1807.[42] Although it is conceivable that the affair was momentarily rekindled a half decade later, there is no evidence that this indeed happened. Neither she nor any of the above are plausible as addressees of Beethoven's letter because they do not meet the necessary requirements of time and place.

Nevertheless, Countess Deym's candidacy has continued to attract advocates.[43] Those advocates are not daunted by her poignant correspondence with Beethoven showing that he could no longer gain entrance to her house after September 1807, or by their own inability to demonstrate any subsequent personal contact between them, or by

Beethoven's proposal of marriage to Therese Malfatti in 1809–10 or his subsequent intimate friendship with Antonie Brentano, or by the absence of the faintest indication that Countess Deym actually was in Prague or any of the Bohemian spas in July 1812. Instead, they continue to search for evidence that they do not doubt will eventually be forthcoming. However, even that faint eventuality can no longer be anticipated.

In a paper published in 1987, entitled "Recherche de Josephine Deym," I called attention to and quoted from three letters dated June 14, July 25, and August 13, 1812, which shed light on the whereabouts and activities of Josephine and her second husband, Baron Christoph von Stackelberg, whom she married in 1810.[44] The first letter, written by the baron to his mother in Talinn, Estonia, describes intimate family matters and extends the hope of a family visit by himself, his wife, and their children to her later in the summer. The second is a business letter from Franz Brunsvik to his sister Josephine requesting a response from her husband regarding an urgent financial matter; the third is a letter from a certain Hager to Josephine, expressing his intention of visiting the Stackelbergs at home on the following day. The letters demonstrate that the Stackelberg marriage was still intact throughout the summer of 1812 and that the countess was actually present in Vienna both shortly before and shortly after July 6–7 of that year, the dates on which Beethoven's letter to the Immortal Beloved was written. The Stackelbergs did eventually separate, but these three letters are powerful evidence that the separation could not have occurred prior to the date on which the Immortal Beloved letter was written. The memoirs of Therese Brunsvik, which are the best source on the breakup of her sister's marriage, clearly indicate that Stackelberg's departure took place the following year, after April 1813.[45]

Thus, these letters undermine the speculations that Josephine was already separated from her husband in early July 1812; that her husband was absent and therefore could not have fathered their last child, Minona (born April 9, 1813); and that her situation at the time of the letter enabled her, unknown to the authorities, to travel to Prague and the north Bohemian spas. At the very least, the new evidence demonstrates that any remaining window of opportunity for her to have actually been in Prague or Karlsbad in late June or early

July is now so small that a prudent scholar ought to rule her out of consideration.[46]

There is one woman who meets not just a few but every one of the primary and secondary requirements. In her case, it is unnecessary to suggest hypothetical possibilities, to speculate that she "might have" been in close contact with Beethoven in Vienna during the first half of 1812, or "could have" been in Prague between July 2 and 4, or "may have" visited Karlsbad. Although this woman is well known in the Beethoven literature, she has, almost unaccountably, never previously been advanced as the possible addressee of Beethoven's letter to the Immortal Beloved.[47] She is Antonie Brentano, born Antonie von Birkenstock (1780–1869), to whom Beethoven later dedicated his Thirty-three Variations on a Waltz by Diabelli, op. 120. The weight of the evidence in her favor is so powerful that it is not presumptuous to assert that the riddle of Beethoven's Immortal Beloved has now been solved.[48]

Let us test the case for Antonie Brentano against each of the prerequisites:

•Item: *The Immortal Beloved was intimately associated with Beethoven, probably in Vienna, during the period preceding the letter.* Antonie Brentano resided continuously in Vienna from the fall of 1809 until the fall of 1812. She became acquainted with Beethoven during a visit with her sister-in-law, Bettina Brentano, to the composer in May 1810 (Antonie was married to Bettina's half brother, the Frankfurt merchant Franz Brentano). It is known that a close friendship developed between Antonie and Beethoven during the next two years. Otto Jahn, who interviewed her in 1867, spoke of their "tender friendship,"[49] and Schindler reported Beethoven's claim that she (and her husband, Franz) were "his best friends in the world."[50] Beethoven was a frequent visitor at the Birkenstock mansion in which the Brentanos lived; in turn she and her family visited him at his lodgings. He consoled Frau Brentano with improvisations on the piano when she was ill and bedridden; he acted as intermediary for her in a proposed sale to his patron, Archduke Rudolph, of rare manuscripts that she owned; and she showed him (or read to him) private letters from Bettina. It is certain that they were in personal contact in Vienna as late as June 26, 1812, when Beethoven wrote out an affectionate dedicatory message on his easy Piano Trio in

B-flat, WoO 39, to Antonie's ten-year-old daughter, Maximiliane, and dated it in his own hand. Additional confirmation that Antonie was in Vienna at this time appears in an entry on the Karlsbad police register, which notes that her passport was issued in Vienna on June 26, 1812.[51] We know, therefore, that Antonie was in Vienna during the latter part of June, and that she was not only in proximity to but in close contact with Beethoven.

•Item: *The Immortal Beloved was in Prague between July 1 and July 4, 1812.* A list of prominent persons arriving in Prague on July 3, 1812, published in the Prague newspaper supplement that was cited above, contains the following entry:

> . . .   DEN 3TEN [JULY]
> . . . . H. Brentano, Kaufmann, von Wien. (woh. im rothen Haus.)
> ["Herr Brentano, merchant, from Vienna. Staying at the Red House Inn."][52]

Franz Brentano, journeying from Vienna to Karlsbad with his wife, Antonie, and one of their children, stopped in Prague on July 3, 1812, and remained there for one or two nights. With this information, it becomes possible for the first time in the voluminous researches on Beethoven's Immortal Beloved to show that one of the women under consideration has been definitely placed in Prague at precisely the same time as Beethoven. There is no proof that Beethoven and Antonie met in Prague, but the presumption that they did is supported by several factors.

First, since we know that they were in touch on June 26 in Vienna, it is reasonable to assume that they then discussed their respective summer vacation plans, and perhaps arranged to meet in Prague. Second, and decisively, they undoubtedly discussed a possible meeting later in the summer, for a reunion actually took place that was possible only through prearrangement. It is unlikely that these close friends—who had just parted in Vienna and were shortly to vacation together at Karlsbad and Franzensbad—would fail to take advantage of the opportunity to meet in Prague as well.

•Item: *The Immortal Beloved was in Karlsbad during the week of July 6, 1812.* The list of departures for July 4 published in the newspaper just cited establishes that Beethoven left Prague before noon on that day.[53] The Brentanos' date of departure does not appear; we know, however, from Max Unger (who cites a guidebook of 1813) that the stagecoach went daily to Karlsbad at eleven A.M. Thus, the Brentanos must have taken the coach from Prague on either the fourth or the fifth of July, because they registered at Karlsbad on July 5, 1812. (If they indeed left on the fourth, they may have traveled with Beethoven on the first leg of the journey.)

The presence of Antonie Brentano in Karlsbad has long been known in the Beethoven literature. Thomas-San-Galli was the first to examine the Karlsbad guest lists and police registers, but he failed to mention the Brentanos' registration. Unger, however, explicitly noted the arrival of Antonie Brentano on July 5. The relevant entry on the guest lists reads:

-33-

CHRONOLOGICAL NO.	NAME, POSITION AND LODGING OF ARRIVING GUESTS	DAY OF ARRIVAL
. . .	. . .	. . .
380	Herr Franz Brentano, banker from Frankfurt with wife and child . . .	July 5

On the following day, the Brentanos—Franz, Antonie, and their youngest child, Franziska (Fanny), who had just turned six—were entered as No. 609 on the Karlsbad police register. The entry gives their place of birth and homeland as Frankfurt, their residence as Vienna, and their Karlsbad address at 311 Aug' Gottes (God's Eye).

The Immortal Beloved was a woman whom Beethoven knew with certainty to be in, or arriving in, Karlsbad during the week of July 6. Antonie Brentano is the only candidate to meet this crucial requirement. We know that Beethoven knew her to be in Karlsbad, because he joined the Brentanos there later in the month. As for the other women who were acquainted with Beethoven and who were also on the Karlsbad guest lists around that time, it cannot be shown that Beethoven knew of any of these women's presence in Karlsbad. Equally important, their arrival dates (June 7 for Frau von der Recke, June 25 for Baroness von Ertmann and Princess Liechtenstein) make it highly unlikely that they could have been in personal contact with Beethoven shortly before the Immortal Beloved letter. Only Antonie Brentano arrived in Karlsbad at a time that parallels Beethoven's own movements from Vienna to Prague to the Bohemian spas.

Antonie Brentano satisfies all of the secondary requirements as well.

•Item: *The Immortal Beloved and Beethoven might soon meet again.* Beethoven left Teplitz around July 25 for Karlsbad.[54] His registration with the police there was delayed, evidently because he had left his passport in Teplitz, but it is certain that he was reunited with Antonie and her family, for, according to the police register dated July 31, he was lodged in the same guesthouse, 311 Aug' Gottes auf der Wiese, where the Brentanos had been living since July 5.[55] They all remained there until August 7 or 8, at which time the Brentano family and their illustrious companion moved from Karlsbad to Franzensbad (Franzensbrunn), where they again occupied neighboring quarters, at the Zwei goldenen Löwen (Two Golden Lions). It is not clear how long the Brentano family remained in Franzensbad; Beethoven's departure from that resort at the beginning of the second week of September presumably marks his separation from them as well. He arrived—alone—back in Karlsbad on September 8 (this is confirmed by Goethe's diary), and by September 16 he returned to Teplitz, where the sisterly ministrations of Amalie Sebald helped to calm him during the aftermath of the turbulent affair of the Immortal Beloved.

•Item: *The Immortal Beloved was probably a woman whom Beethoven had met or become closely acquainted with approximately five years prior to 1816.* Beethoven and Antonie Brentano met in May 1810. They became intimately acquainted shortly thereafter and remained so until the Brentano family's departure for Frankfurt in the fall of 1812.

•Item: *The first initial of the Immortal Beloved's name may have been A.* There are five women to whom this initial could apply: Amalie Sebald, Bettina Brentano, whose married name was Arnim, Antonie Adamberger, Countess Anna Marie Erdödy, and Antonie Brentano. Neither Amalie nor Bettina are possibilities, because they resided in Germany rather than in Austria, and Antonie Adamberger and Marie Erdödy were not in the Bohemian spas during July 1812. Antonie Brentano, therefore, is the only woman of Beethoven's acquaintance whose initial is *A* and who could also be the Immortal Beloved.

•Item: *The initial of the Immortal Beloved's name may have been T.* The following two entries were written in 1816 in Beethoven's Tagebuch:

> With regard to T. there is nothing else but to leave it to God, never to go there where one could do wrong out of weakness; only leave this totally to Him, to Him alone, the all-knowing God!
>
> Nevertheless be as good as possible towards T; her devotion deserves never to be forgotten, although unfortunately advantageous consequences could never accrue to you.[56]

The only women known to Beethoven in this period whose names begin with *T* are Therese Malfatti, "Toni" Adamberger, Therese Brunsvik—none of these three can be seriously considered—and "Toni" Brentano. For thus was Antonie called by all of her intimate friends and relatives, including Beethoven. On February 10, 1811, he wrote to Bettina Brentano, "I see from your letter to Toni that you still remember me";[57] and on February 15, 1817, he wrote to Franz Brentano, "All my best greetings to my esteemed friend Toni."[58] It may be objected that Beethoven would not designate Antonie by both "A" and "T." In fact, he alternately used both her full name and her nickname, as did many of her friends, and she herself alternated between these names in signing her letters, even to the same person.

The existence of Tagebuch references to the Immortal Beloved in 1816 should occasion no surprise, Beethoven's regard and affection (and, if my conclusions are accepted, his love as well) for Antonie at this very time being evident in passages from his four surviving letters to her, three of which are dated early November 1815, February 6, 1816, and September 29, 1816.[59] In addition, the Tagebuch mentions nine letters to either Antonie or her husband or both, written in 1817–18, that have not been found, including one in which a presentation copy of a lied was enclosed.[60] The depth of Beethoven's feeling for Antonie in 1816 is manifested in his letter to her of February 6, 1816:

MY REVERED FRIEND:
I am taking the opportunity afforded me by Herr *Neate* . . . to remind *you* and your kind husband Franz as well of *my* existence.

At the same time I am sending you a copper engraving on which my face is stamped. Several people maintain that in this picture they can also discern my soul quite clearly; but I offer no opinion on that point— . . . I wish you and Franz the deepest joys on earth, those which gladden our souls. I kiss and embrace all your dear children in thought and should like them to know this. But to you I send my best greetings and merely add that I gladly recall to mind the hours which I have spent in the company of both of you, hours which to me are the most unforgettable—

> With true and sincere regards,
> your admirer and friend
> LUDWIG VAN BEETHOVEN[61]

I suspect that Thayer knew of the existence of a love affair between Beethoven and Antonie Brentano, but because he was confused as to the date of the famous letter and regarded Therese Brunsvik as its addressee he did not make the connection between Antonie Brentano and the Immortal Beloved. Thayer's knowledge can be inferred from the following passage concerning the person referred to as "T" in Beethoven's diary:

Now it happens that one of Beethoven's transient but intense passions for a married woman, known to have occurred in this period of his life, has its precise date fixed by these passages in the so-called "Tagebuch" from the years 1816 and 1817. . . . As the family name of *this lady, whose husband was a man of high position and distinction though not noble by birth,* is known, it is certain that the T in the above citations is not Therese Malfatti [italics added].[62]

Thayer's words precisely describe Antonie and Franz Brentano, if we read the phrase I have italicized to imply that the lady was noble, though the husband was not. Antonie was born of the nobility; Franz was a prominent merchant and banker, but not a noble. No other known woman whose name begins with the initial *T* could be the woman referred to by Thayer. He specifically excludes Therese Malfatti; furthermore, she married a nobleman. Therese Brunsvik was never married. "Toni" Adamberger was not married in 1816, and her husband was an aristocrat by birth. It seems probable, therefore, that "Toni" Brentano was the woman whose family Thayer attempted to shield from harmful publicity. Additional evidence for my surmise lies in the fact that Thayer hints at the possibility that this "T" is connected with the "M" of the following handwritten note, first published in facsimile by Schindler:

> Love—yes, love alone can make your life happy! O God, let me find someone whose love I am allowed.
> Baden, 27 July, when M. passed by and, I think, looked at me.[63]

Thayer does not say that "T" and "M" are one person, but only that they "may *indicate* the same person." He says, "The sight of 'M' again, for a moment, tore open a half-healed wound." This opaque passage in Thayer becomes crystal clear if we assume "T" to be "Toni" Brentano and "M" to be her daughter Maximiliane, the sight of whom in 1817 (thought Thayer) revived in Beethoven the image of her mother.

Another item of circumstantial evidence is found on one of Beethoven's manuscripts: in December 1811, he composed a song, "An die Geliebte" ("To the Beloved"), WoO 140, to a poem by J. L. Stoll:

> The tears of your silent eyes,
> With their love-filled splendor,
> Oh, that I might gather them from your cheek
> Before the earth drinks them in.

In the upper-right-hand corner of the first page of the autograph, written in a hitherto unidentified handwriting, are the words:

> Den 2tn März, 1812 mir vom Author erbethen
> [Requested by me from the author on March 2, 1812][64]

A comparison with a large number of Antonie Brentano's manuscript letters shows that this note was written by her. She must, then, have received this love song from Beethoven shortly after its completion. This seems to me a strong indication that, months before the letter of July 6–7, Antonie Brentano was already Beethoven's beloved.

(The song—with an arpeggiated triplet accompaniment—was published as a "Lied ... with piano or guitar accompaniment," the only such designation in Beethoven's lieder output. Since Antonie was an expert guitarist, this can be taken as an additional reason to believe that the song was not only presented to her but was actually composed for her. A second version of the song with a more pianistic accompaniment was composed in December 1812.)

Last among the signs that I have discovered pointing to Antonie Brentano as Beethoven's "*unsterbliche Geliebte*" is another unusual item. Found in Beethoven's personal effects were two portrait miniatures on ivory, which in 1827 came into the possession of the Breuning family. Gerhard von Breuning succeeded in identifying one of these as a portrait of Giulietta Guicciardi.[65] The other miniature remained unidentified by Breuning, but was later deemed (probably by A. C. Kalischer) to be a portrait of Countess Erdödy and has been reprinted many times as such. However, in 1933 Stephan Ley discovered by a detailed comparison of the miniature with an authenticated portrait of the countess made available to him by her great-granddaughter in Vienna that this presumed identification was incorrect.[66] Returning to the subject two decades later, Ley repeated his earlier, fascinating speculation:

> Comparing this portrait with the miniature, the upshot is that the two pictures cannot be delineations of the same person; therefore the miniature is the portrait of an unknown ... and the possibility or indeed probability arises that we may have here a portrait of the "*unsterbliche Geliebte.*"[67]

At the beginning of this chapter the unidentified miniature (now in the H. C. Bodmer collection of the Beethovenhaus in Bonn) is reproduced, along with three authenticated portraits of Antonie Brentano (see p. 208). Figure 1 is a miniature ivory portrait of her at the age of eighteen dating from the time of her marriage, ca. 1798; Figure 3 is a portrait in oils by Joseph Carl Stieler, known to have been painted in 1808; Figure 4 is a portrait in pastels attributed to Nikolaus Lauer that shows her with two of her children; it is one of a pair of family portraits that can be dated to early 1809 by the Brentano correspondence.[68] The miniature that Beethoven owned (Figure 2) can be dated by its subject's costume to somewhere between ca. 1802 and ca. 1805.[69] When viewed in the chronological sequence suggested by this dating, the resemblance of the image on the miniature to Frau Brentano is striking: the color and almond shape of the eyes; the curl and color of the hair; the contour of the eyebrows; the modeling and length of the nose; the long neckline, suggestive of the regal posture for which she was noted; the idiosyncratic curvature of the lips; the facial outline and bone structure; the height of the forehead. Equally significant, the portrait miniature does not resemble any of the other women who have been nominated as Beethoven's Immortal Beloved.

Admittedly, Beethoven's possession of a miniature portrait of one of his closest friends and patrons would not by itself be proof that she was the addressee of the letter to the Immortal Beloved. Nor, despite the close resemblance, is it beyond question that Antonie Brentano is depicted on the miniature. Nevertheless, if it is indeed her image, as seems likely, it would suggest a close or even intimate relationship between her and its recipient, for the gift of such a miniature to a member of the opposite sex was often intended (and regarded) as something more than simply an expression of esteem. Portraits played a not insignificant role in Beethoven and Antonie's personal association: he presented to her in 1816 an engraved copy of his portrait by Blasius Höfel after a pencil drawing by Louis Letronne; in 1819 she commissioned Stieler to do the famous portrait in oils of Beethoven writing the *Missa Solemnis*, and she retained in her possession a miniature copy of it on ivory.

These, then, are the threads in a powerful fabric of circumstantial evidence that, taken as a whole, makes it all but certain that Antonie Brentano was the woman to whom Ludwig van Beethoven wrote his impassioned letter of July 6–7, 1812.

ANTONIE BRENTANO AND BEETHOVEN

Antonie Brentano was born May 28, 1780, in Vienna, the only daughter of the noted Austrian statesman, scholar, and art connoisseur Johann Melchior Edler von Birkenstock and his wife, née Carolina Josefa von Hay. After her mother's death in 1788, young Antonie was placed in the convent of the Ursuline order at Pressburg (Bratislava), where she received a rigorous upbringing for seven years. Returning to Vienna in 1795, she led an equally sheltered existence for several years in her father's mansion until her marriage on July 23, 1798, to a congenial Frankfurt merchant fifteen years her senior, Franz Brentano. Brentano had visited Vienna in late 1796 and asked Birkenstock whether Antonie was available; in August 1797, eight months after his return to Frankfurt, he began his courtship by correspondence and through two intermediaries in Vienna, his half sister Sophia Brentano and his step-mother, Friederike von Rottenhoff. Birkenstock gave Brentano to understand that although he approved of the match the final decision rested with Antonie. In later years, however, Antonie recalled that the marriage had been arranged without consulting her and that she had "obediently yielded" to her father's wishes.[70] She left her beloved Vienna for Frankfurt immediately after the wedding. In her reminiscences, she related that she knew "from rather certain sources" that on the day of her wedding her "true love" remained standing behind a church pillar at St. Stephen's, weeping "bitter tears" of mourning. She still recalled how she had been forced to follow her new husband to a foreign city, and she had by no means forgotten that Franz "was still so alien to her that it was only after months that she grew accustomed to the 'Du' with him."

Antonie found her new home "wholly strange," and she wept "untold hot tears" in solitude, unwilling to let her husband know her feelings. The birth of her first child in 1799 momentarily caused her to "forget all her sorrows," but the child died suddenly early in 1800. She bore four other children by 1806, all of whom survived.

She managed to present a controlled exterior to visitors during the early years. A touring Englishman described her in 1801 simply as "Mad[ame] Brentano, a beautiful Viennese," who graciously took time from her family obligations to initiate him into German poetry.[71] The poet Achim von Arnim's view in 1805 was that "Toni Brentano is, as always, the well-bred hostess."[72] But the cool self-possession implied by those descriptions was not always in evidence. Franz's half brother, the Romantic poet Clemens Brentano, wrote in July 1802 that "Toni is like a glass of water that has been left standing for a long while."[73] Others, too, noticed that all was not well. Clemens's wife, Sophie, wrote to him from Heidelberg, where Antonie was visiting in 1805, that "Toni's appearance . . . astonishes me greatly."[74] Bettina, Franz's younger half sister, expressed her concern in a letter of June 1807 to her brother-in-law, the famous jurist Karl von Savigny, which gives one the impression that Antonie was going through a period of withdrawal and depersonalization. "Toni is in a bizarre correspondence with me," she wrote; "she has rouged and painted herself like a stage set, as though impersonating a haughty ruin overlooking the Rhine toward which a variety of romantic scenes advance while she remains wholly sunk in loneliness and abstraction."[75]

Antonie's malaise soon manifested itself in physical symptoms. In 1806 she wrote to Clemens, "I have a lot of headaches, and my damned irritability doesn't leave me."[76] An undated letter to Savigny refers to a nervous condition that prevents her from traveling.[77] In mid-1808 she wrote to Savigny and his wife, Gunda, "The pains in my chest increased to such a degree that it almost cut my breath off. No position in bed was tolerable, until this terrible seizure dissolved in compulsive crying. . . . I have to look forward to a worsening of my condition rather than to an improvement in my health."[78] She continued, ominously, "A deathly silence [*Todesstille*] reigns within [my] soul."

Antonie's unhappiness centered on her inability to accept the separation from her native city. She longed for Vienna: "Through all difficulties—and these I was never free of—the eternal hope of my journeys to Vienna, which I made regularly every two years, held me erect." Years later she told the writer Karl Theodor Reiffenstein that her father had made her promise to visit him every two years, and that for her "this was the ray of hope in a difficult life, for she indeed had a hard lot during the first years in her new home." Closely related to Antonie's yearning for her "glorious, beloved hometown" was her antipathy toward Frankfurt. One gains the impression that her only moments of happiness in Germany came when she was vacationing or visiting the Brentano country estate, Winkel, on the Rhine, far removed from the family's house on the Sandgasse. Writing from Frankfurt to her son's tutor Joseph Merkel in late 1808, she described her feelings: "Here one is pressed constantly, without enjoyment. There [at Winkel] is enjoyment without stress. There is sunshine; here we follow the will o' the wisp. There truth; here deception. There frugality with little; here debauchery. There present; here past. There rest; here unrest."[79] Drawing back from the implications of this contrast, she added, "But these are not my words, because there means separation for me from the best of all men, and here is beautiful reunion." Nevertheless, in another letter to Merkel she summed up the heartsickness that Frankfurt inevitably engendered in her. "The shadows of the Sandgasse," she wrote, "are the gloomy backdrop to the painting of my life."[80]

In June 1809 Antonie learned that her father was dying. She wrote in a letter of June 16, "When the leaves fall in the autumn, then I will not have a father any more, and before he goes to eternal rest he shall rest in my arms and I near to his heart."[81] Antonie moved to Vienna with the children just prior to her father's death (he died on October 30), and the family took up residence in the imposing Birkenstock house, No. 98 Erdbeergasse in the Landstrasse.[82] Franz followed shortly thereafter and established a branch office of his firm in Vienna, leaving the Frankfurt home office in the care of his half brother Georg.

In May 1810 Bettina Brentano (who was visiting at the Birkenstock house), accompanied by Antonie, sought out the renowned Beethoven at his lodgings at the Pasqualati house, to which he had returned on April 24 after an absence of two years. This visit inaugurated the friendship between Beethoven and the Brentano family. Bettina, who enchanted Beethoven, left Vienna after a few weeks, but Beethoven's friendship quickly extended to Antonie and her husband and children as well. According to Brentano family tradition, "Beethoven often came to the Birkenstock-Brentano house, attended the quartet concerts which were given there by the best musicians of Vienna, and often gave pleasure to his friends with his glorious pianoforte playing. The Brentano children sometimes brought fruit and flowers to him in his lodgings; he in return gave them bonbons and showed the greatest friendliness toward them."[83]

What of Antonie's relationship with her husband at this time? Franz, the bourgeois paterfamilias, apparently did his best to make his aristocratic young wife happy. There are many reports in family correspondence of journeys and vacations during their first decade of marriage. His surrender to her request that they leave his paternal home and business to reside in Vienna for an extended period of time certainly shows that he was prepared to go to great lengths to please her. For her part, Antonie regarded her husband as a good man—she called him

Silhouette by Joseph Neesen (circa 1786).
By permission of the Beethoven-Haus, Bonn.

Dessiné par G. Stainhauser de Treuberg. Gravé par Joh. Neidl.

Louis van Beethoven.

a Vienne chez Jean Cappi.

Engraving by Johann Joseph Neidl after a drawing by
Gandolf Ernst Stainhauser von Treuberg (circa 1801).
By permission of the Beethoven-Haus, Bonn.

Miniature on ivory by Christian Horneman (1802).
By permission of the Beethoven-Haus, Collection H. C. Bodmer.

Portrait in oils by Joseph Willibrord Mähler (circa 1804).
By permission of the Historisches Museum der Stadt Wien.

Portrait in oils by Isidor Neugass (circa 1806).
By permission of the Beethoven-Haus, Bonn.

Pencil drawing by Ludwig Schnorr von Carolsfeld (circa 1810).
Original lost. From Robert Bory, Ludwig van Beethoven: His Life and
Work in Pictures *(London, 1966)*.

Bronze bust by Franz Klein (circa 1812).
By permission of the Beethoven-Haus, Bonn.

Dessiné au Crayon par Louis Letronne et gravé par Blas. Höfel 1814.

LUDWIG van BEETHOVEN.

Engraving by Blasius Höfel after a pencil drawing by Louis Letronne (1814).
Artaria & Co. By permission of the Beethoven-Haus, Bonn.

Portrait in oils by Johann Christoph Heckel (1815).
By permission of the Library of Congress

Portrait in oils by Joseph Willibrord Mähler (1815).
By permission of the Beethoven-Haus, Bonn.

Pencil drawing by August Karl Friedrich Klöber (1818).
By permission of the Beethoven-Haus, Bonn.

Portrait in oils by Joseph Carl Stieler (1820).
By permission of the Beethoven-Haus, Bonn.

Portrait in oils by Ferdinand Waldmüller (1823).
From a copy by Fassbender.
By permission of the Beethoven-Haus, Bonn.

Chalk drawing by Stephan Decker (1824).
By permission of the Historisches Museum der Stadt Wien.

"The Dying Beethoven." Drawing by Joseph Teltscher (March 26, 1827). *By permission of the British Library, Collection Stefan Zweig.*

"Beethoven on His Deathbed." Drawing by Joseph Danhauser
(March 28, 1827).
By permission of the British Library, Collection Stefan Zweig.

"my good Franz" and even "the best of all men"—and it is clear that she respected him for his character and position and was deeply appreciative of his love for her. In her reminiscences, however, she reveals the onesidedness of the relationship: "I did not want to let my husband know how difficult it was for me, because he was always so loving and friendly toward me." One cannot help noting that she does not say "because I loved him"; I haven't found a single forthright expression of her love for Franz in Antonie's correspondence or reminiscences. Evidence of concern and affection abounds, but not of a more profound romantic love. And there are repeated allusions to Franz's total involvement in his business, which are perhaps veiled complaints that she was being neglected. "Even after supper he goes to the office," she wrote to Sophia Brentano. "God, what will come of it?"[84]

Antonie compelled her husband and family to remain in Vienna for three years after the death of her father. Clearly, she prolonged this stay beyond any reasonable length of time in order to postpone returning to Frankfurt, utilizing as her rationale the disposition, which she personally supervised, of her father's huge collection of art objects, manuscripts, and rare antiquities. Her inner conflicts during this period generated a withdrawal into illness. She told Otto Jahn that following her father's death she "was frequently ill for weeks at a time." (She repeatedly went to Karlsbad in search of a cure, but without lasting relief.) The practical effect was to prolong her residence in Vienna—where, despite her illness, she was able to find a happiness not available to her in Frankfurt. "I am kept in my hometown by sweet necessity longer than in the hometown of my children," she wrote, "and I enjoy the real contentment and well-being which are created through circumstances free of compulsion."[85] The bittersweet emotions aroused by her stay in Vienna are described in a letter of June 5, 1811:

> I have lived almost two years here in my father's town, in my father's house, but from which the father was carried off one and a half years ago. Oh, what a father! I have become rich in experiences of several kinds, and I believe that the home feeling which surrounds me even in sad hours I will find nowhere else. But my health is completely shattered, and that prevents me from having a pleasant life, and makes me acquainted with mortality.[86]

The vast Birkenstock collections were surveyed, appraised, and catalogued under Antonie Brentano's supervision, and a series of auctions were held, on February 17, March 18, and April 27, 1812, and March 8, 1813.[87] In this work she was advised by connoisseurs and collectors who had been friends of her father's, and they also helped her to choose many of the most valuable paintings, master drawings, and engravings for herself.[88] It was not an easy task to transform the Birkenstock mansion into what, by early 1813, Clemens Brentano bitterly called "an art-less coffin."[89] Originally, four auctions were scheduled to start on January 15, 1811, the first featuring the library of nearly seven thousand books, maps, and manuscripts, and to run through the autumn of 1811, but the start was postponed for a full year. By the last week of April 1812, by which time everything but a portion of the copper engravings collection had been sold, the end of Antonie's labors was in sight. Toward mid-1812 she faced the imminent prospect of returning to Frankfurt, of being compelled once again to leave her childhood home and all that it represented to her. It is my impression that she may have fled to Beethoven seeking salvation from that prospect—to one who represented for her a higher order of existence, who embodied in his music the spiritual essence of her native city. At the same time, Antonie Brentano may belatedly have been asserting her right to choose her own beloved.

We cannot say precisely when the love affair started. Following Bettina's departure, by early June, Beethoven failed to take his accustomed summer lodgings but instead remained in Vienna and made occasional visits to nearby Baden. He was busy with preparations for the June 15 premiere of his Incidental Music to Goethe's *Egmont*, op. 84, as well as with supervising a good deal of music copying and correction of proofs, because many of his compositions were in press at that time. In October he completed his String Quartet in F minor, op. 95 (marking the autograph "1810 in the month of October"), but the pace of his serious composition had slowed considerably. This slowdown continued into 1811, which saw the completion of just one major work, the "Archduke" Trio, op. 97, which he had sketched the previous year and composed rapidly between March 3 and March 26, as implied by the inscription of these two dates on the autograph.[90] Nevertheless, Beethoven's mood was optimistic; he was apparently content to deal with important musical problems in fewer compositions. His thoughts turned once again to opera; he wrote to Paris "for libretti, successful melodramas, comedies, etc.,"[91] and seriously considered a French melodrama entitled *Les Ruines de Babylon* as an operatic subject. At this time he planned a trip to Italy, but as usual nothing came of his intended journey. Instead, on the recommendation of Dr. Malfatti, he made his first visit to Teplitz, arriving at the very beginning of August 1811, accompanied by his good friend and helper Franz Oliva. There he worked on a revision of *Christus am Ölberge* (*Christ on the Mount of Olives*), op. 85, for publication by Breitkopf & Härtel and rapidly wrote incidental music to both *Die Ruinen von Athen* (*The Ruins of Athens*), op. 113, and *König Stephan* (*King Stephen*), op. 117. The latter was intended for performance in Pest on Emperor Franz's name day, October 4, but was postponed until February 9–11 of the following year, when it served to celebrate both the emperor's birthday and the opening of a new theater there. At Teplitz in 1811 Beethoven initially remained secluded, but through Oliva he found warm companionship with a group of Berlin intellectuals, poets, and musicians that included Karl August Varnhagen von Ense, Rahel Levin, Christoph August Tiedge, Elise von der Recke, and Amalie Sebald. The carefree holiday was soon over, and on September 18 Beethoven left the resort, traveling via Prague to the Lichnowsky estate near Troppau in upper Silesia. There the Mass in C was at last performed for an appreciative audience, and Beethoven and his patron perhaps experienced the contentment of partially recreating the friendly and creative atmosphere of their earlier days.

Thus far there was no sign of a romantic attachment between Beethoven and Antonie Brentano. A letter from Antonie to Clemens of January 26, 1811, however, indicates that she had already begun to revere Beethoven. Clemens had sent her a cantata text that he wanted set to music. She replied:

> I will place the original in the holy hands of Beethoven, whom I venerate deeply. He walks godlike among the mortals, his lofty attitude toward the lowly world and his sick digestion aggravate him only momentarily, because the Muse embraces him and presses him to her warm heart.[92]

At what point this worship was transformed into love is not yet known. My estimate is that this took place in the fall of 1811, when Beethoven first presented her with several of his compositions—the "Drei Gesänge," op. 83, and the piano transcription of *Christus am Ölberge*, op. 85—with dedicatory messages. If, as seems likely, "An die Geliebte" was composed for Antonie, it is clear enough that the love affair was under way by late 1811.

Toward the end of her life, Antonie recalled for Otto Jahn that only one person had been able to console her in her most desolate moments in Vienna. She told Jahn that during her long periods of illness she withdrew from company and remained "in her room inaccessible to all visitors." There was one exception: Beethoven, with whom "a tender friendship" had developed, would "come regularly, seat himself at a pianoforte in her anteroom without a word, and improvise; after he had finished 'telling her everything and bringing comfort' in his language, he would go as he had come, without taking notice of another person."[93] In 1819 Antonie wrote to her spiritual mentor, Bishop Johann Michael Sailer at the University of Landshut, describing Beethoven in the most superlative terms, which can also be interpreted as expressions of love. She characterized him as "this great, excellent person" who "is as a human being greater than as an artist"; she wrote of "his soft heart, his glowing soul, his faulty hearing, with his deeply fulfilling profession as an artist"; of his "warm will and hearty confidence." She concluded, "He is natural, simple, and wise, with pure intentions."[94]

If one rereads the letter to the Immortal Beloved at this juncture, its words take on new colorations. We are now confronted with a document addressed to a real person, rather than to a mysterious unknown whose character and motivations are hidden from us. The overt ethical implications of Beethoven's renunciation become apparent. His desire for Antonie is in conflict not only with his deeply rooted psychological inability to marry, but also with the prospect of the betrayal of a friend, Franz Brentano. Beethoven had warmed himself at the Brentanos' family hearth, partaking vicariously of their family life. He loved them both, and he could not separate them. His anguish and his confusion are apparent in the letter. And his answer becomes clear: he will continue to love both of them, as a single and inseparable unit.

There is no point in speculating about the events that may have occurred during Beethoven's reunion with Antonie and Franz Brentano in Karlsbad and Franzensbad between July and September 1812. It is sufficient to point out that in some way the trio managed to pass through the crisis into a new stage of their relationship. Passion was apparently undergoing sublimation into exalted friendship. Beethoven was visibly elated during these months, as evidenced by his correspondence and his productivity. But the end of the affair may have had a delayed traumatic effect on him.

The precise date of the Brentanos' departure from Vienna for their return to Frankfurt has not yet been reliably established, but it was probably in November 1812. On October 6, Franz wrote to Clemens from Vienna concerning their imminent return to Frankfurt: "Toni as well as I are still not well at all [*sehr leidend*]. . . . If it had not been for my impending journey, which depends on Toni's recovery, I would have invited you to come here, so you could stay with us. But I have a strong impulse to go home, and my errant, unquiet life has lasted much too long."[95] He omitted one germane piece of information, that Antonie had been pregnant since June; she gave birth to her last child, Karl Josef, on March 8, 1813.[96] Beethoven may have prolonged his absence from Vienna until their departure from the capital was assured. Despite occasional revivals of his desire to see his birthplace on the Rhine, Beethoven never made the journey that might have reunited him with the Brentanos, nor, as far as I can determine, did Antonie for her part ever again visit the city of her birth.

In 1827, when she was forty-six, Antonie Brentano began to note down the names of her friends who had died. By the end of her long life, in 1869, the yellowed sheets of paper were filled with names, each followed by the date of death. The first entry reads:

Beethoven, March 26, 1827[97]

On March 28, 1827, and in subsequent letters of April 7 and May 10 (the last wrongly marked "April 10"), a certain Moritz Trenck von Tonder (previously unknown in the Beethoven literature) wrote to Antonie Brentano. "I hesitate to bring you sorrow through the sad news concerning our friend Beethoven," he wrote, but "I know what great interest you, honored lady, take in his fate."[98] Trenck's letters provided her with details of Beethoven's last sufferings along with a full description of the funeral and its attendant ceremonies. He enclosed numerous materials, including a handwritten copy of Grillparzer's funeral address, a packet of poems eulogizing Beethoven, obituary notices, newspaper clippings, and announcements of concerts featuring Beethoven's music. Also included was a report about Beethoven's last days written by his brother Nikolaus Johann. Frau Brentano transcribed and retained many of these, along with copies of dispatches about Beethoven that she gleaned from various European newspapers.

THE MEANING OF THE LETTER

Though there seemed to be an element of amorous charade in several of Beethoven's love affairs, there is also a somewhat sadder implication: in every single one of Beethoven's known passions for a woman, from his youth in Bonn until 1811, he had either been rejected by the woman or had withdrawn in expectation of a rebuff. Magdalena Willmann scorned him as "ugly and half crazy"; Giulietta Guicciardi preferred the shallow Gallenberg to Beethoven as her lover; Marie Bigot reported his "advances" to her husband; Julie von Vering chose Stephan von Breuning; Countess Marie Erdödy wounded his feelings by preferring "the servant to the master"; Therese Malfatti did not respond to his attentions; Bettina Brentano flirtatiously aroused his expectations without revealing that she was then deeply in love with and about to marry Achim von Arnim. And according to Grillparzer, a peasant girl whom Beethoven encountered one summer in Döbling preferred the peasant lads to the supreme composer.[99] Perhaps most afflicting in this series was his rejection by Josephine Deym: she compelled Beethoven to withdraw his passionate demands, insisted upon the spiritualization of their connection, and then turned to Count Wolkenstein.

No one can be rejected so consistently without in some way contributing to the process, perhaps helping to bring about an inwardly desired result. Certainly Beethoven harbored ambivalent attitudes toward women and marriage, which surely were related to lifelong inhibitions about taking his place as the head of a family. Nevertheless, the unbroken series of rejections—several of which he may have regarded as betrayals as well—must have had a devastating cumulative effect on his pride, causing painful doubts and self-questioning. Inwardly he saw himself, not as "Hercules at the crossroads," but, as we know from a letter he wrote to Zmeskall, as Omphale's Hercules, shorn of his power.

For Beethoven, the miraculous significance of the Immortal Beloved affair was that Antonie Brentano was the first (and as far as we know the only) woman ever wholly to accept him as a man, the first to tell him that he was her beloved without reservations of any kind. "Oh continue to love me—never misjudge the most faithful heart of your beloved," he pleads, in the last sentence of the Immortal Beloved letter. It was her love for him that brought to the surface his suppressed ability fully to express his love for a woman. At last a woman had given him her love, offered, apparently, to risk the condemnation of society in order that they might be "wholly united."

The opportunity was at hand to test the strength of his professed desires for domesticity and fatherhood. Gratitude toward and love for Antonie, however, struggled against the ingrained patterns and habits of a lifetime. The power of the letter to the Immortal Beloved stems from the profound honesty with which it reflects this internal conflict. It is not merely a letter of renunciation, but a document in which acceptance and renunciation struggle for domination.

Perhaps Beethoven did not at first regard this romance as essentially different in kind from previous ones. There appeared to be only the slightest possibility of consummation: Antonie was aristocratic by birth, a married woman with four children, and Beethoven was on close terms with her husband. He consoled her during her long periods of illness and melancholy, and he was perhaps wont to proclaim to her the hopelessness of their situation. But if our reconstruction is correct, on July 3, 1812, in Prague, or shortly before, Antonie may well have asserted that the conditions of her existence were not an insuperable bar to their union, and advised Beethoven that she was willing to leave her husband and remain in Vienna, rather than return to Frankfurt. Beethoven, it seems, was unprepared for this sudden turn of events; he responded in confusion, reciprocating her love, desperately attempting to respond in kind, but unable to disguise his ambivalent attitude to the prospect that had emerged so precipitously. Her reaction was one of sorrow and Beethoven attempted to soothe her by expressing his positive feelings, and by holding out a glimmer of hope that her goal was not an unattainable one.

The first part of the letter seeks to bring Antonie comfort while avoiding the commitment she sought. "Why this deep sorrow when necessity speaks—can our love exist except through sacrifices, through not demanding everything." Continue to love me, says Beethoven, but accept the necessity of our separation. "Can you change the fact that you are not wholly mine, I not wholly thine." Antonie had apparently already answered this question in the affirmative, but Beethoven would not recognize the feasibility of so radical a solution. He counsels stoical acceptance, urging, "Look out into the beauties of nature and comfort your heart with that which must be." Momentarily he shows a hint of pique against Antonie for "demanding everything": "You forget so easily that I must live for me and for you." Beethoven desperately wants to keep Antonie's love, but to do so without changing the external circumstances of their lives. He closes the letter with a repetition of his primary motif: "Cheer up—remain my true, my only treasure, my all as I am yours. The gods must send us the rest, what for us must and shall be." "Plutarch has shown me the path of resignation," Beethoven had written on another occasion; here, he is urging the lesson upon his beloved Antonie.

Having completed the letter proper, Beethoven either missed the morning post coach or was unable to carry out so unqualified a rejection. When evening fell, he once again took up the pencil. With the first postscript, his determination to resist begins to disintegrate. The desire to accept Antonie's offer of herself has begun to overpower him. "You are suffering," he writes to her, and he repeats, "You are suffering." Surely the reference is to his own inner conflict and to the anguish that he himself feels. His defenses are crumbling. "I will arrange it . . . that I can live with you," he beseeches. With these words he has accepted the offer, whereupon his thoughts take on a wholly chaotic, free-associational quality, centering, perhaps, on the image of Christ merging with his own personality. "Humility of man toward man—it pains me—and when I consider myself in relation to the universe, what am I and what is He whom we call the greatest—and yet—herein lies the divine in man." Indistinct thoughts flow through

Beethoven's mind, and then the suspicion of another possible betrayal surfaces: "Much as you love me, I love you more—but do not ever conceal yourself from me." He does not pursue the suspicion. He closes rapidly, pleading that he must arise early on the following day.

With the morning, Beethoven has reverted to Plutarch. In the second postscript Beethoven tells how his thoughts drift between joy and sadness as he wonders "whether or not fate will hear us." The light of day has tempered his passion and brought him a new "solution" of the conflict: he will run away, and in his absence the problem may evaporate. "I can live only wholly with you or not at all—Yes, I am resolved to wander so long in distant lands until I can fly to your arms and say that I am really at home with you, and can send my soul enwrapped in you into the land of spirits." But Antonie may take heart at this sorrowful prospect ("unhappily it must be so"), for Beethoven adds that he will remain eternally faithful to her: "You will be the more composed since you know my fidelity to you—no one else can ever possess my heart—never—never—" Momentarily, anger surges through him at the uncomfortable predicament in which Antonie has placed him: "My life in V[ienna] is now a wretched life—your love makes me at once the happiest and the unhappiest of men—at my age I need a steady, quiet life—can that be so in our connection?"

Before the close of the postscript, however, Beethoven's love (and his need for her love of him to endure) once again begins to overpower his resistances. "Be calm, only by a calm consideration of our existence can we achieve our purpose to live together—." "Be calm"—again he is addressing himself, for his conflict has not been resolved. "Love me—today—yesterday—what tearful longings for you—you—you—my life—my all—farewell—Oh, continue to love me—never misjudge the most faithful heart of your beloved L." The last sentence is a plea for forgiveness—for although the letter to the Immortal Beloved contains neither an acceptance nor a rejection, Beethoven knew that he would ultimately be incapable of the breakthrough that Antonie Brentano had offered him.

We do not know whether Beethoven mailed the letter. The sentence "I must close at once so that you may receive the l[etter] at once" makes it likely that he did post it. It is difficult to imagine Beethoven failing to keep his promise to write to her at once, and even more difficult to explain their reunion in the last week of July had he failed to do so. (As we now know, the opportunity to return the letter to its sender shortly arose.) Obviously there is no certainty about the matter: it is also possible that the act of writing the letter externalized the difficult decision that confronted Beethoven, so that once he had written it there was no need to mail it. And it is conceivable that he composed another, more careful and less contradictory letter in its stead, firmly closing the issue.

Our discussion of the letter has so far omitted the symbolism of Beethoven's account of the journey from Prague to Teplitz, which gives the letter much of its aesthetic power, for it touches on mythic and universal categories of experience:

> My journey was a fearful one . . . the post coach chose another route, but what an awful one; at the stage before the last I was warned not to travel at night; I was made fearful of a forest, but that only made me the more eager—and I was wrong. The coach must needs break down on the wretched road, a bottomless mud road. . . . Yet I got some pleasure out of it, as I always do when I successfully overcome difficulties.

We begin to feel that Beethoven is here describing no mundane trip through the rain on a daily post coach, but a symbolic journey through a Dantean *selva oscura*, a dark forest, portraying the danger of his own passage from a fearful isolation into manhood and fatherhood. The letter has resonances of a hero fantasy of grand proportions. In mythology, writes Mircea Eliade, the "road leading to the center is a 'difficult road . . .': Danger-ridden voyages of the heroic expeditions in search of the Golden Fleece, the Golden Apples, the Herb of Life; wanderings in labyrinths; difficulties of the seeker for the road to the self, to the 'center' of his being, and so on. The road is arduous, fraught with perils, because it is, in fact, a rite of the passage from the profane to the sacred, from the ephemeral and illusory to reality and eternity, from death to life, from man to the divinity."[100] Without seeking to burden Beethoven's letter with a heavier freight of interpretation than it may warrant, one surely senses that larger issues are involved than those visible on its surface.

The fear-inspiring forest and the bottomless mud road may be interpreted as symbolizing Beethoven's terror of Antonie's love, of an

engulfing embrace to which he cannot yield because it is somehow forbidden. Conflicting emotions struggle for ascendancy in Beethoven: he
is at once "fearful" and "eager." Although he was spurred to proceed
onward, he felt "I was wrong" to do so. He knew that he should have
remained safely at the last stage until the storm had passed over; he
should have avoided the forest at night and taken the next stage in the
light of day. He had not been able to resist the perilous quest, and at its
close his fear is mingled with a sense of triumph. But he has won a symbolic victory only: he cannot achieve it in reality.

The meeting in Prague was a recognition scene that laid bare to
him a previously unacknowledged aspect of his personality. True, the
unsuccessful outcome of his love for the Immortal Beloved was similar
to the pattern of withdrawal and renunciation in his earlier love affairs,
but the essential difference here was that no rejection—real or imagined—had barred the way. Beethoven could no longer pretend that
external circumstances or pressing creative needs were postponing his
marriage project. Antonie's acceptance (and, apparently, her active pursuit) of Beethoven's love forbade any such rationalizations. The affair
shattered Beethoven's own illusions that he could lead a normal sexual
or family life. Accordingly, we have here the sense of a final renunciation of marriage, and an acceptance of aloneness as his fate. The first
line of his Tagebuch of 1812 to 1818 reads:

You must not be a *human being, not for yourself, but only for others.*[101]

The italics, sad to say, are Beethoven's own.

Now the self-deception of Herculean heroism, the pretense of
romantic masculinity, was at an end; Beethoven's marriage project was
abandoned, and his attitudes toward marriage took on a cheerless character. In 1817 Fanny Giannattasio was dismayed to hear him say that
"he knew of no marriage that sooner or later was not regretted by one
partner or the other" and that, for his part, "he considered it the greatest
good fortune that none of the girls he had desired in earlier years had
become his wife and how good it was that the wishes of mortals were
often not fulfilled."[102]

We should not, however, overlook one basic meaning of
Beethoven's letter, and of the symbolism of the fearful journey.

Beethoven was telling his beloved that he was scared, distraught, and alone following his separation from her in Prague. The letter is a call for a continuation of her love; it is an outcry for her assistance in assuaging his terror, a plea that she not abandon him, no matter what the outcome of her desire to live with him. "Remain my true, my only treasure"; "Love me . . . Oh, continue to love me—." Beethoven understood that for one moment in his life he had within his grasp a woman's unconditional love. His union with Antonie was barred, not by his need for a "steady, quiet life," but by unspecified terrors that overwhelmed the possibility of a fruitful outcome. These terrors were the "terrible circumstances" referred to in a Tagebuch entry dated May 13, 1813:

> To forego what could be a great deed and to stay like this. O how different from a shiftless life, which I often pictured to myself. O terrible circumstances, which do not suppress my longing for domesticity, but [prevent] its realization. O God, God, look down upon the unhappy B., do not let it continue like this any longer.[103]

Beethoven could not overcome the nightmarish burden of his past and set the ghosts to rest. His only hope was that somehow he could make Antonie understand (as he himself did not) the implacable barrier to their union without at the same time losing her love. It is to Antonie Brentano's eternal credit that she was equal to this apparently impossible task. In return she has earned a special sort of immortality.

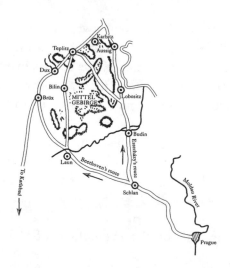

CHAPTER SIXTEEN

THE MUSIC

A T THE TURN OF THE CENTURY, BEETHOVEN was eager to test his abilities in the larger, more popular forms and to reach wider audiences than those of the salons. *Die Geschöpfe des Prometheus* (*The Creatures of Prometheus*), op. 43, written in 1800–01 for a ballet by Salvatore Viganò, was his first major score for the stage; its success may have been a factor in his receipt in 1803 of a commission to write an opera for the Theater-an-der-Wien. Beethoven's ballet music, consisting of a chain of loosely connected dances and mood pieces, is a stylish and accomplished work, skillfully orchestrated and with unusual and colorful instrumental combinations. The popular overture, which was Beethoven's first essay in the genre, is Mozartian in manner, but the ballet's main influence is Haydn in his pastoral, bucolic manner. There are also characteristic Beethovenian touches: the opening Allegro non troppo is virtually a first sketch of the "storm" section of the *Pastoral* Symphony, and the closing dance contains Beethoven's earliest use of the theme of the finale of the *Eroica* Symphony. But this tuneful and engaging score otherwise gives little sign of the dramatic developments to come.

Beethoven's oratorio, *Christus am Ölberge* (*Christ on the Mount of Olives*), op. 85, of early 1803 was his first major work on a religious theme. The choice of this subject, taken together with the composition of the Six Lieder to Poems by Gellert, op. 48, in 1801 or early 1802, and of another pious song, "Der Wachtelschlag" ("The Call of the Quail"), WoO 129, in 1803, gives the impression that there may have been a stirring of religious impulses in Beethoven at this time. Perhaps the deep personal, musical, and ideological crisis that he was undergoing during these years momentarily brought his strong religious feelings to the surface. But with the subsidence of the crisis and the consolidation of his "new path," this tendency apparently waned once again, and religious music disappeared from Beethoven's workshop for half a decade. The oratorio's secular and even operatic style, however, implies that it may

Allegro ma non troppo, *Pastoral* Symphony, op. 68.
First page of autograph full score.

By permission of the Beethoven-Haus, Bonn.

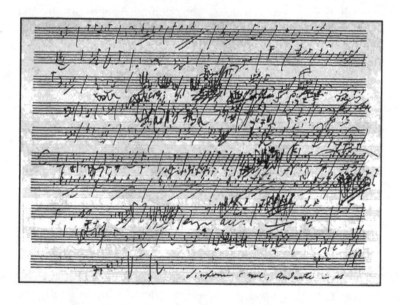

Sketches for Fifth Symphony, op. 67, Andante.

From Paul Bekker, Beethoven *(Berlin, 1911).*

have been conceived less as an expression of faith than as an unorthodox exploration of the psychological presence of Christ.[1] Indeed, one might conclude that Beethoven—not unreasonably—regarded the Crucifixion as a special case of the death of the hero, and that he was attracted to the subject at this time almost as a preparatory study for his most profound instrumental explorations of heroism.

But the subject of death is, by itself, an insufficient precondition for musical heroism. Beethoven wrote a number of lieder and vocal works dealing with death—including "Opferlied," WoO 126, "Klage," WoO 113, "Vom Tode," op. 48, "In questa tomba oscura," WoO 133, and the "Elegischer Gesang," op. 118—which are merely mournful, consoling, or elegiac and do not aspire to express the heroic experience. And though to Beethoven the Adagio affetuoso ed appassionato of his String Quartet in F, op. 18, no. 1, represented the scene in the burial vault of *Romeo and Juliet,* this association leads in that case not to the heroic but to the pathetic and the passionate. Similarly, the "Marcia funebre sulla morte d'un Eroe" movement in the Piano Sonata, op. 26, falls curiously within a context that neither sustains nor effectively contrasts with so weighty a subject. In *Christ on the Mount of Olives* the absence of a counterbalancing theme—whether of heroism, resistance, or transfiguration—leads to a flawed conception, for Beethoven was temperamentally and ideologically disinclined to view Christ's crucifixion as a sorrowful but necessary submission to the Father's will.

The theme of the self-sacrificing Son has its own possibilities of profundity, one that in view of the shape of his own early biography surely touched Beethoven deeply.

> O my Father, oh see, I suffer greatly; have mercy on me . . .
> Father! deeply bowed and weeping, Thy son prays to Thee. . . .
> He is ready to die the martyr's utter death so that man, man, whom
> He loves, may be resurrected from death and live eternally. . . .

That Beethoven set these lines from *Christ on the Mount of Olives* to music in a perfunctory and impersonal manner perhaps indicates that he was not yet ready to explore certain areas of spiritual experience.[2]

The proximity of this work to the Heiligenstadt Testament raises intriguing but unanswerable questions. It is doubtful that it actually was sketched at Heiligenstadt, but it clearly was created in the aftermath of the crisis, and both in its subject matter and in its size it opens, however haltingly and imperfectly, the path to the *Eroica* and *Fidelio*. The "heroic" style seemed to be struggling for emergence, and *Christus* is a step toward that emergence, in which Beethoven returned, almost instinctively, to a form similar to that of the "Joseph" Cantata, in which he earlier treated the subjects of death and heroism. Here, as in that cantata, the discursive oratorio form proved insufficient to the task.

Beethoven rewrote the oratorio extensively in 1804 and again prior to its publication in October 1811. It became extremely popular in England as well as in Vienna during the nineteenth century.

Beethoven's next composition was the Sonata in A for Violin and Piano ("Kreutzer"), op. 47. "Written in a very concertante style, like that of a concerto," he wrote on the title page of the first edition, thus signaling his intention to introduce elements of dynamic conflict into one of the main Classical salon genres and to give equal weight to the collaborating instruments. The "Kreutzer" Sonata's pianistic style looks forward to the middle-period piano sonatas, and the violin has now acquired an urgent, declamatory voice. The work is in three movements: an Adagio sostenuto (the only slow introduction in Beethoven's violin sonatas), leading to a dynamically propulsive Presto; an Andante con variazioni; and a witty Presto Finale, in tarantelle rhythm, that was originally composed for the Sonata for Violin and Piano, op. 30, no. 1. In Tolstoy's novel *The Kreutzer Sonata,* a performance of this sonata precipitates the crucial action: "It seemed that entirely new impulses, new possibilities, were revealed to me in myself, such as I had not dreamed of before," says Tolstoy's tragic hero. "Such works should be played only in grave, significant conditions, and only then when certain deeds corresponding to such music are to be accomplished."

With Beethoven's next work, the Symphony No. 3 in E-flat (*Eroica*), op. 55, we know that we have irrevocably crossed a major boundary in Beethoven's development and in music history as well. The startling and unprecedented characteristics of the *Eroica,* and of many of his subsequent major compositions, were to some degree made possible by Beethoven's perception of new potentialities in the flexible framework of sonata form. Because of its unique ability simultaneously to release and to contain the most explosive musical concepts within binding aes-

thetic structures, sonata form was eminently suited to deal with dramatic and tragic subjects. (The parallels of sonata to drama were noted even
by early observers; Count de Lacépède in 1787 compared "the three
movements of a sonata or symphony to the 'noble' first act, 'more
pathetic' second act, and 'more tumultuous' third act of a drama.")[3] In
terms of the admittedly imperfect analogy between drama and sonata,
we may say, with Tovey, that the sonata cycles of Mozart and Haydn
were frequently musical analogues of the comedy of manners: rational,
unsentimental, objective, witty, satirical treatments of the conventions,
customs, and mores of society. In the comedy of manners, disruptions of
the social fabric are momentary; the loss of love or status is provisional
and temporary; undercurrents of sadness and melancholy are almost
invariably dissolved in a reaffirmation of social norms and in a return to
sanity and wholeness. As Alfred Einstein observed, the symphonies of
Haydn and Mozart "always remained within the social frame," and in
their sonata-form works they "limited themselves to the attainment of
noble mirth, to a purification of the feelings."[4] Hence, however well it
mirrored the rich variety of emotional states and strivings of its composers, patrons, audiences, and the larger collectivity of which these
were constituent parts, the Classical style had as yet failed to map several inescapable and fundamental features of the emotional landscape in
so tumultuous an era. In particular, it rarely plumbed either the heroic
or the tragic levels of experience.

And yet, there were currents stirring in Austrian musical life that
would lead to redress of these omissions. Slowly but inevitably, Viennese
music responded to the reverberations of the French Revolution and the
onset of the Napoleonic Wars. In 1794 Viennese composer Maria
Theresia Paradis wrote a grand funeral cantata on the death of Louis XVI,
which was performed for the widows and orphans of the Austrian soldiers; in 1796 Mozart's disciple Franz Xaver Süssmayr composed a patriotic cantata, *Der Retter in Gefahr*, and other composers began to place their
works—as they said in those days—"on the altar of the Fatherland." The
music of Haydn began to take on a new character: he wrote one symphony (1794) titled *Military*, another (1795) called *Drum Roll*, and in
1796 he wrote the hymnlike anthem "Gott, erhalte Franz den Kaiser"
("God Save Emperor Franz"), which became the rallying cry of Austrian
patriotism. Also in 1796, Haydn composed incidental music to *Alfred*,

oder der patriotische König ("Alfred, or the Patriotic King"), followed several years later by an aria, "Lines from the Battle of the Nile," inspired by Nelson's victory at Aboukir Bay. But it was in two full-scale masses with trumpets and kettledrums, the *Mass in Time of War* (1796) and the *Nelson Mass* (1798), that Haydn approached most closely what would later become Beethoven's heroic style. Another of Beethoven's teachers, imperial kapellmeister Salieri, composed a patriotic cantata in 1799 entitled *Der tyroler Landsturm*, which contains quotations from "La Marseillaise" and Haydn's "Kaiser" hymn; in this work, Erich Schenk found numerous foreshadowings of Beethoven's *Geschöpfe des Prometheus* and *Fidelio*, and even of his Seventh Symphony.[5]

The concept of a heroic music responding to the stormy currents of contemporary history was, therefore, already beginning to take shape. Despite these foreshadowings, however, Beethoven was the first composer fully to fuse the tempestuous, conflict-ridden subject matter of the emerging heroic style with the sonata principle, thus inaugurating a revolution in the history of music. Beethoven took music beyond what we may describe as the pleasure principle of Viennese classicism; he permitted aggressive and disintegrative forces to enter musical form: he placed the tragic experience at the core of his heroic style. He now introduced elements into instrumental music that had previously been neglected or unwelcome. A unique characteristic of the *Eroica* Symphony, and its heroic successors, is the incorporation into musical form of death, destructiveness, anxiety, and aggression as terrors to be transcended within the work of art itself. This intrusion of hostile energy, raising the possibility of loss, is what will make affirmations worthwhile.

It is for reasons such as these that Beethoven's has been called a "tragic" music. But Beethoven's heroic music is not primarily a conventionally tragic, let alone a death-haunted, music, for most of his works in this vein close on a note of joy, triumph, or transcendence. The Funeral March of the *Eroica* yields to an animated, explosive Scherzo and a broad, swinging Finale, marked allegro molto; in *Fidelio*, Florestan and his anonymous fellow prisoners ascend into the light; the precipitating "Fate" theme of the Fifth Symphony is supplanted by the rising march theme of its closing movement; the representation of Egmont's death is followed by a *Siegessymphonie* (victory symphony). In this respect Beethoven remained true to the spirit of classicism and to the Kantian vision of Schiller, who wrote, "The first law of the tragic art was to represent suffering nature. The second law is to represent the resistance of morality to suffering."[6] Furthermore, Beethoven's music does not merely express mankind's capacity to endure or even to resist suffering—the conventional qualities of tragic art. His sonata cycles continue to project, on a vastly magnified scale, the essential features of high comedy: happy endings, joyful reconciliations, victories won, and tragedy effaced. If, as the aesthetician Susanne Langer has observed, tragedy is the image of Fate and comedy the image of Fortune, then Beethoven's music presents the collision of these images, a clash from which Fortune emerges triumphant, so that the hero may continue his quest.[7]

Beethoven's heroism defines itself in conflict with mortality, and mortality is in turn superseded by renewed and transfigured life. Thus, the components of Beethoven's concept of heroism are more extensive than appears at first glance, encompassing the full range of human experience—birth, struggle, death, and resurrection—and these universals are expressed through a fusion of comic and tragic visions of life.

Apart from its extramusical associations, its heroic stance, and its "grand manner," the *Eroica* Symphony marks Beethoven's turn to compositions of unprecedented ambition. He has now chosen to work on a vastly expanded scale, twice that of the symphonic model he had inherited from Haydn and Mozart. The first movement alone spans almost 700 measures. The 250-measure development section, which in earlier Classical sonatas had usually served as a transitional pathway from the exposition to the recapitulation, now exceeds the exposition's length by more than 100 measures and becomes the central battleground on which the harmonic and thematic issues will be fought out. The solution of those issues must, of course, await the recapitulation, which is here most suspensefully delayed by a prolonged transition section, and the lengthy coda, which provides greater rhetorical weight than ever before. The process of formal expansion that was already manifest in the opus 1 Trios and the opus 2 Sonatas here finds fulfillment.

But enlargement of forces and extension of time span do not lead here to a looseness of design and a dilution of content. The *Eroica*'s temporal expansion accompanies—indeed results from—extreme thematic condensation. Early Classical melodies, often based on dance rhythms and forms and generally organized around regular eight-measure periods, were typically symmetrical and balanced, suitable for orderly elaboration, ornamentation, development, and restatement. The thematic materials of the late Classical style were increasingly instilled with a new turbulence and asymmetry through the use of a number of contrasting motifs within a more complex periodic structure. Intensifying this procedure in the *Eroica*'s first movement, Beethoven works with greatly compressed motif cells. Describing this process of "the manipulative extension of a basic or central musical idea," Lang observes, "These sonata subjects are . . . motif cells that in themselves are usually altogether insignificant, but they become cogs in the machinery of design; they are twisted and turned, fragmented and tossed about with infinite inventiveness, only to be reassembled after the battle."[8] Owing to this extreme thematic condensation, critics are on occasion unable to specify what Beethoven's "themes" are. Indeed, in the first movement of the *Eroica*, Riezler believes that what is usually regarded as the main theme or principal motif may actually be "the melodic 'unfolding' of the notes already heard simultaneously in the form of chords."[9] By extension, the "motif" or thematic "cell" may actually consist of the two "curtain-raising" chords in measures 1 and 2:

It is even possible that here Beethoven consciously attempted to "write without themes," to exploit the energy locked within the basic harmonic unit, the chord. The dissonant C-sharp (or D-flat) in measure 7 acts as a fulcrum compelling a departure from the tonic chord, thus creating a dynamic disequilibrium that provides the driving impetus of the movement, an impetus that continues almost unbroken until the restatement of the tonic chord in the final cadence. The result is music that appears to be self-creating, that must strive for its existence, that pursues a goal with unflagging energy and resoluteness, rather than music whose essence is already largely present in its opening thematic statement.[10]

Overlapping with this process is Beethoven's innovative procedure of developing a movement, and even an entire work, out of a single rhythmic motif. These motifs are so powerfully treated that, as Tovey has suggested, many of Beethoven's works "can be recognized by their bare rhythm without quoting any melody at all."[11] Beethoven's unprecedented harmonic procedures were also decisive in shaping his "grand manner" structures. Unorthodox modulatory techniques, shifts of cadential emphases, and multivalent harmonic meanings (which were often perceived as bizarre and whimsical by his contemporaries) served to create, as Leonard Ratner has observed, a "more powerful harmonic leverage than was customary in the music of Beethoven's predecessors and contemporaries . . . a leverage that creates intense harmonic thrusts and broad trajectories."[12]

Innovative features of the *Eroica* (including some anticipated by Haydn and Mozart) are often cited, such as the use of a new theme in the development section of the first movement, the employment of the winds for expressive rather than coloristic purposes, the introduction of a set of variations in the Finale and of a "Marcia funebre" in the Adagio assai, and the use of three French horns for the first time in symphonic orchestration. More fundamentally, Beethoven's style is now informed with a rhetorical fluidity and structural organicism that gives the symphony its sense of unfolding continuity and wholeness within a constant interplay of moods.

With the "Waldstein" and "Appassionata" Sonatas, opp. 53 and 57, composed mainly in 1804 and 1805, Beethoven moved irrevocably beyond the boundaries of the Classical keyboard style to create sonorities and textures never previously achieved. He no longer reined in the technical difficulties of his sonatas to permit performance by competent amateurs, but instead stretched the potentialities of both instrument and performers to their outer limits. The dynamics are greatly extended; colors are fantastic and luxuriant, approaching quasi-orchestral sonorities. For this reason, the critic Wilhelm von Lenz called the "Waldstein" "a heroic symphony for piano."[13] The "Appassionata"—which along with the Sonata in F-sharp, op. 78, was Beethoven's favorite piano

sonata until his opus 106[14]—has evoked comparison with Dante's
Inferno (Leichtentritt), *King Lear* (Tovey), *Macbeth* (Schering), and
Corneille's tragedies (Rolland). Both the "Waldstein" and the
"Appassionata" are in three movements, but in both cases, especially in
the "Waldstein," the slow movements are organically connected with
the finales so as to give the impression of amplified two-movement
works. Whereas the "Waldstein" closes on Beethoven's typical note of
joyous transcendence, the "Appassionata" maintains an unusual tragic
mood throughout. Tovey wrote, "All his other pathetic finales show
either an epilogue in some legendary or later world far away from the
tragic scene . . . or a temper, fighting, humorous, or resigned, that does
not carry with it a sense of tragic doom." Here, however, "there is not a
moment's doubt that the tragic passion is rushing deathwards."[15]

For almost a quarter of a century, beginning in 1803, Beethoven read
countless librettos and considered numerous literary texts in an endless
search for a suitable opera subject.[16] *Vestas Feuer, Macbeth, Melusina, The
Return of Ulysses, The Ruins of Babylon, Bacchus, Drahomira, Romulus and
Remus*—these were only a few of those that interested him seriously but
not sufficiently. He found fault with Mozart's librettos (*Don Giovanni*
being too "scandalous" a subject)[17] and gave high marks only to the
moralistic texts of Cherubini's *Les deux journées* and Spontini's *La
Vestale*. It cannot have been the literary quality of the libretto of *Fidelio*,
the only opera Beethoven ever completed, that attracted him, for it is an
artless text, stagnant in its action, cumbersome in its dramatic development, and awkward in its blending of styles. Clearly, the subject matter
had some special appeal for him.

 Fidelio, whose characters include an imprisoned noble, a faithful
wife, a tyrant-usurper, and a savior-prince, was an ideal vehicle for the
expression of Beethoven's Enlightenment beliefs. The opera's themes
of brotherhood, conjugal devotion, and triumph over injustice are basic
to his ideology, but they do not signal his devotion to a Jacobin outlook.
On the contrary, the 1798 French libretto by Bouilly that was adapted
for Beethoven's use was based on an episode that occurred under the
Terror and can be seen as a critique of the Jacobin persecutions of
the French aristocracy. Perhaps this is why the "rescue opera" or "horror
opera"[18] of which Bouilly's *Léonore* was an example became so
wildly popular in France beginning in the 1790s in works by Nicolas-

Marie Dalayrac, Charles-Simon Catel, Méhul, Henri-Montan Berton, Jean François Le Sueur, and, especially, Cherubini. For the rescue opera appeared to symbolize the reparation for, or even denial of, the persecution or murder of kings and nobles. Audiences may have found cathartic release in the notion that victims of the Terror had been rescued or resurrected, and that in any event all evildoing was attributable to the reprehensible machinations of a villainous and atypical tyrant. Moreover, violent death and arbitrary injustice had become commonplaces of life during the years of revolution and war, yet these terrors were assuaged by the happy endings typical of operas of this genre.

In the rescue opera, and in another rescue form, the Gothic novel of Mrs. Radcliffe and M. G. Lewis, which suddenly gained widespread popularity in the 1790s, there are powerful echoes of the dramas of the German Sturm und Drang, and especially of Schiller's works, which were at that time banned in imperial Vienna. Through the rescue opera Beethoven could now deal with a theme that expressed the ideology he shared with his adored Schiller and that at the same time touched on unresolved areas of his own psychological experience.

With Schikaneder's successful production of Cherubini's *Lodoïska* at the Theater-an-der-Wien in March 1802, the rescue opera reached and conquered Vienna, including Beethoven, who recognized Cherubini as a master composer and who quickly acquired, in Thayer's words, an "ambition to rival Cherubini in his own field."[19] Not only mere rivalry, however, drew Beethoven to the rescue theme. *Fidelio* is a seething compound of contradictory and ambivalent psychological themes and fantasies, lightly disguised by an ethical content and a *Singspiel* surface. It opens in a Mozartian Eden, a sunlit Arcadia in which a good father, Rocco, seeks to bring about the marriage of his daughter, Marcelline, to the young man she loves, Fidelio.

But things are not what they seem. The Edenic surface gives way to a darker substratum: the good father, Rocco, is also a jailor; Fidelio is Leonore in disguise seeking her husband, Florestan, who lies imprisoned by Pizarro for an unspecified "crime" in a dungeon beneath the ground they walk upon. Thus light masks darkness. Marcelline's innocent love unconsciously conceals a forbidden attraction. Rocco, although protesting, agrees to help Pizarro to murder Florestan, hoping thus to obtain the tyrant's approval of Marcelline's marriage. And Leonore's conjugal fidelity leads her to two betrayals: of Marcelline, to whom she falsely pledges her love, and of Florestan, whose wife now embraces another. Rocco and Leonore descend into the tomb to prepare Florestan's grave; in a sense, Leonore is cooperating in the murder of her husband. The rescue fantasy is a version of those ancient myths in which parents and their offspring frequently engage in preemptive or retaliatory homicidal strikes against one another. The impulses behind myths of killing and saving are difficult to differentiate, but in the rescue fantasy the murder is averted by a deus ex machina, here the minister of state, Don Fernando. Florestan's place in the dungeon is then taken by the evil "father," Pizarro, and all the prisoners ascend into the light of freedom while Leonore resumes her sexual identity and receives the plaudits of the multitude for her heroism and fidelity.

Freud believed that a child may conceive a wish to repay his parents for the gift of life, and often he "weaves a phantasy of saving his father's life on some dangerous occasion, by which he becomes quits with him."[20] For Beethoven during the 1780s, father rescue had been a real rather than a fantasy issue: desperately he had tried to safeguard his father, even as he tried to protect the family as a whole from him, until finally his own needs for fulfillment gained ascendancy. As a matter of fact, in later years Beethoven would often seem to be driven by a desire to rescue: he attempted to "save" both of his brothers from their wives and to "save" his nephew from imagined maternal dangers; he even, as Grillparzer observed,[21] interceded with the police on one occasion to save a drunken peasant, Flohberger, from the law. (Was he once again standing between his father and the night watch in Bonn?)

It is also worth noting Beethoven's attraction to *Fidelio*'s theme of gender masquerade. He was drawn to this subject in two other stage works: *Leonore Prohaska*, WoO 96, where the young heroine, disguised as a soldier, fights in a war of liberation; and his Incidental Music to Goethe's *Egmont*, op. 84, where Klärchen wishes that she might dress herself in soldier's uniform and boldly march to join her beloved: "What a joy it would be to be changed into a man!" she sings. In such works, feelings of feminine identification could be freely expressed, while the nobility of these heroines' actions assuaged whatever anxiety might otherwise attach to such feelings. But Beethoven's sympathy for other figures in the opera may well be equally operative: Tyson argues the possibility of the composer's powerful identification with Florestan, imprisoned in the soundless recesses of his cell in the same way that Beethoven was increasingly locked within the prison of his deafness.[22]

A psychoanalyst would not fail to note that the descent into the bowels of the prison, where Florestan lies in a dark cistern—"a ruined well"—carries resonances of birth and rebirth. Viewed on this level, Leonore/Fidelio has gone in search of her/his own mysterious origins, and the freeing of Florestan and his fellow prisoners becomes not only a liberation of the father/husband and brothers but a cleansing repetition of the birth process, a reaching of the ultimate creative mystery. From another standpoint an exponent of myth-criticism would view *Fidelio* as an opera about resurrection as well as rescue. Florestan is not only imprisoned but entombed; Leonore and Rocco descend not to dig his grave but to exhume him from his sepulcher. The winter god (Pizarro) is slain, replacing Florestan in the tomb, and mankind celebrates the arrival of the New Year with hymns to marriage.

Beethoven wrote four separate overtures to his opera. The *Leonore* Overture No. 2 was written for the November 1805 Vienna premiere and was revised into what we know as *Leonore* No. 3 for the revival in May 1806. In preparation for a Prague performance in 1807 that never materialized, Beethoven composed the shorter overture now known, inaptly, as *Leonore* No. 1, op. 138.[23] Where his only previous overture, *Prometheus*, had been composed wholly in the Viennese style, the *Leonore* Overtures continue the amalgamation of Viennese and French influences that is characteristic of Beethoven's heroic style. (In a sense this synthesis is more successful in the overtures than in the opera itself, in which *Singspiel* and *Rettungsoper* characteristics are combined but not wholly integrated.) Beethoven's problem with these overtures was that he summarized and anticipated in them the dramatic action—especially that of the last act—to such an extent that the listener is unprepared for the idyllic character of the first scenes. (Tovey says of *Leonore* No. 3 that it "annihilates the first act.")[24] In 1814, Beethoven abandoned any further attempts at reworking these materials in favor of a festive curtain-raiser, the *Fidelio* Overture.

Beethoven's preoccupation with *Fidelio* from late 1804 until the spring of 1806 had dammed up work on other projects. A month after the last performance of the second version of *Fidelio*, he turned to the composition of three string quartets, later known as the "Razumovsky" Quartets, after their dedicatee, Count Andreas Razumovsky. They are in the keys of F, E minor, and C. They were completed toward the end of 1806 and were published in January 1808 as opus 59.

There is one sense in which the "Razumovsky" Quartets represent a continuation of the heroic impulse: in them Beethoven applied the principles of composition elaborated in the *Eroica* Symphony to another genre, and expanded the quartet form beyond its traditional eighteenth-century boundaries to a point where one may legitimately speak of these quartets as "symphonic quartets." But in another sense these works represent a withdrawal from the heroic impulse, with its insistence upon strength and virtue, its "public" style and affirmative outlook. If the symphonies of 1804 to 1812 are, in Bekker's phrase, "speeches to the nation, to humanity,"[25] then these quartets are interior monologues addressed to a private self whose emotional states comprise a variegated tapestry of probing moods and sensations. It was on a leaf of sketches for these works that Beethoven wrote a phrase already cited in another context: "Let your deafness no longer be a secret—even in art."[26] Here, in these quartets, he will reveal his most inner feelings and strivings.

Although they were conceived of and published as a set, the "Razumovsky" Quartets resemble one another far less than do the six quartets of opus 18, or even the five last-period quartets. They constitute, Kerman writes, "a trio of sharply characterized, consciously differentiated individuals."[27] One unifying element is the use of Russian themes in the finale of no. 1 and in the trio of the scherzo of no. 2, along with the inclusion of a slow movement, Andante con moto quasi Allegretto, in Russian style in no. 3. Some analysts have regarded the quartets as a cycle, seeing the finale of no. 3 (a synthesis of fugue and sonata form) as the climactic counterpart of the opening Allegro of no. 1, and others have stressed the three works' common preoccupation with triumphal finales. Perhaps, however, we can find the unity of the "Razumovskys" in their very diversity of mood and structure as well as in Beethoven's experimentation with many new, and even bizarre, effects and procedures. Among these are the startling use of pizzicato for expressive purposes in the slow movements of nos. 1 and 3; the brilliant string writing and voicing, which refashions the characteristic

Classical style; the rich harmonic patterns and the extraordinary rhythmic drive; and the creation of "flowing and continuous melodies that are capable of being divided at a later stage into smaller, separable units" (Radcliffe),[28] which marks a break with the epigrammatic symphonic style and foreshadows an aspect of Beethoven's (and then Brahms's) later melodic practice. If there are excesses and wayward moments, they are the excesses of sudden discovery and the waywardness of the explorer's vision upon reaching a prospect that stretches in every conceivable direction. Where Beethoven's creative laboratory had at first been the piano and then the symphony orchestra, the focus of his experimental efforts was now transferred to the string quartet. In his enthusiasm for the potentialities of this genre, Beethoven wrote to Breitkopf & Härtel that "I am thinking of devoting myself almost entirely to this type of composition,"[29] a wish that he actually realized twenty years later. But in 1806 Beethoven had not gained the financial independence that would permit him to disregard what he once disdainfully called "the economics of music."[30] Furthermore, the fact is that the "Razumovsky" Quartets did not please everyone; they were found difficult to understand by those who resisted the further evolution of the Classical style. Thayer writes, "Perhaps no work of Beethoven's met a more discouraging reception" from musicians and connoisseurs.[31] But the *Allgemeine musikalische Zeitung* reported in May 1807, "In Vienna Beethoven's most recent, difficult but fine quartets have become more and more popular."[32]

At the same time that the quartets were being composed, Beethoven was also writing his Fourth Concerto for Piano and Orchestra in G, op. 58 (completed in the summer of 1806); the Fourth Symphony in B-flat, op. 60 (completed at Lichnowsky's estate in Silesia in the fall); the Thirty-two Variations for Piano in C minor, WoO 80 (written in the fall); and the Violin Concerto in D, op. 61 (written shortly before its first performance by Franz Clement in December). If Beethoven's "grand manner" symphonic style had partly shaped the Piano Sonatas, opp. 53 and 57, and the "Razumovsky" Quartets, his latest orchestral works, with their temporary retreat from exalted rhetoric into a more lyrical, contemplative, and serene style, appear to have taken on certain qualities of a magnified chamber music. What Bekker wrote of the Fourth Piano Concerto holds in some measure for the Violin Concerto and the Fourth Symphony as well, that they are "characterized by quiet, reflective gravity, by a latent energy, capable from time to time of expressing intense vitality, but usually preserving the mood of tranquility."[33]

As has often been observed, each of Beethoven's works from ca. 1802 onward has a strikingly individual character. Although his predecessors may not have stamped sets of their works from a single die, they often, to borrow an image from Rolland, tended to bake many cakes from the same batch of dough. With Beethoven, there is an apparent refusal (or inhibition) to return to a problem that he considered to be successfully solved. Rather, there is a sense of striving for diverse solutions to each problem. Thus, for example, the Fourth Piano Concerto opens with a sonorous statement of the theme in the solo instrument followed by the *tutti*, whereas in the Violin Concerto the entry of the soloist is deferred for as long as possible, the violin's statement of the *cantabile* first theme is withheld even longer, and it is not permitted to play the full second theme, a lyric theme designed for G-string performance, until the coda. In the one, the *tutti* rises from the solo; in the other the solo emerges from the orchestral fabric and establishes its presence only after an extended process of differentiation. The slow movements are both conceived as dialogues, but the one in the Piano Concerto is a recitative dialogue of disputants, whereas in the Violin Concerto we have a lyrical exchange between agreeable conversationalists. The ebullient Rondo-finales are equally differentiated: Beethoven finds a pastoral solution in the finale of the Violin Concerto, but gives a more urgent, "military" character to that of the Piano Concerto, with its snare-drum rhythms and "bayonet motif" opening theme.

The set of Piano Variations in C minor on an Original Theme, WoO 80, was seriously underrated by Beethoven, who assigned to it no opus number and scoffed at himself ("Oh Beethoven, what an ass you were!") for having composed it.[34] It probably was written in response to the continuing demand for such works by his publishers: like his earlier variations, it was almost immediately printed, appearing in March 1807. But this dynamic and economical work, based on a Baroque theme type and written in Beethoven's heroic/"pathétique" key, has significant structural features, including the use of passacaglia form in a set of variations and the grouping of the variations into larger sections, foreshadowing the "Diabelli" Variations. Rounding out the year is one lied, "Als die Geliebte sich trennen wollte, oder Empfindungen bei Lydiens Untreue" ("When the Beloved Wishes to Part; or, Feelings about Lydia's Unfaithfulness"), WoO 132, which Harry Goldschmidt connects, reasonably enough, with Josephine Deym's withdrawal from Beethoven and her liaison with Count Wolkenstein.

Through some obscure dialectic of Beethoven's creative process, it was characteristic of his heroic impulse that it went into a shorter or longer state of quiescence following each of its major manifestations. It emerged with renewed energy in 1807, with the Overture to Heinrich von Collin's *Coriolan*, op. 62, the *Leonore* Overture No. 1, the Mass in C, op. 86, and the Symphony No. 5 in C minor, op. 67.

Beethoven needed a new overture to open concert programs, to augment his well-worn *Prometheus*. And he evidently wished to demonstrate anew his flair for the theatrical to the princely directors of the Imperial Royal Court Theater, to whom he had made application for a permanent position. The dramatic *Coriolan* Overture, influenced by but far transcending Cherubini's grandiloquent overture style, was the result. It was performed in March 1807 at the Lobkowitz Palace, along with the premiere performances of the Fourth Symphony and the Fourth Piano Concerto. The closing, disintegrating passage, reminiscent of the end of the *Eroica* Funeral March, again symbolizes the death of the hero. Unlike Plutarch's or Shakespeare's hero, Collin's Coriolan chooses death—an action that had more than ordinary resonance to Beethoven in view of his suicidal thoughts. Like the Sonata in F minor, op. 57, *Coriolan* demonstrates that Beethoven did not always insist on joyful conclusions, but was able to locate transcendence in the acceptance of death itself.

Beethoven was less successful with the affirmative stance of his first religious work in a traditional liturgical style, the Mass in C, op. 86. The Mass was begun early in the year and completed at Baden and Heiligenstadt during the summer so that it could be performed at the name day celebration for Princess Maria von Liechtenstein Esterházy on September 13, at Eisenstadt, under Beethoven's direction. It remains an open question whether it was favorably or badly received by its

intended patron; certainly, it was not singled out for special commenda-
tion when sections of it were performed at Beethoven's December 22,
1808, academy. It was published only in October 1812, after much urging by the composer and much hesitation by Breitkopf & Härtel. In this
work, Beethoven relies heavily on his symphonic instincts and on the
precepts of Haydn to carry him through an unfamiliar form.

Beethoven now took up the Symphony No. 5 in C minor, for which
he had jotted down some fragmentary ideas as early as 1804 and which
was fully sketched in the winter of 1806–7 or somewhat later. The
Symphony was written out in the latter half of 1807 and during the first
months of 1808 and was completed by the spring of that year, receiving
its first performance at Beethoven's academy on December 22. The
Fifth Symphony, because of its concentrated energy, its heroic stance,
and, especially, the triumphal—even military—character of all of its
movements save the scherzo, may have carried overtones of patriotic
sentiment to Beethoven's contemporaries: it was completed precisely
during the period that saw an upsurge of German nationalist feeling,
stimulated by the Treaty of Tilsit of July 7–9, 1807, which signaled the
collapse of Prussia and the cession to France of all lands between the
Rhine and the Elbe. The historian Roy Pascal noted that "the philosopher Fichte, the theologian Schleiermacher, poets and writers of all
types, Kleist, Arndt, Görres, called on the Germans not to despair, to
recall their great past, to hate the oppressor, to prepare for liberation."[35]
Beethoven and many of his friends and associates in Vienna echoed and
contributed to this new patriotism. Both Prince Lobkowitz and Count
Razumovsky, to whom the Symphony was jointly dedicated, were
ardent and active enemies of France. Beethoven's own patriotic and
anti-French sentiments reached their height at this time. On April 26,
1807, he wrote to musician and publisher Camille Pleyel: "My dear
Camillus—If I am not mistaken, that was the name of the Roman who
drove the wicked Gauls out of Rome. At that rate I too would like to
bear that name, provided I could drive them away from where they have
no right to be—."[36] Not long thereafter, Beethoven began to sketch two
patriotic songs, "Oesterreich über Alles" and "Jubelgesang auf die
Schlacht" ("Hymn to Battle"), the former to a text by Collin.[37] He did
not complete either song.

Beethoven himself, however, left no programmatic references that would link his Fifth Symphony to contemporary events. Indeed, his only such reported comment indicates that he may have connected the work with antique tragedy. Schindler claimed that in his presence Beethoven explained the opening bars of the first movement with the words "Thus Fate knocks at the door!"[38] The twentieth-century theorist Heinrich Schenker was not impressed by the story; he pointed to the same motif in the G-major Piano Concerto and asked, "Was this another door on which Fate knocked or was someone else knocking at the same door?"[39] Of course this, too, may be wide of the mark, for though the four-note motif became one of Beethoven's "musical fingerprints" for a decade or more, it is never used twice for the same purpose and never in rhetorical contexts remotely similar to those employed in the Fifth Symphony.

After some initial resistance to its unheralded rhythmic concentration, economy of thematic material, and startling innovations—the unexpected oboe cadenza in the first movement, the addition of piccolo and double bassoon to the winds, the "spectral" effects of the double basses in the scherzo and trio, the trombones in the finale, the return of material from the scherzo in the finale—the Fifth Symphony came to be regarded as the quintessential Beethoven symphony, revealing new layers of meaning to each successive generation. Resistance to the symphony has stemmed from its monumental exterior (Goethe said, "It is merely astonishing and grandiose")[40] and from the C-major "yea-saying" of the finale. Spohr found the last movement to be "unmeaning babel," and Berlioz acutely noted that the effect of the transition from the scherzo to the Allegro finale is so stunning that it would be impossible to surpass it in what follows. "To *sustain* such a height of effect is, in fact, already a prodigious effort."[41] In a famous review published in 1810, E. T. A. Hoffmann simultaneously claimed the Fifth Symphony for romanticism and saw in it the consummate hallmarks of an achieved classicism. But twentieth-century criticism has tended to see the Fifth as what Lang called "the consummate example of symphonic logic,"[42] as the ultimate expression of Classic rationality refusing to yield to the violent tremors of impending romanticism. Audiences have learned to identify the work with public virtues (the opening motif was a symbol of resistance to fascism during World War II), perhaps as a means of allaying the untranslatable and inexpressible terrors that this symphony arouses in every listener, despite Beethoven's cathartic C-major effects. Both Hoffmann and Goethe already sensed these terrors.

The Sixth Symphony in F (*Pastoral*), op. 68, followed soon, for Beethoven had been working almost simultaneously on these widely disparate symphonies. Despite the sketching of one of its themes (the 2/4 theme for the trio of the third movement) in 1803, and a few concept jottings in 1807, it was composed almost wholly in 1808, and was completed by late summer in that year.[43] Like the Fifth Symphony, it was jointly dedicated to Lobkowitz and Razumovsky.

With the *Pastoral* Symphony, the working out of Beethoven's post-Heiligenstadt projects seemed to be coming to a close. It was especially fitting that this cycle should terminate in idyllic repose, with an Arcadian conclusion to the heroic quest of the preceding half decade. Beethoven's struggles with fate—which is to say, with every embodiment of authority, domination, and mortality—were not yet at an end, but were temporarily set aside while he rejoiced in a richly deserved return to nature and to childhood, which symbolize, perhaps, the twin realms of the bountiful mother. The return to nature is on the surface of this "characteristic" or genre symphony, which Beethoven variously entitled "Sinfonia pastorella" and "Sinfonia caracteristica." On a violin part prepared according to Beethoven's instructions is written *Sinfonia Pastorella. Pastoral-Sinfonie, oder Erinnerung an das Landleben* (*Pastoral Symphony, or Recollections of Country Life*). The printed score carries the following headings to its movements: "Pleasant, cheerful feelings aroused on approaching the countryside"; "Scene by the brook"; "Jolly gathering of villagers"; "Thunderstorm"; and "Shepherd's song. Grateful thanks to the Almighty after the storm." A nostalgic connection to Bonn is suggested by the fact that Beethoven adapted these movement titles from *Le Portrait musical de la nature* (*The Musical Portrait of Nature*), a symphony by an eighteenth-century Swabian composer, Justin Heinrich Knecht, which was described in the publisher Bossler's advertisement on the back cover of Beethoven's three "Electoral" Sonatas, WoO 47, of circa 1782–83.[44]

This innocent work is exceptional in Beethoven's output, although pastoral moments are frequent in several of his piano sonatas, in his *Prometheus,* in his Variations on a Swiss Air, WoO 64, in the Violin Sonata in G, op. 96, in the Eighth Symphony, and in several of his last works, including the second finale to the String Quartet in B-flat, op. 130. As many have observed, in the *Pastoral* Symphony Beethoven was not only anticipating Romantic program music but was looking back to a long-standing pastoral tradition in the Baroque and Classic periods, as manifested in many works by Bach, Handel, Vivaldi, Mozart, and most famously in Haydn's two oratorios.[45] Beethoven transmuted the pastoral style into a symphonic essence. Although Riezler writes that "it is remarkable how consistently Beethoven avoids all possibility of 'conflict' in the Symphony,"[46] conflict is not really absent. In the fourth movement, "Fate" intrudes as the thunderous voice of the God of wrath, but withdraws without a serious struggle, leaving his children their moment of innocent rejoicing, for which he earns Beethoven's heartfelt gratitude. On a leaf of sketches for the last movement are the words: "Herr, wir danken dir."[47]

With the completion of the *Pastoral* Symphony, Beethoven turned for the remainder of 1808 and 1809 mainly to chamber music and to the sonata, with two major exceptions. The first was the Fantasia for Piano, Chorus, and Orchestra in C minor ("Choral Fantasia"), op. 80, of late 1808. It consists of a fantasy for piano (improvised by Beethoven at the first performance) followed by a set of free variations on a theme, that of the "Gegenliebe" ("Requited Love"), WoO 118, which Beethoven had composed in 1794 or 1795 but never published and which significantly forecasts the melodic shape and harmony of the first phrase of the "Ode to Joy" theme. The alternation of instrumental and choral variations also confirms the impression that Beethoven was groping here toward issues that would occupy him in his last symphony. Stylistically, however, there is nothing advanced or even contemporary in opus 80. The British critic Edward. J. Dent argued that the text expressed "the mystical spirit of eighteenth-century Freemasonry, the new religion of liberty, equality and fraternity."[48] Along somewhat different lines, Stephen Moore Whiting describes the implied protagonist of the work as the

"Artist-Soloist," and hears the work as "a rallying cry and an instruction of the community through the visionary artist."[49] On a simpler level, as Tovey observed, the "Choral Fantasia" is a latter-day ode to Saint Cecilia, in praise of music:[50]

> When music's enchantment reigns
> And the poet's words take flight
> Then marvellous forms arise
> And night and storm turn to light.

The Piano Concerto No. 5 in E-flat, op. 73 (infelicitously dubbed "Emperor" later in the century by the French and English) belongs to the invasion year, 1809, although it may have been begun in the closing days of the previous year. Along with a March in F for Military Band, WoO 18, it may well embody Beethoven's response to the tide of Napoleonic conquest; the bitter remark "Austria rewards Napoleon" ("Östreich löhne Napoleon") is written on page one of the Adagio un poco moto. (Of course, its grandeur and its unparalleled solutions of strictly musical problems far transcend such considerations.) Einstein called this concerto, with its warlike rhythms, victory motifs, thrusting melodies, and affirmative character, the "apotheosis of the military concept" in Beethoven's music.[51] It is a far cry from the military style of Mozart's piano concertos, with their elegance and aestheticism, their mock belligerence, their playful combat, their conversion of the martial into a form of theater, replete with dancing, costumed troops. At its first confirmed public performance, in Leipzig in 1810, the majestic Concerto No. 5 was greeted with ovations. It was published in February 1811 with a dedication to Archduke Rudolph, the son of Emperor Leopold II and Beethoven's composition student since 1809.

The leading tendency of Beethoven's work from late 1808 through 1809, however, was represented by the Piano Trios in D and E-flat, op. 70; the String Quartet in E-flat, op. 74; the three Piano Sonatas in F-sharp, G, and E-flat, opp. 78, 79, and 81a; and the Cello Sonata in A, op. 69, the last of which had been started a bit earlier and was completed by mid-1808. For the first time in almost a decade, Beethoven had no major symphonic projects in progress or in the sketching stage. He considered numerous librettos for an opera during this period, but he rejected all—it is doubtful that he was willing fully to commit to another opera after the travail of *Fidelio*. Beethoven's productivity slackened in 1810 and 1811, the only significant works completed being the String Quartet in F minor, op. 95; the Trio in B-flat ("Archduke"), op. 97; and the Incidental Music to Goethe's *Egmont*, op. 84. The latter was Beethoven's only serious nonchamber music composition of these years. It was not until the later months of 1811, when he began to sketch two new symphonies, that his preoccupation with chamber music moderated for a time.

Beethoven was no longer at pains to apply symphonic ideas to the genres of chamber music, nor was he seeking to create heaven-storming compositions. In a deepening of the trend that began in 1806 with the Fourth Symphony, the Fourth Piano Concerto, and the Violin Concerto, he now seemed to imbue many of his works with a sense of inner repose that did not require turbulent responses to grand challenges. A new, lyrical strain enters his music, along with a pre-Romantic freedom of harmonic motion and of structural design that appears to take up where the fantasy sonatas had left off in 1802.

On the dedication copy of the broad and melodious Sonata in A for Cello and Piano, op. 69, Beethoven wrote "Inter lacrymas et luctus" ("amid tears and sorrow"), which may be a reference to his emotional state, for it may not be altogether appropriate as a description of a work of such quiet solemnity and moderation of emotional expression. Lewis Lockwood observes that it is one of the central works in the cello and piano literature, and he writes that "the solutions found in op. 69 for the problems of range, relative sonority, and matching of importance of the two instruments . . . emerge as an achievement equal to that inherent in the originality and quality of its purely musical ideas."[52]

The Cello Sonata may have been written for his friend Baron Ignaz von Gleichenstein; Beethoven dedicated it to him in April 1809, probably out of gratitude for Gleichenstein's role in negotiating his annuity agreement. In June and August, Beethoven dedicated the Trios, op. 70, to Countess Erdödy, who had been equally helpful in the negotiations. The two works were first performed at two concerts in her home in December 1808, with Beethoven at the piano. The trios were Beethoven's first serious works in this form since his opus 1 of 1795. The first Trio, in D major ("Ghost"), is best known for its powerful

Largo assai e espressivo, whose atmospheric tremolo effects and dynamic contrasts gave rise to the work's nickname. Structurally it is a daring, experimental composition, not only because it is in three rather than the customary four movements, but because the Largo is the work's focus and center of gravity, suggesting that where in other recent works Beethoven had been seeking to condense his slow movements so that they might serve as transitions to a culminating finale, he was here aspiring to something like the centrality that Mozart achieved in the Andantes and Adagio of certain of his piano sonatas and concertos. Accordingly, the first movement functions as an abbreviated overture to the Largo, alternating sonorous and melodious moments with brusque passages in the "learned" style, as though casting about for a direction, and leaving the outcome in suspense. With its rapid contrasts, juxtapositions of style and mood, and "Overtura" character, this movement, marked Allegro vivace e con brio, puts one in mind of the opening of the Grosse Fuge, op. 133, which Beethoven marked "tantôt libre, tantôt recherchée" ("sometimes free, sometimes studied") on its title page. The Presto finale emerges from the spectral Largo (which is almost as long as the two other movements together) in a sweeping ascent from the depths of inwardness, serving to relieve the accumulated tension.

The second trio, in E-flat, one of the masterpieces of the middle period, is so delicately balanced between the traditional Viennese style and Beethoven's own most mature style that a performance given from either of these vantage points can cast a radically different light on the work. In an illuminating passage, Tovey observed that in works such as this trio Beethoven had at last achieved an "integration of Mozart's and Haydn's resources, with results that transcend all possibility of resemblance to the style of their origins."[53] The closing Allegro exemplifies an important tendency: Beethoven's extreme simplification of the exposition, so that its harmonic and thematic implications are not really elaborated until the recapitulation. (Again, though in a different context, the Overtura to the Grosse Fuge comes to mind, for it too will abruptly disclose several themes in rapid succession and will postpone establishing interconnections between them until later in the movement.)

Beethoven's last trio, generally regarded as his masterpiece in this form, was the Trio in B-flat for Piano, Violin, and Cello, op. 97, called "Archduke" because of its dedication to Archduke Rudolph. It is an expansive work both in size (four movements totaling 1,200 measures) and in sonority. Whereas in his heroic symphonies Beethoven had generated the architecture of his compositions from the release and control of energy stored within condensed, explosive germinal motifs and rhythms, he generated the architectural monumentality of the "Archduke" Trio from the development of broad, moderately paced, and flowing melodies. This practice creates a sense of calm, spaciousness, and measured nobility of rhetoric, which we have already encountered in the Cello Sonata, op. 69, the Violin Concerto, and the Fourth and Fifth Piano Concertos. Audacious touches in the Scherzo and moments of brusque wit in the finale contrast effectively with the spaciously lyrical and sublime quality of the opening Allegro moderato. The "Archduke" represents Beethoven's summation of the impulses toward a new type of classicism that characterized his chamber music with piano between mid-1808 and 1811.

In late 1809 Beethoven returned to the piano sonata after an absence of four years and wrote three sonatas in a short space of time. In none of them is there the slightest indication that their immediate predecessors in this genre had been such works as the "Waldstein" and "Appassionata" Sonatas: rather, visible in them is an extension of tendencies in pre-*Eroica* sonatas such as opus 28 and opus 31, no. 1, as well as glimpses of Beethoven's last-period style. The two-movement Sonata in F-sharp, op. 78, dedicated to Therese Brunsvik, was a special favorite of Beethoven's, perhaps because of its serenity, economy of form, and songful expressiveness. The "Sonate facile ou sonatine," op. 79, which bore no dedication upon its publication in November 1810, may have originated as a gift to Therese Malfatti. It has pastoral moments, one authority hearing in it reminiscences of Beethoven's bucolic *Ritterballett* of 1790–91. The beautiful Piano Sonata in E-flat ("Lebewohl" or "Farewell"), op. 81a, was composed for Archduke Rudolph following his departure from Vienna during the French bombardment of 1809, and its expressive movement titles "Lebewohl," "Abwesenheit," and "Das Wiedersehn"—"Farewell," "Absence," "The Return"—may tell us something about the depth of Beethoven's feeling for his young student, even as they suggest that the composer had become interested in the ways in which musical form could mimic narrative patterns—in this case, a circular or parabolic movement emblematic of a leave-taking, a journey, and a return to a transfigured point of departure. The sonata's second movement, Andante espressivo, with its touching chromaticisms, serves as an eloquent introduction to the finale, Vivacissimamente. On the sketches Beethoven wrote, "The Farewell—on May 4th—dedicated to, and written from the heart for, H[is] I[mperial] H[ighness]."[54] A decade later, on the autograph score of the *Missa Solemnis*, Beethoven wrote a similar dedicatory message to Rudolph, for whom the Mass was composed: "From the heart—may it go to the heart!"[55]

On June 2, 1805, Beethoven had written, despairingly, "God knows why my piano music still makes the poorest impression on me."[56] Now, however, with these piano sonatas, the Cello Sonata, op. 69, and the Trios, op. 70, as well as the "Choral Fantasia" and the Piano Concertos, opp. 58 and 73, Beethoven was once again using the piano as his main creative vehicle. Perhaps this is why a feeling of "homecoming" and repose seems to pervade so many of these works. But the questing side of Beethoven's nature, the sense of discontinuity and disequilibrium, of striving and restlessness, would also have to find expression. It did so in the second of the string quartets that he composed in 1809–10. The first, in E-flat, op. 74, called "Harp" because of the striking pizzicato arpeggios in the opening Allegro, is a lyrical, contemplative, and expressive work that, despite its unusual and climactic scherzo, retreats from the innovative thrust of the "Razumovsky" Quartets and returns to the central vocabulary of the Viennese Classical style. Here, as in most of the other chamber and sonata works of this period, one senses that Beethoven was attempting to reestablish contact with styles from which he had largely held himself aloof after 1802. Kerman writes that whereas opus 74 is "an open, unproblematic, lucid work of consolidation," the Quartet in F minor, op. 95, written in the summer of 1810 and withheld from publication for six years, is "an involved, impassioned, highly idiosyncratic piece, problematic in every one of its movements, advanced in a hundred ways."[57] Titled "Quartetto serioso"—the only time Beethoven used this meaningful designation, by which he classified his quartet in the so-called "learned" style—opus 95 is an experimental work that compresses many complex ideas into a compass smaller than that of opus 74 or any of the opus 59 quartets. Beethoven may have been moving here toward his last-period string quartet style, but, for whatever reasons, he turned away from the genre for more than a dozen years. Perhaps he had yet to formulate ways of combining the probing rhetoric and elliptical condensation of opus 95 with the lyricism and open communicativeness of opus 74, a fusion that would be central to the style of the last quartets. Although opus 74 was dedicated to Prince Lobkowitz, the dedication of opus 95 to Zmeskall is another indication that Beethoven was now frequently using dedications as expressions of affection for and gratitude to his friends rather than to discharge patronage obligations.

Beethoven wrote incidental music to three stage works in 1810 and 1811: Goethe's *Egmont*, op. 84 (composed between October 1809 and June 1810); August von Kotzebue's *Die Ruinen von Athen* (*The Ruins of Athens*), op. 113; and to the same author's *König Stephan*, op. 117. The latter two, containing nineteen separate numbers, were written rapidly in the short space of three weeks at Teplitz in late summer 1811. Opuses 113 and 117 were intended to celebrate the opening of an imperial theater in Pest, a patriotic occasion that called for expressions of flattery and adulation. In *The Ruins of Athens*, Minerva awakens from a two-thousand-year sleep to find Athens occupied, the Parthenon in ruins, and culture and reason banished from the Mediterranean, but, happily, still alive in Pest under the enlightened rule of Emperor Franz. Similarly, *King Stephen*, which is subtitled "Ungarns erster Wohltäter" ("Hungary's First Benefactor"—Stephen is the patron saint of Hungary), is a transparent homage to the Austro-Hungarian kaiser. It contains several women's choruses patently derived from Haydn's *Seasons*. These works have not remained in the repertory, although the potpourri overtures (which were found unworthy by the elitist Philharmonic Society of London when it received them in 1816) are occasionally performed. The "Chorus of the Dervishes" and the "*Marcia alla Turca*" of opus 113 are brilliantly orchestrated and effective popular music in the exotic, "Turkish" style.

Beethoven did not have his heart in these compositions, which clearly were done as hackwork to gratify a royal patron. It was otherwise with the music for *Egmont*, which tells of the eponymous hero, a sixteenth-century Flemish aristocrat, who is arrested and condemned by the Spanish conquerors. Klärchen, a burgher's daughter, failing in her effort to rescue Egmont, poisons herself, and Egmont goes proudly to his death, predicting the insurrection that will free his country from Spanish tyranny. The subject had great resonance for Beethoven as an expression of his faith in the *bon prince* and in the ideals of national liberation and individual freedom—perhaps also because it intersected with his own Flemish ancestry. On the surface, the narrative outcome is quite different from that of *Fidelio*, although retaining its linkage of love and freedom, sacrifice and heroism. Here, however, victory is achieved not through a deus ex machina, but through the sacrifice of the protagonists' lives and the perpetuation of their ideals in the communal entity with which they are identified. The theme of national liberation is neatly congruent with the occupation of Vienna in 1809 by the French. Evidently the directors of Vienna's Imperial and Royal Court Theater, who commissioned the work, had contemporary events in mind, for the other possible assignment was also a story of liberation from foreign occupation: Schiller's *Wilhelm Tell*. Beethoven was inspired by Goethe's play to produce his most dramatic theater music, including several songs with orchestra that left their mark on the young Gustav Mahler. The concentrated overture and closing *Siegessymphonie* (victory symphony) are high points of the heroic style.

That the meanings of music are not translatable into language is a philosopher's truism. Kierkegaard wrote that music "always expresses the immediate in its immediacy" and that it was therefore "impossible to express the musical in language."[58] And Nietzsche, in *The Birth of Tragedy*, noted that "language, the organ and symbol of appearance, can never succeed in bringing the innermost core of music to the surface. Whenever it engages in the imitation of music, language remains in purely superficial contact with it."[59] Such warnings, however, have never stopped commentators (including, I fear, this one) from hazarding unprovable speculations as to the "meaning" of one or another of Beethoven's masterpieces. Nowhere has this tendency been more manifest than in nineteenth-century interpretations of Beethoven's Seventh Symphony. Berlioz heard a "ronde des paysans" in the first movement; Wagner called the symphony the "Apotheosis of the Dance"; Lenz saw it as a second *Pastoral* Symphony, complete with village wedding and peasant dances; Nohl visualized a knight's festival, and Oulibicheff a masquerade or diversion of a multitude drunk with joy and wine. For A. B. Marx it was the wedding or festival celebration of a warrior people.[60] More recently, Bekker called it a "bacchic orgy," and Ernest Newman described it as "the upsurge of a powerful dionysiac impulse, a divine intoxication of the spirit."[61]

Quaint as these various interpretations now seem, it may be worthwhile to seek some underlying common denominator in the opinions of so eminent a group of critics. Clearly, a work that so powerfully symbolizes the act of transcendence, with its attendant joyous and liberating feelings, can be represented in language by an infinity of specific transcendent images—which may tell us as much about the free associations of these authors as about Beethoven and his music. But the apparently diverse free-associational images of these critics—of masses of people, of powerful rhythmic energy discharged in action or in dance, of celebrations, weddings, and revelry—may well be variations on a single image: the carnival or festival, which from time immemorial has temporarily lifted the burden of perpetual subjugation to the prevailing social and natural order by periodically suspending all customary privileges, norms, and imperatives. Such are the festivals of the Greek Cronia, the Roman Kalends and Saturnalia, the French "feast of fools," the English "lords of misrule," the medieval folk carnivals and feasts, the German "Fasching," and all other primitive rituals and ceremonies that annually turned society inside out.[62] In the festival there is a joyous lifting of all restraints, a licensed eruption of the profane and the scatological, and an outpouring of mockery, ridicule, and satire expressing a comic vision of life untinged by tragic modalities.

Perhaps it was a festal quality that the nineteenth-century critics sensed in the Seventh Symphony, one that is present in the Eighth, too, for the latter is an offshoot from the same creative impulse. In Ernest Newman's words, it "takes the overspill of the mighty Seventh," voicing, like its companion, "a mood of joyous acceptance of life and the world."[63] Wagner, too, saw the psychological similarity, and the festal character, of the two symphonies: "Their effect upon the listener is precisely that of emancipation from all guilt, just as the aftereffect is the feeling of Paradise forfeited, with which we return to the phenomenal world."[64]

Both symphonies lack the traditional slow movement—the movement of sorrow and contemplation, of mourning and tragedy—present in all other Beethoven symphonies. Indeed, the Eighth, with its Allegretto scherzando followed by a Tempo di Menuetto, goes further in this respect than the preceding symphony: the Seventh has a long slow introduction to the first movement and a dreamlike Allegretto that at least appears slow by contrast with the Vivace and Presto movements that enclose it. Riezler touched on the kinship between these symphonies when he wrote that their professions of faith were "not called upon to fight and conquer a hostile power."[65] They exist in a festal paradise, outside of time and history, untouched by mortality. They transport us into a sphere of laughter, play, and the exuberant release of bound energy. Here, as Bakhtin writes of the medieval festival, "for a short time life came out of its usual, legalized and consecrated furrows and entered the sphere of utopian freedom."[66]

The Seventh and Eighth Symphonies were sketched successively, starting in the closing months of 1811, and were completed the following year, the Seventh by April and the Eighth by October. The main work on the Eighth was done during Beethoven's Bohemian sojourn in the aftermath of the Immortal Beloved letter. To those Viennese who heard the first performances of the Seventh on the same programs as *Wellingtons Sieg* (*Wellington's Victory*) in 1813 (December 8) and 1814 (January 2 and February 27), the Symphony could be heard as a celebration of the victory over Napoleon and the joyous arrival of a long-awaited peace. The Symphony, and especially its Allegretto, became enormously popular and appeared in numerous transcriptions, including arrangements for winds, septet, string quintet, piano quartet, piano trio, piano four hands, piano, and an abridgement for two pianos, which was arranged by Carl Czerny with the composer's approval and dedicated to the Empress Elisabeth Alexievna of Russia. The A-major Symphony was published in orchestral parts and in score by the Viennese music publisher Sigmund Anton Steiner in November 1816, with a dedication to one of Beethoven's most devoted patrons, the banker Count Moritz Fries, who, according to the violinist Karl Holz, paid Beethoven "a regular subsidy" for some years until his bankruptcy in 1825.[67]

The Eighth Symphony was first performed at Beethoven's academy of February 27, 1814, and was published by Steiner in 1817. Not surprisingly, it was overshadowed by both the Seventh Symphony and by

Wellington's Victory. The critic of the *Wiener Allgemeine musikalische Zeitung* wrote that "the applause which it received was not accompanied by that enthusiasm which distinguishes a work which gives universal delight; in short—as the Italians say—it did not create a furor."[68] According to Czerny, Beethoven was angered at this reception, because he considered the Eighth "much better" than the Seventh.[69]

The Violin Sonata in G, op. 96, the tenth and last of Beethoven's sonatas for piano and violin, was sketched and completed in 1812, following the Seventh and Eighth Symphonies, to which it contrasts as a delicate pen-and-ink drawing to a set of major frescos. It has been argued that the Violin Sonata was probably copied out in about May 1815—and may have been revised before its publication in 1816.[70] Where the piano and violin duo had been a vehicle for the inauguration of Beethoven's "new path" in the stormy "Kreutzer" Sonata of a decade earlier, the G-major Sonata abandons the "*stile brillante molto concertante*" of that sonata in favor of a heartfelt, exquisite communicativeness, capped by a refined pastoral finale in which nostalgia and beauty are the twin images of desire, thus providing a quietly imaginative coda to the middle period.

IV

THE FINAL PHASE

Title page, *Wellingtons Sieg*, op. 91, piano arrangement.

S. A. Steiner & Co., Vienna (1816).

CHAPTER SEVENTEEN

THE DISSOLUTION
OF THE HEROIC STYLE

WHEN BEETHOVEN RETURNED to Teplitz from Franzensbad in mid-September 1812, the sustained tension of the previous weeks had passed, and a feeling of despondency came over him. Perhaps as a result of his malaise, he apparently spent much of the remainder of his vacation in bed. On September 17 he wrote to Gottfried Härtel, "I am writing to you from my bed," adding, "I must tell you frankly that people in Austria no longer trust me completely; and no doubt they are right, too."[1] Most of his eight notes to the singer Amalie Sebald, whom he found in Teplitz upon his return, are apologies for his inability to visit her and contain mild complaints about his physical condition, as though he was hoping to evoke a sympathetic response.[2] "Since yesterday I have not been feeling very well," he wrote, "and this morning my indisposition became more serious"; or, "I really feel a little better, dear A[malie]. If you think it proper to visit me alone, you could indeed give me great pleasure." She visited him once or twice, bringing him consolation and chicken soup—for which he insisted on having a bill. He left his bed to see her on at least one occasion, but, he wrote, "After I left you yesterday my condition again deteriorated." It is possible that Amalie felt something more for Beethoven than the platonic, teasing tone of his letters indicates. In the final letter, Beethoven wrote, "What on earth are you dreaming of when you say that you cannot be anything to me? When we meet again, Dear A, we must discuss this point. It was my constant wish that my presence would fill you with calm and peace." Essentially, however, it was Amalie's undemanding tenderness toward the stricken composer that endeared her to him; Beethoven drew comfort and respite from her presence as a welcome relief from the frenzy and pain of the Immortal Beloved relationship. The correspondence with Amalie ended on this note, never to be resumed.

Beethoven did not go directly from Teplitz to Vienna.[3] Instead he traveled to Linz, where his brother Nikolaus Johann was tending his apothecary and living together with Therese Obermayer, who was, as Thayer decorously wrote, "his housekeeper and—something more."[4] Beethoven insisted that his brother break off this affair. His brother refused, whereupon Beethoven, enraged, visited the bishop and the civil authorities, finally obtaining a police order compelling Therese to leave Linz should the illicit relationship continue. Nikolaus Johann's response was to marry Therese on November 8.

Beethoven had probably known of his brother's liaison with Therese for some time, and it seems significant that it was only in the wake of the Immortal Beloved events that he was suddenly motivated to go to Linz, acting under a compulsion so strong that it led to physical violence against his brother. If the eldest brother was unable to have his own woman, why should this be permitted to the youngest? But the matter may be even more complex. Perhaps Beethoven needed to share in the domestic life of his brother, Therese, and her daughter from an earlier relationship; possibly he needed the comfort that closeness to a family member might bring following the harrowing events of the preceding months. And it isn't precluded that Beethoven unwittingly brought about the marriage as a substitute for another union—one that had not taken place.

According to Thayer, Beethoven left Linz after the marriage and "immediately hastened away to Vienna,"[5] but Beethoven's whereabouts between early November and the end of the year are not firmly established. No correspondence survives for the period from late September at Teplitz until shortly before December 29, 1812, in Vienna; Louis Spohr could not find Beethoven at his lodgings during December.

What of Beethoven's productivity during this period? The Seventh Symphony was completed in April 1812; it was followed by the one-movement Trio in B-flat, WoO 39, composed for Maximiliane Brentano, Antonie Brentano's nine-year-old daughter. The Eighth Symphony was written out during the summer months and essentially completed by late August, as we may glean from a reference in the *Allgemeine musikalische Zeitung* for September 2, which announced that

Beethoven had "composed two new symphonies."[6] The autograph, however, reads "Linz in the month of October." In Linz, by November 2,
Beethoven is also known to have composed Three Equale for Four
Trombones, WoO 30. Upon his return to Vienna, Beethoven wrote his
Violin Sonata in G, op. 96, which was first performed on December 29,
by the French virtuoso Pierre Rode and Archduke Rudolph. Soon
thereafter, Beethoven's creativity came almost to a full stop.

Evidence of emotional stress appears in Beethoven's letters of this
time to Archduke Rudolph. In December 1812 he wrote, "Since
Sunday I have been ailing, although mentally, it is true, more than phys-
ically."[7] In January: "As for my health, it is pretty much the same, the
more so as moral causes are affecting it and these apparently are not
very speedily removed."[8] In a letter to Countess Maria Eleonora Fuchs
written just after January 6, 1813, he referred to his "thoroughly lacerat-
ed heart," and on May 27, 1813, he wrote to Rudolph, "A number of
unfortunate incidents occurring one after the other have really driven
me into a state bordering on mental confusion."[9] The severe illness of
his brother Caspar Carl during the late winter caused Beethoven great
concern: Caspar Carl appeared to be in the last stages of consumption,
the disease from which their mother had died. His symptoms soon
remitted, but not before Beethoven had persuaded him to issue a legal
declaration that after his death he desired his brother Ludwig to undertake the guardianship of his son, Karl, a declaration that was to have
fateful consequences a few years later.

During this critical period, Beethoven's feelings of impotence and
despair had brought him to the very edge of an emotional breakdown,
reviving suicidal impulses.[10] In his Tagebuch for early 1814, he wrote,
"For example, the diagnosis of the doctors about my life—If recovery is
no longer possible, then I must use—???"[11] Suicidal thoughts were not
uncommon to Beethoven; he expressed them in the Heiligenstadt
Testament ("I was on the point of putting an end to my life"), and in
letters to Zmeskall ("I often despair and would like to die") and
Wegeler ("I would have left this earth long ago—and, what is more, by
my own hand"), among others.[12] On occasion, he used the threat of suicide as a means of compelling obedience from members of his family or
concern from his friends. It was quite another matter, however, to write
of suicide in his private ruminations.

It was at about this time that the first in a series of lightly disguised references to prostitutes surfaced in Beethoven's correspondence with Zmeskall. Apparently, their code word for prostitutes was *Festungen* (fortresses). On February 28, 1813, Beethoven wrote: "Be zealous in defending the fortresses of the empire, which, as you know, lost their virginity a long time ago and have already received several assaults."[13] Similarly, he wrote on other occasions, "Enjoy life, but not voluptuously— Proprietor, Governor, Pasha of various rotten fortresses!!!!!"; "I need not warn you any more to take care not to be wounded near certain fortresses"; "Keep away from rotten fortresses, for an attack from them is more deadly than one from well-preserved ones."[14] Evidently Zmeskall had frequent recourse to prostitutes, and it appears likely that he was now providing them to Beethoven as well. This seems to be the meaning of several ambiguous lines in other letters to Zmeskall, such as "I thank you most heartily, my dear Z, for the information you have given me concerning the fortresses, for I thought you had the idea from me that I did not wish to stop in swampy places"; "*Yes!* and include me too, even if it's at night"; and, most transparently, "I have seen nothing—I have heard nothing—Meanwhile I am always ready for it. The time I prefer most of all is at about half-past three or four o'clock in the afternoon."[15] Whether experiences with prostitutes deepened the crisis that followed Antonie Brentano's departure is difficult to say, but it was from this period that Beethoven's diary entries began to express his sense of guilt and even revulsion concerning sexual activity. "Sensual gratification without a spiritual union is and remains bestial," he wrote, "afterwards one has no trace of noble feeling but rather remorse."[16] And he was undoubtedly pained by his inability to adhere to his own high standard of moral behavior; some years earlier he had written, "O God, let me finally find the one who will strengthen me in virtue, who will lawfully be mine."[17] One Tagebuch entry, however, has a somewhat stoical quality, implying an acceptance of the demands of the flesh: "The frailties of nature," he wrote, "are given by nature herself and sovereign Reason shall seek to guide and diminish them through her strength."[18]

Beethoven went to Baden on May 27, 1813, and remained there, except for several weeks in July, until mid-September. It was in Baden that his old friends the piano manufacturers Johann Andreas Streicher and his wife, Maria Anna (Nannette), found him, as they told Schindler, "in the most deplorable condition with reference to his personal and domestic comforts. He had neither a decent coat nor a whole shirt, and I must forebear to describe his condition as it really was."[19] They related that "Beethoven's state of mind was at the lowest ebb it had been" in many years. This report is corroborated by another observer, the artist Blasius Höfel, who recalled that at this time he often saw Beethoven at an inn, sitting "in a distant corner, at a table which, though large, was avoided by the other guests owing to the very uninviting habits into which he had fallen. . . . Not infrequently he departed without paying his bill, or with the remark that his brother would settle it. . . . He had grown so negligent of his person as to appear there sometimes positively 'dirty' [*schmutzig*]."[20] Gradually, the Streichers "induced him again to mingle in society . . . after he had almost completely withdrawn himself from it."[21]

By mid-1813, Beethoven had fallen into a state of mental and physical disorder that drastically affected his musical productivity. For the first six weeks of the year, he occupied himself with some thirty-one folk-song settings for the Scottish publisher George Thomson and in early March he sketched the first part of "Meeresstille und glückliche Fahrt" ("Calm Sea and Prosperous Voyage"), op. 112, a brief choral setting of two poems by Goethe, with orchestral accompaniment, which he then set aside until 1815.[22] Thereafter, he composed only a few trifling works—the March and Introduction to Kuffner's *Tarpeja*, WoO 2, written in March, and "Der Gesang der Nachtigall" ("The Nightingale's Song"), WoO 141, dated May 3, 1813—but he did not complete any major work during 1813. For the first time since his adolescence, no momentous new projects were being sketched or actively considered.

It was, therefore, a fortunate day late in that summer when the entrepreneur and inventor of various mechanical devices Johann Nepomuk Mälzel enthusiastically brought to Beethoven the idea and a partial draft for a new composition, *Wellingtons Sieg; oder die Schlacht bei Vittoria (Wellingtons Victory, or the Battle of Vittoria)*, celebrating a British victory over Napoleon in the Peninsular War. Beethoven orchestrated it and the work was performed to sensational acclaim on December 8 and 12, 1813, and repeatedly thereafter.[23]

Mälzel and Beethoven had chosen a most propitious moment for a composition of this kind. The Napoleonic tide had crested with the occupation of Moscow in September 1812; thereafter, Napoleon began to suffer the series of major defeats that eventually led to the termination of the wars that had decimated Europe for almost two decades. The retreat from Moscow, culminating in Napoleon's abandonment of his army and his return to Paris in December 1812, signaled the decline of his fortunes. Wellington's triumph of June 21, 1813, on the Iberian peninsula confirmed the irreversibility of that decline. In June, Austria, which had remained officially neutral since the occupation of Vienna in 1809, became a partner in the Quadruple Alliance, and in August it declared war against France. In October, the Allies scored a decisive victory at the battle of Leipzig. Patriotic feelings, heightened by the anticipation of imminent victory, were given free rein at the December concerts, which were given for the benefit of the Austrian and Bavarian soldiers wounded at the battle of Hanau. Vienna's leading musicians participated in the performances of *Wellingtons Sieg:* Hummel and kapellmeister Salieri played the drums and the cannonades; Schuppanzigh led the violins; and Spohr, Mayseder, and scores of others joined in the festivities—which, in Thayer's words, the musicians viewed "as a stupendous musical joke, and engaged in . . . *con amore* as in a gigantic professional frolic."[24] Beethoven, who had no illusions about the quality of the work, took the occasion to present the debut of his Seventh Symphony, which was also received enthusiastically, the Allegretto being repeated at both concerts. A contemporary newspaper noted that the "applause rose to the point of ecstasy."[25] Overnight, Beethoven attained a level of national popularity that he had never previously experienced, one equal to that achieved by Haydn following the premieres of his oratorios, *The Creation* and *The Seasons.*

Buoyed by this reception, Beethoven resumed composition at a high level of productivity, which lasted through the early months of 1815. He wrote a series of vocal and choral works in celebration of the victorious allies and their princely leaders, among which were such works as "Germania," WoO 94, in commemoration of the capitulation of Paris on March 31, 1814; a chorus entitled "Ihr weisen Gründer glücklicher Staaten" ("You Wise Founders of Happy Nations"), WoO 95, to honor the European monarchs who assembled at the Congress of Vienna in

1814; and, in fawning tribute to the Congress, a full-scale cantata, *Der glorreiche Augenblick* (*The Glorious Moment*), op. 136, composed in the fall of 1814 and received with great enthusiasm. Though this output broadened Beethoven's popularity, it did little to enhance his reputation as a serious composer.

These works, filled with bombastic rhetoric and "patriotic" excesses, mark the nadir of Beethoven's artistic career. In them his heroic style is revived, but as parody and farce. Rather than moving forward to his late style, he here regressed to a pastiche of his heroic manner. The heroic style, forged in doubt, rebellion, and defiance, had ended in conformity.

Of course, this may not have been an occasion for deep thinking about history; hence one cannot altogether blame Beethoven for portraying the historical events of 1812–15 in unmediated terms and raw primary colors—and still less for his inability to foresee the shadows of the oncoming Holy Alliance. With the exception of *Wellingtons Sieg,* which is a monument of trivialities and a forerunner of Tchaikovsky's *1812 Overture* as a noisemaker, these works have disappeared from the repertory.[26] Beethoven has no use for the various sonata forms in these works; instead, he returns to forms favored by the French Revolution's composers, such as the cantata and the hymn, along with instrumental potpourris and medleys.

The "ideological-heroic" manner of these works was not a wholly new development in Beethoven's music. Indeed, one might trace the birth of this style to the "Joseph" and "Leopold" Cantatas of 1790, and even to the two little war songs to texts by Friedelberg of 1796 and 1797. Eventually, the style was sublimated into a subtle and profound form of expression, exemplified by the Third and Fifth Symphonies, *Fidelio,* and the Incidental Music to Goethe's *Egmont.* As we have seen, however, in 1811 Beethoven hastily composed incidental music for *The Ruins of Athens,* op. 113, and *King Stephen,* op. 117, in honor of Kaiser Franz— clear heralds of the mock-heroic topical works of the Congress of Vienna period.

"I had long cherished," wrote Beethoven with reference to *Wellingtons Sieg,* "the desire to be able to place some important work of mine on the altar of our Fatherland."[27] There is no reason to question the genuineness of Beethoven's patriotic feelings or the reality of his desire to celebrate the impending conclusion of the Napoleonic Wars. There is little doubt, however, that the unparalleled popular acclaim and financial reward reaped by *Wellingtons Sieg* tempted him to mine this vein for all it was worth. It was worth a good deal: in all his years in Vienna, Beethoven was able to give only eleven academies (public concerts for his own benefit) and nearly half of these took place in a single year: 1814. Together with the arrears paid on his annuity, the pecuniary benefits soon enabled him to invest more than 4,000 florins in silver—first by lending this sum at a suitable rate of interest to the publisher Steiner and several years later by purchasing eight bank shares.

As Thayer noted, the revival of *Fidelio* in 1814 was a direct consequence "of this sudden and boundless popularity of Beethoven's music."[28] Working with a new librettist, the Romanticist playwright and theater director Georg Friedrich Treitschke, Beethoven made his final revision ("newly written and improved," he wrote)[29] of his twice-failed and apparently forsaken opera between February and mid-May 1814. *Fidelio* was performed on May 23 with such success that many repeat performances were called for; it achieved its sixteenth performance on October 9. At the May 23 performance, Beethoven "was stormily called out already after the first act, and enthusiastically greeted."[30] If in 1805–6 *Fidelio* could be understood as a rescue opera expressive of Enlightenment belief in the triumph of nobility over evil, in 1814 the work unfolded fresh implications that accelerated its popular acceptance. The new version could readily be perceived as a celebration of the victory over the Napoleonic forces and as an allegory of the liberation of Europe from a contemporary tyrant and usurper.

The widespread and thunderous applause for his music was extremely gratifying to a composer who had been stung by the criticism that he was a connoisseur's composer. On July 13 an extraordinary notice was inserted in the *Friedensblätter:*

A WORD TO HIS ADMIRERS

How often, in your chagrin that his depth was not sufficiently appreciated, have you said that van Beethoven composes only for posterity! You have, no doubt, now been convinced of your error, even if only since the general enthusiasm aroused by his immortal opera *Fidelio;* and also that the present finds kindred souls and sympathetic hearts for that which is great and beautiful without withholding its just privileges from the future.[31]

This from the composer who in 1806 angrily withdrew *Fidelio* from theater owner Baron Braun with the words "I don't write for the galleries!" Now he noted in his *Tagebuch*, "One certainly writes nicer music as soon as one writes for the public."[32]

To put it gently, Beethoven had for the moment lost his immunity to the seductions of success and was even willing to suffer charges of opportunism from his fellow musicians. The composer Johann Wenzel Tomaschek wrote, apropos *Wellingtons Sieg*, that he was "very painfully affected to see a Beethoven . . . among the rudest materialists," and was not impressed to hear that Beethoven himself "had declared the work to be folly."[33] Similarly, Schindler claimed that Beethoven "attached no value" to *Der glorreiche Augenblick*[34] (although one wonders, in that case, why Beethoven contemplated writing an overture for it a decade later).[35] But he surely set great store by the profits and praise that such works brought him during the glittering and exhausting festivities that accompanied the convening of the Congress of Vienna from September 1814 to June 1815. All of the crowned heads of Europe were present, along with their entourages and thousands of less exalted visitors. While the actual work of the Congress—the drafting of a peace treaty and the establishment of mechanisms for maintaining European order and stability—went on backstage, a vast program of entertainment intended to divert the throngs of idle notables wholly occupied the foreground. Kaiser Franz appointed a festivals committee, whose members "were driven to distraction by the task of inventing new forms of amusement."[36] There was a multitude of balls, banquets, and gala performances and an endless variety of tournaments, hunts, theatricals, sleighing expeditions, ballets, operas, balloon ascents, and torchlight parades. Byron called the Congress a "base pageant." The historian Ilse Barea wrote, "For the time being, Vienna, the Kaiserstadt, the Imperial City, was the capital of Europe. They, the people of Vienna, strutted the stage as if they had been extras in a vast baroque State gala, acting as the foreigners expected them to act and as they felt like acting in their relief and release."[37]

Beethoven was one such Viennese, and his music was but a single element in the huge program of diversion and amusement. He was presented by Razumovsky and Archduke Rudolph to the assembled monarchs and received both their compliments and their more substantial gifts; distinguished foreign visitors paid him homage; and he obtained an audience with the empress of Russia, to whom he dedicated a Polonaise for Piano, op. 89, receiving in return a present of 50 ducats plus a belated bonus of double that sum for the 1803 dedication to Czar Alexander of the Three Violin Sonatas, op. 30. "He used afterwards to relate, jocosely, how he had suffered the crowned heads to pay court to him, and what an air of importance he had at such times assumed."[38] At least, that is what Schindler claimed. It may well be true that on one level Beethoven was acting a part, playing the haughty, faintly obsequious genius in order to restore his somewhat depleted finances. There seems little doubt, however, that he enjoyed the flattery of the monarchs and princes. Elsewhere, Schindler related that "in later days, the great master would recall not without emotion those days . . . and would say with a tinge of pride that he had allowed himself to be courted by the highest rulers of Europe and had comported himself admirably."[39] Doubtless, however, Beethoven had mixed feelings about the various signs of his new eminence. We know that he was proud to be granted honorary citizenship of Vienna in 1815—and that he also joked about this distinction too from time to time.

Nothing could be more evanescent than such excessive adulation, especially as it was largely founded upon an artificial and atypical aspect of Beethoven's music, one that arose within a unique historical context. It was not surprising, therefore, that the rapidity of this rise was matched by a correspondingly rapid decline, beginning at the end of 1814. Ironically, the first intimations of Beethoven's fall from grace coincided with the peak moment of his popularity, the benefit concert of November 29 in the Redoutensaal where *Der glorreiche Augenblick* (*The Glorious Moment*) was heard for the first time, along with repetitions of *Wellingtons Sieg* and the Seventh Symphony, before a large audience that included two empresses, the king of Prussia, and other eminences, along with the foremost virtuosos of Vienna. The hall was filled, the concert was enthusiastically received, and two repeat concerts were scheduled. But at the repetition of the same program on December 2, nearly half of the seats were empty. The third proposed concert was abandoned, and Beethoven gave no further public concerts for his own benefit until May 1824.

A November 30 report to Baron Franz Hager von Altensteig, head of the secret police, revealed the unstable basis of Beethoven's popularity: "The recital given yesterday did not serve to increase enthusiasm for the talent of this composer, who has his partisans and his adversaries. In opposition to his admirers, the first rank of which is represented by Razumovsky, Apponyi, Kraft, etc., . . . who adore Beethoven, is formed an overwhelming majority of connoisseurs who refuse absolutely to listen to his works hereafter."[40]

In a letter of this period Beethoven poetically summarizes his consciousness of the fragility of eminence. "So all is illusion, friendship, kingdom, empire, all is just a mist which a breath of wind can disperse and shape again in a different way!!"[41] During 1815 he tried to rekindle the fading embers of his popularity by pursuing the musical formulas that had worked so well during the immediately preceding years. In the spring he completed an overture in honor of the kaiser's birthday—*Zur Namensfeier* ("Name Day"), op. 115—which, despite its subject matter, had no appreciable impact on his fortunes. Early in the year he composed incidental music to a drama by Friedrich Duncker, *Leonore Prohaska*, WoO 96, containing a war song, a "*Romanze*," a "*Melodram*," and a funeral march (an orchestration of the third movement of the Piano Sonata in A-flat, op. 26), but no performances materialized. He had greater success with "Es ist vollbracht" ("It Is Accomplished"), WoO 97, a work for bass, chorus, and orchestra inspired by the Battle of Waterloo and the second occupation of Paris. It was performed several times in July, but like all of Beethoven's topical works from the Congress of Vienna period except *Wellingtons Sieg*, it disappeared with the waning of the historical moment that had occasioned it.

One wonders whether certain segments of his audience were not voting with their feet against a composer who, by these works, may have been seen to have compromised his aesthetic and personal integrity. Or was there just a temporary lull in concert activity, inevitable following the cultural ferment at the Congress of Vienna? Whatever the reasons, 1815 was virtually barren of Beethoven performances in Vienna, his only major concert of the year being a benefit for the Children's

Hospital Fund on December 25th. At this concert, he conducted a revival of *Christ on the Mount of Olives* along with the premieres of the "Name Day" Overture, op. 115, and "Meeresstille und glückliche Fahrt" ("Calm Sea and Prosperous Voyage"), op. 112, the last a brief choral setting of two poems by Goethe, with orchestral accompaniment. Opus 112, a small masterpiece of tone painting that treats one of Beethoven's favorite subjects—tranquillity penetrated by agitation, dissolving into joyful triumph—and that is reminiscent in its timbres and moods of the finale of the Ninth Symphony, is sufficient demonstration that the core of Beethoven's musical integrity had not been affected. Indeed, setting aside the politically motivated compositions, 1814 may be regarded more favorably as the year of the final revision of *Fidelio* (including the *Fidelio* Overture), the touching "Elegischer Gesang," op. 118, and the Piano Sonata in E minor, op. 90; and 1815 as the year of "Calm Sea and Prosperous Voyage" and the two Cello Sonatas, op. 102.

It was not altogether apparent even from these significant works that Beethoven had begun to formulate, let alone to explore, a new set of structural and stylistic problems whose solutions would ultimately lead to his last-period style. It was unmistakably clear, however, that the heroic period had ended, even though its reverberations would continue to be heard from time to time in Beethoven's final decade. As J. W. N. Sullivan noted, the music of Beethoven's heroic period was concerned with the "posing and solution of a problem"; now Beethoven "was beginning to realize that the experience was not, for him, a permanent possession."[42] The noted critic and pianist Charles Rosen, approaching the issue from a different perspective, reaches similar conclusions: "It was as if the classical sense of form appeared bankrupt to him, spurring him to search for a new system of expression. [The works of 1807–13] may well have seemed to exhaust beyond renewal the style and the tradition he worked in."[43] The heroic style had in substance ended in 1811–12 with the completion of the Seventh and Eighth symphonies, the Violin Sonata in G, op. 96, and the "Archduke" Trio in B-flat, op. 97. The long-standing problems of Beethoven's heroic opera, *Fidelio*, had been settled at last in 1814. True, the crowning work of the heroic style, the Ninth Symphony, remained to be written, but it was a work that could only be written retrospectively and in a sense even anachronistically, from the vantage point of another world and another style.

The dissolution of the heroic style did not occur suddenly or even dramatically, nor is it altogether certain that Beethoven was conscious of the process that was taking place. Rather, as he developed the implications of the Classical sonata form and sonata cycle and applied the principles of dramatic conflict, symphonic expansion, long tonal trajectories, and condensed motivic development to a succession of genres, each of these genres in turn reached what may have appeared to him to be its maximum potential and was set aside. Beethoven composed no symphonies between 1812 and the completion of the Ninth in 1824; he completed no concerto after 1809 and no piano trio after 1811; and he abandoned the duo sonata after 1815. Five years elapsed between the Piano Sonata in E-flat, op 81a, of 1809, and the Sonata in E minor, op. 90, of 1814. He wrote no sets of variations for piano between 1809 and 1822–23. In 1815 he considered returning to the standard genres, sketching extensively a Piano Concerto in D and a Piano Trio in F minor, but these were abandoned in a fragmentary state.[44]

We have arrived at one of the turning points of music history. However meretricious his productivity, the frenetic activity and acclamation of the Congress period may temporarily have diverted Beethoven from the realization that he had no major creative projects in progress, no challenging musical issues at hand. With the close of the Congress, he faced the necessity of finding new avenues for his creative energies.

Historical circumstances play their role here. From our vantage point in a later age, we can easily see that the mock-heroic style had outlived its—at best temporary—utility. The heroic, exhortatory style had itself lost its historical raison d'être with the end of the Napoleonic Wars, the disintegration of the old connoisseur nobility, and the beginning of a new phase in Austrian national existence. After twenty years of war, many Viennese, returning to a torpid life of peace, stability, and conservatism, began to utilize music not as a stimulant to consciousness, but as a narcotic, perhaps to mask the humdrum reality of post-Napoleonic and post-Enlightenment society. The historian Geoffrey Bruun writes, "A spirit of disillusionment, febrile and confused, succeeded the high certainties of the Age of Reason and the expectations voiced in the revolutionary creed. The philosophy of the Restoration was for many a thing of shreds and patches after the stark and glittering mirror-world the *philosophes* had held before the gaze of humanity, and the reversion to traditional pretensions, petty policies, checks and balances and compromises, though it might mark a return to sanity and repose, still left behind a despairing conviction that humanity had failed itself."[45] The Viennese had always danced; for the moment they apparently wished to do little else. They had added new delicacies to their diet of brown beer and sausages and were increasingly cultivating the Biedermeier comforts, which hid the inadequacies, frustrations, philistinism, and suppressed violence of Viennese life from the consciousness of its citizens. Emerging hedonist trends in Viennese society, along with a turn to melodious and accessible Italian music as well as to idealized dance forms, resulted in a defection of a substantial segment of Beethoven's audience from music that expressed categorical imperatives, that was of an essentially serious, ascetic, conflict-ridden character.

In rapid succession, almost all of Beethoven's most unswerving patrons were lost to him through death, emigration, or personal estrangement. Kinsky died suddenly in late 1812. Lichnowsky, who through his affectionate and steadfast support had for more than twenty years helped to strengthen Beethoven's sense of mission, died in 1814. The Lobkowitz Palace, where so many of Beethoven's works had been performed for two decades, was closed to Viennese musical life with the prince's death in 1816. Razumovsky's magnificent, art-laden palace was destroyed by fire on December 31, 1814, whereupon the count—now elevated to prince—returned to Russia, taking the violinist Schuppanzigh with him. Other early patrons had drifted away or were turning elsewhere (especially to Italian opera) for their musical needs. The support of the faithful and influential Archduke Rudolph became increasingly crucial to Beethoven during these years. Still others of his old patrons were now becoming declassed or finding themselves in economic difficulties. The nobility's private orchestras and ensembles, its salons and palaces, now belonged to the history of the *ancien régime*. The era of the connoisseur aristocracy that had nurtured Gluck, Mozart, Haydn, and Beethoven had come to an end.

It was Beethoven's good fortune that he witnessed the emergence and the perfecting of several fundamental styles that arose during his lifetime in the musical centers of Europe. Instinctively he grasped the implications for his own work in each of these competing styles, which ran the gamut from early classicism to a nineteenth-century modernism that can be called late- or post-classicism or even a sui generis romanticism. Unwilling to stand still, refusing to repeat himself, the result was a rapid acceleration of his stylistic evolution, even though this neccessitated the constant reformulation of his musical ideas and vocabulary.

In 1815 Beethoven faced a situation new in quality. Although there were many new musical trends developing, he was reluctant to explore them. He did not choose to work in the mixture of classicizing and Romantic styles of the new generation in Vienna; he is said to have disparaged the new Italian style exemplified by the meteorically popular Rossini as suitable only to "the frivolous and sensuous spirit of the times."[46] He was then—and remained—unwilling to set supernatural and "gothic" literary texts, which, in the operas of Louis Spohr, Conradin Kreutzer, Heinrich Marschner, and Carl Maria von Weber, were opening the door to one of the most fruitful tendencies of German Romantic music. Beethoven had glimpsed these possibilities well before Spohr wrote his *Faust* (1818) and Weber his *Der Freischütz* (1821); he was perhaps taking the first steps toward romanticism of this type in *Fidelio,* and in Klärchen's songs and the *"Melodram"* of the Incidental Music to *Egmont.* He continued to be attracted to stage projects dealing with the mythical and the magical, the sombre and the supernatural, but he set aside each of these, perhaps because he was too much a child of the Age of Reason to enter wholeheartedly this realm of romanticism. (He remarked to the poet Heinrich von Collin that such subjects have "a soporific effect on feeling and reason.")[47]

Above all, although in his last style Beethoven was to become a master of the evanescent mood, he resisted the impending Romantic fragmentation of the architecturally concentrated and controlled cyclic forms of the Classical era into small forms and lyric mood pieces. The breadth of his ideas remained undiminished. Despite the exhaustion of his heroic style, Beethoven was not yet done with the problems of heroism, tragedy, and transcendence. The task he would set himself in his late music would be the portrayal of heroism without heroics, without heroes.

Beethoven could no longer find inspiration among his contemporaries, among the successors to the Neefes, Haydns, and Cherubinis. He would have to turn elsewhere, to the past, to Bach, Handel, and Palestrina; in his final years he was heard to describe Handel as "the greatest composer who ever lived."[48] For the most part, however, his late music, to an extent never previously seen in the history of music, would be created out of the composer's imagination and intellect rather than through a combination and amplification of existent musical trends. In Beethoven's late style an apparently "unprecedented" style comes into being, one whose tendencies and formative materials are not readily identifiable in the music of his contemporaries or immediate predecessors.

The emergence of the new style was to be a slow and trying process. In the years 1816–19, Beethoven's productivity declined to the lowest level of his adult life. In retrospect, of course, it may seem only natural, in view of the immensity of the task before him, that Beethoven would have to forge his way slowly, almost blindly, one masterpiece at a time, into the world of the last period.[49] But while it was taking place, the process was one of considerable anguish. The exhaustion of the middle-period styles, even more than the shifts in favor and patronage, had painful consequences for Beethoven, for he required constant creative challenges and activity to maintain his psychological equilibrium, to protect himself against powerful regressive tendencies in his personality.

Heightening his vulnerability was a qualitative deterioration in his hearing. Where he had formerly been hard of hearing, Beethoven was now fast becoming clinically deaf. His last public performance as a pianist took place on January 25, 1815, when he accompanied the singer Franz Wild in a performance of "Adelaide" for the Russian empress. In April of the previous year, he had participated in performances of the "Archduke" Trio. But Spohr, who was present, wrote, "On account of his deafness there was scarcely anything left of the virtuosity of the artist which had formerly been so greatly admired. In *forte* passages the poor deaf man pounded on the keys till the strings jangled, and in *piano* he played so softly that whole groups of tones were omitted, so that the music was unintelligible."[50]

These cumulative events had a grievous effect on Beethoven's self-esteem and pride. For now, in a sense, it was not merely his hearing but his music that had "failed" him. The heroic style had served him well: it had helped to ward off anxieties and to defend against internal dangers. Indeed, the style, the birth of which coincided so closely with the onset of Beethoven's hearing difficulties, may have helped for a time to compensate for his deafness and even to ease the pain of his sexual isolation. But now the sense of failure extended beyond Beethoven's deafness and his sexuality. It threatened to derail his creativity.

CHAPTER EIGHTEEN

BEETHOVEN
AND HIS NEPHEW

O N NOVEMBER 15, 1815, BEETHOVEN'S brother Caspar Carl died of tuberculosis, leaving a widow, Johanna, and a nine-year-old son, Karl. Beethoven thereupon moved to assume the exclusive guardianship of the boy. A protracted conflict ensued in which Beethoven and the boy's mother contested the guardianship, with Beethoven eventually emerging as the Pyrrhic victor in 1820. Six years later, in late July 1826, Karl attempted suicide in an ultimately successful effort to break away from the domination of his uncle, whose suffocating embrace had at last become unbearable.

The narrative of Beethoven's life between the end of 1815 and early 1820 is the complex, and occasionally arcane, story of his attempt to surmount—indeed to survive—a personal and creative crisis that threatened to overwhelm him. We may be better able to understand this story if we view the appropriation of his nephew as not merely one manifestation of this crisis but as the primary means by which Beethoven struggled toward a new psychological and creative equilibrium.[1] That he succeeded in his efforts is attested both by the facts of his biography after 1820 and by the crystallization of the late style, fully inaugurated toward the end of 1817 by the commencement of the "Hammerklavier" Sonata, op. 106.

The unwitting but essential ingredients in Beethoven's salvation were, paradoxically, his nephew, Karl, and his sister-in-law Johanna. His obsessive entanglement with them forcibly wrenched his emotional energies from their attachment to the outer world and focused them upon the still unresolved issues of his family constellation. Beethoven was now in the process of converting into a strange form of quasi-reality some of the fantasies that had both veiled and motored his existence,

Karl van Beethoven in cadet's uniform (1827).
Unsigned miniature on ivory.

Historisches Museum der Stadt Wien. Now lost.

bringing into consciousness the delusions of a lifetime so that they could be faced and brought under control.

Caspar Carl van Beethoven married Johanna Reiss on May 25, 1806. In a Conversation Book of 1823, Beethoven wrote, "My brother's marriage was as much an indication of his immorality as of his folly," apparently referring to Johanna's premature pregnancy, inasmuch as their only child, Karl, was born on September 4, 1806.[2] It is probable that Beethoven opposed the marriage, just as he did Nikolaus Johann's in 1812, and as the elder Ludwig had opposed the marriage of Beethoven's parents in 1767. He probably tried to influence his brother against Johanna: a Tagebuch entry of 1815 suggested that Caspar Carl "would still be alive and certainly would not have perished so miserably" had he turned away from his wife "and come wholly to me."[3] But there was no lasting estrangement between the brothers. Caspar Carl continued to perform small duties for his brother from time to time, although important matters were handled by more capable advisers, such as Gleichenstein, Countess Erdödy, Franz Oliva, and Stephan von Breuning. During the French bombardment of Vienna in 1809 Beethoven turned to his brother and sister-in-law for shelter. After 1812 the brothers were in close contact, which, for them, consisted of furious conflicts alternating with passionate reconciliations. In December of 1813 Beethoven wrote to Joseph Reger, a Prague attorney, "My brother, whom I have loaded with benefits, and for whose sake I am now for the most part in misery, is—my greatest enemy!"[4] One report of violence between the brothers, dating from soon before Caspar Carl's death, relates that Johanna on that occasion played the role of peacemaker. Shortly after that "violent quarrel," the nephew remembered, they met on the street, and when Beethoven "noticed the sickly appearance of his brother he embraced him and in the public street covered him with kisses."[5]

Johanna was the daughter of Anton Reiss, a well-to-do Viennese upholsterer, and Theresia Reiss née Lamatsch, the daughter of a wine dealer and burgomaster in Retz, lower Austria. Nothing is known of Johanna's early life, not even the precise date of her birth (which was somewhere between 1784 and 1786).[6] A sole, curious anecdote about her childhood survives: her son recalled that "she often told me that every time she wanted money her father said: 'I won't give you any, but if you can take money without my knowledge it belongs to you!'"[7] Curious, because theft—including the "robbery" by Beethoven of her own child—was to become a leitmotif of her existence. As a young woman, in 1804, she had been accused of stealing from her parents, but charges were not pressed. More fatefully, she was actually convicted in 1811 for falsely reporting as stolen an expensive pearl necklace valued at 20,000 florins that she had taken on consignment and she was sentenced on December 30, 1811, to one year's penal servitude. Her husband tenaciously appealed the sentence, even to the emperor, and it was reduced, first to two months' imprisonment, then to one month of house arrest. Finally it was remitted altogether on July 10, 1812, after she had begun to serve her time.[8] Beethoven later fastened upon the conviction as proof of Johanna's immorality, referring to it as a "horrible crime," and making it the basis for his legal claim that she was unfit to raise her son.[9] A more reasonable observer would take it simply as evidence that Johanna had committed an infraction of the law for which she had paid her debt to society. Brandenburg rightly observes that "no court today would separate a mother from a small child for such a minor offence."[10]

Whether Caspar Carl participated in or had prior knowledge of the scheme to misappropriate the pearls can no longer be determined, but that appears to be what Johanna's relative and attorney Jacob Hotschevar alleged when, in his court testimony of 1818, he described the theft as "a matter where her husband was more at fault than Frau v. Beethofen."[11] Certainly it would not have been easy for Johanna to carry out so complex a set of deceptions involving such a considerable amount of money without her husband's knowledge. It now has become clear that both of them had access to and a need for large sums of money to support a remarkably expensive living standard. Although Johanna had brought a substantial dowry, reportedly 2,000 florins, to her marriage and together with her husband owned a large house in the Alservorstadt, purchased in 1813 for 11,175 florins (in the devalued paper currency), which brought them a rental income from ten or twelve apartments, they were heavily in debt and needed cash to cover their expenses. This background may explain why Caspar Carl's financial probity was questioned on several occasions. Rightly or not, he was suspected of having accepted bribes from Beethoven's publishers, and Stephan von Breuning repeated rumors that Caspar Carl was believed guilty of "sordid behavior" in his official post and supposedly warned Beethoven "not to have any money dealings with his brother."[12] (Indiscreetly, Beethoven revealed to his brother that Breuning had transmitted the report, and this caused a bitter estrangement between the composer and his childhood friend that lasted a full decade.)

It was a turbulent and strife-torn marriage, perhaps inevitably so, for none of the brothers Beethoven was well suited to the married state. Beethoven reported that Caspar Carl had threatened his wife with divorce. Also, according to Beethoven, Caspar Carl repeatedly beat his son in order to render him more tractable (Beethoven did not disapprove of the practice). Nor was Johanna spared: according to her daughter-in-law, Caroline, on one occasion Caspar Carl "stabbed her through the hand with a table knife; she still bore the scar as an old lady."[13]

Much of what we know about Johanna's personality has been filtered through the prejudiced writings of Beethoven, his associates, and early biographers. Only a few of her letters have been published; one was written to Franz Liszt in the early 1840s concerning the proposed sale of Beethoven's Heiligenstadt Testament, which had come into her possession, and it shows her to be a lucid correspondent, capable of dealing diplomatically with a complex situation.[14] Although this letter may have been written by a scribe, four unpublished letters of April 1827 in Johanna's own hand to the attorney Johann Baptist Bach demonstrate her capability and intelligence. Her daughter-in-law described her as a forceful, emotional person. "By her letters," she related, "she moved heaven and earth, and [she] understood how to present her poverty and despair in burning colors and with dramatic effect."[15] But this refers to later years, as does an unspecific report of 1830 that her mode of life was "less than praiseworthy."[16]

Beethoven's attitude toward Johanna prior to Caspar Carl's death was by no means consistently hostile. On one occasion, he even claimed that he had acted as her protector during her marriage: "Although I could never defend, still less approve, *her actions,* yet I warded off my brother's anger from her."[17] Despite his later posture of outrage at her 1811 embezzlement, the three of them entered into a series of complicated financial transactions in 1813, which show Beethoven and

Johanna working cooperatively to help Caspar Carl out of an economic emergency.[18] On April 15, Beethoven lent his brother 1,500 florins in paper currency, repayable in six months, with Johanna as guarantor. Predictably, Caspar Carl failed to pay, whereupon on October 30 Beethoven issued a court claim against Johanna to bring her guarantee into play. Shortly thereafter, however, on December 22, he dropped the claim because he obtained the full 1,500 florins by arranging for his publisher Sigmund Anton Steiner to renew the loan in that precise amount. Steiner paid the money to Beethoven, who in turn promised to grant the publisher rights in three sonatas if the loan was not repaid in full by his sister-in-law within nine months. The net result was that Caspar Carl received 1,500 florins, which he never repaid, and Beethoven received the full amount of his original loan, and Steiner eventually got first publication rights to the Sonatas in E minor, op. 90, and in A, op. 101, though admittedly at a very high price. Inasmuch as Beethoven came to owe Steiner as much as 3,000 florins (plus interest) in loans and advances, it seems clear that while the publisher may have had reason to complain, Beethoven did not intend to leave Johanna in the lurch, and eventually he took at least partial responsibility for her debt.

There was no hint of Beethoven's intention to seize the sole guardianship of his nephew, Karl, until the last minute. On November 14, 1815, no doubt a bit anxious about the "Declaration" he had signed in April of the preceding year naming his brother guardian, the dying Caspar Carl wrote in his testament, "Along with my wife I appoint my brother Ludwig van Beethoven coguardian." Beethoven, learning of this, compelled his brother to alter the sentence to "I appoint my brother Ludwig van Beethoven guardian."[19] Suddenly, to their dismay, Caspar Carl and Johanna realized that Beethoven wanted to exclude Johanna from a joint guardianship. Caspar Carl thereupon composed a codicil to his will, which he signed later on the same day:

> Having learned that my brother, Hr. Ludwig van Beethoven, desires after my death to take wholly to himself my son Karl, and wholly to withdraw him from the supervision and training of his mother, and inasmuch as the best of harmony does not exist between my brother and my wife, I have found it necessary to add to my will that I by no

means desire that my son be taken away from his mother, but that he shall always and so long as his future career permits remain with his mother, to which end the guardianship of him is to be exercised by her as well as my brother.[20]

The next day, November 15, Caspar Carl died. In direct contravention of his brother's last request, Beethoven laid exclusive claim to the guardianship of Karl, the only child of the three Beethoven brothers. On November 28 he wrote to the Imperial and Royal *Landrecht* of Lower Austria, the tribunal having jurisdiction over legal matters affecting the nobility, "I now have the chief claim to this guardianship,"[21] and on December 15 he inquired of the Civil Court (the *Magistrat der Stadt Wien*), "In order to prevent the establishment of an illegal joint guardianship which would be detrimental to the interests of the ward, I . . . require proof of the sentence passed on his mother, Johanna v. Beethoven, who has been tried for embezzlement."[22] A few days later, on December 20, he again petitioned the *Landrecht*, asking that it set aside the provisions of Caspar Carl's will that provided for joint guardianship and claiming that Johanna lacked "moral and intellectual qualities" sufficient to permit her to serve in that capacity.[23] On January 9, 1816, the *Landrecht* ruled in Beethoven's favor, and ten days later Beethoven was appointed legal guardian, empowered to take possession of the boy. On February 2, Karl was taken from his mother and placed in Cajetan Giannattasio del Rio's private school for boys, the Giannattasio Institute in the Landstrasse. Shortly thereafter, Beethoven and Giannattasio petitioned the court to exclude the widow from any direct communication with the boy; the *Landrecht* compromised by permitting her to visit the boy "in his leisure hours," but only if she were accompanied by Beethoven's representative.

On February 6 Beethoven wrote triumphantly to Antonie Brentano, "I have fought a battle for the purpose of wresting a poor, unhappy child from the clutches of his unworthy mother, and I have won the day—Te Deum laudamus."[24] This was only the opening round, however, in a struggle that would increasingly take its toll upon all the protagonists.

Beethoven's conscious view was that he was merely a good uncle striving to rescue an ungrateful child from an unfit mother. Nevertheless, it was clear from the outset that deeper currents were shaping this series of events. Suddenly, and in rapid succession, a number of delusions emerged that suggest that Beethoven was beginning to have trouble distinguishing fantasy from reality. He suspected, without any basis, that Johanna had poisoned her husband, and this fantasy was laid to rest only after he received the assurance of the physician, Dr. Joseph Bertolini, that it had no foundation.[25] He soon began to fear that she was monitoring his movements; early in February he wrote that she had bribed his servant for some unstated purpose unrelated to her son.[26] Later in February he came to believe that Johanna might be a prostitute. "Last night that *Queen of Night* was at the Artists' Ball until three A.M. exposing not only her mental but also *her bodily nakedness*—it was whispered that she—was willing to hire herself—for 20 florins! Oh horrible!"[27] These persecutory and sexual fantasies were subsidiary to a complex rescue fantasy: Beethoven seems to have believed that he was carrying out a sacred task of an unspecified nature. "Disregard all idle talk, all pettiness for the sake of this holy cause," he wrote in his Tagebuch. "Your present condition is hard for you, but the one above, O He is, without Him is nothing. In any event the sign has been accepted."[28] Beethoven had come to regard his "rescue" of Karl as a heroic, divinely authorized mission. By 1816 he had exhausted his symbolic exploration of heroism; now he was enacting a bizarre "heroic" drama in an apparent effort to become the conquistador of his innermost fantasies.

But Beethoven's central delusion in this pathological sequence was even more extraordinary: he began to imagine that he had become a father in reality. On May 13, 1816, he wrote to Countess Erdödy: "I now regard myself as [Karl's] father."[29] "Regard K as your own child," he noted in his Tagebuch.[30] The full import of this was revealed in September, when he wrote to the Prague lawyer Johann Nepomuk Kanka: "I am now the real physical father [*wirklicher leiblicher Vater*] of my deceased brother's child."[31] A few weeks later he wrote to Wegeler, "You are a husband and a father. So am I, but without a wife."[32]

Beethoven's fantasy that he was the real physical father of Karl may have another implication as well: in some mystifying way he may have been participating in an illusory marriage to the "Queen of Night" herself. With the death of Caspar Carl, Johanna became "available" to Beethoven, perhaps activating in him impulses toward union with a mother figure and mobilizing the terror of paternal retribution that often follows from thoughts of such a union. From the start, perhaps, Beethoven's aggression against Johanna can be seen as contending with—or warding off—his desire for her. This would be one way of explaining why he chose to regard her as a prostitute, for such fantasied degradation of a woman may have its source in a wish to make her sexually available to someone who dreads union with a feminine ideal.

In this light, Beethoven's "capture" of his nephew may take on the aspect of a complex ruse that he unconsciously employed in order to remain enmeshed with his brother's widow. At the same time, it is possible that Beethoven's manifest fear of Johanna, especially of being alone with her, and his attribution to her of destructive and corrupting powers clearly far beyond her capabilities arose out of a perception of the implications of taking his brother's place in his own family. In the codicil to his last will and testament, Caspar Carl had in effect urged the union of his wife and his brother: "Only by unity can the object which I had in view in appointing my brother guardian of my son be attained, wherefore, for the welfare of my child, I recommend *compliance* to my wife and more *moderation* to my brother. God permit them to be harmonious for the sake of my child's welfare. This is the last wish of the dying husband and brother."[33] Perhaps Beethoven could avoid the anxieties that this directive implied only by forcefully rejecting Johanna as coguardian.

The negative side of Beethoven's attitude toward Johanna is conspicuous. His letters and Conversation Books are filled with vitriolic and unfounded accusations against her; he reviled her with epithets and applauded Karl when the boy repudiated her. Not surprisingly, the sheer quantity of Beethoven's negative references to Johanna—and his actions in depriving her of her son—has led to the general conclusion that he was implacably hostile toward her. This has been the unqualified view of most previous biographies, from those of Schindler and Thayer, who explain Beethoven's actions in terms of Johanna's supposed unfitness and Beethoven's lofty (if misguided) motivations, to the Sterbas' hostile psychoanalytic study, which portrays the composer as consumed by unalloyed hatred ("blind," "bitter," "relentless") toward his sister-in-law. Several of Johanna's contemporary defenders shared this view. For example, the priest Johann Baptist Frölich, who was

Karl's tutor for a time in 1818, stated to the *Landrecht* that "there is great dislike between Ludwig van Beethoven and the mother" and attorney Jacob Hotschevar spoke of "the enmity which for years, and indeed from the very beginning, prevailed between Herr Ludwig and Frau Johanna v. Beethoven."[34]

Such uncontrolled and passionate feelings of hostility, however, may in themselves be a form of denial, an attempt to stave off powerful positive impulses. Unchecked emotions such as Beethoven's toward Johanna are compounded of a broad range of mixed feelings: the more powerful the manifest emotion, the greater may be the opposite feeling that it strives to keep in check. "In such circumstances," Freud writes, "the conscious love attains as a rule, by way of reaction, an especially high degree of intensity, so as to be strong enough for the perpetual task of keeping its opponent under repression."[35] This holds as well for consciously expressed hatred: "Feelings of love that have not yet become manifest express themselves to begin with by hostility and aggressive tendencies; for it may be that the destructive component in the object-cathexis has hurried on ahead and is only later on joined by the erotic one."[36]

With the death of Caspar Carl and the onset of the guardianship, signs of Beethoven's volatile ambivalence toward Johanna emerged with full force, characterized by alternations between aggressive and conciliatory behavior. Repeatedly, he barred Johanna from access to Karl, but each time he relented, suggesting (and even insisting) that she visit the child in his presence. Throughout 1816 he remained in frequent contact with her, having apparently succeeded in assuring her that his actions were beneficial to her son. On December 28 he asked Kanka to act as curator for the estate of Johanna's cousin for the benefit of Karl, adding that "the mother, too, will probably derive some benefit from the arrangement."[37] In the course of 1817 he drew closer to her, had her meet the child at his house, took Karl to visit her ("His mother wants to place herself on a better footing with her neighbors, and so I am doing her the favor of taking her son to her tomorrow in the company of a third person"),[38] and persuaded her without protest to assign half of her widow's pension "for the education and maintenance" of Karl.[39] Beethoven carefully kept the positive side of his relationship with Johanna well hidden from most of his associates and especially from

Karl's headmaster, Cajetan Giannattasio del Rio. He was somewhat more forthright about his friendly actions toward Johanna in a letter to Zmeskall. "After all," he wrote to him, "it might hurt Karl's mother to have to visit her child at the house of a stranger; and in any case it is a less charitable arrangement than I like."[40]

In August 1817, however, Johanna mortified Beethoven by repeating to Giannattasio certain criticisms of the schoolmaster that Beethoven had confided to her. Regarding this as a betrayal as well as an embarrassment, Beethoven turned against her. "This time I wanted to see whether she could perhaps be reformed by a tolerant and more gentle attitude. . . . But it came to nothing."[41] He thereupon reverted to his "original, strictly severe attitude" and barred her from seeing Karl. Yet in March of 1818 he again moved cautiously toward reconciliation, offering Johanna financial assistance and once again apparently permitting her limited access to her son, whom she had not seen for many months. Then in June, at Mödling, where he had brought his nephew, he discovered that she had persuaded his servants to provide her with information, and at the same time he learned that Karl had secretly been meeting with his mother. Beethoven took these events as constituting a "horrible treachery," was thrown into an ominous state of mental confusion, and reacted with the rage of one who feels utterly betrayed by all concerned. He wrote to his close friend and confidant Nannette Streicher:

> I had been noticing signs of treachery for a very long time; and then on the eve of my departure I received an anonymous letter, the contents of which filled me with terror; but they were little more than suppositions. Karl, whom I pounced on that very evening, immediately disclosed a little, but not all. As I often give him a good shaking, but not without valid reason, he was far too frightened to confess absolutely everything. We arrived here in the middle of this struggle. As I frequently reprimanded him, the servants noticed it; and the old traitress [the housekeeper], in particular, tried to prevent *him from confessing the truth*. But . . . everything came to light. . . . K[arl] has done wrong, but—a mother—a mother—even a bad mother is still a mother. . . . I am not inviting you out here yet, since everything is in confusion. *Still it won't be necessary to take me to the madhouse.*[42]

Despite his fury, Beethoven could not wholly condemn Johanna. But she herself, now convinced that no further reconciliation was possible and alarmed at the harmful effects on Karl of Beethoven's guardianship, filed a lawsuit to recover custody of her son. This inaugurated a period of total confrontation during which Beethoven, now unable to control his actions, described her in the worst possible terms and called for her complete exclusion. He had hoped to have it otherwise. "If the mother could have repressed her wicked tendencies and allowed my plans to develop peacefully," he lamented, "then an entirely favorable result would have been the outcome."[43]

Beethoven's attitude toward his young nephew was similarly riddled with contradictions. Here, too, Beethoven's conscious feelings masked opposing impulses. His repeated protestations of love certainly were not matched by consistently benevolent behavior toward the boy. At first he would fetch Karl from school and take him to lunch, to participate in carnival festivities, or to hear a concert, but this solicitousness did not last long. In the summer of 1816 Karl underwent a hernia operation, performed in Vienna by Dr. Karl von Smetana, but Beethoven did not make the short trip from Baden to Vienna to be at the bedside of his beloved "son." On September 22 he wrote to Giannattasio asking for news: "You will understand that I long to hear how my beloved K[arl] is now progressing. . . . I am beginning to think that you must look upon me as a rather thoughtless barbarian."[44] But a letter to Antonie Brentano, written on September 29, shows that he was genuinely elated by Karl's recovery; Beethoven felt that he had come through a personal trial and described to her "how burdened I am with a father's very real cares."[45] Throughout, he exhibited a torturing tenderness toward his nephew, intense anxiety and constant watchfulness alternating with complaints and reproaches. In November he took the ten-year-old to task for laxness in his studies and punished him by a deliberate show of coldness: "We walked along together more seriously than usual. Timidly he pressed my hand but found no response"[46]—this on the day preceding the first anniversary of the death of the boy's father. In 1817 he authorized, indeed encouraged, Giannattasio to beat Karl "to enforce the strictest obedience." He wrote to the headmaster, "I have already told you how during his father's lifetime he would obey only when he was beaten. Of course that was very wrong, but that was how things were done, and we must not forget it."[47] To make sure that his nephew was fully aware of his attitude, Beethoven added a postscript, "*Please read this letter with Karl.*" In subsequent years, when it became apparent to Beethoven that he had not succeeded in breaking the bond between mother and son, he used physical violence against Karl on more than one occasion.

The depth of Beethoven's hostility toward Karl, however, cannot be gauged by his occasional violence or coldness, or even by his endless reproaches. More extremely, Beethoven deprived the fatherless child of his sole remaining parent—which is to say, he made him an orphan. From the beginning, Beethoven actually referred to Karl as "a poor orphan."[48] Furthermore, it became Beethoven's hope that he could obtain permission from the courts to ship the boy to another city. "It will certainly be best to remove him later on from Vienna and send him to Mölk or somewhere else," he wrote to Giannattasio. "There he will neither see nor hear anything more of his beastly mother; and where everything about him is strange he will have fewer people to lean upon and will be able solely by his own efforts to win for himself love and respect."[49] Beethoven desperately wanted to separate Karl from his mother. At first he meant to bar her from influencing the child, but in later years, especially after the boy reached the age of puberty, Beethoven seems to have suffered from fantasies of incestuous union between Karl and Johanna. He urgently pressed on his nephew the twin imperatives of abstinence and obedience. "You must not hate your mother," wrote Beethoven in a Conversation Book, "but you must not regard her like another good m[other]. . . . If you become *guilty* of further offenses against *me*, you cannot become a good man, that is the same as if you rebelled against your father."[50] Beethoven was able to control Karl by means of such appeals to the boy's guilt over his oedipal stirrings.

Despite his protestations that he was rescuing Karl and that his motives were altruistic ("I do not *need my nephew*, but *he needs me*," he wrote),[51] Beethoven became increasingly dependent upon his nephew. In later years he overvalued him to such an extent that he "would sometimes sing or play him a theme he had thought of for a projected work, in order to get his opinion and preference."[52] Karl was

Beethoven's savior, not the reverse. Beethoven received from the boy the protective warmth of family feeling, relief from loneliness, the pride of (delusory) parenthood, and even a sense of immortality ("I want *by means of my nephew* to establish a fresh memorial to my name"),[53] at a time when numerous leave-takings and losses had left him in a forlorn and lonely state.

In his distraction and confusion, Beethoven frequently was unable to cope with the simple details of everyday existence. For comfort and assistance he turned to Nannette Streicher (née Stein), between early 1817 and the summer of 1818. Born in 1769, Maria Anna Stein rapidly showed signs of becoming a musical prodigy; when she was eight, Mozart wrote of her, "She may succeed, for she has great talent for music."[54] Her talents were to be developed elsewhere, however, as the owner with her brother of a piano factory, in which she was joined by Johann Andreas Streicher after their marriage in January 1794. Beethoven and the Streichers, whose salon was for decades one of the musical centers of Vienna, became fast friends beginning in the 1790s; as we saw earlier, it was they who in 1813 nursed him back to health in a time of great stress. Beginning in the early months of 1817, Beethoven once more called on Frau Streicher to help him, writing to her some sixty letters (as many as he ever wrote to any other person in a comparable period of time) in which he bared his innermost feelings and asked her for guidance. Frau Streicher became, in the Sterbas' apt phrase, his "motherly protectress and counselor,"[55] from whom he sought advice about all his domestic matters—cooking, laundry, the hiring and conduct of servants, the care and purchase of household articles, changes of lodging, and the education and upbringing of nephew Karl. To Frau Streicher Beethoven poured out his deep fears that his servants were in league with Johanna, or deceiving or stealing from him. In the course of the correspondence, which began in good humor and with friendly reserve, Beethoven increasingly expressed his feelings of deep dependency and helplessness:

> The day before yesterday my splendid *servants* took three hours, from seven until ten in the evening, to get a fire going in the stove. The bitter cold, particularly in this house, gave me a bad chill; and

almost the whole day yesterday I could scarcely move a limb. Coughing and the most terrible headaches I have ever had plagued me the whole day. As early as six o'clock in the evening I had to go to bed, where I still am. But I am feeling better. . . . I am in so many respects your debtor that when I think of it I am frequently overcome by a feeling of shame.[56]

Frau Streicher's involvement in Beethoven's domestic affairs and their constant visits to each other inevitably gave rise to suspicions—not, however, on the part of her husband, so far as we know—that they were lovers. At some point in late 1817 they decided that it would be best if he did not see her at her home. "I am glad that you *yourself* realize that it is impossible for me ever to set foot in your house again," wrote Beethoven.[57] He wished to keep this a secret from his servants: "It would be well *for you, as it certainly would be for me, not to let my two servants notice that unfortunately I can no longer have the pleasure of going to see you.* For, if this arrangement were not observed, there might be *very disastrous consequences* for me, because it might seem as if in this respect you wished to detach yourself altogether."[58] Beethoven's servants also had their suspicions that there was a liaison between the two. "They always have their revenge on me whenever they deliver our letters or notice that something is going on between you and me—."[59] By late January Beethoven was again visiting Frau Streicher at her home and salon at Ungargasse 334. The most intense phase of their relationship had now passed, however, and the correspondence itself tapered off, coming to an end in the late spring or early summer of 1818. In one of his last letters, Beethoven tried to revive the feeling of ease that her ministrations had brought him; he wrote, "Please send us soon a comforting letter about the arts of cooking, laundering, and sewing."[60] From Frau Streicher he had received the mothering and comfort he needed and through her had been able freely to regress to the status of a son at the very time that he was affirming his fitness to be a father.

Just as he needed this motherly protectress, so Beethoven needed to feel the warmth of real family experiences. During the two years that Karl was at the Giannattasio Institute, Beethoven made himself at home with the Giannattasio del Rios and their two grown daughters, the elder of whom, Franziska (Fanny), born 1790, kept a touching diary filled with her keen observations.[61] She recalled that Beethoven "seemed to want to consecrate body and soul" to Karl, and that in April 1817 he took lodgings in the neighborhood of the institute so that he could be closer to him. (Frau Streicher also lived nearby.) She remembered, too, how Johanna would disguise herself as a man and come to the school playground so that she could see her son during the gymnastic exercises. She described Beethoven's tears when Karl ran away to his mother, and she wrote down the composer's pathetic outcry, "He is ashamed of me!" Fanny, who had recently had a tragic love affair, fell in love with Beethoven, but in accordance with his usual pattern of being attracted to unavailable women, Beethoven claimed to prefer the younger sister, Anna Maria, born 1792, who was engaged to another. "She has her Schmerling," he would lament, in a reference to her suitor, wholesale merchant Leopold Schmerling. He called Fanny "Madam Abbess," which, she wrote, "pleased me not at all," and he occasionally indulged in "small sarcasms" that hurt her deeply. ("He seemed sometimes so hostile and cold," she wrote.) During some months he was an almost nightly visitor—and a morose one. "Unhappily, interesting evenings were rare. . . . Throughout the evening, he would remain seated at the round table near us, plunged, it seemed, in his thoughts, sometimes throwing us a smiling word, spitting incessantly into his handkerchief and then looking into the handkerchief as though expecting to find blood there." (This might have been worse: others reported that Beethoven "sometimes spat into his hand.")[62]

He was not always so inelegant: one day he brought violets and said to the delighted Fanny, "I bring you spring!" He accompanied the young women at the piano and gave them concert tickets and newly published editions of his lieder. He became friendly with Anna's Schmerling, who, like him, was hard of hearing, and jestingly advised him what to expect: "Schmerling, take it easy, things go from bad to worse!" He composed a "Hochzeitslied" (wedding song), WoO 105, for Anna when she married in 1819. He spoke freely to them of his family affairs, and expressed his negative views on marriage and his newfound notions of free love. That he also told them idealized stories about his youth, his parents, and his revered grandfather suggests that the guardianship struggle had revived his yearning for the past without bringing the actualities of his childhood into consciousness.

BEETHOVEN'S SUSPICIONS CONCERNING THE ADEQUACY of Giannattasio's care for and education of Karl eventually overcame his better
judgment, and on January 24, 1818, he withdrew Karl from the institute
and brought him home to a household that included a new housekeeper, a new housemaid, and a private tutor. Thus Beethoven fulfilled a
long-held desire: as early as May 1816 he had written to Ferdinand
Ries, "I shall have to start a proper household, where I can have him to
live with me," adding later in the same letter, "Unfortunately I have no
wife."[63] In a letter to Countess Erdödy he asked, "What is a boarding
school [Institut] compared with the immediate sympathetic care of a
father for his child?"[64] A diary entry of 1817 expresses his rationale for
raising a child in the bosom of a warm family: "A thousand beautiful
moments vanish when children are in wooden institutions, whereas at
home with good parents they could receive the most soulful impressions
that endure into the most extreme old age."[65] At this very same time,
and perhaps without fully grasping the contradiction, Beethoven was
hoping to send the boy to a foreign city.

Until early 1818, neither Beethoven nor Johanna had lived with
Karl, who remained on neutral ground at the Giannattasio Institute.
This arrangement was tolerable to Johanna, who, despite her difficulties
in gaining access to her son, apparently felt that he was being properly
educated and cared for. It also neutralized the most severe effects of
Beethoven's influence over his nephew. When Beethoven took Karl into
his own disordered home, however, the armed truce was shattered:
Johanna now resumed her efforts to contest the guardianship. It had,
indeed, been a strange kind of counterfeit family, and so fantastic and
unstable a set of relationships could hardly endure for very long. Karl
was torn between obedience toward his uncle and the desire to return to
his mother; Johanna and Beethoven oscillated between mutual rejection
and cooperation. Inexorably the arrangement collapsed, inaugurating a
period of explosive conflict.

In September, Johanna petitioned the *Landrecht* to cancel
Beethoven's authority to direct Karl's future education. Her petition was
denied on September 18, but she persisted, applying to the court for permission to place Karl in a state school, the Imperial Royal Seminary
(Konvikt). This too was rejected, for the *Landrecht*, partly because of the
intervention of Beethoven's influential friends, consistently upheld

the composer's viewpoint, despite the injustice of his actions. Karl was placed in a public school in November, but on December 3 he ran away to his mother and had to be removed from her home by the police; he was placed once again in the Giannattasio Institute. Fortified by her son's love, appalled by new evidence of Beethoven's mistreatment of the child, and fearful that he was about to send Karl out of the country, Johanna made yet another application to the court, returnable on December 11. Her case was ably argued by Jacob Hotschevar, who presented testimony that she had been barred from access to her son, that the boy's moral, educational, and physical condition left much to be desired, and that Beethoven's eccentricity and deafness were sufficient to disqualify him from holding the guardianship. Moreover, Hotschevar now introduced a draft letter written by Caspar Carl confirming that he had not wanted his brother to be the sole guardian and that his will had been entered into under compulsion, and in exchange for the loan of 1,500 florins in 1813:

> *Never* would I have drawn up an instrument of this kind if my long illness had not caused me great expenses; it is only in consideration of these that I could, *under compulsion,* sign this instrument; but at the time I was determined to demand the return of same at an opportune moment or to invalidate it by another instrument, for my brother is too much a composer and hence can *never,* according to my idea, and with my consent, become my son's guardian.[66]

Karl was called as a witness; he testified that he had resisted his mother's attempt to restore him to Beethoven, "because he feared maltreatment," and he told the court that Beethoven had "threatened to throttle him" upon his return.[67] The composer himself then took the stand. An outcome favorable to him was a foregone conclusion, but Beethoven, probably ridden with guilt and reeling from the impact and the implications of Karl's flight to his mother, proved to be his own worst witness. According to the transcript, the court asked him about his plans for Karl's education, and he responded, "After half a year he would send him to the Mölker Konvikt, which he had heard highly commended, or if he were but of noble birth, give him to the Theresianium," a school for sons of the aristocracy. The court, hearing the negative reference to Karl's nobility, pursued the question, asking, "Were he and his brother of the nobility, and did he have documents to prove it?" Beethoven admitted that he had no proof, though he tried to imply that he was indeed noble: "'Van' was a Dutch predicate that was not exclusively applied to the nobility; he had neither a diploma nor any other proof of his nobility." Johanna was then questioned. "Was her husband of noble birth?" "So the brothers had said," she responded; "the documentary proof of nobility was said to be in the possession of the oldest brother, the composer. At the legal hearing on the death of her husband, proofs of nobility had been demanded; she herself had no document bearing on the subject."

On learning of Beethoven's deception in the matter of his nobility, the *Landrecht* dismissed the case from its jurisdiction in a declaration of December 18: "It . . . appears from the statement of Ludwig van Beethoven, as the accompanying copy of the court minutes of December 11 of this year shows, that he is unable to prove nobility; hence the matter of guardianship is transferred to the Magistrat," the civil court that had jurisdiction over cases involving common citizens.[68] Schindler, who was not present and did not join Beethoven's entourage until four years later, claimed that this had a devastating effect on the composer; he wrote that it "drove Beethoven beside himself; for he considered it the grossest insult that he had ever received and . . . an unjustifiable depreciation and humiliation of the artist—an impression too deep to be ever erased from his mind." He was so "deeply mortified" that he "would have quitted the country."[69] A more reliable indication of Beethoven's reaction appears in his already-quoted remark in the Conversation Books: "There is a hiatus here which ought to be filled, for my nature shows that I do not belong with this plebeian M[agistrat]."[70]

With Beethoven's confession the nobility pretense was shattered, but the Family Romance on which it was based continued its tenacious hold on him. It was precisely during the next few years that Beethoven refused to permit any action to be taken to refute the proliferating reports of his royal ancestry. For Beethoven had not been "pretending" to nobility: he felt that he was indeed of noble origin but was unable to demonstrate it because of the mysterious (as he thought) circumstances of his birth. His adoption of Karl had been the adoption of a commoner by a noble: "I have raised my nephew into a higher category," he wrote in 1819; "neither he nor I have anything to do with the M[agistrat]. For only innkeepers, cobblers and tailors come under that kind of guardianship."[71] In some unfathomable way, Beethoven's seizure of his nephew was his delusory method of repairing his own presumed illegitimacy, of fulfilling the prophecy of the Family Romance, of becoming the noble father of a commoner's child. Unable to locate the aristocratic or royal parent of his daydreams, he had created him in his own person.

The *Magistrat* did not sympathize with Beethoven's position in the litigation. Karl was returned to his mother for several weeks early in 1819, and a hearing was held on January 11 that evidently went badly for the composer, for it inspired an excited letter to the *Magistrat* on February 1, in which Beethoven attacked Johanna and defended his own qualifications as guardian. Johanna, he wrote, induced Karl "to dissimulate, ... to bribe my servants, *to tell lies*, ... even *gives him money* in order to arouse lusts and desires which are harmful to him.... [He] has spent several years under her care and been completely *perverted* and *even* made to help her *deceive* his own father." Affirming his own qualifications, he wrote, unabashedly, "I confess that I myself feel that I am better fitted than anyone else to inspire my nephew *by my own example* with a desire for *virtue and zealous activity*."[72] Unmoved by this appeal, the *Magistrat* compelled Beethoven to surrender the guardianship, and on March 26 Councillor Mathias von Tuscher was appointed guardian in his place upon the composer's own recommendation. Through Tuscher, Beethoven attempted to persuade the *Magistrat* to send Karl, who was by now twelve, out of the country to the University of Landshut in Bavaria. The theologian (later Bishop) J. M. Sailer, who headed the university, had agreed to accept the boy after a heartfelt letter of February 22, 1819, from Antonie Brentano.[73] The *Magistrat* rejected the plan, however, and Karl, who had temporarily been placed under the tutorship of a certain Johann Baptist Kudlich during the spring, was entered in late June at Joseph Blöchlinger's Institute in Vienna, where he remained for more than four years.

"I have now taken the necessary steps for the most careful higher education of my ward and nephew," wrote Beethoven to the *Magistrat*, asking that instructions be forwarded to Blöchlinger empowering him "to repel with due severity the mother's untimely and disturbing interruptions."[74] Beethoven was now obsessively concerned to prevent meetings between mother and son: he wrote to his friend the journalist Joseph Karl Bernard, "It is desirable to make Karl realize that he is no longer to see such a vicious mother, who by means of God knows what Circean spells or curses or vows bewitches him and turns him against me."[75] He continued to hope that Karl could be sent abroad, a move that would have minimized Johanna's influence and at the same time would have had the beneficial effect of relieving Beethoven's own anxieties at his proximity to his nephew, against whom he had turned during this period, furiously referring to him as unloving, ungrateful, and callous. "He is an utter scamp and is most fit for the company of his own mother and my *pseudo*-brother," he wrote.[76] And, writing in an even more extreme vein, "He is a monster", "My love for him is gone. *He needed my love.* I do not need his." Yet his ambivalent feelings toward Karl were so prone to sudden reversals that he quickly added, "You understand, of course, that this is not what I *really* think (I still love him as I used to, but without weakness or undue partiality, nay more, I may say in truth that I often weep for him)."[77]

Johanna and Nikolaus Johann Beethoven now entered into an alliance to try to protect Karl from Beethoven's patently pathological behavior, and in the summer Johanna proposed Karl's other uncle to the *Magistrat* as a suitable guardian. Beethoven's rage was now aroused against every perceived adversary—Johanna, Karl, his brother, the *Magistrat* (which he accused of corruption), Councillor Tuscher, and even his loyal friend Bernard, to whom he now wrote, "I must say that I have a suspicion that to me you are just as much an enemy as a bit of a friend— . . . Oh, may the whole miserable rabble of humanity be cursed and damned—."[78]

Beethoven's worst fears were realized on September 17, when the *Magistrat* rendered its decision, accepting Tuscher's resignation and awarding the guardianship to Johanna van Beethoven, with Leopold Nussböck, a municipal official, as joint guardian. Momentarily, Beethoven considered kidnapping Karl and taking him to stay with Aloys Weissenbach, an admirer of Beethoven who lived in Salzburg, but under the steadying influence of his attorney, Johann Baptist Bach, he instead addressed a carefully considered petition to the *Magistrat* on October 30, asking that he be reinstated as guardian and discreetly suggesting for the first time that he would not be opposed to a joint guardianship with his sister-in-law. "[Karl's] whole future depends upon this education, which cannot be left to a woman or to his mother alone," he wrote.[79] But the *Magistrat* was in no mood for compromise: on November 4 and December 20 it twice rejected Beethoven's protest. At this, Beethoven petitioned the Imperial Royal Court of Appeal of Lower Austria on January 7, 1820, for a reversal of the lower court decision. Here again he took a conciliatory position, suggesting a three-way guardianship by himself, his friend Karl Peters, and Johanna. "Since my sole object is the welfare of the boy," he wrote, "I am not opposed to some kind of co-guardianship being granted to his mother. . . . But henceforth to entrust the guardianship to her alone, without appointing an efficient guardian to assist her, such a step would assuredly be tantamount to bringing about the ruin of the boy."[80]

Despite the stream of assaults by Beethoven on Johanna's character and morality, which lasted until the final appeal in 1820, it was at this time that the extraordinary rumor began to circulate that Beethoven was in love with his sister-in-law. This rumor was broadcast by Johanna herself and therefore presumably constituted her own understanding of Beethoven's attitude toward her, her explanation of his uncontrolled and passionate behavior. In November 1819, Bernard wrote in a Conversation Book, "I saw too that the *Magistrat* believes everything that it hears, for example that she said that you were in love with her."[81] Shortly thereafter, Beethoven himself twice noted the story—in a letter to Bernard and in his draft memorandum to the Court of Appeal, where he wrote that Franz Xaver Piuk, one of the members of the *Magistrat*, "retailed the *well-worn complaints of Fr. B about me*, even adding '*that I was supposed to be in love with her, etc.*' and more rubbish of that kind."[82] If anything, these reports may have fortified Beethoven in what was to be his most extreme rejection of Johanna.

On January 10, 1820, the Court of Appeal requested a comprehensive report from the *Magistrat*. This was forthcoming on February 5. The *Magistrat* wrote, in part,

> a. that the appellant, because of his physical defect and because of the enmity which, as the codicil to the will [shows], he entertains toward the mother of the ward, is held unfit to undertake the guardianship.
> b. that the guardianship by law belongs to the natural mother.

c. that her having committed an embezzlement of which she was
guilty against her husband in the year 1811 and for which she
was punished by a police house arrest of one month, is now no longer
an impediment.[83]

In a supplementary report the *Magistrat* was even more forceful, pointing out that the only evidence adduced by Beethoven in support of
depriving Johanna of Karl was her conviction in 1811, and adding,

> Everything else which appears in appellant's statement . . . is unproven
> gossip to which the I. R. *Landrecht* could give no consideration, but
> which is eloquent testimony to how passionately and hostilely appel-
> lant has long since treated the mother and still treats her, how easily he
> falls to reopening her healed wounds, now when, after undergoing
> punishment, she is reinstated in her previous rights, reproaching her
> with a misdemeanor which she expiated many years ago, a mis-
> demeanor which her wronged husband himself forgave her, inasmuch
> as he not only petitioned for leniency in the punishment meted out to
> her but also, in his testamentary dispositions, recognized her as fit and
> worthy to act as guardian of his son.

In a reflection of the passions this case aroused, the *Magistrat* gratu-
itously overstepped the ordinary bounds of judicial restraint and stated
that Beethoven's sole aim was "to mortify the mother and tear the heart
from her bosom."[84]

Beethoven now set about composing a lengthy draft memorandum
marshaling the facts in the case from his point of view. By February
18 he had completed a forty-eight-page document and forwarded it
to Bernard to use as "raw material" in preparing a statement of
Beethoven's position.[85] In this chaotic memorandum, Beethoven agi-
tatedly listed Johanna's transgressions—which boiled down to the misappropriation of the necklace in 1811, having allegedly had "intimate
relations with a lover" after Caspar Carl's death, showing negligence in
caring for her son, and, especially, turning Karl against Beethoven
while scheming to take him for herself.[86] "She did her best by means of
the most horrible intrigues, plots, and defamatory statements to dis-
parage me, his benefactor, mainstay, and support, in short, his father in
the true sense of the word." (That Beethoven was not Karl's father

"in the true sense of the word" seems not as yet to have occurred to him.) At the same time he set forth his own qualifications, although he confessed to occasional errors or weaknesses in his treatment of Karl— including a violent episode in which he had caused the boy some injury in the genital region. "And if, *being human, I have erred now and then or if my poor hearing must be taken into account, yet surely* a child is not taken away *from his father for those two reasons.*" Brief sections of the memorandum are given over to discussions of Karl's education, the cost of maintaining him, and further financial matters. A supplement contains a lurid attack on the moral character of Father Frölich, who had given evidence in support of Johanna during the earlier proceedings. Beethoven's passionate rejection of Johanna is the guiding thread of the memorandum: he portrays her as the embodiment of evil and as his persecutor. He sees himself as beset by schemes, intrigues, and plots, woven by Johanna not out of love for her son but out of a desire for revenge. "I too am a man," he wrote, "harried on all sides like a wild beast, misunderstood, often treated in the basest way by this vulgar authority; with so many cares, with the constant battle against this monster of a mother, who always attempted to stifle any good brought forth."[87]

There is no sign that the memorandum was formally presented to the Court of Appeal. But that, apparently, was not its real purpose. On March 6, Beethoven wrote to Karl Magnus Winter, one of the appellate judges, informing him that he would soon receive from Beethoven "a memorandum consisting of information about Frau van Beethoven, about the *Magistrat*, about my nephew, about myself, and so forth," and grandiosely suggesting that if he were to be denied the guardianship, "such a contingency would certainly provoke the disapproval of our civilized world."[88] In a clear effort to influence the court, Beethoven sent the memorandum to Winter by a messenger who was in the employ of Archduke Rudolph—thus giving unmistakable notice to the judge that a member of the imperial family took an active interest in an outcome favorable to Beethoven. Indeed, as soon as he decided to appeal, Beethoven secured a testimonial from Archduke Rudolph for presentation to the court, and he probably asked him to obtain Archduke Ludwig's intercession as well. Johanna was virtually defenseless against such powerful political influence. Judge Winter, fearful of giving the appearance that he had been bribed or unduly influenced, told

Rudolph's messenger that he would give him no verbal or written response.[89] Meanwhile, a copy of the memorandum was also forwarded to another of the appellate judges, Joseph von Schmerling (the brother of Anna Giannattasio von Schmerling's husband), whom Beethoven was attempting to influence through Karl Bernard and Mathias von Tuscher. "Don't forget about *Schmerling,*" he wrote to the latter, "for by reason of your knowledge you can certainly exert much influence on this affair."[90] Schmerling, formerly a member of the *Landrecht,* had assisted Beethoven in 1816 to limit Johanna's access to Karl at the Giannattasio Institute.[91] Beethoven's attorney, Bach, advised him to make personal calls on both Schmerling and Winter, and a few days before the appellate decision Beethoven brought Karl to see one of them, to demonstrate the boy's desire to remain with his uncle.

A hearing before the *Magistrat* took place on March 29, at the suggestion of the Court of Appeal. The magistrates, aware that political influence had been brought to bear ("Schmerling helped a great deal," wrote Bernard in a Conversation Book),[92] were propitiatory, but refused to reverse themselves. Despite this, Beethoven was now persuaded that a favorable decision from the Court of Appeal was assured: he therefore abandoned his earlier conciliatory position and again insisted on the total exclusion of Johanna from the guardianship. On April 8, the Court of Appeal ruled for Beethoven and appointed him and Peters as joint guardians. Johanna appealed the decision to the emperor, but to no avail. On July 24 the *Magistrat* notified the parties that the case was closed.

Grief-stricken and weary from her long struggle, eager to build a new life, and perhaps to replace her stolen child, Johanna became pregnant in the spring of 1820 by Johann Hofbauer, a "noted, very well-to-do" person,[93] who later freely acknowledged his responsibility. In June, Blöchlinger wrote in the Conversation Book, "It seems to me recently that Frau Beethoven might be in the family way."[94] Perhaps in response to this news, Karl, who had during the preceding period assured his uncle that he had no use for his mother ("She promised me so many things that I could not resist her; I am sorry that I was so weak at the time and beg your forgiveness")[95] again ran away to her. He was quickly returned to Beethoven. Later in the year, Johanna gave her newborn daughter the name Ludovica, the female form of Ludwig—an uncanny testimony to the strength of the bond between the antagonists in this drama, the first act of which had now come to an end.

It is usually taken for granted that Beethoven's creativity was brought almost to a full stop by his total absorption in these events. But the relationship between the guardianship struggle and the graph of Beethoven's productivity is a more complicated one and will not yield to simple assertions of cause and effect. During 1816 and 1817, when his conflicts with Karl and Johanna were relatively minimal, his productivity was extremely low; indeed, following the completion of *An die ferne Geliebte,* op. 98, in April 1816 and the Piano Sonata in A, op. 101, in November, Beethoven wrote nothing of substance for almost a year. Toward the end of 1817 he began work on the Sonata in B-flat ("Hammerklavier"), op. 106 , completing its first two movements by April 1818. The years 1817–18 also saw the sketching of fragmentary ideas for the Ninth Symphony. But the raging litigation, which lasted from the summer of 1818 until early 1820, seems not to have had an adverse effect on Beethoven's productivity; on the contrary, in this period he completed the "Hammerklavier" Sonata, composed twenty-three of the Diabelli Variations, and made very substantial progress on the *Missa Solemnis,* completing the Kyrie and Gloria before the end of 1819 and beginning the Credo in the early months of 1820. Furthermore, Beethoven had other major projects in view: he was at this time commissioned by Johann Wolfmayer, a wealthy textile merchant, to write a Requiem, and by the Gesellschaft der Musikfreunde (Society of Friends of Music) to compose an oratorio on a "heroic" subject. Thus the formulation of Beethoven's late style as well as substantial work on several of its central masterpieces took place in the midst of an emotional firestorm.

Beethoven's involvement in music making was not impaired by his domestic and legal preoccupations. In fact, he was much occupied with performances of his works, for the performance drought of 1815 did not continue into 1816, and the latter year saw a rich harvest of chamber music performances, including renditions of the "Razumovsky" String Quartet, op. 59, no. 3, the Quintet for Piano and Winds, op. 16, and the Septet, op. 20, at Schuppanzigh's concert to mark his departure for Russia; of a piano sonata (probably opus 90) played by Stainer von

Felsburg; and of the Cello Sonata, op. 69, played by Carl Czerny and Joseph Linke (a member of the Schuppanzigh and Razumovsky quartets) at Linke's own farewell concert before joining Countess Erdödy's household in Croatia. In addition, there were performances by the singer Franz Wild of "Adelaide" and "An die Hoffnung" with Beethoven at the piano, and of four of the opus 18 String Quartets at concerts in violinist Joseph Böhm's string quartet series in November and December, held at the hall of the inn Zum römischen Kaiser (the Roman Caesar).

The remarkable resurgence of Beethoven to domination of Vienna's large-scale concert life began at a benefit concert for the Hospital of St. Mark on December 26, 1816, at which the Seventh Symphony was performed, and continued with a rush into 1817, a year in which his music was offered at sixteen separate concerts, produced by such organizations as the Gesellschaft der Musikfreunde and the Tonkünstler-Societät on behalf of a variety of charities, and presented at academies for an array of virtuosos, including the violinists Franz Clement and Pietro Rovelli and the flutist Johann Sedlaczek. The programs of these concerts indicate that certain of Beethoven's works had achieved the status of standard repertory pieces that could attract audiences eager to hear them repeatedly. The "Choral Fantasia" and the *Egmont* Overture were each offered three times, the Seventh Symphony twice (along with a separate performance of the Allegretto), plus performances of *Christus am Öelberge,* the Mass in C, and the overtures to *Prometheus* and *King Stephen.* Chamber music was represented by the "Kreutzer" Sonata and the "Archduke" Trio. In 1818, his music was heard at a minimum of twenty-five concerts, with even more varied selections: again, the Seventh Symphony was featured (both in full and in part), the *Egmont* Overture was given four times; the "Name Day" Overture, op. 115, three times, the *Coriolan* Overture and *Wellingtons Sieg* twice each; plus the Piano Concertos in C minor, op. 37, and in E-flat ("Emperor"), op. 73, the latter played by Czerny on April 12 at an academy for the horn virtuoso Friedrich Hradetzky. A major event was a performance on May 3 of the first movement of the *Eroica* Symphony at a concert of the Gesellschaft der Musikfreunde. In addition, there were performances of the Quintet in C, op. 29, the Septet, op. 20, the "Choral Fantasia," the Triple Concerto, op. 56, and lesser pieces like the ever-popular

"Adelaide" and the Rondo in B-flat for Piano and Orchestra, WoO 6, showing that the Viennese had developed an extraordinarily diverse appetite for virtually the full range of Beethoven's oeuvre. Of course his music also had its detractors. At the December 16, 1816, concert for the Hospital of St. Mark, the Seventh Symphony was faintly applauded and the beloved Allegretto failed to receive its customary encore, facts that Beethoven's friends at the *Wiener Musik-Zeitung* quaintly attributed to the "dense crowding of the audience [which] hindered the free use of their hands."[96] In 1816 Beethoven complained to a visitor, Karl Bursy, "Art no longer stands so high above the ordinary, is no longer so respected, and above all is no longer valued in terms of recompense."[97]

But if some segments of the Viennese populace wanted a different kind of musical fare, these were more than offset by the majority of concertgoers. Perhaps even more significant were the connoisseurs and music lovers who gathered at musicales given at the homes of Carl Czerny, the Ertmanns, the Streichers, and elsewhere, to perform and to hear Beethoven's chamber music and music for solo piano. Beethoven himself often participated in such private concerts. The musician Friedrich Starke recalled that during the years 1816–18 Beethoven was "seldom absent" from the weekly musicales at the Streicher house in the Ungargasse, which had a private concert hall, and that on occasion he brought along his nephew, Karl, to hear his music.[98] Czerny remembered that "in the years from 1818 to 1820 I organized concerts by my pupils every Sunday in my lodgings; they played to quite a select audience, and Beethoven was usually present; he still improvised even then, and did so several times for us; everyone was deeply stirred and moved."[99] In addition, although he no longer performed in public as a pianist, he continued to perform more or less annually as a conductor, even if this was a role for which he had never been well suited. He directed the Seventh Symphony at the concert for the Hospital of St. Mark in 1816, the Eighth Symphony at a Christmas concert for the Hospital Fund in 1817, and the Seventh once again, on January 17, 1819, at another charity concert.

Outside Vienna, Beethoven had moved into a position of extraordinary preeminence and popular appreciation, unmatched by any nonoperatic composer of the era and even surpassing the great popularity of Mozart and Haydn. In Graz, of approximately four hundred separate performances by ninety-three composers of works given at concerts of the Steiermärkischer Musikverein (Styrian Musical Society) between 1815 and 1829, fifty were of music by Beethoven, who was by far the most frequently played composer and author of the weightiest and lengthiest compositions. His symphonies, in whole and in part, were featured on twelve occasions, and the Symphonies Nos. 5, 6, and 7 were repeatedly performed; nineteen symphonic overtures were programmed, including the *Fidelio* Overture nine times and the *Egmont* seven times. Other Graz favorites were *Wellingtons Sieg*, which was offered on seven occasions; the "Choral Fantasia" (five complete performances); "Adelaide" (five); and "Calm Sea and Prosperous Voyage."[100]

Beethoven's popularity continued unabated in England, and in 1817 he was invited by the Philharmonic Society to visit London the following winter. He accepted the offer, which called for him to compose two new symphonies for performance at several concerts for his own benefit. The planned journey never came to fruition, but the offer was the impetus leading to the first serious consideration of the Ninth Symphony and even of plans for another ambitious symphony.

Beethoven's main biographers did not approve of his actions in the guardianship struggle, on either pragmatic or ethical grounds, nor was the eccentricity of his behavior lost upon them. In their influential monograph, *Beethoven and His Nephew*, psychoanalysts Editha and Richard Sterba not only condemned Beethoven's actions but attributed them to "a breakdown of the ethical structure of his personality."[101] The facts of the matter, however, do not compel so extreme an interpretation, one that would force us to believe that the masterpieces of Beethoven's last years were composed by a cruel and unethical human being. In actuality, Beethoven's feelings of guilt at separating Karl from his mother were a constant source of concern and pain to him. As early as 1816, Fanny Giannattasio reported that he cried out, "What will people say, they will take me for a tyrant!"[102] And in his *Tagebuch* of 1817 he quoted the closing lines from Schiller's *Die Braut von Messina*: "This one thing I feel and clearly perceive: life is not the sovereign good, but the greatest evil is guilt."[103] In early 1818, Beethoven revealed in full the agony that his obsessive actions against Johanna were causing him:

I have fulfilled my part, O Lord. It would have been impossible without hurting the widow's feelings but it was not to be. And Thou,
almighty God, seest into my heart, know that I have disregarded my
own welfare for my dear Karl's sake, bless my work, bless the widow,
why cannot I entirely follow my heart and henceforth—the widow—
God, God, my refuge my rock, O my all, Thou seest my innermost
heart and knowest how it pains me to make somebody suffer through
my good works for my dear Karl!!!![104]

His diary then noted the debts with which his sister-in-law was burdened, and Beethoven now addressed Johanna directly, lamenting:
"Lamentable fate! why can I not help you?"[105]

Clearly, in his most private musings Beethoven acknowledged the
unmerciful nature of his actions, showing that his ability to make moral
judgments had not been impaired. He had yielded to impulses that his
conscience rejected, but he yielded with considerable anguish, and
hoped to find forgiveness for his actions. We may condemn his inhu-
manity toward Karl and Johanna, but we should balance this by understanding that he was in the grip of forces that he could not control and
that in his way he ultimately sought atonement.

One cannot hope, amid the multitude of inextricably blended motivations of Beethoven's behavior, to isolate any single one as the main
determinant. On one level, the Sterbas are surely correct in stressing the
pivotal effect of Beethoven's feelings about his brother, in that he appro-
priated Caspar Carl's son and became entangled with his wife.
Perhaps—to extend their thesis somewhat—Beethoven sought thereby
to resurrect (or to take the place of) a brother to whom he was still
ambivalently connected by powerful ties no doubt dating from their
very earliest days as children in Bonn. That is not surprising, for symptoms such as those manifested by Beethoven are most often a continuation of, and are modeled on, archaic conflicts dating from infancy and
childhood. On another level, Beethoven's actions can be understood as a
series of violent alternations between incestuous and matricidal drives.
Some may sense in reading Beethoven's distraught listings of Johanna's
alleged "crimes" (which objectively amount to so little) that he was
unconsciously accusing her of an altogether different set of offenses,
which he was unable to formulate and which had very little to do with

her real presence. Instead, Johanna had come to define for him some negative archetypal essence of the feminine—as taboo object of desire, and as embodiment of carnal sin, maternal neglect, and marital betrayal. To what extent Beethoven's feelings had their ultimate source in his attitude toward his own mother, in which love and desire apparently warred with feelings of neglect and even abandonment, is impossible to determine.[106]

The father, Johann van Beethoven, is not absent in the nephew struggle. On the simplest level, Beethoven had here finally put himself in the place of the father: he had gotten himself a son. Perhaps his rage against Johanna arose from the fact that her motherhood irrefutably contradicted his claim of fatherhood.[107] Furthermore, Beethoven may well have been attempting in his fashion to take upon himself the role of the righteous, "good" father (modeled, perhaps, on his image of his grandfather), which his own father had not been able to fulfill. Paradoxically, his crude behavior toward Karl reveals his unwitting repetition of his father's pattern: perhaps he was simultaneously repeating and repairing his father's ill treatment of himself.

There is abundant evidence that Beethoven's strivings were of a paternal nature. The death of his brother presented Beethoven, perpetually thwarted in his plans for marriage, with an opportunity to become the head of a family. So deep was his desire to accomplish this—especially at this difficult moment of his musical evolution—that his perception of reality blurred and he persuaded himself that he had become a father in fact. We may recall that Beethoven had once before assumed the role of head of the family, following the deaths of his mother and eighteen-month-old sister in 1787 and the descent of his father into terminal alcoholism. It is not impossible that Beethoven's appropriation of his nephew had its root in a compulsion to repeat the experiences of the last, tragic years in Bonn, when he had assumed the primary responsibility to care for his helpless father and young brothers. Perhaps, too, Beethoven was attempting now to make reparation for his abandonment of his family in late 1792, and even to assuage his guilt at the death of his father, which followed so poignantly on his departure for Vienna.

There are many ghosts at the party; indeed, all of the primal figures of Beethoven's life appear to have gathered here in reunion. In his frenzied, almost hallucinatory, state, the leading characters in this domestic tragedy successively and even simultaneously took on the images of the members of Beethoven's original family. His sister-in-law was "split" into fragments of the mother image, alternately perceived as the neglectful, poisoning wife and as the valiant defender of her off-spring, as prostitute and as unattainable love object. Sometimes he even seems to have identified her with his father—as an embezzler and mis-creant, unfit to rear a child. She became the omnipotent and wrathful superego who aroused his terror and awe to such an extent that he variously referred to her as Minerva, Circe, Medea, and, repeatedly, as the "Queen of Night" of Mozart's *Magic Flute*, whose initial mission to rescue her child is overtaken by her own malevolence. (In one letter of 1819, following the exposure of his own nobility pretense, Beethoven even granted Johanna the aristocratic honorific "von," twice writing her name as "Frau *von* Beethoven.")[108]

Beethoven's perception of his nephew was equally fluid: Karl was Beethoven himself, rescued from his false and unworthy parents by the good prince, royal father, and nourishing mother; he was Beethoven's child, narcissistically (divinely) conceived; he embodied the wish that Karl Abraham described, "to have begotten oneself, that is to say, to be one's own father";[109] he was a surrogate for and continuation of Caspar Carl, whose rebirth was reenacted in Beethoven's "rescue" scenario; he was at once Beethoven's hapless father and his partly orphaned younger brothers with whose care the adolescent Beethoven had been charged in 1787; and—even more speculatively—he may also have been a revenant of the firstborn Ludwig Maria, subject, therefore, to the vicissitudes of Beethoven's fratricidal and fraternal impulses.

In this dizzying series of splittings and substitutions, Caspar Carl, Karl, and Beethoven each in turn play the roles of father, brother, and son. As for Beethoven himself, he quite simply united father, mother, brother, and son in a single person—himself. Beethoven had returned to the houses on the Bonngasse, the Wenzelgasse, the Dreieckplatz, and the Rheingasse, there to wrestle with ancient events and relationships in a dreamlike attempt to rewrite the history of his childhood, to create an ideal family in accordance with the strange logic of his desires.

In the course of the formation and dissolution of this fantasy family, Ludwig van Beethoven learned something of the nature of parenthood and touched regions of experience from which he had hitherto been

Karl van Beethoven at a later age. Undated photograph.

From Paul Bekker, Beethoven *(Berlin, 1911).*

excluded. The appropriation of his nephew represented the distorted form through which Beethoven shattered the frozen patterns of a bachelor existence and came to know the passions and tragedies of tumultuous personal relationships. The abstract, spiritualized aspects of conjugal love had been celebrated in *Fidelio;* the *"ferne Geliebte"* had been the ideal beloved precisely because of her unattainability; now Beethoven had penetrated to the tragic substratum that underlies relationships between real human beings.

To what extent these experiences were necessary in shaping the special qualities of Beethoven's last works is difficult to tell. Certainly he emerged from this ordeal a changed person. Beethoven's psychological regression in the years from 1815 to 1820 involved the dissolution of his weakened and malfunctioning defenses, the smashing of his nobility pretense, and the partial emergence of the Family Romance and its attendant fantasies of illegitimacy so that they could be examined in the light of reason. Karl and Johanna had served as catalysts to bring Beethoven's deepest conflicts and desires to the surface, perhaps thereby helping to set the scene for a breakthrough of his creativity into hitherto unimagined territories.

The road to Beethoven's last period was a dangerous one, fraught with anxieties and touching realms of traumatic significance sufficient to undermine—and almost overwhelm—the composer's personality. In the course of this titanic struggle, Beethoven approached the borderline of an irreversible pathology. He turned back both by tapping the resources of his ego and through the assistance—however unwitting—of Johanna van Beethoven, who held up to him the mirror of reality and insisted that his actions be measured against the standards of law and morality. Ultimately Johanna's heroic and passionate struggle for her son and for the preservation of her motherhood may have prevented Beethoven from losing contact altogether with the inner core of his own humanity.

CHAPTER NINETEEN

PORTRAIT
OF AN AGING COMPOSER

THAT BEETHOVEN WAS A MAN OF CONSIDERABLE eccentricity had been known to his contemporaries since Bonn days. After his appropriation of his nephew, Karl, however, the belief that he was something more than eccentric became common currency in Vienna. In 1816, for example, Charlotte Brunsvik wrote, "I learned yesterday that Beethoven had become crazy."[1] The German composer Carl Friedrich Zelter wrote to Goethe in 1819, "Some say he is a lunatic."[2] At that same time Ferdinand Ries, on receiving a startling last-minute request for a revision of the "Hammerklavier" Sonata, "began to wonder if my dear old teacher had really gone daft, a rumor which was going about at various times."[3] During these years, Beethoven railed openly against the nobility, the courts, and the emperor himself, seemingly oblivious of the possible consequences in Metternich's police state. "He defies everything and is dissatisfied with everything and blasphemes against Austria and especially against Vienna," reported Karl Bursy, a medical doctor who visited him in 1816,[4] and young Peter Joseph Simrock, the son of Nikolaus Simrock, heard Beethoven, still smarting from the devaluation of the Austrian currency, say of Kaiser Franz, "Such a rascal ought to be hanged."[5] The police did not disturb Beethoven, in part because he was Beethoven and because he had several friends in imperial circles, but also because he was thought to be a little touched. When Rossini in 1822 implored the Austrian court aristocracy to mitigate Beethoven's financial distress, the universal reply was that there was no point in offering aid; they considered Beethoven not merely deaf, but a misanthrope, a recluse, and mentally unbalanced.

Beethoven was well aware of this reputation. In 1820 he warned his admirer Dr. Wilhelm Christian Müller "not to be misled by the

Beethoven in the Rain.
Undated India ink sketch by Johann Nepomuk Hoechle (ca. 1823).

Original lost.

Viennese, who regard [me] as crazy," and also told him, "If a sincere, independent opinion escapes me, as it often does, they think me mad."[6]

Signs of neurotic disorder—sudden rages, uncontrolled emotional states, an increasing obsession with money, feelings of persecution, ungrounded suspicions—persisted until Beethoven's death, reinforcing Vienna's belief that its greatest composer was a sublime madman. The dramatist Franz Grillparzer, who became closely acquainted with Beethoven in 1823 during a fruitless collaboration on an opera, told Thayer that Beethoven was "half crazy," and on another occasion reported that when Beethoven was irritated "he became like a wild animal."[7] Beethoven's manner and appearance during his later years did nothing to retard the spread of these impressions. Schindler wrote, "His head, which was unusually large, was covered with long, bushy gray hair, which, being always in a state of disorder, gave a certain wildness to his appearance. This wildness was not a little heightened when he suffered his beard to grow to a great length, as he frequently did."[8] His intimate friend Nannette Streicher told the British publishers Mary and Vincent Novello he was "as a beggar he was so dirty in his dress, and in manner like a bear sulky and froward, he laughed like no one else it was a scream, he would call people names as he passed them. . . . he was avaricious and always mistrustful.[9] Her husband added that Beethoven was "always jealous and thinking his friends were deceiving him, even before his deafness attacked him."[10] The story of his arrest by the Wiener Neustadt police in 1821 or 1822 on the grounds that he had been peering into windows and looked like a tramp was surely widely circulated. In the taverns and restaurants he would dicker with waiters about the price of each roll, or would ask for his bill without having eaten. On the street, his broad gestures, loud voice, and ringing laugh made his nephew, Karl, ashamed to walk with him, and caused passersby to regard him as demented. Street urchins mocked the stumpy and muscular figure, with his low top hat of uncertain shape, who walked Vienna's streets dressed in a long, dark-colored overcoat that reached nearly to his ankles, carrying a double lorgnette or a monocle and pausing repeatedly to make hieroglyphic entries in his notebook as he hummed and howled in an off-key voice.

Beethoven's physical health also began to deteriorate after around 1815. By 1820–21 the first symptoms of jaundice, an ominous sign of liver disease, made their appearance. Ultimately he developed cirrhosis of the liver, which was no doubt accelerated by a substantial intake of alcoholic beverages. Thayer, scrupulously following every lead, extracted the cost of Beethoven's wine purchases from his daily house-keeping records, and found that his consumption of wine was far from moderate.[11] But there is no reason to conclude from this that Beethoven had now begun to follow in his father's footsteps. "He drank a great deal of wine at table," said Beethoven's friend Karl Holz to Otto Jahn, "but could stand a great deal, and in merry company he sometimes became tipsy."[12] But he rarely exceeded his one bottle of wine per meal, and when he and Holz once tried to drink Sir George Smart under the table ("We will try how much the Englishman can drink," Smart overheard him say to Holz), it was Beethoven who had the worst of the trial.[13]

It is a measure of Beethoven's character that those who knew him, whether visitors or long-term friends, during his difficult final decade withheld neither their love nor their sympathy from him. The journalist Friedrich Wähner, who resided in Vienna between 1818 and 1825, spoke of Beethoven's "childlike naivete" and likened him to "an amiable boy."[14] Grillparzer, who was no sentimentalist, told of "the sad condition of the master during the latter years of his life, which prevented him from always distinguishing clearly between what had actually happened and what had been merely imagined"—a recognition that did not lessen his compassion. "And yet," he wrote on another occasion, "for all his odd ways, which . . . often bordered on being offensive, there was something so inexpressibly touching and noble in him that one could not but esteem him and feel drawn to him."[15] Many who had been warned of Beethoven's peculiarities feared to visit him, but met instead with a warm and friendly reception, and even received a fond embrace upon their departure.

Beethoven had gradually formed a new circle of friends. These men were for the most part devoted but faintly sycophantic, always ready to serve his needs, whether these were for companionship, advice, small services, or endless small talk. His friends of this sort were quite numerous, and only the leading ones can be mentioned here. Many of them belonged to the world of Viennese music-publishing, including such men as Antonio Diabelli, Sigmund Anton Steiner, and Tobias Haslinger. Beethoven regularly visited Steiner's music shop in the narrow Paternostergassel at the northeast end of the Graben, where many musicians, writers, and admirers—including Schuppanzigh, Czerny, Holz, Böhm, Linke, and Mayseder—gathered to speak with the composer or, like Franz Schubert, worship him from a distance. Beethoven's association with Steiner's firm, which began in 1813 and lasted a full decade, was, despite several business quarrels for which Beethoven was entirely to blame, the most amiable and enjoyable of his associations with publishers. He enlisted Steiner's associates in his private "army," dubbing himself the Generalissimo, Steiner the Lieutenant General, Haslinger the Little Adjutant, and Diabelli the Provost Marshal. Beethoven was fondest of young Haslinger, a trusted employee of Steiner's who ultimately became sole owner of the firm, and engaged in a merry correspondence with him during his last decade; occasional strains in their relationship were readily dissolved in jest.

Another cluster of friends loosely formed what we may term Beethoven's Conversation Book circle. These gathered with him singly and in small groups at favorite taverns and restaurants and discussed everything under the sun—music, politics, gossip, the news of the day, Beethoven's family affairs and career decisions—in the rambling, free-associational fashion one would expect in such situations, after 1818 "conversing" with the deaf man by writing in his Conversation Books. Dr. Müller described him holding court in this fashion at an inn where he took his midday meal: "He would enter into conversation on a variety of topics, and, free of prejudice, express himself critically or satirically about everything: about the government, about the police, about the morals of the aristocracy."[16]

The members of this retinue included some of Vienna's leading journalists and editors, such as Karl Bernard, editor of the *Wiener Zeitung*, Friedrich August Kanne, editor of the *Wiener Allgemeine musikalische Zeitung* from 1820 to 1824 (succeeding Beethoven's friend and colleague Ignaz von Seyfried in that post), Johann Schickh, editor of the *Wiener Zeitschrift für Kunst, Literatur, Theater und Mode*, and Friedrich Wähner, who edited *Janus* from 1818 until its publication was suspended in June 1819. Kanne, a prolific (but unsuccessful) composer as well as a theologian, physician, and poet, was the most interesting—and most eccentric—of this group. He counseled Beethoven on literary and aesthetic matters and may, as Warren Kirkendale argues, have guided him through the abstruse literature on Catholic liturgy and ecclesiastical music during the composition of the *Missa Solemnis*. Wähner, who originally had been a Protestant preacher, was evidently the most radical (or perhaps the least discreet) of this group, and he was expelled from Vienna by the police in the mid-1820s.

Other members of the circle at various times were Karl Peters, tutor of the younger Lobkowitz children; Franz Oliva, who after a long absence from Vienna between 1813 and 1818 became Beethoven's frequent associate from then until December 1820, when he left to take up permanent residence in Russia; Beethoven's lawyer and friend, Johann Baptist Bach, who was a member of the law faculty at the University of Vienna; Joseph Blöchlinger, the director of the institute attended by Karl between June 1819 and August 1823, who could occasionally be seen engaged in a game of chess with Beethoven; and Anton Schindler, a competent musician (formerly a law student), who had briefly met Beethoven in 1814 and became the composer's factotum, amanuensis, and scapegoat for a year and a half from the winter of 1822–1823 to spring 1824 and for three months from late December 1826 until March 1827.[17] Schindler detested Beethoven's relatives and was jealous of many of the composer's close associates. His attitude toward Beethoven himself was compounded of servility, worship, and hatred in more or less equal parts, all of which alternate freely in his influential but unreliable biographical studies of the composer. In addition to these Viennese friends, associates, and cronies, Beethoven was visited by a steady stream of admirers, fellow musicians, music publishers, and foreign luminaries, ranging from Rossini to the young Liszt, and from a variety of Romantic poets to such British music lovers as George Smart and Johann Andreas Stumpff.

The German-speaking countries had entered what historians call the "quiet years," which historian A. J. P. Taylor describes as "the dead period when the Napoleonic storm had blown over and when the new forces which were to disrupt Germany had not established themselves."[18] Although most of Beethoven's friends had secure and even important positions in Viennese life, the Conversation Books reveal that they were disenchanted and dismayed by the regressive aspects of imperial rule, which could no longer be disguised as patriotic necessities. They felt cheated by currency devaluations, certain that they were getting less than their fair share of social and economic privileges. "The aristocrats are again receiving charity in Austria," the musician F. X. Gebauer, a founder of the Gesellschaft der Musikfreunde and guiding force behind the Viennese Concerts Spirituels, wrote in a Conversation Book, "and the republican spirit smolders only faintly in the ashes."[19] Many members of Beethoven's circle—including Oliva, Blöchlinger, Karl, Schindler, Bernard, and Grillparzer—often inveighed against the censorship. Grillparzer, who had recently had an unpleasant encounter with the police, bitterly noted, "The censor has broken me down," causing Holz to remark, "One must emigrate to North America in order to give his ideas free expression."[20] On another occasion Holz observed, "The poets are worse off than the composers with the censor, which works for obscurantism and the introduction of stupidity."[21]

To Beethoven, whose intellectual development took place within the context of the German striving for *Gedankenfreiheit* (freedom of thought), there could be no greater evil than the suppression of ideas and of rational inquiry. Accordingly, he despised the Austrian government, with its network of police agents and its rigid censorship, and, as we have seen, he was not fearful of voicing his sentiments. He summed up his feelings about the government in a succinct phrase, "A paralytic regime."[22] At least one of his friends regarded him (perhaps in jest) as a firebrand: in April 1823 Peters wrote, "You are a *revolutionary*, a *Carbonaro*," a reference to the Carbonari, a quasi-Masonic secret society that originated in Italy and was credited with playing a role in various national uprisings during the 1820s.[23] Nephew Karl, however, feared reprisals and repeatedly urged caution upon Beethoven. "Silence! The walls have ears," he wrote;[24] and he warned, "The Baron [Sigmund Prónay] is a chamberlain of the Emperor. I think that you should not speak against the regime with him."[25]

Nevertheless, these men seem to have led quiet, orderly, and productive lives, and they did not envisage or advocate any radical restructuring of society. In the main, they expressed little but helpless regret and impotent resentment at what they viewed as the decline of an Enlightened Europe. "It seems to me that we Europeans are going backwards, and America is raising itself in culture," wrote Bernard.[26] The group was momentarily stirred by the news of the murder in 1819 in Mannheim of the writer August von Kotzebue by a member of one of the *Burschenschaften,* which were associations of discontented, nationalistic students who pressed for German political unity. The subsequent heightened repression and censorship embodied in Metternich's Karlsbad Decrees of September 1819 only deepened the sense of political futility.

Beethoven and his friends hoped in some vague and undefined way for a return of the Josephinian reform period, which they remembered as having been opposed to entrenched interest. They cherished the past, and looked back to the pre-Napoleonic period as Vienna's Periclean or Augustan age. In May 1820 Bernard wrote, "Before the French Revolution great freedom of thought and political liberty prevailed here."[27] They had no clear social program, and they appeared to pin their tenuous hopes for change on a powerful redeemer who could restore the presumed glories of an earlier time. "The whole of Europe is going to the dogs," wrote Bernard; "N[apoleon] should have been let out for ten years" to set things straight.[28] But such redeemers were not readily at hand. Meanwhile, Beethoven and his associates grumbled and complained, and gazed with envy at the British political system, with its constitutional monarchy and reputed freedom of expression.

But politics and social issues were not the only—or even the central—concerns of the Conversation Book circle.[29] Kanne and Beethoven, until they ultimately tired of endless disputation, engaged in heated debates about musical keys; the former insisted that keys did not convey particular psychological qualities, whereas Beethoven asserted that each had unique emotional characteristics, which were destroyed by transposition. The conversations occasionally turned bawdy. Beethoven remarked, on seeing a passing woman, "What a magnificent behind, from the side!"[30] and customs inspector Franz Janitschek sacrilegiously asked Beethoven whether it was true that Jesus' male organ was exhibited as a relic in a certain woman's convent in Bonn.[31]

Women were totally absent from the circle of Beethoven's close friends during his last years. The extent of this withdrawal is thrown into high relief by a single statistic: of 262 Beethoven letters written between 1787 and the end of 1809, 27 were to women; of approximately 731 between 1810 and 1818, 118 were addressed to women (half of them to

Nannette Streicher), but of 870 letters from the last eight years and three months of Beethoven's life, only 7 were to women—one to Countess Erdödy in 1819, a dedicatory letter to Maximiliane Brentano in 1821, two responses to an invitation from Frau Streicher in August 1824 (his only preserved communications with her after 1818), and one each to Johanna van Beethoven and the singer Henriette Sontag in the same year. Last is a single line agreeing to receive the granddaughter of the music historian Charles Burney in September 1825. I do not count two notes of 1826 to the fishmonger Therese Jonas ordering three pounds of carp and a small pike.

Antonie Brentano and her daughter were honored with dedications of the Sonata in E, op. 109, the "Diabelli" Variations, op. 120, and the English edition of the Sonata in C minor, op. 111—the only women to receive dedications of Beethoven's works during the 1820s.[32] Beethoven no longer indulged in his love pretenses, as he had with Anna Giannattasio and perhaps with the Graz pianist Marie Pachler-Koschak during the latter's Viennese visit in 1817. When Frau Streicher suggested that he needed a "lady to take care of him" and advised him "to marry," he "shook his head bitterly (probably thought no Lady could love one who was so deaf)."[33] Moreover, until a reconciliation with Stephan von Breuning took place in the summer of 1825, he didn't attach himself to any surrogate families after his removal of his nephew from the Giannattasio school led to a separation from the Giannattasios in 1819.

This is not to say that Beethoven now avoided women. He was still capable of teasing the singers Henriette Sontag and Karoline Unger when they visited him in 1822. From a distance, Beethoven repeatedly warned Ries that he would shortly be arriving in London to kiss Ries's wife. "Take care," he wrote, "You think that I am *old*, but I am a *youthful old man.*"[34] Beethoven's sexual activity seems to have continued during this period. In a Conversation Book of 1820, Janitschek explicitly referred to the composer's having been seen looking for prostitutes: he wrote, "Where were you going about 7:00 o'clock today hunting for girls [auf dem Strich gegangen] in the district near the Haarmarkt?" The phrase *"auf dem Strich gehen,"* widespread as early as the eighteenth century, is fairly unambiguously a reference to the pursuit of prostitutes. Beethoven's unrecorded response apparently elicited Janitschek's further remark, in Latin: "*Culpam transferre in alium* [Blame it on someone else]."[35] In a Conversation Book of the previous year Beethoven noted down the title of a book, which in translation reads *On the Art of Recognizing and Curing All Forms of Venereal Disease*, indicating, perhaps, that this was a subject in which he took a more than theoretical interest.[36] (It is speculated that he may once have suffered from a minor venereal disease that responded successfully to treatment.) He was, however, now no longer sleeping only with prostitutes. "Would you like to sleep with my wife?" asked Karl Peters in a Conversation Book of January 1820.[37] Rolland thinks this was said "for the fun of it,"[38] but though the situation may have had its comical aspects there is no reason to assume it was simply an idle question. Peters was about to leave on a trip and generously offered his wife—whom Fanny Giannattasio del Rio described as "very promiscuous"[39]—to Beethoven for a night. Beethoven's reply has not been preserved, but it was apparently affirmative, for Peters wrote that he would go and "fetch his wife." The next day, or a few days later, Janitschek greeted Beethoven with the words "I salute you, O Adonis!" and a few lines later Peters chimed in, "You appear to be very adventurous today. Therefore, why don't you protest against the sole visit to my wife."[40] On several other occasions documented in the Conversation Books, Peters offered a girl to Beethoven. And it appears that Janitschek's wife (from whom he had separated the previous year) was also available. Bernard wrote, "Peters tells us that Frau Janitschek pulled off his mantle as Potiphar did that of Joseph. You also should sleep with Frau von Janitschek."[41] We need not here explore the full import of this apparently free exchange of sexual favors among members of Beethoven's Conversation Book circle: the latent homoerotic implications of this ménage are not far from the surface. What it tells about Beethoven is that he had limited his sexual activity to a succession of loveless relationships that served to discharge his sexual tension but did not engage his deeper feelings.

At every point in his life up to 1820, Beethoven had maintained contact with and depended on one or more mother figures, who helped to maintain his ethical integrity and encouraged or inspired his creativity. This series began with the widows von Breuning and Koch in Bonn and continued with Princess Lichnowsky (and perhaps Countess Wilhelmine Thun) in the early Vienna years and with Countess Erdödy and the women of the Brunsvik-Guicciardi families up to approximately 1810. Antonie Brentano combined this role with that of the saintly, understanding, and beloved woman for a number of years after 1810, even at a distance from Vienna. In 1817 and 1818, the gifted Nannette Streicher served as Beethoven's archetypal self-sacrificing mother substitute. All in all, these women sensed Beethoven's innermost needs and helped him to maintain his commitments both to art and to the categorical imperative.

These commitments were now embedded in Beethoven's nature. The voices of authority and conscience had been internalized. Beethoven now had no Neefe or Lichnowsky to teach and encourage him, and no surrogate mothers to nurture him. But his need for an external source of strength was now being met in another way. Earlier, during the critical years in which he first felt the serious symptoms of his deafness, we saw the signs of a brief religious awakening in Beethoven. Those religious impulses largely disappeared from view for a decade thereafter; apparently, Beethoven's deep worship of nature along with his devotion to Reason managed to serve him as substitutes for religious belief. However, the long crisis that inaugurated Beethoven's late style—a crisis that encompassed both the waning of the Age of Reason and the undermining of Beethoven's rationality in the course of the guardianship struggle—also saw him begin a broad and complex search for a religious faith.[42] He embarked upon a spiritual journey through numerous world religions—Eastern, Egyptian, Mediterranean, and various Christian forms as well—the details of which may be read in his Tagebuch. In that intimate diary he communed with a wide variety of deities and freely gave expression both to his yearnings for solace and to his feelings of dependency on a supernatural being. This is not to say that Beethoven became an adherent of any particular religion in a formal sense; apart, perhaps, from his enfeebled acceptance of the last rites upon the urging of his friends and relatives, he never tempered his disdain for hierarchical religion or for the icons of revealed faith. Nor did he abandon his stalwart adherence to Reason. Rather, he now sought to unite Enlightenment precepts with a conception of an omniscient, omnipotent, ubiquitous, and benevolent father principle reigning in a future peaceable kingdom.

In a letter to Archduke Rudolph in July 1821 Beethoven wrote, "God . . . sees into my innermost heart and knows that as a man I perform most conscientiously and on all occasions the duties which Humanity, God, and Nature enjoin upon me."[43] "Humanity, God, and Nature"—these were Beethoven's spiritual trinity, one that stood as the foundation of an ever-ascending superstructure of faith and expectation, and that would not fail to leave its impress upon his last works.

In order to compose those works, Beethoven now needed conditions of tranquillity that had been absent from his life for too long. "Plea for inner and outer peace," he wrote on sketches of the *Missa Solemnis,* in a phrase of personal as well as of religious significance.[44] Fragile, sickly, rapidly aging, wounded by the events of the previous years, and perhaps stunned by the implications of his own compulsive actions in the guardianship struggle, Beethoven entered the 1820s.

CHAPTER TWENTY

RECONSTRUCTION

T HE LONGEST CRISIS OF BEETHOVEN'S LIFE came to an end with his "victory" in the Court of Appeal in early 1820. In the broadest sense, this crisis, which reached its climax in 1818–20, had begun as early as 1812, in the painful aftermath of the Immortal Beloved affair. Now, battered and torn from the stresses of the intervening experiences, Beethoven set about reconstructing his life and completing his life's work.

Beethoven's output in the next years can be rapidly outlined. He was apparently in no hurry to demonstrate his genius, despite the proliferating rumors that he was written out.[1] Although it had already become clear that the *Missa Solemnis* could not be completed in time for its original deadline—Archduke Rudolph's installation as archbishop of Olmütz on March 9, 1820—the Credo of the Mass was his chief preoccupation from January to midsummer, with time out for the Piano Sonata in E, op. 109, both early and late in the year: the Sonata was the only major work completed in 1820.[2] Continuing on the Mass, he sketched the Benedictus in mid-autumn, but the date when he commenced sketching for the Agnus Dei is uncertain; perhaps it was started before year's end or, more likely, in the following year.[3] The second of the three last piano sonatas, the Sonata in A-flat, op. 110, was finished on Christmas Day 1821, according to a notation on the autograph score, but further work on the finale continued into the first weeks of 1822. Beethoven's last sonata, the Sonata in C minor, op. 111, despite being dated January 13, 1822, apparently occupied him from December 1821 to late March or early April 1822. His unusually meager productivity in 1821 probably should not be ascribed to his complaints of poor health in several letters of that year, for Beethoven achieved a prodigious productivity in 1822, when his letters contained equally frequent complaints about his continuing medical problems. In

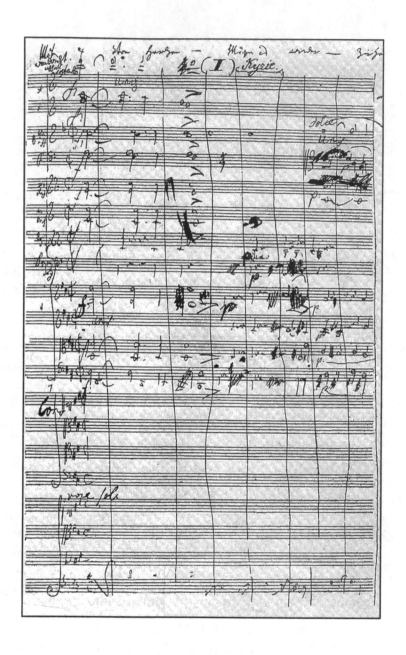

Kyrie of *Missa Solemnis,* first page of autograph full score.
Staatsbibliothek Preussischer Kulturbesitz, Berlin.

1822, in addition to writing opus 111 and finding the definitive form for the last movement of opus 110, he completed the *Missa Solemnis* (save for minor finishing touches), and the Handelian C-major Overture, "Weihe des Hauses" ("Consecration of the House"), op. 124. Between the winter of 1822–23 and May 1823 he also took up and completed the Thirty-three Variations in C on a Waltz by Anton Diabelli, op. 120, and for the first time made substantial progress on the Ninth Symphony. Soon after the Ninth Symphony's completion in 1824 he was already formulating plans for the String Quartet in E-flat, op. 127, which inaugurated the last quartets.

In the intervals between these momentous projects he worked on a number of less significant works, such as his final version of Matthisson's "Opferlied," op, 121b, for soprano, chorus, and orchestra; "Bundeslied," op. 122, for two voices, chorus, and winds, to a text by Goethe; and the Bagatelles for Piano, op. 119, which consists of two distinct groups, nos. 1–6 and 7–11.[4] All of these shorter works have roots in Beethoven's first Vienna decade: the "Bundeslied" initially was sketched as early as the 1790s; the "Opferlied" was the last of a series of settings of this text dating to as early as 1794–95; and the first five of the Bagatelles were written between 1794 and 1802. To these works we should add the Variations in G for Piano, Violin, and Cello on "Ich bin der Schneider Kakadu," op. 121a, because it was initally composed circa 1803, with perhaps additional layers of revisions in 1816 and in the year of its publication, 1824.[5]

Johann Sporschil, a historian and publicist who was then studying in Vienna, described the Beethoven of 1822 and 1823 as "one of the most active men who ever lived" and recalled that "deepest midnight found him still working."[6] He often failed to appear for meals and gatherings, to the dismay of his housekeeper and friends. His absentmindedness increased: he would forget his hat and would be seen bareheaded in inclement weather, his overgrown gray hair dripping in the rain. Everything was subordinated to his work. He no longer strove for heights of personal gratification; the small pleasures of life—walking, eating, drinking, conversation, an occasional pipe—were sufficient. He had reached a stage where he had become wholly possessed by his art. Karl is scarcely mentioned in his correspondence at this time. Beethoven's close Bonn friend Bernhard Romberg gave a cello recital in

February 1822, but Beethoven did not appear, at first pleading an ear-
ache as the cause of his absence, but then giving the real reason—his preoccupation with his work. "If I have not called on you," he wrote, "just
bear in mind the distance of my rooms and my almost ceaseless occupa-
tions, the more so as for a whole year I have been constantly ill and thus
prevented from finishing many compositions which I had begun."[7]

In 1822 the *Allgemeine musikalische Zeitung* reported the news that
Beethoven was improvising at the piano for a small circle of friends, and
could still "handle his instrument with power, spirit, and tenderness."[8]
But he received few visitors. Rossini sought him out in the spring of the
year, was praised for his *Barber of Seville,* and received Beethoven's blunt
opinion that he should not attempt *opera seria,* which the Viennese master considered "ill suited to the Italians. You do not possess sufficient
musical knowledge to deal with real drama."[9] Schubert delivered a set of
variations on a French Song for Piano Four Hands, op. 10, inscribed to
Beethoven from "his Worshipper and Admirer Franz Schubert" but
reportedly did not find Beethoven at home. Johann Friedrich Rochlitz,
the founding editor of the *Allgemeine musikalische Zeitung,* arrived from
Leipzig to survey the Viennese scene and subsequently wrote a
detailed—and almost certainly invented—account of three meetings
with Beethoven. At best, he met the composer on only one occasion, and
did not receive a hearty welcome.[10] His failure to be greeted with open
arms could have been predicted, because Beethoven held Rochlitz
responsible for numerous negative notices in the *Allgemeine musikalische
Zeitung* over the years; he dubbed him "Mephistopheles" and hoped that
Beelzebub would give the editor a warm reception, sooner rather than
later.[11] In 1821, when Beethoven was completing and formulating a
cluster of supreme works, Rochlitz's influential music journal had con-
descendingly written him off: "Beethoven occupies himself, as father
Haydn once did, in the arranging of Scottish songs; for larger undertakings he seems to be completely written out."[12] In a letter to the
Viennese official and composer Ignaz von Mosel of September 14, 1824,
Rochlitz remained skeptical about reports that Beethoven was working
on many ambitious compositions: "After what I saw of him, I no longer
believed this."[13]

But he was wrong. The major projects that had originated during
the guardianship struggle were now coming to fruition. The autograph

score of the *Missa Solemnis* was wholly finished by mid-1823, and the Diabelli Variations by March or April of the same year. The Ninth Symphony then occupied Beethoven for the balance of 1823 and the first two months of 1824.

The remainder of Beethoven's life was devoted to the five String Quartets, opp. 127, 130, 131, 132, and 135. Never before had Beethoven concentrated so exclusively and for so long on a single genre. The String Quartet in E-flat, op. 127, was largely composed during the second half of 1824 and was completed early in the following year. From February to midsummer of 1825 he composed the A-minor Quartet, op. 132. In July and August he wrote most of the first version of the Quartet in B-flat, op. 130—including the monu mental original finale, which was later published separately as the Grosse Fuge, op. 133—and completed it in November. In 1826 he wrote the String Quartets in C-sharp minor, op. 131, and in F, op. 135, ending his creative career in November 1826 with a new finale for opus 130. A few trifles, a fragment of a string quintet, and an arrangement for piano four hands of the Grosse Fuge aside, the quartets were Beethoven's sole preoccupation from February 1824 onward. This is not to say that he had forsaken all future projects: in 1826, when his cycle of quartets was drawing to a close, he briefly began to discuss new ideas for operas, oratorios, concertos, and other works,[14] and on his deathbed Beethoven spoke regretfully of his unfulfilled plans for a Requiem and for a setting of Goethe's *Faust*, and of his ambition to write a piano method. In a letter to Moscheles written a few days before his death he expressed his gratitude for the Philharmonic Society's generosity and pledged to compose for it "either a new symphony, sketches for which are already in my desk, or a new overture, or something else which the Society might like to have."[15] A pocket sketchbook from circa October 1825 contains sketches for both an overture on the letters of Bach's name (B-flat—A—C—B [in German, B—A—C—H]) and for a Tenth Symphony. For the latter Beethoven had begun jotting down ideas as early as October 1822, but he never reached the stage of converting the embryonic concept sketches into continuity drafts, which, as Robert S. Winter observes in a critique of Barry Cooper's so-called "realization" of the first movement, are "the one trustworthy indicator of serious progress on a movement."[16]

This productivity took place against the background of Beethoven's unchallenged position as the most eminent of all living composers, evidenced most convincingly by his continuing popularity on concert programs. At a dozen concerts given during 1819, audiences heard the Second and Seventh symphonies; a movement from the Fourth Symphony; three performances of the *Prometheus* Overture and two of the *Egmont*, plus a scattering of lesser compositions. In 1820, three concerts of the Gesellschaft der Musikfreunde offered the *Eroica*, Fifth, and Eighth Symphonies, as well as a chorus from *Christ on the Mount of Olives*. A benefit concert for widows and orphans, held on April 16, 1820, included one of his overtures, probably the "Name Day," op. 115. A new concert series, F. X. Gebauer's *Concerts spirituels*, featured in its twenty-eight concerts of 1819–21 eight complete performances of Beethoven symphonies plus the Mass in C, *Christ on the Mount of Olives*, and two performances of "Calm Sea and Prosperous Voyage." In 1822 Beethoven was asked to provide music for the opening of the Josephstadt Theater, to take place on October 3, the eve of the Kaiser's name day. The music consisted of a revision of *The Ruins of Athens* to a modified text, with a new chorus, along with a new overture, "Weihe des Hauses" ("The Consecration of the House") in C, op. 124, which, however, was not ready for the premiere. At the opening, which was enthusiastically received, Beethoven shared the conducting responsibilities, and the work was repeated on three succeeding nights.

These numerous and acclaimed performances compel us to doubt Rochlitz's assertion that he heard Beethoven complain in 1822 that he was neglected in Vienna: "*Fidelio?* They cannot give it, nor do they want to listen to it. The symphonies? They have no time for them. My concertos? Everyone grinds out only the stuff he himself has made. The solo pieces? They went out of fashion here long ago, and here fashion is everything."[17] Actually, Beethoven's opera had been staged at least three times annually since 1814,[18] and in the very year of Rochlitz's alleged meeting, Beethoven's ongoing popularity was capped by another revival of *Fidelio* at the Kärntnertor Theater in a benefit performance for the famous soprano Wilhelmine Schröder on November 3, 1822, which enjoyed six repeat performances in the succeeding months. Buoyed by his success at the podium at the Josephstadt Theater opening,

Beethoven tried to conduct the dress rehearsal. Schröder (later Madame Schröder-Devrient) subsequently described the scene:

> The last rehearsals were set, when I learned before the dress rehearsal that *Beethoven* had asked for the honor of conducting the work himself in celebration of the day. . . . With a bewildered face and unearthly inspired eyes, waving his baton back and forth with violent motions, he stood in the midst of the performing musicians and *didn't hear a note!* . . . The inevitable happened: the deaf master threw the singers and orchestra completely off the beat and into the greatest confusion, and no one knew any longer where they were.[19]

Schindler was given the painful task of informing Beethoven of his failure. The latter fled the theater in despair, and, wrote Schindler, "he never wholly recovered from the effect of this blow."[20] (Briefly he was moved to seek treatment for his deafness, first with Dr. Karl von Smetana and then with the priest Pater Weiss, who may have treated—or counseled—him about his hearing infirmity two decades earlier.)

However, Beethoven's productivity was unaffected by the knowledge that, just as he could no longer play the piano in public, so he could no longer conduct. He wrote to Ries in London on December 20, 1822, "Thank God, Beethoven can compose—but, I admit, that is all he is able to do in this world. If God will only restore my health, which has improved at any rate, then I shall be able to comply with all the offers from all the countries of Europe, nay, even of North America; and in that case I might yet make a success of my life."[21]

New proposals came his way. In 1823 the Philharmonic Society of London offered him 50 pounds for a manuscript symphony. The management of the Kärntnertor Theater, encouraged by the success of the *Fidelio* revival, asked Beethoven for a new opera, and he began to examine librettos in search of a fruitful subject. Prince Nikolas Galitzin wrote from St. Petersburg offering Beethoven a generous fee to compose one or more string quartets. On January 25, 1823, Beethoven accepted the offer, promising (optimistically) to complete the first quartet by mid-March at the latest. Visitors now found Beethoven in good spirits, despite eye trouble and other ailments. Carl Maria von Weber wrote in astonishment that "this rough, repellent man actually paid court to me, served me at table as if I had been his lady."[22] Beethoven met several times with Grillparzer, planning their fairy tale opera, *Melusine*, which never reached the sketching stage. Although he despised infant prodigies, he suffered Czerny's student Franz Liszt to play for him and is said to have made appropriate remarks for posterity about the young genius. The musician Louis Schlösser claimed that he found Beethoven, "usually so careless about his attire, dressed with unwonted elegance."[23]

In the winter of 1823–24 Beethoven received an open letter from his most devoted Viennese followers, which laid the groundwork for the greatest public event of this period of his career, the academy of May 7, 1824, at the Kärntnertor Theater. His friends, who knew well his dissatisfaction with Viennese patronage of serious art, hoped to preserve for their city the premieres of the *Missa Solemnis* and the Ninth Symphony. They wrote, in part:

> Out of the wide circle of reverent admirers surrounding your genius in this your second native city, there approach you today a small number of the disciples and lovers of art to give expression to long-felt wishes, timidly to impart a long-withheld entreaty. . . .
>
> Do not withhold longer from popular enjoyment, do not keep any longer from the distressed sense of that which is great and perfect, a performance of the latest masterworks of your hand. We know that a grand sacred composition has been associated with that first one in which you have immortalized the emotions of a soul, penetrated and transfigured by the power of faith and superterrestrial light. We know that a new flower glows in the garland of your glorious, still unrivaled symphonies. For years, ever since the thunders of the victory at Vittoria ceased to reverberate, we have waited and hoped to see you distribute new gifts from the abundance of your wealth to the circle of your friends. Do not disappoint the general expectations any longer! . . .
>
> Need we tell you with what regret your retirement from public life has filled us? Need we assure you that at a time when all glances were hopefully turned towards you, all perceived with sorrow that *the*

one man whom all of us are compelled to acknowledge as foremost among living men in his domain, looked on in silence as foreign art took possession of German soil.[24]

The stilted but heartfelt letter was signed by thirty of the leading musicians, publishers, and music lovers of Vienna. Beethoven was deeply moved by the appeal: "That was very nice of them. It pleases me very much," he reportedly said to Schindler.[25] He and his friends gathered to discuss the proposed concert and to fix its program and performers, and, after much indecision on Beethoven's part, the date and theater were confirmed. Special permission was obtained from the censor to allow the public performance of a sacred work. The size of the orchestra was increased to twenty-four violins, ten violas, and twelve basses and cellos, with doubled winds.

The concert included the "Consecration of the House" Overture, op. 124; the Kyrie, Credo, and Agnus Dei of the *Missa Solemnis,* op. 123, and the Symphony No. 9 in D minor, op. 125. The theater was filled. Zmeskall, crippled by arthritis, was borne to his seat in a sedan chair. Schuppanzigh, who had returned from Russia the previous year, shared the conducting duties with kapellmeister Michael Umlauf. Beethoven stood turning the pages of his score, beating time, but Umlauf had warned the choir and orchestra to pay no attention to the composer, who was so deaf that he could not hear the thunderous applause.

In his review of the concert, the anonymous reviewer for the Leipzig *Allgemeine musikalische Zeitung* pursued the by-now familiar strategy of paying extravagant homage to Beethoven's genius while simultaneously scolding him for his breaches of musical decorum. "Art and truth here celebrate their most brilliant triumph," he wrote about the closing movement of the Ninth Symphony, "and one would be justified in saying: *non plus ultra!* Who can ever surpass these inexpressible heights?" Following this peroration, however, he suggested that even "the composer's most fervent and most impassioned admirers are firmly convinced that this truly unique Finale would be still more imposing if it were in a more concentrated form." And with an unkind thrust he suggested that "the composer himself would share this view, had not cruel fate robbed him of the means of hearing his own creations." In a brilliant review in the *Wiener Allgemeine musikalische Zeitung,* Beethoven's friend Friedrich August Kanne also took a well-worn line of defense, one that had been laid down in E. T. A. Hoffman's pathbreaking review of the Fifth Symphony in 1810: to show, as Kanne put it, the "organic connectedness of all [Beethoven's] musical ideas" and the means by which he succeeded in "bringing manifold diversity into unity." Even the Finale of the Ninth Symphony bears "the stamp of Classicism," he wrote, all of its "diverse, almost contradictory materials . . . linked with great reflectiveness by the chain of imitation," miraculously achieving a state of absolute coherence. Both reviewers had serious reservations about the quality of the performances, the defects of which they attributed to the complexity of the works and an insufficient number of rehearsals. Kanne remarked on the impossibility of holding as many rehearsals as would be necessary in order to achieve the precision and brilliant effects required to perform such "difficult, elaborate music," and he gave way to nostalgia for the old days of enlightened aristocratic patronage, when patrons like Baron van Swieten and his consortium of princes were able to give a full measure of justice to Haydn's most complex works.[26]

Beethoven had high hopes that the concert would be a financial success. (Eager for a large profit, he had, indeed, sought to raise the prices, but was refused permission.) His brother had estimated that with the proceeds Beethoven could pay his long-standing debt to Steiner and "still have 2,000 florins in paper money left over for the summer."[27] His share actually amounted to only a few hundred florins, however. Disappointed, and perhaps overcome by the stresses of the occasion, Beethoven partly spoiled his triumph by charging that the management and Schindler had cheated him. Although Beethoven subsequently withdrew the accusation against Schindler, his anger was unappeased, and Schindler disappeared from the foreground of Beethoven's activities until late in 1826. His place was soon taken by the convivial violinist Karl Holz, the last in the long succession of Beethoven's unpaid and worshipful assistants. ("When I think of the music of Beethoven," he wrote in a Conversation Book, "I am happy to be alive.")[28]

A repetition of the concert on May 23, with a slightly different program, was a failure, partly because it was given at midday on a beautiful Sunday. The house was less than half full, and the receipts were 800 florins short of the actual expenses. Beethoven had to be cajoled into accepting the fee of 500 florins that had been guaranteed to him.

Although these were the last public concerts held for Beethoven's benefit during his lifetime, performances of his works remained frequent. In 1825 alone, in addition to the first performances of the opus 127 and opus 132 String Quartets, there were concerts featuring the Fourth and Seventh Symphonies and the "Archduke" Trio, op. 97. In May, the Ninth Symphony, conducted by Ferdinand Ries, was performed in Aix-la-Chapelle. Many concerts at this time also opened with one or another Beethoven overture. The frequency of performances increased toward the end of the year, with performances of the Mass in C at Vienna's Karlskirche, of both of the Trios, op. 70, and of the *Eroica* Symphony, the "Choral Fantasia," and the Septet, op. 20. On November 29, Beethoven was belatedly elected to honorary membership in the Gesellschaft der Musikfreunde. The society was apparently reconciled to the fact that it would never receive its promised oratorio, although Beethoven continued to hint to Joseph Karl Bernard, the author of the libretto, that it was still in the offing.

Beethoven's greatness had long since become an article of faith in several European countries, and his fame had extended to more distant lands as well. Programs of the Philharmonic Society of London during the decade of the 1820s featured sixty performances of his symphonies and twenty-nine of his overtures. In Vienna, encomiums to his genius in the press were almost excessively flattering. As for Germany, a contemporary traveler reported in 1825 that "the Germans esteem him the most distinguished musical genius of Europe, except Mozart."[29] The German Romantic writers, including such luminaries as Clemens Brentano and E. T. A. Hoffmann, worshiped him to the point of adulation. Schopenhauer regarded his symphonies as expressing the essential nature of music. But acknowledgment of his genius was not universal: a constellation of other eminences—including, on occasion, such writers as Goethe, Hegel, and Grillparzer and such composers as Haydn, Zelter, Weber, Spohr, Cherubini, and even, for a time, Franz Schubert—

found his music deficient when measured against an implicit Classic standard whose ideals included symmetry, objectivity, and moderation. He was denounced for his excessive fancy, his mingling of styles and affects, his infringements of traditional rules.[30] Hegel, an admirer of Mozart and Rossini, maintained his reserve, and his sole comment on Beethoven's music (in which, interestingly, he avoids mention of the composer's name) decries its "powerful contrasts," holding that the "characteristic features of such music readily incur the risk of overstepping the finely drawn boundaries of musical beauty, more especially when the intention is to express force, selfishness, evil, impetuosity, and other extremes of exclusive passion."[31]

During the early 1820s, because of his comparatively low productivity, Beethoven did not earn substantial amounts of money from publications, dedications, or concerts. His main income was the princes' annuity, along with the interest on his eight bank shares (worth 4,000 florins in silver, 10,000 in depreciated currency), but this was not sufficient to meet Beethoven's rather high expenses. He maintained two servants at virtually all times, took a summer residence each year, and had a taste for simple but well-prepared foods and good wines. Furthermore, he had to pay for Karl's board and schooling—2,000 florins per year, he claimed; Johanna's contribution from her pension had long since fallen into arrears. And legal fees, although we do not know their size, must have substantially eroded Beethoven's finances. Like most older people on a fixed income, he feared to touch his capital and insisted that the bank shares had been set aside as Karl's inheritance. It is not surprising, then, that Beethoven began to slip into debt. Over the preceding years, he had borrowed about 3,000 florins from Steiner. Furthermore, the textile merchant Wolfmayer had apparently advanced Beethoven 1,000 florins for the Requiem that Beethoven had promised to write. In 1820, Artaria lent him 750 florins, with repayment guaranteed by Archduke Rudolph. In the preceding year, he had also obtained an advance of 400 florins from the Gesellschaft der Musikfreunde as partial payment for its oratorio. In December 1820, Steiner wrote a restrained but firm letter to Beethoven requesting his money and reminding the composer of his moral obligations. "It is doubly painful to me now to be embarrassed because of my good will and my trust in your word of honor . . . wherefore I conjure you again not to leave me in the lurch and to find means to liquidate my account as soon as possible."[32] Beethoven and Steiner agreed on an extended repayment schedule, and the composer managed to forestall other creditors' demands for several more years, but the pyramiding debts would ultimately lead Beethoven into a complex series of machinations concerning the sale of his *Missa Solemnis* and, more poignantly, to a rupture in his relationship with several close friends and associates.

In 1820 Beethoven offered the publishing rights to the *Missa Solemnis* to Simrock in Bonn, settled on terms, and promised to send it upon completion via Franz Brentano. Simrock was instructed to place 900 gulden in escrow with Brentano, the sum to be released upon delivery of the manuscript. In 1821, however, Beethoven persuaded Brentano to advance to him out of his own pocket the full amount of Simrock's escrow payment. Despite this, he then entered into negotiations concerning the Mass with the Leipzig firm of C. F. Peters, from whom he actually accepted a payment of 1,000 gulden. The full import of Beethoven's dubious conduct became clear with his letters of September 13, 1822, to Brentano and to Simrock, in which he insisted on an increase in the fee, failing which he would "dispatch the Mass to another quarter."[33] Brentano thereupon insisted that Beethoven either fulfill the contract or immediately return the advance. The composer first pledged and then evidently sold off one of his bank shares to meet this and other obligations (even his tailor, Lind, was threatening a lawsuit) and made a partial payment to Brentano in an attempt to renew their friendship. "Command me to undertake whatever task you choose," he wrote, "provided it be within my power to perform it, and I will make every effort to prove to you my regard, my affection, and my gratitude."[34] Brentano, however, apparently demanded full payment, which was not forthcoming, and the friendship ended with Beethoven's words, "I only wish that I were in a position to express my thanks to you in the manner you would most desire."[35]

The vexatious publication history of the *Missa Solemnis* was far from ended. Unknown to Peters, Beethoven was also negotiating with Artaria in Vienna and Schlesinger in Berlin for its publication. Not until the first days of 1825, after further negotiations with Diabelli, Probst, Schlesinger, Peters, and Schott's Sons, did Beethoven settle upon the last of these as worthy of publishing his prize composition. In the interim, he evolved a grandiose plan according to which he would withhold the Mass from publication altogether for a time, and instead offer manuscript copies by subscription to the sovereigns of Europe at 50 gold ducats per copy. Identical letters were sent out in February 1823, along with additional letters to Goethe, Cherubini, and Bernadotte, who was now king of Sweden. Ultimately, ten copies were sold, which took more than a year to copy and deliver. This was not solely or even primarily undertaken as a commercial enterprise, although the profits, after deducting the cost of copying, were more than 1,600 florins. Beethoven had always treasured medals and honors; now he was able freely to acknowledge his need for recognition and appreciation, to reach out to the elevated and royal figures of Europe for tangible signs of their regard. In addition to monetary considerations, that may be why he decided, after seven years, to remind King George IV of England that he had never acknowledged either by sign or hono-rarium Beethoven's dedication to him of *Wellington's Victory*. His letters to Goethe and Cherubini contain unaccustomed expressions of adora-tion for these giants of contemporary culture. "The admiration, love, and esteem which I have cherished since my youth for the one and only immortal Goethe have persisted. . . . I feel constantly prompted by a strange desire to say all this to you, seeing that I live in your writings."[36] To Cherubini he wrote, "I honor and love you—."[37] So great was Beethoven's yearning for recognition that after the Swedish Royal Academy of Music elected him to honorary membership, he wrote to several editors in 1823, asking them to spread the news. "I should con-sider it an honor if you would be kind enough to mention in your so generally esteemed paper my election as foreign member of the Royal Swedish Academy of Music."[38]

At this time the opportunity also arose to fulfill Beethoven's old wish to become associated with the imperial court. The court composer, Anton Teyber, had died on November 18, 1822, and Beethoven applied for the position in a letter to Count Moritz Dietrichstein shortly thereafter, in which he wrote, "I hear that the post of Imperial and

Royal Chamber Music Composer, which Teyber held, is again to be filled, and I gladly apply for it, particularly if, as I fancy, one of the requirements is that I should occasionally provide a composition for the Imperial Court."[39] Beethoven's friends with influence at court—Dietrichstein, Moritz Lichnowsky, and Archduke Rudolph—tried to pave the way for the appointment, evidently obtaining a verbal commitment that the position could be obtained if Beethoven would write a Mass for the emperor to show his homage (to place him, as Thayer wrote, "into the Emperor's good books").[40] At first, Beethoven welcomed the challenge; he wrote to Simrock and to Peters that he was writing two more Masses ("I intend to compose three at least"), with which he could satisfy the court as well as his irate publishers.[41] But writing another Mass was no small task, and Beethoven had other creative projects in progress. Moreover, Beethoven's brother persuaded him that Teyber's position would not be filled. Although Nikolaus Johann surely was not privy to the plans of the imperial court, his prediction turned out to be accurate. In any event, the Mass for the emperor was never written, although there was still talk of it as late as 1826.

That Beethoven's attitude toward honors was occasionally ambivalent is shown by Schindler's well-known, but questionable, story that when, in 1823, Beethoven was offered the choice of a royal decoration or 50 ducats for the Prussian court's subscription to the *Missa Solemnis,* Beethoven unhesitatingly answered "fifty ducats," preferring the cash to the ribbon.[42] Schindler took this as "striking proof how lightly he prized insignia of honor or distinctions in general."[43] Nevertheless, in 1824, when Beethoven received a gold medal weighing the equivalent of 21 louis d'or, personally inscribed by the king of France, Beethoven wrote to Bernard that Louis XVIII's gift showed "that he is a generous King and a man of refined feeling," and asked him to print the news of the royal distinction in the *Wiener Zeitung,* of which Bernard was editor-in-chief.[44] He sent an impression of the medal to Prince Galitzin and wrote proudly to him, "The medal weighs a half pound in gold and [has] Italian verses about me."[45] Soon, indeed, Beethoven, vaunted for his "contempt for aristocrats," as Frau Streicher once put it,[46] was even able to bring himself to ask for a Royal Order from the king of Prussia.

Dedication of Ninth Symphony to King Friedrich Wilhelm III.
Title page, presentation copy of score.

Staatsbibliothek Preussischer Kulturbesitz, Berlin.

That Beethoven's desire for recognition may somehow have been
connected with his Family Romance is suggested by the circumstances
surrounding the dedication of his Ninth Symphony. Not since the
Mass in C had Beethoven vacillated to such an extent about a dedication. At first he promised the dedication to Ries (perhaps thinking
only of a possible edition in London, where Ries actively promoted
Beethoven's works), and then considered in turn the Philharmonic
Society of London, Kaiser Franz, Czar Alexander (who died late in
1825), and the king of France. He was determined that the symphony
"be dedicated," as he wrote, "to a great lord."[47] Finally he settled upon
Friedrich Wilhelm III, the king of Prussia, and on March 28, 1826, he
was happy to learn from the Prussian embassy that "His Royal Majesty
graciously permits me to dedicate to His Supreme Person the D-minor
symphony with choruses."[48] One wonders whether it is altogether acci-
dental that Beethoven chose to dedicate his symphony on the brotherhood of man to the son of the man rumored to be his own father.

CHAPTER TWENTY-ONE

THE "RETURN" TO BONN

B
ENEATH THE SIMPLE, EVEN PROSAIC, "SURFACE" events that we have sketched in the preceding pages, a profound shift in Beethoven's psychological makeup was taking place. In the biographical particulars of his last years we are able to glimpse traces of the course by which he tried to strip away the fantasies and delusions of a lifetime. His attempt to create a fantasy family through the appropriation of his nephew had been accompanied by an unleashing of powerful emotional forces. Although these forces were eventually brought under control—the first years of the 1820s are relatively free of aggressive actions and pathological signs—they seem to have set in motion an irreversible process of self-analysis that affected the deepest layers of the composer's personality.

The shattering of his nobility pretense in December 1818 may well have been a decisive stage in this process. The fact that Beethoven himself confessed his lack of a patent of nobility surely indicated not only that the weight of the long deception had become insupportable but that he was at last beginning to comprehend that he was not "noble" in a literal sense. On the other hand, it was precisely during the next several years that Beethoven refused to refute the proliferating reports of his royal ancestry; in fact, he tenaciously attempted to hold on to this fantasy until almost the very end. Nevertheless, it is very likely that the Family Romance had begun to erode; and it was probably inevitable that the entire structure, once seriously thrown into question, would ultimately give way.

The importance of this process may be stated simply: Beethoven's birth fantasies barred him from fully acknowledging, accepting, and loving his own family. Therefore, they stood in the way of his own self-acceptance, self-love, and self-knowledge. To be rid of these fantasies was not merely to pass from illusion to reality in some abstract sense,

Beethoven's Funeral. In the background is the Schwarzspanierhaus.
Engraving after a watercolor by Franz Stöber.

Private collection.

but to take his place as a member of a family, to "belong" to his own
flesh and blood. A sense of kinship and a sense of personal identity
were simultaneously at stake. Beethoven's capture of Karl may in some
way have been a desperate attempt to hold fast to the slender threads
of kinship, a kinship that his own multiple delusions of nobility had led
him to deny. In becoming Karl's "father," he was giving the lie to his
own Family Romance and affirming that he was indeed a Beethoven
rather than the illegitimate son of a king. Surely the war for possession
of Karl proved that the concept of "family"—more than any other—
could stir Beethoven's passions to their depths.

Just a few weeks after the guardianship litigation came to an end,
Beethoven expressed a desire to return to his birthplace. He wrote to
Nikolaus Simrock, in Bonn, "I cherish the hope of being able perhaps
to set foot next year on my native soil and to visit my parents' graves."[1]
It is a noteworthy fact that this is the first reference to Beethoven's
mother in his correspondence since shortly after her death in 1787,
and the first to his father since the petition of 1793 to the elector.
Beethoven wrote again to Simrock in March 1821, "I am still hoping
to visit Bonn this summer."[2] Events had somehow unearthed this
desire, but Beethoven was not able to make the journey that would
have "reunited" him with his parents, perhaps because he did not wish
to shatter a consciously idealized image of his childhood home, perhaps because such a trip would have meant returning to the site of
early, painful experiences. Moreover, to return to Bonn—to go home—
might have undermined the Family Romance, for it seems doubtful
that this fantasy, already weakened, could have withstood the reality of
walking along the Bonngasse and the Rheingasse or standing in the
courtyard of the Fischer house, reviving memories of early years.

At this critical juncture, Beethoven's birth year fantasy also began to
lose its force. Around 1820, Wilhelm Christian Müller asked him about
his birthday so that he could give him a present. Beethoven replied that
he "didn't know precisely either the day or the year." Müller's daughter
thereupon wrote to Bonn and obtained from the church register a copy
of Beethoven's baptismal certificate, which, as usual, designated the date
as December 17, 1770. Müller eagerly brought this news to the composer, who, instead of rejecting it out of hand, as was his earlier pattern,
"jestingly said that he would not have believed that he was such an old

bloke."³ It is nice to learn that Beethoven had reached a point at which he could joke about his age, but Müller's evidence did not settle the question: a Conversation Book of February 1820 shows Beethoven still speculating about the identity of his godmother. "Bongard must have been the name of the woman who was my godmother—or Baumgarten," he mused.⁴ He still could not accept the validity of the certificate, on which his godmother's name, Frau Gertrud Baum, who lived next door, was clearly set forth.

Apparently, the Family Romance persisted despite the evidence of the baptismal certificate. But simultaneously the yearning for familial reconciliation continued. Beethoven had been largely estranged from his sole surviving brother since 1812, the year of Nikolaus Johann's marriage. In May 1822, soon after Nikolaus Johann and his wife, Therese, took a Viennese winter residence with her relatives at Obere Pfarrgasse 60 in the Windmühle suburb, Beethoven tried to renew their connection, even proposing that they take joint lodgings: "Considered merely from an economic point of view, the scheme would enable us both to save a good deal, apart altogether from the considerable pleasure it would afford us." In the same letter Beethoven expressed his hope "that all life's wretched trivialities need not cause any disturbances between us," and he prayed that "God grant that the most natural bond, the bond between brothers, may not again be broken in an unnatural way."⁵ He hastened to assure his brother, "I repeat that I have nothing against your wife."

Nikolaus Johann thereafter began to take a role in Beethoven's personal and business affairs, and he appeared frequently in the Conversation Books. Rejoicing in this reconciliation, Beethoven wrote twelve letters to his brother during 1822, and he borrowed money from him during the summer, for which Nikolaus Johann was formally given ownership of several compositions as security. At the end of October Beethoven took an apartment right next door to his brother at the corner of Kothgasse. Of course, it was not long before close proximity to his brother's family revived Beethoven's impulse to sabotage the marriage. By 1823 he was strenuously objecting to what he regarded as Therese's less than commendable associations, and he apparently brought these, as he wrote to Schindler, to "the notice of the worthy police authorities."⁶ "Am I to become so degraded as to mix in such low company?" he asked his brother, and he soon abandoned his lodgings, moving in

October to Ungargasse 5 in the Landstrasse suburb. But he assured him, "I hover over you unseen and influence you through others, so that the scum of the earth may not strangle you."[7] The newly formed tie was not broken, however, and the brothers remained closely associated for the rest of Beethoven's life.

Beethoven also needed to be reconciled with Johanna van Beethoven. Following the decision of the Court of Appeal, she had let it be known that she did not wish to see her brother-in-law under any circumstances, and there is no indication of any contact between them for a year or two. But in mid-1822 Beethoven advised his brother that he had undertaken to pay the unpaid interest on the monies she had borrowed from Steiner when her husband was still alive, and he wrote, "I want to do everything I can for her insofar as it isn't against Karl's interest."[8] Early in the following year he was disturbed to learn through writer Karl Bernard that Johanna was ill and unable to pay for her medicines.[9] He determined to assist her, at first with small cash gifts made anonymously through her doctor, and then—much more handsomely—by restoring the half of her pension that she had yielded to Karl in May 1817. Surprisingly, Karl protested vigorously against this proposed generosity toward his mother and maligned her in an attempt to forestall a rapprochement between her and his uncle. Evidently there had been an estrangement between Karl and his mother following the birth of her daughter in 1820. He may have felt that he had been supplanted as the sole object of her love; doubtless he was wounded to learn that his mother had conceived a child out of wedlock, perhaps viewing this as belated "confirmation" of Beethoven's charges of her immorality. Despite Karl's opposition, however, Beethoven would not be dissuaded. He wrote to Bernard, enlisting him as a go-between: "I am sending her herewith 11 gulden. . . . Please have it delivered to her through the *doctor* and, what is more, in such a way that she may not know where it has come from. . . . If we could be fully informed about all the circumstances, then we might see what could still be done for her; and I am prepared to help in every way."[10] Shortly thereafter, Beethoven, no longer hesitant to let Johanna know of his intentions, wrote to Bernard:

> Please do make inquiries today about Frau van Beethoven and, if possible, assure her at once through her doctor that from this month

onwards she can enjoy her full pension *as long as I live*. . . . As she is so ill and in such straitened circumstances, she must be helped at once. . . . I shall make a point of persuading my pigheaded brother also to contribute something to help her.[11]

The following year, 1824, opened on a significant note of reconciliation, which coincided serendipitously with the composition of the "Ode to Joy" choral finale of his Ninth Symphony. On January 8, 1824, in response to Johanna's friendly New Year's greeting, he wrote to formalize his surrender of the pension: "I assure you now in writing that henceforth and for good you may draw Karl's half of your pension. . . . Should I be comfortably off later on and in a position to provide you from my income with a *sum* large enough to improve your circumstances, I will certainly do so."[12] He then offered her his assistance in various matters, wished her "all possible happiness," and assured her that he was "most willing to help you." Clearly, Beethoven no longer consciously regarded Johanna as the incarnation of evil, but had come to see her as an individual, as a member of the family who needed his help. His most dramatic gesture toward Johanna was yet to come.

The ingrained patterns of a lifetime could not be altered easily, however, let alone all at once. Beethoven had invested too much in his fantasies of illegitimacy to abandon them without one last struggle. Inevitably, the issue turned on Karl's entry into manhood and his attempt to achieve a separation from his uncle.

Fittingly enough, Karl had drifted somewhat out of the focus of Beethoven's attention during the early 1820s. Even when he ran away to his mother in mid-1820, it did not arouse his uncle's fury in the old way. Karl's presence is scarcely noted in Beethoven's correspondence of those years, and the relationship between the two was at its most harmonious during this period: Karl functioned as Beethoven's secretary in certain matters and apparently spent a good many weekends, as well as several of his summer vacations, with him. But after his departure from the Blöchlinger Institute and his enrollment at the university in Vienna in the summer of 1823, when he had just turned seventeen, Karl once more came to live with Beethoven, and bitter quarrels between the aging composer and the tearful adolescent are recorded in the Conversation Books of this period. In September Karl turned up at Baden with Joseph Niemetz, his close friend and former classmate at the Blöchlinger Institute. Beethoven strenuously objected to the young man. "He is a burdensome guest," he complained in a Conversation Book for September, "lacking completely in decency and manners. . . . Besides, I suspect that his interests are more with the housekeeper than with me—Besides, I love quiet; also the space here is too limited for several people." Karl steadfastly defended his friend and the right to choose his friends. "For my part I will not stop loving him as I would my brother, if I had one."[13] In the summer of 1824 Karl did not accompany Beethoven to Baden on his holiday, and so became a source of great concern. On October 6 Beethoven wrote urgently to Tobias Haslinger asking that he try to discover where the "missing" Karl had slept on recent nights. Beethoven feared that his nephew, now eighteen, might be having sexual relationships, with all their attendant "dangers." "It is not surprising when one thinks of these wretched institutions that one is anxious about a young fellow who is growing up," he wrote. "And in addition there is that poisonous breath coming from dragons!"[14] Upon his return to Vienna in early November, Beethoven continued quarreling with Karl, to such an extent that his landlady served notice.

In January 1825, Beethoven received and accepted a fresh invitation from the Philharmonic Society to travel to London and supervise a series of concerts of his music, but a grave illness soon made these travel plans academic. On April 18 he wrote to Dr. Anton Braunhofer, "I am not feeling well and I hope that you will not refuse to come to my help, for I am in great pain."[15] Beethoven was suffering from an intestinal inflammation, a condition that aroused the alarm of the doctor as well as the patient. Braunhofer warned Beethoven to control his diet: "No wine, no coffee; no spices of any kind. . . . I'll wager that if you take a drink of spirits, you'll be lying weak and exhausted on your back in a few hours."[16] He also recommended an early departure to the country for "fresh air" and "natural milk." Beethoven moved to Baden on May 7 and remained there until October 15, except for occasional visits to Vienna. His condition remained serious, as we learn from another letter to Braunhofer: "I spit a good deal of blood, but probably only from my windpipe. . . . Judging by what I know of my own constitution, my strength will hardly be restored unaided."[17] He closed the letter with a canon on the words, "Doktor, sperrt das Tor dem Tod, Note hilft auch aus der Not" ("Doctor close the door to Death! Music will also help in my hour of need"). Perhaps it did help. Beethoven was then composing the A-minor String Quartet, op. 132, and in a Conversation Book on May 29 he wrote, "Hymn of Thanksgiving to God of an Invalid on his Convalescence. Feeling of new strength and reawakened feeling"[18]— words that, in slightly altered form, are now found on the Molto adagio of opus 132.

Beethoven's ill health and his premonitions of death apparently overwhelmed his resistances at this time, unloosing a flood of terrors and anxieties, which centered on Karl. Beethoven suspected (perhaps rightly) that Karl had again been meeting with his mother. On May 22 he wrote to him, "So far only suppositions, though indeed someone assures me that you and your mother have again been associating in secret—Am I to experience once more the most horrible ingratitude?"[19] And on May 31 he burst out, "God is my witness that my sole dream is to get away completely from you and from that wretched brother and that horrible family who have been thrust upon me. May God grant my wishes."[20] It was a harrowing time, reminiscent of the bleak days of 1818 and 1819. He poured out his feelings in a letter to Bernard: "I had to face a behavior on [Karl's] part such as I have only experienced in the case of his deceased father, an uncouth fellow. . . . I suspect that that monster of a mother is again involved in this little game and that it is partly an intrigue of that gentleman, my brainless and heartless brother . . . with his overfed whore and bastard." Beethoven's loneliness and sup- pressed longings for a woman's protective love erupted from the depths of his anguish: "That awful fourth floor [referring to his rooms at Johannesgasse 969 in the central city], O God, *without a wife*, and what an existence; one is a prey to every stranger—."[21] Karl, receiving a tor- rent of letters from Baden, was beaten into temporary submission by these outbursts—whereupon Beethoven once again became the loving, protective, and heavy-handed father: "I embrace you. Be my good, hardworking, noble son as I am always your faithful father."[22]

It was to be a precarious truce, for Beethoven had now become obsessed with Karl's sexuality. He exerted every effort to block his nephew from sexual opportunities of any sort; he spied on the boy and continued to attempt to separate him from his friend Niemetz. He alternately berated and pleaded with him, rejected and forgave him. Early in 1826 he wrote to Mathias Schlemmer, a Viennese official with whose family Karl was boarding (near the Polytechnic Institute, to which he had transferred in the spring of 1825):

> One might be led to suspect that perhaps he really is enjoying himself in the evening or even at night in some company which is certainly not so desirable—I request you to pay attention to this and not to let Karl leave your house at night under any pretext whatever, unless you have received something in writing from me through Karl.[23]

Beethoven had gone too far. On one occasion Karl evidently wrote to his uncle threatening some drastic action (suicide, Martin Cooper infers). Beethoven responded, "My beloved Son! Stop, no further— Only come to my arms, you won't hear a single hard word. For God's sake, do not abandon yourself to misery. . . . On my word of honor you will hear no reproaches, since in any case they would no longer do any good. All that you may expect from me is the most loving care and help."[24] But Beethoven could not keep his resolve long enough even to complete his letter: the postscript reads, "If you do not come you will surely kill me."

Beethoven's health was now somewhat restored and he was freely disregarding his doctor's injunction against alcoholic intake. He received a number of visitors, and they found him in excellent spirits— possibly by reason of the great surge of creativity that was carrying the String Quartet in B-flat, op. 130, to completion, and perhaps also because of the renewal of his friendship with Stephan von Breuning. In October, Beethoven settled into his final lodgings, on the second floor in the Schwarzspanierhaus on the Glacis, close to Breuning's residence, and, for the first time in a decade and the last time in his life, he once more tried to attach himself to a warm and loving family. He took many of his meals at the Breunings, sometimes sending over a favorite fish to be prepared by Breuning's wife, and he attended on Frau von Breuning to such an extent that, as her daughter reported to Thayer, it became a source of embarrassment to her. Once again he expressed his longing "for domestic happiness and much regretted that he had never married."[25]

Meanwhile, by the winter of 1825–26 Beethoven's conflicts with his nephew were moving toward their unavoidable climax. Beethoven had continued to keep close watch on the young man's social activities, restricting these to the barest minimum by means of threats, by setting Karl Holz and Mathias Schlemmer to supervise him, and by withholding expense money, thereby forcing Karl to borrow and go into debt. When Karl attended a carnival ball, Beethoven wanted to accompany him and was apparently dissuaded only by Holz's promise that he himself would serve as chaperon. Beethoven received regular reports (presumably from Schlemmer) about Karl's whereabouts ("One night in the Prater. Two nights did not sleep at home").[26] Karl attempted to withdraw from Beethoven, but this only increased Beethoven's reproaches and suspicions. He waited at the Polytechnic Institute at noon, "waiting to escort his nephew home arm in arm."[27] Beset by these pressures, Karl alternated between depression and defiance. When Beethoven tried to compel him to move back in with him, Karl responded diplomatically, "But it is the *last* year [of my schooling]; then we need never be separated any more." Privately, in a letter to Niemetz, he referred to his uncle as "the old fool."[28] His attempts to reason with Beethoven were of no avail, because the aged composer was once again in the grip of forces that he could not understand or acknowledge, let alone control. In one letter to Karl he wrote, "Do not think that I have anything else in mind but your welfare; and judge my actions by this."[29] He was frantically trying to bar his nephew from sexual experience, a pathological effort that carried implications of homoerotic domination, but centered on warped paternal longings and the incest fear that together had impeded Beethoven's lifelong search for a normal family existence. Karl was now regularly visiting his mother, feeding Beethoven's worst fears. Inevitably, violence would prove to be the only means by which this tangled thread could be cut. Toward the summer of 1826 Karl struck Beethoven and fled the house, apparently in terror of his own passions. His only hope for temporary relief was Beethoven's customary departure for the country in the summer. Karl repeatedly emphasizes Beethoven's vacation in the Conversation Books: "In the summer we will not feel the distance as much."[30] But this year, for the first time since the 1790s, Beethoven did not go to the country, not even for a short stay; he delayed, vacillated, offered numerous pretexts. Clearly, he was remaining in Vienna so that he could stand guard over Karl.

At the end of July, Karl escaped from his virtual imprisonment at Schlemmer's house. Schlemmer reported to Beethoven and Holz that he and his wife had discovered loaded pistols in Karl's room and confiscated them. He begged Beethoven, "Be lenient with him or he will despair."[31] Holz found Karl at the Polytechnic Institute, but the youth said, "What good will it do you to detain me? If I do not escape today, I will at another time." Fleeing from Holz, he pawned his watch on August 5, purchased two new pistols with the proceeds, and, either that day or, more likely, the following one, repaired to Baden, where, after writing suicide notes to Beethoven and Niemetz, he climbed a neighboring mountain and shot himself.[32] Wounded, with a bullet in his scalp, he was found by a passing drover and asked to be taken to his mother's house at Innere Stadt 717 in Vienna. Beethoven wrote to Dr. Smetana on August 6, asking him to visit Karl and enclosing Johanna van Beethoven's address.

> A great misfortune has happened, a misfortune which *Karl* has acci-
> dentally brought upon himself. I hope that it is still possible to save
> him, but my hope depends particularly on you, provided you can
> come soon. Karl has a *bullet* in his head. How this has happened you
> will learn in due course.—But come quickly, for God's sake, quickly.[33]

The police, who had jurisdiction over attempted suicides, removed Karl to the General Hospital on August 7, and he remained there until September 25. Beethoven's friends urged him to relinquish the guardianship and to permit Karl to enter the army. "Once with the military," Holz wrote, "he will be under the strictest discipline." Breuning agreed: "A military life will be the best discipline for one who cannot endure freedom; and it will teach him how to live on little."[34] Dr. Bach suggested that he be set to work in a business establishment in another country. As for Karl, his preference now lay with military service. "If my wish concerning a military career can be fulfilled, I will be very happy," he wrote.[35] After the decade-long struggle, Beethoven relinquished his guardianship in favor of Breuning; it was the latter who arranged with his friend Field Marshal Joseph von Stutterheim to accept the youth as a cadet in his regiment. Before Karl could present himself for service, however, it was thought necessary that his hair be given time to grow in to conceal the scars. "I cannot go to the Field Marshal," he wrote in a Conversation Book, "until I am able to appear without any visible sign left of what happened to me."[36] It was decided that Beethoven and Karl should get away from Vienna, and arrangements were made for them to spend some time at Nikolaus Johann's country estate in Gneixendorf in the Danube valley northwest of Vienna. The two left Vienna on September 28, and all of the members of the Beethoven family except for Johanna were united the following day. Beethoven and Karl intended to stay for only a week or two, but they remained in Gneixendorf ("the name resembles to a certain extent a breaking axle," Beethoven wrote to Haslinger)[37] until the first day of December. Neither of the participants in this drama could bring himself to make the move that would result in their final separation. Even Karl postponed his departure from week to week, until Nikolaus Johann and Breuning insisted that he hasten to his new calling.

Despite inescapable quarrels and reproaches, the reunion was not without its nostalgic and idyllic overtones. Beethoven wrote to the Mainz publisher Schott's Sons, "The district where I am now staying reminds me to a certain extent of the Rhine country which I so ardently desire to revisit. For I left it long ago when I was young."[38] Nikolaus Johann and his wife did their best to make Beethoven comfortable, offering him a permanent home with them, providing him with a young servant, Michael Krenn, to whom he became exceedingly attached (perhaps as a substitute for Karl), and attempting to smooth his relations with Karl. Therese, who was able to forgive Beethoven his ill will toward her, wrote consolingly in a Conversation Book, "It seems that [Karl] has some of your rash blood. I have not found him angry. It is you that he loves, to the point of veneration."[39] Beethoven spent a good part of each day rambling through the open fields, and at dawn and in the evenings he worked on what were to be his last compositions. Here he completed the String Quartet in F, op. 135, and the new finale for the String Quartet in B-flat, op. 130. I once thought that these works, with their sense of a confident return to a less conflicted universe, somehow were implicated in the process of separation from Karl, which had lessened the weight of Beethoven's inner burdens. Now I am not so sure, and I have come to prefer Robert Winter's alternative formulation: "The compositional abyss reached by Beethoven in the creation of the C-sharp-minor Quartet was so grave a threat to the composer's fundamental *musical* principles that a return to less radical presuppositions was mandatory if his style was to survive at all."[40]

When asked why he had tried to commit suicide, Karl said he was "tired of life" and "weary of imprisonment." He told the police magistrate that Beethoven "tormented him too much" and that "I grew worse because my uncle wanted me to be better."[41] There is much truth in these explanations, but they are by no means the whole story, nor is it to be expected that Karl would entirely understand his own desperate act. Classically, there are a number of interlocking motives in a suicide attempt. First, and this is clearly present here, there is an assertion of independence from a set of intolerable constraints. Closely linked to this is the process of turning on oneself as a substitute for a desired aggression against another. Hence, Karl's suicide attempt may have been a deflection of his violent impulses against Beethoven.[42] The Sterbas observe that the act "discharged enough aggression to allow him to free himself from the intolerable pressure which his uncle's personality had exercised on him."[43] Karl needed to free himself from his uncle, and it is apparent that he instinctively chose the most effective way to accomplish this, for Beethoven was now suddenly resigned to the necessity of their separation. There may have been another set of motives at work here, however. A suicide sometimes seeks reunion in death with a beloved person; he may want to die in order to join one from whom he has been separated. Here Karl's desire to be reunited with his mother seems fairly evident. He asked to be taken to her, and later, in the hospital, he at last stoutly defended her and firmly asserted his rights as a mother's son:

> I want to hear nothing about her that is derogatory to her, and it is absolutely not my place to pass judgment on her. If I should spend the little time I shall be here with her, it would be no more than a small compensation for all that she has suffered on my account. There can be no question of any harmful influence on me, even if it could occur, simply by reason of the shortness of the time. But in no case will I

treat her more coldly than has hitherto been the case, no matter what anyone may say.[44]

The suicide attempt liberated Karl from his own extreme rejection of his mother—which he had carried out, as he thought, on the instructions of Beethoven, and which for a while even exceeded Beethoven's own negative attitude in intensity. The pistol shots were a cry for help, Karl's way of telling Johanna that he still needed her, wanted her forgiveness and love. Karl's tragedy, however, lay not only in his long, forcible separation from his mother. As we have seen, Beethoven's appropriation of his nephew embodied his desire to be the boy's "real, physical father" and thereby to take Caspar Carl's place. For more than a decade he had tried to train the boy to accept him as his true father, thus initiating a sequence of intolerable conflicts centering on the denial of the boy's real male parent. In this, Karl seems to have been the means by which Beethoven irrationally translated his own Family Romance into reality: he had replaced Karl's real father by a more noble surrogate—himself—and thereby elevated the boy to a noble rank. In a sense, he created an artificial Family Romance for Karl to match his own fantasies of illegitimacy and royal birth. In so doing, he deprived Karl of his father and substituted himself as the youth's begetter and sole parent.

Karl, although ambivalently and painfully acceding to the rejection of his mother, and although he on occasion addressed Beethoven as "My dearest Father," had, it turned out, never accepted the replacement of his father. Beethoven had tried unsuccessfully to mold the boy in his own image: he engaged Carl Czerny and later Joseph Czerny to train him as a pianist, but was forced to abandon the effort for want of sufficient talent in Karl. He then hoped to persuade Karl to enter a career in the humanities, encouraging him to matriculate at the university as a student of philology. But Karl resisted this path also, at first expressing his desire to be a soldier and then, in 1825, insisting on transferring to the Polytechnic Institute to pursue a commercial career. This move may well have been an expression of Karl's desire to follow in the footsteps of his father, who had pursued a career in a variety of posts in the state finance ministry. Ultimately, after his discharge from army service, Karl became, like his father, a minor official in the

Austrian bureaucracy and lived a useful, bourgeois, and apparently contented existence.

Karl's attempt to kill himself thus bespoke his shattering rejection of Beethoven's presumed fatherhood. "All my hopes have vanished," Beethoven wrote to Holz, "all my hopes of having near me someone who would resemble me at least in my better qualities!"[45] The structure of Beethoven's Family Romance was fast disintegrating under the pressure of these events. The separation from Karl would now allow Beethoven himself to come to terms with the facts of his own ancestry.

Beethoven's health began to fail at Gneixendorf. "He would eat nothing at lunch except soft-boiled eggs," Nikolaus Johann wrote in a memorandum, "but then he would drink more wine so that he often suffered diarrhea; thereby his belly became bigger and bigger, and he wore a bandage over it for a long time."[46] He complained of thirst, loss of appetite, and pains in his abdomen. His feet became swollen with fluids. On December 1, he and Karl set out on the return trip to Vienna. Dr. Andreas Ignaz Wawruch, a leading surgeon at the General Hospital, who was soon to become his attending physician, later told how Beethoven "was compelled to spend a night in a village tavern where, besides wretched shelter, he found an unwarmed room without winter shutters. Toward midnight he experienced his first fever chill, a dry, hacking cough accompanied by violent thirst and cutting pains in the sides."[47] On the following day Beethoven arrived at his lodgings in the Schwarzspanierhaus. Drs. Braunhofer and Staudenheim declined to attend Beethoven, possibly because they understood the seriousness of his condition and did not want to preside over his death. Finally, on December 5, Holz called Dr. Wawruch, who described Beethoven's condition thus: "I found Beethoven afflicted with serious symptoms of inflammation of the lungs. His face glowed, he spat blood, his respiration threatened suffocation, and a painful stitch in the side made lying on the back a torment. A severe countertreatment for inflammation soon brought the desired relief; his constitution triumphed and by a lucky crisis he was freed from apparent mortal danger, so that on the fifth day he was able, in a sitting posture, to tell me, amid profound emotion, of the discomforts which he had suffered." It was on that day, December 7, 1826, that Beethoven belatedly replied to Wegeler's letter of December 28, 1825. A brief passage from Beethoven's letter was cited at the beginning of this book. Now the letter can be given in full:

MY BELOVED OLD FRIEND!

Words fail me to express the pleasure which your letter and *Lorchen's* have afforded me. And indeed an answer should have been sent off to you as swiftly as an arrow. But on the whole I am rather slack about writing letters, for I believe that the best people know me well in any case. Often I think out a reply in my head; but when it comes to writing it down, I usually throw away my pen, simply because I am unable to write as I feel. I remember all the love which you have always shown me, for instance, how you had my room whitewashed and thus gave me such a pleasant surprise, and likewise all the kindnesses I have received from the *Breuning* family. Our drifting apart was due to changes in our circumstances. Each of us had to pursue the purpose for which he was intended and endeavor to attain it. Yet the eternally unshakable and firm foundations of good principles continued to bind us strongly together. Unfortunately I cannot write to you today as much as I should like to, for I have to stay in bed. So I shall confine myself to answering a few points in your letter. You say that I have been mentioned somewhere as being the natural son of the late King of *Prussia*. Well, the same thing was said to me a long time ago. But I have adopted the principle of neither writing anything about myself nor replying to anything that has been written about me. Hence I gladly leave it to you to make known to the world the integrity of my parents, and especially of my mother. You mention your son. Why, of course, if he comes to Vienna, I will be a friend and a father to him; and if I can be of use to him or help him in any way, I shall be delighted to do so.

I still possess *Lorchen's silhouette*. So you see how precious to me even now are all the dear, beloved memories of my youth.

As for my *diplomas*, I merely mention that I am an honorary member of the Royal Scientific Society of Sweden and likewise of *Amsterdam*, and also an honorary citizen of Vienna. A short time ago a certain Dr. *Spiker* took with him to *Berlin* my latest grand *symphony* with choruses; it is dedicated to the king, and I had to write the *dedication* with my own hand. I had previously applied to the legation for permission to dedicate this work to the king, which His Majesty then granted. At Dr. *Spiker's* instigation, I myself had to give him the *corrected* manuscript with the alterations in my own handwriting to be delivered to the king, because the work is to be kept in the Royal Library. On that occasion something was said to me about the Order of the *Red* Eagle, Second Class. Whether anything will come of this, I don't know, for I have never striven after honors of that kind. Yet at the present time, for many other reasons, such an award would be rather welcome.

In any case, my motto is always: *Nulla dies sine linea* [No day without a line]; and if I let my Muse go to sleep, it is only that she may be all the more active when she awakes. I still hope to create a few great works and then, like an old child to finish my earthly course somewhere among kind people. You will soon receive some music from the Gebrüder *Schott* at *Mainz*. The portrait I am sending with this letter is certainly an artistic masterpiece, but it is not the latest one which has been done of me. Speaking about my honors, which I know you are pleased to hear of, I must add that the late king of France sent me a *medal* with the inscription: *Donné par le Roi à Monsieur Beethoven*. It was accompanied by a very courteous letter from the *Duc de Chartres, Premier Gentilhomme du Roi*.

My beloved friend! You must be content with this letter for today. I need hardly tell you that I have been overcome by the remembrance of things past and that many tears have been shed while the letter was being written. Still we have now begun to correspond, and you will soon have another letter from me. And the more often you write to me, the greater will be the pleasure you afford me. Our friendship is too intimate to need inquiries from either of us. And now I send you all good wishes. Please embrace and kiss your dear *Lorchen* and your children for me, and when doing so think of me. God be with you all!

Ever your true and faithful friend who honors you,

BEETHOVEN[48]

Dying, given momentary respite from a mortal crisis, Beethoven at last renounced the legend of his noble birth. Perhaps he could begin to take leave of his Family Romance only after his creative career had run its course. He was, however, not yet wholly rid of his birth delusions. As noted in the first chapter, having written this letter to Wegeler authorizing the refutation of the Family Romance, Beethoven neglected to mail it until the latter half of February 1827—a few weeks before his death, and only after the receipt of a reproachful letter from his Bonn friend. And even in the letter to Wegeler Beethoven may have unconsciously restated his lingering adherence to the Family Romance by means of a long recital of his medals and honors, and especially by stressing his dedication of the Ninth Symphony to Friedrich Wilhelm III, the scion of his supposed father.

As we have seen, Beethoven had obtained permission earlier in the year to dedicate the Ninth Symphony to the Prussian king. In September, Haslinger was delegated to have the presentation copy of the score luxuriously bound ("If you would be so kind as to have the score . . . as beautifully bound as befits *a king*, you would do me a great favor"),[49] and Beethoven wrote an appropriate dedicatory message: "Your Majesty is not only the supreme father of your subjects but also the patron of arts and sciences. . . . I too, since I am a native of Bonn, am fortunate enough to regard myself as one of your subjects."[50] Beethoven delayed his departure for Gneixendorf for three days to be certain that all details of the presentation had been attended to. As he informed Wegeler, it was his hope and expectation that a royal order would be conferred on him as a token of appreciation. Approaches intended to achieve this were made through the Prussian ambassador, Prince Hatzfeld, and through Dr. Spiker, the king's librarian. After consulting with the Berlin publisher Adolph Martin Schlesinger, Karl Holz reported to Beethoven that he need have no fear of a slipup. "You will certainly receive it," he wrote.[51] Holz advised that the path was well paved: "[Spiker] says that the decoration will be very easy; the king is very inclined in your favor. . . . The decoration will come sooner than you think."[52] Only Karl saw the matter in its proper perspective: "I believe that a decoration could not make you greater than you are without it," he said, and he told of a certain doctor who had ten decorations but about whom no one gave a second thought.[53]

In any case, this trivial honor, which meant so much to Beethoven and which would have given him so much pleasure, was denied him. The decoration was not forthcoming, and in its stead Beethoven was sent a ring. "I thank you for this gift," wrote the king to Beethoven in late November, "and send you the accompanying diamond ring [*Brillantring*] as a token of my sincere appreciation."[54] Beethoven's disappointment was temporarily assuaged by the expectation of a costly present: he and his friends fluttered with excitement as they awaited its delivery. Beethoven drafted a letter to Aloys Wernhart, the chancery-secretary at the Prussian embassy: "I must ask you to be so kind as to send me the ring which H. M. the King of Prussia has decided to give me—I am very sorry that an indisposition prevents me from receiving in person this token (which is so precious to me) of H. M.'s love of art."[55] The ring turned out to contain, however, not a diamond, but a cheap, "reddish"-looking stone, which Holz took to the court jeweler for appraisal. When he returned with the news that the ring was worth only 160 florins, Beethoven insisted that it be sold. "Holz tried to prevent this with the remark, 'Master, keep the ring, it is from a King.' Beethoven then rose up before Holz and with indescribable dignity and self-consciousness he called out, 'I too am a King!'"[56] In this pronouncement we may have the final and poignant efflorescence of Beethoven's Family Romance fantasy before it yielded to the importunities of reality and to the gathering harbingers of mortality.

Karl remained at Beethoven's bedside throughout December, tending to his needs. Their conflicts were at an end: there were no further quarrels, suspicions, or reproaches, and Karl, at last, could now freely and unreservedly express love for his uncle. On January 2 he left for Iglau (present-day Jihlava) in Moravia to join his regiment. The next day Beethoven wrote a will, declaring that "Karl van Beethoven, my beloved nephew, is the sole heir to all my property" and appointing his attorney, Dr. Bach, as trustee of the estate.[57] On January 13, Karl wrote to Beethoven, "My dear father . . . I am living in contentment, and regret only that I am separated from you."[58] One more letter from Karl to Beethoven has been preserved—written on March 4, asking for news and signed, "Your loving son"—but not a single further letter from Beethoven to his nephew has survived.

Following the temporary remission of his illness during the second week of December, Beethoven's condition rapidly deteriorated. "Trembling and shivering," Dr. Wawruch wrote, "he bent double because of the pains which raged in his liver and intestines, and his feet, thitherto moderately inflated, were tremendously swollen. From this time on dropsy developed, the segregation of urine became less, the liver showed plain indication of hard nodules, [and] there was an increase of jaundice."[59] The abdominal fluids were tapped on December 20, following a consultation between Wawruch and Staudenheim. The fluids weighed 25 pounds, and the subsequent outflow amounted to five times that much. A second operation took place on January 8, and on January 11 a council of physicians—including Beethoven's long-estranged old friend Dr. Malfatti—was held. (According to Gerhard von Breuning, Beethoven "awaited Malfatti's visits as eagerly as those of a Messiah.")[60] Realizing that no medical treatment stood any chance of success, Malfatti recommended that Beethoven be given a frozen punch to relieve his discomfort and to ease his spells of melancholy. At first, attempts were made to limit his intake to one glass per day; following two further abdominal tappings on February 2 and 27, however, all restrictions as to quantity were lifted.

As the news of Beethoven's mortal illness circulated, old friends gathered at the Schwarzspanierhaus to wish him well and to bid him farewell. Schindler, Holz, the Breunings, Nikolaus Johann, and Beethoven's housekeeper, Sali, were in regular attendance. Visitors included Haslinger, Diabelli, the violinist Franz Clement, the music lover Ferdinand Piringer, editor Johann Schickh, Andreas Streicher (but not, apparently, his wife, Nannette), Bernard, the composer Jan Emanuel Doležálek, Schuppanzigh, and Count Moritz Lichnowsky. Ignaz von Gleichenstein made several appearances, bringing his wife and son. Beethoven's old friend and rival Hummel arrived with his wife, Elisabeth, and his young student Ferdinand Hiller. Frau Hummel took her handkerchief and wiped the perspiration from Beethoven's face several times. "Never," Hiller wrote, "shall I forget the grateful glance with which his broken eye looked upon her."[61] (Contrary to legend, Schubert did not visit the deathbed but he and his friends followed the progress of Beethoven's illness with deep concern.) Zmeskall, confined to his house, sent greetings to his old comrade, and Beethoven responded:

A thousand thanks for your sympathy. I do not despair. But what is most painful to me is the complete cessation of my activities. Yet there is no evil which has not something good in it as well. May Heaven grant you, too, an alleviation of your painful condition. Perhaps we shall both be restored to health and then we shall meet and see one another again as friendly neighbors.[62]

Beethoven's amiable former landlord Baron Pasqualati cheered the patient with gifts of Viennese desserts. The Philharmonic Society of London, learning of Beethoven's illness and being informed by him in letters to Smart, the London-based harp manufacturer Johann Andreas Stumpff, and Moscheles that he was in financial distress, unanimously passed a motion to lend him 100 pounds "to be applied to his comforts and necessities during his illness."[63] (Later, learning that he had left a fairly sizable estate, the society felt that it had been deceived, but it decided to take no action to recover its loan.) Beethoven gratefully promised that he would compose a new symphony or overture for the society.

In mid-February, Diabelli brought to Beethoven a lithograph of Haydn's birthplace in Rohrau, which he had just published.[64] Gerhard von Breuning writes, "The picture caused him great pleasure; when I came at noon, he showed it to me at once: 'Look, I got this today. Just see the little house, and such a great man was born in it. Your father must have a frame made for me; I'm going to hang it up.'" Gerhard brought the lithograph to his piano teacher, who made the frame and added in the lower margin, "Joseph Hayden's [*sic*] Birthplace in Rohrau." Beethoven became furious at the misspelling of Haydn's name; his "face turned red with rage and he asked me angrily: 'Who wrote that, anyway? . . . What's that donkey's name? An ignoramus like that calls himself a piano teacher, calls himself a musician, and can't even spell the name of a master like Haydn.'"[65]

He delighted, though, in showing the lithograph to visitors. Hiller related that Beethoven showed it to him and to others with the words, "It gave me a childish pleasure—the cradle of a great man."[66] Can we detect a note of puzzlement in Beethoven's comment, "See the little house, and such a great man was born in it"? Is there here an intimation of Beethoven's sense of wonder that greatness was not incompatible with lowly origins?

In any event, Beethoven had become fully reconciled with Haydn, had transformed him into his good "Papa" once again. Feelings of love had surfaced during these months of Beethoven's final illness and of his long-awaited reconciliations. The lithograph of Haydn's birth house was placed next to his deathbed; on the wall was the oil painting of Ludwig van Beethoven, his grandfather. Images remindful of two kapellmeisters gave Beethoven solace at the end.

The young singers Ludwig Cramolini and his fiancée, Nanette Schechner, paid their respects to the composer whom they worshiped. Beethoven asked Cramolini to sing for him, but the young man was so overcome by the occasion that he could not produce any sounds. When told what had happened, Beethoven burst out laughing and said, "Go ahead and sing, my dear Louis! I can hear nothing, alas! I only want to see you sing."[67] About four days before he died, as Hummel related to Frau Streicher, "He made an effort to overcome the languor that was creeping over him—he arose from his bed and dressed himself—saying to Hummel that it was necessary to make some exertion to stand up against illness and that he would endeavour to overcome his painful and languid sensation." This was said "with great energy and he appeared for the moment to be much better—but unfortunately this flash of his former spirit did not last, his feebleness rapidly returned, and he gradually grew weaker" as he sank toward death.[68]

The end was fast approaching. The last sacraments were rendered, with Beethoven's consent. "Here I have been lying for four months!" he cried out. "One must at last lose patience!"[69] Seeking comfort in tasty foods, he wrote to Pasqualati, "I thank you for the dish of food which you sent me yesterday. An invalid craves like a child for something of that kind. So I am asking you today for the stewed peaches."[70] And again, he asked, "Please send me some more stewed cherries today, but cooked quite simply, without any lemon. Further, a light pudding, almost like gruel, would give me great pleasure."[71] His thoughts turned to the Rhine, and he wrote to Schott in Mainz, on March 10, asking that he send him some Rhine wines: "They will certainly bring me refreshment, invigoration, and good health."[72]

On March 23 Beethoven picked up his pen for perhaps the last time in his life and began to copy a codicil to his will. The codicil, prepared by Breuning, was intended to modify Beethoven's testamentary letter of January 3, 1827, to his attorney, Johann Baptist Bach, whereby his nephew, as sole heir, was bequeathed the "seven bank shares and whatever cash may be available."[73] But Breuning, who regarded the nephew as "very irresponsible," urged Beethoven to limit Karl's "authority to dispose of the capital either for his whole lifetime or at least for several more years . . ."[74] Nikolaus Johann, Schindler, Breuning, and Breuning's son Gerhard all watched as Beethoven painfully transcribed the codicil in a faltering hand. His pen trembled and he was unable to form the words clearly, adding extra letters to several words and omitting others from his signature:

> My nephew Karl shall be my sole legatee, but the capital of my estate
> shall fall to his natural or testamentary heirs.
>   LUWIG VAN BEETHOEN[75]

Possibly Beethoven merely intended to follow Breuning's advice to prevent his nephew from wasting the capital, but by using the phrase "natural or testamentary heirs" he made it possible, whether deliberately or unwittingly we will never know, for the entire capital of his estate to pass to Johanna van Beethoven—the "Queen of Night"—in the event of the death of her son, for she was then the only "natural or testamentary heir" of Karl, who was unmarried and had just entered military service.[76] Despite the protests of the astonished observers, Beethoven refused to make any further alteration, reportedly setting down his pen with the words "There! I won't write another word."[77]

On the following day, March 24, Schindler wrote to Moscheles: "He feels the end coming, for yesterday he said to me and H. v. Breuning, 'Plaudite, amici, comoedia finita est' [Applaud, friends, the comedy is ended]."[78] On the same day, the wines arrived from Schott in Mainz, and Schindler brought the bottles to the bedside table. Beethoven whispered, "Pity, pity—too late!" and spoke no more. He fell into a coma that evening, which lasted until his death on the twenty-sixth. Late in the afternoon of the final day, during a snowfall and thunderstorm, he momentarily opened his eyes, lifted his right hand, and clenched it into a fist. When his hand fell back from this effort, Beethoven was dead.

According to the testimony of composer Anselm Hüttenbrenner of Graz, who witnessed his moment of death, Johanna van Beethoven was the only other person present at the end.[79] This was startling information when Thayer received it in 1860, for Schindler had suppressed

Codicil to Beethoven's will, March 23, 1827.

Archive of Landgericht, Vienna

the identity of the woman in the room. Thayer could not believe that Johanna and Beethoven had been reconciled, and he apparently urged Hüttenbrenner to reconsider his testimony, whereupon Hüttenbrenner substituted Therese van Beethoven's name for that of Johanna.[80] Although there can no longer be any certainty in this matter, Hüttenbrenner's first recollection perhaps remains the best evidence, and it is therefore entirely possible that Johanna was the Frau van Beethoven who cut a lock of hair from Beethoven's head and handed it to Hüttenbrenner "as a sacred souvenir of Beethoven's last hour."[81]

Soon after Beethoven's death, his brother, Breuning, Schindler, and Holz searched his lodgings for the seven remaining bank shares, eventually finding them in a concealed drawer of an old cabinet, which also contained two miniature ivory portraits, one of Giulietta Guicciardi and the other, I have suggested, of Antonie Brentano. Schindler surreptitiously gathered up and removed many items of memorabilia, including four bundles of Conversation Books; many manuscripts and letters; Beethoven's eyeglasses and ear trumpets; numerous statuettes of male figures, including a bust of Brutus; the clock carved in alabaster, which the Princess Lichnowsky had given to Beethoven many years before; and the letter to the Immortal Beloved. Beethoven's remaining manuscripts and scores were taken for appraisal by Johanna's former advocate Jacob Hotschevar, who became Karl's guardian when Stephan von Breuning died in mid-1827. Among these papers was found the Heiligenstadt Testament, which was published in the *Allgemeine musikalische Zeitung* on October 17. Beethoven's belongings were auctioned on November 5, 1827, and brought 1,140 florins. Included were all of his sketchbooks, autographs of his published works, fragments of unpublished works, original manuscripts, parts, scores, printed music, and books. The original autograph of the *Missa Solemnis* sold for only 7 florins, whereas that of the Septet brought 18. The entire estate, including the bank shares, was worth just over 10,000 florins.

The Viennese, who, in addition to having an affection for Beethoven, always enjoyed *"eine schöne Leich"* (a lovely funeral), turned out en masse to bid farewell to their greatest composer. Ten thousand or more (some estimated the throng at double and even triple that number) crowded the streets on March 29 to witness the great procession, which wound through the streets from the courtyard of the Schwarzspanierhaus to the Trinity Church of the Minorites in the Alsergasse and thence to the nearby village of Währing, where the eloquent funeral oration written by Franz Grillparzer was rendered by the actor Heinrich Anschütz and Beethoven was buried in the parish cemetery. The pallbearers were eight kapellmeisters; the torchbearers included many of Beethoven's closest friends as well as Vienna's leading musicians. A choir sang a solemn Miserere, WoO 130, to the somber accompaniment of trombones. Close behind the coffin followed numerous friends and admirers, led by Stephan and Gerhard von Breuning, Nikolaus Johann van Beethoven, and Johanna van Beethoven.

Title page, *An die ferne Geliebte,* op. 98.

First edition, S. A. Steiner & Co., Vienna (1816). Courtesy of Gesellschaft
der Musikfreunde, Vienna.

CHAPTER TWENTY-TWO

THE MUSIC

EETHOVEN CONTINUED TO UPHOLD the ideals of the
Enlightenment, of classicism, and of aristocratic excellence
even after historical conditions had rendered these anachronistic. He also did not abandon his search for a multiplicity of musical
syntheses—rather, he expanded it. In the late works, his archetypal patterns retain their impress: struggle is sublimated into ecstasy, as in the
Arietta of the Sonata in C minor, op. 111; chaos strives for lucid formation, as in the transition to the fugue of the "Hammerklavier" Sonata and
in the opening of the finale of the Ninth Symphony; victorious conclusions are incessantly sought after and discovered, as in the Grosse Fuge,
the Sonata in A-flat, op. 110, and the finale of the Quartet in C-sharp
minor, op. 131. Beethoven could no longer confront such issues, however, with his previous musical vocabulary or procedures. As Parry
observed, Beethoven had by now found "the accepted scheme of organization which he himself had brought to perfection too constraining and
restrictive to the impulse of his thought, and therefore endeavored to
find new types of form and to revive sundry earlier types of organization
and combine them in various ways which departed from the essential
principles upon which composers had been working for generations."[1]

Parry's implication that Beethoven was to create "new" forms in his
late works may well be overstated, because Beethoven never relinquished his reliance upon the Classic structures; rather he imbued
them with greater freedom and fantasy, expanding their boundaries
and maximizing their coherence. Nevertheless, Beethoven's achievement of an unprecedented "modernism" was made possible by his
recognition that in certain respects the received Classical style had
become an impediment to further development, and his realization that
there remained unexplored avenues in earlier stages of musical development that had been bypassed by the composers of the post-Baroque

385

generations. The Classical style had, in the music of Haydn, Mozart, and Beethoven, led to the creation of an extensive and unique body of masterpieces and revolutionized musical forms and vocabulary. In a certain sense, however, the Classical style can also be thought of as constituting a great regression in music history, for at its inception it set aside the entire superstructure of Baroque style, with its advanced harmonic language, its rich polyphonic procedures, its highly organized and complex forms, and its simultaneous dedication to both spirituality and splendor. This regression took place in accordance with the prevailing hedonism of the eighteenth-century aristocratic courts and salons, and with the sanction of the Enlightenment's best theoreticians. It was a regression cloaked in the authority of Reason, opposed to theological contrivances and devoted to rationality and simplicity. Thus, in his *Lettre sur la musique française* (1753), Rousseau wrote, "With regard to counterfugues, double fugues, inverted fugues, ground basses, and other difficult sillinesses that the ear cannot abide and which reason cannot justify, these are obviously remnants of barbarism and bad taste that only persist, like the portals of our Gothic cathedrals, to the shame of those who had the endurance to build them."[2]

With the passing of the Enlightenment and its aesthetic dogmas, Beethoven was free to seek new influences within the very heritage that it had superseded, to create more flexible musical structures and new tonal trajectories by reviving some of the Baroque and pre-Baroque techniques, forms, and procedures that had been thrown overboard by classicism. It is this trend—one that should not be overstated—that feeds the retrospective current in Beethoven's late works, and that paradoxically gives to them a simultaneously archaic and prospective cast of thought.

Late Beethoven is characterized by a highly concentrated exploration of counterpoint and polyphonic textures, a serious interest in Bach and Handel, a new awareness of the church modes, the utilization of Baroque-style "theme types" with specific rhetorical meanings, a turn toward instrumental recitative, a pre-Classic richness of ornamentation employed for expressive purposes, and a heightened preoccupation with monothematic development and variation procedures. These are evidence not of a return to an idealized past in the manner of many German Romantics or of a set of antiquarian researches, but of Beethoven's search for germinating influences and modes of expression that could aid him in the symbolization of new spheres of psychic and social experience, inaccessible to the dramatic and overtly dialectical procedures of sonata form and obbligato style.

So deeply are these influences embedded within Beethoven's personal style that it has taken scholars a century and a half to make a small start on unearthing them. Of course, one cannot dissolve Beethoven's late style into its sources, as some have recently attempted to do, because many of its characteristics, as well as its structures and "sound," are unprecedented in the history of music. One can only hint here at the extraordinary and unique characteristics of the late style (see the excellent discussions in Kerman, Martin Cooper, Riezler, and Tovey): the organic use of the trill for the intensification of emotion; the use of simple, even prosaic musical materials both to contrast with a sublime rhetoric and to reveal the sublimity hidden within the commonplace; the aggressive, dotted-rhythmic polyphonic textures that create a sense of irresistible motion and unbearable strain; the turn to thematic material that is ever more terse and pregnant; the attempt to capture the expressiveness of the human body by a greater use of dance and march forms (this is part of what Martin Cooper calls a "transfigured 'play' element" in Beethoven's last compositions);[3] and, as Kerman has written, a profound yielding to the "vocal impulse" in both his vocal and instrumental music, which makes the late works Beethoven's "crowning monument to lyricism."[4] And not only lyricism, but rhetoric, declamation, and recitative as well: speech and song together press to fulfill Beethoven's drive toward immediacy of communication.

Apart from brief allusions to the six lieder set to poems by Gellert, op. 48, and to the two orchestral songs in the incidental music to *Egmont,* op. 84, Beethoven's lieder were last discussed in the context of his music of the Bonn period. During the intervening years, he continued to show an intermittent interest in this genre, composing more than fifty lieder between 1793 and 1815 and sketching numerous others that he never completed. His main lieder publications were the six Gellert Lieder, op. 48 (1801–2), which included at least two distinguished songs, "Bitten" ("Prayer") and "Vom Tode" ("Death"), the latter with pungent chromaticisms and a Schumannesque quality; Six Songs, op. 75 (published in 1810, composed at various earlier dates), to texts by Goethe, Halem, and Reissig; and Three Songs to poems by Goethe, op. 83

(1811), including the touching "Wonne der Wehmut" ("Rapture of Melancholy"). Several individual lieder are of interest, such as "An die Hoffnung" ("To Hope"), op. 32, and "Gedenke mein!" ("Think of Me!"), WoO 130, both of which were presented to (and subsequently taken back from) Josephine Deym in early 1805; "An die Geliebte" ("To the Beloved"), WoO 140, almost certainly written for Antonie Brentano in 1811; and especially, a second, through-composed setting of "An die Hoffnung," op. 94 (c. 1815), cast as a recitative and aria, a form he had used less persuasively in several early Vienna songs, including the "Seufzer eines Ungeliebten" und "Gegenliebe" ("Sighs of a Despondent Lover" and "Requited Love"), WoO 118, and the popular "Adelaide," op. 46.

Between late 1809 and 1818 Beethoven also composed 179 arrangements of Scottish, Irish, Welsh, and assorted Continental songs for one or more voices with piano, violin, and cello accompaniment.[5] Most of these were commissioned by the Edinburgh publisher George Thomson, who obtained similar work from Pleyel, Leopold Kozeluch, Haydn, Hummel, Weber, and others in a multivolume project that he had commenced as early as 1793. Thomson published 126 of Beethoven's folk-song settings and paid him fairly well for his work—£340, which, together with fees from Continental publishers, brought the composer's total earnings from these settings to approximately 700 gold ducats.[6] The artistic results are of somewhat mixed value: to his chagrin, Beethoven was usually not provided with the texts (or even titles) of the songs—later on he was given titles, scant descriptions, or expressive indications—and was encouraged to keep the piano parts as simple as possible. Moreover, partly because he wanted to cater to conventional tastes, Thomson bowdlerized both the texts and tunes of the traditional folk songs. As a result, Beethoven's settings do not fully explore the harmonic implications of the more archaic melodies, instead translating their sometimes modal language and irregular rhythmic structure into Classical-style harmonies and symmetrical rhythms. His settings of composed songs in putatively national styles (with recent or contemporary texts by Walter Scott, Robert Burns, Thomas Campbell, and others) are much more successful, and several of these, such as that of Scott's "On the Massacre of Glencoe," WoO 152, no. 5, are extremely beautiful. As Barry Cooper has observed, "Beethoven's folksong settings consist of a blending of two very different traditions—folksong and the Classical style. Naturally, traditionalists on both sides of this divide feel uneasy about such a combination."[7]

The theme of yearning for the unattainable is central to many of Beethoven's best lieder. Indeed, he composed six songs called "Sehnsucht" ("Yearning"): there are four such settings to one poem by Goethe (WoO 134); a fifth to a different Goethe poem by the same name (op. 83, no. 2); and a sixth, written in the winter of 1815–16, to a poem by Reissig, WoO 146. Yearning was, of course, the main subject of Beethoven's song cycle, *An die ferne Geliebte* (*To the Distant Beloved*), op. 98, composed in April 1816 to a Romantic pastoral text by Alois Jeitteles, a young poet and medical student who apparently wrote the poems especially for Beethoven, perhaps to his order.

Rolland and others have speculated that the cycle may have been written as a love offering to the Immortal Beloved.[8] Certainly Beethoven was wont to use lieder as love offerings—to Josephine Deym, Therese Malfatti ("Sehnsucht," op. 83 no 2), and Antonie Brentano. Or had the tug of urgent physical desire brought this counterbalancing, Platonic *Liederkreis* into existence? The cycle was dedicated to the dying Prince Lobkowitz in October 1816; perhaps its yearning quality is more generalized, its sense of loss flowing from the numerous leave-takings and deaths of so many of Beethoven's close friends and patrons during the preceding years. A psychoanalyst might object to interpretations grounded in Beethoven's immediate experience and say that the "distant beloved" is unfailingly and fundamentally the image of an idealized mother and that the yearning, renunciatory tone of the song cycle therefore represents the symbolic fulfillment or sublimation of more archaic desires. A literary historian, looking at the same set of facts, would find in the text and in the music's symbolization of longing and nostalgia a classic, rich example of an emergent Romanticist trope. It is impossible to tell which, if any, of these interpretations ought to be stressed, especially since the impulse that gives rise to a work of art may be years or decades old by the time its working out on paper begins.

Still, *An die ferne Geliebte,* which Kerman calls "a quiet herald of the third-period style," occupies a special place in Beethoven's life and work.[9] It seems safe to say that it bids farewell to his marriage project, to romantic pretense, to heroic grandiosity, to youth itself. It is a work that accepts loss without piteous outcry, for it preserves intact the memory of the past and refuses to acknowledge the finality of bereavement:

> For song effaces
> all space and all time,
> and a loving heart attains
> that to which a loving heart consecrates itself.[10]

The musical significance of *An die ferne Geliebte* is that, primitive anticipations by such German composers as Friedrich Heinrich Himmel and Johann Friedrich Reichardt aside, it was the first through-composed song cycle and became the point of departure for the cycles of Schumann and many others (though not for those of Schubert, who maintained a deliberate independence). Beethoven actually carried the process of unification of his material further than the Romantics, for he wove the six songs together so tightly, by means of interconnecting piano passages, that they cannot be sung separately. This may be interpreted as representing sundered Eros achieving reunion, as well as the eternal indissolubility of the bond between lover and beloved, wedded by the emblem of the ring's (or wreath's) circularity. Rolland calls the cycle "one *Lied*, with varied episodes," and Boettcher calls it "a single, prodigiously extended lied."[11] In the forms and keys of the songs, Beethoven established a symmetrical architectonic plan. With a view to still further symmetry, the tune of the first song was originally intended to be used for the sixth one as well, but Beethoven eventually settled on a variant, related melody and then reintroduced the opening melody as a conscious reminiscence (a touch derived from his practice in instrumental works) just prior to the close of the cycle, with heartbreaking effect.

Kerman, in his illuminating study of this work, stresses the ways in which it opens the way to Beethoven's last style: the cyclic form of the *Liederkreis* is the prototype of similar structures in the last works, such as the String Quartet in C-sharp minor, op. 131, and the Grosse Fuge, op. 133 (and, he might have added, the Bagatelles, op. 126). He sees the song cycle as inaugurating the "vocal impulse" that will come to fruition in songful movements of the late sonatas and late quartets, and in the Adagio molto e cantabile and "Ode to Joy" of the Ninth Symphony.

Two further songs close out Beethoven's significant lieder production: the melancholy "Resignation," WoO 149, of 1817, and "Abendlied unterm gestirnten Himmel" ("Evening Song Beneath the Starry Heavens"), WoO 150, a deeply felt dramatic ode to the deity, composed on March 4, 1820, while Beethoven was awaiting the decision of the Court of Appeal.

Beethoven often complained about the limitations of the piano, and he continued to do so up until his last year, when he told Holz, "It is and remains an inadequate instrument."[12] Nevertheless, it was perhaps inevitable that the piano, the earliest vehicle of Beethoven's fantasy, invention, and virtuosity, should now take the lead in the forging of his late style. His song cycle completed, Beethoven turned once again to the piano sonata, composing his last five of these between mid-1816 and the beginning of 1822. These sonatas, along with the Diabelli Variations, op. 120, and the Bagatelles, op. 126, form one of the pillars of Beethoven's creative achievement in his last years. In them, he first worked out the fusion of fugue, variation form, and sonata form that is fundamental to the formulation of his new musical thought. The Sonata in A, op. 101, was completed in November 1816 and published the following February by Steiner with a dedication to Dorothea von Ertmann. The work is similar in design to the fantasy sonatas of earlier years, with its climax reserved for the finale and an expressive Langsam und sehnsuchtsvoll introduction leading to a dramatic, contrapuntally conceived sonata-form movement, the development section of which is a four-part fugue. With the Sonata, op. 101, it became clear that the fugue of the finale of the Cello Sonata in D, op. 102, no. 2, of 1815, was not an isolated musical event but rather the first expression of a veritable contrapuntal obsession during Beethoven's last decade.

Beethoven had received from Albrechtsberger a solid grounding in counterpoint, but, as Nottebohm observed, he did not acquire from him "a thorough training in fugue."[13] During his first two decades in Vienna Beethoven utilized fugal elements and procedures in many works, including the opus 18 quartets and the Mass in C, and occasionally composed fugatos (as in the Funeral March of the *Eroica* Symphony, the Allegretto of the Seventh Symphony, and several choruses of *Christ on the Mount of Olives*). But so far his only really large fugal movements were the finales of the String Quartet, op. 59, no. 3, and of the Variations and Fugue, op. 35. Nottebohm would not grant that even these were proper fugues, and, so Schindler said, neither would many of Beethoven's more pedantic contemporaries, who spread the word: "Beethoven is incapable of writing a fugue."[14] Schindler, in his simplicity, believed that Beethoven's preoccupation with the fugue in his last period was his response to this criticism. But what Ludwig Misch calls "the rebirth of fugue from the spirit of the sonata" arose out of Beethoven's need to create musical motion of a different type than was permitted by the obbligato style,[15] and at the same time expressed his search to expand the possibilities of sonata form itself. More than half of Beethoven's major works would henceforth contain a full-scale fugue, and many others would contain fughettas, fugatos, canons, and other brief contrapuntal passages.[16] In his last decade, Beethoven, who had come to maturity in an antipolyphonic age, reinstated the polyphonic principle as a rival of—and perhaps as the completion of—the sonata principle. The years 1816–17 were a turning point. In 1817 he wrote a string quintet movement in D minor as an introduction to a fugue that he never actually composed; he began an arrangement for string quartet of the B-minor fugue from Bach's *Well-Tempered Clavier*, Book One, BWV 846–69; and he completed a Fugue in D for String Quintet, later published as opus 137.[17]

The first climax of this preoccupation with polyphony occurs in the Sonata in B-flat ("Hammerklavier"), op. 106, of 1817–18. Beethoven's longest sonata (it is almost 1,200 measures), the "Hammerklavier" is in Classic four-movement form. Even more than Beethoven's other late sonatas, it presents technical difficulties that place it far beyond the reach of amateur pianists. (One far-fetched tradition has it that Beethoven composed the work in competition with Hummel's "unplayable" Sonata in F-sharp minor, op. 81.)[18] The sonata apparently received several private performances (reportedly by Czerny, Ries, and Cipriani Potter) in Beethoven's lifetime; eventually, through the efforts of Liszt and Moscheles in particular, it came to be considered one of the greatest and most challenging works of the piano repertory. Beethoven is said to have told Artaria, who published the work in September 1819, "Now there you have a sonata that will keep the pianists busy when it is played fifty years hence."[19]

The fugue in three voices constitutes the entire finale, save for the 15-measure transitional Largo. It is filled with learned contrapuntal devices—Riezler even describes it as "overladen to the point of artificiality with all the arts of the fugue"[20]—which serve to intensify the aggressive, unbridled thrust of the movement, with its defiant and relentless striving (Allegro risoluto) to surmount immense obstacles. Never had Beethoven attempted so difficult an affirmation, and it is this effort that dictates the special nature of the contrapuntal writing. In his earlier years, Beethoven had utilized counterpoint to convey urbane humor (the Scherzo of the String Quartet, op. 18, no. 4) or to introduce a measured and heroic solemnity (the Funeral March of the *Eroica* Symphony), momentarily to disrupt periodicity (the first movement of the String Quartet, op. 18, no. 1) or to create a seamless, powerful rhythmic impulse (the finale of the opus 59, no. 3, String Quartet; the Cum sancto spiritu and the Et vitam venturi of the Mass in C). Here the textures are harsh and angular and the counterpoint rough-hewn and granitic, bursting outward with explosive force, the fugue's jagged qualities accentuated by occasional lyrical passages that interrupt its unremitting advance. Martin Cooper writes, "There is in this finale, as in the Grosse Fuge, an element of excessiveness . . . an instinct to push every component part of the music . . . not just to its logical conclusion but beyond," and he feels that in a sense Beethoven was thereby "doing violence to his listener."[21] The violence is not in Beethoven's intent, however, but in his subject matter, for here, as in the Grosse Fuge, the fugue's closest analogue is the process of creation (or birth), the pain-ridden, exultant struggle for emergence. The passage through the labyrinth, from darkness to light, from doubt to belief, from suffering to joy, cannot be without its unique torments. By the same token, such an emergence is not without its manic raptures—the aspect that led Rolland to stress the mood of turbulent caprice, the laughing spirit that erupts from the fugal texture.[22]

Rosen has demonstrated the organic unity of the "Hammerklavier" Sonata in a detailed analysis showing that all of its movements are built up from a "central idea": a relentless use of chains of descending thirds.[23] It is not altogether clear, however, that Beethoven himself felt he had succeeded in forging an aesthetically whole four-movement Classical work from materials that were disruptive of Classical form. Perhaps he momentarily lost confidence in the value of his effort, for in late March 1819, he authorized Ries to publish the Sonata in England in any one of three forms:

1. The first two movements alone.
2. The Allegro risoluto by itself, without the Largo.
3. The first three movements, with the order of the Scherzo and Adagio sostenuto reversed.

"I leave it to you to do as you think best," Beethoven wrote, and he apologized to Ries for the Sonata's deficiencies, explaining, without a hint of irony, "The *sonata* was written in distressful circumstances, for it is hard to compose almost entirely for the sake of earning one's daily bread; and that is *all* that I have been able *to achieve*."[24]

Subsequently, Ries arranged to publish the English edition as two separate though connected works: a "Grand Sonata for the Piano Forte," consisting of the first three movements in the order 1, 3, 2; and an "Introduction & Fugue for the Piano Forte," consisting of the Largo and Allegro risoluto.[25] Some scholars believe that Beethoven, knowing that the Sonata was being published correctly in Vienna, did not mind what was done with it in London.[26] Actually, plans for drastic revision of certain of Beethoven's late works may instead be circumstantial evidence of the "noninevitability" of his formal structures, suggesting, as I have noted elsewhere, that in late Beethoven, "no work was necessarily final, nor was any form ineluctably the only possible one capable of expressing his central ideas."[27] Mutability became a fixed principle.

In summary, Rosen observed that opus 106 "is not typical of Beethoven, and does not sound it; it is not even typical of his last period. It is an extreme point of his style. He never again wrote so obsessively concentrated a work. In part, it must have been an attempt to break out of the impasse in which he found himself."[28]

Beethoven wrote the three last sonatas following the termination of the guardianship litigation and during the composition of the *Missa Solemnis*. The Piano Sonatas in E, op. 109, in A-flat, op. 110, and in C minor, op. 111, were initially published by the house of Schlesinger in November 1821, about August 1822, and about April 1823, respectively.[29] Here, Beethoven no longer attempted to impart a symphonic breadth to his sonata style, but returned to the smaller dimensions of the Sonatas, op. 90 and op. 101, infusing the new works alternately with a variety of rigorous polyphonic textures and an etherealized improvisatory tone. In each of the three last piano sonatas, the climax has again been shifted to the finale: in opus 110 this is a long and complex fugue, one that, however, has none of the cross-grained quality of opus 106. It is the smoothest of Beethoven's fugal finales and surely also one of the most moving, with its introductory recitative and Arioso dolente ("sorrowful song"), which returns to alternate with the fugue and thus to prepare for the sonata's harmonious conclusion. In the two other sonatas, however, the concluding movements are sets of variations—the first time that Beethoven had utilized variation form in the finale of a piano sonata, although he had done so earlier in the closing movements of the *Eroica* Symphony, the String Quartet, op. 74, and the Violin Sonatas, op. 30, no. 1, and op. 96.

By 1820, Beethoven had written more than sixty sets of variations, either as separate works or as movements of larger cycles. With opus 109 and opus 111, he imbued the form for the first time with a "transfigured," almost ecstatic content and a profundity of expression, which indicated that he had found in this basic musical form a new vehicle for his most imaginative musical thoughts. Thereby, variation form joins fugue as one of the leading features of the late style, and variation movements appear in many of his last masterpieces, including both the Adagio and finale of the Ninth Symphony and crucial movements of the String Quartets, opp. 127, 131, 132, and 135. The crowning work of this new preoccupation is the Thirty-three Variations on a Waltz by Diabelli, op. 120.

In his middle period, the presumptive model for Beethoven's sonata cycle was drama—comedy, tragedy, and the combined forms of these that touch upon mythic and collective levels of experience. This model retained its resiliency and power in the last "public" works: the *Missa Solemnis* and the Ninth Symphony. Perhaps the "Hammerklavier" Sonata embodied Beethoven's powerful desire to hold on not only to classicism and the received sonata style but to the dramatic model as well. Beethoven's aggressive and disruptive contrapuntal procedures had already undermined this model, however, while retaining the dialectical and synthesizing functions that are as characteristic of fugue as of sonata. But with the "grand variation" or "chorale with variations" (as d'Indy alternately names Beethoven's late variation works), a quite different model comes to the fore.

Variation is potentially the most "open" of musical procedures, one that gives the greatest freedom to a composer's fantasy. It mirrors the unpredictability and chance nature of human experience and keeps alive the openness of human expectation. Fate cannot knock at the door in the variation form: such concepts as necessity and inevitability need a dialectical musical pattern within which to express their message, whereas the variation form is discursive and peripatetic, in flight from messages and ideologies. Its subject is the adventurer, the picaro, the quick-change artist, the impostor, the phoenix who ever rises from the ashes, the rebel who, defeated, continues his quest, the thinker who doubts perception, who shapes and reshapes reality in search of its inner significance, the omnipotent child who plays with matter as God plays with the universe. Variation is the form of shifting moods, alternations of feeling, shades of meaning, dislocations of perspective. It shatters appearance into splinters of previously unperceived reality and, by an act of will, reassembles the fragments at the close. The sense of time is effaced—expanded, contracted—by changes in tempo; space and mass dissolve into the barest outline of the harmonic progressions and build up once again into intricate structures laden with richly ornamented patterns. The theme abides throughout as an anchor, as though to prevent fantasy from losing contact with the outer world, but it is ever in process of dissolving into the memories, images, and feelings that underlie its simple reality.

Two thirds of the Diabelli Variations were drafted in 1819, but the set was taken up again in late 1822, completed in the spring of 1823, and published in June 1823 by the firm of Cappi and Diabelli, who perceptively announced it as "a great and important masterpiece worthy to be ranked with the imperishable creations of the old Classics," entitled "to a place beside Sebastian Bach's famous masterpiece in the same form."[30] Bachian and Handelian tendencies are much in evidence here, especially in the devotional fughetta of variation 24, which might have issued from the Goldberg Variations, BWV 988, and in the extended double fugue of variation 32. Beethoven combines melodic and harmonic variation techniques, both as Mozart had done before him and in accordance with his own practice in the "Eroica" Variations, op. 35, and in the finale of the *Eroica* Symphony.

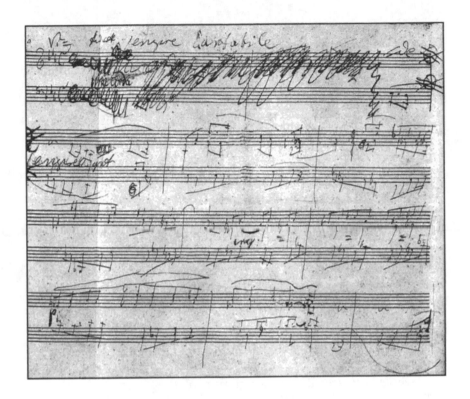

Diabelli Variations, op. 120, variation 30, Andante cantabile.

Private collection. From Georg Kinsky, Manuskripte, Briefe,
Dokumente von Scarlatti bis Stravinsky: Katalog der
Musikautographen-Sammlung Louis Koch *(Stuttgart, 1953).*

In a number of the Diabelli variations, the melodic tie is tenuous, or even effectively absent. Beethoven had become increasingly attached to the harmonic (analytic, structural) variation style during his middle period. The melodic variation was, perhaps, perceived by some as a superficial procedure, and indeed, in the typical ornamental, melodic variation, few risks are taken: the composer strays no farther than the garden gate, reluctant to leave the comforts of home. By his last years, Beethoven was nothing but a risk taker; hence, far from abandoning the melodic variation procedure, he turned to it for the expression of his deepest meditations, as in several of the present variations and in the Piano Sonatas, opp. 109 and 111, the Adagio ma non troppo of the String Quartet, op. 127, and the Adagio molto e cantabile of the Ninth Symphony. In these, increasingly elaborate ornamentation of the theme creates the sense of strophic song whose accompaniment comments on an implied text and magnifies its meaning.

Tovey breaks down Diabelli's theme into its components to show the wealth of implicit ideas ("rich in solid musical facts") in its simple (often called banal) progression of notes: the opening turn, descending fourths and fifths, rising sequences, and simply articulated harmonic and rhythmic framework. He argues that Beethoven's variations on this theme "need no analysis beyond comparison with [it]; their grouping and contrasting explain themselves with dazzling effect."[31] Others have sought to uncover an underlying architecture in the set, some finding a four-movement sonata hidden in it, Halm analyzing it as a work in seven sections, and Geiringer finding an archlike construction in five sections with an epilogue, creating "a strictly symmetrical organization . . . such as that which the Bach period loved to employ."[32] It is even, perhaps, not inappropriate to regard the Diabelli Variations as a gigantic cycle of bagatelles,[33] covering the full range of Beethoven's fantasy and invention. What Ernest Walker wrote of late Beethoven as a whole serves well as a description of this *Pilgrim's Progress* on a Biedermeier waltz: "We find side by side grim uncouthness and unearthly serenity, wild passion and noble majesty, inconsequential antics and delicate charm, tortuous involutions and limpid simplicity."[34] The Diabelli Variations is a work in which extremes meet to an extent previously unknown even in Beethoven's music: here the tawdry and the sublime rub shoulders; Leporello materializes amid music of the spheres; the miniature and the fresco merge into one; the perpetual motion of variation 19 collides with the virtual motionlessness of variation 20; variation 32's constructive synthesis dissolves in a coda in which "the material seems to be gradually broken up and scattered into dust" (Blom).[35]

The Diabelli Variations was Beethoven's last extended work for piano. His only other keyboard compositions of the 1820s—apart from two Waltzes, WoO 84–85, and an Ecossaise, WoO 86, of 1824–25— were the Eleven Bagatelles, op. 119, worked into final form between 1820 and 1822, and Six Bagatelles, op. 126, composed probably in May–June 1824 (not, as formerly believed, during the previous winter). With opus 126 and the Diabelli Variations, Beethoven revealed himself as a master miniaturist, capable of sketching a variety of emotional states in a few quick tone strokes. The opus 126 Bagatelles were conceived as a cycle ("Ciclus von Kleinigkeiten," he wrote on the sketches)[36] and perhaps even as a first sketch of the multimovement form of several of the late quartets. It would not be the first time that the piano, with all its inadequacies ("clavicembalo miserabile," he once called it),[37] had opened the way toward new creative possibilities.

In his last years, according to Schindler, Beethoven's playing at times "was more painful than agreeable. . . . The outpourings of his fancy became scarcely intelligible." Sometimes he would place his left hand flat upon the keyboard "and thus drown, in discordant noise, the music to which his right was feelingly giving utterance."[38] As always, he did not want his private musical thoughts to be overheard. Thus, even at the end, the piano remained Beethoven's most intimate means of communing with his inner self.

Like Beethoven's earlier Mass in C, the *Missa Solemnis,* op. 123, was written for a specific occasion; it was indeed to celebrate the installation of Archduke Rudolph (1788–1831) as archbishop of Olmütz (present-day Olomouc), in Moravia, on March 9, 1820. Rudolph, the son of Emperor Leopold II and the brother of Emperor Franz, was the most important of Beethoven's patrons from circa 1809 onward and was the recipient of eleven major dedications (plus four canons), including those of the Fourth and Fifth piano concertos, the Trio in B-flat ("Archduke"), op. 97, the Piano Sonatas in B-flat and C minor, opp. 106 and 111, and the Grosse Fuge, op. 133. For many years he was Beethoven's only regular piano student in Vienna, as well as his only long-term composition student after Ries left the capital in 1805. Rudolph seems to have worshiped Beethoven, carefully preserving more than 100 letters and collecting first editions, autographs, and fair copies of his compositions. Beethoven, in turn, became deeply attached to him, perhaps in part because Rudolph was the nephew of the revered Joseph II; it was reported that he spoke Rudolph's name "with childlike reverence, as he does no other,"[39] and his letters to him are filled with expressions of adoration. Numerous negative or ambivalent statements about Rudolph to third persons serve only to preserve the privacy of Beethoven's deep feelings for this orphaned and epileptic royal prince.

Rudolph was also important as Beethoven's protector, who provided him with access to the imperial court. And for many years it was apparently Beethoven's expectation that when Rudolph assumed his archbishopric, Beethoven would become his kapellmeister. This, at least, is what Reichardt reported in a letter of March 27, 1809,[40] and in later years, several of Beethoven's letters seem to confirm this impression.[41] Rudolph perhaps kept Beethoven's hopes on this score alive for an unreasonably long time, and it still remains unclear why this expectation—which may have provided one of the motivations behind the composition of the *Missa Solemnis*—was never fulfilled.

The Mass became Beethoven's absorbing passion for four years, replacing *Fidelio* as the great "problem work" of his career. Indeed, there is a sense in which the *Missa Solemnis* came to be regarded by Beethoven as a talismanic composition, whose value to him was so great that (as described earlier) he embarked on a unique series of financial negotiations and manipulations in respect of its publication, which cost him several friendships and gave him an unpleasant, but deserved, reputation for sharp business practice.

None of this, however, speaks to the deeper meaning of the Mass for Beethoven. Beethoven's creativity required repeated musical challenges. In his earlier Vienna years he had methodically set about demonstrating his command of the main genres of the Classical tradition; in the late period, a similar determination is once more evident: in the encyclopedic essays in fugue and in variation technique of the "Hammerklavier" Sonata and the Diabelli Variations, and in the *Missa Solemnis*, which establishes Beethoven's mastery of the highest form of liturgical music.

Although we may be certain that Beethoven poured his deepest religious feelings into the *Missa Solemnis*, we may be equally sure that it was not deference to the Catholic Church that prompted the work. As has often been noted, the piece has never been fully at home in either concert hall or church. On several occasions Beethoven suggested that it could be performed as "a grand oratorio" (adding, parenthetically, "for the benefit of the poor"),[42] and he was not disturbed to learn that in its first performance, in St. Petersburg, it was indeed presented as an oratorio.[43] For his concerts of May 1824, he himself did not hesitate to retitle the Kyrie, Credo, and Agnus Dei of the Mass "Three

Grand Hymns with Solo and Chorus Voices," in order to obtain a waiver from the censor of the ban on performing missal music in a theater.[44] But the clearest evidence of Beethoven's nonsectarian attitude toward his Mass is his offer to provide Simrock with a German-language version to facilitate performances in Protestant communities.[45] As Rolland wrote, Beethoven had "a great need to commune with the Lamb, with the God of love and compassion," but the *Missa Solemnis* "overflows the church by its spirit and its dimensions."[46]

This is not to diminish the religious significance of, or religious intention behind, the Mass. "My chief aim," he wrote to Andreas Streicher, "was to awaken and permanently instill religious feelings not only into the singers but also into the listeners."[47] To Archduke Rudolph he wrote, "There is nothing higher than to approach the Godhead more nearly than other mortals and by means of that contact to spread the rays of the Godhead through the human race."[48]

Beethoven had written the C-major Mass in the Viennese style, with an admixture of grand-manner symphonism. It seems clear that he now felt the Classical tradition to be somehow inadequate for the composition of a major work in this form, or for the expression of a highly sublimated spirituality. As early as 1809 he observed that "in the old church modes the devotion is divine . . . and God permit me to express it someday."[49] Now he systematically and painstakingly set about mastering the rhetorical vocabularies of religious music of earlier periods. Just prior to beginning work on the Mass he wrote in his Tagebuch, "In order to write true church music go through all the ecclesiastical chants of the monks etc. Also look there for the stanzas in the most correct translations along with the most perfect prosody of all Christian-Catholic psalms and hymns in general."[50] He and his friends combed the libraries of Prince Lobkowitz and Archduke Rudolph in search of old music and treatises on liturgical procedures, and Beethoven immersed himself in the music of Palestrina and his Renaissance contemporaries as well as the music of Handel, J. S. Bach, and C. P. E. Bach. ("Don't forget [C. P. E.] Bach's Litanies," he wrote in the Tagebuch.)[51] It is not surprising, then, that the resulting work is an amalgam of archaic and modern styles, more deeply rooted in older traditions than any other work of Beethoven's but retaining the grandeur and dynamic thrust of a symphonism growing out of the sonata style. In a brilliant essay that removes the *Missa Solemnis* from the historical vacuum in which it is ordinarily studied, Warren Kirkendale writes, "Today we see that he not only retained traditional thought to an unexpected degree, but even uncovered much older, buried traditions, and formed musical 'ideas' in the plain and concrete sense of the century in which he was born—naturally with an incomparably freer, personal vocabulary."[52] He demonstrates that Beethoven's Mass achieves its immense power partly through the complex use of conventional images and traditional patterns of musical rhetoric whose associational meanings had been built up through centuries of usage.

The artist's imagination must be given its due as well, however, and though there are many "new roads to old ideas" in the *Missa Solemnis*, its historic importance consists largely in the way in which it reshaped rather than reproduced the traditions of liturgical music. Beethoven did this by very much the same method that created the great religious music of his predecessors, from Dufay and Josquin to Handel and Bach, namely a refusal to accept the received forms and languages as eternal models, instead infusing them with "secular" elements derived from nonliturgical musical styles. This had the effect of expanding the expressive possibilities of the form, giving rise to new referential meanings that in turn became embedded in the matrix of later musical grammar. Beethoven knew that he was not writing his *Missa Solemnis* in the traditional church style; he wrote to the composer Zelter that he regarded the a capella style (of Palestrina and his contemporaries) as "the only true church style,"[53] but he chose to avoid this model, perhaps because he did not wish the work to serve as a comforting assurance of the immutability of faith. In bypassing the Palestrina style (though utilizing it to achieve a specific mystical quality in the Et incarnatus est), Beethoven was rejecting its beatification of hierarchical and, by implication, feudal forms. Instead, Beethoven introduced a restless, questioning element into the received forms of the Mass. "To the Christian whose supreme law is obedience," writes Paul Henry Lang, "the Beethovenian attitude seems repellent, for submission is preceded in him by a struggle with doubts; faith is gained through a Faustian trial."[54]

Beethoven's musical archaisms and reminiscences—Dorian and Mixolydian modes, Gregorian "fossils," quotations from Handel's *Messiah* in the Gloria and Agnus Dei—and his employment of procedures and musical imagery derived from older liturgical styles are, in context, modernistic devices that also serve to stretch the expressiveness of his music beyond the boundaries set for liturgical music by his contemporaries. These devices, as well as the theatrical use of "military" and "pastoral" motifs in the Dona nobis pacem, are also communication shortcuts, rapidly assimilable musical ideographs to ease the process of understanding the grand design of the Mass, which Beethoven called "the *greatest* work which I have composed so far."[55]

Paul Bekker called the *Missa Solemnis* a "Divine Heroic Symphony," asserting that "in the *Eroica* the hero wins culture for humanity as the fruit of his life and death; but here the prize is life everlasting."[56] Contrary to Beethoven's usual practice, however, the *Missa Solemnis* does not strive for a heroic, transcendent, or even necessarily affirmative conclusion. As Ernest Newman observed, "The conclusion of it all is enigmatic. . . . Does Beethoven really believe that the prayer will be answered, or does he leave it all as a kind of question mark projected upon the remote, indifferent sky?"[57] One need not go quite this far; indeed, William Mann has pointed out that one does not ordinarily end a prayer with heroic peroration, but with an "Amen."[58] Nevertheless, one wonders whether Beethoven indeed felt that he, or humanity, would win the prize of life everlasting. There was in him a deep yearning for personal immortality. In 1803 he had written to the painter Alexander Macco, "Continue to paint—and I shall continue to write down notes; and thus we shall live—for ever?—yes, perhaps, for ever."[59] In the Tagebuch he asked Pliny's question, "What greater gift can be conferred on a man than fame and praise and eternal life?"[60] Each of these references to immortality implies a question mark, as does the *Missa Solemnis*. Beethoven hoped for, indeed he yielded to none in his yearning for, resurrection, but this was a desired consummation that came into conflict with his rationalism. In April 1823 his friend Karl Peters wrote in a Conversation Book, "Granted that you don't believe in it you will be glorified, because your music [is] religion."[61] Clearly, Beethoven had expressed his doubts to Peters, who sought to reassure him: "You will arise with me from the dead—because you must. Religion remains constant, only Man is changeable."[62]

Beethoven's ongoing conflict between faith and doubt is revealed in the *Missa Solemnis*. As Riezler knew, in the Dona nobis pacem, with its

sounds of strife and warfare and its anguished cries for peace, both inner
and outer, Beethoven "dared to allow the confusion of the world outside
to invade the sacred domain of church music."⁶³ In this sense, the *Missa
Solemnis* forecasts the theological questions and doubts—along with the
warfare between science and religion—that were to dominate the intellectual battleground of the nineteenth century.

"Utopias are often only premature truths," Lamartine wrote; Victor
Hugo called utopia "the truth of tomorrow." Both aphorisms express
the anticipatory nature of visionary art, its expectation of fulfillment, its
capacity for hovering on the horizon of possibility, its principle of hope.
At the same time, utopian art arises out of the disharmony between the
artist and the conditions of his existence. Thus, in Martin Buber's formulation, "The vision of 'what should be'—independent though it may
sometimes appear of personal will—is yet inseparable from a critical
and fundamental relationship to the existing condition of humanity. All
suffering under a social order that is senseless prepares the soul for
vision."⁶⁴ Finally, if the trajectory of utopian art leads toward a transcendent future, and its origins are in a diseased present, its dreamed-of
alternatives are modeled on memories, fantasies, or artistic representations of an Edenic state.

   We have already encountered utopian elements in Beethoven's
music—in his evocations of a pastoral Arcadia, in his idealization of the
bon prince, in the triumphal *Siegessymphonie* of his *Egmont* music, and in
the emergence of Pizarro's prisoners into the light. In a sense, all of
Beethoven's best music is utopian, in that it holds out images of beauty,
joy, and renewal as models of future possibility. Only with the Ninth
Symphony, however, does the utopian model have a predictive component: the tense of "Alle Menschen werden Brüder"—"All men become
brothers"—is "neither past, present, nor even quite future, but a process
tense, implying what will happen 'if.'"⁶⁵ It contains in addition a hint of
the imperative, a prayer that "All men *should* become brothers" and
should dwell in harmony with a "loving father" under the protection of
that female "*Freude* (Joy), daughter of Elysium," who had eluded
Beethoven's grasp during his lifetime. With the Ninth Symphony, the
anachronistic Enlightenment dream of a harmonious kingdom has
returned to the stage long after the exhaustion of the social and intellec-

tual impulses born of the *philosophes*. Perhaps it could only return—as pure hope—after the apparent historical shipwreck of the dream that Rousseau, Schiller, and the young Beethoven had shared, after Beethoven's separation from the aristocratic and national collectivities that had nourished his sense of communality. Beethoven's Ninth is his refusal to accept the finality of that failure and of that separation.

Although there is a sense in which much of late Beethoven embodies a return to the unrealized projects of an earlier time, in the Ninth Symphony that return is a quite literal one. According to the Bonn humanist Bartholomäus Ludwig Fischenich, who may have introduced Beethoven to Schiller's thought at Bonn University or at the Lesegesellschaft and who also evidently regarded the young composer as his protégé, Beethoven had planned to set to music Schiller's "An die Freude" (usually called in English the "Ode to Joy," written in 1785, published in 1786) before he left Bonn for Vienna.[66] In fact, a brief passage from Schiller's poem already appeared in the "Leopold" Cantata of 1790. A sketchbook of 1798–99 contains music for the poem's "Muss ein lieber Vater wohnen" ("There surely dwells a dear father"), and in 1803 Ferdinand Ries wrote to Simrock in Bonn, offering for publication Beethoven's setting of "An die Freude" as one of eight lieder that had been composed within the preceding "four years."[67] If, as seems to be the case, the song was actually written, it has disappeared without a trace. One wonders whether the censorship that Schiller's works encountered in Vienna during Beethoven's early years there had something to do with that disappearance and with the long postponement of this project. In 1793, the censor banned *Die Räuber* (*The Robbers*) as "immoral" and "dangerous"; not until 1808 did Schiller's works again start to be staged and his books to reappear in the stalls. Thereafter, his popularity became such that in the years from 1813 to 1825 there were 320 performances of his plays at the Theater-an-der-Wien alone.[68]

Beethoven himself told Czerny that Schiller was a difficult poet to set because no musician could surpass his poetry.[69] (Besides "An die Freude," Beethoven set only "Gesang der Mönche" ["Song of the Monks"], WoO 104, from *Wilhelm Tell*, in 1817, and one stanza of the Ballade "Das Mädchen aus der Fremde" ["The Strange Maiden"] in 1810.)[70] In 1812, Beethoven momentarily interrupted the sketching of his Seventh and Eighth Symphonies to jot down some ideas on "Freude schöner Götterfunken" from Schiller's poem, perhaps intended for a D-minor symphony or, more likely, for a choral overture,[71] but in 1814–15 this thematic material was utilized in the "Name Day" Overture, op. 115. In 1818, Beethoven had the idea of using voices in a symphony on mythological themes, but not until 1822–23 did it occur to him that his Schiller project could be fulfilled in his new symphony. He continued to explore alternative instrumental solutions to the choral finale, however, as late as the summer of 1823.

The "Ode to Joy" melody itself was also long in the fashioning. A lilting tune that foreshadows its opening phrase appeared in the song "Gegenliebe," WoO 118, of 1794 or 1795, and again in the vocal finale of the "Choral Fantasia," op. 80, in 1808. Two years later, it is heard once again in the song "Mit einem Gemalten Band" ("With a Painted Ribbon"), op. 83, no. 3, set to a lyric by Goethe. Numerous other anticipations of one or another element of the Ninth Symphony have been traced, including in the "Leopold" and "Joseph" cantatas of 1790, the Second Symphony, *Fidelio* (which incorporates a couplet from Schiller's ode), the "Choral Fantasia," and the closing bars of the Overture to *King Stephen* (which anticipates the Turkish variation of the Ninth's finale). Sketches of what later became the theme of the scherzo date from 1815.[72]

In other ways too the Ninth Symphony stems from a retrospective impulse, and these are perhaps more crucial. For in it, Beethoven returned unreservedly to the heroic style that he had effectively completed by 1812–14. Actually, he retraced his steps still further, turning once again to the *Eroica* Symphony model of 1803–4, with its archetypal patterns and its grand-manner "Empire" style, creating what Martin Cooper terms "a cross between *sinfonia eroica* and *hymne de la république*."[73] It is extraordinary that an apparently superseded style still retained such vitality, and such technical and expressive possibilities. Clearly, the intervening experiences—both biographical and musical— had enriched Beethoven's perception of the potentialities of the conventional sonata-form four-movement symphony. As with the four-movement "Hammerklavier" Sonata, which was conceived almost simultaneously with the Ninth Symphony, he again felt the impulse to test his powers against the restraints of the Classic model—to bring the model to its dynamic and expressive outer limits in one final, perfecting (and destroying) essay.

Yet, the seeming conventionality of the Ninth Symphony's harmonic language and of its forms—sonata form in the first movement, a traditional scherzo (albeit with a fugato and a double repeat), two sets of variations in the Adagio sostenuto and finale—is belied by the fundamental novelty of the symphony, which became the prototype of one branch of nineteenth-century Romantic symphonism, extending from Liszt to Mahler. This resulted from the unprecedented spaciousness and grandeur of the work, from its humanist message—which blends mystical, theological, and utopian/revolutionary strands of thought—and from an organicism of design reminiscent of the Fifth Symphony, but which here repudiates epigrammatic and dynamic condensation in favor of rhetorical sublimity. There has long existed a school of Beethoven analysts—among them Hans Mersmann, Walter Engelsmann, Fritz Cassirer, and Rudolph Réti—who have sought to establish that each of his multimovement works derives from a single motif or theme, as though this would unlock the deepest secrets of his creative process. In the Ninth Symphony, and especially in its first three movements, they have one of their strongest cases. As d'Indy noticed, "*All* the typical themes of the symphony present the arpeggio of the chords of D or B flat, the two tonal bases of the work; one might, therefore, consider this arpeggio as the real cyclic theme of the Ninth Symphony."[74] Réti dwelt on the thematic unity of much of the work, and even urged convincingly that the "Seid umschlungen Millionen" theme of the finale is an inversion of the second subject of the Allegro ma non troppo opening movement.[75]

Such demonstrations notwithstanding, there is a sense in which Beethoven himself set out explicitly to reject the unity of the four movements. Indeed, that is the point of departure of the finale, in which each of the previous movements is recalled only to be dismissed, whereupon the bass soloist recites Beethoven's words, "O friends, not these sounds; rather let us intone pleasanter and more joyful ones," thus inaugurating the main theme of the "Ode to Joy." Of course, this may be regarded as a ruse, a means by which Beethoven achieves a supremely integrated structure through the use of more powerful and individual contrasts than are customary in a sonata finale. And, perhaps more precisely, Beethoven is here setting aside the past, with its memories of strife, tragedy, and loss; he is not repudiating his own music, but rather the states that it symbolizes: "tragedy," "satiric drama," "beauty of an order too sublime for a world of action"— Tovey's shorthand will serve as well as any to describe the central ideas of the first three movements of the symphony.[76] In place of these he sets his joyous affirmation, with its discovery (again Tovey) of "a theme on which the mind could rest as a final solution of typical human doubts and difficulties."[77] In the sketches for the bass recitative, Beethoven made even more explicit this reading of his scenario, writing, "No, this——reminds us of our despair. Today is a day of celebration, let it be celebrated with song and [dance]."[78]

The war between faith and skepticism, which we encountered in the *Eroica* Symphony and in the *Missa Solemnis*, was far from ended: Beethoven has probed the issues, failed to find a permanent solution, and settled upon pure wish as the closest approximation to a provisionally satisfactory outcome. Doubtless this is an "ideological" solution— one that brooks no opposition and admits no nuances of opinion. In this sense, the finale of the Ninth belongs in the line of compositions that extends from the "Joseph" Cantata of 1790 to *Der glorreiche Augenblick* of 1814. However, it succeeds here where all his other avowedly ideological music failed, by compelling its message to emerge from powerful opposing forces—from the tragic, frenzied, and probing modalities of its earlier movements—and by grafting the cantata form into the sonata cycle. It succeeds, primarily, because of the rich ambiguity of a message that manages to transcend the particularities of its origin and to arrive at a set of universal paradigms.

From one point of view, we may say that Beethoven wrote his own text to the Ninth Symphony's "Ode to Joy."[79] He utilized only half of the eighteen sections of Schiller's version of 1803 and freely rearranged them in accordance with his own poetic vision. He omitted all of the verses that made "An die Freude" an elevated, fraternal drinking song—such as

> Brethren, thus in rapture meeting,
> Send ye round the brimming cup.—
> Yonder kindly spirit greeting,
> While the foam to heaven mounts up!

Clearly Beethoven did not see this as an occasion to express literal Dionysian notions. And, in spite of his hatred of despotism, Beethoven chose to ignore Schiller's antityrannical sentiments:

> Safety from the tyrant's power!
> Mercy e'en to traitors base!

Also omitted is Schiller's "Beggars shall be brothers of princes" (a famous line from the 1785 version), which Beethoven had marked for setting in a sketchbook of 1812.[80] In Beethoven's rearrangement of the poem, we are first introduced to Joy, the personification of the nurturing mother ("All creation drinks joy from the breasts of nature"), in whose protective embrace all mankind is reunited ("All men shall become brothers there where thy gentle wings tarry"), thereby opening the way toward reunion with the benevolent father/God ("Brothers, above the starry vault, there surely dwells a loving Father"). It is a simple scenario, which extracts a kernel from Schiller's poem and universalizes it into a condensed parable of familial reconciliation.

Whatever the psychological sources of the "Ode to Joy" may have been, it encompasses larger relevancies and manifold meanings that have given it unassailable status as a model of human transformation. We need not reject Nietzsche's interpretation: "Now the slave emerges as a freeman; all the rigid, hostile walls which either necessity or despotism has erected between men are shattered. Now that the gospel of universal harmony is sounded, each individual becomes not only reconciled to his fellow but actually at one with him."[81] And Rolland's vision remains intact: "In the Ninth Symphony . . . is mingled a scorching mysticism, a passionate intuitive belief in God-in-Nature and in the moral conscience, a German-mythological theosophism, nourished by Schiller, by philosophical readings, perhaps by Schelling, . . . by his contacts with the Orientalists—the whole stirred by a heroic and revolutionary will to action, in the spirit of the time of his youth."[82] For Rolland, as for so many others, the "Ode to Joy" preaches "the kingdom of God on earth, established by the brotherhood of man, in reason and in joy." In the last analysis, Beethoven's private quest and his ideological thrust are identical: a search for an ideal, extended communal family to assuage the inevitability of personal loss, to maintain and to magnify the sanctified memory of his—and everyone's—personal Eden.

Kerman's emphasis on the drive toward songful communicativeness—the vocal impulse—in Beethoven's late works has special relevance in the Ninth Symphony. In the first movement, Beethoven retains the condensed "heroic" thematic technique, developing his materials from an arpeggiated common-chord germ motif; similarly, the scherzo, with its demonic dance character and rhythm-dominated thrust, is far removed from song. With the two expressive and consoling themes of the Adagio molto e cantabile, however, the speech-inflected accents of the human voice enter the Ninth Symphony, and they do so within a variation form that has the character of an extended, through-composed song without words. (The lessons of *An die ferne Geliebte* are not forgotten.) The Adagio also foreshadows the finale in its conscious reminiscences of the arpeggio theme of the opening movement and according to George Grove, in the sketches Beethoven considered the possibility of having the chorus enter (to what words?) with the statement of the movement's second theme, andante moderato, a stepwise, *espressivo* melody that itself forecasts the "Freude" theme of the finale.[83]

This may provide a link between the choral section of the Ninth and one of its forerunners, the planned "Adagio Cantique," which Beethoven had described in 1818:

> Pious song in a symphony in the ancient modes—Lord God, we praise Thee, alleluia!—either alone or as introduction to a fugue. The whole second symphony [two symphonies were envisaged at this time] might be characterized in this manner, in which case the vocal parts would enter in the last movement or already in the Adagio.[84]

Even without words, song enters the Ninth Symphony as prayer and mourning, as consolation and yearning, as thanksgiving and praise.

Kerman calls attention to Beethoven's "determination to touch common mankind as nakedly as possible," and he marvels at "the spectacle of this composer, having reached heights of subtlety in the pure manipulation of tonal materials, battering at the communications barrier with every weapon of his knowledge."[85] In the finale, the vocal impulse overwhelms that barrier, and it does so by introducing the human voice itself into the tonal fabric. Schenker had made much of Beethoven's "logical inconsistency" in following the first sounding of the "Freude" melody by the "terror fanfare" that repudiates everything that preceded it;[86] but there is really no inconsistency: Beethoven thereby affirms that the "Freude" melody in its merely instrumental manifestation was not sufficient to express his vision. Nor, if we are correct in our hearing of this finale, was voice itself sufficient. In the following variations he explores a wide variety of dance and march rhythms that unite the voice with the expressive movements of the human body. Furthermore, in accordance with his late-period practice, he adds a double fugue, with its symbolization of triumphant motion and its religious connotations, to complete the texture. Four of the pivotal characteristics of Beethoven's late style—song, dance, variation, and fugue—are merged in the "Ode to Joy."

"I want to revoke the Ninth Symphony," cried Adrian Leverkühn in Thomas Mann's *Doctor Faustus*. The Ninth has been perceived by later generations as an unsurpassable model of affirmative culture, a culture that by its beauty and idealism, some believe, anaesthetizes the anguish and the terror of modern life, thereby standing in the way of a realistic perception of society. Marcuse writes, "Today's rebels against the established culture also rebel against the beautiful in this culture, against its all too sublimated, segregated, orderly, harmonizing forms. . . . The refusal now hits the chorus which sings the 'Ode to Joy,' the song which is invalidated in the culture that sings it."[87] The fatal (and destructive) misconception underlying such attitudes is this: if we lose our awareness of the transcendent realms of play, beauty, and kinship that are portrayed in the great affirmative works of our culture, if we lose the reconciling dream of the Ninth Symphony, there may remain no counterpoise against the engulfing terrors of civilization, nothing to set against Auschwitz and Vietnam as a paradigm of humanity's potentialities. Masterpieces of art are instilled with a surplus of constantly renewable energy—an energy that provides a motive force for changes in the relations between human beings—because they contain projections of human desires and goals that have not yet been achieved (which indeed may be unrealizable). In Max Raphael's formulation, "The work of art holds man's creative power in a crystalline suspension from which it can again be transformed into living energies."[88] Beethoven was no stranger to such ideas, for he wrote, "Only art and science give us intimations and hopes of a higher life."[89] To the followers of Kant, Schiller, and Goethe, it was clearly the mission of art to lead humanity to an inner harmony and toward a social order that would permit the unfettered development of the universally human, the "fulfillment of beautiful possibilities" (Goethe). The discovery of the prospective and transcendent nature of art was the work of German Classical aesthetics. In the *Critique of Judgment,* Kant maintained that "our own imagination is the agent employed, as in the case of art, where we realize a preconceived concept of an object which we set before ourselves as an end."[90] Schiller thereupon urged that the artist "multiply . . . the symbols of perfection, till appearance triumphs over reality, and art over nature."[91] The symbols of perfection (which Schiller called "the effigies of [the] ideal")—the Ninth Symphony and the late quartets, the trumpet call of *Fidelio,* the *"heiliger Dankgesang,"* the festal paradise of the Seventh Symphony, the Bacchic resurrection of the *Eroica* finale—these keep alive humanity's hopes and sustain faith in the possibilities of renewal. Hegel wrote, "It is the defects of immediate reality which drive us forward inevitably to the idea of the beauty of art."[92] Perhaps so, but Schiller expressed his own, and Beethoven's, view when he perceived the opposite process at work: "To arrive at a solution even in the political problem, the road of aesthetics must be pursued, because it is through beauty that we arrive at freedom."[93]

On November 9, 1822, Prince Nikolas Galitzin, a cellist and a connoisseur of Beethoven's music, wrote from St. Petersburg to ask Beethoven if he would consent "to compose one, two, or three quartets for which labor I will be glad to pay you what you think proper," adding, straightforwardly, "I will accept the dedication with gratitude."[94] Beethoven, deeply occupied with the final stages of the *Missa Solemnis,* delayed his reply until January 25, 1823, at which time he wrote, "You wish to have some quartets; since I see that you are cultivating the violoncello, I will take care to give you satisfaction in this regard."[95] He set the fee at 50 ducats per quartet, and bound himself to complete the first quartet by mid-March at the latest.

Actually, however, it was not Galitzin, but Beethoven himself who initiated this project. The previous May, the Leipzig publisher C. F. Peters had written to Beethoven asking him for some piano quartets and trios, among other works. Beethoven responded on June 5, offering the Mass and some other completed works and setting a price of 50 ducats for a string quartet, "which you could also have very soon."[96] Peters thought the price rather high and, after some further correspondence in July, refused the offer, admitting frankly (and tactlessly) that he really wanted a piano quartet (and "only on the condition that it will not be too difficult") because he already had string quartets in press by Spohr, Bernhard Romberg, and Pierre Rode, "which are all beautiful, excellent works."[97] Beethoven promised to do what he could about a piano quartet, for which—in view of Peters's eagerness and his own reluctance to write one—he raised his fee to 70 ducats. But it was not piano quartets that interested him. As Rolland says, "It is clear that he carried within him a quartet ready to be born"—in fact, more than one.[98] Apparently, as soon as he received Galitzin's commission he wrote to Ferdinand Ries in London asking him to explore the prospects for selling string quartets there. Ries rapidly found a customer, for on February 25, 1823, Beethoven wrote to Neate, "As *Ries* has written to tell me that you would like to have three *quartets* from me, I am writing to ask you to be so kind as to let me know when you would like to receive them. I am satisfied with the *fee* of 100 guineas which you offer."[99] Meanwhile, he continued negotiations with Peters and with Schott's Sons for publication rights. Galitzin's quartets were thus to serve double and triple duty as publishing commodities.

The Russian prince wrote often—and impatiently—in 1823 and 1824 about his quartets, but received nothing beyond Beethoven's reassurances; first the *Missa Solemnis,* the Diabelli Variations, and the Ninth Symphony had to be completed. Only after the grand concerts of May 1824 did Beethoven turn to his string quartets. To recapitulate their chronology: the first, in E-flat, op. 127, was completed in February 1825; the second in order of composition, in A minor, op. 132, was completed by July 1825; the third, in B-flat, op. 130, with the Grosse Fuge as finale, was written more rapidly, between July–August and November 1825; the fourth, in C-sharp minor, op. 131, was begun toward the end of 1825 and was completed by about July 1826; the last, in F, op. 135, occupied Beethoven (with time out to compose an arrangement of the Grosse Fuge for piano four hands, op. 134) from July to October; and in October and November, at Gneixendorf, Beethoven wrote the new finale for the B-flat Quartet, op. 130. Schott's Sons published opus 127 in June 1826, but the remaining quartets were published posthumously in 1827 by Matthias Artaria in Vienna (opus 130 and the Grosse Fuge, op. 133), Schott's Sons in Mainz (opus 131), and Schlesinger in Berlin (opuses 132 and 135).

Title page, Grosse Fuge, op. 133 (1827).

First edition, Mathias Artaria. Courtesy of Gesellschaft der Musikfreunde, Vienna.

One more quartet was apparently planned but never written.[100] The first three were dedicated to Galitzin, the C-sharp-minor Quartet to Field Marshal von Stutterheim, and the F-major to Beethoven's faithful supporter Johann Nepomuk Wolfmayer in compensation for the Requiem that he had commissioned a decade earlier and never received.

It was an opportune time for Beethoven's string quartets to come into existence. In eras when the major avenues of communication are controlled by censorship and an apathetic public tends to utilize art primarily for hedonistic gratification, serious art flees to the margins of society and to the more intimate genres, where it sets up beachheads in defense of its embattled position. Artist and audience rise to defend the sanctity of art at those moments when its social function has become endangered and its aesthetic and ethical purposes called into question.

Such was the case in the aftermath of the Napoleonic Wars, with the breakdown of traditional aristocratic patronage and the erosion of Enlightened attitudes toward the arts. Beethoven's late works seem to have crystallized avant-garde currents among Viennese intellectuals. Audiences isolated from traditional modes of patronage and opposed to normative tastes began to take shape. The late sonatas and quartets, despite their difficulties and their experimental character, were hardly written without an audience in mind. In this Beethoven is quite different from J. S. Bach, who composed his *Art of Fugue*, BWV 1080, in a spirit of solitary inquiry; different also from C. P. E. Bach, who wrote, "Among all my works, especially for the piano, there are only some trios, solos, and concertos that I wrote in all freedom, and for my own use."[101] Beethoven's was now a very special audience, one that had tested its strength against the prevailing artistic currents in its sponsorship of his May 1824 public concerts and found itself wanting in numbers but not in spirit. Drawn from many walks of life—artists and writers, musicians and music lovers, bankers and merchants, along with the remnants of the old connoisseur aristocracy—this audience worshiped Beethoven (not uncritically) and his music as the stalwart symbol of better days past and to come.

The late sonatas were the first works Beethoven composed without the expectation of their being performed in either aristocratic salon or public concert: their audience was in the private musicale—of the Streichers, Ertmanns, and Czerny. Now, a few years later, the number of such music lovers had grown substantially. The violinist Ignaz Schuppanzigh, who twenty years earlier, in the winter of 1804–5, had been the first musician in Austria to undertake regular public quartet concerts,[102] returned from Russia toward the end of April 1823 and resumed his concerts, which at once became major events within this rarefied sphere of Viennese cultural life. For example, Karl reported to

Beethoven about Schuppanzigh's concert of January 25, 1824, which featured a Haydn string quartet in C and Beethoven's Septet, that it was so crowded that "the people had to stand in front of the door."[103] Many of Beethoven's close friends, patrons, and admirers were there: Haslinger, Wolfmayer, Piringer, Schickh, Tuscher, and Kalkbrenner, along with numerous amateurs (*Dilettanten*) who bombarded Nikolaus Johann with questions about the forthcoming academy featuring the Ninth Symphony and the *Missa Solemnis*.

Although as many as five hundred people attended the chamber music concerts, Beethoven was not especially concerned about the size of his audience, and several of the first performances of the last quartets were given privately or semiprivately for small groups of colleagues, disciples, and favored individuals. Nevertheless, despite his occasional claims to the contrary, it was vitally important to Beethoven that his works be understood and appreciated. In this respect the atmosphere was extremely favorable to the late quartets. Schuppanzigh pleaded to be granted the premiere of the first, in E-flat, op. 127: "If [you have] a mind to hand me the *quartet* for a performance," he wrote in a Conversation Book of January 1825, "there may be a big difference in my present *subscription*."[104] The response to the opus 127 Quartet was excellent: after a failed performance by Schuppanzigh, a result of inadequate rehearsal, the quartet was "studied industriously and rehearsed frequently under Beethoven's own eyes" (he could not hear, but followed the motion of the bows),[105] and then was played successfully four times by Böhm, again by Schuppanzigh, and twice more by Mayseder, all within two months. The opus 132 String Quartet was performed first at small private gatherings in September 1825 and twice in public concerts in November, and opus 130, after its public performance by Schuppanzigh on March 21, 1826, was eagerly sought after by Böhm and Mayseder for performance at their string quartet recitals.

Such private performances of the late quartets continued during the next year. The C-sharp-minor Quartet was rehearsed several times at Mathias Artaria's at the beginning of August; Holz wrote in a Conversation Book that Artaria "was enraptured, and the fugue, when he heard it for the third time, he found wholly intelligible."[106] And Holz learned in early September from Schlesinger that the A-minor Quartet, op. 132, had been performed in Berlin: "They have no idea there how

Beethoven should be played."[107] References to rehearsals and projected performances of opus 130 and opus 131 appear in the Conversation Books in December,[108] and Schuppanzigh reported to Beethoven that a recent performance of opus 127 was applauded "with enthusiasm."[109] The new finale of the B-flat Quartet was rehearsed in the latter half of December and was found "altogether heavenly" by the musicians.[110] There were private performances of the quartets in 1826 and 1827. And we know that the Quartet, op. 131, was played expressly for Schubert in November 1828, five days before his death. ("He fell into such a state of excitement and enthusiasm," Holz reported, "that we were all frightened for him.")[111] But none of these were public performances; apparently there had been a rapid falling off of broader interest. The Conversation Books allude to planned public performances by Schuppanzigh and by Linke, but these failed to materialize. (Beethoven's friends may have given the distraught and mortally ill composer false encouragement on this score.)

With the String Quartet in B-flat, op. 130, Beethoven almost certainly had tried to carry his audience with him into a realm that their training and sensibility would not permit them to enter. The Leipzig review that found the Grosse Fuge "incomprehensible, like Chinese . . . a concert that only the Moroccans might enjoy," was by no means a journalistic aberration.[112] Neither Schindler nor Holz appreciated the B-flat-major Quartet as a whole, and Holz reported that the audience at the first performance was "inspired, astonished, or questioning" and failed to find fault with it only because of their "awe" for Beethoven.[113] Perhaps a total acceptance of the late quartets would have required a rebelliousness of spirit, an ability to withstand the shock of the new, that was beyond the reach of even the sensitive and the disaffected in Viennese society. Many of them still preferred the Septet, with its harmless evocation of those better days of long ago.

Accordingly, neither the opus 131 Quartet nor the opus 135 Quartet was performed in concert during Beethoven's lifetime. Indeed, opus 131 did not receive its first public performance in Vienna until 1835, and between 1827 and 1850 the quartets were played there in concert only four times—once each for opus 130 and opus 135, twice for opus 131.[114] The quartets were kept from oblivion during their first decades by performances elsewhere: in Berlin, Leipzig, and, especially, Paris.

At first Beethoven intended to write two, perhaps three, string quartets. The sketches for the first two quartets overlap somewhat: while working on the finale of opus 127 he sketched several sections of opus 132. However, Holz recalled that in the course of composing the first three quartets "new ideas streamed from Beethoven's inexhaustible fantasy in such richness that he almost unwillingly had to write the C-sharp-minor and F-major Quartets."[115] "Again something has occurred to me," Beethoven told Holz as they were out walking, rejoicing in the strength of this creative surge, which made it possible for him to complete five major works in rapid succession.

There is a tension in Beethoven's evolution between adherence to and a rebellious need to dissolve—or at least to reshape—the Classical style. This tension may be seen in his work at all times after 1800, but it becomes clearest after 1815. Classicism remains the touchstone to which Beethoven inevitably returns after each of his (increasingly adventurous) forays into experimental regions. The traditional forms are tacitly undermined in the deceptively transparent song cycle and the opus 101 and opus 102 sonatas of 1815–16, which quietly opens the door to romanticism. The "Hammerklavier" Sonata of 1817–18 constitutes an overreaching attempt to hold on to the traditional arrangement by a magnification of time scale and an intensification of contrast. However, the three sonatas of 1820–22 and the Diabelli Variations (which reached its final form in 1823)[116] are once more departures from precedent. As Martin Cooper observes, Beethoven's conception of sonata form moves away "from the dramatic principle of contrast with its implicit idea of struggle. In its place we find a unified vision where music borrows nothing from the theatre, which had played so important a part in late-eighteenth century musical aesthetics, and aspires to its own unique condition."[117] The Ninth Symphony again restores the four-movement Classic symphonic form, together with contrast, struggle, and a level of theatricality that had been absent from Beethoven's music for almost a decade.

That this alternating pattern would extend to the quartets was, therefore, fairly predictable. Seen from this point of view, the series is introduced by the Quartet, op. 127, in relatively traditional four-movement form, perhaps to reestablish Beethoven's control of the medium. This is followed by three experimental works (opuses 132, 130, 131) that create a variety of new formal structures. The set closes with the more traditional, four-movement String Quartet, op. 135, bringing the cycle to its conclusion. Throughout his career, Beethoven repeatedly bid farewell to the Classic tradition but never said a firm goodbye. There is no reason to believe that, had he lived longer, this quartet would have been his last farewell to the eighteenth century.

Unlike many of the influential earlier commentators, who stressed the stylistic unity of the quartets as a group and drew attention to the many threads that connect each—especially the central three quartets—to the others, Joseph Kerman holds that "each of them provides us with a separate paradigm for wholeness," a "total integrity" that arises out of its individuality of form, feeling, and procedure. Kerman sees in each "the musical image of an underlying psychological progress," and he holds that "the sense of a particular psychological sequence is what gives the late quartets their particular individual intensities—in spite of technical threads crossing from one to the other."[118] In this view he has Beethoven's support, for when Holz asked Beethoven which quartet was the greatest, he answered, "Each in its own way!"[119] At that time he had written but three; later, he chose the C-sharp-minor Quartet, op. 131, as his favorite, again confirming his perception of the works as discrete entities.

Kerman sees lyricism as the guiding impulse of the String Quartet, op. 127, "inspiring the intimate *aveu* of the opening movement, the popular swing of the Finale, and the great stream of melody in the Adagio variations."[120] This quartet can be seen as a natural outgrowth of the last piano sonatas, though it reflects a commitment to Classical structure that the sonatas were tending to disavow. Opus 127 minimizes contrast (the first movement avoids development in favor of ornamentation), with only the Scherzando vivace supplying "the intellectual, mordant note, the note of contrast."[121] Despite its unenigmatic approachability and lyricism, the Quartet is not without its "late-style" characteristics: the driving dotted rhythms of the scherzo; the contrapuntal textures; the fantastic, idealized, occasionally violent dance rhythms of the pastoral Finale; and, especially, the luxuriously ornamental variations of the Adagio, in the course of which the theme itself is transformed into a new entity.

The A-minor Quartet, op. 132, expands the framework to five movements, with a scherzo and a brief, marchlike movement filling both of the usual alternate positions for the dance movement, serving as necessary and "normal" transitions into and out of the unearthly Canziona di ringraziamente, marked Molto adagio, in the archaic Lydian mode. They serve also as elements in what appears to be a consciously wrought arch structure, which is in turn mirrored and capped by the five-sectioned arch construction of the central Molto adagio movement. Beginning with Lenz and Nottebohm, all commentators have noted that the opening theme of the first movement is strikingly similar in shape to the main theme of the Grosse Fuge and to the opening fugue theme of the Quartet, op. 131. Similar themes were occasionally used by Beethoven in several early vocal compositions—"Klage," WoO 113, "Ah! perfido," op. 65, "Vom Tode," op. 48 no. 3—as well as in his last two sonatas, but in the quartets they take on an unprecedented emotional character. Erich Schenk has shown them to be similar to—possibly derived from—a typical thematic configuration of the Baroque period (the similarity to the "royal theme" of Bach's *Musical Offering*, BWV 1079, is especially striking) that symbolized "melancholy conceptions" such as pain, sorrow, trespass, and preparedness for death.[122] This cluster of feelings is apparently communicated by means of an upward-striving, constantly defeated melodic shape and by insistent references to the leading tone. But we do not need a close analysis to tell us that the subject matter of this quartet is pain and its transcendence. Just recovered from a serious illness, Beethoven headed the chorale theme of the slow movement with the words "Heiliger Dankgesang eines Genesenen an die Gottheit, in der Lydischen Tonart" ("Holy Song of Thanksgiving by a Convalescent to the Divinity, in the Lydian Mode"). Music here appears to become an implicit agency of healing, a talisman against death. The contrasting, dancelike (rather, *attempting* to dance) section of the movement is marked "Neue Kraft fühlend" ("Feeling New Strength")—a designation that may also apply to the main character of the remaining movements, the Alla Marcia and the closing rondo, Allegro appassionato, whose urgent, floating waltz melody is an etherealization and dancing fulfillment of the "Feeling New Strength" section, with its haltingly striving 3/8 time.

The B-flat-major String Quartet, op. 130, is the most enigmatic of the late quartets. It was composed in six movements (similar in structure to opus 132, but with a second slow movement, the tearful Cavatina, preceding the finale), the last of which was Beethoven's lengthiest chamber music movement, a colossal, multisectional fugue that was later separated from the work at the suggestion of the publisher in favor of an unproblematic rondo-finale. For some reason Beethoven did not attend the first performance. As soon as the concert was over, Holz rushed to a neighboring tavern, where the composer was awaiting a full report. On hearing that the Presto and the Alla danza tedesca had received such thunderous applause that they had to be encored, he snapped in exasperation: "Yes, these delicacies! Why not the Fugue?"[123] and then allegedly gave his opinion of the audience: "Cattle! Asses!"[124]

Kerman finds the opus 130 Quartet representative of a "drive toward dissociation" in Beethoven's late works, a drive that is the other side of his dominant synthesizing impulses.[125] However, Bekker, who also perceived the kaleidoscopic changes of mood within the total structure and who described the quartet as "a suite, almost a potpourri, of movements without any close psychological interconnection," found an organic explanation to account for this phenomenon. "Each movement," he wrote, "is merely episodic inasmuch as it prepares for the finale"; the movements "do not stand in direct sequence, nor do they represent a continuous line of development; each from a different viewpoint relates directly to the close."[126] Of course, Bekker is referring here to the original finale, the Grosse Fuge; for him, the substitute finale is but "another gem in the multi-colored ornament," which therefore wholly pushes the work into dissociation, for it fails to gather up the threads leading to the Fugue that Beethoven scattered so skillfully and deliberately throughout the earlier movements.

Why did Beethoven agree to separate the Fugue from the Quartet? Most biographers of Beethoven have marveled that this most stubborn of composers should so readily agree to alter the structure of a major composition: some have attributed it to his preoccupation with Karl's suicide attempt; others to his desire for an additional 15-ducat payment; still others to his disdain for those who were unable to grasp his intention. But the fact remains that the Grosse Fuge has struck many sensitive musicians, including its first hearers, as an unsatisfactory close to the quartet. So it is possible that Beethoven too came to feel that the Fugue was too powerful, too strange, to bring the Quartet to an appropriate close. Beethoven must originally have believed that he had accomplished this in the enormous coda of the Fugue, with its dance-like *Siegessymphonie* and its feeling of sunshine after storm. Evidently, however, the reverberations of pain and strife had not yet sufficiently died away, let alone been fully dissipated. And so he may have decided that the Quartet required a catharsis, a return to normality, an epilogue in full daylight, a simple descent to earth, a reversion to classicism such as we find in the new Finale, marked Allegro.

The idea of a new finale was not Beethoven's own, however. The publisher Mathias Artaria (not affiliated with the better-known firm Artaria & Co.) was doubtful about the commercial possibilities of the Quartet because of the difficulties and abstruseness of the Fugue, and it is clear that he wanted a substitute finale, but he did not dare broach the issue openly. Instead, on April 11, 1826, he wrote—flatteringly, and no doubt untruthfully—in a Conversation Book, "There have been already many requests for a four-hand arrangement of the Fugue. Do you permit me to publish it in that form?—Score, the parts, the Fugue *à 4 mains* arranged by you, to be published simultaneously."[127] Beethoven authorized the arrangement for four hands, and he may well have authorized a separate publication of the Fugue in score and parts. Nevertheless, it is clear that he still expected the Quartet to be published with the Fugue, for Artaria thereafter sent it to the engraver in its original form. The proofs were ready in mid-August. Artaria then asked Holz to try to persuade Beethoven to compose a substitute finale. Holz related the story to Lenz in 1857, recalling how he had acted as Beethoven's agent in the affair:

> The publisher Artaria, to whom I had sold the rights for the edition of the Quartet in B-flat for a price of 80 ducats, had charged me with the terrible and difficult mission of convincing Beethoven to compose a new finale, which would be more accessible to the listeners as well as the instrumentalists, to substitute for the Fugue which was so difficult to understand. I maintained to Beethoven that this Fugue, which departed from the ordinary and surpassed even the last quartets in originality, should be published as a separate work and that it merited a designation as a separate opus. I communicated to him that Artaria was disposed to pay him a supplementary hono-

rarium for the new finale. Beethoven told me he would reflect on it, but already on the next day I received a letter giving his agreement.[128]

Beethoven's letter has not survived, but there is sufficient confirmation of Holz's story in the Conversation Books. "You could easily have made two [quartets] from the B-flat Quartet," Holz remarked in early September 1826. "When one thinks so highly of art as you do, it cannot be any other way; but it would be more money for you, and the publisher would have to pay the costs."[129] Shortly thereafter he indicated that the matter was settled. "Artaria is delighted that you have found his proposal so acceptable," he reported; "he will gain much therefrom; the two separate works will be more sought after."[130] In later years, Holz told Lenz that it was the composer's wish that the Rondo follow the fading away of the Cavatina "without a long pause."[131]

We need not enter here into the debate that has raged for the better part of a century as to which finale is the "proper" one: the failure of the debate to settle the issue indicates that Riezler may have been wrong when he asserted that "both endings are 'organic,' and both are in keeping with the 'idea' of the work."[132] There have been attempts to find more in the Allegro than meets the ear, but Kerman may undervalue it in observing that the substitute finale "trivializes the journey which it means to terminate."[133] As for the fugal finale, many have felt that it overshadows—even annihilates—the earlier movements. That there will be no solution to this dilemma is illustrated by Stravinsky's vacillation: at one time he exclaimed, "How right Beethoven's friends were when they convinced him to detach it from opus 130!"[134] But he reversed himself on this issue before his death, realizing not only that the Grosse Fuge was intended as the Quartet's climax, but may have been the work's point of departure as well.[135]

Beethoven's favorite, the String Quartet in C-sharp minor, op. 131, is in seven movements, to be performed virtually without pause, which gives it a greater sense of structural integration than any other work since the song cycle of 1816. A continuity of rhythmic design adds to the feeling that this is one of the most completely seamless of Beethoven's works. At the same time, many pressures toward discontinuity are at work in this Quartet: six distinct main keys, thirty-one changes of tempo (ten more than in opus 130), a variety of textures, and a diversity of forms within the movements—fugue, suite, recitative, variation, scherzo, aria, and sonata form—all of which makes the achievement of unity all the more miraculous. Beethoven is here pressing dissociation so far that it turns into its opposite—perfect coherence and profound integration. Perhaps Beethoven considered this Quartet a summing up, bringing to a close the exploration of the set of musical problems to which the late quartets (and perhaps all of the late works) were devoted, and this may bear on what seem to be numerous references to other works, from the already noted similarity of the opening fugue to themes from opus 132 and the Fugue of opus 130 to what appear to be conscious recollections of the "Heiliger Dankgesang" in the fourth variation of the Andante (measures 1–4), and of the main theme of the opening Allegro of opus 132 in the third variation (measures 1–2, 9–10). The raging, victorious finale is surely the Grosse Fuge revisited—and conquered.

With the Quartet in F, op. 135, Beethoven came "home" at last. This is not to say that it is a conservative or anachronistic work—the hallmarks of the late style are deeply imprinted in it. Radcliffe notes the "astonishing variety of textures" and the "bare, spare contrapuntal writing,"[136] which, despite occasional extreme passages, reflects a withdrawal from the almost baroque luxuriance, fierce drive, and passionate expressiveness of the earlier quartets into a detached, objective irony. Yet if the F-major Quartet avoids the sentimentality of nostalgia, it still, as Kerman writes, "turns sharply back, not forward, more so than any other major work in a decade."[137]

Earlier in this book I related this "homecoming" to the drives toward reconciliation that controlled Beethoven's personality during his last decade (and reached their fulfillment following Karl's suicide attempt, which liberated Beethoven from his pathological fixations quite as much as it freed Karl from his uncle's obsessive domination). A few pages back, however, I was equally certain that the Quartet's provisional return to classicism was part of a recurrent stylistic dialectic in Beethoven's musical development. Seen from yet another standpoint, the withdrawal from the borderlines of musical exploration may well have represented a compromise with a historical milieu unprepared to accept so radical a disruption of its sensibilities. Antonio Bruers and Martin Cooper both find in this Quartet and in the second finale of opus 130 a concession to the bourgeois taste for the unproblematic, a "touch of Biedermeier domesticity" and even "a reduction of visionary power" stemming from the mental climate of Metternich's Vienna.[138] There is no need to accept any of these views, which may appear to place too heavy a freight of interpretation on a fragile musical composition. It does no harm, however, to be aware that every creative act arises at the intersection of a multiplicity of forces and events—the biographical, historical, intellectual, and artistic being only the leading ones. It was Max Raphael who noted the paradox that "the work of art closest to perfection is both most profoundly determined by its time and goes furthest beyond it into timelessness."[139]

And since this book has been devoted to paradoxes and origins, we may as well close with Beethoven's own words on those subjects:

> Let us begin with the primary original causes of all things, how something came about, wherefore and why it came about *in that particular way* and became what it is, why something is *what it is,* why something *cannot be exactly so!!!* Here, dear friend, we have reached the ticklish point which my delicacy forbids me to reveal to you at once. *Consequently it cannot be!*[140]

One does not want wholly to understand this, nor did Beethoven wish us to do so. Better to answer the eternal Hamlet question "Muss es sein?" ("Must it be?")—which is the heading of the last movement of the last Quartet—with Beethoven's simple, ironic reply: "Es muss sein!"

Roman sarcophagus with emblems of the Muses (third century A.D.)

Vatican Museum, Rome. Photo: Deutsches Archäologisches Institut, Rome.

Abbreviations

AMZ   *Allgemeine musikalische Zeitung,* published by the Leipzig music publisher Breitkopf & Härtel.

BB   Beethovenhaus, Bonn.

BF   *Beethoven Forum.* Ed. Christopher Reynolds, Mark Evan Bonds, Lewis Lockwood, James Webster, et al. Lincoln and London: University of Nebraska Press, 1992– . 7 vols. to 1998.

BJ   *Beethoven-Jahrbuch.* 1st series (1908–9), ed. Theodor von Frimmel; 2d series (1953–), vols. 1–8, ed. Joseph Schmidt-Görg and Paul Mies; vol. 9, ed. Hans Schmidt and Martin Staehelin; vol. 10, ed. Martin Staehelin.

Beethoven Remembered   Franz Wegeler and Ferdinand Ries. *Beethoven Remembered.* Trans. Frederick Noonan. Arlington, VA: Great Ocean, 1987. Translation of *Biographische Notizen über Ludwig van Beethoven (see* Wegeler-Ries).

B&H   Breitkopf & Härtel, Leipzig music publisher.

Breuning   Gerhard von Breuning. *Aus dem Schwarzspanierhause.* Vienna: Rosner, 1874.

Breuning-Solomon   Gerhard von Breuning. *Memories of Beethoven: From the House of the Black-Robed Spaniards.* Trans. Henry Mins and Maynard Solomon. Cambridge: Cambridge University Press, 1992. Translation of Breuning, *Aus dem Schwarzspanierhause (see* Breuning).

Briefe   Sieghard Brandenburg, ed. *Ludwig van Beethoven: Briefwechsel, Gesamtausgabe.* Beethovenhaus edition. 8 vols. Munich: Henle, 1996– .

BS   *Beethoven Studies.* Ed. Alan Tyson. 3 vols. New York: Norton, 1973 (vol. 1); London: Oxford University Press, 1977 (vol. 2); Cambridge: Cambridge University Press, 1982 (vol. 3).

DSB   Staatsbibliothek zu Berlin, Preussischer Kulturbesitz, Germany (formerly Deutsche Staatsbibliothek, Berlin/DDR).

Fischer   Joseph Schmidt-Görg, ed. *Des Bonner Bäckermeisters Gottfried Fischer: Aufzeichnungen über Beethovens Jugend.* Bonn: Beethovenhaus, 1971.

Freud, Standard Edition   James Strachey et al., eds. *Standard Edition of the Complete Psychological Works of Sigmund Freud.* 24 vols. London: Hogarth Press, 1953–74.

Frimmel, Handbuch	Theodor von Frimmel. *Beethoven-Handbuch.* 2 vols. Leipzig: Breitkopf & Härtel, 1926.
GM	Goethe Museum of the Freie Deutsche Hochstift, Frankfurt.
Hess	Willy Hess, *Verzeichnis der nicht in der Gesamtausgabe veröffentlichten Werke Ludwig van Beethovens* (Wiesbaden: Breitkopf & Härtel, 1957).
JAMS	*Journal of the American Musicological Society.*
Kastner-Kapp	Emerich Kastner and Julius Kapp, eds. *Ludwig van Beethovens sämtliche Briefe.* 2d ed. Leipzig: Hesse & Becker, 1923.
Kerst	Friedrich Kerst, ed. *Die Erinnerungen an Beethoven.* 2 vols. Stuttgart: Julius Hoffman, 1913.
Kinsky-Halm	Georg Kinsky, *Das Werk Beethovens. Thematisch-bibliographisches Verzeichnis seiner sämtlichen vollendeten Kompositionen.* Completed and edited by Hans Halm. Munich: Henle, 1955.
Konversationshefte	Karl-Heinz Köhler, Grita Herre, Dagmar Beck, et al., eds. *Ludwig van Beethovens Konversationshefte.* 10 vols. Leipzig: VEB Deutscher Verlag für Musik, 1968–93).
Leitzmann	Albert Leitzmann, ed. *Ludwig van Beethoven: Berichte der Zeitgenossen, Briefe und persönliche Aufzeichnungen.* 2 vols. Leipzig: Insel, 1921.
Letters	Emily Anderson, ed. *The Letters of Beethoven.* 3 vols. London: Macmillan, 1961.
Letters to Beethoven	Theodore Albrecht, ed. *Letters to Beethoven and Other Correspondence.* 3 vols. Lincoln: University of Nebraska Press, 1996.
MacArdle *Abstracts*	Donald W. MacArdle, *Beethoven Abstracts.* Detroit: Information Coordinators, 1973.
MQ	*The Musical Quarterly.*
M&L	*Music & Letters.*
MR	*The Music Review.*
NBJ	*Neues Beethoven-Jahrbuch.* Ed. Adolf Sandberger. 10 vols. Augsburg: Benno Filser, and Braunschweig: Litolff, 1924–42.
Nohl	Ludwig Nohl. *Beethovens Leben.* 3 vols. Vol. 1: Vienna: Markgraf, 1864; vols. 2 & 3: Leipzig: Günther, 1867, 1877.
Nottebohm 1	Gustav Nottebohm. *Beethoveniana.* Leipzig: Peters, 1872.

Nottebohm 2   Gustav Nottebohm. *Zweite Beethoveniana*. Leipzig: Rieter-Biedermann, 1887.

Rolland   Romain Rolland. *Beethoven: Les grandes époques créatrices*. Definitive edition. Paris: Albin Michel, 1966.

Schiedermair   Ludwig Schiedermair. *Der junge Beethoven*. Leipzig: Quelle & Mayer, 1925.

Schindler-   Anton Schindler. *Beethoven as I Knew Him*. Ed. Donald W. MacArdle.
MacArdle   Trans. Constance Jolly. Chapel Hill: University of North Carolina Press, 1966. Translation of 3d ed. of Anton Schindler, *Biographie von Ludwig van Beethoven*. Münster: Aschendorff, 1860.

Schindler-   Anton Schindler. *The Life of Beethoven*. Ed. Ignace Moscheles. Boston:
Moscheles   Oliver Ditson, [1841]. Translation of 1st ed. of Anton Schindler, *Biographie von Ludwig van Beethoven*. Münster: Aschendorff, 1840.

Schünemann   Georg Schünemann. *Ludwig van Beethovens Konversationshefte*. 3 vols. Berlin: Hesse, 1941–43.

Solomon,   Maynard Solomon. *Beethoven Essays*. Cambridge, MA: Harvard Univer-
Beethoven   sity Press, 1988.
Essays

Solomon,   Maynard Solomon, "Beethoven's Tagebuch of 1812–1818." *Beethoven*
"Tagebuch"   *Studies* 3 (1982): 193–288. Also in Solomon, *Beethoven Essays* (*q.v.*), pp. 233–95. Translated into German as *Beethovens Tagebuch* (Mainz: Hase & Koehler, 1990); translated into Italian as *Il Diario di Beethoven* (Turin: Mursia Editore, 1992). In the notes, the number refers to the number of the entry as assigned in the foregoing editions.

Sonneck   O. G. Sonneck. *Beethoven: Impressions of Contemporaries*. New York: Schirmer, 1926.

Thayer   Alexander Wheelock Thayer. *Ludwig van Beethovens Leben*. 3 vols. Berlin: Schneider, 1866; Berlin: Weber, 1872, 1879.

Thayer-   A. W. Thayer. *Ludwig van Beethovens Leben*. Ed. Hermann Deiters.
Deiters   Vol. 1, 2d ed. Leipzig: Breitkopf & Härtel, 1901.

Thayer-   A. W. Thayer. *Ludwig van Beethovens Leben*. Edited and enlarged by
Deiters-   Hermann Deiters and Hugo Riemann. 5 vols. Leipzig: Breitkopf &
Riemann   Härtel, 1907–17; reissued 1922–23.

Thayer-   A. W. Thayer. *Thayer's Life of Beethoven*. 2 vols. Ed. Elliot Forbes.
Forbes   Princeton: Princeton University Press, 1964; rev. ed., 1967.

Thayer-   A. W. Thayer, *The Life of Ludwig van Beethoven.* Edited and completed
Krehbiel   by Henry E. Krehbiel. 3 vols. New York: Beethoven Association, 1921;
               reprint, London: Centaur Press, 1960.

TNG   Stanley Sadie, ed. *The New Grove Dictionary of Music and Musicians.*
               20 vols. London: Macmillan, 1980.

Wegeler-   Franz Wegeler and Ferdinand Ries. *Biographische Notizen über Ludwig*
Ries   *van Beethoven.* Coblenz: Bädeker, 1838. Franz Wegeler. Supplement
               (*Nachtrag*). Coblenz: Bädeker, 1845.

WoO   *Werk ohne Opuszahl* (work without opus number). As numbered in Kin-
               sky-Halm (*q.v.*), the works not assigned opus numbers by Beethoven or
               his publishers.

Zu   *Zu Beethoven.* Ed. Harry Goldschmidt. 3 vols. Berlin: Verlag neue Musik,
Beethoven   1979; 1984; 1988.

Notes

PREFACE TO THE FIRST EDITION

1. *Konversationshefte,* vol. 2, p. 24; Schünemann, vol. 2, p. 8.
2. *Letters,* vol. 3, Appendix 1, no. 7, p. 1451.
3. It was long believed that Beethoven's early biographer, Anton Schindler, destroyed two thirds of 400 surviving Conversation Books. Without supporting evidence, Thayer claimed to have been told by Schindler that he had destroyed all but 138 out them, because they were too bulky. Thayer-Deiters-Riemann, vol. 4, p. 152. Herre and Beck scotched the story as perhaps a mishearing of "vier Hundert" for "viel über Hundert"; the story was in any event inherently improbable because of the great monetary value Schindler attributed to these documents, and it has no basis in Schindler's own account, where he referred to "Beethoven's conversation books, of which I preserved a great many more than one hundred." Dagmar Beck and Grita Herre, "Anton Schindlers fingierte Eintragungen in den Konversationsheften," *Zu Beethoven,* vol. 1, pp. 16–17; Schindler, *Biographie von Ludwig van Beethoven* (Münster, 1845), supplement, p. 31.
4. The letters to Beethoven, for the most part previously unpublished or scattered in a variety of often obscure publications, have now been gathered in both German and English editions. See *Letters to Beethoven* and *Briefe.*
5. Solomon, "Tagebuch," no. 136; Leitzmann, vol. 2, p. 262 (no. 148).
6. Johann Aloys Schlosser, *Ludwig van Beethoven: Eine Biographie* (Prague: Stephani & Schlosser, 1828 [1827]), translated by Reinhard G. Pauly as *Beethoven: The First Biography,* ed. Barry Cooper (Portland, OR: Amadeus Press, 1996).
7. Dagmar Beck and Grita Herre, "Einige Zweifel an der Überlieferung der Konversationshefte," *Bericht über den Internationalen Beethoven-Kongress Berlin 1977,* ed. Harry Goldschmidt et al. (Leipzig: VEB Deutscher Verlag für Musik, 1978), pp. 257–74. Beck and Herre, "Anton Schindlers fingierte Eintragungen in den Konversationsheften," *Zu Beethoven,* vol. 1, pp. 11–89, contains a virtually complete listing of the fabricated passages in the already-published volumes; those in later volumes are indicated by asterisks. Earlier suspicions were voiced by A. B. Marx, A. W. Thayer, Georg Schünemann, and in detail by Peter Stadlen, "Schindler's Beethoven Forgeries," *Musical Times* 118 (1977), pp. 549–52; idem., "Schindler and the Conversation Books," *Soundings,* no. 7 (1978): 2–18. Krehbiel wrote: "There are mutilations, interlineations, and erasures in the Conversation Books which it is difficult to believe were not made for the purpose of bolstering up mistaken statements in [Schindler's] biography." Thayer-Krehbiel, vol. 3, p. 281; see also vol. 3, p. 273, and vol. 1, p. 321n.
8. Maynard Solomon, review of Fischer, *Notes* 30, no. 2 (December 1973): 269–72.
9. The standard edition of the Fischhof manuscript, excepting the Tagebuch, is published in Clemens Brenneis, "Das Fischhof-Manuskript in der Deutschen Staatsbibliothek," in *Zu Beethoven,* vol. 2, pp. 27–87.
10. The standard edition of the Tagebuch is Solomon, "Tagebuch."
11. Sigmund Freud, *Delusions and Dreams in Jensen's "Gradiva,"* in Freud, *Standard Edition,* vol. 9, p. 80.

INTRODUCTION
TO THE REVISED EDITION

1. On Schindler's forgeries, see the Preface to the first edition, and note 7, above.

2. Maynard Solomon, "On Beethoven's Creative Process: A Two-Part Invention," *M&L* 61 (1980): 272–83; reprinted in Solomon, *Beethoven Essays*, pp. 126–38. For more on Rochlitz's fabrications, see also Solomon, "The Rochlitz Anecdotes: Issues of Authenticity in Early Mozart Biography," in *Mozart Studies*, ed. Cliff Eisen (Oxford: Clarendon Press, 1991), pp. 1–59.

3. *Konversationshefte*, vol. 10, p. 13.

4. Furthermore, several passages in the Conversation Books for August and September 1826 were thoroughly obliterated, presumably by Schindler, who had the books in his possession and made numerous alterations in them. Expunged passages and missing pages in Conversation Books of the relevant period are referenced in *Konversationshefte*, vol. 10, pp. 173, 178, 183, and 213. For whatever it may be worth, Schindler—who certainly was not predisposed to validate his rival's claim—was himself convinced of the letter's authenticity, claiming to have known about it in 1826, indeed, claiming that Beethoven asked the executor of his estate, Stephan von Breuning, to retrieve the letter, a request that Breuning "refused categorically." Schindler, *Biographie von Ludwig van Beethoven* (Münster, 1860), vol. 2, pp. 323–24; Schindler-MacArdle, pp. 474–75. I rely upon Sieghard Brandenburg (personal communication) for the opinion on Holz's handwriting, and also for the information that the official stamped paper on which it is written is of a type that was available during Beethoven's lifetime.

5. *Letters*, no. 41; *Briefe*, no. 49 (to Franz Anton Hoffmeister, December 15, 1800).

CHAPTER 1. FAMILY BACKGROUND

1. "Forced to become a philosopher already in my 28th year . . ." Thayer-Forbes, p. 305; *Briefe*, no. 106. The translation in *Letters*, Appendix A, takes this as a reference to the past. Compounding the uncertainty surrounding this issue, a diary notation written between December 1793 and early 1794 indicates that Beethoven may at that time have believed that he was born in December of 1768 or 1769. See Dagmar von Busch-Weise, "Beethovens Jugendtagebuch," *Studien zur Musikwissenschaft* 25 (1962): 77.

2. *Letters*, no. 256; *Briefe*, no. 439; translated in Thayer-Forbes, p. 490.

3. Thayer-Forbes, p. 54; *Briefe*, vol. 2, p. 119 n.5.

4. See Solomon, "Beethoven's Birth Year," *MQ* 56 (1970): 702–10; reprinted in Solomon, *Beethoven Essays*, pp. 35–42.

5. *Konversationshefte*, vol. 1, pp. 179, 247; for other references to this matter in the Conversation Books, see Solomon, "Beethoven: the Nobility Pretense," *MQ* 61 (1975): 289–90, n.73.

6. Thayer-Deiters-Riemann, vol. 5, pp. 278–79; *Briefe*, no. 2100.

7. *Letters*, no. 1542; *Briefe*, no. 2236.

8. *Letters*, no. 1551; *Briefe*, no. 2257.

9. Fischer, p. 25; Thayer-Deiters, vol. 1, p. 421.

10. Fischer, p. 27.

11. Schiedermair, p. 101.

12. Fischer, p. 24; translated in Thayer-Forbes, p. 49.
13. See Joseph Schmidt-Görg, *Beethoven: Die Geschichte seiner Familie* (BB, 1964), pp. 210–11 (Document 262); the lease is printed in Thayer-Deiters, vol. 1, p. 103n. 1.
14. Maynard Solomon, "A Papal Dispensation for Cornelius van Beethoven," *BF,* vol. 6 (1998), pp. 129–42.
15. For genealogical details, see Raymond Van Aerde, *Les Ancêtres flamands de Beethoven* (Malines: Godenne, 1927), and Schmidt-Görg, *Beethoven: Die Geschichte seiner Familie.* In the latter, the date of the marriage is variously given as September 7, September 17, and November 17 (see pp. 54, 118, and 152).
16. As the preceding sentences indicate, there are important lacunae in the historical record concerning Beethoven's ancestry: his father's birth year and place of birth, and his paternal grandmother's place of origin and national identity, as well as the nature of her disability.
17. Fischer, p. 23.
18. Johann Jacob Wagner, "Neues über Beethovens Grosseltern mütterlicher Seite," *Kölnische Volkszeitung,* December 8, 1919, p. [21]; Schiedermair, *Der Junge Beethoven,* pp. 101–2; Schmidt-Görg, *Beethoven: Die Geschichte seiner Familie,* p. 219 (Document 342). See also *Zeitschrift für Musikwissenschaft* 1 (1919): 263–64. Between August 1776 and April 1777, Maria Magdalena van Beethoven and her husband fruitlessly pursued a claim for an accounting against the Ehrenbreitstein court bailiff (*Gerichtsvogt*) Georg Friedrich Jenger, who was related by marriage to Frau van Beethoven and had served as guardian of her mother's estate. The suit was unsuccessful, perhaps because it was brought so belatedly, and because there were no documents at hand to confirm suspicions that Jenger had looted the old lady's savings or misappropriated her pension or her allowances of grain, wine, and firewood. Schmidt-Görg, *Beethoven: Die Geschichte seiner Familie,* p. 223 (Documents 366–69), August 5, 1776, August 12, 1776, September 2, 1776, and April 18, 1777. A full discussion, with quotations from the court documents, is in J. J. Wagner, "Beethoven und seine Beziehungen zu Ehrenbreitstein," *Mittelrheinische Geschichtsblätter (monatliche Beilage zur Koblenzer Volkszeitung)* 7, no. 3 (1927). A typed transcript of the published article is in the Beethoven-Archiv. There is no evidence to support Wagner's partisan speculations that Frau Keverich actually left a substantial fortune, either in cash or real estate; and his account is contradictory in other respects.
19. Schiedermair, pp. 101–2; Walter Riezler, *Beethoven,* trans. G. D. H. Pidcock (London: Forrester, 1938), p. 20.
20. Fischer, pp. 61–62.
21. Thayer-Krehbiel, vol. 1, p. 56; Thayer-Forbes, p. 56; see also Wegeler-Ries, pp. 9, 33; *Beethoven Remembered,* pp. 14, 35; Schindler-MacArdle, p. 38; Nohl, vol. 1, p. 245; A. B. Marx, *Beethoven: Leben und Schaffen* (Berlin: Janke, 1859), vol. 1, p. 5. See Maynard Solomon, "Economic Circumstances of the Beethoven Household in Bonn," *JAMS* 50 (1997): 331–51.
22. The average salary in June 1784 of thirty-five musicians, excluding the court kapellmeister, was just under 250 florins, with a median salary of about 300 florins: eleven musicians earned exactly 300 florins and only eight earned more than Johann, the maximum salary being 400 florins. Report of June 27, 1784, Thayer-Deiters, vol. 1, pp. 183–85.
23. Fischer, p. 30.
24. Frimmel *Handbuch,* vol. 2, p. 245.
25. Düsseldorf Archives. Bestand Herzogtum Berg. 1774, pp. 95^v–95^r. This document

from the Herzogtum Berg was discovered by Mr. Theo Molberg and made available courtesy of Sieghard Brandenburg of the Beethoven-Archiv, Bonn, and Dr. J. Joester of the Nordrhein-Westfälisches Hauptstaatsarchiv.

26. For fuller details and references, see Solomon, "Economic Circumstances," pp. 346–47.

27. Fischer, pp. 47–48 and p. 84n. 67. See also Thayer-Deiters-Riemann, vol. 1, p. 167.

28. Fischer, p. 69.

29. Fischer, p. 33.

30. Fischer, pp. 68–71. Thayer learned about the move to the Wenzelgasse from Frau Karth, who was born in 1780 and lived in the very same house on that street, and he was satisfied as to the truth of her statement that she "could not recall to memory any period of her childhood down to the death of Johann van Beethoven, when he and his family did not live in the lodging above that of her parents." Thayer-Krehbiel, vol. 1, p. 75. But see also Frimmel, *Handbuch*, vol. 2, p. 441.

31. Fischer, pp. 21–22.

32. Fischer, p. 25.

33. Jacques-Gabriel Prod'homme, *La Jeunesse de Beethoven* (Paris: Delagrave, 1927), p. 50.

34. Edward Glover, "The Etiology of Alcoholism," in Glover, *On the Early Development of Mind* (London: Imago, 1956), p. 83. See also Karl Abraham, *Selected Papers* (London: Hogarth Press, 1927), pp. 80–89; Nolan D. C. Lewis, "Personality Factors in Alcoholic Addiction," *Quarterly Journal of Alcohol* 1 (1940): 21–44.

35. Decree of April 26, 1768, cited by Thayer-Forbes, p. 21. Other examples of his difficulties with musicians date from 1771 and 1773. See Schmidt-Görg, *Beethoven: Die Geschichte seiner Familie*, p. 220; Schiedermair, pp. 93 f.

36. Fischer, p. 21; Thayer-Deiters, vol. 1, p. 419.

37. Thayer-Forbes, p. 55. Bonn musician and music publisher Nikolaus Simrock wrote that Johann van Beethoven "was a tenor in the court chapel, had a rough voice, was a good musician, but not such a good father." Clemens Brenneis, "Das Fischhof-Manuskript in der Deutschen Staatsbibliothek," in *Zu Beethoven*, vol. 2 (1984), p. 40.

38. Thayer-Forbes, p. 78.

39. Schiedermair, pp. 97–98.

40. Schmidt-Görg, *Beethoven: Die Geschichte seiner Familie*, p. 224; the documents are published and discussed in Schiedermair, "Zur Biographie Johann van Beethovens (Vater)," *NBJ* 3 (1927): 32–41. In an affidavit dated January 31, 1786, Nikolaus Phennings, the lawyer whose name appeared on the claim to elector Maximilian Franz, denied that he had prepared the document: "The above signature is not in my hand and I have not the slightest knowledge of this document, with all its vilenesses [*Schlechtigkeiten*] . . ." (p. 39).

41. Thayer-Forbes, p. 136.

42. Fischer, pp. 38–39.

43. Fischer, p. 61.

44. Fischer, p. 39.

45. Thayer-Forbes, p. 51.

46. Fischer, p. 30.

47. Thayer-Deiters, vol. 1, p. 425; Thayer-Forbes, p. 51; Fischer, p. 30.

48. Fischer, pp. 62–63; Thayer-Deiters, vol. 1, p. 439.

49. Fischer, p. 62; Fanny Giannattasio, diary entry of June 15, 1817; cited in Thayer-Deiters-Riemann, vol. 4, p. 540.

50. Fischer, pp. 37–38; translated in Paul Bekker, *Beethoven* (London: Dent, 1925), p. 5. Translation amended.

CHAPTER 2. CHILDHOOD

1. *Letters*, no. 51; *Briefe*, no. 65 (June 29, 1801).

2. Perhaps by Leopold Radoux, one of a family of artists, originally from Liège, active at the electoral court of Cologne. See Ernest Closson, *The Fleming in Beethoven*, trans. Muriel Fuller (London: Oxford University Press, 1936), pp. 165–66.

3. Wegeler-Ries, p. 8; *Beethoven Remembered*, p. 13. Louis Schlösser, who visited Beethoven in 1823, recalled that the portrait occupied a preeminent place in Beethoven's rooms, and commented on the latter's "childlike reverence" for the elder Ludwig (Thayer-Forbes, p. 849). But Schlösser's account is derived from Wegeler-Ries and has no independent authority. Moreover, the reliability of his Beethoven memoirs has been thrown into question in Maynard Solomon, "Beethoven's Creative Process: A Two-Part Invention," in Solomon, *Beethoven Essays*, pp. 126–38.

4. Kerst, vol. 1, p. 216.

5. Joseph Demmer's petition, dated January 23, 1773, states that "the bass singer van Beethoven is incapacitated and can no longer serve as such." Thayer-Forbes, p. 23.

6. *Letters*, no. 1302; *Briefe*, no. 1855; translated in Thayer-Forbes, p. 918.

7. Thayer-Forbes, p. 57.

8. Fischer, p. 32.

9. F.-J. Fétis, *Biographie universelle des musiciens*, 2d ed. (Paris: Firmin-Didot, 1883), vol. 1, p. 298.

10. Thayer-Forbes, p. 57.

11. Thayer-Krehbiel, vol. 1, p. 61n.

12. Kerst, vol. 1, p. 10.

13. See Schiedermair, p. 130; Thayer-Forbes, pp. 57–58.

14. Fischer, pp. 32–33. The author has combined the translations from Sonneck, p. 4, and Editha and Richard Sterba, *Beethoven and His Nephew* (New York: Pantheon, 1954), pp. 82–83.

15. Otto Erich Deutsch, *Mozart: A Documentary Biography*, trans. Eric Blom et al. (London: A. & C. Black, and Stanford: Stanford University Press, 1965), p. 21.

16. Thayer-Forbes, p. 58n. 8; see Thayer-Deiters-Riemann, vol. 1, p. 132n. 2.

17. Fischer, p. 29.

18. Fischer, p. 33.

19. Thayer-Forbes, pp. 63–64.

20. There are virtually no such references in the correspondence and Conversation Books. Schindler wrote: "Beethoven himself as a rule did not speak of his early youth, and when he did he seemed uncertain and confused." Schindler-MacArdle, p. 46.

21. Schindler-Moscheles, p. 9; Wegeler-Ries, p. 122; *Beethoven Remembered*, p. 109.

22. *Letters*, no. 1; *Briefe*, no. 3 (to J. W. von Schaden, September 15, 1787). For the

only other references to either of his parents in Beethoven's correspondence, see *Letters*, nos. 3, 1028, 1374, 1400, and 1542; *Briefe*, nos. 7, 1403, 1974, 2008, and 2236.

23. Fischer, p. 40.
24. Breuning, p. 13; Breuning-Solomon, p. 29.
25. Wegeler-Ries, p. 122; *Beethoven Remembered*, pp. 109–10.
26. Thayer-Krehbiel, vol. 1, p. 85.
27. The original reads: "von meinem Theuren Vater geschrieben." *BJ*, 2d series, vol. 7 (1971), p. 341 (no. 745). See also Thayer-Forbes, p. 66.
28. Fischer, p. 51.
29. Ludwig Nohl, *Beethoven nach den Schilderungen seiner Zeitgenossen* (Stuttgart: Cotta, 1877), p. 4.
30. Kerst, vol. 1, p. 10.
31. Thayer-Forbes, p. 59.
32. Kerst, vol. 1, pp. 10–11.
33. Thayer-Forbes, p. 58. Translation corrected. A typed transcript of Würzer's memoirs, edited by Franz-Josef Hetjens in 1992, is in the Historisches Archiv des Erzbistums Köln (Nachlass Würzer 20 Teil I); the remarks about Beethoven appear on pp. 65–66.
34. Thayer-Deiters, vol. 1, p. 448.
35. Fischer, p. 32.
36. Thayer-Forbes, p. 58.
37. Phyllis Greenacre, "The Family Romance of the Artist," in Greenacre, *Emotional Growth: Psychoanalytical Studies of the Gifted and a Great Variety of Other Individuals* (New York: International Universities Press, 1971), vol. 2, p. 531.
38. Fischer, pp. 56–57.
39. Sigmund Freud, "The Relation of the Poet to Day-Dreaming," in Freud, *Collected Papers*, 5 vols. (New York: Basic Books, 1959), vol. 4, p. 176; Freud, *Standard Edition*, vol. 4, p. 146.
40. Fischer, pp. 33–34. The original reads, "wenn ich mal ein Herr werde," with implications of becoming "a Lord."
41. Sigmund Freud, "Family Romances" (1909), in Freud, *Collected Papers* (New York: Basic Books, 1959), vol. 5, pp. 74–78; Freud, *Standard Edition*, vol. 4, pp. 237–41; Otto Rank, *The Myth of the Birth of the Hero and Other Writings*, ed. Philip Freund (New York: Vintage Books, [1964]), pp. 65–96. The extensive literature is surveyed and a bibliography provided in Linda Joan Kaplan, "The Concept of the Family Romance," *Psychoanalytic Review* 61 (1974): 169–202.
42. See Phyllis Greenacre, "The Childhood of the Artist," in Greenacre, *Emotional Growth*, vol. 2, pp. 479–504, especially p. 495.
43. J. J. Bachofen, *Myth, Religion, and Mother Right*, trans. Ralph Manheim (Princeton: Princeton University Press, 1967), p. 109.
44. Ludwig Nohl, *Beethovens Brevier* (Leipzig: Günther, 1870), p. 18. According to Otto Jahn, Beethoven also copied this passage into his notebooks (A. C. Kalischer, *Beethoven und seine Zeitgenossen* [Berlin and Leipzig: Schuster & Loeffler, 1908–1910], vol. 2, p. 47).
45. Rank, "Myth of the Birth," p. 66.
46. Nohl, *Beethoven's Brevier*, p. 19; translated in Schindler-MacArdle, p. 310.

CHAPTER 3. THE SECOND DECADE

1. Fischer, pp. 51–52; translated in Sonneck, p. 8.

2. Fischer, p. 43.

3. Thayer-Forbes, p. 66. See [C. G. Neefe], "Nachricht von der churfürstlich-cöllnis-chen Hofcapelle zu Bonn und andern Tonkünstlern daselbst," Cramer's *Magazin der Musik* 1 (March 30, 1783): cols. 377–400; transcription in Schiedermair, pp. 73–82.

4. *Letters*, no. 6; *Briefe*, no. 6.

5. Beethoven was listed as a "student of Neefe" in standard music dictionaries of his time. See Emerich Kastner, *Bibliotheca Beethoveniana*, 2d ed., rev. Theodor Frimmel (Leipzig: B&H, 1925), pp. 3–6.

6. Schiedermair, p. 141; Irmgard Leux, *Chr. Gottlob Neefe* (Leipzig: Kistner & Siegel, 1925), pp. 14–15.

7. Leux, *Chr. Gottlob Neefe*, pp. 188–98; trans. in Paul Nettl, *Forgotten Musicians* (New York: Philosophical Library, 1951), pp. 246–64.

8. For full details, see Maynard Solomon, "Beethoven's Productivity at Bonn," *M&L* 53 (1972): 165–72. As Lewis Lockwood suggested in 1979, it may be better to consider this moratorium as a working hypothesis rather than as a demonstrated fact, even though further scrutiny of the documents and autograph scores has not yet led to the placement of other substantial compositions within those years. See Lockwood, review of *Beethoven*, by Maynard Solomon, *Nineteenth-Century Music* 3 (1979): 76–82, especially 81–82. In the most thorough analysis of the hypothesis, Douglas Porter Johnson brings to bear the evidence of Beethoven's handwriting and his use of various paper types, observing: "Of the *undated* works for which manuscript sources survive, only two [the fragment of the Romance cantabile, Hess 13, and the preliminary draft of a symphonic movement in C minor, Hess 198] can be ascribed with certainty to the years before 1790 . . . Solomon's hypothesis, then, is considerably strengthened by the evidence of handwriting." Johnson, *Beethoven's Early Sketches in the 'Fischhof Miscellany,' Berlin Autograph 28* (Ann Arbor: UMI Research Press, 1980), vol. 1, pp. 219–25 (at pp. 221 and 223). He acknowledges "the problematical distribution of the Bonn works," but suggests "that the explanation for it remains obscure" (p. 225). See also Hans-Günter Klein and Douglas Johnson, "Autographe Beethovens aus der Bonner Zeit: Handschrift-Probleme und Echtheitsfragen," in Kurt Dorfmüller, ed., *Beiträge zur Beethoven-Bibliographie* (Munich: Henle, 1978), pp. 115–24.

9. Nohl, vol. 1, pp. 371–72. Neefe is sometimes blamed for his pupil's deficiencies, but he himself was the first to criticize them. Beethoven complained to Wegeler "of the too severe criticisms made of his first efforts in composition" by Neefe. Wegeler-Ries, p. 113; Thayer-Forbes, p. 65.

10. This was of the Twenty-four Variations for Piano on Righini's "Venni amore," WoO 65, advertised in the *Wiener Zeitung* on August 12, 1791.

11. Thayer-Forbes, p. 79.

12. *Ibid.*

13. Fischer, pp. 58–60, 75; Thayer-Forbes, pp. 62–63. For further details of these summer journeys, see Thayer-Deiters-Riemann, vol. 1, p. 465n. 1.

14. See Luc Van Hasselt, "Beethoven in Holland," *Die Musikforschung* 18 (1965): 181–84; the document appears in translation in *Letters to Beethoven*, no. 3.

15. Thayer-Forbes, p. 63.

16. Fischer, p. 66; Thayer-Krehbiel, vol. 1, p. 66; Thayer-Forbes, pp. 63–64.

17. Fischer, p. 69.

18. Fischer, p. 68; Sonneck, p. 9. Translation amended. For a list of visitors to the Beethoven's lodgings, see Fischer, pp. 75–77.

19. Wegeler-Ries, pp. 18–19, 13; *Beethoven Remembered*, pp. 24, 20. Waldstein's assistance to Beethoven was given in the period between February 1788 and 1792. See Thayer-Forbes, pp. 91–92. Waldstein is said by Frau Karth to have given Beethoven a piano—if true, an expensive gift. Thayer-Forbes, p. 94.

20. Lewis Lockwood, review of *Beethoven*, by Maynard Solomon, *Nineteenth-Century Music* 3 (1979): 82.

21. *Letters*, no. 1; *Briefe*, no. 3 (to J. W. von Schaden, September 15, 1787).

22. *Briefe*, no. 14 (December 23, 1793); Thayer-Forbes, p. 145; *Letters to Beethoven*, no. 17.

23. Ernst Simmel, "Alcoholism and Addiction," in Sandor Lorand, ed., *The Yearbook of Psychoanalysis*, vol. 5 (New York: International Universities Press, 1950), p. 251.

24. Thayer-Forbes, p. 95. Translation corrected.

25. Thayer-Forbes, p. 94.

26. *Letters*, no. 3; *Briefe*, no. 7 (April or May 1793). Translation corrected.

27. *Ibid.* Translation amended.

28. Fischer, p. 72; Schiedermair, p. 130.

29. Helene Deutsch, "Absence of Grief," in Deutsch, *Neuroses and Character Types* (New York: International Universities Press, 1965), p. 235.

30. Thayer-Forbes, p. 105.

CHAPTER 4.
LAST YEARS IN BONN: ENLIGHTENMENT

1. Baron [Caspar] Riesbeck, *Travels Through Germany in a Series of Letters*, trans. Rev. Mr. Maty (London: Cadell, 1787), vol. 3, p. 261.

2. *Ibid.*, vol. 3, p. 286.

3. *Ibid.*, vol. 1, p. 256.

4. A. J. P. Taylor, *The Habsburg Monarchy, 1809–1918* (London: Hamish Hamilton; reprint, New York: Harper, 1965), p. 19.

5. Schiedermair, p. 29.

6. See Winfried Dotzauer, "Freimaurergesellschaften im Rheingebiet. Die Anfänge der Freimaurerei im Westen des Alten Reiches," in *Freimaurer und Geheimbünde im 18. Jahrhundert in Mitteleuropa*, ed. Helmut Reinalter (Frankfurt: Suhrkamp, 1983; reprint, 1986), pp. 162–64; Edith Ennen and Dietrich Höroldt, *Vom Römerkastell zur Bundeshauptstadt: Kleine Geschichte der Stadt Bonn*, 3d ed. (Bonn: Stollfuss, 1976), pp. 158–59; see also the entry "Köln" in Eugen Lennhoff and Oskar Posner, *Internationales Freimaurerlexikon* (Munich: Amalthea, 1932), cols. 848–49. For the "Freimaurerpatent," see Maynard Solomon, *Mozart: A Life* (New York: HarperCollins, 1995), pp. 322–23.

7. Alfred Becker, *Christian Gottlob Neefe und die Bonner Illuminaten* (Bonn: Bouvier, 1969), pp. 12–15.

8. Max Braubach, "Beethoven's Abschied von Bonn: das rheinische Erbe," in Erich Schenk, ed., *Beethoven-Symposion Wien 1970* (Vienna: Böhlaus, 1971), pp. 25–41.

9. Ennen and Höroldt, *Vom Römerkastell zur Bundeshauptstadt*, p. 159. One historian, who neglects the significance of Neefe's anticlericalism, remarks that he "remained politically loyal and conformist, so that his Illuminatism was surely, in the last analysis, without inner conviction," and finds this typical of a split that "may be observed in almost all Illuminist careers." Manfred Agethen, *Geheimbund und Utopie: Illuminaten, Freimaurer und deutsche Spätaufklärung*, vol. 11 in the series Ancien Régime: Aufklärung und Revolution (Munich: Oldenbourg Verlag, 1984), p. 245n. 103. Characteristic of this double aspect, the radical Eulogius Schneider's *Gedichte* was published in 1790 with a dedication to a royal personage, hereditary princess Luise of Wied-Neuwied.

10. Thayer-Forbes, p. 79.

11. Wegeler-Ries, p. 13; *Beethoven Remembered*, p. 19.

12. Wegeler-Ries, p. 18; *Beethoven Remembered*, p. 24.

13. Wegeler-Ries, p. 10; *Beethoven Remembered*, p. 16.

14. Thayer-Forbes, p. 108. See also Schindler's embellished account in Schindler-MacArdle, p. 47.

15. *Letters*, no. 334; *Briefe*, no. 531 (to Joseph von Varena, late November or early December 1811).

16. *Letters*, no. 1306; *Briefe*, no. 1873 (to Nägeli, September 9, 1824).

17. *Letters*, no. 139; *Briefe*, no. 273 (to the Bigots, shortly after March 5, 1807).

18. Schiedermair, p. 31.

19. Wegeler-Ries, *Nachtrag*, p. 9; *Beethoven Remembered*, p. 148.

20. *Letters*, no. 228; *Briefe*, no. 408 (November 22 [not 2], 1809).

21. Heinrich Heine, *Religion and Philosophy in Germany*, trans. John Snodgrass (1834; reprint, Boston: Beacon, 1959), p. 120.

22. *Konversationshefte*, vol. 1, p. 235.

23. Immanuel Kant, *Religion Within the Limits of Reason Alone*, trans. Theodore M. Greene and Hoyt H. Hudson (New York: Harper & Brothers, 1960), p. 3.

24. Herbert Marcuse, *Reason and Revolution* (New York: Oxford, 1941; reprint, Boston: Beacon, 1960), p. 15.

25. Paul Henry Lang, *Music in Western Civilization* (New York: Norton, 1941), p. 19.

26. *BJ*, 1st series, vol. 2 (1909), pp. 331–32; Thayer-Forbes, pp. 120–21.

27. Hans Rosenberg, *Bureaucracy, Aristocracy and Autocracy: The Prussian Experience 1660–1815* (Cambridge, MA: Harvard University Press, 1958; reprint, Boston: Beacon, 1966), pp. 41–42.

28. This does not contradict Beethoven's alleged republicanism, which many biographers, beginning with Schindler, have emphasized. For a republic meant something quite different to Enlightenment thinkers from what it has come to mean to later observers. Rousseau wrote: "I give the name *Republic* to every state that is governed by laws, no matter what its form of administration may be" (*Social Contract*, part 2, chapter 6).

29. Anna Freud, "Adolescence," *Psychoanalytic Study of the Child* 13 (1958): 260.

30. *Letters*, no. 1; *Briefe*, no. 3.

31. Thayer-Forbes, p. 108; Wegeler-Ries, p. 37; *Beethoven Remembered*, p. 39n. 15.

32. *Letters*, no. 9; *Briefe*, no. 4 (summer 1792, not ca. early June 1794).

33. Simrock, cited in Thayer-Forbes, p. 245, from Thayer, vol. 2, p. 76n. 1; Thayer-Deiters-Riemann, vol. 1, p. 267.

34. Simrock to Junker, cited in Nohl, *Beethoven nach den Schilderungen,* p. 12; Kerst, vol. 1, p. 16.

35. Wegeler-Ries, p. 18; *Beethoven Remembered,* p. 23.

36. Transcribed in Nottebohm 1, pp. 138–44; English translation in *Letters to Beethoven,* vol. 1, pp. 14–29 (no. 13a–n); facsimile editions by Hans Gerstinger, ed., *Ludwig van Beethovens Stammbuch* (Leipzig: Velhagen & Klasing, 1927), and Max Braubach, ed., *Die Stammbücher Beethovens und der Babette Koch. Faksimile* (BB, 1970; 2d ed., 1995).

37. See Thayer-Forbes, pp. 100–101 and 105–6; H. C. Robbins Landon, *Haydn: Chronicle and Works,* vol. 3 (Bloomington: Indiana University Press, 1976), pp. 192–93.

38. Thayer-Forbes, p. 121.

39. Fischer, p. 74; see also Thayer-Deiters, vol. 1, p. 443.

40. "According to the Brockhaus *Konversations-Lexikon* which appeared in 1809, Beethoven intended permanently to leave Vienna in 1794 or 1795, the time that coincided with the termination of the studies that were the reason for his voyage" (Prod'homme, *Jeunesse de Beethoven,* p. 166; see also Nohl, vol. 1, pp. 335, 432).

CHAPTER 5. THE MUSIC (BONN)

1. For the musical inventories of the Bonn court chapel and of the electoral music library, see Adolf Sandberger, "Die Inventare der Bonner Hofkapelle," in Sandberger, ed., *Ausgewählte Aufsätze zur Musikgeschichte,* vol. 2 (Munich: Drei Masken, 1924), pp. 109–30; and Sieghard Brandenburg, "Die kurfürstliche Musikbibliothek in Bonn und ihre Bestände im 18. Jahrhundert," *BJ,* 2d series, vol. 8 (1975), pp. 7–47.

2. Thayer-Forbes, p. 101.

3. Sieghard Brandenburg and Martin Staehelin, "Die 'erste Fassung' von Beethovens Righini-Variationen," in *Festschrift Albi Rosenthal,* ed. Rudolf Elvers (Tutzing, Germany: Schneider, 1984), pp. 43–66, refutes the assumption that WoO 65 was revised for its 1802 republication.

4. Schiedermair, p. 274.

5. J.-G. Prod'homme, *Les Sonates pour piano de Beethoven* (1937; reprint, Paris: Delagrave, 1950), p. 26.

6. The copy of the sonata that Beethoven promised Eleanore von Breuning in 1792 (see *Briefe,* no. 4) was not sent until ca. 1798 at the earliest. See Johnson, *Beethoven's Early Sketches in the 'Fischhof Miscellany,'* vol. 1, p. 184.

7. Personal communication. Beethoven's dependence on Mozart's 1781 violin sonatas is further elaborated in Lewis Lockwood, "Beethoven Before 1800: The Mozart Legacy," *BF,* vol. 3 (1994), pp. 47–49.

8. William S. Newman, *The Sonata in the Classic Era* (Chapel Hill: University of North Carolina Press, 1963), p. 507.

9. Joseph Kerman, ed., *Ludwig van Beethoven: Autograph Miscellany from circa 1786 to 1799* (London: British Museum, 1970), vol. 2, p. 283.

10. Thayer-Forbes, p. 119.

11. Thayer-Forbes, p. 106.

12. Thayer-Forbes, p. 120.

13. Max Graf, *Die innere Werkstaat des Musikers* (Stuttgart: Enke, 1910), pp. 155–56.

14. Alfred Heuss, "Die Humanitätsmelodien im 'Fidelio,'" *Neue Zeitschrift für Musik* 91 (1924): 545 ff. See Eduard Hanslick, *Suite: Aufsätze über Musik und Musiker* (Vienna and Teschen: Prochaska, [1885]), pp. 153–62.

15. Hans Gál, "Die Stileigentümlichkeiten des jungen Beethoven," *Studien zur Musikwissenschaft*, 4 (1916): 58–115. See esp. pp. 68 ff.

16. Jules Combarieu, *Histoire de la musique*, vol. 2 (Paris: Armand Colin, 1920), p. 420.

17. Reminiscences of Bernhard Mäurer, in Kerst, vol. 1, p. 11; see also Frimmel *Handbuch*, vol. 1, pp. 248–49. The Cressener Cantata was reportedly composed before Beethoven had learned the rudiments of composition. Some scholars have doubted its existence.

CHAPTER 6. A PIANIST AND HIS PATRONS

1. Max Braubach, ed., *Die Stammbücher Beethovens und der Babette Koch. Faksimile* (BB, 1970; 2d ed., 1995), p. 19; Thayer-Forbes, p. 115; *Letters to Beethoven*, no. 13g.

2. Thayer-Forbes, pp. 103–4.

3. Thayer-Forbes, p. 185.

4. *Letters*, no. 9; *Briefe*, no. 11. The remark is in the postscript of Beethoven's letter of November 2, 1793; Anderson and others mistakenly attach it to his letter to Fräulein von Breuning of summer 1792 (*Briefe*, no. 4).

5. Letters, no. 9, *Briefe*, no. 11. Wegeler names Gelinek as one pianist whom Beethoven accused (Wegeler-Ries, pp. 59–60; *Beethoven Remembered*, p. 56).

6. Czerny, "Recollections from My Life," *MQ* 42 (1956): 304.

7. *Ibid.*, p. 309.

8. The dates of the documented concerts were: March 29, 1795 (Tonkünstler-Societät); March 30, 1795 (Tonkünstler-Societät); March 31, 1795 (Constanze Mozart); December 18, 1795 (Haydn); January 8, 1796 (Maria Bolla); c. late 1796 (the Rombergs); April 6, 1797 (Schuppanzigh); March 29, 1798 (Josepha Duschek); April 2, 1798 (Tonkünstler-Societät); and October 27, 1798 (Schikaneder). See Thayer-Forbes, *passim*; Hermann Reuther, "Beethovens Konzerte," in *Ein wiener Beethoven Buch*, ed. Alfred Orel (Vienna: Gerlach & Wiedling, 1921), pp. 72–107.

9. Wegeler-Ries, p. 109; Thayer-Forbes, pp. 184–85; *Beethoven Remembered*, p. 97.

10. *Letters*, no. 16; *Briefe*, no. 20.

11. To Jahn, cited in Thayer-Forbes, p. 444.

12. Schindler-Moscheles, p. 21.

13. Otto Jahn, *Life of Mozart*, trans. Pauline D. Townsend (London: Novello, Ewer, 1882; reprint, New York: Kalmus, n.d.), vol. 2, p. 385; vol. 3, pp. 218–19; George Grove, *A Dictionary of Music and Musicians*, 1st ed. (London: Macmillan, 1879–90), vol. 4, p. 9.

14. *Letters to Beethoven*, no. 18; *Briefe*, no. 18; Eveline Bartlitz, *Die Beethoven-Sammlung in der Musikabteilung der Deutschen Staatsbibliothek. Verzeichnis* (Berlin: Deutsche Staatsbibliothek, 1970), p. 128 (autograph 35, 37); see also Schindler-MacArdle, p. 49.

15. Thayer-Forbes, p. 211; Kinsky-Halm, p. 22.

16. Holz to Jahn, cited in Thayer-Forbes, p. 258.

17. Thayer-Forbes, pp. 170–71, 187; Wegeler-Ries, p. 28; *Beethoven Remembered*, p. 32.

18. Grove, *Dictionary*, 1st ed., vol. 2, p. 132; Thayer-Forbes, pp. 356–57.

19. Czerny, "Recollections," p. 309.

20. Emily Anderson, ed., *The Letters of Mozart and His Family* (1938; 2d ed., London: Macmillan, 1966), vol. 2, pp. 717–18 (no. 395).

21. Joseph August Röckel, cited in Thayer-Forbes, p. 389.

22. See *Letters*, no. 110; *Briefe*, no. 216 (to Josephine Deym, March or April 1805).

23. The Lichnowskys had a son of their own, Eduard Maria (1789–1845), who became a distinguished agriculturalist and historian.

24. Wegeler-Ries, p. 33; *Beethoven Remembered*, p. 36.

25. Wegeler-Ries, p. 33; *Beethoven Remembered*, p. 36; translated in Schindler-MacArdle, p. 61.

26. *Letters*, no. 51; *Briefe*, no. 65 (June 29, 1801).

27. *Letters*, no. 53; *Briefe*, no. 67 (July 1, 1801).

28. Schindler-MacArdle, p. 50. Translation revised.

29. Alan Tyson, "Beethoven to the Countess Susanna Guicciardi: A New Letter," in *BS*, vol. 1, p. 9; *Letters to Beethoven*, no. 36; *Briefe*, no. 77.

30. *Letters*, no. 254; *Briefe*, no. 445 (to Ignaz von Gleichenstein, spring 1810, perhaps beginning of June).

31. Wegeler-Ries, p. 19; *Beethoven Remembered*, pp. 24–25; translated in Schindler-MacArdle, p. 45.

32. Fischhof Manuscript (DSB), fol. 4ᵛ.

33. Wegeler-Ries, p. 20; *Beethoven Remembered*, p. 25; translated in Schindler-MacArdle, p. 45.

34. Nohl, *Beethoven nach den Schilderungen*, p. 20; Frimmel, *Handbuch*, vol. 2, p. 322.

35. Ernest Newman, *The Unconscious Beethoven* (New York: Knopf, 1927), p. 53.

36. Thayer-Forbes, p. 212.

37. Constant von Wurzbach, *Biographisches Lexikon des Kaiserthums Oesterreich, . . . 1750–1850* (Vienna: K. K. Hof- und Staatsdruckerei, 1856–91), vol. 15, p. 309. In one instance Wurzbach confused the present Prince Lobkowitz with a Lobkowitz of a prior generation; therefore, these reports cannot be accepted as wholly conclusive.

38. Gräfin Lulu Thürheim, *Mein Leben: Erinnerungen aus österreichs grosser Welt, 1788–1819*, ed. René van Rhyn, 2 vols. (Munich: Georg Müller, 1913), vol. 2, pp. 18–19; Nohl, vol. 2, p. 461. See also George Marek, *Beethoven: Biography of a Genius* (New York: Funk & Wagnalls, 1969), p. 108. According to the autopsy report, Lichnowsky's death resulted from "his licentious way of life," presumably venereal disease. See Jürgen May, "Beethoven and Prince Karl Lichnowsky," *BF*, vol. 3 (1994), p. 30.

39. Nohl, *Beethoven nach den Schilderungen*, p. 20.

40. Karl Geiringer, *Haydn: A Creative Life in Music* (New York: Norton, 1946), p. 67.

41. *Ibid.*, pp. 85–86

42. *Ibid.*, p. 55.

43. *Ibid.*, p. 86.

CHAPTER 7. HAYDN

1. A. B. Marx, *Ludwig van Beethovens Leben* (2d ed., Berlin: Janke, 1863), vol. 1, p. 22.

2. For additional details see James Webster, "The Falling-out Between Haydn and

Beethoven: The Evidence of the Sources," in Lewis Lockwood and Phyllis Benjamin, eds., *Beethoven Essays: Studies in Honor of Elliot Forbes* (Cambridge, MA: Harvard University Department of Music, 1984), p. 25.

3. Wegeler-Ries, p. 86; *Beethoven Remembered,* p. 75; Thayer-Forbes, p. 178.

4. H. C. Robbins Landon, ed., *The Collected Correspondence and London Notebooks of Joseph Haydn* (London: Barrie & Rockliff, 1959), p. 128 (to Genzinger, January 17, 1792).

5. Geiringer, *Haydn,* p. 111; Landon, *Collected Correspondence,* p. 132 (letter of March 2, 1792); Webster, "The Falling-out between Haydn and Beethoven," pp. 25–26.

6. Schenk's "Autobiography," cited in Thayer-Forbes, p. 140. Translation amended. For the complete "Autobiography," see Paul Nettl, *Forgotten Musicians* (New York: Philosophical Library, 1951), pp. 265–79. Schenk claimed that his instruction of Beethoven extended until early June 1793, when—he asserted—Beethoven left Vienna with Haydn for Eisenstadt. His claim appears to be confirmed by Beethoven's letter to Zmeskall of June 18, 1793, *Briefe,* no. 0, *Letters to Beethoven,* no. 15. Schenk's assistance therefore lasted for at most five months. For an overview, see Frimmel, *Handbuch,* vol. 2, pp. 102–3.

7. Thayer-Forbes, p. 141.

8. *Ibid.*

9. Schindler-MacArdle, p. 55. The anecdote is not reflected in the *Konversationshefte.*

10. Gustav Nottebohm, *Beethoven's Studien. Beethoven's Unterricht bei J. Haydn, Albrechtsberger und Salieri* (Leipzig & Winterthur: Rieter-Biedermann, 1873), vol. 1, pp. 21–43.

11. Landon, *Collected Correspondence,* p. 117 (letter of August 4, 1791).

12. Geiringer, p. 135.

13. For a cogent modern appraisal of Haydn's effectiveness as Beethoven's teacher, see Alfred Mann, "Beethoven's Contrapuntal Studies with Haydn," *MQ* 56 (1970): 711–26; Mann, "Haydns Kontrapunktlehre und Beethovens Studien," in Carl Dahlhaus et al., eds., *Bericht über den internationalen musikwissenschaftlichen Kongress Bonn 1970* (Kassel: Bärenreiter, 1971), pp. 70–74. See also Vincent d'Indy, *Beethoven: A Critical Biography,* trans. Theodore Baker (Boston: Boston Music Co., 1912), pp. 17–18.

14. Thayer-Forbes, p. 141.

15. Max Unger, "Kleine Beethoven-Studien," *NBJ* 8 (1938): 80.

16. Douglas Porter Johnson, *Beethoven's Early Sketches in the 'Fischhof Miscellany,' Berlin Autograph 28* (Ann Arbor: UMI Research Press, 1980), vol. 1, pp. 303–13, esp. pp. 305 and 311–12. See also Thayer-Forbes, p. 165; Nottebohm 1, p. 51; Nottebohm 2, pp. 27–28; Kerman, ed., *Ludwig van Beethoven: Autograph Miscellany,* vol. 2, p. 276.

17. See Johnson, *Beethoven's Early Sketches in the 'Fischhof Miscellany,'* vol. 1, pp. 87–88, 91, 98–99, 108. The lieder are "Flohlied," op. 75, no. 3, "Selbstgespräch," WoO 114, and "Das Liedchen von der Ruhe," op. 52, no. 3. Contrary to earlier belief, the Rondo in G for Piano and Violin, WoO 41, does not belong to 1793–94, because Beethoven's letter to Eleanore von Breuning with which he enclosed a copy of it dates from ca. summer 1792, before his departure from Bonn. See *Briefe,* no. 4, n.2; Anderson's dating of "early June 1794" (*Letters,* no. 9) may be disregarded.

18. Breuning, p. 97; Breuning-Solomon, p. 97.

19. Thayer-Forbes, p. 144; Landon, *Collected Correspondence,* pp. 141–43.

20. Thayer-Forbes, p. 145. It is very likely, as Unger suggests, that the 400 florins rep-

resenting Beethoven's regular annual salary was retained in Bonn for the support of his two younger brothers, so that as a practical matter "he had only the subsidy of 500 florins for living expenses and also for fees to his teachers." Max Unger, "Beethovens Unterricht bei Josef Haydn," *Kölnische Zeitung*, February 27, 1936, nos. 105–6, p. 19, as summarized in MacArdle, *Abstracts*, p. 376.

21. *Letters*, no. 8; *Briefe*, no. 12 (Beethoven to Elector Maximilian Franz, November 23, 1793); translated in Thayer-Forbes, p. 145. Beethoven's letter was enclosed in the same envelope as Haydn's.

22. See Richard Kramer, *The Sketches for Beethoven's Violin Sonatas, Opus 30. History, Transcription, Analysis* (Ph.D. dissertation, Princeton University, 1974), pp. 145–59. Kramer proposes that "Beethoven's lessons with Salieri were concentrated over a few years, presumably from 1799 through 1801" (p. 158).

23. I. Moscheles, *Recent Music and Musicians* (New York: Henry Holt, 1873), p. 7.

24. *Letters*, no. 192; *Briefe*, no. 350 (Beethoven to B&H, January 7, 1809).

25. Otto Erich Deutsch, ed., *Schubert: A Documentary Biography*, trans. Eric Blom (London: Dent, 1946), p. 64; Frimmel, *Handbuch*, vol. 2, pp. 95–96.

26. Printed in Andreas Weissenbäck, "Drei noch unveröffentlichte Briefe Albrechtsbergers an Beethoven," *Musica divina* (Vienna), January–February 1921, pp. 10–11; *Briefe*, nos. 24, 29, and 31; trans. *Letters to Beethoven* nos. 21, 25, and 26. Present location unknown. Brandenburg sees reasons to question the authenticity of the letters. See *Briefe*, vol. 1, p. 34. For Albrechtsberger's negative view of newer musical developments in Vienna in 1798, possibly implying his repudiation of Beethoven, see Martin Staehelin, "A Veiled Judgment of Beethoven by Albrechtsberger?" in Lockwood and Benjamin, eds., *Beethoven Essays: Studies in Honor of Elliot Forbes*, pp. 46–52.

27. Thayer-Deiters-Riemann, vol. 2, p. 200; Kerst, vol. 2, p. 191.

28. Wegeler-Ries, p. 86; trans. *Beethoven Remembered*, p. 75; see also Thayer-Forbes, p. 149.

29. Rosemary Hughes, ed., *A Mozart Pilgrimage: Being the Travel Diaries of Vincent and Mary Novello in the year 1829*, transcribed and compiled by Nerina Medici di Marignano (London: Novello, 1955), p. 194. But see memoirs by Karl Friedrich Hirsch and Cipriani Potter recalling Beethoven's praise of Albrechtsberger. Kerst, vol. 1, pp. 225–26, 231.

30. Wegeler-Ries, p. 84; *Beethoven Remembered*, p. 74. In a fragmentary letter of December 28, 1796, to Lorenz von Breuning, Beethoven appears dismayed by Haydn's evident hesitation to contribute one of his symphonies for performance at a Romberg academy. See *Briefe*, no. 25; *Letters to Beethoven*, no. 22. The letter is speculatively reconstructed by Martin Staehelin in "Unbekannte oder wenig beachtete Schriftstücke Beethovens," *BJ*, 2d series, vol. 10 (1983), pp. 24–33.

31. Wegeler-Ries, p. 85; *Beethoven Remembered*, p. 74; translated in Thayer-Forbes, p. 164. Because Ries's account contains several inconsistencies, Landon considers it to be "pure fiction." See H. C. Robbins Landon, *Haydn: Chronicle and Works*, vol. 4, *Haydn: The Years of "The Creation," 1796–1800* (Bloomington: Indiana University Press, 1977), p. 61.

32. Thayer-Forbes, pp. 237–38.

33. Reported by Aloys Fuchs, cited in Kerst, vol. 1, p. 109.

34. Kerst, vol. 2, p. 192.

35. For a brief but thorough summary of the literature dealing with Haydn's influence on Beethoven, see Georg Feder, "Stilelemente Haydns in Beethovens Werken," in Carl Dahlhaus et al., eds., *Bericht über den internationalen musikwissenschaftlichen Kongress Bonn 1970* (Kassel: Bärenreiter, 1971), pp. 65–70.

36. Czerny, "Recollections," p. 305.

37. *AMZ* 1 (1798–99): 252, translated in Otto Jahn, *The Life of Mozart* (London: Novello, Ewer, 1882), vol. 2, p. 384. A music yearbook for 1796 referred to Beethoven the virtuoso performer as a "musical genius," but described him as only a promising novice in composition: "He has become a student of our immortal Haydn, to be initiated into the sacred mysteries of composition." Johann Ferdinand Ritter von Schönfeld, *Jarbuch der Tonkunst Wien und Prag 1796*, ed. Otto Biba (Munich-Salzburg: Katzbichler, 1976); trans. Kathrine Talbot as "A Yearbook of the Music of Vienna and Prague, 1796," as an appendix to Elaine Sisman, ed., *Haydn and His World* (Princeton: Princeton University Press, 1997), pp. 293–94.

38. *AMZ* 1 (1798–99): 366, 570; see Schindler-MacArdle, pp. 76–77.

39. Ignaz von Seyfried, *L. v. Beethovens Studien* (1832; trans. H. H. Pierson, Leipzig: Schuberth, 1853), Supplement, p. 17.

40. *Ibid.*

41. *Ibid.*

42. Letter of December 14, 1803, in *Haydn-Studien* 1, no. 2 (February 1966): 99–100.

43. Letter of January 4, 1804, in *ibid.*: 100.

44. Thayer-Forbes, p. 430.

45. Geiringer, *Haydn*, p. 170.

46. *Letters*, no. 376; *Briefe*, no. 585 (to Emilie M., July 17, 1812).

47. *Letters*, no. 59; *Briefe*, no. 97 (July 13, 1802). Italics omitted.

48. Doležálek, cited in Kerst, vol. 2, p. 192; Thayer-Forbes, p. 259.

49. Giuseppe Carpani, *Le Haydine ovvero Lettere su la vita e le opere del celebre maestro Giuseppe Haydn* (Milan, 1812), p. 253; the passage is quoted in Giuseppe Bertini, *Dizionario, storico-critico degli scrittori di musica* (Palermo, 1814), vol. 1, p. 96. Landon dates the friendship of Haydn and Carpani to the years 1796–97 and 1804–9. See Landon, *Haydn: Chronicle and Works*, vol. 4, p. 126.

50. These are the reminiscences of Louis Drouet, printed in Thayer-Deiters-Riemann, vol. 2, pp. 197–200; translated in Landon, *Haydn: Chronicle and Works*, vol. 4, pp. 63–64.

51. According to Moscheles, "Haydn heard that Beethoven had spoken in a tone of depreciation of his oratorio *The Creation*. 'That is wrong of him,' said Haydn; 'What has he written then? His Septet?'" Haydn then added, "Certainly that is beautiful, nay, splendid!" (Moscheles, *Recent Music and Musicians*, p. 23). Tovey observes that the Septet "is perhaps the only work of Beethoven's which earned Haydn's unqualified and enthusiastic praise." Donald Francis Tovey, *Beethoven* (London: Oxford University Press, 1965), p. 88.

52. In a lengthy essay, valuable for its comprehensive survey of contemporary materials concerning the relationship between Beethoven and Haydn, James Webster reviews the foregoing evidence and dismisses as unreliable the testimony of all but one of the contemporary commentators, including several with good reputations for veracity and accuracy. Webster, "The Falling-out between Haydn and Beethoven," pp. 3–45. Thus, Carpani, Moscheles, Ries, Seyfried, and others were retailing "hearsay"; Czerny's testimony is "lurid, highly exaggerated"; Doležálek is an author of "naughty one-liners"; Schenk's account "beggars reason," and, because errors persist in Beethoven's surviving exercises for Haydn, Schenk's story of having corrected those exercises for Beethoven "is most likely a pure fabrication" (see pp. 9–12). Furthermore, all those reports of contemporaries that were written down or related long after the fact must on that account alone "be treated with

great skepticism." The only witness who "entirely satisfies" Webster's criteria for credibility is Georg August Griesinger, who reported his observations to Gottfried Härtel of Breitkopf & Härtel within hours or days after they were made.

But even if one were to grant these objections—and all biographers know that the testimony of memoirists and eyewitnesses must be used with caution— evidence sufficient to demonstrate what I call the "complex and tangled character" of the relationship from the beginning exists even outside the anecdotal materials, especially in the crucial letter from Elector Maximilian Franz to Haydn. Webster's speculations about the elector's letter—that though it was drafted it may not have been sent, or may not have reached Haydn (p. 21)—cannot be tested; and his suggestion that Haydn knew Beethoven's compositions to have been written in Bonn and "assigned" their revision as homework does not withstand scrutiny, because in his own letter Haydn proudly referred to the compositions as new works—"evidence of his diligence beyond the scope of his own studies"—and because Beethoven's anxious letter to the elector of November 23, 1793, apologizes for the quality of the materials Haydn had mailed to Bonn on that same day by pledging to send worthier products of his talents "during the coming year." *Letters,* no. 8; *Briefe,* no. 12 (Beethoven to Elector Maximilian Franz, November 23, 1793).

CHAPTER 8.
PORTRAIT OF A YOUNG COMPOSER

1. Nohl, *Beethoven nach den Schilderungen,* pp. 19–20; Sonneck, pp. 20–21.
2. Sonneck, p. 155.
3. Nohl, *Beethoven nach den Schilderungen,* p. 20; Sonneck, p. 21.
4. Schindler-MacArdle, p. 120.
5. Seyfried, English translation, Supplement, p. 22.
6. *Ibid.*
7. Thayer-Forbes, pp. 466 and 537.
8. Sonneck, p. 31. Two memoirists of questionable reliability left vivid descriptions: Schindler pictured Beethoven as "comical, lively, and sometimes even loquacious" (Schindler-MacArdle, p. 120), and Rochlitz wrote that "once he is in the vein, rough, striking witticisms, droll conceits, surprising and exciting paradoxes suggest themselves to him in a continuous flow" (Thayer-Forbes, p. 802; Sonneck, p. 128).
9. Nohl, *Beethoven nach den Schilderungen,* pp. 41–42.
10. *Letters,* no. 296; *Briefe,* no. 485 (February 10, 1811).
11. Seyfried, English translation, Supplement, p. 16.
12. Breuning, p. 98; Breuning-Solomon, pp. 97–98.
13. Seyfried, cited in Nohl, *Beethoven nach den Schilderungen,* p. 43.
14. On a folio sheet at present on loan from the heirs of Stefan Zweig to the British Library, Department of Manuscripts. See *Führer durch die Beethoven Zentenar-Austellung der Stadt Wien 1927* (Vienna, 1927), no. 529. First published in Ludwig Nohl, *Beethoven's Brevier* (Leipzig, 1870), p. 104n. For another translation, see Thayer-Forbes, p. 501.
15. *Letters,* no. 258; *Briefe,* no. 442 (to Therese Malfatti, ca. late May 1810).
16. Solomon, "Tagebuch," no. 126; Leitzmann, vol. 2, p. 261 (no. 140).
17. Seyfried, English translation, Supplement, p. 17.

18. Braubach, *Die Stammbücher Beethovens und der Babette Koch*, p. 5; Thayer-Deiters-Riemann, vol. 1, p. 496; *Letters to Beethoven*, no. 13a.

19. Thayer-Forbes, pp. 223–24. See also Amenda's extravagantly devoted letter to Beethoven following his departure, with its expressions of heartfelt love and friendship. "See, beloved" ("Sieh, Geliebter"), he wrote, commenting that "these remarks might appear excessively rapturous (schwärmerisch) to you. . . . Whoever knows you as I do, and only loved you in a normal manner, is unworthy of the divine feeling of love." *Letters to Beethoven*, no. 31; *Briefe*, no. 31 (1800 or 1801). Translation amended. For an unwarranted speculation that as a Protestant Amenda could not have been employed by the Lobkowitzes, see Jaroslav Macek, "Franz Joseph Maximilian Lobkowitz: Musikfreund und Kunstmäzen," in *Beethoven und Böhmen* (BB, 1988), p. 151.

20. Thayer-Forbes, p. 261.

21. *Letters*, no. 94; *Briefe*, no. 186 (July 24, 1804).

22. *Letters*, no. 202; *Briefe*, no. 367 (ca. March 12, 1809).

23. *Letters*, no. 248; *Briefe*, no. 435 (April 1810) and *Letters*, no. 291; *Briefe*, no. 450 (1810, perhaps summer).

24. *Letters*, no. 12; *Briefe*, no. 17 (August 2, 1794).

25. Thayer-Forbes, p. 232.

26. Wegeler-Ries, p. 43; *Beethoven Remembered*, p. 43.

27. *Letters*, no. 16; *Briefe*, no. 20 (February 19, 1796).

28. Holz to Jahn, cited in Kerst, vol. 2, p. 186. It is not known when this reported incident took place.

29. *Konversationshefte*, vol. 1, p. 211.

30. Seyfried, English translation, Supplement, p. 22.

31. Letter to his sister, July 9, 1808, in Kerst, vol. 1, p. 123; Thayer-Forbes, p. 439.

32. *Letters*, no. 7; *Briefe*, no. 11 (November 2, 1793); trans. Thayer-Forbes, p. 162.

33. Dagmar von Busch-Weise, "Beethovens Jugendtagebuch," *Studien zur Musikwissenschaft* 25 (1962): 77; Thayer-Forbes, p. 182.

34. *Letters*, no. 6; *Briefe*, no. 6 (between October 1792 and October 26, 1793).

35. Ernest Walker, *Beethoven* (New York: Brentano's, 1905), p. 141.

36. Thayer-Forbes, p. 864.

37. *Letters*, no. 48; *Briefe*, no. 59.

38. *Letters*, no. 4 (to Theodora Johanna Vocke, May 22, 1793). From Schiller, *Don Carlos*, Act II, scene 2.

39. *Letters*, no. 30; *Briefe*, no. 35.

40. *Letters*, no. 53; *Briefe*, no. 67 (to Amenda, July 1, 1801). Beethoven refers to his audience as "the rabble" in *Letters*, no. 57; *Briefe*, no. 84 (to Hoffmeister, April 8, 1802).

41. *Letters*, no. 12; *Briefe*, no. 17 (August 2, 1794).

42. In Selected Bibliography, see "Freemasonry" (p. 500).

43. Kerst, vol. 2, p. 187. The original reads, "Beethoven war Freimaurer, aber in späteren Jahren nicht in Tätigkeit."

44. Solomon, *Beethoven Essays*, p. 78.

45. See Maynard Solomon, "Beethoven: The Nobility Pretense," *MQ* 61 (1975): 272–94.

46. W. A. Thomas-San-Galli, *Die unsterbliche Geliebte Beethovens. Amalie Sebald. Lösung eines vielumstrittenen Problems* (Halle: Otto Hendel, 1909), p. 65; Martin Cooper, *Beethoven: The Last Decade* (London: Oxford, 1970), p. 16.

47. Eduard Hanslick, *Geschichte des Concertwesens in Wien* (Vienna: Braumüller, 1869), pp. 50ff.
48. *Konversationshefte*, vol. 1, p. 252.
49. *Letters*, no. 979; *Briefe*, no. 1348 (to Johann Baptist Bach, October 27, 1819).
50. Otto Fenichel, *Collected Papers*, ed. Hanna Fenichel and David Rapaport (London: Routledge & Kegan Paul, 1954–55), vol. 2, p. 158.
51. Kerst, vol. 1, p. 215.
52. *Letters*, no. 1194; *Briefe*, no. 1680 (end of June 1823). See Kotzebue, *Vom Adel: Bruchstück eines grösseren historisch-philosophischen Werkes über Ehre und Schande, Ruhm und Nachruhm aller Völker, aller Jahrhunderte* (Leipzig: Paul Gotthelf Kummer, 1792).
53. Schindler-Moscheles, p. 70.
54. *Konversationshefte*, vol. 1, p. 219.

CHAPTER 9. VIENNA: CITY OF DREAMS

1. A. J. P. Taylor, *The Habsburg Monarchy, 1809–1918* (New York and Evanston: Harper & Row, 1965), p. 38.
2. For a fuller discussion of class subdivisions in Viennese society, see my "Beethoven's Class Position and Outlook," in Harry Goldschmidt, Karl-Heinz Köhler, and Konrad Niemann, eds., *Bericht über den internationalen Beethoven-Kongress 20. bis 23 März in Berlin 1977* (Leipzig: VEB Deutscher Verlag für Musik, 1978), pp. 67–79, 501–12.
3. Riesbeck, *Travels through Germany*, vol. 1, pp. 251, 244.
4. *Ibid.*, vol. 2, p. 4.
5. John Owen, *Travels into Different Parts of Europe, in the Years 1791 and 1792* (London: Cadell & Davies, 1796), vol. 2, p. 473.
6. Henry Reeve, *Journal of a Residence at Vienna and Berlin in the Eventful Winter of 1805–1806* (London: Longmans Green, 1877), p. 119.
7. John Russell, *A Tour in Germany, and Some of the Southern Provinces of the Austrian Empire, in the Years 1820, 1821, 1822* (Boston: Wells & Lilly, 1825), p. 396.
8. Russell, *A Tour in Germany*, p. 398.
9. Reeve, *Journal of a Residence at Vienna*, p. 25.
10. Ilse Barea, *Vienna* (New York: Knopf, 1966), p. 151.
11. Taylor, *Habsburg Monarchy*, p. 12.
12. Hanns Sachs, *The Creative Unconscious* (Cambridge, MA: Sci-Art Publishers, 1942), pp. 11–54.

CHAPTER 10. THE MUSIC (EARLY VIENNA)

1. *Letters*, no. 228; *Briefe*, no. 408 (to B&H, November 22, 1809).
2. Rolland, p. 112n. 2; translated as *Beethoven the Creator* (New York: Harper, 1929), p. 367.
3. Tovey, *Beethoven*, p. 7.
4. Thayer-Forbes, p. 209. Lockwood observes that Beethoven proceeded from "imitation" to "appropriation" of his Mozartian models and eventually to an assimilation of the Mozart legacy, not by attacking it "from an outside perspective but by

growing up as its inheritor and then exploding it from within." Lewis Lockwood, "Beethoven Before 1800: The Mozart Legacy," *BF,* vol. 3 (1994), pp. 39–52, especially pp. 49, 52.

5. Wegeler-Ries, p. 101; *Beethoven Remembered,* pp. 88–89; Thayer-Forbes, p. 348. The mutual influence of Beethoven and Clementi on each other's piano music has been often remarked. See Frimmel, *Handbuch,* vol. 1, pp. 97–98, and especially Leon Plantinga, *Clementi: His Life and Music* (London: Oxford University Press, 1977), pp. 103–5, 307–13. Beethoven admired Clementi's piano method, *Introduction to the Art of Playing on the Piano Forte* (London, 1801) and obtained a copy of the Vienna edition (T. Mollo, 1807) for young Gerhard von Breuning in 1826. See *Letters,* no. 1532; *Briefe,* no. 2203 (to Stephan von Breuning, after September 20, 1826).

6. *Letters,* no. 18; *Briefe,* no. 22. For an illuminating study, see William S. Newman, "Beethoven's Pianos versus his Piano Ideals," *JAMS* 23 (1970): 484–504.

7. *Letters,* no. 66; *Briefe,* no. 116 (November 1802).

8. *Letters,* no. 67; *Briefe,* no. 123 (ca. December 18, 1802).

9. *Letters,* no. 72; *Briefe,* no. 133 (to B&H, April 8, 1803).

10. Thayer-Forbes, p. 164.

11. Lockwood has persuasively shown that it was Jean Louis Duport rather than his brother, Jean Pierre Duport, for whom the Sonatas were composed. See Lewis Lockwood, "Beethoven's Early Works for Violoncello and Contemporary Violoncello Technique," in Rudolf Klein, ed., *Beiträge '76–78, Beethoven-Kolloquium 1977: Dokumentation und Aufführungspraxis* (Kassel: Bärenreiter, 1978), p. 176.

12. Walter Riezler, *Beethoven,* p. 126.

13. Kinsky-Halm, p. 22.

14. Alfred Mann suggests that Beethoven may have studied quartet composition with Haydn (*MQ* 56 [1970]: 725n. 10). It is also possible that Beethoven studied quartet composition with Emanuel Aloys Förster (1748–1823). See Thayer-Forbes, pp. 261–62.

15. Nottebohm 2, p. 494; Sieghard Brandenburg, "The First Version of Beethoven's G major String Quartet, Op. 18 No. 2," *M&L* 58 (1977): 127–52.

16. Joseph Kerman, *The Beethoven Quartets* (New York: Knopf, 1967), p. 55.

17. The Septet was first performed, under Schuppanzigh's direction, in the hall at Jahn's restaurant on December 20, 1799. See Harry Goldschmidt, "Beethoven in neuen Brunsvik-Briefen," *BJ,* 2d series, vol. 9 (1977), p. 109.

18. Charles Rosen, *The Classical Style* (New York: Viking, 1971), p. 381.

19. Beethoven wrote out a complete autograph of opus 19 with its original finale, the present Rondo in B-flat, WoO 6, in 1793 or early 1794; some cadenza sketches date from early 1795; a revision of the finale was composed in haste in late 1794 or early 1795; and the first and last movements underwent another revision in 1798. See Johnson, *Beethoven's Early Sketches in the 'Fischhof Miscellany,'* vol. 1, pp. 88, 100, 202–3, and 217.

20. *Ibid.,* pp. 118, 152.

21. *Letters,* no. 48; *Briefe,* no. 59 (to B&H, April 22, 1801).

22. The Concerto in C minor, op. 37, is plausibly assigned to 1802–3 by Leon Plantinga, "When Did Beethoven Compose His Third Piano Concerto?," *Journal of Musicology* 7 (1989): 275–307. It is proposed that the concerto was written for the academy of April 5, 1803, at which it was first performed. But although there is a growing consensus that the work was completed in 1803, several scholars,

including Alan Tyson and Hans-Werner Küthen, believe the concerto was probably first written down in 1799–1800.

23. Kerman, ed., *Ludwig van Beethoven: Autograph Miscellany*, vol. 2, pp. 166–74,
190–91; Johnson, *Beethoven's Early Sketches in the 'Fischhof Miscellany,'* vol. 1,
pp. 131, 466.

24. Hanslick, *Geschichte des Concertwesens*, pp. 34–35.

25. Donald Francis Tovey, *Essays in Musical Analysis*, vol. 1 (London: Oxford University Press, 1935), p. 21.

26. *AMZ* 3 (1800–1801): 49.

27. *Letters*, no. 44; *Briefe*, no. 54 (to Hoffmeister, January 15, 1801). Translation
revised.

28. Paul Bekker, *Beethoven*, p. 106.

29. Jürgen Uhde, *Beethovens Klaviermusik*, vol. 2, *Sonaten 1–15* (Stuttgart: Reclam,
1970; 4th ed., 1985), p. 336.

30. Eric Blom, *Beethoven's Pianoforte Sonatas Discussed* (London: Dent, 1937; reprint,
New York: Da Capo, 1968), p. 123.

31. Ludwig Misch, *Beethoven Studies*, trans. G. I. C. de Courcy (Norman: University
of Oklahoma Press, 1953), p. 53.

32. Carl Czerny, *On the Proper Performance of All Beethoven's Works for the Piano*
(reprint, Vienna: Universal, 1970), p. 13; Kerst, vol. 1, p. 46.

CHAPTER 11. CRISIS AND CREATIVITY

1. *Letters*, no. 263; *Briefe*, no. 454 (received July 9, 1810, according to Zmeskall's
notation).

2. *Letters*, no. 51; *Briefe*, no. 65. Transcription amended.

3. *Letters*, no. 53; *Briefe*, no. 67. Transcription amended.

4. *Letters*, no. 54; *Briefe*, no. 70.

5. *Letters*, no. 51; *Briefe*, no. 65 (letter of June 29, 1801).

6. *Letters*, no. 53; *Briefe*, no. 67.

7. *Letters*, no. 51; *Briefe*, no. 65.

8. Thayer-Forbes, p. 96.

9. Thayer-Forbes, p. 291.

10. *Letters*, no. 57; *Briefe*, no. 84.

11. *Letters*, no. 58; *Briefe*, no. 86 (letter of April 22, 1802).

12. It is sometimes stated that Ries arrived in Vienna for the first time in September or
October 1801, but this contradicts his plain statements and makes it difficult to
account for several of his reminiscences of events in 1800. I follow the suggestion
of Ludwig Ueberfeldt in his book *Ferdinand Ries' Jugendentwicklung* (Bonn: Rost,
1915), p. 12. In his "Ferdinand Ries (1784–1838): The History of his Contribution
to Beethoven Biography," *Nineteenth-Century Music* 7 (1984): 217, Alan Tyson
argued for 1801, but he has since opted for 1800 (personal communication).

13. Wegeler-Ries, pp. 98–99; *Beethoven Remembered*, pp. 86–87; Thayer-Forbes, p. 304.

14. *Letters*, Appendix A, vol. 3, pp. 1351–54; *Briefe*, no. 106; translated in Thayer-
Forbes, pp. 304–6.

15. The Sterbas speculate that the Testament was directed solely to Caspar Carl, and

that Beethoven was so angry with Nikolaus Johann that he could not write his name (*Beethoven and His Nephew*, p. 32). See also A. C. Kalischer, *The Letters of Beethoven*, trans. J. S. Shedlock (London: Dent, 1909), vol. 1, p. 62, for a wholly improbable speculation.

16. George Grove, *Beethoven and His Nine Symphonies* (3d ed., 1898; reprint, New York: Dover, 1962), p. 45n.

17. *Letters*, no. 16; *Briefe*, no. 20 (February 19, 1796); *Briefe*, no. 1485 (July 30, 1822).

18. *Letters*, no. 1151; *Briefe*, no. 1606.

19. *Letters*, Appendix C (nos. 1, 5, 6, and 11).

20. *Letters*, no. 205; *Briefe*, no. 369 (March 28, 1809); cf. *Letters*, no. 148; *Briefe*, no. 287 (to Gleichenstein, after July [not June] 23, 1807).

21. Nohl, vol. 3, p. 812. A passport application dated September 1795 in Bonn is signed "Jean van Beethoven" (information from Sieghard Brandenburg).

22. *Letters*, no. 3; *Briefe*, no. 7.

23. Sisman observes that the Heiligenstadt Testament "suggests the structure, elevated tone, and figures of a rhetorically conceived letter or speech." Elaine Sisman, "Pathos and the *Pathétique*: Rhetorical Stance in Beethoven's C-Minor Sonata, Op. 13," *BF*, vol. 3 (1994), p. 83.

24. Thayer-Forbes, p. 1059.

25. See G. Bilancioni, *La Sordità di Beethoven* (Rome: Formíggini, 1921), pp. 132ff.; Waldemar Schweisheimer, *Beethovens Leiden* (Munich: Müller, 1922), pp. 62ff.; Schweisheimer, "Beethoven's Physicians," *MQ* 31 (1945): 289; Walther Forster, *Beethovens Krankheiten und ihre Beurteilung* (Wiesbaden: B&H, 1955), *passim*; Edward Larkin, "Beethoven's Medical History," in Martin Cooper, *Beethoven: the Last Decade*, pp. 440–41.

26. Sonneck, p. 26; Czerny, "Recollections," p. 306.

27. Thayer-Forbes, pp. 370–71.

28. Wegeler-Ries, p. 98; *Beethoven Remembered*, p. 86.

29. Wegeler-Ries, *Nachtrag*, p. 10 (letter of November 13, 1804); *Beethoven Remembered*, p. 149; Thayer-Forbes, p. 358. Breuning and Beethoven shared an apartment for a short time in early 1804, but the stresses of their proximity led to a violent quarrel, followed by a passionate reconciliation in the fall of the same year.

30. Thayer-Forbes, p. 690.

31. Kerst, vol. 2, p. 186.

32. Nohl, *Beethoven, Liszt, Wagner* (Vienna: Braumüller, 1874), p. 112.

33. Thayer-Forbes, p. 373.

34. See *Letters*, nos. 51 and 53; *Briefe*, nos. 65 and 67; Thayer-Forbes, p. 850; Thayer-Forbes, p. 252; Nohl, *Beethoven nach den Schilderungen*, p. 185; George Smart, *Leaves from the Journal of Sir George Smart*, ed. H. B. Cox and C. L. E. Cox (London: Longmans, Green, 1907), p. 124; Thayer-Forbes, p. 187.

35. Thayer-Krehbiel, vol. 1, pp. 263–64.

36. Solomon, "Tagebuch," no. 88; Leitzmann, vol. 2, p. 257 (no. 100).

37. *Letters*, no. 53; *Briefe*, no. 67.

38. *Letters*, no. 60; *Briefe*, no. 98 (July 14, 1802).

39. Nottebohm 1, p. 89; Thayer-Forbes, p. 400.

CHAPTER 12. THE HEROIC DECADE (I)

1. Moscheles, *Recent Music and Musicians*, pp. 3–4. As early as 1797, Beethoven's works were second in quantity only to Mozart's on a list of music owned by the young pianist Dorothea Graumann (later Baroness von Ertmann). See Hellmut Federhofer, "Ein thematischer Katalog der Dorothea Graumann," in Dagmar Weise, ed., *Festschrift Joseph Schmidt-Görg zum 60. Geburtstag* (BB, 1957), pp. 100–110. Not all young musicians were Beethoven's partisans, however. The young Carl Maria von Weber called Beethoven's post-1800 works "a confused chaos, an unintelligible struggle after novelty" (Letter of May 1, 1810, to Hans Georg Nägeli, cited in Ludwig Nohl, ed., *Letters of Distinguished Musicians*, trans. Lady Wallace [London: Longmans, Green, 1867], p. 209).

2. For the full Haydn reference, see chapter 7, n.49, above; for Dionys Weber, see Nohl, *Beethoven nach den Schilderungen*, p. 82.

3. Czerny, "Recollections," p. 311; *AMZ* 7 (1804–1805): 321, 501.

4. *Letters*, no. 132; *Briefe*, no. 254 (to B&H, July 5, 1806).

5. Arthur Loesser, *Men, Women, and Pianos: A Social History* (New York: Simon & Schuster, 1954), p. 116.

6. Thayers-Deiters-Riemann, vol. 3, p. 77; Thayer-Forbes, p. 445. Translation corrected.

7. See O. E. Deutsch, *Beethovens Beziehungen zu Graz* (Graz: Leykam, 1907), especially pp. 4–11.

8. Nicholas Temperley, "Beethoven in London Concert Life, 1800–1850," *MR* 21 (1960): 207–14.

9. Seyfried, English translation, Supplement, p. 21.

10. William S. Newman, *Sonata in the Classic Era*, p. 528, citing Schindler *Biographie* (1860), vol. 1, p. 240; H. Earle Johnson, *Musical Interludes in Boston, 1795–1830* (New York: Columbia University Press, 1943), p. 144; see Hanslick, *Geschichte des Concertwesens*, p. 278.

11. See Alan Tyson, *The Authentic English Editions of Beethoven* (London: Faber, 1963), p. 39. Several of these were first editions: see *ibid.*, p. 19, and MacArdle, "First Editions of Beethoven Published in England," *Monthly Musical Record* 90 (1960): 228ff.

12. See Thayer-Forbes, pp. 309–13; Donald W. MacArdle, "Beethoven, Artaria, and the C major Quintet," *MQ* 34 (1948): 567–74.

13. *Letters*, no. 82; *Briefe*, no. 157 (ca. September 20, 1803).

14. This and the following references are from Erich H. Müller, "Beethoven und Simrock," *Simrock Jahrbuch* 2 (1929): 24–28; *Briefe*, nos. 152, 165, and 173; *Letters to Beethoven*, nos. 65, 71, and 75. I am indebted to Alan Tyson for raising the possibility that Beethoven intended to leave Vienna permanently at this time.

15. *Letters*, no. 88; *Briefe*, no. 177 (to Joseph Sonnleithner). I no longer advocate redating this letter to late 1804. It belongs, as Anderson says, probably in February or March 1804, evidenced by the fact that on August 31, 1804, Sonnleithner retired from direction of the theater and Schikaneder was reinstated, following his reconciliation with theater manager Baron Braun. See Anton Bauer, *150 Jahre Theater an der Wien* (Zürich, Leipzig, and Vienna: Amalthea, 1952), p. 70.

16. The rehearsals for both the Symphony and the "Triple" Concerto evidently took place in late May and/or June 1804, according to evidence cited in Tomislav Volek and Jaroslav Macek, "Beethoven's Rehearsals at the Lobkowitz's," *Musical Times* 127 (1986): 79, and Reinhold Brinkmann, "Kleine 'Eroica'-Lese," *Österreichische Musikzeitschrift* 39 (1984): 636–37. For the first performances of the *Eroica* Symphony, see chapter 13, n.3.

17. The more precise dating of the opera's preliminary stages, primarily as reflected in the sketchbook entitled Mendelssohn 15, has long been a matter of scholarly contention, with Thayer and Alan Tyson arguing that the main sketching was done in 1805 and Nottebohm and Theodore Albrecht assigning the relevant sketches to 1804. See Thayer, vol. 2, pp. 393–403; Nottebohm 2, pp. 409–60; Alan Tyson, "Beethoven's *Leonore* Sketchbook (Mendelssohn 15): Problems of Reconstruction and of Chronology," in Stephen Spector, ed., *Essays in Paper Analysis* (Washington, D.C., 1987), pp. 168–90, translated into German as "Das Leonoreskizzenbuch (Mendelssohn 15): Probleme der Rekonstruktion und der Chronologie," *BJ*, 2d series, vol. 9 (1977), pp. 469–99; Theodore Albrecht, "Beethoven's *Leonore*: A New Compositional Chronology," *Journal of Musicology* 7 (1989): 165–90. None of the arguments on either side are decisive, although it seems to me that the weight of the evidence favors the Thayer-Tyson view rather than that of Nottebohm-Albrecht. Albrecht credits Beethoven with an improbably high level of productivity between March and October 1804, thereby creating a corresponding gap in Beethoven's productivity for the months from October 1804 to June 1805, a gap that cannot be satisfactorily filled with rehearsals for the *Eroica* Symphony and the scoring of the first two acts of *Leonore*. It is safe to say that the dates of the commencement and conclusion of the opera are firmly established, and that the composition of the first version of *Leonore* was Beethoven's primary project from the beginning of 1804 until the fall of 1805, but that the dates on which he sketched and scored many of the numbers cannot yet be fixed with certainty. See also the related discussion of the sketches for the Sonata, op. 57, in Martha Fröhlich, *Beethoven's 'Appassionata' Sonata*, Studies in Musical Genesis and Structure, ed. Lewis Lockwood (Oxford: Clarendon Press, 1991), pp. 44–49. The departure of Sonnleithner on August 31, 1804, and his replacement by Schikaneder as director of the theater management may well have marked the occasion for a renewal of the contract between Beethoven and the Theater-an-der-Wien.

18. *Letters*, no. 90; *Briefe*, no. 181 (July 6, 1804).

19. La Mara [Marie Lipsius], *Beethoven und die Brunsviks* (Leipzig: Siegels Musikalienhandlung, 1920), p. 51; see also André Hevesy, *Beethoven: The Man* (London: Faber & Gwyer, 1927), p. 77. Joseph Schmidt-Görg persuasively assigns this letter to December 1804; see Schmidt-Görg, ed., *Dreizehn unbekannte Briefe an Josephine Gräfin Deym geb. v. Brunsvik* (BB, 1957), pp. 15, 23.

CHAPTER 13.
BONAPARTE: THE CRISIS OF BELIEF

1. Wegeler-Ries, p. 78; *Beethoven Remembered*, p. 68; Thayer-Forbes, pp. 348–49.

2. In view of several conspicuous errors in Schindler's account of the genesis of the *Eroica* Symphony, there is no reason to accept his claim that he heard the same story from Moritz Lichnowsky, whom he cited as his main authority for material on Beethoven's middle years in Vienna (see Schindler-MacArdle, p. 116; Schindler-Moscheles, pp. 34–35).

3. Macek has discovered a Lobkowitz accounting record dated August 14, 1804, which refers to "performance of the new symphony by Beethoven," thus placing the first performance of the *Eroica* in the first half of that month. See Jaroslav Macek, "Musik bei Lobkowitz und Kinsky und Ludwig van Beethoven," in *Ludwig van Beethoven: Leben und Nachleben in den böhmischen Ländern*, ed.

Oldrich Pulkert (Prague: forthcoming). The place of the performance is not definitely fixed, Macek opting for Lobkowitz's Vienna palace but Walther Brauneis arguing that it was performed—without Beethoven present—at Schloss Eisenberg, where Lobkowitz customarily spent his summers. See Walther Brauneis, "'. . . composta per festeggiare il sovvenire di un grand Uomo': Beethoven's 'Eroica' als Hommage des Fürsten Franz Joseph Maximilian von Lobkowitz für Prinz Louis Ferdinand von Preussen," *Jahrbuch des Vereins für Geschichte der Stadt Wien*, vols. 52–53 (1996–97), pp. 53–88. The symphony may have been performed at the Lobkowitz Palace on January 23, 1805, three days after a separate performance at Herr von Würth's, and the first public performance was given on April 7, 1805, at the Theater-an-der-Wien. The program of the last of these announced it as a "new grand symphony in D-sharp" (Thayer-Forbes, p. 375).

4. *Letters*, no. 96; *Briefe*, no. 188.

5. I follow the readings of Nottebohm in *Ein Skizzenbuch von Beethoven aus dem Jahre 1803* (Leipzig: B&H, 1880), p. 76, and J.-G. Prod'homme in *Les Symphonies de Beethoven* (Paris: Delagrave, 1906), pp. 83–84. See also Thayer-Forbes, p. 349; Grove, *Beethoven and His Nine Symphonies*, p. 55; Ludwig Nohl, *Die Beethoven-Feier und die Kunst der Gegenwart* (Vienna: Braumüller, 1871), p. 33.

6. Erich H. Müller, "Beethoven und Simrock," *Simrock Jahrbuch* 2 (1929): 27; Kinsky-Halm, p. 131.

7. Emile Zola, *Les Romanciers naturalistes* (Paris, 1923), pp. 94–95; translation in George Steiner, *Tolstoy or Dostoevsky* (New York: Vintage, 1961), p. 23.

8. Barea, *Vienna*, pp. 123–24.

9. Goethe, *Conversations with Eckermann*, trans. [J. Oxenford] (New York & London: Walter Dunne, 1901), p. 304; Hegel, cited in Karl Löwith, *From Hegel to Nietzsche* (Garden City, NY: Anchor, 1967), p. 214.

10. Heine, *Religion and Philosophy in Germany*, p. 145.

11. J. Christopher Herold, ed., *The Mind of Napoleon* (New York: Columbia University Press, 1955), p. 273.

12. Mary Shelley, ed., *The Poetical Works of Percy Bysshe Shelley* (1839; reprint, Boston: Little, Brown, 1857), vol. 1, p. 137.

13. *Letters*, no. 57; *Briefe*, no. 84.

14. For further discussion of this proposed trip, see Max Unger, "Zur Enstehungs- und Aufführungsgeschichte von Beethovens Oper 'Leonore,'" *Neue Zeitschrift für Musik* 105 (1938): 130ff.

15. *Letters*, no. 51; *Briefe*, no. 65.

16. *Letters*, no. 44; *Briefe*, no. 54 (ca. January 15, 1801). For the utopian sources of Beethoven's phrase "Magazin der Kunst," see Maynard Solomon, "Beethoven's *Magazin der Kunst*," in Solomon, *Beethoven Essays*, pp. 193–204.

17. In some instances, for example the dedication to Baron van Swieten and the numerous dedications to Freemason Prince Lichnowsky, it is difficult to disentangle patronage requirements and ideological affinities. For Swieten, see E. Wangermann, *Aufklärung und staatsbürgerliche Erziehung: Gottfried van Swieten als Reformator des österreichischen Unterrichtswesens 1781–1791* (Munich: Oldenbourg, 1978), pp. 12–16. Among Beethoven's other dedicatees, Goethe and Friedrich Wilhelm II were Masons.

18. E. J. Hobsbawm, *The Age of Revolution, 1789–1848* (New York: Mentor Books, 1964), p. 109.

19. *NBJ,* vol. 2 (1925), pp. 104–18; see also Schmitz, *Das romantische Beethovenbild* (Berlin and Bonn: Dümmler, 1927), pp. 163–76.

20. Boris Schwarz, "Beethoven and the French Violin School," *MQ* 44 (1958): 431–47.

21. See Riezler, *Beethoven,* p. 89.

22. Thayer-Forbes, p. 403.

23. Sonneck, pp. 74–75; see *MQ* 6 (1920): 378.

24. Thayer-Forbes, p. 442. A possible explanation lies in the fact that Beethoven's intimate Bonn friend Karl August von Malchus served for five years beginning in January 1808 in several high offices at the Westphalian court. See Max Braubach, ed., *Die Stammbücher Beethovens und der Babette Koch; Faksimile* (BB, 1970), p. 154; Theodore Albrecht, *Letters to Beethoven,* vol. 1, p. 17n. 1.

25. *Letters,* no. 414; *Briefe,* no. 633 (April 8, 1813).

26. Thayer-Forbes, pp. 470–71.

27. "Die Messe könnte vielleicht noch dem Napoleon dedizirt werden," cited in Max Unger, "Beethovens vaterländische Musik," *Musik im Kriege,* nos. 9 and 10 (1943–44): 171. See also MacArdle, *Abstracts,* p. 156, and *BJ,* 2d series, vol. 7 (1971), p. 207 (no. 494).

28. Grove, *Beethoven and His Nine Symphonies,* p. 54.

29. Czerny, *On the Proper Performance,* p. 8.

30. Schindler-MacArdle, pp. 111–12, 115–16.

31. Kerst, vol. 1, p. 55; vol. 2, p. 194; Czerny, *On the Proper Performance,* p. 13.

32. Georg Brandes, *Main Currents in Nineteenth-Century Literature,* vol. 2 (London: Heinemann, 1902), p. 27.

33. Ernst Cassirer, *The Philosophy of the Enlightenment* (Princeton: Princeton University Press, 1951), pp. 136, 147.

34. *Ibid.,* p. 136.

CHAPTER 14. THE HEROIC DECADE (II)

1. For full details see Thayer-Forbes, pp. 381–87.

2. *Ibid.,* p. 388.

3. Reeve, *Journal of a Residence at Vienna,* pp. 64–65.

4. Thayer-Forbes, p. 393.

5. In Denis Arnold and Nigel Fortune, eds., *The Beethoven Reader* (New York: Norton, 1971), p. 364.

6. Thayer-Forbes, p. 397.

7. *Letters,* no. 481; *Briefe,* no. 709 (before April 5, 1814).

8. See the letters of Caspar Carl van Beethoven to B&H of October 10, 1804, and November 24, 1804 (Thayer-Deiters-Riemann, vol. 2, pp. 623–24; *Briefe,* nos. 194 and 199; *Letters to Beethoven,* nos. 86 and 91).

9. Kinsky-Halm, p. 141.

10. Walker, *Beethoven,* p. 181. That is not the only possible interpretation. The acacia has significance as a Masonic symbol of innocence, mourning, immortality, and resurrection. See the "Acacia" entry in Arthur Edward Waite, *A New Encyclopaedia of Freemasonry,* 2 vols. in 1 (London: W. Rider & Son, 1921; reprint, New York:

University Books, 1970) vol. 1, pp. 1–4. In that case, "brother" in Beethoven's notation could also be read as a Masonic reference, as in Jacques Henry, *Mozart frère maçon: La symbolique maçonnique dans l'oeuvre de Mozart* (Aix-en-Provence, 1991), p. 38.

11. Schindler-MacArdle, p. 60.
12. Prod'homme, *Jeunesse de Beethoven*, p. 176.
13. Reeve, *Journal of a Residence at Vienna*, p. 79.
14. Seyfried, cited in Thayer-Forbes, p. 403; letter of Ries to Wegeler, December 28, 1837, in Stephan Ley, ed., *Beethoven als Freund der Familie Wegeler–v. Breuning* (Bonn: Cohen, 1927), pp. 252–53.
15. Schindler appears to have invented a parallel story about a break between Prince Nikolaus Esterházy and Beethoven at the premiere of the Mass in C, op. 86, at Eisenstadt, on September 13, 1807. According to Schindler, Esterházy remarked cuttingly, "But, my dear Beethoven, what is this that you have done again?" while Hummel, his kapellmeister, laughed, leading Beethoven to quit Eisenstadt in anger on that day (see Schindler-Moscheles, p. 50; Thayer-Forbes, p. 423). Documentary evidence shows that Beethoven did not leave Eisenstadt prematurely, but stayed until September 16 (Thayer-Forbes, p. 424). Moreover, on January 18, 1809, Esterházy contributed 100 florins toward the cost of Beethoven's December 1808 academy (Thayer-Forbes, p. 449n. 32). Though the prince did not receive the dedication of the Mass, there is a corrected copy of it in the Esterházy-Archiv in Budapest (Kinsky-Halm, p. 239).
16. Beethoven changed the inscription on the title page from "son Excellence Monseigneur le Comte de Rasoumoffsky" to "son Altesse Monseigneur le Prince Charles de Lichnowsky." Later on, Razumovsky was restored as the dedicatee. See Alan Tyson, "The 'Razumovsky' Quartets: Some Aspects of the Sources," *BS*, vol. 3 (1982), pp. 134–35.
17. A list of Beethoven's clavier pupils in Vienna would include Carl Czerny, Ferdinand Ries, Archduke Rudolph, Therese and Josephine von Brunsvik, Giulietta Guicciardi, Dorothea von Ertmann, Princess Barbara Odescalchi, Beethoven's nephew, Karl, and the son of composer Emanuel Aloys Förster. Ries and Rudolph also studied composition with him. When asked by Xaver Schnyder von Wartensee if he accepted students, he responded in the negative, calling it "vexatious work." Wartensee to Hans Georg Nägeli, *Letters to Beethoven*, no. 157 (December 17, 1811).
18. Wegeler-Ries, *Nachtrag*, p. 12; *Beethoven Remembered*, p. 150.
19. *Letters*, Appendix 1 (1), vol. 3, pp. 1444–45; *Briefe*, no. 302 (before December 4, 1807). Unger argues that it should be dated not earlier than fall 1807. See Max Unger, "Beethoven und das Wiener Hoftheater im Jahre 1807," *NBJ*, vol. 2 (1925), pp. 76–83.
20. *Briefe*, no. 302n. 1.
21. *Letters*, no. 143; *Briefe*, no. 281 (May 11, 1807 [not 1806, as dated by Beethoven]). Translation amended.
22. J. F. Reichardt, *Vertraute Briefe*, ed. G. Gugitz (Munich: Müller, 1915), vol. 1, p. 205; see also Nohl, *Beethoven nach den Schilderungen*, p. 51.
23. Thayer-Forbes, p. 439.
24. *Letters*, no. 169; *Briefe*, no. 331 (after July 16, 1808).
25. *Letters*, no. 170; *Briefe*, no. 303 (before December 4, 1807).
26. Thayer-Deiters-Riemann, vol. 2, p. 125; Thayer-Forbes, p. 457. Translation amended.

27. Thayer-Forbes, p. 456.

28. *Letters,* no. 202; *Briefe,* no. 367.

29. *Letters,* no. 220; *Briefe,* no. 392.

30. *Letters,* no. 228; *Briefe,* no. 408 (formerly dated November 2, 1809).

31. André Hevesy, *Les petites amies de Beethoven* (Paris: Champion, 1910), p. 29; Hevesy, *Beethoven: The Man,* p. 56. Hevesy misdated the letter "August 2, 1800," despite its clear reference to the August 4, 1803, performance of opus 85. The composition referred to by Countess Guicciardi is the Lied ("Ich denke dein") and Six Variations for Piano Four Hands in D, WoO 74, which was presented to Therese and Josephine von Brunsvik on May 23, 1799, and revised in summer 1803.

32. *Konversationshefte,* vol. 2, pp. 365–66; Schünemann, vol. 2, pp. 363–64; Thayer-Forbes, p. 290.

33. Quoted by Widmann in Albert Dietrich and Joseph Viktor Widmann, *Recollections of Johannes Brahms* (London: Seeley and Co., 1899), p. 116. Translation amended.

34. *Letters,* no. 54; *Briefe,* no. 70.

35. *Konversationshefte,* vol. 2, p. 367; Schünemann, vol. 2, p. 365.

36. Thayer-Forbes, p. 358.

37. Schmidt-Görg, *Dreizehn unbekannte Briefe,* pp. 15–16; Hevesy, *Beethoven: The Man,* pp. 75 and 77; Thayer-Forbes, pp. 359 and 377.

38. Romain Rolland, *Beethoven the Creator,* trans. Ernest Newman (New York: Harper & Brothers, 1929), p. 318. From Marianne Czeke, ed. and trans., *Tagebücher und Aufzeichnungen der Gräfin Therese Brunsvik* (n.p., n.d.). Originally published in Hungarian (Budapest: Ungarischen Historischen Gesellschaft, 1938).

39. Hevesy, *Beethoven: The Man,* p. 212.

40. Schmidt-Görg, *Dreizehn unbekannte Briefe,* pp. 24–25; *Briefe,* no. 265; Thayer-Forbes, p. 379. I lean toward Schmidt-Görg's conclusion that the letter dates from 1804–5 rather than Brandenburg's proposed date of winter 1806–7. See also *Letters to Beethoven,* no. 100, which assigns a date of early 1805.

41. *Letters,* no. 110; *Briefe,* no. 216 (March or April 1805).

42. *Ibid.*

43. Undated draft letter, *BJ,* 2d series, vol. 6 (1969), p. 207.

44. Schmidt-Görg, *Dreizehn unbekannte Briefe,* p. 28; translated in George Marek, *Beethoven: Biography of a Genius,* p. 244; *Briefe,* no. 250; *Letters to Beethoven,* no. 102. Harry Goldschmidt, *Um die Unsterbliche Geliebte: Eine Bestandsaufnahme* (Leipzig: VEB Deutscher Verlag für Musik, 1977 [1978]), p. 149, establishes the probable date of the letter as April 24, 1806.

45. La Mara, *Beethovens unsterbliche Geliebte,* p. 67.

46. Siegmund Kaznelson, *Beethovens ferne und unsterbliche Geliebte* (Zürich: Standard-Buch, 1954), pp. 181–82; La Mara [Marie Lipsius], *Beethoven und die Brunsviks* (Leipzig: Siegel, 1920), pp. 70–72.

47. *Letters,* no. 151; *Briefe,* no. 294 (September 20, 1807).

48. *Letters,* no. 153; *Briefe,* no. 297 (probably after September 20).

49. *Letters,* no. 156; *Briefe,* no. 404.

50. Thayer-Forbes, p. 425.

51. *Letters,* no. 139; *Briefe,* no. 273 (shortly after March 5, 1807); the other letter of apology is *Letters,* no. 138a; *Briefe,* no. 272 (March 5, 1807).

52. See Joseph Schmidt-Görg, "Wer war 'die M.' in einer wichtigen Aufzeichnung Beethovens?" *BJ,* 2d series, vol. 5 (1966), pp. 75–79. See p. 229 below.

53. Breuning, p. 24; Breuning-Solomon, p. 38.

54. J.-G. Prod'homme, *Beethoven, raconté par ceux qui l'ont vu* (Paris: Stock, 1927), p. 89.

55. Nottebohm 2, p. 261; Kalischer, *Beethoven und seine Zeitgenossen,* vol. 2, p. 229; *Briefe,* no. 360 (between March 4 and 7, 1809).

56. *Letters,* no. 208; *Briefe,* no. 364 (after March 8, 1809).

57. The first reconciliation is probably evidenced by the performance of the String Quartet, op. 74, at Countess Erdödy's palace on March 31, 1810; a second rupture occurred, perhaps as early as the summer of the same year, and was not healed until February 1815, evidenced by Beethoven's letter to the countess of February 29, 1815, and her gift of wine to him. See *Letters,* no. 531; *Briefe,* no. 785. For Brandenburg's well-founded conclusions about the date of the second rift, see *Briefe,* vol. 2, p. 47n. 1.

58. *Letters,* no. 258; *Briefe,* no. 442 (May 1810). Translation amended. The Bagatelle in A minor, WoO 59, known as "Für Elise" and composed in either 1808 or 1810, is thought to have been written for Therese Malfatti. See Kinsky-Halm, p. 505, and Cooper, *Beethoven and the Creative Process,* p. 266.

59. Thayer-Forbes, p. 490.

60. *Letters,* no. 254; *Briefe,* no. 445 (beginning of June 1810); trans. Thayer-Forbes, p. 488. Translation amended.

61. Paul Scudo, "Une Sonate de Beethoven," *Revue des deux mondes,* new series, 15, no. 8 (1850): 77–97 (see p. 94 for the quotation). Scudo reassures his readers that what they have read is "not a figment of my imagination" (p. 95). Nevertheless, numerous details of his article are invented; he does not even refrain from inserting the words "ma Giulietta" into the text of the Immortal Beloved letter (p. 94).

62. Schindler, *Biographie* (1860), vol. 1, p. 94; translated in Thayer-Krehbiel, vol. 1, p. 324; for another translation, see Schindler-MacArdle, pp. 101–4. Jedlersee should be Jedlesee.

63. Thayer-Krehbiel, vol. 1, p. 325. Frimmel, too, thought it "a highly improbable story that Beethoven had wanted to starve himself in the park at Jedlersee because of his grief over his love for Giulietta Guicciardi." Frimmel, *Handbuch,* vol. 1, p. 58.

64. Nohl, vol. 3, p. 897. Röckel could not fix the date, recalling only that it was "several years" after 1806, and thus may conceivably be related to the mortifying finale of Beethoven's courtship of Josephine Deym. By the time of his interview, Röckel could have read Scudo's and Schindler's accounts.

65. *Letters,* no. 256; *Briefe,* no. 439 (May 2, 1810). Translation amended

66. *Letters,* no. 259 (May 1810); *Briefe,* no. 430 (April 18, 1810).

67. Schindler-MacArdle, p. 365; Thayer-Forbes, pp. 481–82. Leitzmann located an almost identical citation of the passage in a Masonic text by Brüder Decius [Karl Leonhard Reinhold, pseud.], *Die hebräischen Mysterien oder die älteste religiöse Freimaurerei* (Leipzig: Georg Joachim Göschen, 1788), pp. 53–54. See Leitzmann, vol. 2, p. 374 (no. 182); see also Frimmel, *Handbuch,* vol. 1, pp. 178–79; Schmitz, *Das romantische Beethovenbild,* pp. 85–88. Baensch pointed out that the word order of the first passage as given in Reinhold is slightly different from that given by Schiller and Beethoven. See Otto Baensch, *Aufbau und Sinn des Chorfinales in Beethovens neunter Symphonie* (Berlin and Leipzig: Walter de Gruyter, 1930), p. 27n. 3. The leaf containing Beethoven's copy of the inscriptions is in the Wegeler Collection, Beethoven-Haus, Bonn; facsimile in Stephan Ley, *Beethovens Leben in authentischen Bildern und Texten* (Berlin: Cassirer, 1925), p. 129.

CHAPTER 15: THE IMMORTAL BELOVED

1. Wegeler-Ries, p. 117; *Beethoven Remembered*, p. 104.

2. Thayer-Forbes, p. 293.

3. Thayer-Forbes, p. 289.

4. *Letters*, no. 373; *Briefe*, no. 582; translated in Thayer-Forbes, pp. 533–34. Translation amended. The transcription in *Briefe* mistakenly includes Schindler's addition of "auch" in "Ach, wo ich bin, bist [auch] du mit mir."

5. Schindler-Moscheles, p. 39.

6. Schindler-MacArdle, p. 105.

7. Nohl, vol. 2, pp. 477–78.

8. *Letters*, no. 143; *Briefe*, no. 281 (May 11, 1807).

9. Thayer-Forbes, p. 291.

10. O. G. Sonneck, *The Riddle of the Immortal Beloved* (New York: Schirmer, 1927), p. 21.

11. Thayer-Krehbiel, vol. 1, p. 332.

12. *Ibid.*, p. 333.

13. Bonn, 1890. English translation by Gertrude Russell as *Recollections of Countess Therese Brunswick* (London: T. Fisher-Unwin, 1893), and by Caroline T. Goodloe in *Music* 4 (1893 [Chicago]).

14. A. C. Kalischer, *Die "Unsterbliche Geliebte" Beethovens: Giulietta Guicciardi oder Therese Brunswick?* (Dresden: Bertling, 1891), pp. 1–29.

15. Grove, *Beethoven and His Nine Symphonies*, pp. 112, 140, and 154–56.

16. Paul Bekker, "Beethoven an die Unsterbliche Geliebte—ein unbekannte Brief des Meisters," *Die Musik* 10, no. 21 (1911): 131–42. The tune is from the finale of the String Quintet in C, op. 29—"evidence" that the letter originated in 1801. See also Bekker, "Schlusswort," *Die Musik* 11, no. 7 (1912): 40–45.

17. Thomas-San-Galli, *Die unsterbliche Geliebte Beethovens. Amalie Sebald. Lösung eines vielumstrittenen Problems* (Halle: Hendel, 1909).

18. Sonneck, *Riddle*, p. 16.

19. Thayer-Krehbiel, vol. 1, p. 332.

20. *Letters*, no. 375; *Briefe*, no. 586 (the letter was first published in 1906; Thayer died in 1897).

21. Unger, *Auf Spuren von Beethovens "Unsterblicher Geliebten"* (Langensalza, Germany: Beyer, 1911).

22. Thomas-San-Galli, *Beethoven und die unsterbliche Geliebte: Amalie Sebald/Goethe/ Therese Brunsvik und Anderes* (Munich: Wunderhorn, 1910).

23. A traveler leaving on the evening coach would arrive on the morning of the third day. Possibly, however, Beethoven left Vienna on the morning of June 29.

24. *Beilage zur kaiserlich-königlich-privilegirten Prager Oberpostamts-Zeitung*, no. 80, Friday, July 3, 1812, col. 1. The earliest use I have located of this newspaper supplement to establish Beethoven's arrival in Prague is in Jan Racek, *Beethoven a České Země* (Brno, 1964), p. 31. See also Marek, *Beethoven: Biography of a Genius*, pp. 302–3.

25. *Letters*, no. 374; *Briefe*, no. 583 (July 14, 1812). Translation amended.

26. *Beilage zur . . . Prager Oberpostamts-Zeitung*, no. 81, Monday, July 6, 1812, col. 2. See Racek, *Beethoven a České Země*, p. 31. The earliest documentation of the date of Beethoven's departure from Prague is in Max Unger, "The 'Immortal Beloved,'" *MQ* 13 (1927): 253. Unger found this information in what he calls the *Prager Post-Zeitung*, which I assume to be the *Prager Oberpostamts-Zeitung*.

27. *Beilage zur . . . Prager Oberpostamts-Zeitung*, no. 81, Monday, July 6, 1812, col. 2. The newspaper supplement mistakenly gives Esterházy's destination as Karlsbad.

28. According to Goethe's diaries, cited in Unger, *Auf Spuren*, p. 21.

29. Unger, *Auf Spuren*, pp. 115–16. Bohumil Plevka argues that the routes are actually reversed; see Plevka, *Beethovenuv Dopis Nesmrtelné Milence* (Beethoven's Letter to the Immortal Beloved) (Teplitz, 1965), pp. 12–14, as summarized in Harry Goldschmidt, *Um die Unsterbliche Geliebte: Eine Bestandsaufnahme* (Leipzig, 1977 [1978]), pp. 48–50. I do not have sufficient information to decide this question.

30. *Letters*, no. 375; *Briefe*, no. 586 (July 17, 1812); translated in Thayer-Forbes, p. 535.

31. Sonneck, *Riddle*, p. 42. For a transcription of Beethoven's entry on the Teplitz *Anzeigsprotokoll*, see Racek, *Beethoven a České Země*, p. 43n. 64.

32. *Letters*, no. 380; *Briefe*, no. 591 (to B&H, August 9, 1812).

33. Unger, *Auf Spuren*, pp. 22–23.

34. *Ibid.*, p. 24.

35. *Ibid.*

36. In a personal communication published in Racek, *Beethoven a České Země*, pp. 49–50, Schmidt-Görg reported locating twenty letters written by Beethoven with similar watermarks dating from the years 1812 to 1818, including four letters dated July 14, July 17, August 9, and August 12, 1812 (*Letters*, nos. 374, 375, 380, and 381; *Briefe*, nos. 583, 586, 591, and 592).

37. Unger, *Auf Spuren*, p. 15, was the first to observe the logic of this.

38. Thomas-San-Galli, *Beethoven und die unsterbliche Geliebte*, p. 35. Harry Goldschmidt informs me that this requirement had been in effect for some years prior to 1812, and that the police registers were not necessarily exhaustive (personal communication). I have been unable to locate any proof of the latter assertion.

39. Solomon, "Tagebuch," no. 1; Leitzmann, vol. 2, p. 242 (no. 8)

40. Thayer-Forbes, p. 646. Translation amended.

41. *Letters*, no. 632; *Briefe*, no. 923. Translation amended.

42. Schmidt-Görg, *Dreizehn unbekannte Briefe*. As noted in chapter 14, the relationship was effectively over by September 20, 1807, when Beethoven came to understand clearly that he would no longer find the countess at home. See *Letters*, no. 151; *Briefe*, no. 294. In a subsequent, final exchange, she asked for news of him and he rejected her friendly overture: "You want me to tell you how I am. A more difficult question could not be put to me—and I prefer to leave it unanswered, rather than—to answer it too truthfully." This undated exchange of letters between them is placed in 1807 in Schmidt-Görg, *Dreizehn unbekannte Briefe*, pp. 33–34, and *Letters*, no. 156, and "perhaps in 1809" in *Briefe*, nos. 403 and 404.

43. The leading proponents of Josephine Deym-Stackelberg are La Mara, *Beethoven und die Brunsviks*; Kaznelson, *Beethovens ferne und unsterbliche Geliebte*; Jean and Brigitte Massin, *Recherche de Beethoven* (Paris: Fayard, 1970); Goldschmidt, *Um die Unsterbliche Geliebte*; and Marie-Elisabeth Tellenbach, *Beethoven und seine "unsterbliche Geliebte" Josephine Brunswick: Ihr Schicksal und der Einfluss auf Beethovens Werk* (Zürich: Atlantis Musikbuch-Verlag, 1983). Their most prestigious, if uncritical, supporter has been Carl Dahlhaus: "Even though the external evidence remains hypothetical, internal evidence [innere Gründe] makes it probable that Josephine Brunswick was the intended recipient of the letter." *Ludwig van Beethoven: Approaches to his Music*, trans. Mary Whittall (Oxford: Clarendon Press, 1991), p. 247. See also pp. xxii, 10–11. The nature of the "internal evidence" is not specified.

44. Maynard Solomon, "Recherche de Josephine Deym," Solomon, *Beethoven Essays,* pp. 157–65.
45. The memoirs, written in 1846 and 1855, discuss Minona's birth and other events of 1813 on the pages immediately *prior* to describing the breakup of the marriage. La Mara [Marie Lipsius], *Beethovens unsterbliche Geliebte: Das Geheimnis der Gräfin Brunsvik und ihre Memoiren* (Leipzig: B&H, 1909), pp. 101–3. Kaznelson, in order to maintain the notion that Stackelberg separated from Countess Deym in mid-1812, arbitrarily rearranged all the conflicting dates offered in Therese's memoirs. See Kaznelson, *Beethovens ferne und unsterbliche Geliebte,* pp. 239–40.
46. Tellenbach is reluctant to credit the plain meaning of the documents, characterizing them as "questionable," reading them in unreasonable ways, and flatly refusing to "give credibility" to the letter dated June 14, 1812, from Baron von Stackelberg to his mother describing an intact family making plans for the summer of that year. See Marie-Elisabeth Tellenbach, "Psychoanalysis and the Historiocritical Method: On Maynard Solomon's Image of Beethoven (Part 2)," *The Beethoven Newsletter* 9 (Summer–Winter 1994): 120.
47. In the older literature, Unger was the first to mention her name in this connection, but dismissed her candidacy without stating his reasons (*Auf Spuren,* p. 74), as did Rolland (p. 1488), Jean and Brigitte Massin (*Ludwig van Beethoven,* p. 240), and Marek (*Beethoven: Biography of a Genius,* pp. 306–7). In his *Um die Unsterbliche Geliebte,* Harry Goldschmidt acknowledged the strength of my evidence in her favor, but did not abandon his advocacy of Josephine Deym. Early support for my position came from Alan Tyson and Joseph Kerman in *TNG,* vol. 2, pp. 367–68. Writing in 1992, Landon observed that "Solomon's proposal . . . now has gained nearly complete acceptance" (H. C. Robbins Landon, ed., *Beethoven: His Life, Work and World* [London: Thames and Hudson, 1992], p. 168). More recently the case for identifying Frau Brentano as the Immortal Beloved is favored by Sieghard Brandenburg in *Briefe,* vol. 2, p. 272n. 1 and in his letter to *Beethoven Journal,* vol. 12, no. 2 (1997), p. 94; and Theodore Albrecht in *Letters to Beethoven,* vol. 1, p. 242n. 3 and vol. 2, p. 157n. 1.
48. There is still room for a reasonable doubt. However, in order to follow the implications of my proposed identification somewhat further, I have in the later sections of this chapter acted on the assumption that Frau Brentano has been proved to have been the Immortal Beloved.
49. [Otto Jahn], "Ein Brief Beethovens," *Die Grenzboten: Zeitschrift für Politik und Literatur* 26, no. 2 (1867): 100–101. Partly reprinted in Thayer-Forbes, p. 492, and Thayer-Deiters-Riemann, vol. 3, pp. 214–15.
50. Schindler-MacArdle, p. 259. We have only Schindler's word for this characterization, since no letter containing this phrase has survived.
51. See also Wilhelm Grimm's letter to Achim von Arnim, June 21, 1812, in Reinhold Steig, *Clemens Brentano und die Brüder Grimm* (Stuttgart and Berlin: Cotta, 1914), p. 174n. 2.
52. *Beilage zur . . . Prager Oberpostamts-Zeitung,* no. 81, Monday, July 6, 1812, col. 1. The Brentanos' presence in Prague is confirmed by Franz Brentano's letter of July 15, 1812, to Clemens Brentano (GM).
53. *Beilage zur . . . Prager Oberpostamts-Zeitung,* no. 81, Monday, July 6, 1812, col. 2.
54. The exact date of his arrival is not known. He did not register with the police until July 31. Goethe's diary for July 27, 1812, notes, "Beethoven left here several days ago for Karlsbad." (Cited in Thomas-San-Galli, *Beethoven und die unsterbliche Geliebte,* p. 37; see also Thomas-San-Galli, *Die unsterbliche Geliebte Beethovens,* p. 65.)
55. See Theodor Frimmel, *Beethoven-Forschung* 10 (January 1925): 45.

56. Solomon, "Tagebuch," nos. 104 and 107; Leitzmann, vol. 2, pp. 258–59 (nos. 115 and 119).

57. *Letters*, no. 296; *Briefe*, no. 485.

58. *Letters*, no. 758; *Briefe*, no. 1083. Translation corrected. See also *Letters*, no. 1064; *Briefe*, no. 1451 (December 20, 1821).

59. *Letters*, nos. 570, 607, and 660; *Briefe*, nos. 850, 897, and 978. The fourth letter (*Letters*, no. 659; *Briefe*, no. 763) is undated, but probably belongs to late 1814, despite Anderson's assignment of it to 1816. (See *BJ*, 1st series, 2 [1909], p. 214.)

60. Solomon, "Tagebuch," nos. 123, 133, 139, and 141.

61. *Letters*, no. 607; *Briefe*, no. 897. Translation amended.

62. Thayer-Deiters-Riemann, vol. 4, pp. 62–63; Thayer-Forbes, p. 686; italics added.

63. Facsimile in Schindler-MacArdle, pp. 102–4. See above, Chapter 14, n.52.

64. The manuscript is in the Bibliothèque Nationale, Paris. Goldschmidt conducted a separate handwriting comparison and found my identification "indisputable" (Harry Goldschmidt, *Um die Unsterbliche Geliebte*, p. 108). Helga Lühning offers no basis for her dissenting opinion (see *Beethoven. Werke, XII/1: Lieder und Gesänge. Kritischer Bericht*, p. 90n. 1).

65. Breuning, p. 124; Breuning-Solomon, p. 113.

66. Stephen Ley, "Ein Bild von Beethovens unsterblicher Geliebten?" *Atlantis* 5 (1933): 766–67. See Maynard Solomon, "New Light on Beethoven's Letter to an Unknown Woman," *MQ* 58 (1972): 585n. 39.

67. Stephen Ley, *Wahrheit, Zweifel und Irrtum in der Kunde von Beethovens Leben* (Wiesbaden: B&H, 1955), pp. 24–25. See also *NBJ*, vol. 6 (1935), pp. 30–31; Stephen Ley, *Aus Beethovens Erdentagen* (Bonn: Glöckner, 1948), pp. 254–56.

68. "We are . . . making two family portraits. In the first, Franz, together with Finus [Josefa] and Maxe—that means 6 blue eyes; on the other Georg and Franziska—that means 6 black eyes." Antonie Brentano to Joseph Merkel, January 18, 1809 (GM).

69. Deirdre Donohue of the Costume Institute at the Metropolitan Museum of Art, New York, dates the miniature to the early years of the nineteenth century, noting that the cut, materials, and construction of the dress, the colors of the shawl, and the pearl belt are from the vocabulary of 1802–5 fashion. "I believe that the miniature, although her hairstyle may imply a simpler time, is no earlier than 1802. Her dress is distinctly later than 1800." As for the hairstyle, she observes that "it is the most likely thing to be anachronistic." (Letter to the author, June 4, 1997.) See also Sieghard Brandenburg, *Der Brief an die unsterbliche Geliebte* (BB, 1986), p. 32.

70. Here and in the following I quote, without repeating the source for each citation, from Frau Brentano's reminiscences as written down following two series of conversations with her on May 4, 1865, and January 25, 1866, by Karl Theodor Reiffenstein. These are partly reprinted in Rudolf Jung, ed., *Goethes Briefwechsel mit Antonie Brentano, 1814–21* (Weimar: Böhlhaus, 1896), pp. 5–12, and Hubert Schiel, ed., *Frankfurter Beiträge, Arthur Richel gewidmet* (Frankfurt: Hauserpresse [Schaefer], 1933), pp. 68–72. The extensive courtship correspondence of 1797–98 reveals that Birkenstock drove a hard bargain for his daughter's hand and also that he postponed the conclusion of the marriage arrangements for some months because he feared for his daughter's safety in the war-torn Rhineland. (I am grateful to Harry Goldschmidt for making extracts from this correspondence, located in DSB, available to me.)

71. Henry Crabb Robinson, *Diary, Reminiscences, and Correspondence* (Boston: Fields, Osgood, 1870), vol. 1, p. 55.

72. Letter of September 1, 1805, to Sophia Brentano, cited in Reinhold Steig, *Achim von Arnim und Clemens Brentano* (Stuttgart: Cotta, 1894), p. 144.

73. Wilhelm Schellberg and Friedrich Fuchs, eds., *Das unsterbliche Leben: unbekannte Briefe von Clemens Brentano* (Jena: Eugen Diederichs, 1939), p. 268.

74. Letter of August 10, 1805, cited in Heinz Amelung, ed., *Briefwechsel zwischen Clemens Brentano und Sophie Mereau* (Leipzig: Insel, 1908), vol. 2, p. 163.

75. Bettina von Arnim, *Werke und Briefe*, ed. Gustav Konrad (Frechen/Cologne: Bartmann, 1959–61), vol. 5, p. 265.

76. Letter of July 10, 1806, to Clemens Brentano (GM).

77. Letter of October 3 (no year) to Karl von Savigny (Handschriftenabteilung/Literaturarchiv, Savigny Collection, DSB).

78. Letter of June 21, 1808, to Kunigunde (Gunda) and Karl von Savigny (Savigny Collection, DSB).

79. Letter of December 14, 1808, to Joseph Merkel (GM).

80. Letter of November 21, 1808, to Merkel (GM).

81. Letter to Merkel (GM).

82. Antonie and the children arrived in Vienna between September 1 and the middle of October 1809.

83. Thayer-Deiters-Riemann, vol. 3, p. 216.

84. Letter of November 22, 1799, to Sophia Brentano (DSB). Even before her marriage she complained of Franz's immersion in his work: "For such an unimportant person as I am, he will not undertake a journey [to Vienna], and then he is now so occupied with business" (quoted in letter from Franz to Sophia Brentano, October 4, 1797).

85. Letter of January 9, 1812, to Clemens Brentano (GM).

86. Letter to Merkel (GM).

87. See *Catalogue des tableux et desseins des maitres célèbres des différentes écoles ... qui composent le cabinet de feu Mr. J. M. de Birckenstock* (Vienna: Artaria & Co., 1810), and *Catalogue Raisonné de la Collection d'Estampes anciennes et modernes de toutes les écoles de feu Mr. J. M. de Birckenstock*, 2 vols. (Vienna: André Schmidt, [1811–1813?]). Two additional catalogues (Schmidt, 1810) covered the contents of Birkenstock's library. For the dates of the auctions, see *Wiener Zeitung* for December 26, 1810; November 2, 1811; March 11, 1812; April 15 and 18, 1812; and March 2, 1813. On January 9, 1812, Antonie wrote to Clemens Brentano, "The sale will definitely begin the 14th [*sic*] of February this year, as the newspapers have stated. First the books together with the first two schools of copper engravings; in April, the paintings will follow, and other art collections as the small catalog shows" (GM).

88. F. A. C. Prestel, *Catalogue de la célèbre collection d'estampes de feu Madame Antonia Brentano, née de Birckenstock, ... Franckfort S. M., Lundi, 16 May 1870 et jours suivants* (Frankfurt: Kruthoffer, 1870), p. vii.

89. Clemens Brentano letter to Ludwig Tieck, early 1813, cited in Johannes B. Diel, *Clemens Brentano: ein Lebensbild*, vol. 1 (Freiburg im Breisgau: Herder, 1877), pp. 388–89. For some details of Birkenstock's estate and the amounts realized from the auctions, see Franz Gräffer, *Kleine wiener Memoiren und wiener Dosenstücke*, ed. Anton Schlossar and Gustav Gugitz (Munich: Müller, 1918), vol. 2, p. 355n.

90. On evidence derived from their paper types, and because publication of both the "Archduke" Trio and the F-minor String Quartet was delayed until 1816, it has been claimed that their autographs were revised and written out three or four years after the dates Beethoven inscribed on them. See Sieghard Brandenburg, "Die Quellen zur Entstehungsgeschichte von Beethovens Streichquartett Es-dur Op.

127," *BJ*, 2d series, vol. 10 (1983), pp. 223–24, and Alan Tyson, in a chapter of Douglas Johnson, Robert S. Winter, and Alan Tyson, *The Beethoven Sketchbooks: History, Reconstruction, Inventory*, ed. Douglas Johnson (Berkeley and Los Angeles: University of California Press, 1985), p. 198. However, Seow-Chin Ong's researches now strongly suggest that there was no later revision of the "Archduke" Trio and that Beethoven's datings for both works—and presumably for the Violin Sonata in G, op. 96, as well—are to be taken seriously. See Ong, "The Autograph of Beethoven's 'Archduke' Trio, Op. 97," in proceedings (forthcoming) of the conference "Austria, 996–1996: Music in a Changing Society" held in Ottawa, January 1996.

91. *Letters*, no. 308; *Briefe*, no. 499 (to B&H, May 20, 1811). Translation amended.

92. Letter of January 26, 1811, to Clemens Brentano (GM).

93. Thayer-Forbes, p. 492.

94. Sandberger, *Ausgewählte Aufsätze zur Musikgeschichte*, vol. 2, pp. 255–56; translation in Solomon, *Beethoven Essays*, pp. 178–80.

95. Letter of October 6, 1812, to Clemens Brentano (GM). Another letter from Franz to Clemens Brentano, written from Frankfurt and dated January 28, 1813 (GM), provides the *terminus ad quem*.

96. In my "Antonie Brentano and Beethoven," *M&L* 58 (1977): 162n. 50, I predicted that the issue of the paternity of Karl Josef would "undoubtedly give rise to much fruitless speculation as to the father's identity." See also my *Beethoven Essays*, pp. 183–84. It is in the nature of such matters that they will always remain open questions. The British writer Susan Lund has argued the case for Beethoven's paternity, claiming that numerous allusions in his letters to his fatherhood are somehow references to Karl Joseph rather than to his guardianship of his nephew, Karl. See Susan Lund, "Beethoven: A True 'Fleshly Father,'" in Lund, *Raptus: A Novel About Beethoven* (Melstamps, England: published by the author, 1995), pp. vii–xli. To demonstrate Beethoven's consciousness of literally being a father, Lund neglects evidence to the contrary; for example, she quotes from Beethoven's letter to Amenda of April 12, 1815, "You live *happily*, you have *children*," but she omits the telling phrase "neither of which is true of me," although it follows without pause in Beethoven's letter. See Lund, *Raptus*, p. xiii; *Letters*, no. 541; *Briefe*, no. 803. See also Ernst Pichler, "Beethovens unsterbliche Geliebte: Thema mit Variationen," *Neue Zürcher Zeitung*, "Literatur und Kunst" section, April 15–16, 1995, p. 70. For a critique, see Barry Cooper, review of *Raptus*, by Susan Lund, *M&L* 77 (1996): 618–19.

97. Maria Andrea Goldmann, *Im Schatten des Kaiserdomes: Frauenbilder* (Limburg: Steffen, 1938), p. 100. A more detailed discussion of Frau Brentano, with an account of her later life and additional bibliographical information, is in Maynard Solomon, "Antonie Brentano and Beethoven," *M&L* 58 (1977): 153–69, enlarged in Solomon, *Beethoven Essays*, pp. 166–89.

98. These documents, formerly in the Louis Koch Collection and now in the Beethoven-Archiv, Bonn, were kindly made available to me by Martin Staehelin during his tenure as director of the Beethoven-Archiv.

99. Kerst, vol. 2, p. 44; Sonneck, pp. 156–57.

100. Mircea Eliade, *Cosmos and History: The Myth of the Eternal Return*, trans. Willard R. Trask (New York: Harper & Row, 1959), p. 18.

101. Solomon, "Tagebuch," no. 1.

102. Fanny Giannattasio, diary entry of June 15, 1817; cited in Thayer-Deiters-Riemann, vol. 4, p. 540.

103. Solomon, "Tagebuch," no. 3; Leitzmann, vol. 2, p. 242 (no. 10).

CHAPTER 16: THE MUSIC (MIDDLE PERIOD)

1. "At the same time," Tyson wrily comments, "it was a work calculated to entitle him to a Holy Week benefit concert at the Theater-an-der-Wien" (personal communication).

2. See Alan Tyson, "Beethoven's Heroic Phase," *Musical Times* 110 (1969): 141, in which he points to the time pressures under which the work was completed, and to the obsessive rewriting of the line "Take this cup of sorrow from me" in the March 1804 revision.

3. William S. Newman, *Sonata in the Classic Era*, p. 27.

4. Alfred Einstein, *Music in the Romantic Era* (New York: Norton, 1947), p. 42.

5. Erich Schenk, "Salieris 'Landsturm'-Kantate von 1799 in ihren Beziehungen zu Beethovens 'Fidelio,'" in S. Kross and H. Schmidt, eds., *Colloquium Amicorum, Joseph Schmidt-Görg zum 70. Geburtstag* (BB, 1967), pp. 338–54.

6. Schiller, "The Pathetic" ("Über das Pathetische"), in *The Works of Friedrich Schiller: Aesthetical and Philosophical Essays*, ed. N. H. Dole (New York: Bigelow, Brown & Co., 1902), vol. 1, p. 142.

7. Susanne K. Langer, *Feeling and Form* (New York: Scribner's, 1953), p. 333.

8. *High Fidelity*, December 1974, p. 98.

9. Riezler, *Beethoven*, pp. 247–48.

10. Beethoven perhaps first achieved this kind of effect in the opening of the Piano Sonata in D minor, op. 31, no. 2. Later, Beethoven utilized a similar technique in the first movements of the Fifth and Ninth Symphonies; the Fifth Piano Concerto, op. 73; the Piano Sonatas, opp. 53 and 57; and the Overture to *Egmont*. In his celebrated essay on the Fifth Symphony, Tovey argues the absurdity of analyzing Beethoven's middle-period symphonies in terms of the development of motif cells, emphasizing that the first movement of the Fifth Symphony, for example, "is really remarkable for the length of its sentences rather than for the brevity of its initial figure" (*Essays in Musical Analysis*, vol. 1, p. 38).

11. Tovey, *Essays in Musical Analysis*, vol. 1, p. 39. See also Curt Sachs, *Rhythm and Tempo* (New York: Norton, 1953), p. 329.

12. Leonard G. Ratner, "Key Definition—A Structural Issue in Beethoven's Music," *JAMS* 23 (1970): 483.

13. Wilhelm von Lenz, *Beethoven et ses trois styles* (Paris: G. Legouix, 1909; reprint, New York: Da Capo, 1980), p. 210.

14. Czerny wrote: "Beethoven himself considered [opus 57] his greatest" (Thayer-Forbes, p. 407).

15. Donald Francis Tovey, *A Companion to Beethoven's Pianoforte Sonatas* (London: Associated Board of the Royal Schools of Music, 1931), p. 169.

16. See Otto Erich Deutsch, "Beethovens Theaterpläne," *Schweizerische Musikzeitung*, no. 3 (March 1, 1945): 76–78; Giovanni Biamonti, *Catalogo cronologico e tematico delle opere di Beethoven* (Turin: ILTE, 1968), pp. 1062–68; Winton Dean, in Arnold and Fortune, *The Beethoven Reader*, pp. 381–85.

17. Seyfried, cited in Sonneck, p. 44.

18. Ernst Bücken, in *Der heroische Stil in der Oper* (Leipzig: Kistner & Siegel, 1924), p. 77, sees "horror opera" ("*Schreckensoper*") as the primary category, with three subdivisions: "Rescue," "Outlaw," and "Revolutionary" opera. See also R. Morgan Longyear, "Notes on the Rescue Opera," *MQ* 45 (1959): 49–66.

19. Thayer-Forbes, p. 381.

20. Freud, "A Special Type of Choice of Object Made by Men," in *Collected Papers*, vol. 4, p. 200; Freud, *Standard Edition*, vol. 11, p. 172; see also Karl Abraham, "The Rescue and Murder of the Father in Neurotic Phantasy-Formations," in Abraham, *Clinical Papers and Essays on Psychoanalysis* (New York: Basic Books, 1955), pp. 68–75.

21. Kerst, vol. 2, p. 44; Sonneck, pp. 156–57.

22. See n. 2, above. Tyson observes that "the provision of bread and wine to the starving prisoner Florestan also has sacramental (Eucharistic) overtones" (personal communication).

23. See Joseph Braunstein, *Beethovens Leonore-Ouvertüren* (Leipzig: B&H, 1927). The date of *Leonore* No. 1 is firmly established in Alan Tyson, "The Problem of Beethoven's 'First' Leonore Overture," *JAMS* 28 (1975): 292–334. A further revision of *Leonore* No. 2 was sketched in 1814, but abandoned. (See Alan Tyson, "Yet Another Leonore Overture?" *M&L* 58 [1977]: 192–203.)

24 Tovey, *Essays in Musical Analysis*, vol. 4, p. 42.

25. Bekker, *Beethoven*, p. 147.

26. Thayer-Forbes, p. 400; Nottebohm 2, p. 89.

27. Kerman, *Beethoven Quartets*, p. 118.

28. Philip Radcliffe, *Beethoven's String Quartets* (New York: Dutton, 1968), p. 50.

29. *Letters*, no. 132; *Briefe*, no. 254 (July 5, 1806).

30. *Letters*, no. 272; *Briefe*, no. 465 (to B&H, August 21, 1810). Translation amended.

31. Thayer-Forbes, p. 409.

32. *Ibid.*

33. Bekker, *Beethoven*, p. 122.

34. Thayer-Forbes, p. 410.

35. Roy Pascal, *The Growth of Modern Germany* (London: Cobbett, 1946), p. 12.

36. *Letters*, no. 140; *Briefe*, no. 277.

37. Nottebohm 2, pp. 262–63.

38. Schindler-MacArdle, p. 147.

39. Heinrich Schenker, *Beethoven: V. Sinfonie* (Vienna: Tonwille, [1925]), p. 7.

40. Cited in Grove, *Beethoven and His Nine Symphonies*, p. 137.

41. Hector Berlioz, *Beethoven's Symphonies*, trans. Edwin Evans (London: Reeves, 1958), p. 67.

42. Lang, *Music in Western Civilization*, p. 764.

43. Nottebohm, *Ein Skizzenbuch . . . aus dem Jahre 1803*, p. 55; Nottebohm 2, pp. 369–71.

44. Grove, *Beethoven and His Nine Symphonies*, pp. 191–92.

45. F. E. Kirby, "Beethoven's Pastoral Symphony as a *Sinfonia caracteristica*," *MQ* 56 (1970): 605–23, with further references.

46. Riezler, *Beethoven*, p. 152.

47. Nottebohm 2, p. 375.

48. Edward J. Dent, "The Choral Fantasia," *M&L* 8 (1927): 111–22.

49. Steven Moore Whiting, "'Hört ihr wohl': Zu Funktion und Programm von Beethovens 'Chorfantasie,'" *Archiv für Musikwissenschaft* 45 (1988): 144.

50. Tovey, *Essays in Musical Analysis*, vol. 2, p. 135.

51. Alfred Einstein, *Essays on Music* (London: Faber & Faber, 1958), p. 247. The marginal reference to Napoleon noted above was deciphered by Hans-Werner Küthen, *Beethoven Werke, Gesamtausgabe, Abteilung III, Bd. 3, Klavierkonzerte II, Kritischer*

Bericht (Munich: Henle, 1996), p. 41; facsimile in Küthen, ed., *Beethoven Klavierkonzerte* II, Abbildung 5.

52. Lewis Lockwood, "The Autograph of the First Movement of Beethoven's Sonata for Violoncello and Pianoforte, Opus 69," *The Music Forum*, vol. 2, ed. W. J. Mitchell and Felix Salzer (New York and London: Columbia University Press, 1970), p. 34.

53. Tovey, *Beethoven*, p. 88.

54. Nottebohm 2, p. 100.

55. Kinsky-Halm, p. 361.

56. Nottebohm 2, p. 446.

57. Kerman, *Beethoven Quartets*, p. 156.

58. Søren Kierkegaard, *Either/Or: A Fragment of Life*, trans. David F. Swenson and Lillian Marvin Swenson, 2 vols. (Princeton: Princeton University Press, 1944), vol. 1, p. 56.

59. Friedrich Nietzsche, *The Birth of Tragedy out of the Spirit of Music*, trans. Francis Golffing (Garden City, NY: Anchor, 1956), p. 46.

60. See Michel Brenet [Marie Bobillier, pseud.], *Histoire de la symphonie à orchestre* (Paris: Gauthier-Villars, 1882), pp. 146–47; see also Prod'homme, *Les Symphonies de Beethoven (1800–1827)*, pp. 332–33.

61. Bekker, *Beethoven*, p. 185; Ernest Newman, notes to the Klemperer recording (Angel H-3619).

62. See Robert C. Elliott, *The Shape of Utopia: Studies in a Literary Genre* (Chicago and London: University of Chicago Press), 1970, pp. 12ff; see also A. L. Morton, *The English Utopia* (London: Lawrence & Wishart, 1952), and Mikhail Bakhtin, *Rabelais and His World* (Cambridge, MA: MIT Press, 1968). All of these derive in large part from Sir James George Frazer, *The Golden Bough: A Study in Magic and Religion*, abridged edition (New York: Macmillan, 1939), *passim*, and/or Sigmund Freud, *Group Psychology and the Analysis of the Ego*, in Freud, *Standard Edition*, vol. 18, *passim*.

63. Ernest Newman, notes to the Klemperer recording (Angel H-3619).

64. Richard Wagner, *Beethoven* (1870), trans. A. R. Parsons (New York: Schirmer, 1883), p. 65.

65. Riezler, *Beethoven*, p. 153.

66. Bakhtin, *Rabelais*, p. 89.

67. Frimmel, *Handbuch*, vol. 1, p. 156; Thayer-Deiters-Riemann, vol. 2, p. 311.

68. Thayer-Deiters-Riemann, vol. 3, p. 414; translated in Thayer-Forbes, p. 575.

69. Thayer-Forbes, p. 576.

70. Sieghard Brandenburg, "Bemerkungen zu Beethovens Op. 96," *BJ*, 2d series, vol. 9 (1977), pp. 11–25. But see chapter 16, note 90 above. Beethoven wrote on the first page of the autograph, "Sonata. in February 1812 or 13," and its first performance was given on December 19, 1812 (see Kinsky-Halm, p. 270, and Thayer-Forbes, p. 545).

CHAPTER 17:
THE DISSOLUTION OF THE HEROIC STYLE

1. *Letters*, no. 383; *Briefe*, no. 594.

2. *Letters*, nos. 382, 384–90; *Briefe*, nos. 593, 595–601 (September 16–22, 1812).

3. In an undated letter to Gleichenstein, Beethoven asks, "How can one get to Linz *most quickly* and *most cheaply?*" *Briefe*, no. 448; *Letters*, no. 391. The letter is incor-

rectly assigned by Anderson to "end of September, 1812"—an impossible date for various reasons. Brandenburg assigns it to "probably early summer 1810," but it may be still earlier.

4. Thayer-Forbes, p. 542.

5. *Ibid.*

6. Thayer-Forbes, p. 543. For dates of these symphonies, see Nottebohm 2, pp. 101–18; see also *NBJ*, vol. 5 (1933), pp. 45–46.

7. *Letters*, no. 394; *Briefe*, no. 618.

8. *Letters*, no. 402; *Briefe*, no. 615. Translation amended.

9. *Letters to Beethoven*, no. 169; *Briefe*, no. 616 (translation amended); and *Letters*, no. 426; *Briefe*, no. 656.

10. In earlier editions of this book, I speculated, on the basis of Schindler's report, that Beethoven may have attempted suicide at the Erdödy estate in 1813, in the aftermath of the Immortal Beloved affair. But Beethoven and Countess Erdödy were almost certainly estranged during that year, a rift that was not healed until early 1815, so that the account of such an attempt, if it is to credited at all, could not have derived from the period in question. For a more skeptical view of the suicide account, see chapter 14.

11. See Solomon, "Tagebuch," no. 20; Leitzmann, vol. 2, p. 245 (no. 30). Rolland comments: "The missing words have been suppressed. . . . [O]ne may ask himself whether Beethoven was not contemplating suicide" (Rolland, p. 1459).

12. *Letters*, Appendix A, vol. 3, pp. 1352–53; no. 805 (to Zmeskall, August 21, 1817); and no. 256 (to Wegeler, May 2, 1810). The German equivalents are *Briefe*, nos. 106, 1161, and 439.

13. *Letters*, no. 407; *Briefe*, no. 625. The Sterbas were the first to grasp the implications of these references (Sterba and Sterba, *Beethoven and His Nephew*, p. 110).

14. *Letters*, nos. 562 (October 16, 1815), 653 (September 5, 1816), and 681 (December 16, 1816); *Briefe*, nos. 841, 970, and 1014. Brandenburg writes, "The expression 'Festung' . . . is understood by many interpreters as a synonym for 'prostitute.'" *Briefe*, vol. 3, p. 332. Similarly, the phrase "sumpfigten Gegenden" ("swampy places," or "marshy grounds" in Anderson's translation) can serve in every language as a metaphor for arenas of sexual activity. Thus, Cellini writes of passing his time and catching venereal diseases "in marshy grounds." See Benvenuto Cellini, *Memoirs* (Oxford: Oxford University Press, 1927), chapter 11.

15. *Letters*, no. 715 (end of 1816), no. 597 (January 21, 1816), and no. 846 (probably spring 1811, judging by the watermark); *Briefe*, nos. 1008, 881, and 490. See also *Letters*, nos. 333, 347, 349, and 368; *Briefe*, nos. 530, 550, 553, and 558. For *Letters*, no. 715, I use the translation in A. C. Kalischer, ed., J. S. Shedlock, trans., *The Letters of Beethoven*, 2 vols. (London: Dent, 1909), vol. 2, p. 33, slightly modified.

16. Solomon, "Tagebuch," no. 122; Leitzmann, vol. 2, p. 261 (no. 135).

17. Thayer-Forbes, p. 685.

18. Solomon, "Tagebuch," no. 138; Leitzmann, vol. 2, p. 262 (no. 150); Nohl, vol. 3, p. 828.

19. Schindler-Moscheles, p. 55; see also Schindler-MacArdle, pp. 164–65.

20. Thayer-Forbes, p. 590.

21. Schindler-Moscheles, p. 55.

22. Barry Cooper, *Beethoven's Folksong Settings: Chronology, Sources, Style* (Oxford: Clarendon Press, 1994), pp. 36–37; Barry Cooper, *Beethoven and the Creative Process* (Oxford: Clarendon Press, 1990), pp. 217–18.

23. For Mälzel's and Beethoven's respective contributions to this work, see Hans-Werner Küthen, "Neue Aspekte zur Enstehung von *Wellingtons Sieg,*" *BJ,* 2d series, vol. 8 (1975), pp. 73–92.

24. Thayer-Forbes, p. 565.

25. Thayer-Forbes, p. 566.

26. But, for a spirited defense of the work as the best exemplar of its genre, see Ludwig Misch, "The Battle of Victoria," *Beethoven Studies* (Norman: University of Oklahoma, 1953), pp. 153–62.

27. *Letters,* Appendix H (no. 6), vol. 3, p. 1438.

28. Thayer-Forbes, p. 571.

29. Solomon, "Tagebuch," no. 22; Leitzmann, vol. 2, p. 246 (no. 32).

30. *Der Sammler,* cited in Thayer-Forbes, p. 583.

31. Thayer-Forbes, pp. 586–87. Translation amended.

32. Solomon, "Tagebuch," no. 16; Leitzmann, vol. 2, p. 245 (no. 26); Thayer-Forbes, p. 561. In 1827, Ferdinand Hiller heard Beethoven exclaim: "They say 'Vox populi, vox dei'—I have never believed in it" (Kerst, vol. 2, p. 229).

33. Thayer-Forbes, p. 565.

34. Schindler-Moscheles, p. 64.

35. See Nottebohm 2, p. 577; *Letters,* no. 1388; *Briefe,* no. 1992 (to Haslinger, June 12, 1825).

36. Harold Nicholson, *The Congress of Vienna: A Study in Allied Unity* (New York: Viking, 1946; Compass Books, 1961), p. 160.

37. Barea, *Vienna,* p. 130.

38. Schindler-Moscheles, p. 64.

39. Schindler-MacArdle, p. 205.

40. M. H. Weil, ed., *Les dessous du congrès de Vienne,* 2 vols. (Paris: Payot, 1917); cited in Edouard Herriot, *The Life and Times of Beethoven* (New York: Macmillan, 1935), p. 217.

41. *Letters,* no. 540; *Briefe,* no. 802 (to J. N. Kanka, April 8, 1815).

42. Sullivan, *Beethoven,* p. 166.

43. Charles Rosen, *The Classical Style* (New York: Viking, 1971), p. 404.

44. Lewis Lockwood, "Beethoven's Unfinished Piano Concerto of 1815: Sources and Problems," *MQ* 56 (1970): 624–47; see especially p. 626. For the F-minor Trio, see Nottebohm 2, pp. 345, 348; Johnson, Winter, Tyson, *The Beethoven Sketchbooks,* pp. 245–46.

45. Geoffrey Bruun, *Europe and the French Imperium, 1799–1814* (New York: Harper Torchbooks, 1963), p. 202.

46. Thayer-Forbes, pp. 804 and 956.

47. *Letters,* no. 175; *Briefe,* no. 332 (before August 6, 1808).

48. See Solomon, *Beethoven Essays,* p. 291; skeptics who doubt that Beethoven ranked Handel above Bach, Haydn, and Mozart may observe that these remarks were usually made to and reported by British visitors. But see also the statement by Frau Streicher: "The only three musicians he liked were Handel, Sebastian Bach and Mozart." Hughes, *A Mozart Pilgrimage,* p. 189.

49. See W. S. Newman, *Sonata in the Classic Era,* p. 527.

50. Thayer-Forbes, pp. 577–78. Spohr's hostility to Beethoven's music should be taken into account.

CHAPTER 18: BEETHOVEN AND HIS NEPHEW

1. Viewed psychoanalytically, Beethoven at this time faced a "danger situation," which gave rise to an array of neurotic and even quasi-psychotic symptoms. According to Freud, such symptoms "are created in order to remove the ego from a situation of danger." Symptom formation is a "defensive process . . . analogous to flight by means of which the ego removes itself from a danger that threatens it from outside," and represents, indeed, "an attempt at flight from an instinctual danger." Freud, *Inhibitions, Symptoms and Anxiety*, in Freud, *Standard Edition*, vol. 20, pp. 144–45.

2. *Konversationshefte*, vol. 3, p. 157; Schünemann, vol. 3, p. 158.

3. Solomon, "Tagebuch," no. 69; Leitzmann, vol. 2, p. 255 (no. 82); Sterba and Sterba, *Beethoven and His Nephew*, p. 51.

4. *Letters*, no. 441; *Briefe*, no. 679 (Beethoven to Joseph Reger, December 18, 1813). Translation amended.

5. Nohl, vol. 3, p. 34; Thayer-Forbes, p. 551. Translation amended.

6. See Frimmel, *Handbuch*, vol. 2, p. 484.

7. Nohl, vol. 3, p. 814; Sterba and Sterba, *Beethoven and His Nephew*, p. 54.

8. For full details, based on the recent rediscovery of relevant documents and the unpublished researches of Robert Franz Müller, see Sieghard Brandenburg, "Johanna van Beethoven's Embezzlement," in Brandenburg, ed., *Haydn, Mozart, and Beethoven: Essays in Honor of Alan Tyson* (Oxford: Oxford University Press, 1998), pp. 237–51.

9. *Letters*, Appendix C (no. 15), vol. 3, p. 1389.

10. Brandenburg, "Johanna van Beethoven's Embezzlement," p. 246. Nevertheless, Brandenburg describes her as "this financially—and perhaps also morally—destitute woman" and questions whether she ought to have been entrusted with the upbringing of her own child. *Ibid.*, p. 248.

11. Thayer-Deiters-Riemann, vol. 4, p. 545; Brandenburg, "Johanna van Beethoven's Embezzlement," p. 236n. 6, p. 242.

12. Breuning, p. 46; Breuning-Solomon, p. 53.

13. Nohl, vol. 2, p. 482.

14. Hedwig M. von Asow, *Ludwig van Beethoven: Heiligenstädter Testament* (Vienna: Döblinger, 2d ed., 1969), pp. 4–5.

15. Nohl, ed., *Neue Briefe Beethovens* (Stuttgart: Cotta, 1867), p. 243n.; Kalischer-Shedlock, *Letters of Beethoven*, vol. 2, p. 304.

16. Dagmar Weise, ed., *Beethoven: Entwurf einer Denkschrift an das Appellationsgericht . . .* (BB, 1953), p. 31; Nohl, vol. 3, p. 849n. 68.

17. *Letters*, no. 1009; *Briefe*, no. 865 (undated and unaddressed draft of letter to the Imperial and Royal *Landrecht* of Lower Austria, probably ca. December 20, 1815).

18. For the following account, see Max Reinitz, *Beethoven im Kampf mit dem Schicksal* (Vienna: Rikola, 1924), pp. 35–39; Reinitz, "Beethovens Prozesse," *Deutsche Rundschau* 162 (1915): 248ff; Thayer-Forbes, p. 551—the date of the settlement should be December (not October) 22, 1813.

19. Thayer-Forbes, p. 624; *Letters to Beethoven*, no. 213.

20. Thayer-Forbes, p. 625; *Letters to Beethoven*, no. 213.

21. *Letters*, Appendix C (no. 1), vol. 3, p. 1360; *Briefe*, no. 857.

22. *Ibid.* (no. 2), vol. 3, p. 1361; *Briefe*, no. 861.

23. *Ibid.* (no. 3), vol. 3, p. 1362; *Briefe*, no. 866.

24. *Letters*, no. 607; *Briefe*, no. 897.

25. Kerst, vol. 2, p. 193.

26. *Letters*, no. 603; *Briefe*, no. 893 (to Giannattasio, February 1, 1816).

27. *Letters*, no. 611; *Briefe*, no. 904 (to Giannattasio, February 15, 1816).

28. Solomon, "Tagebuch," nos. 80–81; Leitzmann, vol. 2, p. 256 (no. 92); for another translation, see Michael Hamburger, ed., *Beethoven: Letters, Journals, and Conversations* (Garden City, NY: Anchor, 1960), p. 139.

29. *Letters*, no. 633; *Briefe*, no. 934.

30. Solomon, "Tagebuch," no. 80; Leitzmann, vol. 2, p. 256 (no. 92).

31. *Letters*, no. 654; *Briefe*, no. 971 (September 6, 1816). Translation amended.

32. *Letters*, no. 661; *Briefe*, no. 979 (September 29, 1816). Translation amended.

33. Thayer-Forbes, p. 625; *Letters to Beethoven*, no. 213.

34. Sterba and Sterba, *Beethoven and His Nephew*, pp. 146 and 317.

35. Freud, "Notes Upon a Case of Obsessional Neurosis," in Freud, *Standard Edition*, vol. 10, p. 239.

36. Freud, *The Ego and the Id*, in Freud, *Standard Edition*, vol. 19, p. 43.

37. *Letters*, no. 686; *Briefe*, no. 1019.

38. *Letters*, no. 876; *Briefe*, no. 1153 (to Giannattasio, August 9, 1817).

39. *Letters*, Appendix C (no. 6) (contract between Johanna van Beethoven and Ludwig van Beethoven, May 10, 1817).

40. *Letters*, no. 793; *Briefe*, no. 1149 (July 30, 1817).

41. *Letters*, no. 800; *Briefe*, no. 1157 (to Giannattasio, August 14, 1817).

42. *Letters*, no. 904; *Briefe*, no. 1260 (June 18, 1818).

43. *Letters*, Appendix C (no. 9) (to the *Magistrat der Stadt Wien*, February 1, 1819), vol. 3, pp. 1375–76.

44. *Letters*, no. 658; *Briefe*, no. 976.

45. *Letters*, no. 660; *Briefe*, no. 978.

46. *Letters*, no. 672; *Briefe*, no. 997 (to Giannattasio, November 14, 1816).

47. *Letters*, no. 871; *Briefe*, no. 1152.

48. *Letters*, nos. 618 (to Archduke Rudolph, February 1816) and 636 (to Neate, May 18, 1816); *Briefe*, nos. 887 and 937.

49. *Letters*, no. 598; *Briefe*, no. 1276 (to Giannattasio, end of January 1816). Brandenburg assigns this letter to between December 1818 and June 22, 1819. *Briefe*, vol. 4, p. 220n. 1.

50. *Konversationshefte*, vol. 2, p. 156; Schünemann, vol. 2, p. 157; Sterba and Sterba, *Beethoven and His Nephew*, p. 200.

51. *Letters*, no. 937; *Briefe*, no. 1287 (to Franz Tschischka [not J. B. Bach], ca. February 1, 1819).

52. Breuning, pp. 77–78; Breuning-Solomon, p. 82.

53. *Letters*, no. 937; *Briefe*, no. 1287.

54. Anderson, *The Letters of Mozart*, 2d ed., vol. 1, p. 340 (no. 228b).

55. Sterba and Sterba, *Beethoven and His Nephew*, p. 112.

56. *Letters*, no. 839; *Briefe*, no. 1206 (December 28, 1817).

57. *Letters*, no. 860; *Briefe*, no. 1201 (shortly before December 27, 1817, or perhaps January 1818).

58. *Letters,* no. 841; *Briefe,* no. 1200 (shortly before 17 December 1817, or perhaps between January 13 and 25, 1818).

59. *Letters,* no. 885; *Briefe,* no. 1223 (shortly before January 12, 1818).

60. *Letters,* no. 904; *Briefe,* no. 1260 (June 18, 1818).

61. The relevant sections of her diary are reprinted in Thayer-Deiters-Riemann, vol. 4, pp. 513–41, and in Nohl, *Eine stille Liebe zu Beethoven* (1875; 2d ed., Leipzig: Seeman, 1902); further reminiscences by her are in Prod'homme, *Beethoven, raconté,* pp. 81–93.

62. Frimmel, *Beethoven Studien: Bausteine zu einer Lebensgeschichte des Meisters,* vol. 2 (Munich and Leipzig: Müller, 1906), p. 116.

63. *Letters,* no. 632; *Briefe,* no. 923 (to Ferdinand Ries).

64. *Letters,* no. 633; *Briefe,* no. 934 (to Marie Erdödy, May 13, 1816).

65. Solomon, "Tagebuch," no. 125; Leitzmann, vol. 2, p. 261 (no. 139).

66. Thayer-Deiters-Reimann, vol. 4, p. 544; translated in Sterba and Sterba, *Beethoven and His Nephew,* p. 315.

67. The following citations from the court records appear in Thayer-Deiters-Riemann, vol. 4, pp. 550–54; Thayer-Forbes, pp. 708–11; and Sterba and Sterba, *Beethoven and His Nephew,* pp. 311–13.

68. Thayer-Deiters-Riemann, vol. 4, p. 554; Sterba and Sterba, *Beethoven and His Nephew,* p. 148.

69. Schindler-Moscheles, pp. 70–71; see Schindler-MacArdle, pp. 220–21.

70. *Konversationshefte,* vol. 1, p. 219.

71. *Letters,* no. 979; *Briefe,* no. 1348 (to J. B. Bach, October 27, 1819).

72. *Letters,* Appendix C (no. 9), vol. 3, pp. 1375–77; *Briefe,* no. 1286.

73. *Briefe,* no. 1289; *Letters to Beethoven,* no. 256; translated in Solomon, *Beethoven Essays,* pp. 178–80.

74. *Letters,* Appendix C (no. 10), vol. 3, p. 1381.

75. *Letters,* no. 951; *Briefe,* no. 1314 (to Joseph Karl Bernard, probably July 19, 1819).

76. *Letters,* no. 954; *Briefe,* no. 1321 (to Bernard, August 19, 1819). *Briefe,* no. 1321 is reconstructed from what were formerly regarded as three separate letters (*Letters,* nos. 956, 960, and 954).

77. *Letters,* nos. 960 and 956; both contained in *Briefe,* no. 1321 (to Bernard, August 19, 1819).

78. *Letters,* no. 964; *Briefe,* no. 1315 (to Bernard, ca. July 22, 1819).

79. *Letters,* Appendix C (no. 11), vol. 3, pp. 1382–83.

80. *Letters,* Appendix C (no. 14), vol. 3, pp. 1387–88.

81. *Konversationshefte,* vol. 1, p. 115.

82. *Letters,* no. 1008; *Briefe,* no. 1362 (between November 1819 and early January 1820); *Letters,* Appendix C (no. 15), vol. 3, p. 1400. Martin Cooper observes that Beethoven "was certainly not the first bachelor of high moral principles" to "vent his bad conscience on women in general, and in particular on any woman who thwarted his wishes (and perhaps aroused his desires?) as did Beethoven's sister-in-law Johanna." Cooper, *Beethoven: The Last Decade,* p. 31.

83. Sterba and Sterba, *Beethoven and His Nephew,* p. 175; Thayer-Deiters-Riemann, vol. 4, p. 563.

84. Sterba and Sterba, *Beethoven and His Nephew,* pp. 185–86; Thayer-Deiters-Riemann, vol. 4, p. 565.

85. *Letters,* no. 1007; *Briefe,* no. 1367.

86. *Letters,* Appendix C (no. 15); the original, in facsimile and transcription, is in Dagmar Weise, ed., *Beethoven: Entwurf einer Denkschrift an das Appellationsgericht . . . Facsimile* (BB, 1953); a translation from Kastner-Kapp is in Sterba and Sterba, *Beethoven and His Nephew,* pp. 319–34.

87. See Weise, *Denkschrift,* p. 44n. 1; Kastner-Kapp, pp. 553–54; and Sterba and Sterba, *Beethoven and His Nephew,* p. 324; omitted from *Letters,* vol. 3, p. 1393, apparently in error.

88. *Letters,* no. 1010; *Briefe,* no. 1369.

89. *Konversationshefte,* vol. 1, p. 330.

90. *Letters,* no. 941; *Briefe,* no. 1304 (to Mathias Tuscher, perhaps as early as May 1819, but probably ca. February 1820).

91. Thayer-Forbes, p. 635; *Letters,* no. 611; *Briefe,* no. 904 (to Giannattasio, February 15, 1816).

92. Sterba and Sterba, *Beethoven and His Nephew,* p. 190; *Konversationshefte,* vol. 1, p. 398.

93. Joseph Schmidt-Görg, *Beethoven, die Geschichte seiner Familie,* p. 232n. 54, and Schmidt-Görg, personal communication, March 20, 1973.

94. *Konversationshefte,* vol. 2, p. 153; Schünemann, vol. 2, p. 153.

95. Thayer-Forbes, p. 754.

96. Nohl, *Eine stille Liebe,* p. 124.

97. Thayer-Forbes, p. 644.

98. Frimmel, *Handbuch,* vol. 2, p. 265.

99. Czerny, *Proper Performance,* p. 16.

100. The data on Graz concert life are derived primarily from Erika Eisbacher, "Das Grazer Konzertleben v. 1815 bis März 1839" (Ph.D. dissertation, Karl-Franzens Universität, Graz, 1956), and Ferdinand Bischoff, *Chronik des steiermärkischen Musikvereines* (Graz: Verlag des steiermärkischen Musikvereines, 1890). See also Otto Erich Deutsch, ed., *Schubert: A Documentary Biography* (London: Dent, 1946), and Till Gerrit Waidelich, ed., *Franz Schubert Dokumente 1817–1830,* vol. 1 (Tutzing, Germany: Schneider, 1993).

101. Sterba and Sterba, *Beethoven and His Nephew,* p. 211. For a dissent from the Sterbas' interpretation of Beethoven's character, see Maynard Solomon, "Beethoven and His Nephew: A Reappraisal," *BS,* vol. 2 (1977), pp. 138–71.

102. Kerst, vol. 1, p. 214.

103. Solomon, "Tagebuch," no. 118; Leitzmann, vol. 2, p. 260 (no. 130).

104. Solomon, "Tagebuch," nos. 158–60; Leitzmann, vol. 2, p. 264 (no. 171).

105. Solomon, "Tagebuch," no. 164; Leitzmann, vol. 2, p. 265 (no. 174).

106. The Sterbas connect his harsh condemnation of Johanna to his presumed "disillusionments in the first exemplary love-object." Sterba and Sterba, *Beethoven and His Nephew,* p. 100.

107. Of course, on some level Beethoven knew well the difference between adoption and physical parentage; in his copy of *Othello,* he placed three question marks next to Brabantio's "I had rather to adopt a child than to get it" (Nohl, *Beethoven's Brevier,* p. 3).

108. *Letters,* no. 979; *Briefe,* no. 1348 (to J. B. Bach, October 27, 1819).

109. Abraham, *Clinical Papers,* p. 288.

CHAPTER 19:
PORTRAIT OF AN AGING COMPOSER

1. Frimmel, *Handbuch*, vol. 1, p. 233.
2. Thayer-Forbes, p. 738.
3. Wegeler-Ries, p. 107; translated in *Beethoven Remembered*, p. 95. Translation amended.
4. Thayer-Forbes, p. 644.
5. Thayer-Forbes, p. 647.
6. Nohl, *Beethoven nach den Schilderungen*, p. 141.
7. Henry Edward Krehbiel, *Music and Manners in the Classical Period* (Westminster: Constable, 1898), p. 210; Frimmel, *Handbuch*, vol. 1, p. 237.
8. Schindler-Moscheles, p. 187.
9. Hughes, *A Mozart Pilgrimage*, p. 188.
10. *Ibid.*, p. 189.
11. Krehbiel, *Music and Manners*, pp. 199–200, 209.
12. Thayer-Forbes, p. 944.
13. Thayer-Forbes, p. 965.
14. Kerst, vol. 2, pp. 97–98; Frimmel, *Handbuch*, vol. 2, p. 394.
15. Nohl, *Beethoven nach den Schilderungen*, p. 166; Breuning, p. 40; Breuning-Solomon, p. 49.
16. Dr. Wilhelm Christian Müller, "Etwas über Ludwig van Beethoven," *AMZ* 29 (May 23, 1827): 345–54. Rochlitz, a better writer, retells and expands Müller's description as though he had himself witnessed the scene, which is disputable. See Thayer-Forbes, pp. 800–801; Sonneck, pp. 123–24.
17. Max Unger, "Beethovens Konversationshefte als biographische Quelle," *Musik im Kriege*, nos. 11–12 (February–March 1944): 211; Donald W. MacArdle, "Anton Felix Schindler, Friend of Beethoven," *Music Review* 24 (1963): 53.
18. A. J. P. Taylor, *The Course of German History* (1946; reprint, New York: Capricorn, 1962), p. 54.
19. *Konversationshefte*, vol. 1, p. 346.
20. *Konversationshefte*, vol. 9, p. 168; Nohl, vol. 3, p. 609; J.-G. Prod'homme *Cahiers de conversation de Beethoven* (Paris: Corrêa, 1946), p. 410. For a summary of Conversation Book and other materials of this nature, see Jean Boyer, *Le "romantisme" de Beethoven* (Paris: Didier, 1938), pp. 400–405; see also Frida Knight, *Beethoven and the Age of Revolution* (London: Lawrence & Wishart, 1973), pp. 139–44.
21. *Konversationshefte*, vol. 8, p. 148; Boyer, *Le "romantisme" de Beethoven*, pp. 404–5.
22. *Konversationshefte*, vol. 1, p. 300.
23. *Ibid.*, vol. 3, p. 158; Schünemann, vol. 3, p. 159. Schünemann misreads "Carbonaro" as "Carlomane." See Boyer, *Le "romantisme" de Beethoven* p. 400.
24. *Konversationshefte*, vol. 2, p. 279; Schünemann, vol. 2, p. 286.
25. *Konversationshefte*, vol. 3, p. 298; Schünemann, vol. 3, p. 284.
26. Thayer-Forbes, p. 774.
27. *Konversationshefte*, vol. 2, p. 172.
28. Thayer-Forbes, p. 775.
29. For a wide range of topics in the Conversation Books, see Luigi Magnani, *I Quaderni di conversazione di Beethoven* (Milan and Naples: Ricciardi, 1962), *passim*.
30. Köhler, "Beethoven's Conversation Books," *High Fidelity*, January 1970, p. 59.

31. *Konversationshefte,* vol. 1, p. 212.

32. Marie Pachler-Koschak received a few measures, "Das Schöne zum Guten," WoO 202, during a visit to Beethoven on September 27, 1823. Beethoven intended to dedicate the Sonatas, opp. 110 and 111, to Antonie Brentano.

33. Hughes, *A Mozart Pilgrimage,* p. 191.

34. *Letters,* no. 1175; *Briefe,* no. 1641 (April or early May 1823).

35. Nohl, vol. 3, pp. 827–28n. 30. "Wohin sind Sie heute gegen 7 Uhr beym Haarmarkt auf dem Strich gegangen?" The Latin phrase, as written in Heft 7, 54ᵛ (January 22–February 23, 1820) is also transcribed thus in *Konversationshefte,* vol. 1, p. 254, and Schünemann, vol. 1, p. 249, but is wrongly rendered as "Culpam trans Ge—alium" (i.e., "Blame it on the genitals") in Walther Nohl, ed., *Ludwig van Beethoven: Konversationshefte* (Munich: Allgemeine Verlagsanstalt, 1924), p. 323. Grita Herre reconfirms the reading as *"Culpam transferre in alium"* (personal communication, July 3, 1996). Janitschek is sometimes also spelled Janschickh.

36. *Konversationshefte,* vol. 1, p. 55 and n. 92. L. V. Lagneau, *Die Kunst, alle Arten der Lustseuche zu erkennen, zu heilen, und sich dafür zu sichern,* advertised in *Intelligenzblatt* for April 14, 1819.

37. *Konversationshefte,* vol. 1, p. 184 (the entry was partly obliterated). "Wollen Sie bey meiner Frau schlafen? Es ist so [sehr] kalt." One authority implausibly suggests the entry could be read, "Would you like to sleep over at my wife's place?"

38. Rolland, p. 840.

39. Nohl, vol. 3, pp. 827–28n. 30.

40. *Konversationshefte,* vol. 1, pp. 207–8; Schünemann, vol. 1, p. 205. The former attributes this line to Janitschek.

41. *Konversationshefte,* vol. 1, p. 262.

42. I have dealt with this question in more detail in "Beethoven: The Quest for Faith," *BJ,* 2d series, vol. 10 (1983), pp. 101–19; reprinted in Solomon, *Beethoven Essays,* pp. 216–29.

43. *Letters,* no. 1054; *Briefe,* no. 1436 (July 18, 1821).

44. Nottebohm 2, p. 151.

CHAPTER 20: RECONSTRUCTION

1. *AMZ* 23 (1821): 539; cited in Schindler-MacArdle, p. 231.

2. The date of commencement of opus 109 is the subject of some debate, for on the evidence of the sketches it it difficult to decide whether he commenced work on it in January or, somewhat more likely, in March or April of 1820. On the difficulties in dating the Sonata, see Robert S. Winter, "Reconstructing Riddles: The Sources for Beethoven's *Missa solemnis,*" in Lockwood and Benjamin, *Beethoven Essays,* pp. 234–38; William Meredith, "The Origins of Beethoven's op. 109," *Musical Times* 126 (1985): 713–16, who opts for the earlier date; and Nicholas Marston, "The Origins of Beethoven's op. 109: Further Thoughts," *Musical Times* 127 (1986): 199–201. Johnson, Winter, and Tyson, in *The Beethoven Sketchbooks,* place the commencement in April 1820 (p. 258). Re the later sonatas, they regard the date on opus 110 as its date of completion, and the date on opus 111 as the date the composer began to write out the autograph of the first movement (p. 268). Finally, unlike earlier scholars, who accepted Beethoven's statement that opus 109 was done by September 20, 1820, the authors of *The Beethoven Sketchbooks* suggest that work on it extended until later in the year (p. 374).

3. William Kinderman, in the commentary to his forthcoming edition of the Artaria 195 sketchbook, "Beethoven's Sketchbook for the *Missa solemnis* and the Piano Sonata in E, Op. 109 (Artaria 195)," presented at the annual meeting of the American Musicological Society, Phoenix, 1997, proposes that the autograph scores of the Credo, Sanctus, and Benedictus date from the summer and autumn of 1820; that substantial progress was also achieved at that time on sketching the Agnus Dei and Dona nobis pacem; and that sketches and drafts for the Sonata, op. 110, are datable to August–September 1820. However, the supporting arguments, while eminently plausible, are based on evidence that is somewhat equivocal and tends to reduce Beethoven's already meager productivity in 1821 to an unlikely level.

4. "You are also receiving six bagatelles or *trifles, and again another five,* which belong together, in two parts." *Letters,* no. 1143; *Briefe,* no. 1580 (to Ferdinand Ries, February 25, 1823). As Barry Cooper has shown, all but one of the first group were drawn from a portfolio of "Bagatellen" in which Beethoven deposited various unpublished short piano pieces; from this miscellany he chose five (op. 119, nos. 1–5) written between 1794 and 1802, modified and programmed them to provide a sense of unity, and completed an integral set of six by composing opus 119, no. 6, as a finale in ca. 1822. The newly composed second group, consisting of opus 119, nos. 7–11, and dated January 1, 1821, on the autograph, was published separately in 1821. For full details, see Cooper, *Beethoven and the Creative Process,* pp. 263–82. The early sketches for "Bundeslied" (in Gesellschaft der Musikfreunde, Vienna, manuscript A 64) were first noted in Hans Boettcher, *Beethoven als Liederkomponist* (Augsburg: Benno Filser, 1928), Plate 4; see also Johnson, *Beethoven's Early Sketches in the 'Fischhof Miscellany,'* vol. 1, p. 136.

5. The probability that a complete draft was ready by early 1803 is convincingly argued in Alan Tyson, "Beethoven's 'Kakadu' Variations and their English History," *Musical Times* 104 (1963): 108–10.

6. Kerst, vol. 2, p. 72.

7. *Letters,* no. 1072; *Briefe,* no. 1457 (February 12, 1822).

8. *AMZ* 24 (1822): 310; cited in MacArdle, *Abstracts,* p. 6.

9. Francis Toye, *Rossini: A Study in Tragi-comedy* (New York: Knopf, 1947), p. 86.

10. See Maynard Solomon, "Beethoven's Creative Process: A Two-Part Invention," in Solomon, *Beethoven Essays,* pp. 135–37. Martin Kopitz has seen an entry in Rochlitz's Leipzig diary in which there is a brief entry referring to the day on which he met "poor Beethoven" in a restaurant (personal communication from Sieghard Brandenburg). Rochlitz's "letter" about Beethoven was first published in his *Für ruhige Stunden* (Leipzig, 1828}, and reprinted in Rochlitz, *Für Freunde der Tonkunst* (Leipzig, 1824–32; 3d ed., ed. A. Dörffel, Leipzig, 1868), vol. 4, pp. 222–37; it is reprinted as "Der Besuch des Hofrats Friedrich Rochlitz bei Ludwig van Beethoven in Wien," in *Der Bär. Jahrbuch von B&H* (1927), pp. 166–73.

11. *Letters,* no. 1415; *Briefe,* no. 2043 (to Karl Holz, August 24, 1825); see also Theodor Frimmel, "Ein Konversationsheft Beethovens aus dem Jahre 1825," *BJ,* 1st series, vol. 2 (1909), p. 166.

12. *AMZ* 23 (1821): 539.

13. Wiener Stadt- und Landesarchiv Handschriftensammlung 7/130/12, cited in Rita Steblin, "The Newly Discovered Hochenecker Portrait of Beethoven (1819): 'Das ähnlichste Bildnis Beethovens,'" *JAMS* 45 (1992): 481n. 41.

14. Thayer-Forbes, pp. 983–86.

15. *Letters,* no 1566; *Briefe,* no. 2284 (March 18, 1827).

16. Robert S. Winter, "Of Realizations, Completions, Restorations and Reconstructions: From Bach's *The Art of Fugue* to Beethoven's Tenth Symphony," *Journal of the Royal Musical Association* 116 (1991): 108. Winter deconstructs Cooper's pastiche of the first movement, which has been inappropriately marketed as "Beethoven's Tenth Symphony" (*ibid.*, pp. 101–25). Inasmuch as the work never existed as an organized composition, it is inaccurate for Cooper to describe the movement as a "reconstruction"; rather, it is his own construction utilizing Beethoven's concept sketches among its ingredients.

17. Thayer-Forbes, p. 801.

18. Nohl, vol. 3, p. 308.

19. Thayer-Forbes, p. 811.

20. Schindler-MacArdle, p. 237.

21. *Letters*, no. 1110; *Briefe*, no. 1517.

22. Thayer-Forbes, p. 872.

23. Thayer-Forbes, p. 851.

24. Thayer-Forbes, pp. 897–99; Thayer-Deiters-Riemann, vol. 5, pp. 67–69. Translation amended. Also *Letters to Beethoven*, no. 344.

25. Schindler-MacArdle, p. 275. As scholar Shin Augustinus Kojima has shown, Schindler exaggerated his prior knowledge of the petition (see *Letters to Beethoven*, vol. 3, p. 8).

26. *AMZ* 26 (1824): 437–42; *Wiener AMZ* 8 (1824): 120, 149–51, 157–60, 173–74, reprinted in Stefan Kunze, ed., *Ludwig van Beethoven: Die Werke im Spiegel seiner Zeit: Gesammelte Konzertberichte und Rezensionen bis 1830* (Laaber: Laaber-Verlag, 1987), pp. 426–27, 470–85.

27. *Konversationshefte*, vol. 5, p. 122.

28. Prod'homme, *Cahiers de conversation de Beethoven*, p. 346.

29. Henry E. Dwight, *Travels in the North of Germany in the Years 1825 and 1826* (New York: Carvill, 1829), p. 145.

30. For examples and discussion, see Maynard Solomon, "Beethoven: Beyond Classicism," in Robert S. Winter and Robert Martin, eds., *The Beethoven Quartet Companion* (Berkeley and Los Angeles: University of California Press, 1994), pp. 59–76.

31. Hegel, *The Philosophy of Fine Art*, trans. F. P. B. Osmaston (London: Bell, 1920), vol. 3, p. 417.

32. Thayer-Forbes, p. 767; *Briefe*, no. 1422 (December 29, 1820).

33. *Letters*, nos. 1098 and 1099; *Briefe*, nos. 1494 and 1495.

34. *Letters*, no. 1152; *Briefe*, no. 1608 (March 10, 1823).

35. *Letters*, no. 1226; *Briefe*, no. 1722 (August 2, 1823).

36. *Letters*, no. 1136; *Briefe*, no. 1562 (February 8, 1823). Translation amended.

37. *Letters*, no. 1154; *Briefe*, no. 1611 (March 12–15, 1823). Goethe did not reply; according to Holz, Cherubini replied (see Kerst, vol. 2, p. 184) but his letter has not survived.

38. *Letters*, no. 1217; *Briefe*, no. 1589 (to Pilat, perhaps end of February 1823).

39. *Letters*, no. 1121; *Briefe*, no. 1511.

40. Thayer-Forbes, p. 841.

41. See *Letters*, nos. 1153 (to Simrock, March 10, 1823) and 1158 (to Peters, February 20, 1823, though dated March 20); *Briefe*, nos. 1607 and 1575.

42. Schindler-MacArdle, p. 241. Holz said flatly: "The story . . . is not true" (Kerst, vol. 2, p. 183).

43. Schindler-Moscheles, p. 81.
44. *Letters*, no. 1271; *Briefe*, no. 1812 (April 12 [not early March] 1824). Schindler himself described it as "the greatest distinction conferred upon the master during his lifetime." Schindler-MacArdle, p. 242.
45. *Letters*, no. 1292; *Briefe*, no. 1841 (May 26, 1824).
46. Hughes, *A Mozart Pilgrimage*, p. 189.
47. *Letters*, no. 1407; *Briefe*, no. 2022 (to Schotts Söhne, August 2, 1825).
48. *Letters*, no. 1472; *Briefe*, no. 2136. See reminiscences of Samuel Heinrich Spiker in Prod'homme, *Beethoven raconté*, pp. 228–29.

CHAPTER 21: THE "RETURN" TO BONN

1. *Letters*, no. 1028; *Briefe*, no. 1403 (August 5, 1820). This seems to be the first of these rare references to Bonn since a Tagebuch entry of 1815 (see Solomon, *Tagebuch*, no. 50).
2. *Letters*, no. 1051; *Briefe*, no. 1429 (March 14, 1821).
3. From a letter of April 22, 1827, by Wilhelm Christian Müller, in Theodor Frimmel, "Notizen," *Beethoven-Forschung* 1 (1911): 27.
4. *Konversationshefte*, vol. 1, p. 237; see also vol. 1, p. 225.
5. *Letters*, no. 1078; *Briefe*, no. 1461 (beginning of May 1822).
6. *Letters*, no. 1247; *Briefe*, no. 1693 (after July 3, 1823).
7. *Letters*, no. 1231; *Briefe*, no. 1731 (August 19, 1823).
8. *Letters*, no. 1087; *Briefe*, no. 1486 (July 31, 1822); translated in Thayer-Forbes, p. 799.
9. For details on this and what follows, see *Konversationshefte*, vol. 2, p. 335; vol. 2, pp. 324–30; Schünemann, vol. 2, pp. 307–8; vol. 3, pp. 115–22.
10. *Letters*, no. 1259; *Briefe*, no. 1539 (January 26, 1823).
11. *Letters*, no. 1256; *Briefe*, no. 1538 (January 26, 1823).
12. *Letters*, no. 1257; *Briefe*, no. 1771 (January 8, 1824).
13. *Konversationshefte*, vol. 4, pp. 137–39; Thayer-Forbes, p. 922. The conversation took place in Baden in September 1823 (not 1824, as Schindler assumed).
14. *Letters*, no. 1316; *Briefe*, no. 1894 (October 7, 1824). The reference is to Johanna van Beethoven, whom Beethoven was again starting to demonize. In a Conversation Book of April 1824 he called her "a maternal monster." *Konversationshefte*, vol. 6, p. 20.
15. *Letters*, no. 1359; *Briefe*, no. 1958.
16. *Konversationshefte*, vol. 7, p. 222; Thayer-Forbes, p. 945.
17. *Letters*, no. 1371; *Briefe*, no. 1967 (May 13, 1825).
18. *Konversationshefte*, vol. 7, p. 291; Thayer-Forbes, p. 947.
19. *Letters*, no. 1377; *Briefe*, no. 1978.
20. *Letters*, no. 1379; *Briefe*, no. 1980.
21. *Letters*, no. 1387; *Briefe*, no. 1991 (June 10, 1825).
22. *Letters*, no. 1390; *Briefe*, no. 1996 (June 15, 1825).
23. *Letters*, no. 1380; *Briefe*, no. 2114 (January 22–February 7, 1826; Anderson incorrectly assigns this letter to May 1825).
24. *Letters*, no. 1445; *Briefe*, no. 2074 (October 15, 1825–early August 1826).

25. Memorandum by Marie von Breuning, cited in Thayer-Forbes, p. 968.

26. Thayer-Forbes, p. 999.

27. *Ibid.*, p. 994.

28. Thayer-Deiters-Riemann, vol. 5, p. 353n. 3; Thayer-Forbes, p. 995.

29. *Letters*, no. 1489; *Briefe*, no. 2075 (October 15, 1825–early August 1826; probably June 1826).

30. Thayer-Forbes, p. 991.

31. *Konversationshefte*, vol. 10, pp. 84–85; Thayer-Forbes, p. 995.

32. Formerly, biographies placed the suicide attempt on July 30; the correction stems from fixing the date on which Karl purchased pistols with proceeds from the sale of his watch. See *Konversationshefte*, vol. 10, pp. 67, 89, 95, and 359nn. 290 and 299.

33. *Letters*, no. 1495; *Briefe*, no. 2181 (August 6, 1826).

34. *Konversationshefte*, vol. 10, pp. 89, 95; Thayer-Forbes, p. 1001.

35. *Ibid.*, p. 193; Thayer-Forbes, p. 1003.

36. Thayer-Forbes, p. 1014.

37. *Letters*, no. 1534; *Briefe*, no. 2219 (October 2, 1826).

38. *Letters*, no. 1535; *Briefe*, no. 2223 (October 13, 1826).

39. Thayer-Forbes, p. 1015.

40. Robert Winter, review of Solomon, *Beethoven*, in *Notes: Journal of the Music Library Association* 34 (1978): 849–50.

41. Thayer-Forbes, p. 999.

42. Sterba and Sterba, *Beethoven and His Nephew*, p. 282.

43. *Ibid.*; see also R. Gruneberg, "Karl van Beethoven's 'Suicide,'" *Musical Times* 97 (May 1956): 270.

44. *Konversationshefte*, vol. 10, p. 205; Thayer-Deiters-Riemann, vol. 5, p. 378; Thayer-Forbes, pp. 1003–1004; translated in Sterba and Sterba, *Beethoven and His Nephew*, p. 286.

45. *Letters*, no. 1521; *Briefe*, no. 2197 (September 9, 1826).

46. Thayer-Deiters-Riemann, vol. 5, p. 410; Thayer-Forbes, p. 1013.

47. Wawruch's account of Beethoven's last illness is cited from Thayer-Forbes, pp. 1016–18.

48. *Letters*, no. 1542; *Briefe*, no. 2236 (December 7, 1826). Transcription amended.

49. *Letters*, no. 1526; *Briefe*, no. 2204 (ca. September 22, 1826).

50. *Letters*, Appendix D (no. 6); *Briefe*, no. 2214 (September 27–28, 1826).

51. *Konversationshefte*, vol. 10, p. 190; Prod'homme, *Cahiers de conversation*, p. 426, where the remark is attributed to A. M. Schlesinger.

52. *Konversationshefte*, vol. 10, p. 214; Prod'homme, *Cahiers de conversation*, p. 427.

53. Prod'homme, *Cahiers de conversation*, pp. 426–27; not located in *Konversationshefte*, but see vol. 10, p. 195, where Karl writes, "The decoration, I believe, won't do any good. . . ."

54. Thayer-Deiters-Riemann, vol. 5, p. 369; *Briefe*, no. 2231; *Letters to Beethoven*, no. 445 (November 25, 1826).

55. *Letters*, no. 1546; *Briefe*, no. 2238 (ca. December 12, 1826). Formerly this letter was believed to have been addressed to Prince Franz Ludwig Hatzfeld.

56. Holz to Fanny Linzbauer, cited in Nohl, vol. 3, p. 749, and Nohl, *Beethoven, Liszt, Wagner*, p. 111. See also Holz to Jahn, in Kerst, vol. 2, p. 183.

57. *Letters,* no. 1547; *Briefe,* no. 2246 (to J. B. Bach).

58. Thayer-Forbes, p. 1027; *Briefe,* no. 2250; *Letters to Beethoven,* no. 455.

59. Thayer-Forbes, p. 1022; *Briefe,* no. 2269; *Letters to Beethoven,* no. 464.

60. Breuning, p. 92; see also p. 103; Breuning-Solomon, pp. 95 and 101.

61. Thayer-Forbes, p. 1047.

62. *Letters,* no. 1552; *Briefe,* no. 2258 (February 18, 1827).

63. Minutes of the Philharmonic Society of London for February 28, 1827, cited in Thayer-Forbes, p. 1036.

64. I located Diabelli's unsigned lithograph, long considered lost, in the Bildarchiv of the Österreichische Nationalbibliothek; it is reproduced in Breuning-Solomon, p. 98.

65. Breuning, pp. 98–99; Breuning-Solomon, pp. 98–99.

66. Kerst, vol. 2, p. 230; Sonneck, p. 218.

67. Prod'homme, *Beethoven raconté,* p. 245.

68. Hughes, *A Mozart Pilgrimage,* p. 204.

69. Hiller, cited in Thayer-Forbes, p. 1045.

70. *Letters,* no. 1564; *Briefe,* no. 2279 (March 13, 1827).

71. *Letters,* no. 1569; *Briefe,* no. 2274 (after March 7, 1827).

72. *Letters,* no. 1561; *Briefe,* no. 2278 (March 10, 1827).

73. *Letters,* no. 1547; *Briefe,* no. 2246.

74. Breuning to Beethoven, *Letters to Beethoven,* no. 452; *Briefe,* no. 2247 (after January 3, 1827).

75. *Letters,* no. 1568; *Briefe,* Anhang. See Nohl, vol. 3, p. 781; facsimiles in Ley, *Beethovens Leben in authentischen Bildern und Texten,* p. 140, and *Briefe,* vol. 6, p. 383. Schindler alleged that Breuning's draft of the codicil provided that the capital of Beethoven's legacy was to be held in trust, with his nephew to "draw the interest, and the principal to pass to the nephew's legitimate offspring after his death." Schindler-MacArdle, p. 328.

76. This ironic possibility was first noted by the legal scholar Rudolf Stammler, "Rechtliche Verwicklungen Beethovens," *Welhagen und Klasings Monatshefte* 43, no. 2 (1929): 153; cited in MacArdle, "The Family van Beethoven," *MQ* 35 (1949): 544n. 9.

77. Schindler-MacArdle, p. 328. On March 27, 1827, Dr. Bach filed the testamentary letter of January 3, 1827, with the Vienna *Magistrat.* See *Letters to Beethoven,* no. 471; *Briefe,* vol. 6, p. 335. The codicil was filed with the Vienna Provincial Court (Landgericht).

78. Ley, *Beethoven als Freund der Familie Wegeler–v. Breuning,* p. 236 (Schindler to Moscheles, letter of March 24, 1827); Thayer-Forbes, p. 1048.

79. Krehbiel, *Music and Manners,* p. 204.

80. Thayer-Deiters-Riemann, vol. 5, pp. 490–91; Thayer-Forbes, pp. 1050–51.

81. Thayer-Forbes, p. 1051.

CHAPTER 22: THE MUSIC (LAST PERIOD)

1. C. H. H. Parry, *Style in Musical Art* (London: Macmillan, 1911), p. 95.

2. J.-J. Rousseau, *Écrits sur la musique* (reprint, Paris, 1838), pp. 288–89.

3. Barry Cooper, *Beethoven and the Creative Process,* p. 133.

4. Kerman, *Beethoven Quartets,* p. 196.

5. For full details, see Barry Cooper, *Beethoven's Folksong Settings: Chronology, Sources, Style* (Oxford: Clarendon Press, 1994). Beethoven wrote, "The Scottish songs show how unconstrainedly the most unstructured melody can be treated by harmonic means" (Solomon, *Tagebuch,* no. 34).

6. Adding in fees for Beethoven's instrumental variations on national airs, his total remuneration from these sources amounts to c. 955 ducats. Cooper remarks that the fees "seem fairly generous when placed in context." Barry Cooper, *Beethoven's Folksong Settings,* pp. 99–100.

7. Barry Cooper, *Beethoven's Folksong Settings,* p. 196.

8. Rolland, pp. 527–28.

9. Kerman, *"An die ferne Geliebte," BS,* vol. 1 (1973), p. 154.

10. Philip L. Miller, ed. and trans., *The Ring of Words* (Garden City, NY: Anchor, 1966), p. 147.

11. Rolland, p. 545; Boettcher, *Beethoven als Liederkomponist,* p. 67.

12. Thayer-Forbes, p. 984.

13. Nottebohm, *Beethoven's Studien,* p. 200.

14. Schindler-MacArdle, p. 212.

15. Ludwig Misch, *Neue Beethoven-Studien und andere Themen* (BB, 1967), p. 59.

16. See Kerman, *Beethoven Quartets,* pp. 270–72; d'Indy, *Beethoven,* p. 98; John V. Cockshoot, *The Fugue in Beethoven's Piano Music* (London: Routledge & Kegan Paul, 1959), pp. 145–78. See the comprehensive list in the authoritative work by Warren Kirkendale, *Fuge und Fugato in der Kammermusik des Rokoko und der Klassik* (Tutzing, Germany: Schneider, 1966), pp. 263–64, translated by Margaret Bent and the author as *Fugue and Fugato in Rococo and Classical Chamber Music* (Durham, NC: Duke University Press, 1979), pp. 225–27.

17. See Nottebohm 2, pp. 349 ff.; Hess, p. 24.

18. Wilhelm von Lenz, *Beethoven: Eine Kunst-Studie* (Hamburg: Hoffman & Campe, 1860), vol. 5, p. 32. The suggestion is highly improbable, not least because Hummel's sonata was first published in 1819.

19. *Ibid.* For a summary of reported early performances, see W. S. Newman, "Some Nineteenth-Century Consequences of . . . Opus 106," *Piano Quarterly* 67 (Spring 1969): 12.

20. Riezler, *Beethoven,* p. 227; for analyses of the fugue, see Cockshoot, *The Fugue in Beethoven's Piano Music,* pp. 73–94, and Tovey, *A Companion to Beethoven's Pianoforte Sonatas,* pp. 230–42.

21. Martin Cooper, *Beethoven: The Last Decade,* p. 172.

22. Rolland, pp. 650–51.

23. Rosen, *The Classical Style,* pp. 406–33.

24. *Letters,* no. 939; *Briefe,* no. 1295.

25. Tyson, *Authentic English Editions of Beethoven,* p. 102; Kinsky-Halm, p. 296.

26. But see also Martin Cooper, *Beethoven: The Last Decade,* p. 164, and Rolland, pp. 594–95.

27. Solomon, "Beethoven's Ninth Symphony: The Sense of an Ending," *Critical Inquiry* 17 (Winter 1991): 292.

28. Rosen, *The Classical Style,* p. 434.

29. See Kinsky-Halm, pp. 311–19, which is now somewhat out of date.

30. Cited in Tovey, *Essays in Musical Analysis: Chamber Music* (London: Oxford University Press, 1944), p. 124.

31. *Ibid.*, pp. 126–27.

32. Karl Geiringer, "The Structure of Beethoven's Diabelli Variations," *MQ* 50 (1964): 496–503. See August Halm, *Beethoven* (Berlin: Max Hesse, 1927), pp. 176–203, 263–302. Uhde sees a four-movement variation-symphony, but concludes that "a general consensus concerning this is scarcely possible, for the work permits so much elbow room for interpretations that other orderings appear also possible. Beethoven's own conception remains a mystery. And this mystery is one ingredient of the work." Jürgen Uhde, *Beethovens Klaviermusik I: Klavierstücke und Variationen* (Stuttgart: Philipp Reclam, 1968; 2d ed., 1980), p. 556.

33. The Bagatelles, op. 119, nos. 7 and 8, have been regarded as spin-offs from opus 120.

34. Walker, *Beethoven*, p. 149.

35. Eric Blom, *Classics: Major and Minor* (London: Dent, 1958), p. 78.

36. Nottebohm 2, p. 196.

37. Comment on a leaf of sketches of 1824, cited in Nohl, vol. 3, p. 512.

38. Schindler-Moscheles, pp. 179–80.

39. Weissenbach, cited in MacArdle, "Beethoven and the Archduke Rudolph," *BJ*, 2d series, vol. 4 (1962), p. 41; Nottebohm 1, p. 152.

40. J. F. Reichardt, *Vertraute Briefe*, ed. G. Gugitz (Munich: Müller, 1915), vol. 2, p. 95; Thayer-Deiters-Riemann, vol. 3, p. 189.

41. See *Letters*, nos. 938 (to Ries, March 8, 1819), 939 (to Ries, ca. March 20, 1819), 948 (to Archduke Rudolph, March 3, 1819), and 1016 (to Rudolph, April 3, 1820); *Briefe*, nos. 1294, 1295, 1292, and 1378.

42. See *Letters*, nos. 1134, 1135, and 1136; *Briefe*, nos. 1550, 1563, 1562, and Anhang (all early February 1823). Also *Letters*, no. 1292; *Briefe*, no. 1841 (to Prince Galitzin, May 26, 1824).

43. Schmitz sees no contradiction here, because the oratorio is also one of the main forms of religious music (Schmitz, *Romantische*, pp. 100–101).

44. *Letters*, no. 1278; *Briefe*, no. 1810 (to the Imperial Censor, Franz Sartori, after April 10, 1824).

45. *Letters*, no. 1029; *Briefe*, no. 1407 (August 30, 1820); see also Schmitz, *Romantische*, p. 100n. 3.

46. Rolland, pp. 674 and 677.

47. *Letters*, no. 1307; *Briefe*, no. 1875 (September 16, 1824).

48. *Letters*, no. 1248; *Briefe*, no. 1438 (July–August 1821).

49. Cited in Warren Kirkendale, "New Roads to Old Ideas in Beethoven's *Missa Solemnis*," *MQ* 56 (1970): 676.

50. Solomon, "Tagebuch," no. 168; Leitzmann, vol. 2, p. 265 (no. 177); Thayer-Forbes, p. 715.

51. Solomon, "Tagebuch," no. 155; Leitzmann, vol. 2, p. 263 (no. 167). C. P. E. Bach's "Zwei Litaneyen . . . für acht Singstimmen in zwei Chören," published in Copenhagen, 1786 (Nottebohm, *Ein Skizzenbuch von Beethoven aus dem Jahre 1803*, p. 77n. 3).

52. Kirkendale, "New Roads to Old Ideas," p. 666.

53. *Letters*, no. 1161; *Briefe*, no. 1621 (March 25, 1823).

54. Lang, *Music in Western Civilization*, p. 768.

55. *Letters*, no. 1079; *Briefe*, no. 1468 (to Carl Friedrich Peters, June 5, 1822).

56. Bekker, *Beethoven*, p. 274.

57. Ernest Newman, notes to the Toscanini recording (RCA LM 6013).

58. William Mann, notes to the Klemperer recording (Angel B-3679).

59. *Letters*, no. 85; *Briefe*, no. 169 (November 2, 1803).

60. Solomon, "Tagebuch," no. 114; Leitzmann, vol. 2, p. 260 (no. 126). The quotation is from Pliny, *Epistles*, book 3, letter 21, line 6.

61. *Konversationshefte*, vol. 3, pp. 158–59; Schünemann, vol. 3, p. 160.

62. *Ibid.*

63. Riezler, *Beethoven*, p. 198.

64. Martin Buber, *Paths in Utopia* (Boston: Beacon, 1960), p. 7.

65. Solomon, *Beethoven Essays*, p. 30.

66. *BJ*, 1st series, vol. 2 (1909), pp. 331–32; Thayer-Forbes, pp. 120–21; letter to Charlotte Schiller, January 26, 1793. For a full discussion, see Maynard Solomon, "Beethoven und Schiller," *Beiträge zur Musikwissenschaft* 23 (1981): 91–103, abridged as "Beethoven and Schiller," in Solomon, *Beethoven Essays*, pp. 205–15.

67. Nottebohm 2, p. 479; *Simrock Jahrbuch* 2 (1929): 26 (letter of September 13, 1803); *Briefe*, no. 155; *Letters to Beethoven*, no. 67. See also Willy Hess, *Beethoven-Studien* (BB, 1972), pp. 113–14.

68. Bauer, *150 Jahre Theater an der Wien*, pp. 80–82.

69. Boettcher, *Beethoven als Liederkomponist*, p. 45; Thayer-Forbes, p. 472.

70. Nottebohm 2, p. 282; Boettcher, pp. 44–45. Also the canons, WoO 163 and WoO 166.

71. Nottebohm 1, p. 41; Nottebohm 2, p. 168.

72. Nottebohm 2, pp. 328–29.

73. Martin Cooper, *Beethoven: The Last Decade*, p. 281.

74. D'Indy, *Beethoven*, p. 114.

75. Rudolph Reti, *The Thematic Process in Music* (New York: Macmillan, 1951), p. 22.

76. D. F. Tovey, *Beethoven's Ninth Symphony* (1922; rev. ed., London: Oxford, 1928), pp. 24 and 36.

77. *Ibid.*, p. 36.

78. Nottebohm 2, pp. 189–90, with slight alterations based on the presumptive reading in A. C. Kalischer, "Die Beethoven-Autographe der Königl. Bibliothek zu Berlin," *Monatshefte für Musik-Geschichte* 28 (1896): 19.

79. As Max Rudolf has shown, the designation of the poem as an "Ode to Joy" does not derive from Schiller, who called it simply "An die Freude" (To Joy). Rudolf, "Beethoven's 'An die Freude' and Two Mysterious Footnotes," *Beethoven Newsletter* 5 (1990): 29–33. Beethoven was not the first to use the designation: Carl Immanuel Engel set Schiller's poem under that title as one of the Masonic songs in *XII Lieder mit Begleitung des Claviers* (Leipzig, [1789]) and an early collection of settings is titled *Vierzehn Compositionen zu Schiller's Ode an die Freude von Anonymus, von Dalberg, Christmann, J. C. Müller, W. Schulz, A. B. Schulz, C. F. Schulze, Seidel, Rellstab, Willing, Zelter, und zwey Ungenannten* (Hamburg, ca. 1799–1800).

80. Nottebohm 1, p. 41.

81. Nietzsche, *The Birth of Tragedy*, p. 23.

82. Rolland, pp. 977 f.; see also Otto Baensch, *Aufbau und Sinn des Chorfinales in Beethovens neunter Symphonie* (Berlin and Leipzig: Walter de Gruyter, 1930), pp. 94–95.

83. Grove, *Beethoven and His Nine Symphonies*, p. 364; Kalischer, "Die Beethoven-Autographe," p. 19, lends itself to a different reading.

84. Thayer-Forbes, p. 888.

85. Kerman, *Beethoven Quartets*, p. 194.

86. Heinrich Schenker, *Beethovens neunte Sinfonie* (Vienna: Universal, 1912), p. 268; translated and edited by John Rothgeb as *Beethoven's Ninth Symphony* (New Haven and London, 1992), p. 243.

87. Herbert Marcuse, *An Essay on Liberation* (Boston: Beacon, 1969), pp. 46–47.

88. Max Raphael, *The Demands of Art* (Princeton: Princeton University Press, 1968), p. 187.

89. *Letters*, no. 1308; *Briefe*, no. 1881 (to Schotts Söhne, September 17, 1824).

90. Immanuel Kant, *The Critique of Aesthetic Judgement*, trans. James Creed Meredith (Oxford: Clarendon Press, 1911), p. 34.

91. Schiller, *Letters on the Aesthetic Education of Man*, in *The Works of Friedrich Schiller: Aesthetical and Philosophical Essays*, ed. N. H. Dole (New York: Bigelow, Brown, 1902), letter 9.

92. Hegel, *The Philosophy of Fine Art*, vol. 1 (London: Bell, 1920), p. 208.

93. Schiller, *Letters on the Aesthetic Education of Man*, letter 2.

94. Thayer-Forbes, p. 815; *Briefe*, no. 1508; *Letters to Beethoven*, no. 299.

95. *Letters*, no. 1123; *Briefe*, no. 1535. Due to Galitzin's later financial difficulties, Beethoven never received full payment for the dedications.

96. *Letters*, no. 1079; *Briefe*, no. 1468. The earliest sketches of opus 127 contain the legend "Quartet for Peters" (Nohl, vol. 3, p. 512).

97. Rolland, p. 1030; Lenz, *Beethoven: Eine Kunst-Studie*, vol. 5, p. 221; see also Max Unger, "Neue Briefe an Beethoven," *Neue Zeitschrift für Musik* 81 (1914): 409ff.; *Briefe*, nos. 1475 and 1480; *Letters to Beethoven*, nos. 294–95 (July 3 and 12, 1822).

98. Rolland, p. 1029.

99. *Letters*, no. 1144; *Briefe*, no. 1581. Transcription amended.

100. *Letters*, Appendix G (no. 17) (to Schlesinger, September 10, 1825).

101. Nohl, *Letters of Distinguished Musicians* (London: Longmans, Green, 1867), p. 56.

102. See Eduard Hanslick, *Geschichte des Concertwesens in Wien* (Vienna: Braumüller, 1869), pp. 202–7; Rolland, p. 1036.

103. *Konversationshefte*, vol. 5, p. 120; see also Anton Schindler, *Biographie von Ludwig van Beethoven*, 2d ed. (Münster: Aschendorff, 1845), Supplement, p. 64, and Rolland, p. 1040.

104. *Konversationshefte*, vol. 7, p. 82; translation in Thayer-Forbes, p. 938.

105. Böhm, cited in Thayer-Forbes, p. 940.

106. *Konversationshefte*, vol. 10, p. 104.

107. *Ibid.*, p. 185.

108. *Ibid.*, p. 307.

109. DSB, Heft 126, fol. 14^v (unpublished).

110. DSB, Heft 126, fol. 13^v (unpublished).

111. Nohl, vol. 3, p. 964.

112. Stefan Kunze, ed., *Ludwig van Beethoven: Die Werke im Spiegel seiner Zeit*, pp. 559–60; Schindler-MacArdle, p. 307.

113. Lenz, *Beethoven: Eine Kunst-Studie*, vol. 5, p. 218.

114. See Ivan Mahaim, *Beethoven: Naissance et renaissance des derniers quatuors* (Paris: de Brouwer, 1964), vol. 2, pp. 442–71, for performances to 1875.

115. Lenz, *Beethoven: Eine Kunst-Studie*, vol. 5, pp. 216–17.

116. The authoritative treatment of the autograph sources is William Kinderman,

Beethoven's Diabelli Variations. Studies in Musical Genesis and Structure, ed. Lewis Lockwood (Oxford: Clarendon Press, 1989), pp. 3–60; Kinderman, "The Evolution and Structure of Beethoven's 'Diabelli' Variations," *JAMS* 35 (1982): 306–09.

117. Martin Cooper, *Beethoven: The Last Decade,* p. 421.

118. Kerman, *Beethoven Quartets,* pp. 229, 265–66; see also Rolland, p. 1071.

119. Kerst, vol. 2, p. 188; Lenz, *Beethoven: Eine Kunst-Studie,* vol. 5, p. 217.

120. Kerman, *Beethoven Quartets,* p. 239.

121. *Ibid.,* p. 241.

122. Erich Schenk, "Barock bei Beethoven," in *Beethoven und die Gegenwart,* ed. Arnold Schmitz (Berlin and Bonn: Dümmler, 1937), pp. 210–16.

123. Lenz, *Beethoven: Eine Kunst-Studie,* vol. 5, pp. 218–19.

124. Mahaim, p. 419. (I cannot locate an earlier source for this quotation, which may be apocryphal.)

125. Kerman, *Beethoven Quartets,* p. 268.

126. Bekker, *Beethoven,* p. 331.

127. Thayer-Deiters-Riemann, vol. 5, p. 298; O. G. Sonneck, *Beethoven Letters in America* (New York: Beethoven Association, 1927), p. 79; Mahaim, p. 422.

128. Lenz, *Beethoven: Eine Kunst-Studie,* vol. 5, p. 219; Mahaim, p. 436n. 11; see also Holz to Jahn, in Thayer-Deiters-Riemann, vol. 5, p. 298n. 3.

129. *Konversationshefte,* vol. 10, p. 185.

130. *Ibid.,* p. 197.

131. Lenz, *Beethoven: Eine Kunst-Studie,* vol. 5, p. 216.

132. Riezler, *Beethoven,* p. 239.

133. Kerman, *Beethoven Quartets,* p. 322; see also p. 374.

134. Cited in Mahaim, p. 417.

135. *The New York Review of Books,* September 26, 1968, pp. 3–4.

136. Radcliffe, *Beethoven's String Quartets,* p. 173.

137. Kerman, *Beethoven Quartets,* p. 354.

138. Martin Cooper, *Beethoven: The Last Decade,* pp. 413–14; Antonio Bruers, *Beethoven: Catalogo storico-critico di tutte le opera,* 3d ed. (Rome: Giovanni Bardi, 1944), p. 317.

139. Max Raphael, *Prehistoric Cave Paintings* (New York: Pantheon, 1945), p. 17.

140. *Letters,* no. 1068; *Briefe,* no. 1216 (to Treitschke, 1818–22). Translation amended.

Selected Bibliography

(For abbreviated items, see pages 427–30.)
The bibliography is arranged by topic, as follows:

BEETHOVEN'S WORKS AND WRITINGS

COLLECTED WORKS

A modern complete edition, *Ludwig van Beethoven. Werke,* edited by Joseph Schmidt-Görg, Martin Staehelin, Sieghard Brandenburg, and Ernst Herttrich on behalf of the Beethoven Archiv in Bonn, has been in progress since 1961 (28 vols. to 1998). Many volumes are expertly annotated and others lack any critical apparatus. The older standard edition, *Beethovens Werke: Kritische Gesamtausgabe,* 25 vols. (Leipzig: B&H, 1862–65, 1888), is still widely used despite its numerous inaccuracies. Omissions from the latter are listed in Willy Hess, *Verzeichnis der nicht in der Gesamtausgabe veröffentlichten Werke Ludwig van Beethovens* (Wiesbaden: B&H, 1957). Hess edited the *Supplemente zur Gesamtausgabe,* 14 vols. (Wiesbaden: B&H, 1959–71).

SKETCHES AND AUTOGRAPHS

The publication, reconstruction, and analysis of Beethoven's sketches has been the most active and fruitful field in late-twentieth-century Beethoven scholarship. About eight thousand pages of sketches survive, in more than seventy desk and pocket sketchbooks, score sketches for the late quartets and other works, and some 350 individual pages, bifolia, and sketch miscellanies. A provisional inventory of these is in Hans Schmidt, "Verzeichnis der Skizzen Beethovens," *BJ,* 2d series, 6 (1969): 7–128. An earlier brief list is in Josef Braunstein, *Beethovens Leonore-Ouvertüren* (Leipzig: B&H, 1927), pp. 159–60.

The authoritative catalogue raisonée and reconstruction of the sketchbooks—but not, apart from some special cases, of the individual sketch leaves or miscellanies of sketches—is the encyclopedic Douglas Johnson, Robert S. Winter, and Alan Tyson, *The Beethoven Sketchbooks: History, Reconstruction, Inventory,* ed. Douglas Johnson (Berkeley and Los Angeles: University of California Press, and Oxford: Oxford University Press, 1985), an indispensable reference work. Gustav Nottebohm published commentaries with copious music examples of two sketchbooks, including that of the *Eroica* Symphony, and provided more selective excerpts from a wide variety of sketches in shorter essays gathered into two seminal volumes, *Beethoveniana* (Leipzig: Peters, 1872) and the posthumous *Zweite Beethoveniana* (Leipzig: Rieter-Biedermann, 1887).

Other significant early descriptions are in Nohl, *Beethoven, Liszt, Wagner* (Vienna: Braumüller, 1874), pp. 95–101, and two series of articles by J. S. Shedlock in *Musical Times* 33–35 (1892–94). Transcriptions (sometimes accompanied by facsimiles) of about a dozen sketchbooks and autograph miscellanies have been published in the twentieth century, prepared by Cecilio de Roda, Arnold Schmitz, M. Ivanov-Boretsky, K. L. Mikulicz, Nathan L. Fishman (or Fischman), Wilhelm Virneisel, Dagmar Busch-Weise, Joseph Schmidt-Görg, Joseph Kerman, Sieghard Brandenburg, Clemens Brenneis, and Richard Kramer. A large-scale edition, *Skizzen und Entwürfe,* Veröffentlichungen des Beethovenhauses in Bonn, neue Folge, erste Reihe, has long been under way, but is proceeding at a deliberate pace.

The basic modern literature on the sketches includes Alan Tyson, "Sketches and Autographs," in Denis Arnold and Nigel Fortune, eds., *The Beethoven Reader* (New York: Norton, 1971), pp. 443–58; Alan Tyson and Douglas Johnson, "Reconstructing

Beethoven's Sketchbooks," *JAMS* 25 (1972): 137–56; Lewis Lockwood, "On Beethoven's Sketches and Autographs: Some Problems of Definition and Interpretation," *Acta Musicologica* 42 (1970): 32–47, reprinted in Lewis Lockwood, *Beethoven: Studies in the Creative Process* (Cambridge, MA: Harvard University Press, 1992), pp. 4–16; Joseph Kerman, "Beethoven's Early Sketches," *MQ* 56 (1970): 515–38; and Kerman, "Beethoven Sketchbooks in the British Museum," *Proceedings of the Royal Musical Association* 93 (1966–67): 77–93. An influential paper on Beethoven's revisions of his autograph scores is Emil Platen, "Beethovens Autographen als Ausgangspunkt morphologischer Untersuchungen," in Carl Dahlhaus, et al., eds., *Bericht über den internationalen musikwissenschaftlichen Kongress Bonn 1970* (Kassel: Bärenreiter, 1971), pp. 534–36. The authoritative monograph on the chronology of the Bonn and early Vienna works is Douglas Porter Johnson, *Beethoven's Early Sketches in the "Fischhof Miscellany," Berlin Autograph 28,* 2 vols. (Ann Arbor: UMI Research Press, 1980). In his "Beethoven Scholars and Beethoven's Sketches," *Nineteenth-Century Music* 2 (1978–79): 3–17, Johnson questioned the utility of sketch studies for a critical understanding of the music. See also *Nineteenth-Century Music* 2 (1978–79): 270–79; and *Nineteenth-Century Music* 3 (1979): 187–88, for rejoinders from Sieghard Brandenburg, William Drabkin, and Richard Kramer, with further comment from Johnson. See also Lewis Lockwood, "The Beethoven Sketchbooks and the General State of Sketch Research," in William Kinderman, ed., *Beethoven's Compositional Process,* North American Beethoven Studies, I (Lincoln: University of Nebraska Press and American Beethoven Society, 1991), pp. 6–13, and Joseph Kerman, "Sketch Studies," in D. Kern Holomon and Claude V. Palisca, eds., *Musicology in the 1980's* (New York: Da Capo, 1982), pp. 53–66. A wide-ranging stylistic interpretation is Paul Mies, *Beethoven's Sketches* (London: Oxford, 1929; reprint, New York: Johnson Reprint, 1969). Barry Cooper, *Beethoven and the Creative Process* (Oxford: Clarendon Press, 1990) contains commendable studies of sketches for a variety of selected works but is less valuable for insight into Beethoven's artistic aims.

For comparative textual problems in Beethoven's autographs and original editions, see Hubert Unverricht, *Die Eigenschriften und die Originalausgaben von Werken Beethovens in ihrer Bedeutung für die moderne Textkritik* (Kassel: Bärenreiter, 1960), and Paul Mies, *Textkritische Untersuchungen bei Beethoven* (BB, 1957).

Now in need of minor updating are William Drabkin's trustworthy lists of published facsimiles and/or transcriptions of sketch manuscripts and facsimile editions of Beethoven autograph scores in *TNG,* vol. 2, p. 414, and *The New Grove Beethoven,* (New York: Norton, 1983), pp. 208–9; compare the lists in Barry Cooper, William Drabkin, Anne-Louise Coldicott, and Nicholas Marston, *Beethoven Compendium: A Guide to Beethoven's Life and Music* (London: Thames and Hudson, 1991), pp. 185–90.

LETTERS

The standard English edition is Emily Anderson, ed. and trans., *The Letters of Beethoven,* 3 vols. (London: Macmillan, 1961), a model of elegant translation and succinct annotation. The first collection of letters to Beethoven, along with some Beethoven letters omitted from Anderson, is Theodore Albrecht, ed., *Letters to Beethoven and Other Correspondence,* 3 vols. (Lincoln: University of Nebraska Press, 1996); thoroughly annotated, though in sometimes awkward translation, it now serves as a worthy supplement to Anderson. Anderson's edition superseded A. C. Kalischer, ed., *The Letters of Ludwig van*

Beethoven, 2 vols. (London: Dent, 1909), trans. J. S. Shedlock—a first-rate translation. About five hundred items omitted from Kalischer-Shedlock appear in *New Beethoven Letters,* ed. and trans. Donald W. MacArdle and Ludwig Misch (Norman: University of Oklahoma Press, 1957) in sure translation and with superb annotations.

The state-of-the-art German edition, featuring many previously uncollected letters, expert annotations, and highly accurate transcriptions based on the original autographs where available, is Sieghard Brandenburg, ed., *Ludwig van Beethoven: Briefwechsel, Gesamtausgabe,* Beethovenhaus edition, 8 vols. (Munich: G. Henle-Verlag, 1996–), of which all but a volume of documents are already published. A preliminary volume for that edition is *Der Briefwechsel mit dem Verlag Schott* (Munich: Henle, 1985). Earlier German collected editions include A. C. Kalischer and Theodor Frimmel, eds., *Beethovens sämtliche Briefe,* 2d ed., 5 vols. (Berlin and Leipzig: Schuster & Loeffler, 1908–11); Fritz Prelinger, ed., *Ludwig van Beethovens sämtliche Briefe und Aufzeichnungen,* 5 vols. (Vienna and Leipzig: Stern, 1907–11); and Emerich Kastner and Julius Kapp, eds., *Ludwig van Beethovens sämtliche Briefe* (Leipzig: Hesse & Becker, [1923]); although the text of Kastner-Kapp is not annotated and the transcriptions have been slightly modernized, it was until 1996 the most complete and convenient German edition. Other pioneering collections include Ludwig Nohl, ed., *Briefe Beethovens* (Stuttgart: Cotta, 1865) and *Neue Briefe Beethovens* (Stuttgart: Cotta, 1867); Leopold Schmidt, ed., *Beethoven-Briefe* (Berlin: Simrock, 1909); Max Unger, ed., *Ludwig van Beethoven und seine Verleger S. A. Steiner und Tobias Haslinger in Wien, Adolf Martin Schlesinger in Berlin* (Berlin and Vienna: Schlesinger, 1921); O. G. Sonneck, ed., *Beethoven Letters in America* (New York: Schirmer, 1927); and Joseph Schmidt-Görg, ed., *Dreizehn unbekannte Briefe an Josephine Gräfin Deym geb. v. Brunsvik* (BB, 1957; reprint, 1986). Three volumes of a complete edition in Russian translation, *Pisma Betchovena,* edited by the noted scholar Nathan L. Fischman with Larissa Kirillina, have been published (Moscow, 1970, 1977, 1986); vol. 4 is in preparation. The watermarks of numerous letters are described in Joseph Schmidt-Görg, "Wasserzeichen in Beethoven-Briefen," *BJ,* 2d series, 5 (1966): 7–74. For Beethoven's handwriting, see Max Unger, *Beethovens Handschrift,* Veröffentlichungen des Beethovenhauses in Bonn, no. 4 (Leipzig: Quelle & Meyer, 1926), and Max Unger, "Beethovens Handschrift," *Die Musik* 17 (1925): 432–41. Guidelines for editing Beethoven's collected letters are set forth in Alan Tyson, "Prolegomena to a Future Edition of Beethoven's Letters," *BS* 2: 1–19.

CONVERSATION BOOKS

The monumental edition, *Ludwig van Beethovens Konversationshefte,* Karl-Heinz Köhler, Grita Herre, Dagmar Beck, at al., eds. (Leipzig: VEB Deutscher Verlag für Musik, 1968–), is nearing completion. Of eleven projected volumes plus a comprehensive index, ten carefully and expertly annotated volumes have appeared up to 1993, though vols. 4 and 5 lack individual indexes. An earlier edition of vols. 1–3 is Georg Schünemann, ed., *Ludwig van Beethovens Konversationshefte,* 3 vols. (Berlin: Hesse, 1941–43). In many instances, Schünemann's readings and handwriting identifications vary from those of *Konversationshefte.* A French edition of excerpts from the entire range of Conversation Books is J.-G. Prod'homme, ed. and trans., *Cahiers de conversation de Beethoven, 1819–27* (Paris: Corrêa, 1946). Schindler's falsified entries are identified and listed in Herre and Beck, "Anton Schindlers fingierte Eintragungen in den Konversationsheften," *Zu Beethoven* 1 (ed. Harry Goldschmidt, published by Neue

Musik, Berlin, 1979): 11–89, and are marked with an asterisk in the later volumes; an eight-page *Verzeichnis der fingierten Eintragungen Anton Schindlers* was issued by the publishers of the complete edition and provides a convenient guide to the forgeries as published in vols. 1, 2, 4, 5, and 6. There is no English edition of the Conversation Books. Schünemann, Prod'homme, and an earlier edition of volume 1, edited by Walther Nohl (Munich: Allgemeine Verlaganstalt, 1924) are indexed in Donald Mac-Ardle, *An Index to Beethoven's Conversation Books* (Detroit: Information Service, 1962). Unsystematic excerpts from the Conversation Books appear in various biographical writings, especially those by Schindler, Nohl, Thayer, Kerst, Volkmann, and Kalischer. A loose commentary on some of the subjects discussed in the Conversation Books is Luigi Magnani, *I Quaderni di conversazione di Beethoven* (Milan and Naples: Ricciardi, 1962), translated into German by Ragni Maria Gschwend (Munich: Piper, 1967).

OTHER SOURCE WRITINGS

A fundamental source is Beethoven's *Tagebuch, 1812–18*, published in a bilingual edition with extensive commentary in Maynard Solomon, "Beethoven's Tagebuch of 1812–1818," *BS* 3 (1982): 193–288; a revised edition in English translation only is in Solomon, *Beethoven Essays*, pp. 233–95. The Italian and German translations of Solomon, *Tagebuch*, with complete facsimiles of the copyist's autograph are *Il Diario di Beethoven*, trans. Claudio Salone (Milan: Mursia Editore, 1992), and *Beethovens Tagebuch*, translated under the supervision of S. Brandenburg (Mainz: Hase & Koehler, 1990); the latter requires laid-in errata pages for the "Author's Foreword" and a serious typographical mishap on p. 184. Superseded older editions are in Ludwig Nohl, *Die Beethoven-Feier und die Kunst der Gegenwart* (Vienna: Braumüller, 1871), pp. 52–74, and Albert Leitzmann, ed., *Ludwig van Beethoven: Berichte der Zeitgenossen, Briefe und persönliche Aufzeichnungen*, 2d ed., 2 vols. (Leipzig: Insel, 1921), vol. 2, pp. 241–66, the latter using the third-generation copy of the Tagebuch preserved in a collection of materials for a projected early biography, the so-called Fischhof Manuscript in the DSB.

The notebook that Beethoven kept from late 1792 to early 1794 is transcribed in Dagmar von Busch-Weise, ed., "Beethovens Jugendtagebuch," *Studien zur Musikwissenschaft* 25 (published by Hermann Böhlaus, Graz, 1962): 68–88. A collection of Beethoven's excerpts and marked passages from several of his favorite authors (Homer, Goethe, Sturm, Shakespeare, etc.) is in Ludwig Nohl, ed., *Beethoven's Brevier* (Leipzig: Günther, 1870). No systematic collection exists of Beethoven's prose notations written on autographs and leaves of sketches, but see Nottebohm 1 and Nottebohm 2, *passim.*, and Friedrich Kerst, ed., *Beethoven im eigenen Wort* (Berlin: Schuster & Loeffler, 1904); an English edition was translated by H. E. Krehbiel (New York: Huebsch, 1905). Annotated facsimiles of other important documents include Hedwig Müller v Asow, *Beethoven. Heiligenstädter Testament, Faksimile* (Vienna: Doblinger, 1969); Max Braubach, ed., *Die Stammbücher Beethovens und der Babette Koch. Faksimile* (BB, 1970; 2d ed., 1995); Hans Gerstinger, ed., *Ludwig van Beethovens Stammbuch* (Leipzig: Velhagen & Klasing, 1927); Dagmar Weise, ed., *Beethoven: Entwurf einer Denkschrift an das Appellationsgericht . . . Faksimile* (BB, 1953). The Fischhof manuscript, excepting the Tagebuch, is transcribed in Clemens Brenneis, "Das Fischhof-Manuskript in der Deutschen Staatsbibliothek," *Zu Beethoven* 2 (1984): 27–87; see also Brenneis, "Das Fischhof-Manuskript. Zur Frühgeschichte der Beethoven-Biographik," *Zu Beethoven* 1 (1979): 90–116.

REFERENCE WORKS

CATALOGUES

Thematic catalogues of Beethoven's works by B&H (1851), A. W. Thayer (1865), Gustav Nottebohm (1868), and Antonio Bruers (1951) were superseded by the standard work, Georg Kinsky and Hans-Halm, *Das Werk Beethovens. Thematisch Bibliographisches Verzeichnis* . . . (Munich: Henle, 1955). It contains a systematic, thematic list of all the completed published works, together with detailed descriptions of the autographs, early editions, and published arrangements as well as cross-references to the published sketches, correspondence, and critical literature. A supplementary volume, Kurt Dorfmüller, ed., *Beiträge zur Beethoven-Bibliographie* (Munich: Henle, 1978), contains addenda and corrigenda to Kinsky-Halm, several articles on watermarks, manuscript holdings, and authentic or authoritative editions. A more modest but still useful catalogue is Giovanni Biamonti, *Catalogo Cronologico e Tematico delle Opere di Beethoven* (Turin: ILTE, 1968). A valuable special catalogue is Alan Tyson, *The Authentic English Editions of Beethoven* (London: Faber, 1963). The final four volumes of Wilhelm von Lenz, *Beethoven: Eine Kunst-Studie* (Hamburg: Hoffman & Campe, 1860) are a database of catalogue listings, analyses, and historical detail, entitled *Kritischer Katalog sämmtlicher Werke Ludwig van Beethovens mit Analysen derselben.*

Beethoven manuscript holdings in various collections have been catalogued as follows: The Beethovenhaus Bonn: Hans Schmidt, "Die Beethovenhandschriften des Beethovenhauses in Bonn," *BJ*, 2d series, 7 (1971): 1–443; Schmidt, "Addenda and Corrigenda," *BJ*, 2d series, 8 (1975): 207–20. The H. C. Bodmer collection, now in the Beethovenhaus Bonn, is catalogued in Max Unger, ed., *Eine schweizer Beethovensammlung: Katalog* (Zürich: Corona, 1939).

The Staatsbibliothek zu Berlin (formerly, Deutsche Staatsbibliothek, East Berlin): Eveline Bartlitz, *Die Beethoven-Sammlung in der Musikabteilung der Deutschen Staatsbibliothek: Verzeichnis* (Berlin: Deutsche Staatsbibliothek, 1970).

The Staatsbibliothek Preussischer Kulturbesitz, Berlin: Hans-Günter Klein, *Ludwig van Beethoven: Autographe und Abschriften*. Katalog (Berlin, 1975).

Bibliothèque Nationale, Paris: Max Unger, "Die Beethovenhandschriften des Parisien-Konservatoriumsbibliothek," *NBJ* 6 (1935): 87–123.

The British Library: Augustus Hughes-Hughes, *Catalogue of Manuscript Music in the British Museum* (London: British Museum, 1964), and Pamela J. Willetts, *Beethoven and England* (London: British Museum, 1970), pp. 62–69.

A catalogue of Beethoven holdings in Viennese public collections, *Musikautographe Ludwig van Beethovens in öffentliche Wiener Sammlungen*, is in preparation (Tutzing: Schneider), edited by Ingrid Fuchs on behalf on the Wiener Beethovengesellschaft.

The former Soviet Union: see Nathan Fishman, "Verzeichnis aller in der UdSSR ermittelten und registrierten Beethoven-Autographe. Stand: 1. January 1980," *Zu Beethoven* 3 (1988): 113–40.

Holdings in the United States, Slovakia, and Berlin are the subject of essays by Otto E. Albrecht, Luba Ballová, and Rudolf Elvers and Hans-Günter Klein, in Kurt Dorfmüller, ed., *Beiträge zur Beethoven-Bibliographie* (Munich: Henle, 1978).

The Louis Koch Beethoven collection is catalogued in Georg Kinsky, ed., *Manuskripte, Briefe, Dokumente von Scarlatti bis Stravinsky. Katalog der Musikautographen-Sammlung Louis Koch* (Stuttgart: Hoffmannsche Buchdruckerei Felix Krais, 1953), pp. 50–138.

For an abbreviated and now outdated guide to public and private holdings, see Kinsky-Halm, pp. 777–78. The present locations of the sketchbooks are given in Douglas Johnson, ed., *The Beethoven Sketchbooks* (Berkeley and Los Angeles: University of California Press, and Oxford: Oxford University Press, 1985), pp. 599–610.

HANDBOOKS

An invaluable standard work is Theodor Frimmel, *Beethoven-Handbuch,* 2 vols. (Leipzig: B&H, 1926). Largely abridged from Frimmel is Paul Nettl, *Beethoven Encyclopedia* (New York: Philosophical Library, 1956), 2d ed., retitled *Beethoven Handbook* (New York: Frederick Ungar, 1967). *The Beethoven Compendium: A Guide to Beethoven's Life and Music* (London: Thames and Hudson, 1991), edited by Barry Cooper, and written by Cooper, William Drabkin, Anne-Louise Coldicott, and Nicholas Marston, is an admirable reference work, wide-ranging and especially strong in its work lists and as a swift and accurate guide to the sketches, autograph scores, and publications. The typescript of a projected encyclopedia by Donald W. MacArdle, incomplete at his death in 1964, is in the Library of Congress. A handy compilation of the texts of Beethoven's completed vocal compositions is Kurt E. Schürmann, ed., *Ludwig van Beethoven. Alle vertonten und musikalisch bearbeiteten Texte* (Münster: Aschendorf, 1980).

BIBLIOGRAPHIES

No up-to-date cumulative bibliography of writings about Beethoven exists. For some of the older literature, see Emerich Kastner, *Bibliotheca Beethoveniana* (1913), 2d ed., enlarged by Theodor Frimmel (Leipzig: B&H, 1925), and listings in various volumes of *NBJ* and *BJ,* 2d series. Much of the periodical literature to ca. 1962 is surveyed in MacArdle, *Beethoven Abstracts* (Detroit: Information Coordinators, 1973). Further MacArdle abstracts of the book literature are on deposit at the Library of Congress, the British Library, and the New York Public Library.

See also the bibliographies in the "Beethoven" entries in the following works: *Die Musik in Geschichte und Gegenwart,* vol. 1 (Kassel: Bärenreiter, 1949–51), cols. 1954–65; *Riemann Musik Lexikon,* 12th ed., vol. 1 (Mainz: B. Schott's Söhne, 1959), pp. 129–30; *TNG,* vol. 1, pp. 410–14. Many post-1980 listings are evaluated in William Kinderman, *Beethoven* (Berkeley and Los Angeles: University of California Press, 1995), pp. 339–50.

The researcher will find copious Beethoven listings in the volumes of *The Music Index* and listings and abstracts of the scholarly literature in *rilm Abstracts of Music Literature* (1967–).

An on-line bibliography is in its early stages of preparation by the Ira F. Brilliant Center for Beethoven Studies at San Jose State University. Scheduled for completion in 2004, as of 1998 it contained about one third of a projected 23,000 entries. Its web page can be reached at http://www.sjsu.edu/music/Beethoven (Telnet capability required).

SERIALS, PERIODICALS, YEARBOOKS

The main periodicals devoted exclusively to Beethoven studies are the following:

Beethovenjahrbuch, ed. Theodor Frimmel, 2 vols. (Munich and Leipzig: Müller, 1908–09).
Beethoven-Forschung, Lose Blätter, ed. Theodor Frimmel, 10 issues (Vienna, 1911–25).

Neues Beethoven-Jahrbuch, ed. Adolf Sandberger, 10 vols. (Augsburg, Braunschweig, 1924–42).

Beethoven-Jahrbuch, 2d series, ed. Joseph Schmidt-Görg, Paul Mies, et al., 10 vols. through 1983 (Bonn, 1954–).

Beethoven Studies, ed. Alan Tyson, 3 vols. (New York: Norton, 1973; Oxford: Oxford University Press, 1977; Cambridge: Cambridge University Press, 1982)

Zu Beethoven, ed. Harry Goldschmidt, 3 vols. (Berlin: Verlag Neue Musik, 1979, 1984, 1988).

The Beethoven Newsletter, ed. William Meredith, 1986– . Retitled *The Beethoven Journal* in 1995.

Beethoven Forum, ed. Christopher Reynolds, Lewis Lockwood, James Webster, Mark Evan Bonds, et al., 7 vols. to 1998 (Lincoln and London: University of Nebraska Press, 1992–).

Two important series of Beethoven monographs are Veröffentlichungen des Beethoven-Hauses in Bonn, ed. Ludwig Schiedermair, 10 vols. (BB, 1920–34), and Veröffentlichungen des Beethovenhauses in Bonn, Neue Folge, Schriften zur Beethovenforschung, ed. Joseph Schmidt-Görg and Sieghard Brandenburg, 12 vols. through 1995 (Bonn: BB, and Munich: Henle).

SPECIAL JOURNAL ISSUES

The following journals have devoted special issues to Beethoven: *MQ* 13 (April 1927); *M&L* 8 (April 1927); *La Revue Musicale* 8 (April 1927); *JAMS* 23 (Fall 1970); and *MQ* 56 (October 1970), published in book form as Paul H. Lang, ed., *The Creative World of Beethoven* (New York: Norton, 1971); *M&L* 58 (April 1977). *Die Musik* frequently published special Beethoven issues. See MacArdle, *Abstracts* for contents of these and other special issues of periodicals and for yearbooks of the publishers B&H, Peters, and Simrock.

SYMPOSIUMS, CONGRESS REPORTS, FESTSCHRIFTS

The principal Beethoven symposiums include the following: Alfred Orel, ed., *Ein Wiener Beethoven Buch* (Vienna: Gerlach & Wiedling, 1921); *Beethoven-Zentenarfeier internationaler musikhistorischer Kongress* (Vienna: Universal, 1927); Gustav Bosse, ed., *Beethoven-Almanach der deutschen Musikbücherei* (Regensburg: Bosse, 1927); Arnold Schmitz, ed., *Beethoven und die Gegenwart* (Berlin and Bonn: Dümmler, 1937); Dagmar Weise, ed., *Festschrift Joseph Schmidt-Görg zum 60. Geburtstag* (BB, 1957); Siegfried Kross and Hans Schmidt, eds., *Colloquium Amicorum: Joseph Schmidt-Görg zum 70. Geburtstag* (BB, 1967); Erich Schenk, ed., *Beethoven-Symposion Wien 1970* (Vienna: Böhlaus, 1971); Erich Schenk, ed., *Beethoven-Studien* (Vienna: Böhlaus, 1970); H. A. Brockhaus and K. Niemann, eds., *Bericht über den internationalen Beethoven-Kongress 10–12. Dezember 1970 in Berlin* (Berlin: Verlag Neue Musik, 1971); Carl Dahlhaus et al., eds., *Bericht über den internationalen musikwissenschaftlichen Kongress Bonn 1970* (Kassel: Bärenreiter, 1971); Harry Goldschmidt et al., eds., *Bericht über den internationalen Beethoven-Kongress 20. bis 23. März 1977 in Berlin* (Leipzig: VEB Deutscher Verlag für Musik, 1978); Rudolf Klein, ed., *Beiträge*

'76–78: *Beethoven-Kolloquium 1977, Dokumentation und Aufführungspraxis* (Kassel: Bärenreiter, 1978); Robert Winter and Bruce Carr, eds., *Beethoven, Performers, and Critics: The International Beethoven Congress, Detroit, 1977* (Detroit: Wayne State University Press, 1980); Martin Staehelin, ed., *Divertimento für Hermann J. Abs: Beethoven-Studien* (BB, 1981); Lewis Lockwood and Phyllis Benjamin, eds., *Beethoven Essays: Studies in Honor of Elliot Forbes* (Cambridge, MA: Harvard University Department of Music, 1984). William Kinderman, ed., *Beethoven's Compositional Process*, North American Beethoven Studies, no. 1 (Lincoln: University of Nebraska Press and American Beethoven Society, 1991), documents the 1986 conference at the University of Victoria, with outstanding contributions by Lewis Lockwood, William Drabkin, William Kinderman, and Barry Cooper, among others; Sieghard Brandenburg, ed., *Haydn, Mozart, and Beethoven: Essays in Honor of Alan Tyson* (Oxford: Oxford University Press, 1998), contains Beethoven essays by Lockwood, Solomon, Kerman, Kramer, Brandenburg, Brenneis, and others.

ESSAYS

Among collections by individual Beethoven scholars are the following: Theodor Frimmel, *Neue Beethoveniana* (Vienna: Gerold, 1888); Frimmel, *Beethoven-Studien*, 2 vols. (Munich & Leipzig: Müller, 1905–06); Alfred C. Kalischer, *Beethoven und seine Zeitgenossen*, 4 vols. (Berlin: Schuster & Loeffler, [1908–10]); Adolph Sandberger, *Ausgewählte Aufsätze zur Musikgeschichte*, vol. 2 (Munich: Drei Masken, 1924); Ludwig Misch, *Beethoven Studies* (Norman: University of Oklahoma Press, 1953); Ludwig Misch, *Neue Beethoven-Studien und andere Themen* (BB, 1967); Willy Hess, *Beethoven-Studien* (BB, 1972); Harry Goldschmidt, *Die Erscheinung Beethoven*, Beethoven-Studien, no. 1 (Leipzig: VEB Deutscher Verlag für Musik, 1974; 2d ed. [expanded], 1985); Maynard Solomon, *Beethoven Essays* (Cambridge, MA: Harvard University Press, 1988); Lewis Lockwood, *Beethoven: Studies in the Creative Process* (Cambridge, MA: Harvard University Press, 1992); and Carl Dahlhaus, *Ludwig van Beethoven und seine Zeit* (Laaber: Laaber-Verlag, 1987), the latter in an English translation (whose title more accurately describes the book's contents), Mary Whittall, trans., *Ludwig van Beethoven: Approaches to His Music* (Oxford: Clarendon Press, 1991).

Four major papers by Joseph Kerman are collected in his *Write All These Down: Essays on Music* (Berkeley and Los Angeles: University of California Press, 1994), pp. 153–238. This collection does not include his much-cited "Notes on Beethoven's Codas," *Beethoven Studies* 3 (1982), 141–59. Still valuable for their unique materials and interpretations are Hans Volkmann, *Neues über Beethoven* (Berlin and Leipzig: Seemann, 1904 [1905]); Stephen Ley, *Wahrheit, Zweifel und Irrtum in der Kunde von Beethovens Leben* (Wiesbaden: B&H, 1955); and Stephan Ley, *Aus Beethovens Erdentagen* (Bonn: Glöckner, 1948).

Of great interest are the uncollected writings of Wilhelm Altmann, Sieghard Brandenburg, Otto Erich Deutsch, Carl Dahlhaus, William Drabkin, William Kinderman, Georg Kinsky, Richard Kramer, Klaus Kropfinger, Hans-Werner Küthen, Albert Leitzmann, Donald MacArdle, William S. Newman, Emil Platen, Jan Racek, Ludwig Schiedermair, Joseph Schmidt-Görg, Georg Schünemann, Alan Tyson, Max Unger, and Wilhelm Virneisel, among others. These must be consulted in the journals, Festschriften, symposiums, and congress proceedings. A fine international anthology is Ludwig Finscher, ed., *Ludwig van Beethoven*, published as vol. 428

in the series Wege der Forschung (Darmstadt: Wissenschaftliche Buchgesellschaft, 1983).

BEETHOVEN'S LIFE

REMINISCENCES OF CONTEMPORARIES

Apart from the numerous reminiscences printed in Thayer-Krehbiel and Thayer-Forbes, the only significant selections available in English are O. G. Sonneck, ed., *Beethoven: Impressions of Contemporaries* (New York: Schirmer, 1926), and H. C. Robbins Landon, *Beethoven: A Documentary Study* (New York: Macmillan, 1970; abridged ed., 1975); the latter contains numerous snippets of memoirs and reminiscences but has no useful guide to its contents. See also the imprecise translations in Michael Hamburger, ed., *Beethoven: Letters, Journals and Conversations* (reprint, Garden City, NY: Anchor, 1960). Although now outdated, the most comprehensive German editions are Friedrich Kerst, ed., *Die Erinnerungen an Beethoven*, 2 vols. (Stuttgart: Julius Hoffman, 1913), and Leitzmann (see Abbreviations, p. 428). These may be augmented by J.-G. Prod'homme, *Beethoven, raconté par ceux qui l'ont vu* (Paris: Stock, 1927), and Ludwig Nohl, *Beethoven nach den Schilderungen seiner Zeitgenossen* (Stuttgart: Cotta, 1877). An English edition of Nohl, E. Hill, trans., *Beethoven. Depicted by his Contemporaries* (London, 1880), is faultily translated. Unique and detailed memoirs of Beethoven's early years are in Joseph Schmidt-Görg, ed., *Des Bonner Bäckermeisters Gottfried Fischer: Aufzeichnungen über Beethovens Jugend* (BB, 1971). The diary of Fanny Giannattasio is published in Ludwig Nohl, *Eine stille Liebe zu Beethoven*, 2d ed. (Leipzig: Seemann, 1902); a defective English translation is *An Unrequited Love. An Episode in the Life of Beethoven* (London: Reeves, 1876); for a reliable edition see Thayer-Deiters-Riemann, vol. 4, pp. 513–41. See also the well-known anecdotes in the supplement to Ignaz von Seyfried, *L. v. Beethovens Studien* (Vienna: Haslinger, 1832), and the English edition, H. H. Pierson, trans. (Leipzig: Schuberth, 1853). For Czerny's reminiscences of Beethoven, see Carl Czerny, "Recollections from My Life," *MQ* 42 (1956), 302–17, and Czerny, *On the Proper Performance of All Beethoven's Works for the Piano* (Vienna: Universal, 1970), pp. 4–18.

Several of the early biographies (see Biographies, below) also contain important individual reminiscences, especially Wegeler-Ries and the several editions of Anton Schindler's *Biographie von Ludwig van Beethoven*. See also Gerhard von Breuning, *Aus dem Schwarzspanierhause* (Vienna: Rosner, 1874), and the English version, Henry F. Mins and Maynard Solomon, trans., Maynard Solomon, ed., *Memories of Beethoven: From the House of the Black-Robed Spaniards* (Cambridge: Cambridge University Press, 1992).

BIOGRAPHIES

There exists no comprehensive documentary study of Beethoven comparable to those that have been done for Bach, Handel, Haydn, Mozart, and Schubert. The standard biography is Alexander Wheelock Thayer, *Ludwig van Beethovens Leben*, 3 vols. (Berlin: Schneider, 1866; Weber, 1872, 1879). The five-volume second edition was expanded and edited by Hermann Deiters and/or Hugo Riemann (Leipzig: B&H, 1901–11). Volume 1 was later reedited by Riemann (Leipzig: B&H, 1917). Thayer's original

English manuscript, which carried the biography to ca. 1816, was completed and edited by Henry E. Krehbiel from Thayer's notes and the German editions and published as *The Life of Ludwig van Beethoven*, 3 vols. (New York: Beethoven Association, 1921). This was scrupulously revised, updated, and edited by Elliot Forbes as *Thayer's Life of Beethoven*, 2 vols. (Princeton: Princeton University Press, 1964; rev. ed., 1967). All editions of Thayer are now in need of further updating in the light of more recent scholarship.

A pioneering biographical study is Franz Wegeler and Ferdinand Ries, *Biographische Notizen über Ludwig van Beethoven* (Coblenz: Bädeker, 1838), with a *Nachtrag* (Supplement) by Wegeler (Coblenz, 1845). This was serviceably translated by Frederick Noonan as *Beethoven Remembered* (Arlington, VA: Great Ocean Publishers, 1987), but with a hopelessly inadequate scholarly apparatus (an edition initiated by Alan Tyson is eagerly awaited). Anton Schindler, *Biographie von Ludwig van Beethoven*, appeared in three versions. The first (Münster: Aschendorff, 1840) was translated as *The Life of Beethoven*, ed. Ignace Moscheles (London, 1841; Boston: Oliver Ditson, [1841]). The second edition (Münster: Aschendorff, 1845) contains several supplementary sections, including extensive quotations from the Conversation Books and an essay on Beethoven in Paris. The greatly expanded third edition (2 vols., Münster: Aschendorff, 1860) was translated by Constance Jolly and edited by Donald W. MacArdle as *Beethoven as I Knew Him* (Chapel Hill: University of North Carolina Press, 1966).

Ludwig Nohl, *Beethovens Leben*, 3 vols. in 4 (Vienna: Markgraf & Müller, 1864; Leipzig: Günther, 1867–77), is a pathbreaking work utilizing original sources and interviews. A second edition of Nohl, edited by Paul Sakalowski, 4 vols. (Berlin, 1909–13), tacitly omits 330 pages of valuable notes and close documentation. J.-G. Prod'homme, *La Jeunesse de Beethoven* (Paris: Payot, 1920; Librairie Delagrave, 1927), and Ludwig Schiedermair, *Der junge Beethoven* (Leipzig: Quelle & Meyer, 1925), are the standard works on Beethoven's early years. Martin Cooper, *Beethoven: The Last Decade, 1817–27* (London: Oxford University Press, 1970), and Editha and Richard Sterba, *Beethoven and His Nephew* (New York: Pantheon, 1954), are important studies of his final years. Romain Rolland, *Beethoven: Les grandes époques créatrices*, 5 vols. in 7 (Paris: Sablier, 1928–57)—and a one-volume *Édition définitive* (Paris: Albin Michel, 1966)—though incomplete, is a brilliant, wide-ranging study of the life and major works; there are English translations of the first two volumes as *Beethoven the Creator*, trans. Ernest Newman, and *Goethe and Beethoven*, trans. G. A. Pfister and E. S. Kemp (New York: Harpers, 1929, 1931).

Numerous general biographies are of interest, of which a few can be singled out for their historical importance or new information: Adolph Bernhard Marx, *Ludwig van Beethoven: Leben and Schaffen*, 2 vols. (Berlin: Janke, 1859); Wilhelm von Lenz, *Beethoven: Eine Kunststudie*, vol. I (Kassel: Hoffman & Campe, 1855; new edition, A. C. Kalischer, ed., Berlin: Schuster & Loeffler, 1921); Alexandre Oulibicheff, *Beethoven, ses critiques et ses glossateurs* (Leipzig: Brockhaus, and Paris: Gavelot, 1857); Victor Wilder, *Beethoven, sa vie et son oeuvre* (Paris: Charpentier, 1883); W. J. v. Wasielewski, *Ludwig van Beethoven*, 2 vols. (Berlin: Brachvogel & Ranft, 1888); Paul Bekker, *Beethoven*, (Munich: Schuster & Loeffler, 1911), trans. M. M. Bozman (London: Dent, 1925); André de Hevesy, *Beethoven: Vie intime* (Paris: Émile-Paul Frères, 1927), translated by F. S. Flint as *Beethoven the Man* (London: Faber & Gwyer, 1927); Edouard Herriot, *Vie de Beethoven* (Paris: Gallimard, 1929), translated by Adelheid I. Mitchell and William J. Mitchell as *The Life of Beethoven* (New York: Macmillan, 1935); Walter Riezler, *Beethoven* (Berlin: Atlantis, 1936; 9th ed., 1966), trans. G. D. H. Pidcock (London: Forrester, 1938); Willy Hess, *Beethoven* (Zürich: Gutenberg, 1956); Jean and Brigitte Massin, *Ludwig van Beethoven* (Paris: Fayard, 1967); George Marek, *Beethoven: Biography of a Genius* (New York: Funk & Wagnalls, 1969); Denis Matthews, *Beethoven*, Master Musicians Series (London: Dent, 1985). See also Konrad Küster, *Beethoven* (Stuttgart: Deutsche Verlags-Anstalt, 1994). There are worthy older biographies by Richard Specht, W. A. Thomas-San-Galli, Gustav Ernest, Theodor Frimmel, Hans Volkmann, Marion M. Scott, W. J. Turner, J. N. Burk, and Arnold Schmitz.

Among shorter biographies, the most valuable remains George Grove, the "Beethoven" entry in *Grove's Dictionary of Music and Musicians,* vol. 1 (London: Macmillan, 1879), pp. 162–209, reprinted in the second, third, and fourth editions and in George Grove, *Beethoven, Schubert, Mendelssohn* (New York: Macmillan, 1951). The "Beethoven" entry in the fifth edition of *Grove's,* by William McNaught, and that in *Die Musik in Geschichte und Gegenwart* by Joseph Schmidt-Görg are both routine, but students should not overlook the extraordinary entry by Donald Francis Tovey in *Encyclopaedia Britannica,* 11th ed., and the lucid, insightful account by Alan Tyson and Joseph Kerman in *TNG,* vol. 2, pp. 354–414, published separately as *The New Grove Beethoven* (New York: Norton, 1983).

PSYCHOLOGICAL STUDIES

A number of interpretative studies have significantly shaped or altered the received view of Beethoven's inner life or character: Richard Wagner, *Beethoven* (Leipzig: Fritzsch, 1870), trans. A. R. Parsons (New York: Schirmer, 1872); Romain Rolland, *Beethoven* (Paris: Cahiers de la Quinzaine, 1903), trans. B. Constance Hull (London: Kegan Paul, 1917); Max Graf, *Die innere Werkstatt des Musikers* (Stuttgart: Ferdinand Enke, 1910), translated into English and revised by the author as *From Beethoven to Shostakovich* (New York: Philosophical Library, 1947); Ernest Newman, *The Unconscious Beethoven: An Essay in Musical Psychology* (New York: Knopf, 1927); J. W. N. Sullivan, *Beethoven: His Spiritual Development* (London: Jonathan Cape, 1927); Richard and Editha Sterba, *Beethoven and His Nephew* (New York: Pantheon, 1954). See also Alan Tyson's influential "Beethoven's Heroic Phase," *Musical Times* 110 (1969): 139–41, and the present author's psychoanalytic efforts, "The Dreams of Beethoven," *American Imago* 32 (1975): 113–44 (also in Solomon, *Beethoven Essays,* pp. 56–76), and Solomon, "The Posthumous Life of Ludwig Maria van Beethoven," in Solomon, *Beethoven Essays,* pp. 77–92.

SPECIAL TOPICS

GENEALOGY AND FAMILY BACKGROUND

Raymond Van Aerde, *Les Ancêtres flamands de Beethoven* (Malines, Belgium: Godenne, 1927); Joseph Schmidt-Görg, *Beethoven: Die Geschichte seiner Familie* (BB, 1964); Joseph Schmidt-Görg, "Stand und Aufgaben der Beethoven-Genealogie" in Schmitz, ed., *Beethoven und die Gegenwart,* pp. 114–61; Donald W. MacArdle, "The Family van Beethoven," *MQ* 35 (1949): 528–550, with definitive bibliography. See also Maynard Solomon, "A Papal Dispensation for Cornelius van Beethoven," *Beethoven Forum* 6 (1998): 129–42, and Ernest Closson, *The Fleming in Beethoven,* trans. Muriel Fuller (London: Oxford University Press, 1936).

LODGINGS

Kurt Smolle, *Wohnstätten Ludwig van Beethovens von 1792 bis zu seinem Tod* (BB, 1970); Rudolph Klein, *Beethoven Stätten in Oesterreich* (Vienna: Lafite, 1970). For a concise conspectus, see Thayer-Forbes, pp. 1108–1109.

MEDICAL HISTORY

Waldemar Schweisheimer, *Beethovens Leiden* (Munich: Müller, 1922); Schweisheimer, "Beethoven's Physicians," *MQ* 31 (1945): 289–98; Walther Forster, *Beethovens Krankheiten und ihre Beurteilung* (Wiesbaden: B&H, 1955); G. Bilancioni, *La Sordità di Beethoven* (Rome: Formíggini, 1921); Edward Larkin, "Beethoven's Medical History," in Martin Cooper, *Beethoven: The Last Decade* (London: Oxford University Press, 1970), pp. 439–66 (with select bibliography); Hans Bankl and Hans Jesserer, *Die Krankheiten Ludwig van Beethovens: Pathographie seines Lebens und Pathologie seiner Leiden* (Vienna: Wilhelm Maudrich, 1987). See also Maynard Solomon, "On Beethoven's Deafness," in Solomon, *Beethoven Essays*, pp. 93–98.

IDEOLOGY AND INTELLECTUAL OUTLOOK

Arnold Schmitz, *Das romantische Beethovenbild* (Berlin and Bonn: Dümmler, 1927); Schiedermair, *Der Junge Beethoven* (Leipzig: Quelle & Mayer, 1925), pp. 316–36; Martin Cooper, *Beethoven: The Last Decade* (London: Oxford University Press, 1970), pp. 86–98; Adolf Sandberger, "Beethovens Stellung zu den führenden Geistern seiner Zeit in Philosophie und Dichtung," in Sandberger, ed., *Ausgewählte Aufsätze zur Musikgeschichte*, vol. 2 (Munich: Drei Masken, 1924), pp. 263–91; J.-G. Prod'homme, "Beethoven's Intellectual Education," *MQ* 13 (1927): 169–82; Hans Joachim Marx, "Beethoven als politischer Mensch," in Luba Ballová, ed., *Tagungsbericht des 2. internationalen musikologischen Symposiums* (Piešťany: Slovakisches National Museum, 1970), pp. 173–85, with further bibliographical references; reprinted in *Ludwig van Beethoven 1770–1970* (Bonn: Inter Nationes, 1970), pp. 24–34. See also Maynard Solomon, "Beethoven and Schiller," in Solomon, *Beethoven Essays*, pp. 205–15.

Siegfried Kross, ed., *Beethoven: Mensch seiner Zeit* (Bonn: Ludwig Röhrscheid Verlag, 1980), includes several useful papers, especially Kross, "Beethoven und die rheinisch-katholische Aufklärung," and Bernhard Höfele, "Beethoven und der Krieg." The informative essays by Hans-Werner Küthen, Michael Ladenburger, and Thomas Röder in Helga Lühning and Sieghard Brandenburg, eds., *Beethoven: Zwischen Revolution und Restauration* (BB, 1989), center particularly on the Congress of Vienna period. An oversimplified view of Beethoven's political outlook is Frida Knight, *Beethoven and the Age of Revolution* (London: Lawrence & Wishart, 1973). Beethoven's identification with an ideal, Enlightened aristocracy is argued in Maynard Solomon, "Beethoven, Sonata, and Utopia," *Telos*, no. 9 (Fall 1971): 32–47; Solomon, "Beethoven and the Enlightenment," *Telos*, no. 19 (Spring 1974): 146–54, and in Solomon, "Beethoven's Class Position and Outlook," in Harry Goldschmidt et al., eds., *Bericht über den internationalen Beethoven-Kongress, 20. bis 23. März 1977 in Berlin* (Leipzig: VEB Deutscher Verlag für Musik, 1978), pp. 67–79, 501–12.

Beethoven's attraction to a particular utopian and Babouvist idea of patronage is explored in Maynard Solomon, "Beethoven's *Magazin der Kunst*," in Solomon, *Beethoven Essays*, pp. 193–204. Solomon, "Beethoven's Aesthetic Views" (forthcoming) surveys Beethoven's views on the nature of art, creativity, and the responsibilities of the artist. An inventory of Beethoven's personal library prepared by the authorities after his death is printed in Leitzmann, vol. 2, pp. 379–83.

FREEMASONRY

Theodor Frimmel, *Handbuch*, vol. 1, pp. 151–52; Arnold Schmitz, *Das romantische Beethovenbild* (Berlin and Bonn: Dümmler, 1927), pp. 86–88; Daniel Legou, ed., *Dictionnaire de la Franc-Maçonnerie* (rev. ed., Paris: Presses Universitaire de France, 1987), p. 118; Alberto Basso, *L'invenzione della gioia: Musica e massoneria nell'età dei Lumi* (Milan: Garzanti, 1994), pp. 421–53; and Hans-Werner Küthen, *Ein unbekanntes Notierungsblatt Beethovens aus der Entstehungszeit der "Mondscheinsonate"* (Prague: Resonus, [1996]).

ICONOGRAPHIES AND ILLUSTRATED CATALOGUES

Robert Bory, *Ludwig van Beethoven: His Life and Work in Pictures* (London: Thames & Hudson, 1966), offers fine black-and-white reproductions. Superbly printed in full color is H. C. Robbins Landon, *Beethoven: A Documentary Study* (New York: Macmillan, 1970), which may be supplemented by Joseph Schmidt-Görg and Hans Schmidt, eds., *Ludwig van Beethoven* (New York: Praeger, 1970). The deluxe folio edition of Paul Bekker, *Beethoven* (Berlin: Schuster & Loeffler, 1911), features a 160-page appendix of black and white facsimiles and illustrations.

Stephan Ley, *Beethovens Leben in authentischen Bildern und Texten* (Berlin: Cassirer, 1925), reproduces many unique images in routine black and white. The best scholarly survey of Beethoven portraits is Theodor Frimmel, *Beethoven im zeitgenössischen Bildnis* (Vienna: Karl König, 1925); see also Frimmel, *Beethovens äussere Erscheinung*, vol. 1 of *Beethoven-Studien* (Munich and Leipzig: Müller, 1905–06). Outstanding among many Beethoven exhibition catalogues are *"Die Flamme Lodert," Beethoven Ausstellung der Stadt Wien*, ed. Fritz Racek et al. (Vienna: Historisches Museum der Stadt Wien, 1970); *Ludwig van Beethoven 1770–1827: Ausstellung der Bayerischen Staatsbibliothek München*, ed. Kurt Dorfmüller et al. (Tutzing, Germany: Schneider, 1977), which includes reproductions of title pages of the symphonies and concertos; *Monument für Beethoven: zur Geschichte des Beethoven-Denkmals (1845) . . . Katalog zur Ausstellung des Stadtmuseums Bonn und des Beethoven-Hauses*, ed. Ingrid Bodsch (Bonn: Stadtmuseum, 1995); and *Ludwig van Beethoven*, ed. Adelbert Schusser, in the series Musikergedenkstätten (Vienna: Historisches Museum der Stadt Wien, 1995). Alessandra Comini's copiously illustrated monograph, *The Changing Image of Beethoven: A Study of Mythmaking* (New York: Rizzoli, 1987), surveys nineteenth-century Beethoven iconography. *Mythos Beethoven*, ed. Rainer Cadenbach (Laaber, Germany: Laaber Verlag, 1986), catalogues a striking Beethovenhaus exhibition of materials illustrating shifting popular and artistic conceptions of Beethoven.

BEETHOVEN'S TEACHERS

A scrupulous work on Beethoven's musical instruction is Gustav Nottebohm, *Beethovens Unterricht bei J. Haydn, Albrechtsberger und Salieri*, vol. 1 of *Beethovens Studien* (Leipzig and Winterthur: Rieter-Biedermann, 1873).

On Neefe: Irmgard Leux, *Christian Gottlob Neefe* (Leipzig: Kistner & Siegel, 1925); Leux, "Neue Neefeiana," *NBJ* 1 (1924): 86–114; Alfred Becker, *Christian Gottlob Neefe und die bonner Illuminaten* (Bonn: Bouvier, 1969); and Schiedermair, *Der junge Beethoven*, pp. 140–62. Neefe's "Autobiography" is available in translation in Paul Nettl, *Forgotten Musicians* (New York: Philosophical Library, 1951), pp. 246–64.

On Haydn: The encyclopedic standard work is H. C. Robbins Landon, *Haydn: Chronicle and Works,* 5 vols. (Bloomington: Indiana University Press, 1976–80). A reliable brief biography is Karl Geiringer, *Haydn: A Creative Life in Music* (New York: Norton, 1946; rev. ed., Geiringer and Irene Geiringer (Berkeley and Los Angeles: University of California Press, 1968). James Webster, "The Falling-out between Haydn and Beethoven: The Evidence of the Sources," in Lewis Lockwood and Phyllis Benjamin, eds., *Beethoven Essays: Studies in Honor of Elliot Forbes* (Cambridge, MA: Harvard University Department of Music, 1984), pp. 3–45, grants the ambivalent nature of the relationship between Haydn and Beethoven for the half dozen years until 1804 but is not persuaded by the evidence for the earlier period, 1793–95. See also Fritz von Reinöhl, "Neues zu Beethovens Lehrjahr bei Haydn," *NBJ* 6 (1935): 35–47. For an able defense of Haydn's instruction, see Alfred Mann, "Beethoven's Contrapuntal Studies with Haydn," *MQ* 56 (1970): 711–26; for Beethoven's relations with Albrechtsberger and Salieri, see the entries in Frimmel, *Handbuch.* See also Richard Kramer, "Notes to Beethoven's Education," *JAMS* 28 (1975): 72–101.

RELATIONSHIPS WITH SIGNIFICANT INDIVIDUALS

These may most easily be consulted in Frimmel, *Handbuch;* Alfred C. Kalischer, *Beethoven und seine Zeitgenossen* (Berlin: Schuster & Loeffler, 1908–10); and the articles indexed in MacArdle, *Abstracts.* Among MacArdle's own important special studies of such relationships, see esp. "Beethoven and the Czernys," *Monthly Musical Record* 88 (1958): 124–35; "Beethoven and George Thomson," *M&L* 37 (1956): 27–49; "Beethoven and Grillparzer," *M&L* 40 (1959): 44–55; "The Brentano Family in Its Relations with Beethoven," *MR* 19 (1958): 6–19; "Beethoven and the Archduke Rudolph," *BJ,* 2d series, 4 (1962): 36–58; "Beethoven and Ferdinand Ries," *M&L* 46 (1965): 23–34; "Anton Felix Schindler, Friend of Beethoven," *MR* 24 (1963): 50–74; "Beethoven and Schuppanzigh," *MR* 26 (1963): 3–14; and "Beethoven und Karl Holz," *Musikforschung* 20 (1967): 19–29. All of the preceding require some updating in light of subsequent scholarship.

Members of Beethoven's circle of friends in Bonn are succinctly described in Max Braubach, ed., *Die Stammbücher Beethovens und der Babette Koch. Faksimile* (BB, 1970; 2d ed., 1995), pp. 133–59. For professors at Bonn University, including Eulogius Schneider, Bartholomäus Fischenich, and Franz Wegeler, see Max Braubach's superb *Die erste bonner Hochschule, Maxische Akademie und kurfürstliche Universität, 1774/77 bis 1798* (Bonn: Bouvier and Röhrscheid, 1966).

For trustworthy data on Beethoven's Viennese publishers, see Friedrich Slezak, *Beethovens Wiener Originalverleger,* Forschungen und Beiträge zur Wiener Stadgeschichte, Bd. 17 (Vienna: Deuticke, 1987) and numerous monographs on the various publishers by Alexander Weinmann.

Informative studies of major patrons are Josef Heer, *Der Graf von Waldstein und sein Verhältnis zu Beethoven,* Veröffentlichungen des Beethoven-Hauses in Bonn, ed. Ludwig Schiedermair, vol. 9 (BB, and Leipzig: Quelle & Meyer, 1933); Jürgen May, "Beethoven and Prince Karl Lichnowsky," *Beethoven Forum* 3 (1994): 29–38; Jaroslav Macek, "Franz Joseph Maximilian Lobkowitz: Musikfreund und Kunstmäzen," in Sieghard Brandenburg and Martella Gutiérrez-Denhoff, eds., *Beethoven und Böhmen. Beiträge zu Biographie und Wirkungsgeschichte Beethovens* (BB, 1988), pp. 147–201; Tomislav Volek and Jaroslav Macek, "Beethoven's Rehearsals at the Lobkowitz's," *Musical Times* 127 (1986): 75–80; and Susan Kagan, *Archduke Rudolph, Beethoven's Patron,*

Pupil, and Friend (Stuyvesant, NY: Pendragon Press, 1988); see also Sieghard Brandenburg, "Die Beethoveniana in der Musikaliensammlung des Erzherzogs Rudolph," *Zu Beethoven* 3 (1988): 141–76.

On Ferdinand Ries, the dissertation by Ludwig Ueberfeldt, *Ferdinand Ries' Jugendentwicklung* (Bonn: Rost, 1915), remains valuable. It is supplemented by the exemplary article by Alan Tyson, "Ferdinand Ries (1784-1838): The History of his Contribution to Beethoven Biography," *Nineteenth-Century Music* 7 (1984): 209–21. A modern biography of Schindler would be a valuable desideratum; in the meanwhile we rely upon the uncritical Eduard Hüffer, *Anton Felix Schindler, der Biograph Beethovens* (Münster: Aschendorff, 1909). For Zmeskall, see Hermann Ullrich, "Nikolaus Zmeskall von Domanowetz," *Mozartgemeinde Wien, Wiener Figaro* 43 (1976): 19–25. For Countess Erdödy and J. X. Brauchle, see Günther Haupt, "Gräfin Erdödy und J. X. Brauchle," *Der Bär: Jahrbuch von Breitkopf & Härtel* (1927), pp. 70–99.

For Clementi, see Leon Plantinga's elegant standard biography, *Clementi: His Life and Music* (London: Oxford University Press, 1977), especially pp. 307–15.

See also entries under The Immortal Beloved, below.

NEPHEW KARL

Editha and Richard Sterba's *Beethoven and His Nephew* (New York: Pantheon, 1954). For a critique, see Maynard Solomon, "Beethoven and His Nephew: A Reappraisal," *Beethoven Studies* 2 (1977): 138–71, excerpted in Solomon, *Beethoven Essays* pp. 139–54. Stefan Wolf, *Beethovens Neffenkonflikt*, Veröffentlichungen des Beethoven-Hauses in Bonn, neue Folge, vierte Reihe: Schriften zur Beethoven-Forschung, ed. Sieghard Brandenburg, no. 12 (Munich: Henle, 1995), offers a thorough and fair-minded review of the biographical literature, but its narrative of the conflict itself does not substantially improve on the accounts available in Thayer and the Sterbas.

THE IMMORTAL BELOVED

The most lucid summary of the problem and the criteria for its solution is O. G. Sonneck, *The Riddle of the Immortal Beloved* (New York: Schirmer, 1927). The basic works are the following: W. A. Thomas-San-Galli, *Die unsterbliche Geliebte Beethovens. Amalie Sebald. Lösung eines vielumstrittenen Problems* (Halle: Otto Hendel, 1909); Thomas-San-Galli, *Beethoven und die unsterbliche Geliebte: Amalie Sebald/Goethe/ Therese Brunsvik und Anderes* (Munich: Wunderhorn, 1910); Max Unger, *Auf Spuren von Beethovens "Unsterblicher Geliebten"* (Langensalza, Germany: Hermann Beyer, 1911); La Mara [Marie Lipsius], *Beethovens Unsterbliche Geliebte: Das Geheimnis der Gräfin Brunsvik und ihre Memoiren* (Leipzig: B&H, 1909); André de Hevesy, *Petites amies de Beethoven* (Paris: Champion, 1910); La Mara [Marie Lipsius], *Beethoven und die Brunsviks* (Leipzig: Siegel, 1920); Siegmund Kaznelson, *Beethovens ferne und unsterbliche Geliebte* (Zürich: Standard-Buch, 1954); Jean and Brigitte Massin, *Recherche de Beethoven* (Paris: Fayard, 1970); Harry Goldschmidt, *Um die Unsterbliche Geliebte: Eine Bestandsaufnahme* (Leipzig: VEB Deutscher Verlag für Musik, 1977 [1978]); Marie-Elisabeth Tellenbach, *Beethoven und seine "unsterbliche Geliebte" Josephine Brunswick: Ihr Schicksal und der Einfluss auf Beethovens Werk* (Zürich: Atlantis Musikbuch-Verlag, 1983).

The present author's identification of Antonie Brentano was first announced in *The New York Times*, May 21, 1972, section 2, p. 19, and presented in detail in "New Light on Beethoven's Letter to an Unknown Woman," *MQ* 58 (1972): 572–87, and "Antonie Brentano and Beethoven," *M&L* 58 (1977): 153–69, which was considerably expanded in Solomon, *Beethoven Essays*, pp. 166–89. My critique of the advocacy of Josephine von Deym-Stackelberg, with new evidence, is in my "Recherche de Josephine Deym," Solomon, *Beethoven Essays*, pp. 157–65. For a facsimile, accurate transcription, and discussion of the letter see Sieghard Brandenburg, ed., *Beethoven: Der Brief an die Unsterbliche Geliebte*, Jahresgabe des Vereins Beethoven-Haus 1986, no. 5 (BB, 1986; reprint, 1989); the transcription in *Briefe* is not altogether accurate. For a revival of the hypothesis that Amalie Sebald was Beethoven's second beloved, see Harry Goldschmidt, *"Auf diese Art mit A geht alles zu Grunde':* Eine umstrittene Tagebuchstelle in neuem Licht," *Zu Beethoven* 3 (1988): 8–30. For Therese Malfatti, see Albert Leitzmann, "Beethoven und Therese Malfatti: Eine kritische Studie," *Deutsche Rundschau* 38 (1911): 267–90.

REPUTATION AND RECEPTION

A standard work is Hans Heinrich Eggebrecht, *Zur Geschichte der Beethoven-Rezeption*, Abhanglungen der Geistes- und Sozialwissenschaftlichen Klasse, Jahrgang 1972, no. 3 (Mainz: Akademie der Wissenschaften und der Literatur, 1972); 2d enlarged edition, Series: Spektrum der Musik, 2 (Laaber, Germany: Laaber Verlag, 1994). Helmut Loos, ed., *Beethoven und die Nachwelt: Materialien zur Wirkungsgeschichte Beethovens* (BB, 1986), surveys an imposing variety of interesting topics in such papers as Sieghard Brandenburg, "Künstlerroman und Biographie: Zur Entstehung des Beethoven-Mythos im 19. Jahrhundert"; Helmut Loos, "Zur Texturierung Beethovenscher Instrumentalwerke: Ein Kapitel der Beethoven-Deutung"; Heribert Schröder, "Beethoven im Dritten Reich: Eine Materialsammlung"; and Jürgen Pfeiffer, "Beethoven im Film: Eine kommentierte Filmographie." Two informative monographs are David B. Dennis, *Beethoven in German Politics, 1870–1989* (New Haven and London: Yale University Press, 1996), and Andreas Eichhorn, *Beethovens Neunte Symphonie: Die Geschichte ihrer Aufführung und Rezeption*, Kasseler Schriften zur Musik, no. 3 (Kassel: Bärenreiter, 1993). An outstanding reception study is Ruth A. Solie, "Beethoven as Secular Humanist: Ideology and the Ninth Symphony in Nineteenth-Century Criticism," in Eugene Narmour and Ruth A. Solie, eds., *Explorations in Music, the Arts and Ideas: Essays in Honor of Leonard B. Meyer* (Stuyvesant, NY: Pendragon Press, 1988), pp. 1–42.

For the origins of a dominant trope in Beethoven reception, see Scott Burnham, "Criticism, Faith, and the *Idee:* A. B. Marx's Early Reception of Beethoven," *Nineteenth-Century Music* 13 (1990): 183–92. Tia DeNora, *Beethoven and the Construction of Genius: Musical Politics in Vienna, 1792–1803* (Berkeley and Los Angeles: University of California Press, 1995), and the same author's "Beethoven, the Viennese Canon, and the Sociology of Identity, 1793–1803," *Beethoven Forum* 2 (1993):, 29–54, aims to undermine the canonic status of Beethoven's music by ascribing his eminent reputation to his aristocratic connections and his patrons' capacity to dominate musical taste. The argument starts from the dubious premise that Beethoven's music had already attained a dominant position in Viennese concert life during his first decade there. See also Charles Rosen's critique in *New York Review of Books*, November 14,

1996, pp. 57–63. Elisabeth Eleonore Bauer, *Wie Beethoven auf den Sockel kam: Die Entstehung eines musikalischen Mythos* (Stuttgart and Weimar: Metzler, 1992), examines the formation of a Beethoven myth in the writings of A. B. Marx and others associated with the *Berliner Allgemeine musikalische Zeitung*. Beethoven's effect on subsequent symphonic composers is considered in Mark Evan Bonds, *After Beethoven: Imperatives of Originality in the Symphony* (Cambridge, MA: Harvard University Press, 1996).

See also works cited under Classicism and Romanticism, below.

LOCAL STUDIES

Typical and exemplary studies include Leo Schrade, *Beethoven in France: The Growth of an Idea* (New Haven: Yale University Press, 1942); Nicholas Temperley, "Beethoven in London Concert Life, 1800–1850," *MR* 21 (1960): 207–14; Otto Kinkeldey, "Beginnings of Beethoven in America," *MQ* 13 (1927): 217–48, which is now superseded by Anne Chan, "Beethoven in the United States to 1865" (Ph.D. dissertation, University of North Carolina, Chapel Hill, 1976); Luba Ballová, *Beethoven a Slovensko* (Osveta, Slovakia, 1972); Samuel Geiser, *Beethoven und die Schweiz* (Zurich and Stuttgart: Rotapfel-Verlag, 1976); Jan Racek, *Beethoven a České Země* (Brno, 1964); Sieghard Brandenburg and Martella Gutiérrez-Denhoff, eds., *Beethoven und Böhmen: Beiträge zu Biographie und Wirkungsgeschichte Beethovens* (BB, 1988); Victor Papp, *Beethoven és a Magyarok* (Budapest, 1927); O. E. Deutsch, *Beethovens Beziehungen zu Graz* (Graz: Leykam, 1907); and Hans Volkmann, *Beethoven in seinen Beziehungen zu Dresden* (Dresden: Deutscher Literatur Verlag, 1942). For reception in and relation to other places, see the extensive listings in the bibliographies in *NBJ* and *BJ*, 2d series.

RELIGION

Arnold Schmitz, *Das romantische Beethovenbild* (Berlin and Bonn: Dümmler, 1927), pp. 82–101, and Jean Boyer, *Le 'romantisme' de Beethoven* (Paris: Didier, 1938), pp. 359–81; Martin Cooper, *Beethoven: The Last Decade* (London: Oxford Unviersity Press, 1970), pp. 105–19; Romain Rolland, *Beethoven: Les Grandes Époques créatrices* (Paris: Albin Michel, 1966), pp. 667–749; see also Arnold Schmitz, "Zur Frage nach Beethovens Weltanschauung und ihrem musikalischen Ausdruck," in Schmitz, ed., *Beethoven und die Gegenwart* (Berlin and Bonn: Dümmler, 1937), pp. 266–93; Schiedermair, *Der junge Beethoven*, pp. 327–29; Schiedermair, *Die Gestaltung weltanschaulicher Ideen in der Vokalmusik Beethovens* (Leipzig: Quelle & Meyer, 1934). See also Wilfrid Mellers, *Beethoven and the Voice of God* (London: Oxford University Press, 1983), and Maynard Solomon "Beethoven: The Quest for Faith," *BJ*, 2d series, 10 (1983): 101–19; reprinted in Solomon, *Beethoven Essays*, pp. 216–29.

See also listings under *Missa Solemnis*, below.

FINANCES

See Maynard Solomon, "Economic Circumstances of the Beethoven Household in Bonn," *JAMS* 50 (1997): 1–21, for a review of the Bonn documents. There is no adequate calculation of Beethoven's Viennese finances such as those done for Mozart. Julia Moore, "Beethoven and Musical Economics" (Ph.D. dissertation, University of Illinois, Urbana-Champaign, 1987), contains useful data on the costs of goods and inflation rates, but calculates neither Beethoven's income nor expenses, drastically underestimates his living standard during his final decade, and overstates the economic motivations of his late compositions. See also Julia Moore, "Beethoven and Musical Economics," *Beethoven Forum* 1 (1992): 191–223. Max Reinitz, *Beethoven im Kampf mit dem Schicksal* (Vienna: Rikola, 1924), is a detailed study of Beethoven's legal entanglements, including his efforts to restore the value of his annuity. A documented overview of the annuity payments is Martella Gutiérrez-Denhoff, "'O Unseeliges Dekret.' Beethovens Rente von Fürst Lobkowitz, Fürst Kinsky und Erzherzog Rudolph," in Sieghard Brandenburg and Gutiérrez-Denhoff, eds., *Beethoven und Böhmen* (BB, 1988), pp. 91–146. For annuity payments from Prince Kinsky see V. Kratochvil, "Beethoven und Fürst Kinsky," *Beethoven-Jahrbuch*, 1st series, 2 (1909): 3–47; summarized in Donald W. MacArdle and Ludwig Misch, eds. and trans., *New Beethoven Letters* (Norman: University of Oklahoma Press, 1957), pp. 72–73. For Lobkowitz's payments, see Schindler-MacArdle, p. 339n. 144. For the official evaluation of Beethoven's estate, see Theodor Frimmel, *Beethoven-Studien*, vol. 2 (Munich & Leipzig: Müller, 1906), pp. 169–201, and Thayer-Forbes, pp. 1061–76.

CRITICISM

SURVEYS AND OVERVIEWS

Two classic works are Walter Riezler, *Beethoven* (Berlin; Atlantis, 1936; 9th ed. 1966), trans. G. D. H. Pidcock (London: Forrester, 1938), and Paul Bekker, *Beethoven* (Munich: Schuster & Loeffler, 1911), trans. M. M. Bozman (London: Dent, 1925), alongside which we may also place Joseph Kerman's synoptic discussion of the music in Alan Tyson and Joseph Kerman's "Beethoven" entry, *TNG*, vol. 2, 376–89. William Kinderman, *Beethoven* (Berkeley and Los Angeles: University of California Press, 1995), is always informative and provides impressive narrative and symbolic interpretations in its extended discussions of the main works. Much of the music is brilliantly analyzed in Donald Francis Tovey, *Essays in Musical Analysis*, 7 vols. (London: Oxford University Press, 1935–44); Tovey, *The Mainstream of Music* (Cleveland and New York: Meridian, 1959); and Tovey, *Beethoven* (London: Oxford University Press, 1944; reprint, 1965).

High-level descriptive commentary on the entire oeuvre may be found in Albrecht Riethmüller, Carl Dahlhaus, and Alexander L. Ringer, eds., *Beethoven, Interpretationen seiner Werke*, 2 vols. (Laaber, Germany: Laaber-Verlag, 1994), a reference work written by seventy collaborators. For the Bonn music, see Schiedermair, *Der junge Beethoven*; J.-G. Prod'homme, *La Jeunesse de Beethoven* (Paris: Payot, 1920; reprint, Librairie Delagrave, 1927); Thayer-Deiters-Riemann; specialized studies by Hans Gál, "Die Stileigentümlichkeiten des jungen Beethoven," *Studien zur Musikwissenschaft* 4 (1916): 58–115; and Heinrich Jalowetz, "Beethovens Jugendwerke in ihren melodischen Beziehungen zu Mozart, Haydn und Ph. E. Bach," *Sammelbände der internationalen Musik-Gesellschaft* 12 (1910–11): 417–74. Martin Cooper, *Beethoven: The Last Decade* (London: Oxford University Press, 1970), offers serious discussions of the late works. An intelligent and fresh survey is Denis Arnold and Nigel Fortune, eds., *The Beethoven Reader* (New York: Norton, 1971), published in England as *The Beethoven Companion* (London: Faber and Faber, 1971). Joseph Schmidt-Görg and Hans Schmidt, eds., *Ludwig van Beethoven* (New York: Praeger, 1970), contains handy but uneven surveys of individual genres. Thomas K. Scherman and Louis Biancolli, eds., *The Beethoven Com-*

panion (Garden City, NY: Doubleday, 1972), is an unreliable anthology of previously published criticism and program notes, some newly translated. See also Harry Goldschmidt, *Beethoven: Werkeinführungen* (Leipzig: Reklam, 1975); Karl Schönewolf, *Beethoven in der Zeitenwende,* 2 vols. (Halle: Mitteldeutscher, 1953), and Wilfrid Mellers's challenging *Beethoven and the Voice of God* (London: Oxford University Press, 1983). For recurrent patterns in the music, see Ernest Newman, *The Unconscious Beethoven: An Essay in Musical Psychology* (New York: Knopf, 1927), and Rudolph Réti, *Thematic Patterns in Sonatas of Beethoven,* ed. Deryck Cooke (London: Faber and Faber, 1967).

For a survey of the literature on Beethoven's "three styles" and suggestions for an approach to periodization, see Maynard Solomon, "The Creative Periods of Beethoven," *MR* 34 (1973): 30–38, also in Solomon, *Beethoven Essays,* pp. 116–25; Kerman's alternative approach to the style periods may be found in Alan Tyson and Joseph Kerman, "Beethoven," *TNG* 2, pp. 376–78. A fine survey of the chamber music is Hans Mersmann, *Die Kammermusik,* vol. 2 (Leipzig: B&H, 1930); this continues the late-Romantic series begun by Hermann Kretzschmar, *Führer durch den Konzert-Saal,* 3 vols. (Leipzig, 1887–90). An enduring survey is Vincent d'Indy, "Beethoven" entry in *Cobbett's Cyclopaedic Survey of Chamber Music* (London and New York: Oxford, 1929). Sieghard Brandenburg and Helmut Loos, eds., *Beiträge zu Beethovens Kammermusik: Symposion Bonn 1984,* Veröffentlichungen des Beethovenhauses in Bonn, neue Folge, vierte Reihe, no. 10 (Munich: Henle, 1987), features worthy contributions by Wolfgang Osthoff, Martin Staehelin, Stefan Kunze, Reinhold Brinkmann, Richard Kramer, William Kinderman, Emil Platen, William Drabkin, Hans-Werner Küthen, Rudolf Bockholdt, Lewis Lockwood, and others, and an especially penetrating paper by Klaus Kropfinger, "Das gespaltene Werk–Beethovens Streichquartett Op. 130/133."

SYMPHONIES

A comprehensive modern treatment is much needed. The standard older monographs are George Grove, *Beethoven and His Nine Symphonies,* 3d ed. (1898; reprint, New York: Dover, 1962); J.-G. Prod'homme, *Les Symphonies de Beethoven* (Paris: Librairie Delagrave, 1906); and Karl Nef, *Die neun Sinfonien Beethovens* (Leipzig: B&H, 1928).

For the Third Symphony see Heinrich Schenker, "Beethovens 3. Sinfonie zum erstenmal in ihrem wahren Inhalt dargestellt," in Schenker's series *Das Meisterwerk in der Musik,* vol. 3 (Munich, 1930; reprint, Hildesheim: Olms, 1974); Walter Riezler, *Beethoven* (London: Forrester, 1938), pp. 247–81; Romain Rolland, *Beethoven: Les grandes époques créatrices,* (Paris: Albin Michel, 1966), pp. 49–80; and David Epstein, *Beyond Orpheus: Studies in Musical Structure* (Cambridge, MA: MIT Press, 1979), pp. 111–38, the latter on the impulse toward integration in the first movement of the *Eroica* Symphony. Four exemplary papers in Lewis Lockwood, *Beethoven: Studies in the Creative Process* (Cambridge, MA: Harvard University Press, 1992), pp. 118–80, explore the compositional genesis and design of the Symphony. Michael C. Tusa's discovery of the earliest surviving orchestral performance parts is described in "Die authentischen Quellen der 'Eroica,'" *Archiv für Musikwissenschaft* 42 (1985): 121–50.

For the Fifth Symphony, see Heinrich Schenker's monograph, *Beethoven: V. Sinfonie* (Vienna: Tonwille, [1925]; 2d ed., Vienna: Universal, 1970); Elliot Forbes, ed., *Beethoven, Symphony No. 5 in C Minor* (New York: Norton, 1971), with essays by Heinrich Schenker (excerpt), Donald Francis Tovey, E. T. A. Hoffmann, and others;

and Peter Gülke, *Zur Neuausgabe der Sinfonie Nr. V von Ludwig van Beethoven* (Leipzig, 1978).

For the Sixth Symphony: F. E. Kirby, "Beethoven's Pastoral Symphony as a *Sinfonia caracteristica*," *MQ* 56 (1970): 605–23; Philip Gossett, "Beethoven's Sixth Symphony: Sketches for the First Movement," *JAMS* 27 (1974): 248–84; Alan Tyson, "A Reconstruction of the Pastoral Symphony Sketchbook," in Alan Tyson, ed., *Beethoven Studies* 1 (1973): 67–96; and David Wyn Jones, *Beethoven: Pastoral Symphony*, Cambridge Music Handbook (Cambridge: Cambridge University Press, 1996).

The canonic writings on the Ninth Symphony include Donald Francis Tovey, *Beethoven's Ninth Symphony* (London: Oxford, 1928); Heinrich Schenker, *Beethovens Neunte Sinfonie* (Vienna: Universal, 1912; 2d ed., 1969), translated and edited by John Rothgeb as *Beethoven's Ninth Symphony* (New Haven and London: Yale University Press, 1992); Otto Baensch, *Aufbau und Sinn des Chorfinales in Beethovens neunter Symphonie* (Berlin and Leipzig: Walter de Gruyter, 1930); and Romain Rolland, *Beethoven. Les grandes époques créatrices* (Paris: Albin Michel, 1966), pp. 863–1024. The literature has been augmented in recent decades by a spate of writings that explore a wide range of interpretative perspectives, including Leo Treitler, "History, Criticism, and Beethoven's Ninth Symphony," *Nineteenth-Century Music* 3 (1980): 193–210, and "'To Worship That Celestial Sound': Motives for Analysis," *Journal of Musicology* 1 (1982): 153–70, both reprinted in Treitler, *Music and the Historical Imagination* (Cambridge, MA: Harvard University Press, 1989), pp. 19–66; Maynard Solomon, "Beethoven's Ninth Symphony: A Search for Order," *Nineteenth-Century Music* 10 (1986): 3–23; reprinted in Solomon, *Beethoven Essays*, pp. 3–32; Solomon, "Beethoven's Ninth Symphony: The Sense of an Ending," *Critical Inquiry* 17 (Winter, 1991): 289–305; and Richard Taruskin, "Resisting the Ninth," *Nineteenth-Century Music* 12 (1989): 241–56, reprinted in Taruskin, *Text and Act: Essays on Music and Performance* (New York: Oxford University Press, 1995), pp. 235–61. Seven papers on the Ninth, by Gülke, Küthen, Andreas Eichhorn, Lockwood, Sigrid Bresch, Solomon, and Webster, appear in Siegfried Kross et al., eds., *Probleme der symphonischen Tradition im 19. Jahrhundert: Internationales Musikwissenschaftliches Colloquium Bonn 1989, Kongressbericht* (Tutzing, Germany: Schneider, 1990), pp. 37–186.

Four papers are devoted to analyzing the form of the "Ode to Joy": Ernest Sanders, "Form and Content in the Finale of Beethoven's Ninth Symphony," *MQ* 50 (1964): 59–76; William Kinderman, "Beethoven's Compositional Models for the Choral Finale of the Ninth Symphony," in Kinderman, ed., *Beethoven's Compositional Process*, North American Beethoven Studies, no. 1 (Lincoln: University of Nebraska Press and American Beethoven Society, 1991), pp. 160–88; James Webster, "The Form of the Finale in Beethoven's Ninth Symphony," *Beethoven Forum* 1 (1992): 25–62; and Michael Tusa, "'Noch einmal': Form and Content in the Finale of Beethoven's Ninth Symphony," *Beethoven Forum* 7 (1998, in press). Full-scale discussions of the Ninth are provided by Johannes Bauer, *Rhetorik der Überschreitung: Annotationen zu Beethovens neunter Symphonie*, Musikwissenschaftliche Studien, no. 8 (Pfaffenweiler: Centaurus, 1992); Nicholas Cook, *Beethoven: Symphony No. 9* (Cambridge: Cambridge University Press, 1993), in the convenient Cambridge Music Handbook series; and David Benjamin Levy, *Beethoven: The Ninth Symphony*, Monuments of Western Music, ed. George B. Stauffer (New York: Schirmer Books, 1995). For the sketchbook sources of the Ninth, see Douglas Johnson, Alan Tyson, and Robert S. Winter, *The Beethoven Sketchbooks*

(Berkeley and Los Angeles: University of California Press, 1985), esp. pp. 275–303 and 397–414; Robert Winter, "The Sketches for the 'Ode to Joy,'" in Robert Winter and Bruce Carr, eds., *Beethoven, Performers, and Critics: The International Beethoven Congress, Detroit, 1977* (Detroit: Wayne State University Press, 1980), pp. 176–214; and Sieghard Brandenburg, "Die Skizzen zur Neunten Symphonie,"*Zu Beethoven* 2 (1984): 88–129.

Surviving sketches for the first movement of a tenth symphony are identified and surveyed in Barry Cooper, "Newly Identified Sketches for Beethoven's Tenth Symphony," *M&L* 66 (1985): 9–18; Cooper's questionable claims for his "realization" of the first movement of the Tenth Symphony are ably contested in Robert S. Winter, "Of Realizations, Completions, Restorations and Reconstructions: From Bach's *The Art of Fugue* to Beethoven's Tenth Symphony," *Journal of the Royal Musical Association* 116 (1991): 96–125.

CONCERTOS

Paul Badura-Skoda, "Text und Interpretationsprobleme in den fünf Klavierkonzerten Beethovens," *Piano-Jahrbuch* 3 (1983): 9–28; Leon Plantinga, "When Did Beethoven Compose His Third Piano Concerto?" *Journal of Musicology* 7 (1989): 275–307; Plantinga, *Beethoven's Concertos* (New York: Norton, in press), bids fair to become a standard work. See Hans-Werner Küthen's detailed critical reports for the Neue Gesamtausgabe editions: *Beethoven: Werke*, III/3, *Klavierkonzerte*, 2 vols. (Munich: Henle, 1984 and 1996). See also listings in Programmatic Interpretations, below.

STRING QUARTETS

The brilliant modern account is Joseph Kerman, *The Beethoven Quartets* (New York: Knopf, 1967); also laudable is Philip Radcliffe's concise *Beethoven's String Quartets* (London: Hutchinson, 1965; New York: Dutton, 1968). The pioneering study is Theodor Helm, *Beethovens Streichquartette* (Leipzig: Fritsch, 1885; reprint, Leipzig: Siegel, 1921). Ivan Mahaim, *Beethoven: Naissance et renaissance des derniers quatuors*, 2 vols. (Paris: de Brouwer, 1964), offers rich details on the performances and reputation of the late quartets in the nineteenth century. A major symposium is documented in Christoph Wolff, ed., *The String Quartets of Haydn, Mozart and Beethoven: Studies of the Autograph Manuscripts,* Isham Library Papers, no. 3 (Cambridge, MA: Harvard University Department of Music, 1980), with contributions by Richard Kramer, Robert Winter, Sieghard Brandenburg, and Martin Staehelin. Context, analysis, and reception of the quartets are covered by contributors to Robert S. Winter and Robert Martin, eds., *The Beethoven Quartet Companion* (Berkeley and Los Angeles: University of California Press, 1994).

For the revisions of the early quartets, see Sieghard Brandenburg, "The First Version of Beethoven's G major Quartet, Op. 18 No. 2," *M&L* 58 (1977): 127–52; Janet M. Levy, *Beethoven's Compositional Choices: The Two Versions of Opus 18, No. 1, First Movement* (Philadelphia: University of Pennsylvania Press, 1982); and Hans Josef Wedig, *Beethovens Streichquartett Op. 18 Nr. 1 und seine erste Fassung* (BB, 1992).

Several studies of sources and compositional process are Alan Tyson, "The 'Razumovsky' Quartets: Some Aspects of the Sources," *BS* 3 (1982): 107–40; Bruce Campbell, "Beethoven's Quartets Opus 59: An Investigation into Compositional Process" (Ph.D. dissertation, Yale University, 1982); Sieghard Brandenburg, "Die Quellen zur Entstehungsgeschichte von Beethovens Streichquartett Es-dur Op. 127," *Beethoven-Jahrbuch,* 2d series, 10 (1983): 221–76; and Robert S. Winter, "Plans for the Structure of the String Quartet in C Sharp Minor, Op. 131," *Beethoven Studies* 2 (1977): 106–37. An authoritative full-length account of the voluminous sketches for opus 131 is Robert Winter, *Compositional Origins of Beethoven's Opus 131* (Ann Arbor: UMI Research Press, 1982).

Other stimulating interpretations of the string quartets include Warren Kirkendale, "The 'Great Fugue' Op. 133: Beethoven's 'Art of Fugue,'" *Acta Musicologica* 35 (1963): 14–24; Leonard G. Ratner, *The Beethoven String Quartets: Compositional Strategies and Rhetoric* (Stanford: Stanford Bookstore, 1995); Jeremy Yudkin, "Beethoven's 'Mozart' Quartet," *JAMS* 45 (1992): 30–74; Richard Kramer, "Between Cavatina and Ouverture: Opus 130 and the Voices of Narrative," *Beethoven Forum* 1 (1992): 165–89; and Daniel K. L. Chua, *The "Galitzin" Quartets of Beethoven: Opp. 127, 132, 130* (Princeton: Princeton University Press, 1996).

TRIOS

Rudolf Bockholdt and Petra Weber-Bockholdt, eds., *Beethovens Klaviertrios: Symposion München 1990,* Veröffentlichungen des Beethovenhauses in Bonn, neue Folge, vierte Reihe: Schriften zur Beethovenforschung, no. 11 (Munich: Henle, 1992). See also Seow-Chin Ong, "Source Studies for Beethoven's Piano Trio in B-flat Major, Op. 97 ('Archduke')" (Ph.D. dissertation, University of California, Berkeley, 1995), and Ong, "The Autograph of Beethoven's 'Archduke' Trio, Op. 97," in proceedings (forthcoming) of the conference held in Ottawa in January 1996 entitled "Austria, 996–1996; Music in a Changing Society."

The literature on the "Kakadu" Variations, op. 121a, includes Lewis Lockwood, "Beethoven's 'Kakadu' Variations, Op. 121a: A Study in Paradox," in a forthcoming Festschrift for Jacob Lateiner; Bernt Edelmann, "Wenzel Müllers Lied vom 'Schneider Wetz' und Beethovens Trio-Variationenen Op. 121a"; and Wolfgang Osthoff, "Die langsamen Einleitungen in Beethovens Klaviertrios (Op. 1 Nr. 2; Op. 121a; Op. 70 Nr. 2)." The latter two are in Bockholdt and Bockholdt, *Beethovens Klaviertrios: Symposion München 1990* (see above), pp. 76–102 and 119–29.

PIANO SONATAS

For a learned conspectus of the sonatas and their literature, with thorough bibliography, see William S. Newman, *The Sonata in the Classic Era,* History of the Sonata Idea, vol. 2 (Chapel Hill: University of North Carolina Press, 1963; 2d ed., New York: Norton, 1972), pp. 501–43. Newman counts more than fifty separate books devoted to the sonatas. Valuable pioneering works include Wilhelm von Lenz, *Beethoven et ses trois styles* (St. Petersburg, 1852; Paris: Legouix, 1909), and Wilibald Nagel, *Beethoven und seine Klaviersonaten,* 2 vols. (1903–5; 2d ed., Langensalza, Germany: Hermann Beyer, 1923–24). Volumes 2 and 3 of Jürgen Uhde, *Beethovens Klaviermusik,* 3 vols. (Stuttgart: Phillip Reclam, 1968–74; reprint, 1980–91) contain illuminating and sensitive accounts of the thirty-two sonatas and other piano works. Other monographs include Kenneth Drake, *The Beethoven Sonatas and the Creative Experience* (Bloomington: University of Indiana Press, 1994), and Joachim Kaiser, *Beethovens 32 Klaviersonaten und ihre Interpreten* (Frankfurt: Fischer Verlag, 1975). The most useful older studies remain Jacques-Gabriel Prod'homme, *Les Sonates pour piano de Beethoven* (Paris: Librairie Delagrave, 1937); Eric Blom, *Beethoven's Pianoforte Sonatas Discussed* (London: Dent, 1938; reprint,

New York: Da Capo, 1968); and Donald Francis Tovey, *A Companion to Beethoven's Pianoforte Sonatas (Bar-to-bar Analysis)* (London: Associated Board of the Royal Schools of Music, 1931). Hugo Riemann's structural analysis, *L. van Beethovens sämtliche Klavier-Solosonaten*, 3 vols. (Berlin: Max Hesse, 1917–19), retains its authority. For the last sonatas, except for opus 106, see Heinrich Schenker, ed., *Die letzten fünf Sonaten von Beethoven: Kritische Ausgabe mit Einführung und Erläuterung*, 4 vols. (Vienna: Universal, 1913–21; new ed., 1971–72).

Monographs on the sources for individual sonatas include William Drabkin's outstanding "A Study of Beethoven's Opus 111 and Its Sources" (Ph.D. dissertation, Princeton University, 1977); Martha Fröhlich's study of opus 57, *Beethoven's 'Appassionata' Sonata*, Studies in Musical Genesis and Structure, ed. Lewis Lockwood (Oxford: Clarendon Press, 1991); Nicholas Marston's *Beethoven's Piano Sonata in E, Op. 109*, Studies in Musical Genesis and Structure, ed. Lewis Lockwood (Oxford: Clarendon Press, 1995); and Allen Forte's Schenkerian study of the sketches for opus 109, *The Compositional Matrix* (Baldwin, NY: Music Teachers National Association, 1961; reprint, New York: Da Capo, 1974). Nicholas Marston, "Approaching the Sketches for Beethoven's 'Hammerklavier' Sonata," *JAMS* 44 (1991): 404–50, offers a chronology of the loose sketch leaves and identifies previously unknown desk sketches for opus 106.

William Kinderman, "Integration and Narrative Design in Beethoven's Piano Sonata in A-flat major, Opus 110," *Beethoven Forum* 1 (1992): 111–45, is a superlative reading of that sonata's long-range narrative implications. Elaine R. Sisman, "Pathos and the *Pathétique:* Rhetorical Stance in Beethoven's C-Minor Sonata, Op. 13," *Beethoven Forum* 3 (1994): 81–105, is a first-rate essay on sonata-form analogies to rhetorical tropes and patterns.

STRING SONATAS

Descriptive analyses may be found in J. H. Wetzel, *Beethovens Violinsonaten*, vol. 1 (Berlin: Max Hesse, 1924), and Marcel Herwegh, *Technique d'Interprétation . . . appliqué aux sonates pour piano et violon de Beethoven* (Paris: Magasin Musical, 1926). For thoughts of several eminent violinists on performance details, see Joseph Szigeti, *The Ten Beethoven Sonatas for Piano and Violin* (Urbana, IL: American String Teachers Association, 1965), and Max Rostal, *Beethoven: The Sonatas for Piano and Violin*, trans. Horace and Anna Rosenberg (London: Toccata Press, 1985). Richard A. Kramer, "The Sketches for Beethoven's Violin Sonatas, Opus 30: History, Transcription, Analysis," 3 vols. (Ph.D. dissertation, Princeton University, 1974), is a major dissertation, deserving of more frequent citation. Carl Schachter, "The Sketches for the Sonata for Piano and Violin, Op. 24," *Beethoven Forum* 3 (1994): 107–25, persuasively discloses how the final work is already implicit in its initiating impulse.

VARIATIONS

Jürgen Uhde, *Beethovens Klaviermusik I: Klavierstücke und Variationen* (Stuttgart: Philipp Reclam, 1968; 2d ed., 1980), is the outstanding account, combining keen analytic insights with perspectives influenced by Ernst Bloch's utopian "philosophy of hope." Elaine Sisman, *Haydn and the Classical Variation* (Cambridge, MA: Harvard University Press, 1993), pp. 235–62, 272–75, is a thoughtful survey, also containing a handy tabulation of Beethoven's works in variation form. A useful list of variation movements in the instrumental works may be consulted in Norbert Stich, "Satzgattungen in Beethovens

Instrumentalwerken," in Siegfried Kross and Hans Schmidt, eds., *Colloquium Amicorum: Joseph Schmidt-Görg zum 70. Geburtstag* (BB, 1967), p. 385. See also Henry Hadow, "Variation-Form," *M&L* 8 (1927): 127–31; Willy Hess, "Von Dressler bis Diabelli," in Erich Schenk, ed., *Beethoven-Studien* (Vienna: Böhlaus, 1970), pp. 72–79; and Otto Klauwell, *Ludwig van Beethoven und die Variationenform,* Musikalisches Magazin, no. 3 (Langensalza, Germany: Hermann Beyer & Söhne, 1901).

For the Diabelli Variations, the starting point is the superb monograph by William Kinderman, *Beethoven's Diabelli Variations,* Studies in Musical Genesis and Structure, ed. Lewis Lockwood (Oxford: Clarendon Press, 1989), and Kinderman, "The Evolution and Structure of Beethoven's 'Diabelli' Variations," *JAMS* 35 (1982): 306–28. Highlights of the critical literature on opus 120 include Donald Francis Tovey, *Essays in Musical Analysis: Chamber Music* (London: Oxford University Press, 1944), pp. 124–35; Eric Blom, "Beethoven's Diabelli Variations," in Blom, *Classics Major and Minor* (London: Dent, 1958), pp. 48–78; Karl Geiringer, "The Structure of Beethoven's Diabelli Variations," *MQ* 50 (1964): 496–503; Arnold Münster, *Studien zu Beethovens Diabelli-Variationen* (Munich: Henle, 1982); Uhde, *Beethovens Klaviermusik,* vol. 1 (see above), pp. 503–56; and August Halm's brilliant post-Nietzschean approach in *Beethoven* (Berlin: Max Hesse, 1927), pp. 176–203, 263–302. See also Maynard Solomon, "Beethoven's Diabelli Variations: The End of a Beginning," *Beethoven Forum* 7 (in press).

EARLY VARIATIONS

Steven Moore Whiting, "To the 'New Manner' Born: A Study of Beethoven's Early Variations" (Ph.D. dissertation, University of Illinois, 1991), is a stylish treatise; Whiting's reliable essays on the variations WoO 40, WoO 63–67, and WoO 71, may be consulted in Albrecht Riethmüller, Carl Dahlhaus, and Alexander L. Ringer, eds., *Beethoven, Interpretationen seiner Werke* (Laaber, Germany: Laaber-Verlag, 1994). The sources of the opus 35 Variations are examined in Christopher Reynolds, "Beethoven's Sketches for the Variations in E-flat Op. 35," in *Beethoven Studies* 3 (1982): 47–84. The connection between the variations and the finale of the *Eroica* Symphony is discussed in Kurt von Fischer, "Eroica-Variationen Op. 35 und Eroica-Finale," *Schweizerische Musikzeitung* 89 (1949): 282–86. See also Glenn Stanley, "The 'wirklich gantz neue Manier' and the Path to It," *Beethoven Forum* 3 (1994): 53–79, which argues for the innovative quality of the earlier Viennese variations.

BAGATELLES

Sieghard Brandenburg, ed., *Sechs Bagatellen für Klavier, Op. 126,* facsimile and transcription, with Brandenburg's commentary (BB, 1984). Edward T. Cone, "The Late Bagetelles: Beethoven's Experiments in Composition," in Cone, *A View from Delft: Selected Essays,* ed. Robert P. Morgan (Chicago and London: University of Chicago Press, 1989), pp. 179–200. On the chronology and compositional history of opus 119, see Barry Cooper, *Beethoven and the Creative Process* (Oxford: Clarendon Press, 1990), pp. 263–82. A wide-ranging but unrigorous hermeneutic interpretation is Heinrich Poos, "Beethoven ars poetica: Die Bagatelle op. 119,7," *Musik-Konzepte* 56 (1987): 3–45.

FIDELIO/LEONORE

A scholarly model is Winton Dean, "Beethoven and Opera," in Denis Arnold and Nigel Fortune, eds., *The Beethoven Reader* (New York: Norton, 1971), pp. 331–86. A standard work on the three versions of the opera is Willy Hess, *Beethovens Oper Fidelio und ihre drei Fassungen* (Zürich: Atlantis, 1953). Now superseded is Maurice Kufferath, *Fidelio* (Paris: Fischbacher, 1913). The texts of Bouilly's *Léonore* and Sonnleithner's adaptation are in Adolf Sandberger, *Ausgewählte Aufsätze zur Musikgeschichte*, vol. 2 (Munich: Drei Masken, 1924), pp. 281–365. The classic study of the overtures is Josef Braunstein, *Beethovens Leonore-Ouvertüren* (Leipzig: B&H, 1927), which must be modified in light of Alan Tyson, "The Problem of Beethoven's 'First' *Leonore* Overture," *JAMS* 28 (1975): 292–334. For the compositional chronology of the first version, see Chapter 12, n.16. Two papers by Michael Tusa explore contextual, structural, and tonal issues: "The Unknown Florestan: The 1805 version of 'In des Lebens Frühlingstagen,'" *JAMS* 46 (1993): 175–220, and "Beethoven and Opera: The Grave-digging Duet in *Leonore* (1805)," *Beethoven Forum* 5 (1996): 1–63. The Cambridge Opera Handbook *Ludwig van Beethoven: "Fidelio"* (Cambridge: Cambridge University Press, 1996) is ably edited by Paul Robinson.

THE BONN CANTATAS

The pioneering essay is Eduard Hanslick, "Zwei neu aufgefundene Cantaten von Beethoven," in *Suite: Aufsätze über Musik und Musiker* (Vienna: Prochaska, n.d. [1885?]); see also Elliot Forbes, "Stürzet nieder, Millionen," in Harold Powers, ed., *Studies in Music History: Essays for Oliver Strunk* (Princeton: Princeton University Press, 1968), pp. 449–57; Jürgen Mainka, "Beethovens bonner Kantaten," in H. A. Brockhaus and K. Niemann, eds., *Bericht über den internationalen Beethoven-Kongress 10.–12. Dezember 1970 in Berlin* (Berlin: Verlag Neue Musik, 1971), pp. 315–26; and William Kinderman, *Beethoven* (Berkeley and Los Angeles: University of California Press, 1995), pp. 20–27.

MISSA SOLEMNIS

A rich literature on the *Missa Solemnis* has emerged, inaugurated by Warren Kirkendale's major study of its musical and liturgical sources, "New Roads to Old Ideas in Beethoven's *Missa Solemnis*," *MQ* 56 (1970): 665–701, reprinted in Paul Henry Lang, ed., *The Creative World of Beethoven* (New York: Norton, 1971). William Kinderman, "Beethoven's Symbol for the Deity in the *Missa solemnis* and the Ninth Symphony," *Nineteenth-Century Music* 9 (1985): 102–18, brilliantly explores rhetorical and musical tropes, especially those related to the representation of contrasts between height and depth. Outstanding brief commentaries are to be found in Bekker, *Beethoven*; Riezler, *Beethoven*; Martin Cooper, *Beethoven: The Last Decade*; and in Ernest Newman's notes to the Toscanini recording (RCA, LM 6013, 1954). See also Romain Rolland, *Beethoven: Les grandes époques créatrices* (Paris: Albin Michel, 1966), pp. 667–750; T. W. Adorno, "Verfremdetes Hauptwerk: zur Missa solemnis," in his *Moments musicaux* (Frankfurt: Suhrkamp, 1964), translated as "Alienated Masterpiece: The *Missa Solemnis*," *Telos*, no. 28 (Summer 1976): 113–24; Willy Hess, *Beethoven-Studien* (BB, 1972), pp. 232–62. William Drabkin, *Beethoven: Missa solemnis*, Cambridge Music Handbooks (Cambridge: Cambridge University Press, 1991), is a model handbook, combining original insights with full control of the literature; see also Drabkin, "The Agnus Dei of Beethoven's *Missa solemnis:* The Growth of its Form," in William Kinderman, ed., *Beethoven's Compositional Process*, North American Beethoven Studies, no. 1 (Lincoln: University of Nebraska Press and American Beethoven Society, 1991), pp. 131–59.

　　For the sketches and autographs of the *Missa Solemnis*, see Robert S. Winter, "Reconstructing Riddles: The Sources for Beethoven's *Missa solemnis*," in Lewis Lockwood and Phyllis Benjamin, eds., *Beethoven Essays: Studies in Honor of Elliot Forbes* (Cambridge, MA: Harvard University Music Department, 1984), pp. 217–50; for an essay on the significance of the *Missa Solemnis*, see Ernest H. Sanders, "Beethoven's Treatment of Form and Content in his *Missa Solemnis*," in Christoph-Hellmut Mahling and Ruth Seiberts, eds., *Festschrift Walter Wiora zum 90. Geburtstag* (Tutzing, Germany: Schneider, 1997), pp. 398–418. See also Gene P. Strayer, "The Theology of Beethoven's Masses" (Ph.D. dissertation, University of Pennsylvania, 1991). Bathia Churgin, "Beethoven and Mozart's Requiem: A New Connection," *Journal of Musicology* 5 (1987): 457–77, discusses a newly discovered copy of a Mozart fugue made by Beethoven evidently in connection with the composition of the *Missa Solemnis*.

CHORAL FANTASIA

Edward J. Dent, "The Choral Fantasia," *M&L* 8 (1927): 111–22; Steven Moore Whiting, "'Hört ihr wohl': Zu Funktion und Programm von Beethovens 'Chorfantasie,'" *Archiv für Musikwissenschaft* 45 (1988): 132–47; Wilhelm Seidel, "Fantaisie c-Moll für Klavier, Chor und Orchester," in Albrecht Riethmüller, Carl Dahlhaus, and Alexander L. Ringer, eds., *Beethoven, Interpretation seiner Werke*, (Laaber, Germany: Laaber-Verlag, 1994), vol. 1, pp. 618–25.

LIEDER

The standard work is Hans Boettcher, *Beethoven als Liederkomponist* (Augsburg: Benno Filser, 1928). See also the brief study by Henri de Curzon, *Les Lieder et airs détachés de Beethoven* (Paris: Fischbacher, 1905); Romain Rolland, *Beethoven: Les grandes époques créatrices* (Paris: Albin Michel), pp. 527–69; Joseph Kerman, "*An die Ferne Geliebte,*" *Beethoven Studies* 1 (1973): 123–57, and Lewis Lockwood, "Beethoven's Sketches for *Sehnsucht* (WoO 146)," *Beethoven Studies* 1 (173): 97–122.

For a well-considered bibliographic and stylistic study of Beethoven's folk-song arrangements see Barry Cooper, *Beethoven's Folksong Settings: Chronology, Sources, Style* (Oxford: Clarendon Press, 1994); this is complemented by Petra Weber-Bockholdt's interpretative monograph, *Beethovens Bearbeitung britischer Lieder,* Studien zur Musik, vol. 13 (Munich: William Fink Verlag, 1994). See also Cecil Hopkinson and C. B. Oldman, *Thomson's Collection of National Song, with Special Reference to the Contributions of Haydn and Beethoven* (Edinburgh: Clark, 1940); Kinsky-Halm, pp. 627–28; and Richard Hohenemser-Halensee, "Beethoven als Bearbeiter schottischer und anderer Volksweisen," *Die Musik* 10, no. 6 (December 1910): 323–38.

STYLE

Among specialized studies of Beethoven's styles and forms, see Arnold Schmitz, *Beethovens 'zwei Prinzipe'* (Berlin and Bonn: Dümmler, 1923); Hans Mersmann, *Beethoven: Die Synthese der Stile* (Berlin: Julius Bard, [1922]); Walter Engelsmann, *Beethovens Kompositionspläne* (Augsburg: Benno Filser, 1931); Fritz Cassirer, *Beethoven und die Gestalt* (Stuttgart: Deutsche Verlags-Anstalt, 1925); and Kurt von Fischer, *Die Beziehungen von Form und Motiv in Beethovens Instrumentalwerken* (Strasbourg: Heity, 1948; 2d ed., Hildesheim: Olms, 1972). See also writings by Otto Baensch, Romain Rolland, Walter Krug, Gustav Becking, August Halm, Donald Francis Tovey, Rudolph Réti, Hugo Leichtentritt, Erwin Ratz, and T. W. Adorno. For a convenient tabulation of Beethoven's instrumental forms, see Norbert Stich, "Satzgattungen in Beethovens

Instrumentalwerken," in Siegfried Kross and Hans Schmidt, eds., *Colloquium Amicorum: Joseph Schmidt-Görg zum 70. Geburtstag* (BB, 1967), pp. 379–85.

Two books on Beethoven's so-called heroic style are Michael Broyles, *The Emergence and Evolution of Beethoven's Heroic Style* (New York: Excelsior, 1987), and Scott Burnham, *Beethoven Hero* (Princeton: Princeton University Press, 1995), the former grounded in formal theory, the latter largely devoted to hermeneutic implications of Beethoven's rhetoric.

LATE STYLE

For a seminal essay on late Beethoven, see Ernest Newman, "Beethoven: The Last Phase," in Newman, *Testament of Music* (London: Putnam, 1962), pp. 240–52. T. W. Adorno's most famous discussions of late Beethoven, apart from his contributions to Thomas Mann's *Doctor Faustus* (New York: Knopf, 1948), are "Spätstil Beethovens" and "Verfremdetes Hauptwerk: zur *Missa Solemnis*, both in his *Moments musicaux* (Frankfurt: Suhrkamp, 1964), pp. 13–17, 167–85. His fragmentary Beethoven writings are posthumously published in Theodor W. Adorno, *Beethoven: Philosophie der Musik; Fragmente und Texte,* T. W. Adorno, Nachgelassene Schriften, Part 1, vol. 1, ed. Rolf Tiedemann (Frankfurt: Suhrkamp, 1993). For an informed discussion see Stephen Hinton, "Adorno's Unfinished *Beethoven*," *Beethoven Forum* 5 (1996): 139–53. For an influential exegesis, see Rose Rosengard Subotnik, "Adorno's Diagnosis of Beethoven's Late Style: Early Symptom of a Fatal Condition," *JAMS* 29 (1976): 242–75. A conference, "Rethinking Beethoven's Last Period," was held at Harvard University in November 1996; portions of the proceedings are to be published as a Festschrift for Lewis Lockwood in *Beethoven Forum* 7 (ca. 1998). Other recent investigations of the late style include Kevin Korsyn, "Integration in Works of Beethoven's Final Period" (Ph.D. dissertation, Yale University, 1983); Korsyn, "J. W. N. Sullivan and the *Heiliger Dankgesang:* Questions of Meaning in Late Beethoven," *Beethoven Forum* 2 (1994): 133–74; and Sylvia Imeson, "'The time gives it proofe': Paradox in the Late Music of Beethoven" (Ph.D. dissertation, University of Victoria, 1993).

For several studies exemplifying a variety of modern analytic approaches, see Lawrence Kramer, "Beethoven's Two-Movement Piano Sonatas and the Utopia of Romantic Esthetics," in Kramer, *Music as Cultural Practice, 1800–1900* (Berkeley and Los Angeles: University of California Press, 1990), pp. 21–71; V. Kofi Agawu, "A Semiotic Interpretation of the First Movement of Beethoven's String Quartet in A Minor, Op. 132," in Agawu, *Playing with Signs: A Semiotic Interpretation of Classic Music* (Princeton: Princeton University Press, 1991), pp. 110–26, which proposes a fusion of Schenkerian and Ratnerian models; Robert S. Hatten, *Musical Meaning in Beethoven: Markedness, Correlation, and Interpretation* (Bloomington: Indiana University Press, 1994), a set of Piercean analyses; and Daniel K. L. Chua, *The "Galitzin" Quartets of Beethoven: Opp. 127, 132, 130* (Princeton: Princeton University Press, 1996), which subjects these works to keen ideological scrutiny informed by Adorno's analytic categories. The Beethoven chapter in Warren Kirkendale, *Fugue and Fugato in Rococo and Classical Chamber Music,* trans. Margaret Bent and the author (Durham, NC: Duke University Press, 1979), pp. 203–71, remains a definitive study of Beethoven as the inheritor of traditional contrapuntal practices.

CLASSICISM AND ROMANTICISM

For classicism and romanticism, see Friedrich Blume, *Classic and Romantic Music* (New York: Norton, 1970); Charles Rosen, *The Classical Style: Haydn, Mozart, Beethoven* (New York: Viking, 1971; rev. ed., 1997); and Alfred Einstein, *Music in the Romantic*

Era (New York: Norton, 1947). For the growth of the Romantic image of Beethoven, see Arnold Schmitz, *Das romantische Beethovenbild* (Berlin and Bonn: Dümmler, 1927), and Jean Boyer, *Le 'romantisme' de Beethoven* (Paris: Didier, 1938), with comprehensive bibliography. See also William S. Newman, "The Beethoven Mystique in Romantic Art, Literature, and Music," *MQ* 69 (1983): 354–87. For Beethoven's receptivity to Romantic and modernist trends, see Maynard Solomon, "Beethoven: Beyond Classicism," in Robert S. Winter and Robert Martin, eds., *The Beethoven Quartet Companion* (Berkeley and Los Angeles: University of California Press, 1994), pp. 59–76; Solomon, "Some Romantic Imagery in Beethoven," in Sieghard Brandenburg, ed., *Haydn, Mozart, and Beethoven: Essays in Honour of Alan Tyson* (Oxford: Oxford University Press, 1998), pp. 253–81. See also Hans Heinrich Eggebrecht, "Beethoven und der Begriff der Klassik," in Erich Schenk, ed., *Beethoven-Symposion Wien 1970* (Vienna: Böhlaus, 1971), pp. 43–60; Rey M. Longyear, "Beethoven and Romantic Irony," *MQ* 56 (1970): 647–64; Carl Dahlhaus, "E. T. A. Hoffmanns Beethoven-Kritik und die Aesthetik der Erhabenen," *Archiv für Musik-Wissenschaft* 38 (1981): 79–92.

PROGRAMMATIC INTERPRETATIONS

Arnold Schering, in *Beethoven in neuer Deutung* (Leipzig: C. F. Kahnt, 1934), *Beethoven und die Dichtung* (Berlin: Junker und Dünnhaupt, 1936), and other writings, claimed to be able to identify a single literary source as Beethoven's underlying poetic idea for each of his major sonatas and string quartets. For a listing of Schering's proposed literary sources for twenty-five of the sonatas, see William S. Newman, *The Sonata in the Classic Era*, History of the Sonata Idea, vol. 2 (Chapel Hill: University of North Carolina Press, 1963; 2d ed., New York: Norton, 1972), pp. 504–5.

An intimate connection between the *Eroica* Symphony and the *Creatures of Prometheus* ballet scenario is argued in Constantin Floros, *Beethovens Eroica und Prometheus-Musik* (Wilhelmshaven: Heinrichshofen's Verlag, 1978), and by Martin Geck and Peter Schleuning, *"Geschrieben auf Bonaparte"—Beethovens "Eroica": Revolution, Reaktion, Rezeption* (Hamburg: Rowohlt Verlag, 1989). The view of the *Eroica* as a "Prometheus" symphony was largely anticipated by Harry Goldschmidt, *Beethoven: Werkeinführungen* (Leipzig: Reclam, 1975), pp. 29–33, 287–300. See also the discussion of Floros and Schleuning in Thomas Sipe, "Interpreting Beethoven: History, Aesthetics, and Critical Reception" (Ph.D. dissertation, University of Pennsylvania, 1992).

Extramusical mythic and literary plots have been proposed for several of Beethoven's instrumental works by Owen Jander, most notably for the Piano Concerto No. 4, pursuing an idea first proposed by A. B. Marx: see especially Jander, "Beethoven's 'Orpheus in Hades,'" *Nineteenth-Century Music* 8 (1985): 195–212, and "Orpheus Revisited: A Ten-Year Retrospect on the Andante con moto of Beethoven's Fourth Piano Concerto," *Nineteenth-Century Music* 19 (1995): 31–49. Notable caveats to this approach have been entered, by Edward T. Cone, "Beethoven Orpheus—or Jander's?" *Nineteenth-Century Music* (1985): 283–86, and Joseph Kerman, "Representing a Relationship: Notes on a Beethoven Concerto," *Representations* 39 (1992): 80–101.

PERFORMANCE PRACTICES

The very extensive literature goes back to writings and memoirs by Beethoven's students and associates, including Schindler, Holz, and Czerny, and to editions and treatises by contemporary keyboard pedagogues and critics. A brief selection of exemplary studies includes Carl Czerny, *The Art of Playing the Ancient and Modern Piano Forte Works* (London: R. Cocks & Co., n.d.), chapters 2 and 3 reprinted in *On the Proper Performance of All Beethoven's Works for the Piano* (Vienna: Universal, 1970); William S. Newman, *Beethoven on Beethoven: Playing His Piano Music His Way* (New York: Norton, 1988); Rudolf Kolisch, "Tempo and Character in Beethoven's Music," *MQ* 77 (1993): 90–131, 268–342; Peter Gülke, "Zum Verhältnis von Intention und Realisierung bei Beethoven," *Musik-Konzepte 8: Beethoven: Das Problem der Interpretation* (Munich, 1979), pp. 34–53; Robert Winter, "Performing Beethoven's Early Piano Concertos," *Early Music* 16 (1988): 214–30; and the essays by various hands in Robin Stowell, ed., *Performing Beethoven*, Cambridge Studies in Performance Practice, no. 4 (Cambridge: Cambridge University Press, 1994). A list prepared by Bathia Churgin of the probing and eminently sensible Beethoven essays by the conductor Max Rudolf is in *Beethoven Newsletter* 10 (1995): 42; see especially the following Rudolf essays: "Inner Repeats in the Da Capo of Classical Minuets and Scherzos," *Journal of the Conductors' Guild* 3 (1982): 145–50; "The Metronome Indications in Beethoven's Symphonies," *Journal of the Conductors' Guild* 1 (1980): 1–13; and the perceptive "Scores and Parts: Remarks on Current Editions of Mozart and Beethoven Symphonies," *Journal of the Conductors' Guild* 3 (1982): 118–22. See also Eva Badura-Skoda, "Performance Conventions in Beethoven's Early Works," in Robert Winter and Bruce Carr, eds., *Beethoven, Performers, and Critics: The International Beethoven Congress, Detroit, 1977* (Detroit: Wayne State University Press, 1980), pp. 52–76; and the relevant pages of Sandra P. Rosenblum, *Performance Practices in Classic Piano Music* (Bloomington and Indianapolis: Indiana University Press, 1988). Rudolf Klein, ed., *Beiträge '76–78, Beethoven-Kolloquium 1977: Dokumentation und Aufführungspraxis* (Kassel: Bärenreiter, 1978), ranges widely over issues of performance practice, particularly in contributions by Sieghard Brandenburg, Peter Stadlen, Emil Platen, Hans Schmidt, Vera Schwarz, Siegfried Kross, Shin Augustinus Kojima; Günther Massenkeil, Richard Kramer, Lewis Lockwood, Herbert Seifert, and Hubert Unverricht.

GENERAL BACKGROUND

HISTORICAL BACKGROUND

Among standard histories of music, see Paul Henry Lang, *Music in Western Civilization* (New York: Norton, 1941); Jules Combarieu, *Histoire de la Musique*, vol. 2, 2d ed. (Paris: Armand Colin, 1920); and Hugo Leichtentritt, *Music, History, and Ideas* (Cambridge, MA: Harvard University Press, 1947). An elegant sociology of the piano is Arthur Loesser, *Men, Women, and Pianos: A Social History* (New York: Simon & Schuster, 1954). For the evolution of the symphony orchestra, see Paul Bekker, *The Orchestra* (New York: Norton Library, 1963), and Adam Carse, *The Orchestra from Beethoven to Berlioz* (New York: Broude Bros., 1949).

The standard history of the sonata, its styles, forms, and development, is William S. Newman, *A History of the Sonata Idea*, 3 vols. (Chapel Hill: University of North Carolina Press, 1959–69); see also Philip T. Barford, "The Sonata-Principle," *MR* 13 (1952): 255–63.

For a compact history of Bonn, see Edith Ennen and Dietrich Höroldt, *Vom Römerkastell zur Bundeshauptstadt: Kleine Geschichte der Stadt Bonn*, 3d ed. (Bonn: Stollfuss, 1976), with a bibliography. For more detailed studies of the Bonn social and historical context, see a large variety of writings by the eminent historian Max Braubach.

For background on Vienna and the Habsburg empire: Ilse Barea, *Vienna* (New York: Knopf, 1966), is a superb social and cultural history. A late-eighteenth-century guidebook with valuable information on Viennese life, culture, and institutions is Johann Pezzl, *Skizze von Wien*, 2 vols. (Vienna, 1786–90); an abridged translation is in H. C. Robbins Landon, *Mozart and Vienna* (New York, 1991), pp. 53–191. Two notable books by Ernst Wangermann, *The Austrian Achievement: 1700–1800* (London: Thames & Hudson, 1973), and *From Joseph II to the Jacobin Trials*, Oxford Historical Series, 2d series, ed. R. W. Southern et al. (London: Oxford University Press, 1959), pp. 133–87, provide background on the Josephinian period and the subsequent decline into repression. See also Denis Silagi, *Jakobiner in der Habsburger-Monarchie*, Wiener historische Studien, no. 6 (Vienna and Munich: Verlag Herold, 1962).

CONTEMPORARY TRAVELS AND MEMOIRS

A selection of keenly observed travel writings includes the following: Baron Caspar Riesbeck, *Travels Through Germany in a Series of Letters*, trans. Rev. Mr. Maty, 3 vols. (London: T. Cadell, 1787); John Owen, *Travels into Different Parts of Europe, in the Years 1791 and 1792* (London: Cadell & Davies, 1796); Henry Reeve, *Journal of a Residence at Vienna and Berlin in the Eventful Winter of 1805–1806* (London: Longmans Green, 1877); John Russell, *A Tour in Germany, and Some of the Southern Provinces of the Austrian Empire, in the Years 1820, 1821, 1822* (Boston: Wells & Lilly, 1825). Several memoirs by Beethoven's contemporaries include Charlotte Moscheles, *Life of Moscheles*, trans. A. D. Coleridge, 2 vols. (London: Hurst and Blackett, 1873), also published as Moscheles, *Recent Music and Musicians* (New York: Henry Holt, 1873); Rosemary Hughes, ed., *A Mozart Pilgrimage: Being the Travel Diaries of Vincent and Mary Novello in the year 1829*, trans. and comp. Nerina Medici di Marignano (London, 1955), which contains recollections of Beethoven by the Streichers and Abbé Stadler; J. F. Reichardt, *Vertraute Briefe*, ed. G. Gugitz, 2 vols. (reprint, Munich: Müller, 1915); and Ignaz Franz Castelli, *Memoiren meines Lebens* (Vienna, 1861, reprint, ed. Joseph Bindtner, 2 vols., Munich: Müller, 1914).

CONCERT LIFE

Eduard Hanslick's *Geschichte des Concertwesens in Wien* (Vienna: Braumüller, 1869), is rather unsystematically packed with data on Viennese concert life from the founding of the Tonkünstler-Societät in 1772 until the 1860s. For a comprehensive, but inevitably incomplete, listing of public and private concerts in Vienna to 1810 and an informative discussion of the economics of Viennese concert life, see Mary Sue Morrow, *Concert Life in Haydn's Vienna: Aspects of a Developing Musical and Social Institution* (Stuyvesant, NY: Pendragon Press, 1989). Two valuable discussions are Otto Biba, "Concert Life in Beethoven's Vienna," in Robert Winter and Bruce Carr, eds., *Beethoven, Performers, and Critics* (Detroit: Wayne State University Press, 1980), pp. 77–93, and Biba, "Beethoven und die 'Liebhaber Concerte' in Wien im Winter 1807/08," in Rudolf Klein, ed., *Beiträge '76–78, Beethoven-Kolloquium 1977: Dokumentation und Aufführungspraxis* (Kassel: Bärenreiter, 1978), pp. 82–93. Alice M. Hanson, *Musical Life in Biedermeier Vienna* (Cambridge: Cambridge University Press, 1985), is excellent on concert venues, musical institutions, and the social context between 1815 and 1830.

CONTEMPORARY CRITICISM

For Beethoven's contemporary critics: an indispensable but not exhaustive compendium of reviews in contemporary periodicals, organized by opus numbers, and only sparsely annotated, is Stefan Kunze, ed., *Ludwig van Beethoven: Die Werke im Spiegel seiner Zeit: Gesammelte Konzertberichte und Rezensionen bis 1830* (Laaber, Germany: Laaber-Verlag, 1987). A fine edition of writings by Beethoven's greatest contemporary critic is David Charlton, ed., *E. T. A. Hoffmann's Musical Writings: "Kreisleriana," "The Poet and the Composer," Music Criticism,* trans. Martyn Clarke (Cambridge: Cambridge University Press, 1989). See also A. B. Marx, *Musical Form in the Age of Beethoven: Selected Writings on Theory and Method,* ed. and trans. Scott Burnham (Cambridge: Cambridge University Press, 1997), and Robin Wallace, *Beethoven's Critics* (Cambridge: Cambridge University Press, 1987).

For the aesthetic and critical context, see Peter le Huray and James Day, eds., *Music and Aesthetics in the Eighteenth and Early-Nineteenth Centuries,* Cambridge Readings in the Literature of Music (Cambridge: Cambridge University Press, 1981); Ian Bent, ed., *Music Analysis in the Nineteenth Century,* 2 vols. (Cambridge: Cambridge University Press, 1994); Oliver Strunk, ed., *Source Readings in Music History,* rev. ed., Leo Treitler, general ed. (New York: Norton, 1998). See also listings under Reputation and Reception, above.

Index of Compositions

The index contains a complete numerical list of works with opus numbers plus lists of works without opus numbers (WoO and Hess) and of projected works mentioned in this book. The index is preceded by a "classified list" of major compositions referring the reader to the relevant opus, WoO, or Hess numbers.

CLASSIFIED LIST

BAGATELLES FOR PIANO

op. 33; op. 119; op.126; WoO 59 ("Für Elise")

BALLETS

Die Geschöpfe des Prometheus, op. 43; *Ritterballett,* WoO 1.

CONCERTOS

For Piano: in E-flat, WoO 4; No. 1, op. 15; No. 2, op. 19; No. 3, op. 37; No. 4, op. 58; No. 5, op. 73; unfinished concerto of 1815, Hess no. 15.

For Violin: in C, fragment, WoO 5; in D, op. 61.

For Piano, Violin and Cello, op. 56.

CANTATAS, ORATORIOS, AND OTHER CHORAL WORKS

"Joseph" Cantata, WoO 87; "Leopold" Cantata, WoO 88; *Der glorreiche Augenblick,* op. 136; *Christus am Ölberge,* op. 85; "Choral Fantasia," op. 80; "Meeresstille und glückliche Fahrt," op. 112; "Elegischer Gesang," op. 115; "Germania," WoO 94; "Ihr weisen Gründer," WoO 95.

CHAMBER MUSIC, MISCELLANEOUS

String Quintets, op. 4 and op. 29; Septet, op. 20; Octet, op. 103; Quartets for

Piano and Strings, WoO 36; Rondino, WoO 25.

LIEDER

Six Gellert Lieder, op. 48; Eight Lieder, op. 52; Six Lieder, op. 75; Three Goethe Lieder, op. 83; *An die ferne Geliebte,* op. 98.

MASSES

Mass in C, op. 86; *Missa Solemnis,* op. 123.

OPERA AND INCIDENTAL MUSIC

Fidelio/Leonore, op. 72; *Egmont,* op. 84; *Die Ruinen von Athen,* op. 113; *König Stephan,* op. 117; *Leonore Prohaska,* WoO 96; *Vestas Feuer,* Hess 115.

OVERTURES

Coriolan, op. 62; *Egmont,* op. 84; *Fidelio,* op. 72; *Leonore,* opp. 72 and 138; *König Stephan,* op. 117; "Name Day," op. 115; *Prometheus,* op. 43; *Die Ruinen von Athen,* op. 113; "Weihe des Hauses," op. 124.

SONATAS

For Piano: op. 2; op. 7; op. 10; op. 13 ("Pathétique"); op. 14; op. 22; op. 26 ("Funeral March"); op. 27 ("Quasi una Fantasia"); op. 28; op. 31; op. 49; op. 53 ("Waldstein"); op. 54; op. 57 ("Appassionata"); op. 78; op. 79; op. 81a ("Lebewohl"); op. 90; op. 101; op. 106 ("Hammerklavier"); op. 109; op. 110; op. 111; WoO 47 ("Electoral"); WoO 51.

For Violin and Piano: op. 12; op. 23; op. 24; op. 30; op. 47 ("Kreutzer"); op. 96.

For Cello and Piano: op. 5; op. 69; op. 102.

For Horn and Piano: op. 17.

STRING QUARTETS

op. 18, 1–6; op. 59, 1–3 ("Razumovsky"); op. 74; op. 95; op. 127; op. 130; op. 131; op. 132; op. 135; Grosse Fuge, op. 133.

SYMPHONIES

No. 1, op. 21; No. 2, op. 36; No. 3, op. 55; No. 4, op. 60; No. 5, op. 67; No. 6, op. 68; No. 7, op. 92; No. 8, op. 93; No. 9, op. 125; *Wellingtons Sieg*, op. 91.

TRIOS

For Piano, Violin and Cello: op. 1; op. 70; op. 97; WoO 38; WoO 39.

For Violin, Viola, and Cello: op. 3; op. 8; op. 9.

VARIATIONS

For Piano: on a March by Dressler, WoO 63; on a Swiss Air, WoO 64; on "Venni amore," WoO 65; on "Es war einmal ein alter Mann," WoO 66; on a Theme by Count Waldstein, WoO 67; on "Quant' è più bello," WoO 69; on a Russian Dance, WoO 71; on "La stessa, la stessissima," WoO 73; on "God Save the King," WoO 78; on "Rule Britannia," WoO 79; on an Original Theme in C minor, WoO 80; Six Variations in F, op. 34; Fifteen Variations (*Eroica*) in E-flat, op. 35; on a Waltz by Diabelli, op. 120.

WORKS WITH OPUS NUMBERS

Opus 1: Three Trios for Piano, Violin, and Cello in E-flat, G, and C minor, 83, 84, 89, 94, 99, 104, 130, 131, 133, 136, 140, 269

Opus 2: Three Piano Sonatas in F minor, A, and C, 66, 99, 135, 137

Opus 3: Trio for Violin, Viola, and Cello

Opus 4: String Quintet in E-flat (a revision of the Octet, op. 103), 134

Opus 5: Two Sonatas for Piano and Cello in F and G minor, 79, 131–32, 166, 449n. 11

Opus 6: Sonata for Piano, Four Hands

Opus 7: Piano Sonata in E-flat, 111, 137–38

Opus 8: Serenade for Violin, Viola, and Cello in D

Opus 9: Three Trios for Violin, Viola, and Cello in G, D, and C minor, 82, 133, 134, 136, 140

Opus 10: Three Piano Sonatas in C minor, F, and D, 65, 82, 136, 137–38

Opus 11: Trio for Piano, Clarinet (or Violin) and Cello in B-flat, 83, 135

Opus 12: Three Sonatas for Piano and Violin in D, A, and E-flat, 98, 101, 132, 134

Opus 13: Piano Sonata in C minor ("Pathétique"), 65, 66, 80, 83, 128, 136, 137–38

Opus 14: Two Piano Sonatas in E and G, 130, 137–38

Opus 15: Piano Concerto No. 1 in C, 111, 135–36, 145

Opus 16: Quintet for Piano and Wind Instruments in E-flat, 135, 322

Opus 17: Sonata for Piano and Horn in F, 135

Opus 18: Six String Quartets in F, G, D, C minor, A, and B-flat, 98, 110, 130, 133–34, 136, 140, 141, 150, 249, 260, 323, 391, 393

Opus 19: Piano Concerto No. 2 in B-flat, 94, 135–36, 449n. 19

Opus 20: Septet in E-flat, 100, 101, 103,

WORKS WITHOUT OPUS NUMBERS

PROJECTED WORKS (UNCATALOGUED)

Index

Note: page numbers in *italics* indicate illustrations. Captions for pictorial biography of Beethoven have not been indexed.